GREAT LIVES

THE TIMES

GREAT LIVES

A CENTURY IN OBITUARIES

EDITED BY IAN BRUNSKILL

TIMES BOOKS

First published in hardback in 2005
This paperback edition first published in 2007 by Times Books

HarperCollins Publishers
77–85 Fulham Palace Road
London w6 8jb

www.harpercollins.co.uk
Visit the book lover's website

1 3 5 7 9 10 8 6 4 2

The Times is a registered trademark of Times Newspapers Ltd

ISBN-13 978–0–00–720169–3
ISBN-10 0–00–720169–9

British Library Cataloguing in Publication Data

A catalogue record for this book is available from the
British Library.

Designed by Mark Thomson

Typeset in FF Nexus by
Rowland Phototypesetting Ltd, Bury St Edmunds, Suffolk

Printed and bound in Great Britain by
Clays Ltd, St Ives plc

CONTENTS

* * *

INTRODUCTION

Ian Brunskill
Obituaries Editor of *The Times*

FROM ITS BEGINNINGS in 1785 *The Times* has recorded significant deaths, paying tribute to victims of the French Revolution, for instance, in much the same way as, more recently, it has remembered those killed in London by terrorist bombs. For the first half century or more, however, the paper's obituary coverage was neither consistent nor systematic. Often it amounted to little more than a list of names of people who had died, and on more than one occasion *The Times* simply plagiarized a notice from another paper if it had none of its own.

It was under John Thadeus Delane, Editor of *The Times* from 1841 to 1877, that this began to change. There was still no attempt to match in *The Times* the standard set by John Nichols at the *Gentleman's Magazine*, who in the account of one recent historian had, from 1778, 'expanded the calendar of deaths ... into a full-blown obituaries column' which 'established a standard of necrology for modern times'. But Delane clearly recognized that the death of a leading figure on the national stage was an event that would seize the public imagination as almost nothing else could, and that it demanded more than just a brief notice recording the demise. 'Wellington's death,' Delane told a colleague, 'will be *the only topic*'.

Delane instituted the practice of preparing detailed, authoritative – and often very long – obituaries of the more important and influential personalities of the day while they were still alive. The resulting increase in the quality and scope of the major notices ensured that, even if the paper's day-to-day obituary coverage remained erratic, *The Times* in the second half of the 19th century rose to the big occasion far better than its rivals could. The investment of effort and resources was not hard to justify. The Victorian public had an extraordinary appetite for all kinds of biographical writing, to the point where it sometimes seemed that no public school headmaster or cathedral dean could depart this world without inspiring a fat two-volume *Life*. The *Times* obituaries not only found a ready following among readers of the paper but were soon being collected and republished in book form too. Six volumes of 'Biographies of Eminent Persons' covered the period 1870–1894.

The benefits of the advances made in the 19th century under Delane – the combination of broad historical sweep with the accumulation of telling detail;

the striving for balance and subtlety of judgment – are evident in the best of the 20th-century obituaries collected here. It was not until 1920, however, that *The Times* appointed its first obituary editor, and it was some years later still before the paper began to run a daily obituary page. As late as 1956, the publisher Rupert Hart-Davis could complain in a letter to the retired Eton schoolmaster George Lyttelton: 'The obituary arrangements at *The Times* are haphazard and unsatisfactory. The smallest civil servant – Sewage Disposal Officer in Uppingham – automatically has at least half a column about him in standing type at the office, but writers and artists are not provided for until they are eighty.'

That was a little unfair, even at the time, but if matters have improved since then, it is in large part due to the efforts of the late Colin Watson, who took over as obituaries editor in the year Hart-Davis expressed that disparaging view and who remained in the post for 25 years. He built up and maintained the stock of advance notices so that there were usually about 5,000 on file at any one time, a figure that has remained more or less constant ever since.

Watson, in an article written on his retirement, gave a revealing and only half-frivolous account of what the whole business involves. It was – is – a relentless, if rewarding, task: 'You may read and read and read,' he wrote, 'particularly history; turn on the radio; listen for rumours of ill-health (never laugh at so much as a chesty cold); and you may write endless letters – but never dare say you are on top.'

Many *Times* obituaries are written in house; others are commissioned from distinguished outside contributors with expert knowledge of the subject. 'Just as every man is said to have a book in him,' Watson thought, 'so most people have one obit in them, except actors and musicians, who can't or won't write.' The only problem with these 'notable men and women in the outside world', Watson observed, is 'a/ to find them, b/ to persuade them to write and c/ to get them actually to deliver'. The difficulty is compounded by the far from generous rates of pay – a guinea per hundred words in Watson's time and scarcely better, I blush to admit, today. There is also the absence of a byline, a factor which probably counts for more in today's celebrity culture than it did a few decades ago.

The tradition of anonymity in *Times* obituaries has its advantages, nevertheless. Signed notices by well-known names are seldom quite free of that comic solipsism so neatly caught in the title of Spike Milligan's *Adolf Hitler: My Part in his Downfall*. An unsigned piece is much more likely to be read – and written – as an account of the subject's life, and not of his relations with the author. There are practical merits too. *Times* notices may be elaborate composites, updated over many years, sometimes by more than one hand. The obituary of Queen Elizabeth The Queen Mother, for instance, would have needed half a dozen bylines, some of them for writers who had predeceased their subject by several years.

If Watson may in many respects be said to have brought the obituary department into the modern world, it fell to his successors, particularly John Higgins and Anthony Howard, to show how effectively the paper could respond when other newspapers, from the mid-1980s, began to expand their obituary coverage to match that of *The Times*. There were some elsewhere who claimed, in the course of this expansion, to have invented or reinvented the newspaper obituary in its modern form – chiefly, it often seemed, by treating all their subjects like amusing minor characters in the novels of Anthony Powell. In fact, as I hope this collection shows, the obituary form as practised for more than a century in *The Times* had at its best always been both broader in range and livelier in approach than may generally have been assumed. Hart-Davis's Sewage Disposal Officer in Uppingham doubtless had his day, or may have it even yet. But almost from the start *Times* obituarists have written – and written well – about foreign firebrands as well as British worthies, women as well as men, villains as well as heroes, artists and entertainers as well as heads of state.

Obituaries are about lives, not death. 'Read no history', Disraeli famously enjoined in his early novel *Contarini Fleming*: 'nothing but biography, for that is life without theory.' That's slightly misleading, of course. For biography to serve as a prism through which history is viewed, biographers must shape unruly lives into tidy narratives of virtue rewarded or promise unfulfilled. Newspaper obituarists mostly have to do that faster than they would like, and without much benefit of hindsight. Yet on the whole, and to a remarkable degree, the first drafts of history collected here seem to have stood the test of time.

These 'Great Lives' are a frustratingly small selection. For every notice included, there were half a dozen others reluctantly left out. Even so, between them, these obituaries cover fields from showbiz to science and from politics to sport. They span a century from the Boer War, through the First and Second World Wars, to the end of Communism and the continuing global conflicts of today. Taken together, I hope these lives of exceptional individuals may be a revealing, distinctive history of the exceptional times in which they lived – a history, too, of *The Times* itself and its changing relationship with its readers and with the world.

LORD KITCHENER

5 JUNE 1916

HORATIO HERBERT KITCHENER was born at Gunsborough House, near Listowel, in County Kerry, on June 24, 1850. He was the second son of Lieutenant-Colonel H. H. Kitchener, of Cossington, Leicestershire, by his marriage with Frances, daughter of the Rev. John Chevallier, DD, of Aspall Hall, Suffolk, and was therefore of English descent though born in Ireland.

He was educated privately by tutors until the age of 13, when he was sent with his three brothers to Villeneuve, on the Lake of Geneva, where he was in the charge of the Rev. J. Bennett. From Villeneuve, after some further travels abroad, he returned to London, and was prepared for the Army by the Rev. George Frost of Kensington Square. He entered the Royal Military Academy at Woolwich in 1868 and obtained a commission in the Royal Engineers in January, 1871. During the short interval between passing out of Woolwich and joining the Engineers he was on a visit to his father at Dinan, and volunteered for service with the French Army. He served under Chanzy for a short time, but was struck down by pneumonia and invalided home. He now applied himself vigorously to the technical work of his branch, and laboured incessantly at Chatham and Aldershot to succeed in his profession.

Palestine and Cyprus

His first chance of adventure arose owing to a vacancy on the staff of the Palestine Exploration Society. Kitchener was offered the post in 1874 and at once accepted it. He remained in the Holy Land until the year 1878, engaged first as assistant to Lieutenant Conder, RE, in mapping 1,600 square miles of Judah and Philistia, and then in sole charge during the year 1877 surveying that part of Western Palestine which still remained unmapped. The work was done with the thoroughness which distinguished Kitchener's methods in his subsequent career. He rejoined Conder in London in January, 1878, and by the following September the scheme of the Society was carried through, and a map of Western Palestine on a scale of one inch to a mile was satisfactorily completed. The work entailed considerable hardship, and even danger. Kitchener suffered from sun-stroke and fever. He and his surveying parties were frequently attacked by bands of marauders, and on one of these occasions both Conder and he barely escaped with their lives. On another occasion Kitchener pluckily rescued his comrade from drowning. His survey work in Palestine led directly to his nomination for similar work in Cyprus, where he began the map of the island which was eventually published in 1885.

Egypt and the Red Sea

Realising that trouble was brewing in Egypt, Kitchener managed to be at Alexandria on leave at the time of Arabi's revolt. He served through the campaign of 1882, and, thanks largely to his knowledge of Arabic, became second in command of the Egyptian Cavalry when Sir Evelyn Wood was made Sirdar of the Egyptian Army. He left Suez in November, 1883, to take part in the survey of the Sinai Peninsula, but almost immediately returned for service in the Intelligence branch. He was sent southward after the defeat of Hicks Pasha in order to win over the tribes and prevent the further spread of disaffection. His personality and influence did much. The Mudir of Dongola in response to Kitchener's appeal, fell upon the dervishes at Korti and defeated them. But the tide of Mahdi-ism was still flowing strongly. By July, 1884, Khartum was invested, and upon Kitchener fell the duty of keeping touch between Gordon and the expedition all too tardily dispatched for his relief.

Kitchener was now a major and DAA and QMC on the Intelligence Staff. In December, 1884, Wolseley and his troops reached Korti. Kitchener accompanied Sir Herbert Stewart's column on its march to Metemmeh, but only as far as Gakdul Wells, and consequently he was not at Abu Klea. When the expedition recoiled, it became Kitchener's painful duty to piece together an account of the storming of Khartum and the death of Gordon. For Kitchener's services in this arduous and disappointing campaign there came a mention in dispatches, a medal and clasp, and the Khedive's star. In June, 1885, he was promoted lieutenant-colonel. In the summer the Mahdi died and the Khalifa Abdullahi succeeded him. Kitchener had resigned his commission in the Egyptian Army and had returned to England, but he was almost at once sent off to Zanzibar on a boundary commission and was subsequently appointed Governor-General of the Red Sea littoral and Commandant at Suakin in August, 1886. Here he soon found himself at grips with the famous Emir Osman Digna.

After some desultory fighting round Suakin Kitchener marched out one morning, surprised Osman's camp at Handont, and carried it with the Sudanese. But in the course of the action he was severely wounded by a bullet in the neck, and was subsequently invalided home. The bullet caused him serious inconvenience until it was at last extracted. In June, 1888, he became colonel and ADC to her Majesty Queen Victoria, who had formed a high and just estimate of Kitchener's talents and ever displayed towards him a gracious regard. He rejoined the Egyptian Army as Adjutant-General, and was in command of a brigade of Sudanese when Sir Francis Grenfell stormed Osman Digna's line at Gemaizeh. Toski, in the following summer, was another success, and Kitchener's share in it at the head of 1,500 mounted troops won for him a CB.

Three less eventful years now went by while the Egyptian Army, encouraged by its successes in the Geld, grew in strength and efficiency. In 1892 Kitchener succeeded Grenfell as Sirdar, and in 1894 was made a KCMG.

The Reconquest of the Sudan

Lord Salisbury's Government decided on March 12, 1896, that the time had come for a forward movement on the Nile. Their immediate object was to make a diversion in favour of Italy, whose troops had just been totally defeated by the Abyssinians at Adowa, but the natural impetus of the advance carried the Sirdar and his army eventually to Khartum. Kitchener was ready when the order to advance was given. He had 10,000 men on the frontier, rails ready to follow them to Kerma, and all preparations made for supply. At Firket he surprised the dervishes at dawn, and at a cost of only 100 casualties caused the enemy a loss of 800 dead and 1,000 prisoners. A period of unavoidable inactivity ensued to admit of the construction of the railway, the accumulation of supplies, and the preparation of a fleet of steamers to accompany the advance. Cholera ravaged the camp and sandstorms of a furious character impeded operations, but the advance was at last resumed, and after sharp fights at Hafir and Dongola, the latter town was occupied on September 23, and the first stage of the reconquest of the Sudan was at an end. Kitchener was promoted major-general, with a very good, but not yet assured, prospect of completing the work which he had begun so well.

From the various lines of further advance open to him Kitchener chose the direct line from Wady Halfa to Abu Hamed, and formed the audacious project of spanning this arid and apparently waterless desert, 230 miles broad, with a railway, as he advanced. The first rails of this line were laid in January, 1897, and 130 miles were completed by July. Abu Hamed was captured on August 7 by Hunter with a flying column from Merowi, and Berber on August 31. The remaining 100 miles of the desert railway were then completed. Fortune favoured Kitchener at this period. Water was found by boring in the desert, but the construction of the line was still a triumph of imagination and resource. There were risks in the general situation at this moment, for the position of the army was temporarily far from favourable. There was a specially difficult period towards the close of 1897, when large dervish forces were massed at Metemmeh and a dash to the north seemed on the cards. But the Khalifa delayed his stroke, and when in February, 1898, the Khalifa's lieutenant Mahmud began to march to the north Kitchener was ready for him.

The Atbara

Mahmud and Osman Digna, with some 12,000 good fighting men and several notable Emirs, had concentrated on the eastern bank of the Nile round Shendy, and marching across the desert had struck the Atbara at Nakheila, about 35 miles from its confluence with the Nile. Kitchener, while holding the junction point of the rivers at Atbara Fort, massed the remainder of his force at Res el Hudi on the Atbara, prepared either to attack the dervishes in flank if they moved north or to fall on them in their camp if they remained inert. The reconnaissances showed that the dervishes had fortified their camp in the thick scrub, and that the *dem* could best be attacked from the desert side. An attack seemed likely to be costly, and Kitchener hoped that the dervishes, who were short of food, would either attack the Anglo-Egyptian *zariba* or offer a fight in the open field. The dervishes did not move, and not even a successful raid on Shendy by the gunboats carrying troops affected their decision. After some telegraphic communications with Lord Cromer, Kitchener drew nearer to his enemy, advancing first to Abadar and then to Umdabia. Here he was within striking distance, and in the evening of April 7 the whole force marched silently out into the desert, and after a well-executed night march came within sight of Mahmud's lines at 3 a.m. on the morning of Good Friday, April 8. A halt was made about 600 yards from the trenches and the artillery opened fire, while the infantry was reformed for the assault, Hunter's Sudanese on the right and the British on the left. At 7.40 a.m. Kitchener ordered the advance. A sustained fire of musketry broke out from the dervish entrenchments and was returned with interest by the British and Sudanese, who advanced firing without halting and as steadily as on parade. The din was terrific and the attack irresistible. In less than a quarter of an hour the dervish *zariba* was torn aside and Kitchener's troops inundated the defences. The dervishes stood well and even attempted counter-attacks, but they were swept out of the *dem* into the river and the bush, leaving 1,700 dead in the trenches, including many Emirs. The wily Osman escaped, but Mahmud was made prisoner, while comparatively few of the dervishes who escaped regained Khartum. In this brief but fierce and decisive action the Anglo-Egyptian force suffered 551 casualties.

As Kitchener rode up to greet and to thank the regiments while they were reforming the men received him with resounding cheers. He may not have won their love, for no man, not even Wellington, ever less sought by arts and graces to cultivate popularity among his men, but he had given them a fight after their own hearts, and their confidence in him was unbounded and complete.

Omdurman

By June, 1898, the rails reached the Atbara, and preparations were continued for the final advance at the next high Nile. The army was gradually concentrated by road and river at Wad Hamed, on the west bank of the Nile, 60 miles from Khartum. From this point, 22,000 strong, it set out in gallant array, on a broad front, covered and flanked by the gunboats and the mounted troops. The sun was scorching and the marching hard, but the men were in fine condition and their spirit was superb.

By September 1 the plain of Kerreri was reached – the plain which, according to prophecy, was to be whitened by skulls – and the cavalry now reported that the enemy was advancing. Kitchener drew up his troops in crescent formation, their flanks resting on the river, the British brigades on the left. A night attack by the dervishes was expected and might have proved dangerous, but fortunately it was not attempted, and when dawn came on September 2 the fate of the Khalifa's host was sealed. Kitchener had ridden forward at dawn to Jebel Surgam, a high hill which concealed the two armies from each other, and returned in serious mood, for he had seen some 52,000 dervishes advancing in ordered masses to the attack, and their aspect was formidable. Well marshalled and well led, they swept away the Egyptian cavalry and camel corps, hurling them down the hill, and then turned towards the river and came down upon Kitchener with flags waving, shouting their war cries, and led right gallantly by their Emirs. It was very brave but very hopeless. Kitchener gave the order to open fire when the dervish masses were within 1,700 yards. There was a clear field of fire with scarcely cover for a mouse. The hail of bullets from guns, rifles, and maxims smote the great host of barbarism and shattered it from end to end. The dervish fire was comparatively ineffective, and though individual fanatics struggled up to within short range no formed body came near enough to charge. Completely repulsed with frightful losses the masses melted away, the survivors reeled back, and the fire temporarily ceased.

Kitchener now ordered an advance upon Omdurman in *échelon* of brigades from the left, and this brought on the second phase of the battle. In the *échelon* formation Macdonald's Egyptian brigade on the right was farthest out in the desert, and, as the advance began, the dervish reserves and other masses which had been recalled from the pursuit of the cavalry closed upon Macdonald and delivered a furious attack. The coolness of the commander and the steadiness of his troops saved the situation. Wauchope hurried to his support, while the other brigades wheeled to their right and drove the remnants of the Khalifa's army away into the desert. A gallant attack by the 21st Lancers under Colonel Martin upon a large body of dervishes in a *khor* was a stirring incident of the fight on the left, but placed the Lancers out of court for pursuit. The army resumed its march, halted at the Khor Sambat to reform, and then entered Omdurman without allowing time for the enemy to recover and line the walls. Kitchener and his staff, after wandering about the town in some danger from fire, which continued intermittently throughout the night, sought shelter with Lyttelton's brigade, which bivouacked in quarter-column protected by pickets on the desert side of the town, and from this bivouac 'à la belle étoile' the commander wrote the dispatch announcing the victory.

In this great spectacular, but all too one-sided battle there fell 10,700 gallant dervishes, while twice as many more left the field with wounds. The Anglo-Egyptian losses were 386 all told. The Khalifa's great black flag, now at Windsor

Castle, was captured, and if the Khalifa himself escaped for the time being it was not long before he and his remaining Emirs fell victims to Wingate's troops. Mahdi-ism was smashed to pieces, Gordon was avenged, and the intolerable miseries of a rule which had reduced the population by some seven million souls were brought at last to an end. Two days after the victory a memorial service was held amidst the ruins of Gordon's old Palace at Khartum. The British and Egyptian flags were hoisted on the walls close to the spot where Gordon fell. As Kitchener stood under the shade of the great tree on the river front to receive the congratulations of his officers, all the sternness had died out of him, for the aim of 14 long years of effort had been attained. He returned home to receive the honours and rewards which England does not stint to those who serve her well in war. He was raised to the peerage under the title of Baron Kitchener of Khartum, received the GCB, and was granted £30,000 and the thanks of both Houses of Parliament. The total cost of the campaigns of 1896–98 was only £2,354,000, of which £1,355,000 was spent on railways and gunboats. Of the total sum, rather less than £800,000 was paid by the British Government.

South Africa

Kitchener was not long left to enjoy his well-merited honours in peace. The Black Week of December, 1899, in South Africa caused Lord Roberts to be appointed Commander-in-Chief in the field, and with him there went out Lord Kitchener as Chief of Staff. During the time that Lord Roberts remained in South Africa Kitchener as much as possible effaced himself, and though always ready with counsel and assistance never gave a thought to his own aggrandizement. He was a model lieutenant and gave throughout a fine example of loyalty to his chief. He took part in all the marches and operations which carried the British flag from the Orange River by Paardeberg to Bloemfontein and Pretoria, and displayed energy in performing every duty that Lord Roberts saw fit to confide in him.

Paardeberg

When Cronje left his lines at Magersfontein and retreated eastward up the Modder, Lord Roberts was temporarily indisposed and Kitchener was virtually in command. When the morning of February 18, 1900, found Cronje still in laager at Wolvekraal, in a hollow encircled by commanding heights, upon Kitchener, in co-operation with French, devolved the duty of tackling him. Kitchener decided to strike while the enemy was within reach and issued orders for an advance upon the laager from east and west and by both banks of the river. The Boer position was bad. But the river bed afforded excellent cover and there was a good field of fire on both banks. Moreover, large bodies of Boers came up from the south and east throughout the day in order to extricate Cronje, and interfered materially with the orderly conduct of the fight. A long, wearing, and somewhat disconnected fight raged throughout the day, at the close of which the British troops had suffered 1,262 casualties without having penetrated the enemy's lines. Kitchener rode rapidly during the day from one point of the battlefield to another endeavouring to electrify all with his own devouring activity. If the conduct of the fight was open to criticism it had this supreme merit – namely, that it was furiously energetic, and if it did not succeed in its immediate object it glued Cronje to his laager and drove away the Boers who were attempting to succour a comrade in distress. There are incidents in this fight which are still remembered with regret so far as Kitchener's leading is concerned, but it is fair to say that in looking only to the main object set before him – namely, the destruction of Cronje's force before it could escape or be reinforced – Kitchener was guided by correct principles, and that the subsequent surrender of the Boer force was largely due to the energetic manner in which Kitchener had smitten and hustled the enemy from the first.

The Guerilla War

When Lord Roberts handed over the command to Kitchener in November, 1900, it was generally supposed that the war was at an end. All the organized forces of the Boers had been dispersed, and nearly all the chief towns were in British occupation. But under the guidance of enterprising leaders the spirit of resistance rose superior to misfortune. On all sides guerilla bands sprang up and began a war of raids, ambuscades, and surprises with which a regular army is rarely fitted to cope on equal terms. There were still about 60,000 Boers, foreigners, and rebels in the field, and although they were not all, nor always, engaged in fighting, a fairly accountable force could usually be collected for any specific enterprise by a local leader of note. Their resolution, their field-craft, and the help of every kind which they drew from the countryside made them most formidable enemies. Their subjugation, in view of the wide area over which they operated, was one of the most arduous tasks that has ever been entrusted to a British commander. Of the 210,000 men under Kitchener more than half were disseminated along the railways and in isolated garrisons. The new commander did not possess that numerous force of efficient mounted troops which was indispensable to bring the war to a conclusion.

Into the active conduct of the war, and into the reorganization of his army, Kitchener threw the whole weight of his immense personal influence. He instilled a new spirit into the war when he dashed off to Bloemfontein to hurry along columns for the pursuit of De Wet, and he left no stone unturned to improve the quality of his army. He raided clubs, hotels, and rest camps to beat up loiterers, appealed to all parts of the Empire for mounted men, stimulated the purchase of remounts, raised mounted men from his infantry and artillery, created a new defence force in Cape Colony, and in every possible way prepared to meet like with like and to impart a new spirit of energy and enterprise into the conduct of the war.

The first months of 1901 were marked by the invasion of Cape Colony by De Wet and other leaders, and by a great driving operation in the Eastern Transvaal under French. Both movements failed to entrap the main Boer forces engaged, but the active conduct of the operations, and the losses suffered by the Boers, began that process of moral and material attrition by which the war was ultimately brought to an end.

The winter campaign from May to September, 1901, eliminated about 9,000 Boer fighters, leaving 35,000 still in the field, but this number was much underestimated at the time. With the spring rains there was a general renewal of the war on the part of the burghers, their leading idea consisting of diversions in Cape Colony and Natal. Severe fighting followed in many places. As the months wore on both the offensive and the defensive virtues of Kitchener's system became more striking. The blockhouse lines became more solid and began to extend over fixed areas of the country. Strengthened by infantry, they flanked the great drives, and became the nets into which the Boer commandos were driven. There came at last a dawning of perception in the Boer mind that further resistance, however honourable, was hopeless.

The Peace

An offer of mediation made by the Netherlands Government on January 25, 1902, gave an excuse to both sides for ending the war. Though this offer was not accepted, a copy of the correspondence which followed it was transmitted to the Transvaal Government on March 7, without any covering letter, explanation, or suggestion. It produced an immediate effect. President Schalk Burger asked for a safe-conduct for himself and others to enable them to meet the Free State Government to discuss terms, and a meeting took place in Kitchener's house on April 12. A Convention at Vereeniging was arranged. Sixty Boer delegates there assembled on May 15. Terms were at last agreed to by the delegates in concert with Lord Kitchener and Lord Milner, and, after revision by the British Government, were finally accepted by 54 votes to 6 on May 31, only half an hour before the expiry of the time of grace.

Returning once more to England Kitchener was made a Viscount, and received the Order of Merit, the thanks of both Houses of Parliament, and a substantial grant of public money. Once again he was not allowed to enjoy for long his new honours in peace, and was appointed Commander-in-Chief in India in the same year that he had returned home.

Work in India

At the time when Kitchener reached India, the army in India, though possessing many war-like qualities, was suffering from serious organic and administrative defects. It did not present the offensive value which might have been expected from its numbers and its cost. It did not exploit all the martial races available for its service. The distribution of the troops had not been altered to correspond with new railway facilities and a changed strategical situation. It was not self-supporting in material of war, and the armament of the troops was behind the times. There was scarcely a single military requisite that had been completely supplied to the four poorly-organized divisions which formed the inadequate field army, and scarcely any provision had been made for maintaining the army in the field. The content of the Indian Army had not been inspired by adequate provision for its material well-being. Lastly, the higher administration of the Army was under a system of dual control, which produced conflicts between the responsibility pertaining to the Commander-in-Chief and the power which rested in the Military Department.

The history of Kitchener's seven years in India is a history of sustained and in the end almost completely successful efforts to overcome these serious defects. He did not act in a hurry. He began by making extended tours over India, including a journey of 1,500 miles on horseback and on foot round the North-West frontier, and he consulted every officer of eminence and experience in India. Lord Curzon, who had urged Kitchener's appointment, was heartily with him in his plans for Army reform up to the unfortunate moment when a difference of opinion arose between Viceroy and Commander-in-Chief on the question of the Military Department and the higher administration of the Army. The difference gave rise at last to a serious crisis. Kitchener fought his own battle alone and unsupported in the Governor-General's Council, and the decision of Mr Balfour's Government and the settlement finally made by Lord Morley were in his favour. Mr Brodrick's dispatch of May 31, 1905, placed the Commander-in-Chief in India in charge of a newly-named Army Department, which became in the end invested with most of the rights and duties of the old Military Department, but large powers were reserved for the Secretary to the Army Department. Lord Curzon resigned in 1905.

Kitchener's projects for the reform of the Army had begun to take shape in 1904. On October 28 of that year an Army Order divided the country into nine territorial divisional areas, and arranged the forces contained in them into nine divisions and three independent brigades, exclusive of Burma and Aden. The plan was to redistribute the troops according to the requirements of the defence of India, to train all arms together at suitable centres, and to promote decentralization of work and devolution of authority. Kitchener proposed to secure thorough training for war in recognized war formations, to enable the whole of the nine divisions to take the field in a high state of efficiency, to expand the reserve which would maintain them in the field, and to have behind them sufficient troops to support the civil power with garrisons and mobile columns. In May, 1907, another Army Order created a Northern and a Southern Army. The commanders of these Armies became inspectors whose duty was to ensure uniformity of training and discipline. The administrative work was delegated to officers commanding divisions.

Kitchener's plan for the redistribution of the Army was much attacked because it was misrepresented and misunderstood. The cantonments given up were those which no longer required troops. The troops were not massed by divisions but by divisional areas, and in drawing up his plans for obligatory garrisons and the support of the civil power Kitchener worked closely with the civil authorities and left unguarded no likely centre of disaffection. The new distribution corresponded with strategical exigencies, and the various divisions were échelonnéd behind each other in a manner to utilize to the full the carrying capacity of the railways. There was no concentration on the frontier as was popularly supposed. The point of both Armies was directed to the North-West frontier, but there was nothing to prevent a concentration in any other direction.

Kitchener's scheme was not one for increasing the Army, but for utilizing better existing material. He improved and widened the recruiting grounds of the Army. He did much for the pay, pensions, and allowances of the Indian Army, established grass and dairy farms all over India, and was very successful through his medical service in combating disease. It was his object, as it was that of Lord Lawrence, not only to make the Army formidable, but to make it safe. The principle of keeping the artillery mainly in the hands of Europeans was maintained. By creating the Quetta Staff College Kitchener enabled India to train her own Staff Officers, and by building factories he rendered the Army self-supporting in material of war. The total cost of these reforms was £8,216,000.

Australasian Defence

Kitchener, who was made Field Marshal on September 10, 1909, returned home by way of Australasia, having been invited to examine the land forces and the new Military laws of Australia and New Zealand and to suggest improvements in them. He did his work as thoroughly as usual. He left behind him a memorandum of a very impressive character, and had the satisfaction to learn that his recommendations were approved. On his return home he was made a KP, and was appointed High Commissioner and Commander-in-Chief in the Mediterranean in succession to the Duke of Connaught, who had resigned. Kitchener only accepted this post at the desire of King Edward, and when the King released him from the obligation, he resigned the appointment. In 1911 he purchased Broome Park, with 550 acres, near Canterbury, and occupied his unaccustomed leisure in beautifying and rearranging the house and grounds. The failure of the Government to employ Kitchener aroused unfavourable public comment, but in 1911 the death of Sir Eldon Gorst created a vacancy in Egypt, and Kitchener was offered, and accepted, the post of British Agent and Consul-General.

Egypt and the Sudan

Kitchener landed at Alexandria on September 27, 1911. He arrived in a cruiser, and this fact did not fail to make an impression (upon which he had doubtless calculated) on the natives, who had already been somewhat chastened by the news of his appointment as British Agent.

When Kitchener assumed office at Kasr-el-Doubara, he found a fierce religious controversy still raging between the Copts and the Moslems, and political unrest and seditious journalism still sufficiently active to cause some anxiety. Scarcely had he had time to take stock of his surroundings than there broke out the Italo-Turkish War, which, since its seat was at Egypt's door, threatened to create in this country a situation which might at any moment have become very serious owing to the large Italian colony and the community of religion, and in many cases of interest, that binds the Egyptians to Turkey.

There seems little doubt that Kitchener's presence and his prestige were solely responsible for the safe passage of Egypt through the critical periods of the Tripoli and the two Balkan Wars. But for him, the Egyptian Government would not have been able to prevent collisions between the Greek and Italian colonies and the natives, and certainly it would not have succeeded in forcing the Egyptian Moslems to maintain the neutrality which was obviously so essential to the country's welfare. From the very outset he dealt most firmly with the malcontents and the seditious Press. The tone and the higher standard of the vernacular Press today are an all-sufficient justification of his ruthless enforcement of the Press Law.

Whilst the adoption of a strong policy had a great deal to do with the pacification of the country, there was undoubtedly one other important determining factor. Kitchener came to the conclusion that the best means of counteracting the exciting influence of the Turkish wars and of cutting the ground from under the feet of the sedition-mongers was to keep the country occupied with the contemplation of matters of a more personal and local nature. He therefore initiated a policy of economic reform which, owing to its far-reaching character, should make its beneficial effects felt generations hence.

A beginning was made with the savings bank system, which was extended to the villages, where the local tax collector was authorized to receive deposits, the idea being to encourage the fellaheen to pay in part of the proceeds of their crops against the day when the taxes fall due, and so prevent their squandering the money and having to borrow to pay the imposts. A Usuary Law was introduced forbidding the lending of money at more than three per cent and empowering the courts to inflict fines and imprisonment on infringers of the law. Kitchener also caused Government cotton halekas (markets) to be opened all over the country, which remedied the exploiting of the fellah by the local dealers in the matter of short weight and market prices of cotton. Next he introduced the Five Feddan or Homestead Law, which briefly laid down that distraint could not be levied on the agricultural property of a cultivator, consisting of five feddans or less, and which thus tended to create a system of homesteads. As a companion to his schemes for improving the material lot of the fellah Kitchener caused to be created a new form of jurisdiction, called the Cantonal Courts, which dispense to the fellaheen justice according to local custom. Local notables sit on the bench and this system of village justice for the people by the people has proved a great success.

With a view to protecting the country from the evil results of the fellah's ignorance, Kitchener gave much attention to the consideration of the agricultural question. He supported through thick and thin the then newly formed Department of Agriculture, and in due course had it transformed into a Ministry. Since Egypt depends entirely on the cotton crop, every aspect of the question was studied. Cotton seed was distributed on a large scale by the Government in order to stop adulteration. Laws were introduced for combating the various pests that attack the crop; demonstration farms were created at strategic points to show the fellah the best means of cultivating the land, and a hundred and one measures have been, and are being, taken to safeguard and effect a permanent improvement in the agricultural position of the country. The remainder of Kitchener's economic policy is represented by the gigantic drainage and land reclamation work that is being carried out in the Delta. For years a scheme had been talked of, but it remained for Kitchener to put it into execution. The cost will be about £2,500,000, but most of this will be reimbursed from the sale of land and the increase in the rate of taxation.

On the political side Kitchener was no less successful. He attempted what every one admitted to be an urgent necessity, but what all his predecessors had feared to undertake – viz., the reform of the management of the Wakfs – Moslem endowments – and he transferred the control from the hands of a Director-General nominated by the Khedive to those of a Minister directly responsible to the Council of Ministers and controlled by a superior board nominated by the Government. The reform was hailed with unbounded delight by the entire population. His other great achievement was the reform of the system of representative government.

Meanwhile, Kitchener did not neglect the military situation. He pushed to the utmost the construction of roads throughout the Delta, thus increasing the mobility of the troops; he stopped the Khedive from selling the Mariut Railway to a Triple Alliance syndicate, and by enabling the Egyptian Government to purchase it placed at its disposal (and at that of Great Britain) a line of communication of great potential strategic value in the future. The army of occupation was increased by the bringing of every battalion up to full strength. Points of vantage for strategic purposes were secured in Cairo under the guise of town-planning reforms.

Secretary of State for War

On August 5, 1914, Kitchener, who happened to be in England at the moment, was appointed Secretary of State for War. The post, as will be remembered, had been held since the end of the previous March by Mr Asquith, who now, 'in consequence of the pressure of other duties', handed it over to a man in whom the country at large placed perfect confidence. The fact that, for the first time, a soldier with no Cabinet experience was to become War Minister was seen to be an advantage rather than otherwise. What was needed was not a politician but an organizer – and organization was believed to be Kitchener's especial gift. He was, too, exceptional in not under-rating his enemy. His first act as Minister was to demand a vote of credit for £100,000,000, and an increase of the Army of half a million men. In an interview with an American journalist, published in December, he was reported to have expressed his opinion that the war would last at least three years. In an official denial next day, 'the remarks attributed to the Secretary of State' were declared to be 'imaginary'. In any case, it is certain that in the appeal which he issued, within two days of his appointment, for 100,000 men, the terms of service were given, as 'for a period of three years or until the war is concluded'. In an article published in *The Times* of August 15, the reason why his plans had been based upon a long war were explained, and the wisdom of this recognition, at a moment when the world in general, including the Germans, cherished the belief that the war would be soon over, should always be remembered in forming any estimate of Kitchener's work as Minister of War.

The curious inability of the authorities to come straight to the point, which was to dog the steps of the voluntary system as long as it lasted, at first concealed the fact that these 100,000 men were to be not an expansion, it was supposed, of the Territorial Force, nor even an addition to the Regular Army, but the beginning of an entirely new Army, to which common parlance quickly gave the name of 'Kitchener's'. Considerable difference of opinion existed in military circles as to the wisdom of Kitchener's method of creating it. Many eminent officers, including Lord Roberts, considered that he would have been better advised if he had merely expanded the Territorial Force, the cadres of which would have provided a ready-made organization. But Kitchener preferred to do things in his own way.

In spite of the difficulties inevitable in the absence of machinery capable of coping with a rush some 50 times greater than any contemplated in normal circumstances, he was able by August 25, on his first appearance as a Minister of the

Crown, to inform the House of Lords that his 100,000 recruits had been 'already practically secured'. He added:

'I cannot at this stage say what will be the limits of the forces required, or what measures may eventually become necessary to supply and maintain them. The scale of the Field Army which we are now calling into being is large and may rise in the course of the next six or seven months to a total of 30 divisions continually maintained in the field.'

It would be an ungrateful task to recall the series of appeals, misunderstandings, and recriminations which attended the course of the recruiting campaign. Its varying fortunes seem trivial enough today, when the task is complete. Kitchener was a sincere believer in the voluntary service which had given him the Armies with which he had won his fame. And amid the chaos of political controversies which surrounded him in the Cabinet he applied himself unsparingly to the task of raising men.

At the beginning of the war he lived at Lady Wantage's house in Carlton House Terrace, but early in 1915 he went into residence at York House, St James's Palace, which was placed at his disposal by the King. He worked all day and every day, only spending a few hours occasionally at Broome Park. Of relaxation he took practically none, unless the inspecting of troops may be described by that name.

As time went on it became evident that Kitchener was attempting more than lay in the power of any one man. In May of last year the disclosures of the Military Correspondent of *The Times* as to the shortage of shells at the front came as a sudden shock to the country, although they were merely the culmination of a series of previous warnings. It is proof of the immense belief which Kitchener inspired in the country that *The Times* was falsely accused of 'attacking' him in calling attention to an admitted deficiency. But the prompt institution of the Ministry of Munitions relieved him of that part at least of his heavy burden, and enabled him to devote himself more strenuously than ever to the attempt to maintain under the voluntary system the enormous Army gradually assembling in the field. With the reconstitution at the beginning of October, 1915, of the General Staff Kitchener was relieved of yet another part of his overgrown duties, and the War Office gradually assumed shape and organization.

Kitchener naturally paid several visits to France on tours of inspection. He was also present at the Allied Conferences at Calais and Paris, where his knowledge of French, superior to that of most of his colleagues, gave him a certain advantage in the discussions.

In November last the announcement that, 'at the request of his colleagues', Kitchener had left England for a short visit to the Eastern theatre of war brought home to the general public the seriousness of the situation in Gallipoli. The part played by him in the military aspects of the decisions arrived at before and during the Dardanelles Expedition can only be conjectured. After a short stay in Paris, he visited the Dardanelles, and later had an audience of King Constantine in Athens, returning home by way of Rome, the Italian front, and Paris. The result of Kitchener's investigations, confirming as they did the recommendations of General Monro, was the evacuation of Gallipoli.

The remarkable and unprecedented occasion on which, five days ago, he received a considerable proportion of the members of the House of Commons, making a statement to them and replying to recent criticisms of Army administration, is fresh in the public memory.

Kitchener was made a KG in 1915. During the war he also received the Grand Cordon of the Legion of Honour and of the Order of Leopold. He was never married. The earldom which was conferred on him in July, 1914, passes by special remainder to his elder brother, Colonel Henry Elliott Chevallier Kitchener, who was born in 1846. The new peer served in Burma and with the Manipur Expedition in 1891, being mentioned in dispatches. At the outbreak of the present war he offered his services to the Government, took part in the campaign in South-West Africa, and is now on his way home. He is a widower, and has one son, Commander H. F. C. Kitchener, RN; and a daughter.

V. I. LENIN

Dictator of Soviet Russia.
World revolution as goal.

21 JANUARY 1924

NIKOLAI LENIN, whose death is announced on another page, was the pseudonym of Vladimir Ilyich Ulianov, the dictator of Soviet Russia. His real name has almost passed into oblivion. It was under his *nom de guerre* that he became famous. It is as Lenin that he will pass into history.

This extraordinary figure was first and foremost a professional revolutionary and conspirator. He had no other occupation; in and by revolution he lived. Authorship and the social and economic studies to which he devoted his time were to him but the means for collecting fuel for a world conflagration. The hope of that calamity haunted this cold dreamer from his schooldays. His is a striking instance of a purpose that from early youth marched unflinchingly towards a chosen goal, undisturbed by weariness or intellectual doubt, never halting at crime, knowing no compunction. The goal was the universal social revolution.

Lenin was born on April 10, 1870, at Simbirsk, a little town set on a hill that overlooks the middle Volga and the eastward rolling steppes. His father, born of a humble family in Astrakhan, had risen to the position of district director of schools under the Ministry of Education. The atmosphere of the home was that of the middle-class urban intelligentsia, which ardently cultivated book-learning, was keenly interested in abstract ideas, but had little care for the arts and was at best indifferent to the Russian national tradition.

Of Lenin's early life little is known. He attended the local high school, the headmaster of which was Feodor Kerensky, father of Alexander Kerensky, whom Lenin was one day to overthrow from political power. The boy appears to have been diligent in his studies, but retiring and morose. In 1887 his elder brother was executed for taking part in an attempt on the life of Alexander III. This event may possibly have intensified Lenin's revolutionary sentiments, though emotion never played a great part in his personal life. He was guided by cold logic though he well knew how to work on the feelings of others and to transform them into the motive power he required for his own purposes.

From the high school he passed on into the University of Kazan where he became a student in the faculty of law. Here he came under the suspicion of the authorities, and was expelled from the university on account of his 'unsound political views'. He continued his studies privately, and finally took his degree at the University of St Petersburg.

Marxism in Action

In the early 'nineties the radical intellectual circles in St Petersburg were stirred by a new development of the Socialist movement. From the 'forties onward Socialism had been the accepted creed of a large proportion of Russian intellectuals, but it was a romantic Socialism, mainly of an agrarian character, and based on an extraordinary sympathy for an idealized peasantry. At the beginning of the 'nineties a small group of young men became enthusiastic advocates of what was known as the scientific Socialism of Karl Marx, and, in articles in reviews and in the theoretical public debates on economic subjects that the autocracy permitted at that time they raised a revolt against the 'Populist' Socialism that had become traditional in the intelligentsia. Peter Struve, who later became a Liberal, and even developed Conservative leanings, and Michael Tugan-Baranovsky, who in the end became a popular and highly respected Professor of Political Economy, were the leaders of the Marxian group. Lenin joined them and was greatly assisted by them in his early, literary, efforts, which consisted of polemical articles on the aspects of Socialism that were then in debate. At that time he wrote under the pseudonym of Ilyin.

Lenin never wrote a first-class scientific work. He was not primarily a theorist or a writer but a propagandist. For him articles and books were but means to an end. It was when the Marxists turned from theoretical discussion to the organization of party effort that Lenin found his true vocation. In 1898 the Russian Social Democratic Party came into being. It was of course a conspirative organization. Political activities were under the ban. No political parties, whether Liberal, Conservative, or Socialist, were permitted publicly to exist. The secret parties, or rather clubs, organized by the revolutionaries, recruited their adherents among the intelligentsia, and only to a very small extent among the workmen and peasants. The Marxists organized among the workmen of St Petersburg and other towns clandestine classes for instruction in Socialist doctrine.

It was dangerous work, but Russian revolutionaries were never deterred by the fear of imprisonment or exile. Lenin began his career as an active revolutionary in this comparatively innocuous form of effort. He was caught by the police, as many others were, imprisoned, and sent to Siberia. As compared with many others, his experience of police persecution was brief indeed, but it is significant that during his banishment in Siberia his character as a deliberate fomenter of discord among the revolutionary parties was already, sharply, revealed. The older exiles, who held fast to the 'Populist' tradition, were for the most part gentle, humane, and easy going. They formed a class apart with a strong *esprit de corps*, with fixed habits of comradely intercourse. When Lenin and the other Marxists came, the peace was broken, a new aggressive tone was introduced, and perpetual intrigue led to perpetual dissension and suspicion.

How Bolshevism Began

Lenin escaped from Siberia to Western Europe in 1900, and took up his abode in Switzerland. Here he became one of the leaders in the revolutionary activities of the band of refugees organized under the name of the Russian Social Democratic Party, and in 1901 he joined the editorial staff of their review, *Iskra* (the Spark). The party retained until the Bolshevist Revolution the title of 'The One (or United) Russian Social Democratic Party'. As a matter of fact it was not long before Lenin himself split the party into two warring sections. At the second congress of the party, held in London in 1903, a fierce discussion arose over questions of tactics, and ended in a vote which yielded a majority (*bolshinstvo*) for the view advocated by Lenin. The supporters of the majority view came to be known as Bolsheviki, while the adherents of the minority (*menshinstvo*) were called Mensheviki. Lenin stood at this conference for an extreme centralization of the party organization and for the adoption of direct revolutionary methods, as opposed to the educational and evolutionary tactics advocated by the other side. He displayed then the temperament that moulded his career. A man of iron will and inflexible ambition, he had no scruple about means and treated human beings as mere material for his purpose. Trotsky, then Lenin's opponent on the question of tactics, and later his chief colleague in the Council of People's Commissaries, has given a vivid description of Lenin's conduct on this occasion.

At the second congress of the Russian Social Democratic Party (he wrote) this man with his habitual talent and energy played the part of disorganizer of the party … Comrade Lenin made a mental review of the membership of the party, and came to the conclusion that the iron hand needed for organization belonged to him. He was right. The leadership of Social Democracy in the struggle for liberty meant in reality the leadership of Lenin over Social Democracy.

Dictatorship as a Principle

It is unnecessary to dwell at length on the theoretical side of the controversy between Lenin and the Menshevists. Both sides published in support of their views a large number of fiercely polemical articles and pamphlets, which for the uninitiated make extremely dull reading, though for the patient historian they may provide a vivid illustration of revolutionary mentality. Lenin's idea was that the Central Committee should absolutely dominate every individual, and every local group in the party. He was opposed to any sort of democratic equality or local autonomy in the party organization. Dictatorship by a compact central group was the principle on which he worked. 'Give us an organization consisting of true revolutionaries,' he wrote, 'and we will turn Russia upside down.' He regarded his opponents in the party as opportunists and no true revolutionaries. He was for direct action, for cutting loose from all entangling compromise with Liberals and more cautious Socialists.

The Social Democrats argued vehemently and incessantly, but this did not prevent them from agitating, organizing, and conspiring in Russia. While the rival party, the Socialist Revolutionaries, agitated among the peasantry and planned and carried out a series of terrorist acts, of which several Ministers, Governors, and the Grand Duke Serge were the victims, the Social Democrats developed their propaganda among the factory workmen, with but slight success until 1906, when the discontent caused by the Japanese War and the shooting of workmen in St Petersburg on Red Sunday, January 22, provoked an openly revolutionary movement throughout Russia. The movement culminated in the granting of a Constitution on October 30, 1905. During the months immediately preceding and following this event the Socialist agitation was at its height. Then, for the first time, the masses of the Russian people became acquainted with Socialist principles, and the agitators gained experience in dealing with the masses.

Propaganda at Work

Lenin's name was not prominent during the first Revolution. He was very active behind the scenes, organizing, directing, pushing things in his own direction, noting the readiness of the masses to respond to extreme and demoralizing watchwords, sneering at all hints of compromise, at every stage forcing a disruption between the Social Democrats and the *bourgeois* parties. It is curious that he refused to become a member of the first short-lived St Petersburg Council of Workmen's Deputies, formed after the promulgation of the Constitution. Trotsky played a prominent part in this Soviet. It is characteristic of Lenin that he only adopted the Soviet idea at the moment – 12 years later – when it suited his own purposes.

From 1905 to 1907 Lenin lived in Russia under an assumed name, endeavouring to keep alive and to organize the revolutionary movement, which, in the end, the Stolypin Government ruthlessly suppressed. His name is connected with several cases of 'expropriation'. Apparently he did not personally organize these armed raids on banks and post-offices, but considerable sums seized in such robberies were handed over to the Bolshevists and used by Lenin to develop his propaganda at home and abroad. He left Russia when the collapse of the 1905 Revolution became apparent and resumed his activities in Geneva. On the whole his position among the revolutionaries had been greatly strengthened and among the mixed crowd of new exiles who had been thrown out of Russia by the failure of the first revolutionary offensive he found many instruments suitable for his unscrupulous purpose.

In 1912 he moved to Cracow so as to be in closer touch with his agents in Russia. A singular episode, characteristic of his contempt for *bourgeois* morality, was his intrigue, in collusion with the Secret Police, to split the small Social Democratic Party in the Duma through a certain Malinovsky, who visited him in Cracow with the knowledge of the Head of the Department of Police.

In 1914, at the outbreak of war, Lenin was in Galicia. As a Russian subject he was arrested by the Austrian authorities, but he was released when it was discovered that he would be a useful agent in the task of weakening Russia. He returned to Switzerland, where he carried on defeatist propaganda with the object of transforming the war between the nations into a revolutionary civil war within each nation. He was joined by defeatist Socialists from various countries. The funds for these operations were perhaps provided by Germany, since the sums Lenin had received from expropriations during the first revolution were exhausted. The activities of this little group of Socialists were hardly noticed amid the great events of the war. The conferences of Zimmerwald and Kienthal in 1915 had the appearance of insignificant gatherings of crazy fanatics. Yet they drafted the defeatist revolutionary programme and framed the watchwords which later acquired enormous power in Russia and influenced the working classes throughout Europe. Lenin regarded the vicissitudes of the war purely from the standpoint of revolutionary tactics. He noted the lessons of war, industry, and State-control, and the effects of war on mass-psychology.

The Revolution of 1917

The revolution that suddenly broke out in Russia in March, 1917, gave Lenin his long-sought-for opportunity. The Provisional Government formed after the abdication of the Emperor Nicholas proclaimed unrestricted liberty and encouraged the return of the political exiles, who came flocking back in thousands. There was some difference of opinion in the Government about permitting the return of such a notorious defeatist as Lenin. He came nevertheless, transported through Germany with the help of the German General Staff. Ludendorff considered that he was likely to be a most effective agent in disorganizing the Russian Army, and wrecking the Russian front. In this he was not mistaken; what he did not foresee was that Lenin would provoke a violent revolutionary movement that was later to react on Germany herself.

Lenin was received in Petrograd with all revolutionary honours. Searchlights from armoured cars lighted up the Finland railway station, which was thronged with people. Socialists of all parties made speeches, but Lenin was not to be led away by any external success. He wanted real power. On April 14, the day after his arrival, he laid his programme before the Social Democratic Conference, a programme which six months afterwards he carried out to the letter in his decrees.

At the time his speech was ridiculed by the moderate Socialists. Only a small group of Bolshevists applauded their leader when he declared that peace with the Germans must be concluded, at once, a Soviet Republic founded, the banks closed, that all power must be given to the workers, and that the Social-Democrats must henceforth call themselves Communists. His motion was rejected by 115 to 20.

Lenin had at his back a compact organization well equipped with money. The Bolshevists displayed extraordinary activity in demoralizing the Army and the workmen and in provoking riots among the peasantry. There was no power to restrain them. In Petrograd, Lenin took up his quarters in the house of the dancer Kaszesinska, and from the balcony addressed large crowds day after day. In July he attempted a *coup d'état*, but failed. He went into hiding, but continued to direct subversive movement. The Provisional Government under Kerensky shrank from coercive measures. The Socialist Revolutionaries and Social-Democrats who controlled the Petrograd Soviet partly sympathized with the Bolshevists, partly feared them, but in their appeals to the masses they were always outbid by Lenin's followers, and speedily they lost ground.

After the failure of Korniloff's attempt in August to re-establish law and order the general demoralization increased. The Army went to pieces and, taking advantage of this disorganized host of armed men, to whom he promised immediate peace, Lenin effected a *coup d'état* on November 7, 1917, this time without any difficulty. Lenin appeared with his followers in a Congress of Soviets, and was acclaimed as Dictator. The members of the Provisional Government were imprisoned, all but Kerensky, who escaped. There was a sharp struggle in Moscow, where for several days boys from officers' training schools defended the Kremlin, but they finally succumbed.

Master of the Terror

Lenin took up his residence in the Kremlin, and from that ancient citadel of autocracy and orthodoxy launched his propaganda, of world-revolution. Outwardly he lived as modestly as when he had been an obscure political refugee. Both he and his wife – he had married late in the 'nineties Nadiezhda Krupskaya – had the scorn of sectarians for *bourgeois* inventions and comforts. Short and sturdy, with a bald head, small beard, and keen, bright, deep-set eyes, Lenin looked like a small tradesman. When he spoke at meetings his ill-fitting suit, his crooked tie, his generally nondescript appearance, disposed the crowd in his favour. 'He is not one of the gentle-folk,' they would say, 'he is one of us.'

This is not the place to describe in detail the terrible achievements of Bolshevism – the shameful peace with Germany, the plundering of the educated and propertied classes, the long-continued terror with its thousands of innocent victims, the Communist experiment carried to the point of suppressing private trade, and making practically all the adult population of the towns servants and slaves of the Soviet Government; the civil war, the creation and strengthening of the Red Army, the fights with the border peoples, the Ukraine, with Koltchak and Denikin and with Poland, culminating in 1920 in the defeat of the White Armies and the conclusion of peace with Poland. Never in modern times has any great country passed through such a convulsion as that brought about by Lenin's implacable effort to establish Communism in Russia, and thence to spread it throughout the world.

In the light of these world-shaking events Lenin's personality acquired an immense significance. He retained control. He was the directive force. He was in effect Bolshevism. His associates were pygmies compared with him. Even Trotsky, who displayed great energy and ability in organizing the Red Army, deferred to Lenin. Both the Communist Party and the Council of People's Commissaries were completely under Lenin's control. It happened sometimes that after listening to a discussion of two conflicting motions in some meeting under his chairmanship Lenin would dictate to the secretary, without troubling to argue his point some third resolution entirely his own. He had an uncanny skill in detecting the weaknesses of his adversaries, and his associates regarded him with awe as a supreme tactician. His judgment was final.

He was ultimately responsible for the terror as for all the other main lines of Bolshevist policy. He presided over the meeting of the Council of People's Commissaries which, in July, 1918, approved the foul murder of Nicholas II and his family by the Ekaterinburg Soviet.

The Communist experiment brought Russia to economic ruin, famine, and barbarism. Under Soviet rule the Russian people suffered unheard of calamity. To Lenin, this mattered little. When the famine came in 1921 he remarked, with a scornful smile, 'It's a trifle if twenty millions or so die.'

He did realize, however, that the effort to maintain undiluted Communism was endangering the existence of his Government. In March, 1921, he called a halt. Against the wishes of the majority of his followers he proclaimed a new economic policy, consisting of a temporary compromise between Socialism and Capitalism, with the Communist movement in complete control. His hope was that this policy would secure a breathing space during which the Communists might rally for a new attack on world capitalism.

The famine raged. Russia sank deeper and deeper into the mire. The resources of the Soviet Government, the gold reserve of the Imperial Government which they had squandered in their wild propaganda and in their feeble pretence of foreign trade, were almost exhausted. Their one hope lay in bluffing Europe, and to this task they set themselves with great zest and incomparable skill.

Last Illness

In the midst of the rapid crumbling of all his plans, Lenin fell ill towards the end of 1921, and for many weeks was unable to take any public part in affairs. The nature of his complaint was obscure. Experts were summoned from Germany, and a bullet was extracted that had been fired on Lenin when an attempt was made on his life by the Jewish socialist revolutionary, Dora Kaplan, in 1918. There was a brief interval, during which Lenin's health was apparently restored, and he made speeches declaring that the new economic policy would go no farther, and that concessions to capitalists were at an end. He was unable to attend the Genoa Conference, and shortly after the conclusion of the Conference the reports as to his health became more alarming. German specialists were again summoned, and his condition became so grave that steps were taken by his associates to establish a directorate, to carry on his functions.

One paralytic stroke followed another, and it became clear that Lenin would never return to affairs, that his days were numbered. He was removed to a country house near Moscow, where, under the care of nurses, he lingered on till his name grew shadowy and his party was divided by an open dispute for the succession.

GIACOMO PUCCINI

A famous opera composer

29 NOVEMBER 1924

GIACOMO PUCCINI, whose death is announced on another page, had held first place among the composers of opera in his generation so decisively that to the majority of opera-goers he seemed to stand alone. Musicians may find among his contemporaries a dozen or more names whose works for the stage they will prefer before his. Humperdinck, Strauss, Charpentier, Bruneau, and Debussy have all displayed qualities which in their different ways are beyond the range of Puccini's art, yet no one of them competes for his position of favour in the eyes of the general public. A conservative operatic management such as we have known in London may try experiments in one or other; ever since the success of *La Bohème* there have been no experiments in Puccini. The only question was how quickly each new work could be hurried on to the stage. In fact, an opera of his entitled *Turandot* was announced for production next spring; and he had almost finished it.

Once he was regarded as a member of a group of brilliant and sensational representatives of Young Italy. The comparatively early death of Leoncavallo, the failure of Mascagni to follow up the meteoric success of *Cavalleria*, and the lack of any decisive characteristics in Giordano enabled Puccini to outdistance his companions in that group, and Italian opera still has the advantage in the world over that of any other country in that it rallies to its standard the great voices, whether those voices are the product of Italy or of Australia, or Ireland or America.

Puccini was born at Lucca in the same year as Leoncavallo (1858) and was, like Bach and Mozart, the inheritor of a family tradition of musicianship. He represented the fifth generation of musical Puccinis, the earliest of whom, his great-great-grandfather, bore the same Christian name, Giacomo, and, was a friend of Martini, the master of Mozart. Puccini's father dying when the boy was six years old, it was through the determination and sacrifice of his mother, who was left poor, that he was given the opportunity of study at the Milan Conservatory. There he worked at composition with Bazzini and with Ponchielli, the composer of *La Gioconda*. The production of a student work, a Capriccio for orchestra, called forth praise of his possibilities as a symphonic writer, but Puccini never mistook that as an indication that he should write symphonies. He subsequently put his powers in this direction to good use in devising those running orchestral commentaries

Giacomo Puccini

which, supporting the dialogues of his characters on the stage, form the links between the great lyrical outbursts.

For some time Puccini lived in Milan with his brother and a fellow-student, enjoying the delights and sorrows of a Bohemian existence, enduring a sufficient amount of hardship to give him a place in the long roll of struggling geniuses, and incidentally storing up memories which were to give him the right local colour for his first accepted masterpiece.

His first opera, *Le Villi*, a modest work suggested to him by Ponchielli, was given at the Teatro dal Verme in Milan in 1884. Its production was an important moment in his career and the success was considerable, even if one discounts something from the tone of the telegram which he sent off to his mother after the first performance: 'Theatre packed, immense success; anticipations exceeded; 18 calls; finale of first act thrice encored.' The substantial part of it was that *Le Villi* was bought for a small sum by Messrs. Ricordi, who published it eventually, but not until Puccini's fame had been established by his subsequent works.

Le Villi in an enlarged form brought Puccini on to the stage of La Scala in the following year, but it was not until 1889 that his second opera, *Edgar*, arrived and was actually produced there. *Edgar* was a failure, the one decisive and permanent failure which Puccini ever encountered. Possibly it helped him, as many such failures have helped, to realize the necessity of making 'every stroke tell', as Weber said in another connection. At any rate, Puccini must have seen in it the error of accepting too readily a weak libretto, for he became exceedingly fastidious, and each one of the works by which he is known is the result of a personal choice of subject framed to his wishes by his librettists, of whom L. Illica and G. Giacosa have been the chief.

The first was *Manon Lescaut*, which was produced at Turin in 1893, the drama of which, like its successor, *La Bohème*, is treated rather as a series of episodes than as a whole. Considering how well known the Abbé Prevost's novel was, the operatic version might have carried this treatment further. Indeed, the attempt to remodel the story so as to make the deportation of Manon in the third act consequent upon the events of the second produces considerable incongruity. As the opera stands there is either too much or too little connection between its parts to be dramatically satisfactory. Outside Italy it had at first to contend with the popularity of Massenet's opera, but in this country at any rate it has steadily increased in popularity, and its success rests largely on the skilful musical handling of details, such as the scene of Manon's *levée*, and on the passionate love music of the last act, which Caruso first realized to the full.

From the time of the production of *Manon* onwards Puccini's most famous operas follow in a series with three to four years between each. *La Bohème*, also at Turin, came in 1896, *La Tosca* at Rome in 1900, *Madama Butterfly* at Milan in 1904. The Carl Rosa Opera Company first brought *La Bohème* to England and performed it in English a couple of years before it was produced at Covent Garden at the instigation of Mme Melba. Puccini came to England for the first performance of *The Bohemians* at the Theatre Royal in Manchester, on which occasion, it may be remarked, he was much amused by the makeshift fashion in which the brass and drums of the orchestra had to be accommodated in boxes. *La Bohème* having won its way both in London and the provinces, *La Tosca* was quickly secured and was given at Covent Garden in 1900 with Mme Ternina in the principal part. The extraordinary ill treatment which *Madama Butterfly* received from the Milanese public on its production at *La Scala* in 1904 really had very little effect on Puccini's position with the wider public. The performance under Signor Campanini had scarcely begun when it was interrupted by hisses and cries of disapproval; it was carried through in spite of continued disturbance, and at the end Puccini took the score away with him, refusing to risk a second performance there. Yet so firmly fixed was he in the estimation of the English public that the Covent Garden authorities did not hesitate to stage it in the following year with the distinguished cast (Mme Destinn and Signori Caruso and Scotti) who were its most famous interpreters.

It is on these three works that Puccini's fame most principally rests, and, while each of them possesses to the full his salient characteristics of glowing melody and strong characterization, the variety of their subject matter brings wide differences of musical treatment. There is a freshness and simplicity about *La Bohème* which does not fade with frequent repetition. *La Tosca*, at first rather looked askance at by serious musicians for the crudity of its melodrama, yet contains some of the most forcible musical moments in the whole of Puccini's work. The broad tune with which the orchestra pictures Tosca's sense of horror after the murder of Scarpia is in itself enough to proclaim Puccini's genius for emotional melody. The whole of the music of the later scenes of *Madama Butterfly*, depicting the phases of hope, fear, disillusionment, heroism, shows an insight for which neither of the previous operas prepares us.

After this there was an interval of seven years before Puccini wrote another opera. He was said to have considered a number of subjects, including the story of Marie Antoinette. When one thinks of the increasing power with which he had delineated the characters of women, it seems a pity that he turned aside from his subject. When the opportunity came of a production in America he was seized by a play of David Belasco's, which had been successful in New York, one of those hectic romances of California, in which rascality and sentiment alternate with bewildering rapidity. *La Fanciulla del West* was announced in the autumn of 1910 for simultaneous production in New York, Boston, and Chicago, and the composer went to New York to superintend the performance there, for which Mme Destinn and Caruso were engaged. In the circumstances it is hardly necessary to say that the arts of advertisement were used to the full and that the work was clamoured for in the principal opera houses of Europe. It is refreshing to find that the benefits of advertisement are, after all, comparatively short lived, for the boom given to *The Girl of the Golden West*, to quote the original title, did not blind anyone to the fact that, in spite of moments of beauty and a wealth of striking detail, it was not to be placed in the same class with its predecessors.

A still longer interval divided it from the set of three one-act operas which was completed in 1919 and which was given at Covent Garden in 1920 after performance in Italy and America. In planning his triptych, Puccini sought an opportunity to display again his power of dealing with widely different situations, involving strongly contrasted types of emotion. *Il Tabarro* is one of those pieces of sordid violence which have attracted all Italian composers since Mascagni's *Cavalleria Rusticana*. *Suor Angelica* aims at an atmosphere of religious mysticism, and *Gianni Schicchi* is caustic comedy. In the first he was doing again what he and others had already done with success. In the second he failed by mistaking a self-conscious sentiment for a real emotion. In the third he succeeded in what for him was an entirely new genre and produced a masterpiece of *opera buffa* which captivated every one; that this was the general opinion in England was shown by what happened at Covent Garden. For the first few performances the three were given in sequence, and it was pointed out that Puccini wished them to be given together; then *Suor Angelica* was dropped, and finally *Gianni Schicchi* alone remained, the places of the others being filled by performances of the Russian Ballet.

In one respect Puccini set a practical example by which other composers might profit. He always gave his personal supervision to the first productions of his works, and he never conducted them. In this way he was able to assure himself that the regular conductors had a sympathetic understanding of his musical intentions and could secure what he wanted in his absence. He was ready to acknowledge the great debt which he owed to his interpreters, both conductors and singers, and his appreciation of their efforts went hand in hand with an unerring instinct for gauging their capabilities. By writing music which it was a joy to sing he could be certain that the singer would convey his own pleasure in it to the hearers. Puccini could use his orchestra for any thing that he wanted to say, either to describe the draught by which Mimi's candle was extinguished or to enhance the first ardours of Rodolfo's love. Even in the most lurid moments of *La Tosca* and *Il Tabarro* he handled the orchestra without a sense of effort. He knew all the tricks of modern orchestration, yet rarely, save in some passages of *La Fanciulla del West*, seemed to set much store by them. His unerring sense of what would be effective in the theatre was a power shared by most composers of his country, but he employed it to finer purpose than the majority in his generation. If Puccini's was not the greatest music, at least there could never be any doubt that it was music.

RUDOLPH VALENTINO

A film 'star'

23 AUGUST 1926

MR RUDOLPH VALENTINO, one of the foremost cinema actors in the United States, died this morning from pleurisy following an operation for appendicitis, upon which peritonitis had supervened. By the death of Mr Valentino the film world loses one of its most popular 'stars', for, although he only became first known a very few years ago, his rise was remarkably rapid, and within a few months his face was familiar all over the world. He was first seen in a film in this country in *The Four Horsemen of the Apocalypse*, when it was shown in London for a long season at the Palace Theatre four years ago. His performance in this piece was probably his best, but it was not until later in the same year, when he appeared in *The Sheik*, that he became extraordinarily popular. His acting started the 'Sheik' type of film, which has remained so popular ever since. In his last production, finished just before he was taken ill and not yet seen in England, he appeared again in a similar part. This film is called *The Son of the Sheik*, and is to be shown in London next month. *The Sheik* was followed by *Blood and Sand* and *The Young Rajah*, and then, two years ago, Mr Valentino made another great popular success in the film version of *Monsieur Beaucaire*. This was first shown in London at the London Pavilion, and in it he gave a most entertaining performance. His popularity with all types of audiences continued to grow, and his last productions have proved that he shared an equal popularity with Mr Charlie Chaplin, Mr Douglas Fairbanks, and Miss Mary Pickford. His film personality was remarkable, and it is difficult to think of any other film actor who can quite take his place.

CLAUDE MONET

The great painter of light

5 DECEMBER 1926

JUDGED BY THE NATURE and extent of his influence, Claude Oscar Monet, whose death is announced on another page, was the most important artist within living memory. Others, such as Manet and Renoir, may have excelled him in personal achievement and even in the number of their evident followers, but for what may be called infective and pervasive effects upon the body of painting there is nobody to compare with him except Cézanne, whom he long outlived, and Cézanne was not his equal in accomplishment. Monet did not invent a new thing; he would hardly have had such a widespreading influence if he did; but, happening to be born at the right moment with an instinctive bent for that expression of light which both Turner and Constable had attempted, he carried it on to fulfilment and dominated the field of painting until Cézanne, inheriting his gains, recalled the attention of artists to the claims of solid earth. He may be said to have irradiated landscape painting, and the gleams penetrated into quarters where any conscious acceptance of his influence would have been hotly disclaimed.

Though he came to be associated with the North of France, Normandy in particular, Monet was actually born in Paris, in the Rue Laffitte, on November 14, 1840 – the same day as his future friend, Auguste Rodin – his mother being a member of a Lyons family. His childhood was spent at Havre, where caricatures drawn by him and exhibited in a shop window attracted the attention of Eugène Boudin, who initiated him into painting in the open air. As early as 1856 the two were exhibiting together at Rouen, and Monet always spoke of Boudin with gratitude, saying that he had 'dashed the scales from his eyes and shown him the beauties of land and sea painting'. The following year Monet went to Paris, but without immediate results, and in 1860 he left for Algeria to complete his military service in the Chasseurs d'Afrique. He returned invalided, with his instinct for light further confirmed. Back at Havre he fell in with Jongkind, the Dutch artist, who, like Boudin, may be said to have prepared the way for Impressionism, and the three of them worked together.

In 1863 Monet went again to Paris with the intention of entering the studio of Gleyre, and here he made the acquaintance of Renoir, Sisley, and other painters, who, with differences, were carrying on the tradition of the Barbizon group, Corot in particular. Monet quickly decided to work out his own salvation. He made his first appearance in the Salon of 1865 with two marine subjects – 'Pointe de la Hève' and 'Embouchure de la Seine à Honfleur'. His work at this period showed affinities with both Boudin and Jongkind, and also with Manet – a broadening of the facts under the influence of light into atmospheric values, but without any decided attempt to realize light itself on the canvas. Its characters may be seen in 'Plage de Trouville', in the Courtauld collection at the Tate Gallery, though that picture was not painted until 1870.

Monet's first attempt to paint a large landscape with figures in the open air bore the same title as a famous picture by Manet, 'Déjeuner sur l'herbe'. It introduced him to Courbet and the two men became fast friends. An amusing story is told of a visit paid by them to Alexandre Dumas the Elder, who was stopping in Havre. This was in 1866, when Monet's 'Camille', afterwards known as 'Dame en Vert', was attracting attention in the Salon. Neither of the artists had met Dumas, but Courbet insisted that they should call. At first they were told that Dumas was not at home, but Courbet said: 'Tell him that it is Courbet who asks for him; he will be in.' Dumas came out in shirt and trousers; he and Courbet embraced with tears; and the two painters were invited to lunch, cooked by Dumas himself, who afterwards paraded them through the streets of Havre in his carriage.

The following year Monet's 'Women in a Garden' was rejected by the Salon, and its exhibition in a shop window brought him the acquaintance of Manet and introduced him to the group of writers, including Zola, who were then championing Manet and his friends. It was between this date and the outbreak of the Franco-Prussian War that the informal association of artists began which, consolidated by the attitude of the Salon, led to the Impressionist school. They included Monet, Camille Pissarro, Manet, Degas, Renoir, Sisley, Cézanne, Berthe Morisot, who was Manet's sister-in-law, and Mary Cassatt among others. Not all these artists were Impressionists, as the word came to be understood, but they had common sympathies in refusing to be bound by authority.

Visit to England

During the siege of Paris, in 1870–71, Monet and Pissarro paid a visit to England, and there can be little doubt that the acquaintance with Turner and Constable which they made then had considerable influence in confirming their aims – just as the exhibition of Constable's 'Hay Wain' in Paris had profoundly affected an earlier generation of French painters. It was in 1874 that the word 'Impressionism' was first coined, and by accident. Under the title of 'Société anonyme des artistes peintres, sculpteurs et graveurs du 15 avril au 15 mai 1874', the artists already named, with others, arranged a collective exhibition at Nadar's, in the Boulevard des Capucines. Among the works by Monet there was one entitled 'Sunrise, an Impression', merely by way of description. The word 'Impressionists' was seized upon as a term of ridicule for the whole group, and though many of them had nothing in common with Monet they cheerfully accepted it as a battle-cry. Financially the exhibition was a disaster, the works being sold by auction the following year at prices averaging about 100 francs. It was at this time that Manet, who was well off, suggested to Duvet a way of helping Monet, then very poor, by buying ten of his pictures between them for 1,000 francs without disclosing the purchasers.

The Impressionists, as they were now called, continued to hold exhibitions, being supported by Durand-Ruel and other dealers with the courage of their convictions, and little by little, with the aid of intelligent criticism, hostility was overcome and the aims of Monet and his associates began to be understood. It was not, however, until 1889, when he shared an exhibition with Rodin at the Georges Petit Gallery, that Monet had a substantial success, his first one-man show in 1880 having been a failure.

With his studies of the Gare Saint Lazare in the third group exhibition of 1877, Monet had already begun the series of the same or similar subjects – railway stations, cathedrals, hay-ricks, river banks, poplars, water-lilies – under different conditions of light which were to establish his fame, and from 1889 onward his artistic reputation steadily increased. In 1883 he had settled at Giverny, in the department of the Eure, Normandy, and he remained there for the rest of his life, with occasional visits abroad, quietly and happily producing his pictures. Monet never received any honour from the State, though a tardy offer was made to him of a seat on the Académie des Beaux Arts, which he declined, and such pictures of his as are to be found in French national collections, at the Luxembourg Museum and elsewhere, are gifts or bequests. He himself presented to the French nation a series of 19 'Water-Lily' paintings, and in 1923, at the age of 83, in the company of his old friend, M. Clemenceau, who was a supporter of the Impressionists in the stormy days of the 'seventies, Monet visited the Tuileries Gardens to inspect the building which was being specially constituted to contain them.

London Views

His work has been frequently shown in London, at the Goupil Gallery, the Leicester Galleries, the Lefèvre Galleries, the French Gallery, the Independent Gallery, and elsewhere, and some years ago an association of English and foreign artists was formed in London called the 'Monarro Group', combining the names of Monet and Pissarro as heads of the movement with which they found themselves in sympathy. In connection with Monet's visits to England his views of the Thames, including 'Waterloo Bridge' and 'The Houses of Parliament', must not be forgotten. He is represented in the Modern Foreign Section of the Tate Gallery by two pictures only: 'Plage de Trouville', painted in 1870, purchased in 1924 by the Trustees of the Courtauld Fund; and 'Vetheuil: Sunshine and Snow', painted in 1881, included in the Lane Bequest of 1917.

Monet's artistic progress may be described as the more and more purely æsthetic organization of his technical conquest of light and atmosphere. He did not follow the so-called neo-Impressionists into the formal dotting which was the logical outcome, or scientific application, of his own system of laying strokes or touches of pure colour side by side, eliminating all browns from the palette, but contented himself with a method which produced the effects he desired; and it was the æsthetic value, the poetry, rather than the mere realization of light that inspired him. Nor, though he was a pioneer in the discovery of 'colour in shadow', was he a decorative colourist by intention; he painted colour for the sake of light rather than light for the sake of colour. His work has been called lacking in design, but the charge cannot be supported. It stands to reason that if an artist is designing in atmospheric values, in veils of light, the design will not be so emphatic, so easily grasped, as if he were designing in solid forms, but nobody can look with attention at a picture by Monet and regard it as a mere representation of the facts and conditions. In this respect his work might well be compared to the music of his countryman Claude Debussy, in which, under an atmospheric shimmer, the melodies are not so immediately recognizable as they are in the works of Bach or Beethoven, but are nevertheless present to the attentive ear.

At the same time it must be allowed that the aim and methods of Monet were better adapted to some subjects than others, and with due appreciation of his cathedrals, railway stations, and Venetian scenes, we find his happiest expression in those river subjects in which a leafy garland of poplars reflects the influence of sky and water, such as the beautiful 'Poplars on the Epte', in the National Gallery of Scotland, Edinburgh, or in the arabesques of water lilies. A fair description of the emotional effect of a typical work of Monet at his best would be that of a 'sunny smile'. It was inevitable that after so much trafficking in airy regions painting should come to earth again, and the concern for plastic volumes and a more emphatic design instituted by Cézanne and other leaders of the movement conveniently known as Post-Impressionism was as natural a sequence to the Impressionism of Monet, as is the desire for physical exercise after loitering in a garden. But, so far as it is humanly possible to judge, Monet left a gleam upon the surface of painting which will never entirely disappear. Monet has been the subject of many writings, including an exhaustive study by M. Camille Mauclair.

EMMELINE PANKHURST

A pioneer of woman suffrage

14 JUNE 1928

MRS EMMELINE PANKHURST, whose death is announced on another page, was born in Manchester on July 14, 1858. In her early childhood she was brought into close touch with those who had inherited the spirit of the Manchester reformers. Her father, Mr Robert Goulden, a calico-printer, was keenly interested in the reform question and the dawn of the movement for woman's suffrage; her grandfather nearly lost his life in the Peterloo franchise riots in 1819. At the age of 13, soon after she had been taken to her first woman suffrage meeting by her mother, she went to school in Paris, where she found a girl-friend of her own way of thinking in the daughter of Henri Rochefort. In 1879 she married Dr R. M. Pankhurst, a man many years older than herself. An intimate friend of John Stuart Mill and an able lawyer, he shared and helped to mould his wife's political views. She served with him on the committee which promoted the Married Women's Property Act, and was at the same time a member of the Manchester Women's Suffrage Committee. In 1889 she helped in forming the Women's Franchise League, which, however, was discontinued after a few years. She remained a Liberal until 1892, when she joined the Independent Labour Party. After being defeated for the Manchester School Board, she was elected at the head of the poll for the board of guardians and served for five years. When her husband died, in 1898, she was left not well off, and with three girls and a boy to bring up. Accordingly she found work as registrar of births and deaths at Chorlton-on-Medlock, but her propaganda activities were considered inconsistent with her official position and she resigned.

In 1903 her interest in the cause of woman suffrage was reawakened by the enthusiasm of her daughter Christabel and she formed the Women's Social and Political Union, the first meeting of which was held in her house in Manchester in October of that year. Two years later the militant movement was started as the immediate result of the treatment received by Miss Christabel Pankhurst and Miss Annie Kenney, two members of the union who endeavoured to question Sir Edward Grey on the prospects of woman suffrage, at a political meeting held in Manchester. In 1906 Mrs Pankhurst and her union began a series of pilgrimages to the House of Commons, which resulted in conflicts with the police and the imprisonment of large numbers of the members. In October, 1906, she was present at the first of these demonstrations, when 11 women were arrested. In January, 1908, she was pelted with eggs und rolled in the mud during the Mid-Devon election at Newton Abbot, and a month later she was arrested when carrying a petition to the Prime Minister at the House of Commons, but was released after undergoing five of the six weeks' imprisonment to which she was sentenced. Some months later, in October, a warrant was issued for her arrest, together with Miss Pankhurst and Mrs Drummond, for inciting the public to 'rush' the House of Commons. During her three months' imprisonment in Holloway Gaol she led a revolt of her followers against the rules of prison discipline, demanding that they should be treated as political prisoners. In 1909, the year in which the 'hunger strike' and 'forcible feeding' were first practised in connection with these cases, she was once more arrested at the door of the House of Commons, and after her trial, and pending an appeal founded on the Bill of Rights and a statute of Charles, dealing with petitions to the Crown, she went to America and Canada on a lecturing tour; two days before her return her fine was paid by some unknown person, so that she did not go to prison.

As soon, however, as she was back in England, she again devoted her energies to the encouragement of the campaign of pin-pricks and violence to which she was committed and by which she hoped to further the cause which she had at heart. In 1912, for her own share in those lawless acts, she was twice imprisoned, but in each case served only five weeks of the periods of two months and nine months – for conspiracy to break windows – to which she was sentenced. A year later she was arrested on the more serious charge of inciting to commit a felony, in connection with the blowing-up of Mr Lloyd George's country house at Walton. In spite of the ability with which she conducted her own defence the jury found her guilty – though with a strong recommendation to mercy – and she was sentenced by Mr Justice Lush to three years' penal servitude. On the tenth day of the hunger strike which she at once began (to be followed later on by a thirst strike) she was temporarily released, under the terms of the measure introduced by Mr McKenna commonly known as the Cat and Mouse Act, because of the condition of extreme weakness to which she was reduced. At the end of five months, during which she was several times released and rearrested, she went to Paris, and then to America (after a detention of 2½ days on Ellis Island), having served not quite three weeks of her three years' sentence. On her return to England the same cat-and-mouse policy was resumed by the authorities – and accompanied by more and more violent outbreaks on the part of Mrs Pankhurst's militant followers – until at last, in the summer of 1914, after she had been arrested and released nine or ten times on the one charge, it was finally abandoned, and the remainder of her term of three years' penal servitude allowed to lapse.

Whether, but for the outbreak of the Great War, the militant movement would have resulted in the establishment of woman suffrage is a point on which opinions will probably always differ. But there is no question that the coming of the vote, which Mrs Pankhurst claimed as the right of her sex, was sensibly hastened by the general feeling that after the extraordinary courage and devotion shown by women of all classes in the nation's emergency there must be no risk of a renewal of the feminist strife of the days of militancy. When the War was over it was remembered that on its outbreak Mrs Pankhurst, with her daughter Christabel and the rest of the militant leaders, declared an immediate suffrage truce and gave herself up to the claims of national service and devoted her talents as a speaker to the encouragement of recruiting, first in this country and then in the United States. A visit to Russia in 1917, where she formed strong opinions on the evils of Bolshevism, was followed by a residence of some years in Canada and afterwards in Bermuda for the benefit of her health. Since she came home, at the end of 1925, she had taken a deep interest in public life and politics, and had some thoughts of standing for Parliament, though she declined Lady Astor's offer to give up to her her seat in Plymouth.

Whatever views may be held as to the righteousness of the cause to which she gave her life and the methods by which she tried to bring about its achievement, there can be no doubt about the singleness of her aim and the remarkable strength and nobility of her character. She was inclined to be autocratic and liked to go her own way. But that was because she was honestly convinced that her own way was the only way. The end that she had in view was the emancipation of women from what she believed, with passionate sincerity, to be a condition of harmful subjection. She was convinced that she was working for the salvation of the world, as well as of her sex. She was a public speaker of very remarkable force and ability, with a power of stimulating and swaying her audience possessed by no other woman of her generation, and was regarded with devoted admiration by many people outside the members of her union. With all her autocracy and her grievous mistakes, she was a humble-minded, large-hearted, unselfish woman, of the stuff of which martyrs are made. Quite deliberately, and having counted the cost, she undertook a warfare against the forces of law and order the strain of which her slight and fragile body was unable to bear. It will be remembered of her that whatever peril and suffering she called on followers to endure, up to the extreme indignity of forcible feeding, she herself was ready to face, and did face, with unfailing courage and endurance of body and mind.

D. H. LAWRENCE

A writer of genius

2 MARCH 1930

DAVID HERBERT LAWRENCE, whose death is announced on another page, was born at Eastwood, near Nottingham, on September 11, 1885. His novel *Sons and Lovers* and his play *The Widowing of Mrs Holroyd* are at least so far biographical as to tell the world that his father was a coalminer and his mother a woman of finer grain. At the age of 12 the boy won a county council scholarship; but the sum was scarcely enough to pay the fees at the Nottingham High School and the fares to and fro. At 16 he began to earn his living as a clerk. When his ill-health put an end to that, he taught in a school for miners' boys.

At 19 he won another scholarship, of which he could not avail himself, as he had no money, to pay the necessary entrance fee; but at 21 he went to Nottingham University College, and after two years there he came to London and took up teaching again. It was in these years that he wrote, under the name of Lawrence H. Davidson, some books on history. He had begun also the writing of fiction, and his first novel, *The White Peacock*, was published about a month after his mother's death had robbed him of his best and dearest friend.

Sons and Lovers, published when he was 28, brought him fame. Many years of poverty were to pass before his work began to make him financially comfortable; and even then the collapse of a publishing firm in America deprived him of some of the fruits of his labours. But this revolt against society which fills his books had its counterpart in his life, in his travels, and especially in his attempt to found, in 1923, an intellectual and community settlement in New Mexico.

Undoubtedly he had genius. He could create characters which are even obtrusively real. His ruthless interpretation of certain sides of the nature of women was recognized by some women to be just. Every one of his novels, as well as his books of travel, contains passages of description so fine that they command the admiration of people whom much of his work disgusts. His powers range from a rich simplicity, a delicacy almost like that of Mr W. H. Davies, to turbulent clangour, and from tenderness to savage irony and gross brutality. There was that in his intellect which might have made him one of England's greatest writers, and did indeed make him the writer of some things worthy of the best of English literature. But as time went on and his disease took firmer hold, his rage and his fear grew upon him. He confused decency with hypocrisy, and honesty with the free and public use of vulgar words. At once fascinated and horrified by physical passion, he paraded his disgust and fear in the trappings of a showy masculinity. And, not content with words, he turned to painting in order to exhibit more clearly still his contempt for all reticence.

It was inevitable (though it was regrettable) that such a man should come into conflict with the law over his novel *The Rainbow*, over some manuscripts sent through the post to his agent in London and over an exhibition of his paintings. But a graver cause for regret is that the author of *Sons and Lovers*, of *Amores*, and the other books of poems, of *Aaron's Rod*, the short stories published as *The Prussian Officer*, *Ladybird*, and *Kangaroo* should have missed the place among the very best which his genius might have won.

In 1914 Lawrence married Frieda von Richthofen, who survives him. He left no children.

* * *

NELLIE MELBA

A great prima donna

23 FEBRUARY 1931

MELBA, to use the name by which she was universally known until the prefix of Dame Nellie was attached to it, whose death we regret to announce this morning, was born near Melbourne in 1859, and began her career as Helen Porter Mitchell. Her Scottish parents, who had settled in Australia, had themselves some musical proclivities. But it was not until after her early marriage to Mr Charles Armstrong that it became clear that her gifts must be taken seriously.

It was largely by her own efforts that she came to England in 1885 with the intention of cultivating her voice. When she arrived the experts to whom she appealed in London did not realize her possibilities. It is amusing to record that she was refused work in the Savoy Opera Company by Sullivan, though probably he did her and the world at large the greatest service by his refusal. She went to Paris, and to Mme Mathilde Marchesi belongs the credit of having instantly recognized that, to quote her own phrase, she 'had found a star'.

A year of study and of close companionship with this great teacher was all that was needed to give Nellie Armstrong a brilliant *début* at 'La Monnaie' in Brussels as Mme Melba. She made her first appearance there on October 13, 1887, in the part of Gilda in *Rigoletto*. Her second part was Violetta in *La Traviata*, so that from the first she was identified with the earlier phases of Verdi, in which she has been pre-eminent ever since. Although, contrary to the traditions of the Brussels theatre, she sang in Italian, she aroused such enthusiasm that when a little later she was to sing *Lakmé*, and the question arose as to whether her French accent was sufficiently secure, the composer Délibes, is said to have exclaimed, 'Qu'elle chante *Lakmé* en français, en italien, en allemand, en anglais, ou en chinois, cela m'est égal, mais qu'elle la chante.'

Her first appearance at Covent Garden on May 24, 1888, in *Lucia di Lammermoor*, was a more qualified success. Curiously enough, she was more commended at first for some supposed dramatic power than for the only two things which have ever really mattered in her case – the exquisite voice and the perfect use of it. From London she returned to the more congenial atmosphere of Brussels, and in the following year, 1889, proceeded to the conquest of Paris, where she triumphed as Ophélie in Ambroise Thomas's *Hamlet*. In Paris Mme Melba had the advantage of studying the parts of Marguerite in *Faust* and of Juliette with Gounod, and she took part in the first performance of *Roméo et Juliette* in French at Covent Garden in 1889.

From this time onward Mme Melba had only to visit one country after another to be acclaimed. From St Petersburg, where she sang before the Tsar in 1891, to Chicago, where in 1893 her singing with the de Reszkes was one of the features of the 'World's Fair', the tale of her triumphs was virtually the same. But from the musical point of view a more important episode was her prolonged visit to Italy between these two events. Here she met the veteran Verdi and the young Puccini. Verdi helped her in the study of Aïda and of Desdemona (*Otello*). She made the acquaintance of Puccini's *Manon*, but *La Bohème*, the only one of his operas with which she was to be identified, was not yet written. Another young composer who begged leave to be presented was Leoncavallo. She sang Nedda in the first London performance of *I Pagliacci* a little later.

Mme Melba's early American appearances recall her few experiments with Wagner. She sang Elisabeth in *Tannhäuser* at the Metropolitan Opera House, New York, during her first season there, and it was later in America that she made her single appearance as Brünnhilde. She had previously sung Elsa (*Lohengrin*) at Covent Garden, but she quite rightly realized that Wagner's music was not for her. The only pity, when one recalls her repertory, is that either lack of opportunity or of inclination prevented her from turning to Mozart instead.

Her actual repertory amounted to 25 operas, of which, however, only some 10 parts are those which will be remembered as her own. *La Bohème* was the last of

Dame Nellie Melba in one of her last appearances in England, in the British National Opera production of Gounod's *Faust*, 1923.

these to be added, and she first sang in it at Philadelphia in 1898, having studied it with the composer in Italy earlier in the year. She was so much in love with the music that she would not rest until she had brought it to London, and it was largely by her personal influence that it was accepted at Covent Garden. Indeed, she persuaded the management to stage *La Bohème* with the promise to sing some favourite scena from her repertory in addition on each night that she appeared in it until the success of the opera was assured. She kept the promise, though the rapid success of the opera soon justified her faith. To most of the present generation of opera-goers 'Melba nights' meant *La Bohème* nights, and, for several seasons before the War and when Covent Garden reopened after it, there could not be too many of them for the public. She bade farewell to Covent Garden on June 8, 1926, when, in the presence of the King and Queen, she sang in acts from *Roméo et Juliette*, *Otello*, and *La Bohème*. Actually her last appearance in London was at a charity concert in 1929.

It is difficult now to realize that 30 years or so ago *La Bohème* seemed to offer few opportunities for the special characteristics of Mme Melba's art, intimately associated as it then was with Donizetti, the earlier Verdi, and Gounod. But those characteristics in reality had full play in all music based on the expression of a pure vocal *cantilena*, and could appear in the simply held note at the end of the first act of

La Bohème as completely as in the *fioritura* of 'Caro nome' or 'The Jewel Song'. The essence of her power was due to such an ease in the production of pure tone in all parts of the voice and in all circumstances that there was no barrier between the music and the listener.

It is unnecessary to enlarge on the personal popularity of Melba here, or the almost passionate devotion which she inspired among her own countrymen on the various occasions when she revisited Australia. Her book of reminiscences, *Melodies and Memories* (1925), was disappointing, for it contained too little about her methods and experiences. She was generous in giving her services for good causes, and her work for War charities is remembered in the title conferred in 1918. She was then created DBE, and GBE in 1927.

* * *

SIR EDWARD ELGAR

The laureate of English music

23 FEBRUARY 1934

THE NUMBER OF musicians of whom it can safely be said that the general public needs no explanation of their importance and asks for no justification of the place which their fellows accord them is small. Among composers this country has possessed two in the last century – Sullivan and Elgar. Of these the case of Elgar, who died yesterday at his home at Worcester at the age of 76, is the more remarkable because his genius was devoted to the larger forms of the musical art with which the ordinary man is supposed to sympathize least readily – the symphony, the concerto, and the oratorio. He never associated himself with the theatre in any close way; he never held any dominating official position in the musical life of the country, he rather stood aloof from institutions of any sort. Through nearly half his working life he was entirely unknown; during the remainder he was unhesitatingly accepted as our musical laureate.

In these days when the term 'British composer' is on everyone's lips it is worth while remarking that Elgar by descent, upbringing, and education was entirely English. His father, a native of Dover, had settled in Worcester, where he kept a music shop and was organist to the Roman Catholic church of St George. His mother, Ann Greening, came from Herefordshire.

Edward William Elgar (he entirely dropped the second name in later years) was born at Broadheath, a village about four miles from Worcester, on June 2, 1857, and spent his youth in the typically English environment of the cathedral town and its surrounding country. Much has been said of Elgar's upbringing as a member of the Roman Catholic Church and of the inspiration which it brought to his greatest choral work, *The Dream of Gerontius*, all of which is natural and true. But Elgar used to resent the idea that these influences in any way cut him off from others. As a boy he was constantly in and out of the cathedral listening to the music of its daily services and drawing many of his earliest and most treasured experiences from them. The Three Choirs Festivals at Worcester were sources of the most vivid delight to him. Indeed, it was characteristic of him at all times, that he loved to show himself knowledgeable on whatever others were inclined to think might lie a little outside his sphere of interest.

Early Compositions

Young Elgar had no systematic musical education, but he entered into all the musical activities of his father, which were many. He played the organ at St George's, and, indeed, succeeded his father as regular organist there; he played the bassoon in a wind quintet (which perhaps accounts for the bassoon solo in the 'Enigma' Variations No. 111), but more particularly the violin, his thorough knowledge of which certainly had something to do with the brilliant passage-work of the famous concerto. He took an active part in all local music, particularly the concerts of the Worcester Glee Club, whose members gave him a bow for his violin in recognition of his services. Above all, he composed constantly, and some of the music now known in the orchestral suites, *The Wand of Youth*, dates from his boyhood. Pieces for violin and piano, part-songs, a motet, slight essays for the orchestra, are chief among such early works as survive. The interesting thing about them is that among much that is obvious and some that is trite one comes across turns of melody and harmony which are unmistakably the voice of Elgar. Even the first phrase of 'Salut d'Amour' must be allowed to be one of them.

Elgar was 32 years of age when he married, in 1889, Caroline Alice, only daughter of General Sir Henry Gee Roberts. This is hardly the place to write particularly of his wife's influence on his career, but beyond question her unfaltering faith in him both as man and as artist sustained him through all the disappointments of his isolated position and enabled him to hold the difficult course towards success to which his helm was set.

In one respect his marriage rather emphasized the difficulties, for it caused him to live in London for the first time, and to discover how unready were musicians, publishers, and concert givers to take any interest in his music. The neglect of genius is always a fruitful theme for commentators who are wise after the event. Elgar was a genius, he lived two years in London unrecognized; these commentators cry 'shame!' but it is difficult to see what there was to recognize between 1889 and 1891. He had written none of the great works which have made him famous since. It may be remarked that Mr Bernard Shaw's recently published *Music in London, 1890–1894* does not contain the name of Elgar. True his overture 'Froissart' was produced at the Worcester Festival in 1890, and some people realized that here was something fresh and original.

Festival Works

In 1891 Elgar returned to the West Country and settled at Malvern, where he began his serious work in the composition of a number of pieces for choir and orchestra which were produced at various festivals in the succeeding years. *The Black Knight*, characteristically described as 'a symphony for chorus and orchestra', came out in 1893. *Scenes from the Saga of King Olaf, Scenes from the Bavarian Highlands* and an oratorio, *The Light of Life*, all appeared in 1896, the first at the North Staffordshire Musical Festival, the other two at Worcester. Here indeed was proof positive of the new voice in music, more than a hint of that mystical imagination, that sensitiveness to tone-colour, and that elusive yet individual gift of melody which were to seize his hearers so powerfully a little later. A patriotic cantata, *The Banner of St George*, for the Diamond Jubilee year, and *Caractacus*, written for the Leeds Festival of 1898, emphasized another side of Elgar's musical character, an alert and nervous energy, the love of pageantry, the discovery of the poetry underlying external splendour. One finds here the Elgar of the 'Pomp and Circumstance' marches, the Coronation march, and the Scherzo of the Second Symphony.

The invitation to write for the Leeds Festival (this was the last festival conducted by Sullivan) was in Elgar's case, as in that of several other English composers, the sign that he had 'arrived'. A still more decisive landmark in his career was the production by Richter of the 'Enigma' Variations for orchestra in London in the following year, and it is indeed difficult to understand how, amid these signal proofs of his qualities, *The Dream of Gerontius* could have missed fire as it did at Birmingham in 1900. No doubt its very originality stood in its way. Choral singers accustomed to solid oratorio choruses could not understand these paeans of angels and frenzied outcries of demons. It was held to be extremely difficult. Common opinion declared that while it had beautiful moments it was a failure as a whole. That opinion has now been reversed. Every one realizes that *The Dream of Gerontius* has some perilously weak moments, but that as a whole it is one of the great imaginative creations of musical art.

The failure at Birmingham, however, was a step towards Elgar's recognition outside his own country. A. J. Jaeger, an early enthusiast for Elgar's music, and at that time reader to Messrs. Novello and Co., was instrumental in getting *Gerontius* accepted for performance at the Lower Rhine Festival at Düsseldorf, where it was most enthusiastically acclaimed. The approval of a keenly critical German public led to its revival at Worcester in 1902, with the result that everyone knows. Birmingham made amends by producing the two companion oratorios, *The Apostles* and *The Kingdom*, at its two subsequent festivals (1903 and 1906); the London Choral Society was formed to give the first public performance of *The Dream of Gerontius* in London (1903), and a special festival consisting entirely of Elgar's music was arranged at Covent Garden in 1904. In the following year he paid his first visit to the United States, where his works were received with enthusiasm.

The Symphonies: Public Acclaim

With these triumphs the first period of Elgar's success as a composer of choral and orchestral works on the largest scale was completed. A second and equally brilliant instrumental period was to begin with the production of the first symphony in 1908. The Variations and several concert overtures, notably the popular 'Cockaigne' and 'In the South', together with the beautiful 'Introduction and Allegro' for strings, had contributed to the assurance that Elgar would reach his most individual expression in some work of the symphonic type; but he was even slower than Brahms in committing himself to a symphony. When the first symphony in A flat was announced for a concert of the Hallé Orchestra under Richter at Manchester excitement ran high. The broad melody with which it opens, the restless surge of its first *allegro*, the delicate merging of the *scherzo* into the slow movement and the triumphant progress of the *finale* to an apotheosis of the opening theme, would have carried away an audience less thrilled with expectancy than was that which crowded the Free Trade Hall on December 3, 1908.

Never has a symphony become so instantly 'the rage' with the ordinary British public as did this. For some time the regular orchestras of London could not play it often enough, special concerts were arranged for it, enterprising commercialists even engaged orchestras to play it in their lounges and palm courts as an attraction to their winter sales of underwear. The 'boom' was as absurd as such things usually are, and as short-lived, but it was based on something real. Here at last the public had found a composer whom experts acknowledged to be a master and whom they could understand. Elgar had caught the ear of the public for big music, apart from words or voice or drama.

That the violin concerto produced by Kreisler in 1910 should have been received in the same spirit is less remarkable, for the solo work has all the advantage of personal virtuosity which the symphony lacks. Both it and the second symphony in E flat, dedicated to the memory of King Edward VII, were felt by musicians to be of a finer fibre than the first, but the quiet, reflective ending of the second symphony was in itself sufficient to prevent the work being sought for as the first had been. The majestic funeral march of this symphony and the lofty but restrained dignity of the *finale* make it rank very high, however, in the estimation of musicians.

The War and After

It is not surprising that a period of comparative unproductiveness should have followed on these years. *The Music Makers*, a short choral work of a sentimental cast, in which themes from all Elgar's chief works were freely quoted, rather emphasized his decline in energy. One further orchestral work, the symphonic poem 'Falstaff', however, showed that his invention was by no means exhausted. The War came, and various *pièces d'occasion*, sincerely felt and fervently expressed, occupied him. Such were the music to Cammaerts's poem 'Carillon' and three commemorative odes (Laurence Binyon), of which 'For the Fallen' was the most impressive. He turned also to the composition of chamber music, and brought out together several works of that class, a violin sonata of rather unequal texture, a delicate string quartet, and a fine quintet for piano and strings. With these came in 1919 the concerto for violoncello, which though scored for a normally full orchestra has more in common with the intimate mood of the chamber works than with that of his big orchestral period.

In the spring of 1920 the death of Lady Elgar broke the composer's life. For some time he lived very much in retirement; but among the few occasions on which he was willing to make a public appearance were always the Three Choirs Festivals of his native West Country. But for him those festivals might not have been restored after the War, and certainly could never have enjoyed the prosperity of the last decade without the attraction of Elgar's music given under his own direction. In 1924 the King appointed him to the traditional office, without specific duties, of Master of the King's Musick.

There was presently some talk of his finishing the trilogy of oratorios begun with *The Apostles*, possibly for a Gloucester festival, but that scheme did not mature. A few minor compositions, however, were thrown off, and in the summer of 1932 Elgar mentioned casually in conversation the existence in his desk of a Third Symphony. He was persuaded to promise it to the BBC Orchestra, and it was announced for production this year. The Third Symphony, however, was not in his desk, but in his head, when he spoke of it, and, like many a great composer before him, he spoke of it as 'practically written' when he had made only a few sketches. Though Elgar made considerable progress with it after the offer of the BBC was accepted, ill-health last year prevented him from bringing it into a condition from which it could be finished by anyone else. During his last illness he spoke of his anxiety lest an attempt should be made by another hand to finish his work. His wishes in regard to the fragments must be respected. There is not a single movement which is near completion, though some passages have been fully scored.

Elgar was a man of many interests outside music, and as years increased they tended to absorb more of his time and attention. He loved travel, experimental chemistry, heraldry, literature, and the racecourse. Sometimes he seemed to take a whimsical pleasure in persuading himself (though he could never persuade others) that these were the serious preoccupations of his life and that the writing of symphonies was only a frivolous hobby. He was fond of saying that he knew very little about music, was not particularly interested in the performances of his works, and never read what the papers said of them. This sometimes seemed an affectation, but was really an armour of defence. He suffered much from the adulation of indiscriminate admirers and often yearned to get out of the limelight at the very moment when he deliberately walked into it. He was like his music, essentially simple and spontaneous, though the simplicity might be occasionally clouded, by decorative details. Indeed it was his power of expressing himself in his music which made so extraordinarily direct an appeal. Through all the diversity of the subjects he treated the same mind speaks. A tune of two bars or a progression of two chords is enough to reveal him. It is impossible to imagine him writing like anyone else or even purposely maintaining a disguise through a page of score.

Many Honours

Elgar received many honours both at home and abroad. He was knighted in 1904 by King Edward, and on the occasion of King George's coronation the Order of Merit was conferred on him, a distinction never previously bestowed on a musician. In 1928 he was made KCVO, in 1931 he was created a baronet, and he was promoted to GCVO last year. The University of Cambridge led the way in the many offers of academic distinctions, *honoris causa*. It was at the instance of Stanford that Elgar became a Doctor of Music of Cambridge on November 22, 1900. Academic institutions of France, Italy, Belgium, Holland, Sweden, and the United States of America have paid him their several tributes. But the greatest tribute is the extent to which his music has travelled to foreign countries and has been performed by artists of the first rank. While there have been plenty of critics able to discover that his music is not a thousand things which the ideal symphony or the ideal oratorio ought to be, Elgar has been everywhere appreciated as one of the most individual composers of modern times, and distinguished from many of his contemporaries in the fact that music for him was always first and foremost beautiful sound.

Sir Edward Elgar leaves an only daughter, Carice Irene, who was married to Mr S. H. Blake in 1922.

MARIE CURIE

The discoverer of radium

4 JULY 1934

MME CURIE, whose death we announce with regret on another page, had a world-wide reputation as the most distinguished woman investigator of our times. Her claim to fame rests primarily on her researches in connection with the radioactive bodies and particularly for her discovery and separation of the new element radium, which showed radiating properties to a marked degree. This was a discovery of the first importance, for it provided scientific men with a powerful source of radiation which has been instrumental in extending widely our knowledge not only of radioactivity but of the structure of atoms in general. Radium has also found an extensive application in hospitals for therapeutic purposes, and particularly for the treatment of cancerous growths by the action of the penetrating radiation emitted spontaneously from this element.

Marie Sklodowska, as she was before her marriage, was born on November 7, 1867, at Warsaw, and received her education there. She early showed a deep interest in science, and went to Paris to attend lectures in the Sorbonne. She had small financial resources, and had to teach in schools to earn sufficient money to pay her expenses. In 1895 she married Pierre Curie, a young scientist of great promise, who had already made several notable discoveries in magnetism and in the physics of crystals. Mme Curie continued her scientific work in collaboration with her husband, but the direction of their work was changed as the result of the famous discovery of Henri Becquerel in 1896, who found that the element uranium showed the surprising property of emitting penetrating types of radiation, which blackened a photographic plate and discharged an electrified body.

Examination of Pitchblende
Mme Curie made further investigations of this remarkable property using the electric method as a method of analysis. She showed that the radioactivity of uranium was an atomic property, as it depended only on the amount of uranium present and was unaffected by the combination of uranium with other elements. She also observed the striking fact that the uranium minerals from which uranium was separated showed an activity four to five times the amount to be expected from the uranium present. She correctly concluded that there must be present in uranium minerals another substance or substances far more active than uranium.

With great boldness she undertook the laborious work of the chemical examination of the radioactive mineral pitchblende, and discovered a new strongly active substance which she named polonium, after the country of her birth. Later she discovered another new element, allied in chemical properties to barium, which she happily named radium. This element is present in minerals only in about one part in 3,000,000 compared with uranium, and shows radioactive properties more than a million times that of an equal weight of uranium. The Austrian Government presented Mme Curie with the radioactive residues necessary for the separation of radium in quantity, and she was in this way able to obtain sufficient material to determine the atomic weight and physical and chemical properties of the new element.

The importance of this discovery was at once recognized by the scientific world. In 1903 the Davy Medal of the Royal Society was awarded jointly to Professor and Mme Curie, while in 1904 they shared a Nobel Prize with Henri Becquerel. After the death of Pierre Curie in a street accident in Paris in 1906 Mme Curie was awarded in 1911 the Nobel Prize in Chemistry for the discovery and isolation of the element radium. In 1906 she was appointed to a special Chair in the Sorbonne and was the first woman to obtain this distinction. Later a special Radium Institute, called the Pierre Curie Institute, was founded for investigations in radioactivity, and Mme Curie became the first director. She held this post at the time of her death.

Classes at the Sorbonne

In the course of the last 20 years this institute has been an important centre of research, where students of many nationalities have carried out investigations under her supervision. Mme Curie was a clear and inspiring lecturer, and her classes at the Sorbonne were widely attended. Her scientific work was all of a high order. She was a careful and accurate experimenter, and showed marked power of critical judgment in interpreting scientific facts. She retained an enthusiastic interest in her science throughout her life, and was a regular attendant at international conferences, taking an active and valuable part in scientific discussions.

She had a deep interest in the application of radium for therapeutic work both in France and abroad, and during the War actively helped in this work. She was twice invited to visit the United States and was received with acclamation, while the women of that country presented her with a gram of radium, to allow her to extend her researches. In 1922 she was appointed a member of the International Committee for Intellectual Cooperation of the League of Nations and took an active part in their deliberations.

Mme Curie left two children. The elder, Irene, early showed marked scientific ability and married a co-worker in the Radium Institute, M. Joliot. It was a source of great satisfaction and pride to Mme Curie in her later years to follow the splendid researches made by her daughter and her husband, for they have made notable contributions to our knowledge of neutrons and transformations. During the present year, they observed that a number of elements became radioactive by bombardment with the particles from radium, and have thus opened up a new method for study of the transformation of the atoms of matter.

The many friends of Mme Curie of all nations, and the scientific world as a whole, will greatly lament the removal of one who was held in such great honour for her splendid discoveries in science, and one who by strength of character and personality left a deep impression on all those who met her.

* * *

SIGMUND FREUD

Psycho-analysis

23 SEPTEMBER 1939

PROFESSOR SIGMUND FREUD, MD, originator of the science of psycho-analysis, died at his son's London home at Hampstead on Saturday night at the age of 83. From 1902 until recently he was Professor of Neurology in the University of Vienna. When the Germans violated Austria last year he was compelled to fly to England, where he had lived ever since.

Freud was one of the most challenging figures in modern medicine. Indeed, though his work was primarily medical, there is something incongruous in speaking of him as a doctor. Rather he was a philosopher, using the methods of science to achieve therapeutic ends. Philosophy, science, and medicine all paid him the tributes of excessive admiration and excessive hostility.

The truth would seem to be that even at this late date the time has not yet arrived when a just estimate of psycho-analysis and its founder is possible. The atmosphere is too highly charged with controversy. Supporters and opponents are still in too bitter a mood. One can neither affirm that Freud's teaching will stand the test of time, nor deny that it may change permanently the whole conception of the operations of the human mind. Psycho-analysis, whatever it may have become

49

in alien hands, possesses at least the merit of having been given to the world as a treatment of disease and not as a moral law. Freud, indeed, though he took great liberties with philosophy, though he was himself a philosopher *malgré lui*, always wrote and spoke as a man of science. He did not pretend to have invented his remarkable view of mental processes: he asserted that he had discovered it.

But Freud, the man, was clearly bigger than his detractors are usually ready to admit. His influence has pervaded the world within the space of but a few years. It can be discerned today in almost every branch of human thought, and notably in education, and some of his terms have become part of everyday language, 'the inferiority complex' for example.

Misunderstanding dogged Freud's steps from the beginning. He spoke of sex in that large sense which includes the love of parents for their children, the love of children for their parents, the labours of a man to provide for his family, the tenderness of a grown man towards his mother, and so on: and immediately his intention was narrowed by his critics to their own partial view. They accused him of attempting to undermine the moral law. Again, he indicated his belief that natural impulses which have been suppressed have not, by that act, been annihilated. They remain in what he called the 'unconscious mind' to vex and trouble their possessors. At once the cry was raised that this man preached a doctrine of unbridled libertinism. Those raising it overlooked the fact that Freud had placed side by side with his doctrine of repression his doctrine of 'sublimation'. We must not, he taught, regard a natural impulse as, of itself, wrong or unworthy. To do so is to abhor the law of Nature and so the order of the universe. Rather we must take that impulse and apply it to the noblest purposes of which we are capable.

This, it may be admitted, was a little like saying that a negative produces a positive, and that man owes his spiritual development to racial and social taboos. It was a doctrine which appealed strongly to Puritanical minds, with the result that Freud's supporters, like his opponents, included persons of the most diverse views. Psycho-analysis thus became not one but a dozen battle-grounds on which the combatants fought with the fierceness of zealots. There is indeed, in all Freud's writing, a haunting echo of theological controversy. His conception included, under other names, many ancient doctrines and dogmas. Thus there is but little real distinction between 'original sin' and the 'natural impulse' of the Viennese professor. Freud, too, adjured his patients to recognize their human nature as the necessary first step to cure; not merely the knowledge but the conviction of sin was essential to a change of heart. Again, he bade his followers know themselves by every means and devised astonishing new methods of self-knowledge or 'self-analysis'. Thus was the evil spirit of a suppressed emotion or desire unmasked and released to be transmuted into the good spirit serving as a mainspring of action.

The famous theory of dreams and the various 'complexes' resolve themselves, when viewed as Freud meant them to be viewed, into observations of the activities of the 'natural man' imprisoned and ignored yet always alive within us. This original sin, if denied, possesses, he believed, the power to 'attach' itself to or 'associate' itself with other, apparently good and innocent thoughts, lending them, thereby, its own passionate energy. Hence the innumerable 'anxieties' and fears ('phobias') of the mentally sick: hence their strange apings of physical disease, their perverted ideas, their unreasoning prejudices. To resurrect this natural man and yoke his powers to fresh and useful enterprises was the life-aim of the physician.

There are those, today, who deny the very existence of the 'unconscious mind' – though their numbers are diminishing. There are others who see in nervous ailments only the failure of will power, whereby they think we hold our instincts in wholesome restraint. Finally, there are many who believe that an actual physical lesion, a disease of the body, underlies every abnormality of the mind. Freud's doctrine is anathema to all such. His doctrine, moreover, has been modified and changed, notably by Jung, who laid far less stress than Freud on the sexual character of emotional impulse. The controversy is apt to become a barren one.

Freud was born at Freiberg, in Moravia, on May 6, 1856, and studied in Vienna and at the Salpêtrière in Paris, graduating MD in 1881. Most of his numerous works have been translated into English and other languages, and he was editor of *Internationale zeitschrift für Psychoanalyse* and of *Imago*, and director of the *International Journal of Psycho-Analysis*. Last year he was elected a Foreign Member of the Royal Society, and many years ago he received the honorary degree of LL.D from Clark University, Worcester, Massachusetts. Professor Freud married in 1886, and had three sons and three daughters.

AMY JOHNSON

A great airwoman

6 JANUARY 1941

MISS AMY JOHNSON, CBE, whose death is now confirmed, will always be remembered as the first woman to fly alone from England to Australia. That flight took place in 1930 and her name at once became world-famous.

In the early days of the war she was employed in 'ferrying' material to France for the RAF. Her cool courage, flying unarmed through the danger zone, was much admired by the RAF pilots. Since that time she had flown a variety of aircraft many thousands of miles and she met her death while serving her country.

Amy Johnson was of Danish origin. Her grandfather, Anders Jörgensen, shipped to Hull when he was 16, settled there, changed his name to Johnson, and married a Yorkshire woman named Mary Holmes. One of their sons, the father of Amy, became a successful owner of Hull trawlers. Amy graduated BA at Sheffield University, and then went to London to learn to fly at the London Flying Club at Stag Lane, Edgware. After taking her 'A' licence she passed the Air Ministry examination to qualify as a ground engineer. Before starting on her flight to Australia her only considerable experience of cross-country flying was one flight from London to Hull.

Having acquired a secondhand Moth with Gipsy engine, she started from Croydon on May 5, 1930, on an attempt to beat the light aeroplane record of 15½ days from England to Australia. Considering her lack of experience at that time as a navigator, it was a marvel that she found her way so well. She arrived safely at Darwin on May 24. Thence she flew to Brisbane, where, probably through her exhausted condition, she overshot the aerodrome and crashed her Moth rather badly. Australian National Airways Limited arranged for her to fly as a passenger in one of their machines to Sydney, and in the pilot of that machine she met her future husband, Mr J. A. Mollison. She was accorded a great reception in Australia, and was received at Government House. King George V conferred on her the CBE and the *Daily Mail* made her a present of £10,000. On her return to England she was met at Croydon by the Secretary of State for Air, the late Lord Thomson, in person.

In 1931 she made a fine flight to Tokyo across Siberia, and then back to England, and in 1932 she started off in another Puss Moth, Desert Cloud, to beat her husband's record to the Cape, which she did by nearly 10½ hours. The skill with which she crossed Africa proved that she had become a first-class pilot. In 1933 she and

Amy Johnson with her new plane in September 1938.

her husband acquired a D. H. Dragon aeroplane and set out to fly to New York. They successfully crossed the Atlantic, Newfoundland, Nova Scotia, Maine, and Massachusetts, but when they were approaching New York their petrol ran short and they therefore landed at Bridgeport, 60 miles short of New York, in the dark. The Dragon ran into a swamp, and overturned. It was extensively damaged, and both of them were bruised and scratched. Her flight to the Cape and back in May, 1936, will rank as one of her greatest achievements. She beat the outward and the homeward records, the record for the double journey, and the capital to capital record. The Royal Aero Club conferred its gold medal upon her in October, 1936, in recognition of her Empire flights. Her book *Sky Roads of the World* was published in September, 1939.

Her marriage took place in 1932, but in 1936 she resumed her maiden name for the purposes of her career, and in 1938 the marriage was dissolved.

VIRGINIA WOOLF

Novelist, essayist, and critic

28 MARCH 1941

THE DEATH OF Mrs Virginia Woolf, which must now be presumed, and is announced on another page, is a serious loss to English letters. As a novelist she showed a highly original form of sensitivity to mental impressions, the flux of which, in an intelligent mind, she managed to convey with remarkable force and beauty. Adeline Virginia Stephen was born at Hyde Park Gate, London, in 1882, the daughter of Sir Leslie Stephen (then editor of the *Cornhill* and later of the *DNB*) by his second wife, Julia Prinsep Duckworth (a widow, born Jackson). She was related to the Darwins, the Maitlands, the Symondses, and the Stracheys; her godfather was James Russell Lowell; and the whole force of heredity and environment was deeply literary. Virginia was a delicate child, never able to stand the rough-and-tumble of a normal schooling. She was reared partly in London and partly in Cornwall, where she imbibed that love of the sea which so often appears in her titles and her novels. Her chief companion was her sister Vanessa (later to become Mrs Clive Bell, and a distinguished painter). Her home studies included the unrestricted use of Sir Leslie's splendid library, and as she grew up she was able to enjoy the conversation of distinguished visitors like Hardy, Ruskin, Morley, and Gosse. She devoured Hakluyt's *Voyages* at a very juvenile age, and early acquired a love of the whole Elizabethan period that never left her. Her mother died when she was 13 and her father in 1904, when she was 22. After Sir Leslie Stephen's death Virginia, Vanessa, and two brothers set up house together at Gordon Square, Bloomsbury, and as time went on the sisters, with Mr Clive Bell, the late Lytton Strachey, Mr T. S. Eliot, and some others, formed a group with which the name of that London district was associated, sometimes with ill-natured implications. But, so far as Virginia Woolf was concerned, she would have done honour to any district. She very soon displayed a keen and catholic critical sense which found expression in those brilliant and human articles written for *The Times Literary Supplement*, many of which are contained in her book, *The Common Reader*. In 1912 she married Mr Leonard Woolf, the critic and political writer, and went to live at Richmond, Surrey.

The marriage led to much joint work, literary and in publishing; but Mrs Woolf's private interests remained primarily artistic rather than political. Despite friendships with Mrs Fawcett, the Pankhursts, and Lady Constance Lytton, she took no active part in the movement for woman suffrage, though as she showed in

A Room of One's Own, she passionately sympathized with the movement to secure for women a proper place in the community's life. It was not until she was 33 (in 1915) that she published her first novel, *The Voyage Out*, which was a recension of a manuscript dating back some nine years. It was an immature work, but very interesting prophetically, as can be seen by comparing it with *To the Lighthouse*. By this time Mr and Mrs Woolf had set up as publishers at Hogarth House, Richmond, calling their firm the Hogarth Press. The high level of the works published by this press is universally recognized. Among them are some of the best early works of Katherine Mansfield, Middleton Murry, T. S. Eliot, E. M. Forster, besides the works of Mrs Woolf herself. Later transferred to Bloomsbury, the Press acquired an additional reputation for the issue of books having a political trend to the Left.

In 1919 Mrs Woolf brought out a second novel, *Night and Day*, which was still by way of being 'prentice work, but with *Jacob's Room* (1922) she became widely recognized as a novelist of subtle apprehensions and delicate reactions to life, with a method of her own and a finely wrought and musical style. Her subsequent novels, *Mrs Dalloway*, *To the Lighthouse*, *Orlando*, and *The Waves*, rightly earned her an international reputation. These books broke away from the orderly narrative style of the traditional English novel, and are sometimes baffling to minds less agile than hers: but their subtle poetry and their power of inspiring intense mental excitement in imaginative minds are qualities which far outweigh occasional obscurity. The flux of perceptions and the inexorable movement of time were two of her chief themes; and if there is some truth in the criticism that her characters are little more than states of mind, it is also true that they are very highly individualized by the author's remarkable power of observation. Above all, she had a perfect sense of form and of the unity – even if its expression were unattainable – underlying the whole strange process which we call human life. Mrs Woolf's last book, published in 1940, was a profoundly interesting biography of Roger Fry.

DAVID LLOYD GEORGE

National leadership in war and peace. A pioneer of social reform.

26 MARCH 1945

THE DEATH OF Earl Lloyd George of Dwyfor, which is announced on another page, marks the loss of one of the most controversial and commanding figures in British political life. Though for many years he had been out of office, he left an indelible mark on his country's history both as a protagonist of social reform and as an indomitable leader during the war of 1914–18.

The Right Hon. David Lloyd George, PC, OM, first Earl Lloyd George of Dwyfor, and Viscount Gwynedd, of Dwyfor in the county of Caernarvon, in the Peerage of the United Kingdom, was born in Hulme, Manchester, on January 17, 1863. His father, William, came of a stock of substantial farmers in South Wales, but, preferring books to the plough, left the farm and became a wandering missionary of education, teaching in many places, of which Manchester was the last. His mother was a Lloyd, daughter of a Baptist minister who lived at Llanystumdwy, near Criccieth, in Caernarvonshire. The father died when he was 42, leaving the mother to bring up David, then a baby of 18 months, a daughter, who was older, and another son, who was born posthumously. Hearing of her plight her brother, Richard Lloyd, at once left his workshop – he was a master bootmaker – and took his sister and her children back to live with him at Llanystumdwy. He treated his sister's children as his own, and sent them to the village school. David at school is said to have been quick rather than industrious, and his best subjects were geography and mathematics.

Start as a Lawyer

The Georges had known Mr Goffey, a Liverpool solicitor, and in the family councils about the boy's future it was finally decided, thanks mainly to his mother's insistence, to make him a lawyer. At 16 he was articled to a firm of solicitors in Portmadoc. Five years later he had started as a solicitor on his own account at Criccieth, to which the family had by then removed, and his uncle's back parlour was his first chambers. He began to get work, and in 1885 he and his younger brother William had offices in the main street of Portmadoc. Three years later – just after his twenty-fifth birthday – the young solicitor was doing well enough to marry Margaret Owen, who belonged to a prosperous yeoman family just outside Criccieth. The marriage was happy and helpful.

Lloyd George's boyhood was cast in the great days of the Welsh national revival, which for tactical reasons looked to the Liberal rather than to the Conservative Party. Always a Nationalist and a Democrat, in this respect a typical Welshman, he had no part in the traditions of either party, and his politics were rooted in incidents and accidents of the early struggles of Welsh Nationalism. He said later in life that the chapel was his secondary school and university, and with the sap of the new national life rising in its services and in its institutions it was one not to be despised. 'How the past holds you here!' he exclaimed when he visited Oxford after the South African War, 'I am glad I never came here.'

At an early age, when most boys are content to reflect the commonplaces of their school-books, he was the Hampden of the village politics. At 18 he was writing over the name 'Brutus' in a local newspaper articles showing a curious detachment of political judgment, but inclining strongly to the Radical wing of the Liberals. Early in 1886 he was on the first Irish Home Rule platform at Festiniog, and greatly impressed Michael Davitt by his speech. Two years later he was adopted as the Liberal candidate for Caernarvon Boroughs, and in 1890 was elected at a by-election by a narrow majority.

He did not speak frequently, and at first men noted chiefly the pleasant softness of his voice and his turn for personal quips. It was a platform speech on Welsh Disestablishment at the Metropolitan Tabernacle that first made him famous outside Wales, but he wisely stuck to his Parliamentary work, and presently became the most active among the Welsh Parliamentary rebels. He made an unsuccessful effort to create an independent Welsh Nationalist Party, with an organization of its own, and he used every device of the mutinous Parliamentarian to force the Rosebery Government to bring in a Welsh Disestablishment Bill and pass it through the Commons.

South African War

After the cordite vote of 1895, when the Liberal Government was defeated by a chance vote on the insufficiency of small-arm ammunition, the Liberals were in opposition for 10 years. Up to then a Welsh Nationalist, hardly interested in party controversy except in so far as it served Wales, Lloyd George in the 1896 Parliament became the leader of the Left Wing Liberals. Foiled in his ambition to be the Parnell of all Wales, he now threw himself with ardour into English politics. He opposed the Agricultural Rates Bill with such vigour that he got himself suspended. This was the opposition of the peasant, 'cottage-bred' man to the landlord who, he alleged, was subsidized by this measure.

Local feeling had run very high in his election in 1892 and 1895, but his resistance to the South African War made him the most unpopular man in the country. He conducted a campaign for the conclusion of peace, and it was almost the rule for him to have his meetings broken up. But the worst riot, and one which brought him within peril of his life, was that in Birmingham in the week before Christmas, 1901, from which he only escaped under escort by dressing in the uniform of a policeman. Yet it may be doubted whether he was ever so thoroughly happy as he was at this period of his life. He took the risks quite deliberately, believing that he was right; and he had his reward in the reputation for courage and constancy acquired at this time.

The end of the South African War marked also the end of the long period during which he had bothered or opposed his own party almost as much as their rivals. The Conservative Education Bill of 1902 gave him his first real chance to emerge as a leader of the whole Liberal Party. The Bill, which proposed to give public assistance to all voluntary schools, whether sectarian or not, offended the cardinal principle of the Nonconformists that denominational teaching should not be fostered by the State, and rallied practically all Liberals against the principle of granting public funds without imposing public control. He had full scope for his gifts of industry and oratory during every stage of the Bill, and he used them to such purpose that he won a tribute during the closing stages from Balfour himself. His efforts during 1902 procured for him a position and reputation which made his inclusion in the next Liberal Government certain.

From 1906, when the Liberals came into power, he held office continuously for more than 15 eventful years. His conduct of the Board of Trade, to which office he was appointed in 1906, was a complete surprise to all his old enemies who knew him only by his agitation in the South African War and expected to find him an intransigent, unpractical extremist. On the contrary, he was accessible to argument, ingenious in compromise, and much more independent of his officials than most Ministers. Not only was he ready to hear what the interests affected had to say on a measure that he was preparing, but he made it a practice – and here his procedure was quite original – himself to seek them out, call them in conference, and embody their criticisms, if he thought them valid, while the measure was still in the drafting stage. In this way he not only secured the more rapid passage of Bills through Parliament, but when they became law he had the cooperation of the interests affected in making them a success.

The Merchant Shipping Act, the Port of London Act, and the Patents Act (which, by the way, offended the strait-laced free-traders) were all remarkable products of this new method of legislation, which completely broke with bureaucratic tradition. Broadly, it would probably be true to say that he always had an imperfect sympathy with the orthodox Civil Service habit of mind, and, while he relied on it to administer existing law, he despaired of its giving him new ideas and looked elsewhere for them. Here was the germ of what was later known as the new bureaucracy. While he was at the Board of Trade, too, he showed his ingenuity as a mediator by settling the railway strike of 1907. His industrial settlements, however, had a way of being opportunist rather than permanent. The loss of his eldest daughter a few weeks after the strike ended was a sore grief to him.

Chancellor of the Exchequer

The 1909 Budget

In 1908 Campbell-Bannerman died. Asquith succeeded him as Prime Minister and was succeeded as Chancellor of the Exchequer by Lloyd George. At this time, and for some years later, Lloyd George was in very close association with Mr Winston Churchill. Mr Churchill, who succeeded Lloyd George at the Board of Trade, contributed a minimum wage in sweated industries, a weekly half-holiday for shop workers, and the Labour Exchanges. Lloyd George, on going to the Treasury, found an Old Age Pensions Bill already drafted by his predecessor, and after he had carried this through he turned his thought towards schemes of national insurance against sickness and unemployment, and visited Germany in the autumn of 1908 to study the German insurance system. The combination in one pair of hands of responsibility for national finance and of directing a vigorous policy of social reform was unique.

His first Budget, brought in on April 29, 1909, was described by its author as a 'war budget', the war being against poverty and squalor, and it dominated politics for the next two years. The speech in which it was introduced was the longest and one of the least successful that he ever made, and with its central idea of taxing the increment on land values, or at any rate with the machinery for doing this, his advisers at the Treasury are believed to have been in very imperfect sympathy, and the Bill was very badly pulled about during the eight months of unclosured debate that it consumed in passing through the Commons. Fierce as was the controversy in the Commons, it was still fiercer in the country, and rarely in our modern politics have such hard words been used on both sides. A speech at Limehouse, made by Lloyd George in July which added a new verb to the English language, is probably the best statement of his case; another at Newcastle in November described the proposals as fraught with 'rare and refreshing fruit for the parched lips of the multitude'.

In invective and abuse Lloyd George was surpassed by his critics, and future generations re-reading the speeches of 1909 will marvel that so much sound and fury should have been generated over taxes whose yield never approached the cost of collection and which disappeared almost unregretted 10 years later. Lloyd George undoubtedly thought that the country was with him, and when the Lords threw out the Finance Bill he is alleged to have exclaimed: 'I have them now.' But the comparatively small majority of 124 at the first election of 1910 was almost equivalent to a defeat, for the Liberals had lost 115 seats, or 230 votes.

Leaders' Conference

This election had a profound effect on his future. Perhaps it was now that he was converted to coalition. At any rate, it was he who, after the death of King Edward VII, made the first suggestion of the conference of party leaders that followed. It is known that Lloyd George and Balfour were in agreement at the conference, and, had their views been accepted, something like the party truce that was concluded in 1914 would have been concluded at the end of 1910. Among the terms of the concordat it is believed that Lloyd George was willing to withdraw his opposition to McKenna's shipbuilding programme, and even to consent to some form of compulsory service. During the General Election at the end of 1910 (the second of the year) Lloyd George had the throat trouble which impaired the early beauty and flexibility of his voice.

In the next year he introduced and carried his Insurance Bill. There could be no doubt of the genuineness of his sympathy with the trials of poverty; and he was astonished at the strength of the opposition aroused. It remains, however, the most important of his legislative achievements. He proposed in the next years to attack the problem of the reform of land tenure, but his studies were interrupted by the shadows of the coming war with Germany and of the Marconi scandal. This last was the worst trouble of his political life, but no one imputed worse to him than carelessness and an imperfect sense of what was expected from one holding his high office.

Foreign Policy

It remains to gather up the threads of Lloyd George's views on foreign policy before war came. He entered the Liberal Government in 1906 with a violent prejudice against the Liberal League and all its works, and with some good personal reason, for it had been founded as a check on the Liberal Left, of which he was the leader. He belonged to the Campbell-Bannerman wing of the party and adopted without questioning the old Liberal objections to expenditure on armaments, and pleaded for its diversion to social reform.

On this as on other matters the conference of 1910 seems to have induced a certain change of opinion. At any rate, in 1911, after the dispatch of the Panther to Agadir, he made at the Guildhall banquet a remarkable speech, in the course of which he declared that if Germany were to treat this country as of no account in the comity of nations then peace at such a price would be an intolerable humiliation for our great country. But he remained fundamentally unconvinced of the German menace. As late as January 1, 1914, in a newspaper interview, the authenticity of which was never denied, he said that he felt convinced that if Germany ever had any idea of challenging our supremacy at sea, the exigencies of the military situation must necessarily put it out of her head. He said that our relations with her were more friendly than they had been for years, and he looked forward to the spread of a revolt against militarism all over western Europe.

When the crisis began in July Lloyd George was the leader of the peace party, which was in an actual majority as late as July 31. By August 2, after (and doubtless in consequence of) the letter from the Conservative Party leaders, the Cabinet had agreed to a limited intervention in case the German fleet came into the Channel to conduct operations against the French coasts. It was to weaken this resolve that von Kühlmann issued his statement to the Press that if Great Britain remained neutral Germany would not conduct naval operations against the French coast, and this promise made some impression on Lloyd George. He told an interviewer that after such a guarantee 'I would not have been a party to a declaration of war had Belgium not been invaded, and I think I can say the same thing for most, if not all, of my colleagues.' In his opinion, a poll of the electors on Saturday (August 1) would have shown 95 per cent against embroiling this country in hostilities, whereas by the Tuesday after a poll would have resulted in a vote of 99 per cent in favour of war. Equally logical and equally consistent with his reluctance to enter the war was his determination that once in the war we could not afford to come out of it except as unequivocal victors.

He soon emerged as the most ardent war spirit in the Government. His early war speeches lacked Asquith's fine mastery of phrase, but were more stirring, and two speeches, one at the Queen's Hall in September and another at the City Temple in November, are fit to be included in any anthology of militant British oratory. Lloyd George was a member of a committee formed in October to advise the War Office on the best means of providing the guns and ammunition that were required. All countries, including Germany, had under-estimated the expenditure of shells, and, though progress was made in increasing the supplies, it fell far short of our requirements, particularly after trench war had begun. Lloyd George was at first disposed to put the blame on the 'lure of drink'. We were fighting, he said on March 17, Germany, Austria, and drink, and the greatest enemy was drink. The final result of the offensive against this antagonist was the appointment of the Liquor Control Board.

Munitions for the Troops; Policy for Ministry
But it was evident that, however hard men worked, the output of guns and shells could only be assured by relaxation of union restrictions. 'This is an engineers' war,' said Lloyd George on February 28, and on March 17 he urged a conference of trade union leaders to accept certain proposals for the dilution of labour, including

the admission of women to workshops. Thus early was outlined the policy which three months later led to the formation of the Ministry of Munitions and the Munitions Act.

His energy was so much valued by the Army that when French decided in May to appeal to Caesar for a better supply of munitions, and in particular of high explosives, he sent copies of his correspondence with the Government through Captain Guest, one of his ADCs and formerly a Junior Whip in the Government, to Lloyd George, and also to Bonar Law and Balfour. Colonel Repington, then Military Correspondent of *The Times*, was the vehicle of the appeal to the nation as a whole. It is almost forgotten that Lloyd George in a speech to the House of Commons on April 21 said much the same about our manufacture of war munitions as Asquith in his much-criticized speech at Newcastle the day before, but French's reason for choosing Lloyd George was a just one. He had, as he said, shown by his special interest in this subject that he grasped the military nature of our necessities. There may have been other reasons, too, for the choice, for Lloyd George, a coalitionist at heart since 1910, very early in the war began to doubt whether a party Government could do everything that was required for victory.

Coalition Formed

Lloyd George, who from the South African War days took a very keen interest in military campaigns, was one of the first to shed the facile optimism which was fashionable in the first year of the war, and the likelihood that conscription and grinding taxation would be necessary soon began to oppress him. How could a party Government propose such measures? Was it not necessary to form a coalition of parties if the Government was to have the requisite moral authority? This new crisis matured about the same time as the failure, attributed to lack of munitions, of the attack on the Aubers Ridge. On May 12, 1915, Mr Handel Booth – whose relations with Lloyd George had been fairly close – suggested that the time had come when leaders of the other two parties should be admitted to the Government; three days later Lord Fisher resigned, and on May 17 Asquith, in a letter to Bonar Law, consented to the formation of a Coalition Government. There can be little doubt that Lloyd George inspired this change, which was both necessary for the successful prosecution of the war and accorded with Lloyd George's political views, and it was certainly he who quelled the Liberal opposition. In the new Ministry, completed by the end of the first week in June, Lloyd George was Minister of Munitions, and a year later we had definitely established an ascendancy over Germany in the manufacture of munitions.

The formation of the Ministry of Munitions and the substitution of a Coalition for a Liberal Government did not exhaust Lloyd George's energies in this wonderful first year of the war. He also had views on strategy. He saw the incipient weakness of Russia, and was one of the few who appreciated the magnitude of Hindenburg's victories over Russia at Tannenberg and in the spring of 1915 at its true value. Mackensen's victory over Russia at Gorlice sharpened his opinion that the chief danger was in the East, and that our sound strategy was to concentrate our offensive efforts against the weaker member of the Central Alliance. He and Mr Churchill thought alike, but whereas Mr Churchill worked for the Dardanelles enterprise, Lloyd George, as early as January, 1915, advocated the dispatch of an expedition to the Balkans to cooperate with Serbia. Briand was of the same general opinion. But the project of a French Army of the East, which it was at first intended should cooperate on the Asiatic shores of the Dardanelles, was opposed by Joffre, and by the time Briand had succeeded the military situation in Serbia was so bad, owing to the entry of Bulgaria, that our General Staff advised that there was no possibility of saving Serbia. It also advised that the employment of troops at Salonika was a dissipation of our strength. In this, however, the Cabinet was over-persuaded by Lloyd George and by the urgent appeals of the French, and the decision to land at Salonika was taken.

Prime Minister
The Change of Office

On the death of Lord Kitchener in June 1916, Lloyd George became War Minister, though it was understood that Asquith made the appointment not without reluctance. There was already widespread dissatisfaction with Asquith's Government. It is unnecessary to consider whether or not Lloyd George now deliberately planned to supplant Asquith as Prime Minister. He did not believe that Asquith possessed the vigour and vision necessary to win the war, whereas he was confident that he himself did; and he sincerely believed, not without justification, that he was the one man best able to push the war through to victory.

The breach between the two men arose out of negotiations for the formation of a War Committee of the Cabinet, the control of which Lloyd George already wished to keep out of Asquith's hands. On December 4, 1916, *The Times* published an accurate account of these negotiations in a leading article. Asquith seems to have believed that the article was inspired by Lloyd George, though in fact its contents were quite familiar in the inner circle of politics. In any case he at once wrote a letter insisting that the Prime Minister, while not a member of the Committee, must have 'supreme and effective control of war policy', by supervising the agenda of the Committee and having all its conclusions subject to his approval or veto. Lloyd George repudiated this interpretation of what was afoot, and accepted Asquith's construction of the arrangement, 'subject to *personnel*', a proviso inserted partly in the interests of Carson, who shared Lloyd George's views on Balkan strategy. In spite of this letter, Asquith, having consulted his Liberal colleagues, wrote that evening insisting that the Prime Minister must be chairman. Lloyd George then resigned. Asquith followed suit, and with the active support of Bonar Law a new Government was constituted under Lloyd George as Prime Minister, and from then on his will was practically supreme in the conduct of the war. His energy, his own buoyant confidence and courage, and his ability to impart confidence and courage to others were of immense importance.

The end of the war left Lloyd George in a position of commanding, almost dictatorial power; and that position he proceeded at once to consolidate by getting a new mandate from the constituencies for the continuance of the Coalition. The same Government which had won the war, the people were told, was necessary to reconstruct the country and make sure that the new England was to be a fit land for heroes to live in.

Whatever may have been his intention, he allowed the General Election of 1918 to degenerate into an outburst of hysteria. He returned to power with the two potential embarrassments of extravagant promises and an immense majority. They caused him moments of annoyance from the very beginning, but it was fully three years before they seriously impaired a position of personal supremacy such as no British Prime Minister had ever before enjoyed. He dominated the Government of England at a moment when, probably, England's power in the world was greater than it had ever been.

The Versailles Treaty

Meanwhile the Peace Conference assembled in Paris. This is not the place to examine the faults or the merits of the provisions of the Versailles Treaty, but it must be noted that the longer the conference continued the more did the world lose faith in Lloyd George. All observers paid tribute to his courage in debate, his versatility, his power to win over the other negotiators and to smooth out differences between them, his extraordinary nimbleness and dialectical skill; and all alike grew to disbelieve in the fixity of his convictions or the permanence of any position which he might take up. This impression, which incidents of the next few years did little to dispel, was no less unfortunate for the reputation of Great Britain and of British diplomacy than it was for Lloyd George himself.

At home, Lloyd George attacked the problems of peace in precisely the same spirit as he had attacked those of the war. In his letter to Bonar Law of November 2, 1918, inviting the cooperation of the Unionist Party in the continuation of the Coalition, he said that the problems of peace would be 'hardly less pressing and will require hardly less drastic action' than those of the war itself; and for that action the unity of the Coalition was as necessary as ever.

His speeches at this time reflected a mind filled with generous visions of the new and splendid world which was to be built up on the ruins of the war. But like most men of imagination he was inclined to be contemptuous of awkward facts.

Deepening Depression

Only slowly did it become evident how completely the fabric of all societies had been shattered. Lloyd George and his colleagues were not alone in dreaming of a world turning eagerly to the pursuits of peace, and (what was of the first importance for Great Britain's prosperity) crying hungrily for all those manufactured goods which during the war they had been compelled to deny themselves. But as month after month and year after year the financial conditions of the world grew more chaotic, and the purchasing power of the peoples of the world smaller, commercial depression in England deepened until by 1922 there were normally from 1,250,000 persons unemployed, and the burden of unemployment insurance became heavy alike upon industry and upon the taxpayer.

The Government attempted to struggle on with its schemes of national regeneration and at the same time to parry the onset of economic depression. It showed the utmost fertility in devising palliatives, and there was no branch of public effort directed towards the encouragement of trade or the relief of unemployment during the years between the two wars which did not owe its inception to the Coalition Government. But some portions of the Government's policy, such as the Agriculture Act and the Addison Housing Scheme, had to be abandoned. Others were allowed to wither, and the general impression was created that the Government was being forced into economy, which was indeed no solution whatsoever, rather than leading the nation towards it.

Dissatisfaction with the foreign policies of the Coalition was even deeper than with its conduct of affairs at home. The costly adventure into Mesopotamia was extremely unpopular. The early encouragement of the Greeks in their operations against Turkey and the half-hearted policy – neither entire abandonment nor a continuance of active help – after King Constantine's return showed irresolution and lack of any guiding principle. Above all, our relations with France grew less and less friendly. Neither Lloyd George nor the Coalition was to blame for the withdrawal of the United States from the pact to guarantee the security of France or for the German recalcitrancy in the matter of reparation payments, any more than they were to blame for the worldwide unrest and disorganization which followed the war.

No Prime Minister and no Government could, probably, have kept the confidence of the country through these troubled years of disillusionment and distress. All Governments must bear the blame for many things which are beyond their control, and never were Lloyd George's better qualities more conspicuously displayed. His courage, his versatility, his buoyancy of spirit, and, almost more than all, his amazing physical energy were the wonder of his enemies and the delight of his friends. He had largely superseded the established methods of diplomatic negotiation through the recognized channels by round-table discussions by the heads or plenipotentiary representatives of the various Governments. Over each of the conferences summoned in pursuance of this plan he established an extraordinary personal ascendancy which was something more than the respect necessarily paid to the man who stood for the might of Great Britain. The conferences never attained anything like the objects for which they had been called, but, making the most of what little achievement there was, Lloyd George succeeded in representing each as better than a failure and in keeping hope alive to the next; and at critical moments his speeches in the House of Commons were triumphs. Read in print, the speeches lose much of their magic. In his treatment of France, of Germany, of Russia, of Greece, of the League of Nations, of the Treaty of Versailles itself, Lloyd George was always ready to put everything aside in favour of his own inspiration of the moment.

The Irish Troubles; Discontent with Government

Among the various causes which contributed to the growing discontent with the Coalition Government were the troubles in Ireland. For some reason the Irish question seems never to have especially interested Lloyd George. Soon after the Armistice he spoke vaguely of the Government's intention to 'satisfy Irish aspirations', without injury to the rights and claims of Ulster: but he seems to have been far from comprehending how far Irish sentiment had travelled since the days of 1914. Prudence demanded that the Irish question should be taken up at once and in the most liberal spirit. *The Times* strongly advocated a measure of self-government for Ireland, without compulsion upon Ulster, and was the first to urge this measure on a reluctant Government. But the Cabinet (certainly its hands were full) dallied and postponed action while every month made the situation more difficult. It was the old fable of the Sibylline books. The price at which Irish peace might have been bought immediately after the war was contemptuously rejected at the beginning of 1920. Then followed one of the most terrible chapters of Ireland's terrible history, a chapter of civil war, of murder, of repression and reprisals and when the final 'settlement' was made it was on terms and in a spirit which would have been incredible three years earlier.

The importance of the influence of the Irish settlement on the fate of the Lloyd George Government was not so much that it aroused any especial popular disapproval as that it definitely alienated an influential section of the Unionist Party. Lloyd George, when he superseded Asquith, had split the Liberal Party in two and he had no more embittered enemies than that half of the party which still followed Asquith. In spite of the concessions which he had made to the wage-earners during and immediately after the war, he had now lost the confidence of Labour as a whole, by a policy which, as in other spheres, lacked consistent principle. The predominant partner in the Coalition was the Unionist Party. On his ability to hold Conservative support the fate of his Government rested. The antagonism aroused among Conservatives by his Irish policy, therefore, was of serious importance. Its extent, however, should not be exaggerated. The policy which culminated in the Treaty of 1922 was loyally supported and indeed largely created by Conservative Ministers; and although a certain section of Conservatives doubtless found in it justification for a revival of their traditional mistrust of Lloyd George, the malcontents would not have been strong enough to overthrow him without allies from quite a different part of the Conservative camp.

Fall of the Coalition

What precipitated Lloyd George's fall was the crisis in the Near East, with the Kemalist victory over the Greeks, the capture of Smyrna, and the Turkish threat to Constantinople and the little British force, now deserted by its allies, on the Dardanelles. The first intimation that the general public had of the seriousness of the situation was from a clumsily worded communication from the Government to the self-governing Dominions asking them whether Great Britain could count on their military support in case of war. The country was alarmed, and inevitably turned its wrath against the Government, which, outside of Parliament, had by now few friends.

In spite of the endeavours of Austen Chamberlain to keep the party in line, a conference of the Unionist members of the House of Commons held at the Carlton Club in November, 1922, decided by a vote of 186 to 87 in favour of party independence, and Bonar Law, recently recovered from serious illness, consented to act as the party leader. The decisive nature of this vote was due to the growing belief among a number of the younger Conservatives that the choice before them was neither more nor less than whether or not Lloyd George should become the leader of the Conservative Party. They were not in close personal touch with him and not under the spell of his personality. They were repelled rather than attracted by his dramatic and dictatorial methods of doing business. Bonar Law's emergence gave them an alternative leader and their mistrust of Lloyd George became revolt. At the General Election, which followed immediately, the Coalition Liberals (now calling themselves National Liberals) returned less than 60 members against 344 Unionists. When the new Parliament assembled Lloyd George found himself in the corner seat behind the gangway, at the head of the smallest of the four parties. The official representation of the Opposition passed to the Labour Party.

Re-entry into Party

The result of the election undoubtedly surprised and wounded Lloyd George, who appears to have expected that he would be able to assert over a vast electorate that personal supremacy which he had consistently exercised for so long over smaller bodies. He lost little time, however, in repining, and was soon buoyantly at work trying to effect his re-entry into the Liberal Party. Although he had antagonized many to whom the Coalition was anathema, he was still in a strong position. He had his own powerful organization, equipped with the Coalition Liberal share of the party funds which had been collected to finance a national campaign, and his hold on the Welsh electorate gave him a strong territorial basis for claiming the leadership of a revived Liberal Party.

His efforts to reidentify himself with Liberalism continued to the end of his career with a success which was more apparent than real. He was readmitted to the fold, and, after the transference of Asquith to the House of Lords, consistently elected leader of the Liberal Parliamentary Party. But his leadership was always subject to fragmentary challenges and widespread distrust. The fund which came to be associated with his name was hated by a large section of Liberals even though it was being employed for the use of the Liberal Party. His failure to establish himself as a sectional leader was perhaps due to the same faults of character as had led to his downfall as a national leader, but it is at least doubtful whether the task would not have been beyond any man's powers. He had to make an effective political force out of a party subject to suction both from the Right and from the Left, every item of whose policy might be claimed as its own by the one or the other of two parties, both of which had clearly a much better chance of carrying it out. The task before him was not merely to overcome prejudice against him within the Liberal Party; it was to transform a centre party into a focus of recruitment for itself rather than a source of recruitment for its rivals.

In this task he never succeeded. His committees of political research produced an agricultural and an urban policy in 1923. He himself produced an unemployment policy in 1929. In all these social and economic schemes he was undoubtedly the anticipator of the agreed and accepted policies of today, as he was the successor of the Liberal policies of the years before the war of 1914–18: but the only real electoral success – that of 1923 – was due not to new plans but to the old associations of Liberals with free trade. Between 1931 and the outbreak of the present war, he gradually retired into the position of an elder statesman, whose occasional irruptions into active politics continued to command more interest than agreement. Perhaps some of this shadow was due to the fact that his voice did not come well over the wireless. But in conversation his personality and his tongue remained as vivid as ever. For example, when asked what he thought of Mr Chamberlain's visit to Munich, he grimly remarked: 'In my day they came to see me.' But it would not be unfair to say that he viewed all Governments with almost equal disfavour, and that he never felt that he himself could usefully fit into any possible team. At least he played no great part in public life either in the years immediately preceding the present war or in the war itself. He was greatly affected by the death of his first wife, Dame Margaret Lloyd George, in 1941. One source of great pleasure to him, however, was the success of his two children, Major Gwilym Lloyd George and Miss Megan Lloyd George, in their political careers. Between them and him there existed the very closest bonds of affection and devotion.

Looking back over Lloyd George's remarkable career, it appears to fall quite clearly into three parts. In the first he appears as the crusading Radical, finding his inspiration in an ever-widening circle of problems and opportunities. In the second he is still a crusader, but a crusader on behalf of the whole nation. In the third he is trying to persuade himself that he is still a crusader, when he has become in fact a tactician. In every one of these phases his gifts of charm, of wit, of courage moved and attracted audiences, but in the last the prophetic power and hold had vanished. None the less, one of his political opponents once said of him that throughout the bitterest times of their controversy he had always felt that Lloyd George was on the side of the underdog, and this remained true to the end.

His countrymen at least will remember that he wrought greatly and daringly for them in dark times, in peace and in war, and will admit without distinction of class or party that a great man has passed away.

In 1919 he received the OM, in 1920 the Grand Cordon of the Legion of Honour, and he was an honorary DCL of Oxford and an honorary LL.D of Edinburgh. He married, in 1888, Margaret, daughter of Richard Owen, of Mynyddednyfed, Criccieth. She was created a GBE, and died in 1941, leaving two sons and two daughters. Secondly he married, in 1943, Miss Frances Louise Stevenson, CBE, who had been his private secretary from 1913.

Earl Lloyd George's elder son, Viscount Gwynedd, known until recently as Major Richard Lloyd George, now succeeds as second earl. In 1917 he married Roberta Ida Freeman (fifth daughter of Sir Robert McAlpine, first baronet), who divorced him in 1933, having had a son and a daughter. He married a second time, and his present wife is a line controller of the London Transport Welfare Department. The first earl's second son is Major the Right Hon. Gwilym Lloyd George, Minister of Fuel and Power; his elder daughter is Lady Olwen Carey-Evans, wife of Major Sir Thomas Carey-Evans, MC, FRCS; and his younger daughter is Lady Megan Lloyd George, MP for Anglesey.

PRESIDENT FRANKLIN
D. ROOSEVELT

Four times chief executive of United States.
Service in freedom's cause.

12 APRIL 1945

THE DEATH OF President Roosevelt from cerebral haemorrhage on Thursday afternoon at Warm Springs, Georgia, as announced in the later editions of *The Times* yesterday, robs the United States of its Chief Executive within less than six months of his election to serve a fourth term of office at the White House – a term without precedent in American history. Throughout yesterday the people of the United States, of the United Nations, and of all peace-loving States mourned the passing of a leader whose influence for good had extended far beyond his national boundaries.

Franklin Delano Roosevelt, the thirty-first President of the United States, was, as his whole life attested, a man of destiny. From one fate to another he was called. Through two great and prolonged crises in his country's history he set its course and steered it through. Each of them provided a searching test of character and statecraft, and each made its own demands upon the Chief Executive. In both of them, however, he retained the confidence and was upheld by the support of an immense majority of his fellow-countrymen. The place in history which he will fill in relation to the greatest of his predecessors has yet to be decided but one of the determining factors in regard to it will be that he alone of them was invested by his fellow-countrymen with a fourth term of office and at his elections secured more decisive votes than any Presidential candidate before him. It will be remembered also that his pre-eminence was by no means due to lack of opposition, for many of his policies were carried in the teeth of a resistance by powerful and vocal sections of the American public. He was in fact during his first three terms master of Congress for only one comparatively brief period, and after that was opposed as strongly by some important groups in his party as by the Republicans. He had often, therefore, to use outside opinion to force his own supporters to follow him. His ability to do so was one of the truest measures of his stature. His like can, indeed, only be sought among those whose idealism made a comparable appeal to his people, and whose actions were equally justified in the event.

Rights of Democracy

The world was first to hear of Franklin Roosevelt, the second of his blood and familiar name to occupy the White House, as a champion of the rights of democracy. In this he was a true heir to the traditions of his country. Sensitive as he always was to the feelings of those near him he seemed able to enlarge the range of his sympathy and understanding until it embraced a huge and diversified nation. To him, a man of generous though sometimes hasty instincts, distress, suffering, and insecurity were standing challenges. He had an aristocrat's magnanimity and angry inability to see unnecessary pain inflicted, and the 'New Deal' was a supreme assertion of the claim of all mankind to life, liberty, and the pursuit of happiness. 'Every man has the right to live; and this means that he has the right to a comfortable living' was both the expression of a genuine belief and a continuing directive of policy. To many millions of Americans it became a sufficing and unquestioned gospel. Even if the Fates had had no more to ask of him than the mighty struggle against the depression of the early 1930s which it inspired, his place in the first rank of Presidents would be secure. At the end of four years of it faith in his leadership had actually increased, and even after four more survived in a remarkable degree.

Roosevelt was required, however, not only to protect the fruits of his advanced Liberalism from internal enemies, but also against a far more formidable menace from without. His aims demanded that he should be a man of peace. Peace, however, was not to continue in his time. He did within the limitations of his position all he could to avert the calamity of war, and both before and after its outbreak displayed, in addition to an astonishing gift of judging his own people, almost as remarkable a one for seeing deep into the Axis leaders. Totalitarianism was the antithesis of all he stood for. He never concealed his personal hatred of it; but he determined with cautious statesmanship to move only as fast as his own countrymen could be led to travel with him. There were in the early stages of the war cross currents in American opinion, and it was not until Pearl Harbour that he had a united people behind him. In foresight he was from the first far ahead of most of them: but he understood the American temper much too well to force the pace, and in this way he succeeded in maintaining the position of a trusted interpreter of world events. When, therefore, Japan struck and he was free from the restrictions which had fettered him, he moved instantaneously into that not merely of a commander-in-chief in war, but of a national war-leader as well. He had, moreover, by this time not only armed his country, but had insured the capacity of Great Britain to hold Germany. It was, in fact, in the years immediately before Japan's attack no less than in the years after it that his life's battle for democracy was won.

Atlantic Crossings

It is true that, when pressed by his own party in 1940 to seek a third term and opposed by Mr Wendell Willkie, he failed to register as tremendous a victory as in 1936; but it is true also that it was a contest chiefly upon domestic issues, for Mr Willkie was broadly in agreement with him on the wider and more pressing ones of war. Thus during the years of America's belligerency he was in fact the supreme head of an embattled people, and in authority the equal in vital matters of the great national figures with whom he cooperated. When, therefore, in the course of the long conflict he crossed the Atlantic to join in allied councils of war he went with all the prestige of his standing in the nation he represented as well as that of his own transcendent personality.

Roosevelt was a statesman in virtually every direction open to a truly democratic leader. As President he had immense powers and exercised them freely. Thus at times he would initiate and act with daring, and at others hold and caution. Occasionally he would move ahead of his people: but, if he found he had gone too far he would fall quietly into step with them again. He thus displayed the resiliency of his fibrous strength. Sprung of long lines of American ancestors, he was so deep rooted in the American soil and so steeped in American sentiment that he had no sense of inferiority to any man or people upon earth and could therefore be completely spontaneous. So American was he, indeed, that he seemed instinctively to realize the ideals which, however inarticulately, were stirring in his fellow-countrymen, and, since they were usually his own as well, it became his delight to translate them into concrete political forms. He became, moreover, in virtue chiefly of the accuracy of his intuitions, the shrewdest and most adroit of politicians. He had also the rare power of making government appear interesting and exciting, especially to the younger generation. He had, of course, his weaknesses and incapacities, though they were perhaps the inevitable concomitants of his virtues. He was assailed, for example, as a reckless spender, a plotter against the Constitution, a dictator, and an enemy of sound finance; but when due allowance is made for political animus, the substance of such charges seems small indeed beside his achievements. Added, moreover, to his many other qualifications for his exalted office he had an abounding vitality and exuberance of spirit, and, by no means least of his powers, he was a sound judge and a natural attractor of men. No doubt he was a favoured child of fortune; and yet the man who had fought and conquered a fell disease had, it seemed, wrung from that grim struggle the secret of all human victories.

Early Life
Wish to Be a Sailor

Franklin Delano Roosevelt was born at Hyde Park, in Dutchess County, New York, on January 30, 1882. He was the only son of an affluent and long-established family well and widely related. President Theodore Roosevelt was his distant cousin. In him Dutch, French, Scottish, and Irish strains were mingled, but all of them had been seasoned for generations in the United States. His father, James Roosevelt, was both a man of business and a country gentleman. His mother, a remarkable woman who was to exert a great influence upon his life, was Sara Delano, a member of a French family which had left Leyden in the early seventeenth century. Although delicate he had a happy childhood, during which he was taken a number of times to Europe. Then rather late he was sent to school at Groton. As a boy he had wanted to enter the Navy – his love of ships remained with him always – but instead he went to Harvard. There, although he moved in a largely Republican set, he was known as a strong Democrat, the political faith of his immediate family; he also gained distinction by being managing editor of *The Crimson*, an undergraduate newspaper. After taking a full share in the university life and sports he graduated in 1904.

On St Patrick's Day, 1905, when he was studying law at Columbia University he married Eleanor Roosevelt, the niece of the famous Republican President. She was only a girl: but he seemed to have divined the quality of one who, herself a woman of remarkable ability, was to become a potent factor in his career and the most prominent and active mistress the White House has ever known. The young couple settled in New York, and in 1907 he was admitted to the Bar and joined the important legal firm of Carter, Ledyard and Milburn, of that city. Then in 1910 he yielded to the suggestion that he should stand for the State Senate as candidate for the Dutchess County District which for years had been a Republican stronghold. At the election his immense vitality, charm, and good humour won the day and his brilliant political career began. At its outset he made his name, for he became the central figure in a courageous and successful revolt against Tammany Hall over the election of a Senator to Washington.

Navy Assistant Secretary

When in 1912 Woodrow Wilson became President, Roosevelt was offered a choice of two places in the administration; but neither appealed to him. Then, however, Josephus Daniels, the new Secretary of the Navy, asked him if he would take the congenial post of Navy Assistant Secretary and he readily consented. Daniels was a pacifist of puritanical mind, but the two men got on well together, and Roosevelt, who was much the more popular with the service, was, in his capable and vigorous way, able to do a great deal to increase the efficiency of the fleet. He found, however, that the President was less helpful than he might have been. Wilson liked and admired Roosevelt, who continued to hold him in deep regard, but he hesitated to give signs of preparation for war. It was indeed only in 1916 that he consented to an increased navy, and thus gave the Assistant Secretary his chance. In June, 1918, Roosevelt was offered a nomination for the governorship of New York but refused it. Then in the next month he went in pursuit of his duties to England and afterwards to France. He was eager at the time to play a combatant's part, but this was not to be. In London he created an admirable impression and made many friends. After the Armistice he went to Europe again.

At the Democratic Convention of 1920, which was held at San Francisco, Governor Cox, of Ohio, was nominated to succeed Wilson, and, much to his surprise and pleasure, the convention agreed that Roosevelt should go forward for the Vice-Presidency. It was a strenuous campaign; but the fate of the Democrats was sealed, and he retired into private life with good humour and, in spite of the defeat of his party, a high reputation. He thereupon resumed his legal practice, and as an occupation for his spare time undertook to reorganize the Boy Scout movement in New York. He had, however, been subjected to a long and unbroken strain, and in the next year was smitten with poliomyelitis, a form of infantile paralysis. It might well have ended his career, but, bearing its pain and deprivation with superb courage, he triumphed first over the disease itself and then by degrees over the physical incapacity it left. 'I'll beat this thing,' he said. He was never in fact to regain the full use of his legs, and to him, who had the physique and habit of an athlete, swimming was to remain his only locomotive exercise. Owing, however, to his iron will and magnificent resistance he was able to do some work in 1922, and in 1924 played a prominent part in the Democratic Convention of that year. All who knew him seemed to have agreed that his ordeal had deepened as well as strengthened a character already strong.

Governor of New York

By 1928 much benefited by prolonged treatment at Warm Springs, in Western Georgia, where he later established a foundation for the treatment of infantile paralysis, he was able to stand without crutches, and once again to bear the strain of active politics. It was he, therefore, who nominated his old friend 'Al' Smith as Democratic candidate to the Presidency, and himself on Smith's strong persuasion stood for the governorship of the State of New York. His election to it was in the circumstances of the time a triumph, for even Smith himself failed for the first time to carry his Empire State. This important office, which raised him to Presidential status, he was to hold for two terms of two years each. His was in many ways a notable administration, for he found himself in a laboratory in which he could test the reforms he was afterwards to apply to the country as a whole. He also developed his own political technique, and it was at this period that he was among the first to exploit the political uses of the broadcast, a medium of which he became perhaps the most skilled and effective exponent of his time. Perhaps the greatest of his many problems was the administration of New York City, and when in view of certain scandals he instituted an extensive investigation into its municipal affairs, events were to show that his action had been justified. By the end of the second period of office he had greatly increased his reputation in the country at large by the just and fearless performance of his official duties.

Elected President

New Deal Promised

Meanwhile the economic condition of the nation, gripped in the ever-deepening depression of those years, was going from bad to worse. The unemployment figures, in so far as they could be estimated, ran to many millions. Values were sinking to fantastic levels, factories were without orders, and a dreadful paralysis was encroaching on every normal national activity. It was against this background of gloom and widespread sense of hopelessness that the Presidential election of 1932 was held. At it the Republicans, who felt bound to vindicate their President by their votes, decided to put Herbert Hoover forward for a second time. At the Democratic Convention at Chicago there was a good deal of initial manoeuvring, but eventually Roosevelt was nominated, and once his campaign had started there was little question of the result. In it he was helped immensely by the work of the group of chosen experts known as the 'Brain Trust', whom he had employed to advise him, and to ensure that the votes his policy might gain would not be obtained by false pretences. Apart from the fact that the Hoover regime had failed to master the depression, there were many circumstances in his favour. The Democratic platform was, in defiance of all precedent, brief and definite; conditions generally could scarcely have been more desperate; and the refusal of prohibition was a popular Democratic plank. Moreover, as the campaign progressed Roosevelt's inspired nomination pledge of 'a new deal for the American people' began to catch the public imagination: Hoover, indeed, was beaten from the first; but the result when it came was unparalleled in American history – a majority of 4,000,000 votes and 480 out of 531 in the electoral college. On this there followed the four months of impotence which the constitution imposed when there was nothing for him to do except to watch the increasing difficulties of the country and to mature the Brain Trust's plans. In February, when he was in Florida, a crazy Italian made an attempt upon his life, and his companion, Anton Cermak, the Mayor of Chicago, was killed.

On the eve of his inauguration the nation long lost to hope was on the point of panic. Banks had been closing all over the country and it was rumoured that those of New York and Chicago would shut the next day. It was a moment of culmination at which Roosevelt alone seemed to stand between the people and complete despair. At such a time he was at his greatest, and as he drove with his tired predecessor through the streets of the capital to the inauguration ceremonies, he appeared to radiate courage and assurance. His speech was brief and foreshadowed immediate and strenuous action. Before evening every member of his Cabinet was sworn in, and almost at once came his proclamation of a four-day banking holiday. He called Congress together at the earliest possible moment and with his overwhelming support there was able to pass through a vast programme of reform. His plans for national recovery covered the whole range of industry. Huge schemes of public relief works were launched and the Budget rose to a total unprecedented even in the years of war. Since taxation could not cover it, he had to borrow. In finance his plan was to move towards a managed currency, and his aim a dollar which would not change in its purchasing or debt-paying power during the succeeding generation. There was to be constant talk of a balanced Budget in some year not too far ahead, but the figures and estimates were scarcely to point in that direction. With the huge defence programme which developed later all hope of it expired.

Fireside Chats

There were three aspects of the President's 'New Deal'. The first was to avert abuses by imposing drastic limitations on all big industrial organizations; the second to develop national resources by such means as huge dams and hydro-electric plants; the third to establish social security in one grand sweep. Nothing in regard to it was particularly new except the immensity of its scale and speed with which it was attempted to put it through. At every stage, moreover, he sought to carry the country with him, and to this end kept it informed of both his aims and achievements by his 'Fireside Chats', a system of direct personal contact which developed into an unprecedented intimacy between President and people.

There were, of course, loud complaints from business and other interests, and those who felt themselves to be prejudiced or endangered by the new legislation. But apart from some checks and some dissension the President's proposals were carried through on a broad tide of popular support. Even after what has been called the first 'honeymoon' year everything continued to go smoothly enough. Then, however, the 'codes' which Roosevelt's National Industrial Recovery Act of 1933 had imposed upon employers were condemned by the Supreme Court and rendered invalid. His Agricultural Adjustment Act was also to suffer the same fate. It was the beginning of a sharp constitutional conflict. In spite, however, of a tendency in some quarters to make it a political issue, the President, to whom opposition was always a stimulant, faced the difficulty calmly, and, in trying to save what he could, succeeded beyond expectation. In spite, therefore, of the loss of legislation which incidentally had served a great deal of its purpose, the 'New Deal' went on.

The new President had also been faced with serious problems of foreign policy. War debts provided one of them and disarmament another. In April, 1933, Mr Ramsay MacDonald went to see him at Washington to discuss the whole world situation, and in May he issued an important message to the heads of the 54 States concerned in the disarmament and economic conferences of that year. In it he appealed for a common understanding and suggested a definite non-aggression pact. It appeared indeed at the time that he contemplated a closer participation of representatives of the United States in international conferences, and as a step in that direction made Mr Norman Davis his Ambassador at large to various countries of Europe. Unfortunately, however, owing to American failure to see eye to eye with some of the European countries in regard to the stability of international exchange, the high hopes which had been formed were to remain unrealized, for the economic conference proved abortive. Thereafter for some years the United States was to lapse into an increasing detachment.

Plea for Broader Outlook

By 1935 the President was able to claim that his basic programme was substantially complete. Apart from its material effects it had undoubtedly exerted a remarkable educative influence on the people, and in the same year he stated that the objective of the nation had greatly changed, and that clearer thinking and understanding were leading to a broader and therefore a less selfish outlook. By that year also the economic skies had begun to lighten. It was, therefore, with the confidence of great achievements and substantial hopes that he entered his campaign of 1936. The Republicans had chosen Mr Alfred Landon, the Governor of Kansas, to oppose him – by no means a formidable champion. It was, none the less, a bitter combat, in which, except for his party organization, the President seemed to stand alone. Against him were arrayed all the massed strength and resources of financial and industrial leadership, some of the clergy, more than three-quarters of the nation's newspapers, and the film industry. Relying, however, upon the record of his administration he toured the country. The result was remarkable indeed. All that his opponents could do and say counted, as *The Times* said, for no more than Mrs Partington's mop. It was observed at the time that everybody was against him except the electorate; but it returned him with a majority of 8,593,130 popular votes and with only Maine and Vermont against him in the Electoral College. It was a victory beyond all precedent and a supreme vindication of American democracy.

Second Term

A Remarkable Prophecy

Entering upon his second term in January, Roosevelt put forward proposals for a radical reorganization of the Executive Branch directed towards increasing the effectiveness of the office of President. He also turned to the Supreme Court, which had proved so great an obstacle to his plans, and proposed to elect an additional judge above the nine who were then sitting for every one of them who had passed the age of 72. He was at once accused of tampering with the constitution, and the storm which followed was by no means confined to the Opposition. He had, therefore, to forgo his scheme. Fate was, however, to come to his assistance, for several judges were soon to die, and in a few more years the Bench was to be composed of men with greater sympathy for his social legislation.

The second term, however, was to be full of other than domestic preoccupations. In his Inaugural Address he did not mention foreign affairs; but in the next October he sounded a warning note and said that the epidemic of world lawlessness was spreading. 'Let no one imagine,' he added, 'that America will escape, that America may expect mercy; that this Western Hemisphere will not be attacked; and that it will continue tranquilly and peacefully to carry on the ethics and the arts of civilisation.' It was remarkable prophecy; but perhaps even more remarkable, the prophet himself proceeded to act upon it.

Dictators Denounced

With, therefore, all the prestige of his election behind him, he proceeded to take what steps he could to reinforce the cause of peace. One of them was to continue patiently to foster his 'good neighbour' policy in regard to the South American countries. When in 1941 Japan struck her blow he was to reap the advantage of the wise course Washington in his days had pursued towards the Latin American nations and of the established machinery of Pan-American cooperation. Nine Caribbean republics joined in at once in North America's war of defence, and what had formerly been an almost hostile attitude on the part of South America towards its northern neighbour was as time passed to be one of increasing friendliness. As a result, America as a whole was to become the most disappointing of all continents to the Axis, and what might have been a fruitful field for the tares of Nazi diplomacy was very largely denied to it. Neither, however, the 'good neighbour' policy nor his desire to prevent war was to keep him from forceful comment on the increasingly aggressive and tyrannical acts of the German and Italian dictators, and he denounced Germany's disregard of treaties soundly. When, moreover, he went to Canada in 1938 to open the new international bridge over the St Lawrence he made the historic pledge: 'I give you the assurance that the people of the United States will not stand idly by if Canadian soil is threatened by any other Empire.'

In 1938 also Roosevelt began more fully to employ his influence in the affairs of Europe. Consequently when the crisis in regard to Czechoslovakia was at its height he addressed messages to both sides begging them to reach a peaceful solution by negotiation: and not to break off their deliberations. He sent, too, a second appeal to Hitler urging the maintenance of peace and then, when all negotiations seemed to have broken down at Godesberg, he established touch with Mussolini and had a hand in bringing about the Munich Conference, thus delaying war for a season. Throughout, however, the several critical years before it came he had no illusions in regard to the sinister nature of the dictators' policies. 'It is no accident,' he had said, when he visited Buenos Aires for the Pan-American Conference, 'that the nations which have carried the process of erecting trade barriers the farthest are those which proclaim most loudly that they require war as an instrument of policy.' Incidentally, he concluded on that occasion with the remarkable words, 'We took from our ancestors a great dream. We offer it back as a great unified reality. We offer hope for peace and more abundant life to the peoples of the world.'

Opposition to Hitler

Roosevelt saw far too deeply into the European situation to be set at rest by the achievement of Munich. At the beginning of 1939 he told Congress that he would go to any length short of war to stop the aggressor, and added that there were effective means of doing so. His speeches during the months which followed contained strong declarations for peace, but still more powerful vindications of democracy. His policy, he declared, was the defence of civilization against militarism. Thus he opposed to the morbid race theory and overweening demands of Hitler the broad and humane sanity of his democratic faith. At the same time he proceeded to strengthen the material defences of the United States and, as a precaution, ordered a comprehensive survey of American industry.

When in March Hitler seized what remained of Bohemia he sent messages to him and Mussolini as a 'friendly intermediary' asking them to give a guarantee not to attack for 10 years a specified list of nations. If they agreed he said he would be prepared to ask for reciprocal guarantees and call an international conference to which the United States would give every support in order to try to reach a settlement of all international difficulties. It was, in fact his last great bid; but Hitler would have none of it.

During the summer of 1939 the King and Queen toured Canada and took the opportunity of visiting the United States. The President and Mrs Roosevelt received them at Washington and were their hosts at the White House and then for a weekend at Hyde Park. It was a happy interlude in grave and anxious days. Then, as towards the end of August war drew nearer, Roosevelt appealed twice to Hitler to preserve peace and to the President of Poland to continue negotiations. He also sent a personal message to the King of Italy asking him to use his influence in promoting negotiations. Next, on September 1 when war seemed inevitable, he begged the Powers concerned to declare publicly that they would not bomb civilian populations or unfortified cities. The German answer was the devastation of open Polish towns and villages. After this there was nothing for him to do except to fulfil his obligation to proclaim neutrality, and, under the laws which had been adopted in recent years with the purpose of keeping America out of war, he had to forbid American ships to enter the zone of combat, to warn Americans not to travel there, and to preclude the supply of ammunition or armaments to the belligerents and the raising of loans by those who still owed war debts in America. In the autumn, however, on his urgent insistence, the ban on armaments was relaxed so as to permit the sale of aeroplanes, munitions, and weapons to France and Great Britain under the 'cash and carry' plan. In this country it was a very welcome amendment, and was the beginning of the pro-allied legislation which he was determined to enact. He had indeed many weapons in his armoury and was prepared to use them all. He could warn and thunder and impose embargoes and trade sanctions but he lacked the only one to which Hitler might have paid attention, for he could not offer the threat of war. A biographer has written of him that at this time he was 'a crusader wielding a sheathed sword'.

National Defence

With the overrunning of Europe and the fall of France the attitude of the people of the United States began to change. Demands for a vast programme of national defence arose, and Roosevelt, responsive as ever to national feeling, announced that there could only be peace 'if we are prepared to meet force with force if the challenge is ever made'. The last despairing appeal of France moved him deeply; but he was compelled to point out that assistance by armed forces was not for him but for Congress to give. By June, 1940, American opinion had moved so far that he was able to say of Italy that 'the hand that held the dagger had struck it into the back of its neighbour' and to add that America sent forward her prayers and hopes 'to those beyond the seas who are maintaining with magnificent valour the battle for freedom'. In July, 1940, at a Press conference he defined the 'five freedoms', the aims to be realized if peace were to return to the earth.

In the election of 1940 Mr Wendell Willkie was the Republican candidate. There was an honoured and unbroken tradition which forbade a third term to any President, and for a long time Roosevelt refused to say whether he would be prepared to stand. At last, however, having made it clear that he had no desire to do so, he yielded to a unanimous request from the convention at Chicago. Willkie was a strong opponent of the New Deal and of most of Roosevelt's internal legislation. He was, however, in general agreement with him on a more vigorous defence policy and fuller aid for Britain. It was therefore to those matters that the President confined his attention, inaugurating meanwhile a huge programme for the production of munitions with the aid of leading businessmen whom he called in to assist and advise. He also took two leading Republicans, Colonels Knox and Stimson, into the Cabinet, transferred 50 destroyers to Great Britain in return for naval bases, and worked out a defence policy with Canada. He thus fulfilled his slogan 'Full speed ahead' in war production. In the campaign itself, however, he took little part and made only a few speeches towards its close, when he said he had been misrepresented.

Third Time President

Once again, although Mr Willkie did better against him than either Mr Hoover or Mr Landon, he won handsomely – he was elected by a majority of some 5,000,000 on the popular vote – and thus opened up new fields of leadership. Almost immediately he brought forward his lend-lease proposals, which were embodied in a measure entitled 'An Act to promote the defense of the United States'. These proposals were to enable him to provide war supplies for Great Britain and in fact for 'the government of any country whose defense the President deems vital to the defense of the United States'. Thereafter he kept on enlarging his production plans and stated that America would be 'the arsenal of democracy'. He also pushed her naval patrols farther into the ocean than they had gone in defence of neutrality, and, after the Italians had been driven from Eritrea, sent American supply ships to the Red Sea. Calling for 'unqualified immediate all-out aid for Britain, increased and again increased until total victory has been won', he urged that there should be no idle machine and that they should operate 24 hours a day and seven days a week. Speaking in May at the birthplace of Woodrow Wilson, he said: 'He taught us that democracy could not survive in isolation. We applaud his judgment. We applaud his faith.' Thus, by arming his country for its own defence and in the meantime sustaining the resistance of Great Britain, he served what was in fact the single purpose of saving democracy.

On May 27, 1941, Roosevelt delivered one of the most momentous broadcasts of his career. He reasserted the American doctrine of the freedom of the seas and announced that he had issued a Proclamation to the effect that an unlimited national emergency existed which required strengthening of the defences of the United States to the extreme limit of national power and authority. He pointed to the sinkings of merchant shipping, and said that all measures necessary to the delivery to Great Britain of the supplies she needed would be taken. 'This can be done. It must be done. It will be done.' In June, Lord Halifax, as Chancellor of Oxford University, conferred the degree of DCL upon him, the first time that a Chancellor had officiated at a Convocation outside the walls of Oxford.

Pearl Harbour; Entry into the War

As the year progressed the President became even more assertive in word and action. American troops were sent to Iceland, and in August he met Mr Churchill at sea. The Atlantic Charter recorded their agreement. There were attacks upon the American Navy, and he replied to them with a warning that Axis warships would enter American defensive waters at their peril. A little later he went to Congress to seek a revision of the Neutrality Act. Meanwhile German hatred of him found expression in a crescendo of abuse. Ever since the attack upon Russia he had shown his determination to uphold her resistance, and in November a credit of $100,000,000 was extended to her. Thus as the situation in both the Western and Eastern Hemispheres grew tenser he appeared to be gathering his strength against an inevitable collision. It came on December 7. He had just sent a message to the Emperor of Japan couched in persuasive terms, but protesting against the flooding of Japanese forces into Indo-China. One hour before the reply was delivered by the Japanese Ambassador Pearl Harbour was in smoke and ruin. The next day he gave in person a message to Congress and called for a declaration of war. Except for one member of the House of Representatives the answer was unanimous. 'With confidence,' he said, 'in our armed forces, with the unbounded determination of our people, we will gain the inevitable triumph, so help us God.' And so when a few days later Congress no less readily accepted the challenge of Germany and Italy, Roosevelt entered upon the war leadership supported by the national confidence to which his wise and patient handling of a long-drawn crisis had so richly entitled him.

Hotfoot upon the belligerency of the United States Mr Churchill went to Washington to plan for unity of action, and stayed at the White House. It was the beginning of a wartime association founded upon a well-established mutual regard and doubly proofed against external efforts to break it. Never before in history had the leaders of two great democracies worked together on the fraternal terms which came to exist between the President and the Prime Minister. Each stood high in the opinions of the other's people, and as a result each strengthened the other's hand. Roosevelt and Churchill together were a combination of scarcely precedented power.

Faith and Courage; All Resources Mobilized

The President's message to Congress at the beginning of 1942 showed that the attack by Japan had not only failed to stun him but that he had reacted in much the same way as to the economic perils of 1932. In both cases his response was a programme of immediate action on a nationwide scale. All the vast resources of the United States were mobilized for war. A people which justly prided itself upon the largeness of its conceptions was given an almost unlimited scope for effort. The estimated cost was staggering, but the nation accepted it. He was close on 60 and his birthday at the end of the month brought many messages which indicated the regard of the allied peoples for him. He was already in the ninth year of the immense labours in which his own faith and courage had been his chief sustenance.

As Commander-in-Chief of the United States it was Roosevelt's task to make a peaceful and largely self-centred people strategically minded, and to interpret the war to them as a world conflict rather than an opportunity for the counter-strike they longed to deal Japan. Isolationism was his greatest obstacle, and he said of those who still proclaimed its merits that they wanted the American Eagle to imitate the ostrich. Thus in firm but good-humoured fashion he led his people on, and the fact that the great majority were brought to take the broad, patient, and unselfish view which the character of the war demanded was due primarily to him. Despite, however, the huge measure of support he commanded, he continued to be exposed to a running fire of criticism from sections of the public and the Press.

In April he proposed a seven-point programme to combat the rise which had taken place in the cost of living and included a large increase in taxation. The fear of inflation had begun and was to continue to haunt him, but he was to find Congress somewhat reluctant to incur electoral unpopularity by supporting him in drastic measures. Another danger which he sought to avert was a light-hearted but, as he knew, unfounded optimism on the part of the people. By the summer, however, he was in a position to say that America's reservoir of resources was reaching a flood stage, and vast amounts of material were being sent over-sea to the assistance of the allies. It was a vindication of his own far-sightedness. His lend-lease agreements were already taking shape as key instruments of national policy and he was beginning to realize his world statesman's aim of distributing the financial burdens of the war. In June he welcomed Mr Churchill once again and found that they were still at one upon the major problems of the war. In September he made a quick tour of 11 States in order to test the spirit of the nation and reported it 'unbeatable'. In November came the landing in North Africa – Mr Churchill attributed the authorship of it to him – and what he regarded as the turning point of the war.

Casablanca

The President's New Year address in 1943 to a new Congress will probably rank among the greatest of many great utterances, for in it he was the inspired realist. He looked backward with a well justified satisfaction and forward with a lively hope. He said it was necessary to keep in mind not only the evil things against which America was fighting but the good things she was fighting for. Never indeed did he stand forth so clearly as the leader of his people's thought as well as the ruler of their actions or as the possessor of a grasp wide enough to encompass the whole of the struggle for civilization. Then hard upon this call to thought and action came the bill for it – a Budget of $100,000,000,000. These preliminaries to the year performed, he was before the month had ended at Casablanca, when he conferred with Mr Churchill and the Fighting French at what, remembering General Grant, he called the 'Unconditional Surrender Meeting'. The momentous conversations lasted for some 10 days and every aspect of the war was reviewed at them. Nothing like this had ever happened before, for he was the first President who had ever left his country in wartime. On the way home he stopped at Brazil for a discussion with the President. By thus breaking with tradition and adopting Mr Churchill's practice of going himself to a vital centre of action Roosevelt achieved a master-stroke of leadership, for not only did he enhance his own authority as war leader but drew the beam of national interest after him. Paramount, however, though his authority was he continued to be engaged by efforts to keep prices down in spite of the hesitancy of Congress and the recalcitrance of active labour interests. In April he went to Mexico to discuss post-war cooperation. It was the first time the chief executives of the two countries had met. At the same time he visited the American forces in the Southern States.

In May Mr Churchill, at the President's invitation, paid his fourth wartime visit to the United States, and it was widely noted that such occasions were the presage of great events. In this case the communiqué announced a full agreement on all points 'from Great Britain to New Britain and beyond'. At the same time Roosevelt found himself in one of his recurrent troubles with labour – in this case, the miners – and handled it with characteristic firmness. He was not, however, to receive the support he desired from Congress, for late in June an Anti-Strike Bill which he vetoed was passed in spite of him. It was one of a series of setbacks in domestic policy. They were offset by occasional victories; but his supreme task of directing American strategy continued to be complicated by distractions due to the attitude of an increasingly difficult Legislature.

With the collapse of Italy the war entered on a new, and hopeful phase; but he refused to limit his aims even to a total victory over the Axis, and looked beyond it to another over all the forces of oppression, intolerance, insecurity, and injustice which had impeded the forward march of civilization. In August he went to Quebec for yet another meeting with Mr Churchill in which his old friend Mr Mackenzie King sat with them. Then, he travelled westwards to Ottawa, where he addressed the two Houses of the Canadian Parliament. It was the first time an American President had been there, and in his speech he stated that during the Quebec Conference things had been talked over and ways and means discussed 'in the manner of members of the same family', a phrase in true accord with both the theory and practice of the 'good neighbour' policy.

In November, 1943, Roosevelt left the United States for the series of historic conferences by which the leaders of the Allied Nations sought to consolidate their aims and efforts. At the first meetings in Cairo he and Mr Churchill met Generalissimo Chiang Kai-shek and discussed future military operations against Japan. They declared that she should be stripped of all her island gains in the Pacific as well as the territories she had stolen from China and other spoils of her aggression. To this end it was agreed to continue to persevere in the serious and prolonged efforts necessary to secure her unconditional surrender. The President with the Prime Minister moved next to Teheran, where for four intensive days they were in council with Marshal Stalin, whom Roosevelt then met for the first time. There in most amicable discussion the three leaders shaped and confirmed their international policy and announced jointly that they recognized their responsibility for a peace that would command the good will of the overwhelming masses of the peoples of the world. Thereupon the President with Mr Churchill went back to Cairo for discussions with M. Ismet Inönü, the President of the Turkish Republic. On the return journey Roosevelt visited both Malta and Sicily, arriving eventually at the White House bronzed and cheerful. One of his last actions of the year was to order the Secretary of State for War to take over the railways where trouble had been threatening.

In early January, 1944, Mr and Mrs Roosevelt presented their homestead at Hyde Park to the United States Government as a historical national site with a proviso that the immediate family might use it. It followed upon an earlier gift of the Roosevelt Library there. Then a few days later the President's message to Congress embodied his programme for still further mobilization of the resources of the nation. In it he referred scathingly to the 'pressure groups' and others who, while he had been abroad, had been busy in the pursuit of interests which he regarded as only secondary to the supreme task of winning the war. This corrective he accompanied by yet another Budget for $100,000,000,000.

In the New Year there were to be still further difficulties with Congress. In late February he vetoed the Tax Bill, and thereby lost one of his staunchest supporters, Senator Barkley, of Kentucky, the Democratic Leader in the Senate, only to be overridden by large majorities in both Houses. It was a protest against what were regarded as the encroachments of the Administration. The obedient Legislature of his earlier years had long since been replaced by one largely hostile to his social policy. The result was the cat and dog relationship between President and Congress which the American Constitution permits, and his caustic description of the Bill as relief 'not for the needy but for the greedy' was an appeal over the head of the legislators to the people.

Senator Truman

As the spring lengthened the probability of his running for a fourth term seemed steadily to grow greater. In April, 1944, he had to take a rest, but in May he was back at the White House, himself again, clear of eye and voice. Simultaneously with his return to it the chairman of the Democratic National Committee asserted that he would accept the party's nomination; but he himself refused to be drawn. At the end of the month, when reminded on one occasion of his support of President Wilson, he stated that he contemplated a new and better League of Nations in the post-war world and a little later outlined the American plan for a world security organization. On July 11 he broke his silence and announced that if elected he would serve a fourth term as President. The news was received calmly because it was widely expected. On July 20 the Democratic Convention at Chicago nominated him with loud applause and the waving of many banners ensigned with his name. Senator Truman was, however, chosen instead of his associate, Mr Wallace, to run for the Vice-Presidency.

In July the President was in Honolulu for a three days' conference. On his way back he visited the Aleutians and Alaska, and dramatically broadcast from a warship on the Pacific coast. Then in September he went to Quebec to meet Mr Churchill. The discussions, which ranged over a wide field, were conducted, as Mr Churchill said, 'in a blaze of friendship'. It was only after his return from Quebec that he made the first political speech of his campaign; but his wartime activities as Commander-in-Chief pleaded as strongly for him with the electorate as any words he could have uttered. Things were, indeed, beginning to go well for him, and on October 16 the *New York Times* came down in his favour. On October 22 he made a 51-mile tour of the City of New York in cold and rain. Meanwhile, his opponent, Mr Dewey, sought to mobilize every hostile and dissentient element against him. The President, however, standing foursquare upon his record, but dealing chiefly with foreign affairs, hit back upon occasion as hard as he had ever done.

Fourth Term

A Landslide Victory

The result of the election was once again a victory for Roosevelt so decisive as to be in fact a landslide. Such strength as Mr Dewey showed was in the rural districts; the workers in the great towns and cities were overwhelmingly for the President. In both the Senate and the House of Representatives he had comfortable majorities. Thus, not only unique in American history but triumphantly so, he prepared himself to enter on his fourth term.

No sooner was Roosevelt back at the White House than suggestions that he would shortly confer with Mr Churchill and Marshal Stalin filled the American

Press, but arrangements had still to be made. In the meantime, therefore, he attended to the preparations for his fourth term, and spent a holiday at Warm Springs, in Georgia. On his return he took occasion to allay some disquietude in regard to the validity of the Atlantic Charter by declaring that its objectives were sound and as valid as when they were framed.

Early in 1945 his message on the state of the Union was read to a joint session of Congress. It was of exceptional length and great significance, and, after a masterly and comprehensive review of the military situation, in which he paid a vigorous personal tribute to General Eisenhower, went on to state that his country could not and would not shrink from the responsibilities which follow in the wake of battle. He followed it on January 20 by his fourth inaugural address, delivered from the south portico of the White House. On this occasion he spoke for only 14 minutes, though it was historical indeed as the first wartime Presidential inauguration since that of Abraham Lincoln. Then the next important news of him came from the Black Sea, when on February 8 the Press announced that he, Mr Churchill, and Marshal Stalin had reached complete agreement for joint military operations in the final phase of the war against Germany. In a few days the famous Yalta declaration, which disclosed the full extent of the agreement reached among the three national leaders, was given to the world. For him personally, no less than for the other two, it was a crowning triumph of wisdom and political capacity.

Crimea Conference

On March 1 Roosevelt made what he called his 'personal report' of the Crimea conference to the Senate and the House of Representatives and, by broadcast, to the American people. He had, so far as any United States President could, accepted joint responsibility with Great Britain and Russia for the solution of the political problems in Europe – a responsibility, he said, the shirking of which would be 'our own tragic loss' – and he asked for approval of the decisions made by political leaders and public opinion. He looked forward with hope to the San Francisco conference. He believed that the three great centres of military power would be able to achieve their aims for security; and in this mood of confidence he approached the full and intricate problems involved in America's collaboration with the rest of the world. Thus he worked to the end.

Roosevelt was a tall and handsome man with a fine head. In compensation for his weakened lower limbs he had developed a great torso and immense strength in his arms. A direct speaker of remarkable precision and clarity, he had a clear voice with a ring of music in it, which helped him particularly in broadcasting. Instinctively friendly and sympathetic, he was the most approachable of men and had an engaging smile for all. At his Press conferences, which he managed in a fashion of his own, he was the familiar of all who attended them; but nowhere were his immense skill and clever touch in human relationships more apparent. At them he was open to direct *viva voce* examination and permitted himself a frankness which only the observance by the American Press of the strict code of honour embodied in the words 'Off the record' could have rendered possible. He had many interests. In his latter days he was particularly fond of deep sea fishing, and often went for long fishing trips; but his chief hobbies were ships – he had a remarkable collection of prints of them – and philately.

He leaves four sons, James, Elliot, Franklin, and John, all of whom have served in the armed forces, and a daughter who is married to Mr John Boetiger, a journalist, who is now on war service.

* * *

ADOLF HITLER

Dictator of Germany. Twelve years of force and tyranny.

30 APRIL 1945

FEW MEN in the whole of history and none in modern times have been the cause of human suffering on so large a scale as Hitler, who died in Berlin yesterday. If history judges to be greatest those who fill most of her pages, Hitler was a very great man; and the house-painter who became for a while master of Europe cannot be denied the most remarkable talents. He found Germans depressed, bewildered, aimless. After five years in office he had united the German race in a single Reich, abolished regional diversities of administration, and got rid of unemployment. But these achievements were merely instruments of an overwhelming lust for power. Nazi domination over Germany was a stepping stone towards the domination of Nazi Germany over the world. The process was continuous, and the methods were the same. Hitler effected the triumph of the Nazi Party in Germany by a mixture of deceit and violence; he then employed the same devices to destroy other nations. From the time he became master of Germany he made lies, cruelty, and terror his principal means to achieve his ends; and he became in the eyes of virtually the whole world an incarnation of absolute evil.

Hitler was unimpressive to meet on informal occasions, but became transformed when he was face to face with a crowd, especially if it was an audience of his followers. He would speak to them like a man possessed and give the appearance of utter exhaustion when his speech was over. His speeches betrayed few if any original ideas, and even his belief in the suggestive power of reiteration scarcely justified the repetitions of past history with which most of his public orations were overladen. He was, however, a propagandist of the first order, and his uncannily subtle and acute understanding of the mind of his own people was the ultimate source of his power for evil.

Early Years

Adolf Hitler was born on April 20, 1889, at Braunau-am-Inn, on the frontier, as he said himself, of the two German States, the reunion of which he regarded as a work worthy to be accomplished by any and every means. His parents were of Bavarian, and perhaps Bohemian, peasant descent, and his father – who until his fortieth year was known as Schicklgruber – was a Customs officer in the Austrian service and married three times – Adolf being the only son of his young third wife. Adolf was sent to the best school available, being intended for the Government service, though he himself had artistic inclinations. In 1902 his father died suddenly, leaving no resources available for the continued education of his son.

From 1904 to 1909 the young Hitler lived a life of hardship. He moved after the loss of his mother to Vienna where he had dreams of becoming an architect, but could earn only a hazardous livelihood as assistant to a house-painter and by selling sketches. For three years he lived the life of the poorest man in Vienna, sleeping in a men's hostel, eating the bread of charity at a monastery, occasionally reduced to begging. The food for thought also presented gratuitously by life in a great city, to such as care to receive it, was not left untasted by him. Hazy legends like the Nordic saga jostled in his mind with illusions regarding the ennobling effect of war and with more rational dreams of German national unity. He saw and hated the growing Slav ascendancy and the enfeeblement of the German elements in the racially mixed Austro-Hungarian Monarchy. He drank in the pan-Germanism of Luege, in which all the original elements of 'Hitlerism' are to be found. He read assiduously the works of Marx and his disciples, and thoroughly disagreed with their conclusions. He discovered the Jews and acquired a fanatical aversion to them. By 1910 he had so far improved his professional position as to be able to set up as an independent draughtsman; and, still hoping to become an architect, removed to Munich thinking to find wider scope in the Bavarian capital.

A year or two later the 1914–18 war broke out, and Hitler, preferring to enrol himself in the German national army rather than in the polyglot forces of the Hapsburgs, although he was an Austrian subject, joined the 16th Bavarian Reserve Regiment as a volunteer. His war service was meritorious, but not distinguished.

He won the Iron Cross, and rose to the rank of corporal. He was wounded in the battle of the Somme in 1916, and badly gassed in the later stages of the war. It was while lying in a Berlin hospital, temporarily blinded, that he learned of the events known as the November Revolution of 1918.

Political Career Begun

On leaving hospital he returned to Munich. That pleasant city soon became the prey of his enemies the Marxists. The reaction against their regime made a breeding-ground for Fascism. It was at that moment that Hitler began his political career. Thousands of bewildered and workless young Germans were meeting and talking and propounding every sort of theory and scheme. Hitler possessed what most of these fumblers lacked, a few definite ideas and a knowledge of the value and of the art of propaganda. One night he attended in Munich a meeting of a newly formed German Workers' Party, and decided to join it. He was its seventh member, and was not long in making himself its leader and his nationalist and anti-Marxist creed its programme. The movement soon took hold in Bavaria.

Hitler discovered his remarkable oratorical powers and proved himself an adept in the management of large meetings. He realized to the full the value of repetition and of reiterating a single theme over and over again in a slightly different form. 'All propaganda,' he said, 'should adapt its intellectual level to the receptive ability of the least intellectual of those whom it is desired to address.' A pillar of strength in these days was Captain Röhm, a staff officer at Munich and a valued organizer in the councils of his military superiors. He won for Hitler the tacit approval of the local high command and certain financial resources without which two-fold help little progress could have been achieved.

Thus supported and encouraged, Hitler, in conjunction with Röhm, Göring, General Ludendorff, and others, made his first attempt to seize power in the notorious Munich *Putsch* of November 10, 1923. They were met outside the Feldherrnhalle by police, who fired upon them, killing Hitler's nearest companion and 15 others. Hitler lay flat on his face. Only Ludendorff marched straight on. As soon as the firing slackened Hitler, with a dislocated shoulder, fled in a motor-car, but was arrested two days later and imprisoned in the fortress of Landsberg. During the nine months he spent there he wrote the greater part of *Mein Kampf,* that turgid, rambling, remarkable book of nearly 1,000 pages, which became the Bible of the Nazi movement.

Hitler's authority declined after the fiasco of Munich, and for a while Gregor Strasser, the creator of the Nazi Party in North Germany, counted for more than he in the party ranks, whose strength in the Berlin Reichstag was no more than 12. Hitler gradually reasserted himself, however, and in the elections of 1930, when Dr Brüning was Chancellor, and when the economic crisis was already creating widespread unemployment and distress, the number of National-Socialist Deputies jumped to 107.

The political situation rapidly deteriorated. Faced by the growth of the extremist vote and the chaotic state of the party system, the Chancellor was forced increasingly to govern by decree, and though his intentions were most genuinely liberal, he led Germany far along the road to dictatorship. On May 30, 1932, he fell after dealing Hitler two shrewd blows – the dissolution of the Brown Army and the re-election of Field Marshal Paul von Hindenburg as Reichspräsident in face of the fully mobilized Nazi vote in support of Hitler's own candidature. Hitler regarded himself as heir to the Chancellorship. But he had still 10 months to wait, 10 months of crisis during which he was thwarted, not by the now impotent Liberal and Socialist vote, not even by the vociferous Communists, who by their threats to the bourgeoisie were indirectly a help, but by the veiled resistance of the Right Wing of the old regime, with its backing of Junkers, trade magnates, Monarchists, and the *entourage* of the now senile Reichspräsident.

The appointment of the shifty von Papen as Chancellor to succeed Brüning was followed by the rescinding of the latter's ban on the Brown Army as a bait to catch the Nazi support, and by a general election. At the polls Hitler more than doubled his vote, being returned with 230 followers, the largest party in the Reichstag. He demanded the Chancellorship, but Papen manoeuvred him into an interview with the Field Marshal, where Hitler, who was nervous and showed to little advantage, received a pre-arranged rebuff. His prestige suffered considerably thereby, but worse was to follow. After three months of hopeless struggle in a hostile Reichstag Papen held another election. The Nazis lost 2,000,000 votes. A feeling of defeat spread throughout the party. Some of the leaders were in despair. In Germany and abroad it was thought that Hitler had passed his zenith.

In the meantime the affairs of Germany prospered little better than those of the Bavarian ex-corporal. Papen had to resign in November, 1932, and was followed by General Kurt von Schleicher, the last Chancellor of the old regime, a clever man, who came near to destroying Hitler and paid the forfeit on June 30, 1934. Schleicher had the confidence of the Army, and, as far as anyone could, that of President von Hindenburg, but he had no Parliamentary support, and was threatened by Papen, who regarded him as the cause of his own fall from power. Schleicher in December made a bid for independence. He thought to propitiate the Nazi strength by attracting to himself in a semi-Socialist administration Gregor Strasser.

Chancellor at Last

Reichstag Fire

It was a critical moment. Hitler, who had borne the recent setbacks with surprising calm, now lost heart. 'If the party breaks up,' he confided to Goebbels, 'I'll end matters with my pistol in three minutes.' Schism indeed seemed imminent. But Strasser himself spoilt the scheme. He dallied and hesitated. The discussions were deferred, and before they could be resumed Schleicher had fallen. The tables had been suddenly turned by von Papen, who in January made an alliance with Hitler in order to overthrow Schleicher. The Nazi leader, whom he regarded as humbled by recent ill-fortune, was to be Chancellor and he himself Vice-Chancellor, with a majority of non-Nazi colleagues, the good will of the President, and, he confidently hoped, the real power. The plan took shape, and on January 30, 1933, Adolf Hitler was formally invested with the seals of office as Reichskanzler.

The new Government was a minority one, and decided to dissolve the Reichstag and hold another election, the third in nine months. In an unparalleled propaganda campaign, in which the opposition parties had to remain passive observers, voters were belaboured with the Communist menace. Yet the voting gave an absolute majority only to the combined Nazi and Nationalist Parties, and the uneasy alliance between Hitler and Hugenberg, the Nationalist leader, would perhaps have continued but for an event of the first importance, the Reichstag fire. Whoever lit the match, it was the Nazis who arranged and profited by this act of incendiarism. Interpreted by them as a Communist act of terrorism, it was made the pretext for the suspension of all constitutional liberties and the setting up of the Nazi dictatorship under Hitler.

The seizure of power by the Nazis in March, 1933, brought to an end the hollow alliance with the Nationalists under Hugenberg, who was forced to resign shortly afterwards. At the same time the German Press was muzzled and put under the control of Goebbels. Unhampered by Parliamentary restrictions or Press criticism, Hitler and his lieutenants pushed on with the Nazi revolution. Force and unity were the guiding ideals, and every element within or outside Germany which withstood the overriding claims of German nationalism was marked down for destruction.

The long struggle for power was now ended. The National-Socialist Party was faced with the task of consolidation, and this was set about with more zeal than unity of conception or purpose. The position of Röhm's Brown Army in the State and its relation to the Reichswehr and the position of the Stahlhelm, the armed organization of the Nationalists, were among the most thorny problems and involved much bitterness and heart-burning.

The 'Blood Bath'; Shooting of Röhm

On July 1, 1934, the civilized world learnt with horror of the killings that had taken place the day before and have since been known as the purge or the 'blood bath'. How many people lost their lives will never be known. The outstanding victims were Röhm, Schleicher, and Strasser. On the night of June 29 Hitler flew from the Rhineland to Munich and on to the place where Röhm was staying. Röhm was taken from his bed to Munich and shot. All over Germany similar scenes were being enacted. Leading officials of the party and comparative nonentities alike lost their lives. Many an act of private revenge was carried out that night. Hitler, in his statement to the Reichstag, said he had saved Germany from a plot of reactionaries, dissolute members of the Brown Army and the agents of a foreign Power. The reason for the massacre of June 30 may never be exactly known, but apart from private rancours and rivalries it is generally believed that Röhm aimed at having the Reichswehr embodied in his SA organization – which Hitler had the sense to refuse.

The 'blood bath' was officially approved by Field Marshal von Hindenburg, who probably understood nothing of it. A month later, on August 2, the old man died, and within an hour Adolf Hitler was declared his successor. He abjured the title of Reichspräsident and elected to be known as Führer and Kanzler. The poor man of Vienna was now the master of Germany, absolute lord of 60,000,000 Europeans.

Armaments

Hitler's advent heralded a series of increasingly grave breaches of treaty obligations and challenges to European opinion. Dr Brüning had already claimed equality in armaments. This claim was vigorously repeated by Hitler, and it was on the pretext that it had been too tardily admitted by the Powers that he abruptly left the League of Nations in October, 1933. Franco-British discussions in London in February, 1935, for a general settlement were brusquely forestalled by Hitler's announcement of conscription for an army of half a million and the creation of an Air Force. The British Government joined the French and Italian Governments in condemning the unilateral repudiation of treaty obligations, but a few weeks later, in June, 1935, it concluded a naval agreement with Hitler granting him 35 per cent of the naval strength of Great Britain and equality in submarines. To 'his people', as he now called the Germans, it looked as though their Führer's tactics paid, while Europe could no longer ignore the fact that Germany was again a great Power.

In March, 1936, Adolf Hitler, taking advantage of the embroilment of Great Britain and France with Italy over Abyssinia, suddenly occupied the demilitarized zone of the Rhineland, at the same time denouncing the Treaty of Locarno, which he claimed had already been abrogated by the formation of the Franco-Russian

Alliance. The military occupation of the Rhineland was the most serious as well as the most spectacular breach made so far in the facade of the Versailles Treaty. In conjunction with the introduction of conscription it transformed the military situation. It deprived the Western Powers in one moment of the strongest weapon in their armoury, one that had been used in early post-war years, the freedom of entry into German territory. Henceforward Hitler could hope to hold off an attack on his western front with one hand, while the other was free elsewhere.

The occupation of the Rhineland was accompanied by a series of proposals addressed by Hitler to the world at large, and for the special attention of the French and British peoples. He offered a 25-year non-aggression pact, an aid pact for Western Europe, non-aggression pacts with his eastern neighbours, and he even announced his readiness to return to the League of Nations under certain conditions. None of these proposals was taken seriously enough by the outside world for any concrete result to follow.

Suspicion of Hitler was now growing, though the world did not yet grasp the full baseness of Nazi technique, with its deliberate use of the lie as an instrument of policy whereby to lull future victims into a sense of security while some nefarious scheme was being developed elsewhere. Yet the Führer and Chancellor himself had asserted that the bigger the lie the better the chance of its being believed.

The Rhineland coup was followed by two years of digestion and consolidation, during which time German military preparations were pushed forward with increasing activity, and an economic reorganization aiming at self-sufficiency was undertaken. Events outside Germany in 1936 and 1937 increased the nervous tension in Europe and did much to strengthen Hitler's position. The policy of sanctions against Italy incompletely carried out through the machinery of the League of Nations made the worst of both worlds. It fell short of what was needed to save Ethiopia, but served to turn Mussolini from friendship and collaboration with the Western Powers to an increasingly close connection with Hitler, the foremost critic in Europe of the League of Nations. This understanding was given substantive form by the support accorded by the two totalitarian States to General Franco's cause in Spain, and was finally registered by the official establishment in September, 1937, of the Rome–Berlin Axis. By this diplomatic revolution Hitler won an important European ally at the expense of the Powers of the Versailles 'Diktat', whose prestige, both moral and material, had as a result of these various events suffered a considerable diminution.

Seizure of Austria

Entry into Vienna

In the early weeks of 1938 the storm centre of Europe shifted back to Berlin. Hitler engineered an abrupt crisis in Austro-German relations, which ended on March 11 by the violation of the frontier by the German Army and the forcible incorporation of Austria in the Reich. Mussolini, who in 1934, on the murder of Herr Dollfuss, had massed troops on the Brenner frontier, made no move, and received the effusive thanks of the Führer: '*Mussolini: Ich soll es Ilnen nie vergessen.*' Hitler's dramatic entry into Vienna a few days later, after nearly a quarter of a century's absence, during which he had experienced every vicissitude of hope, despair, and triumph, was watched with curiosity and even sympathy by millions of people outside the Reich, whose Governments had in the past resoundingly refused to the constitutional requests of both Berlin and Vienna the union which the German Dictator had now achieved by force.

The union of the Reich and the Ostmark, as Austria was now called, immediately raised the problem of Czechoslovakia, which contained a minority of some 3,500,000 Germans and was now surrounded by German territory on three sides. The question asked all over Europe was how soon would Bohemia share the fate of Austria. Hitler's assurance to the Czech Government that it had nothing to fear did not allay suspicion. A series of communal elections throughout Czechoslovakia in May raised to fever-pitch the excitement created in the German minority by the inclusion in the Reich of their Austrian co-racialists. At the annual meeting in September of the National-Socialist Party at Nuremberg Hitler stood as the avowed champion of the Sudeten Germans, and their demands immediately precipitated an acute European crisis involving the imminent risk of general war. Hitler, with the German Army mobilized, his western front approaching a state of impregnability, faced by potential opponents who were mentally bewildered and militarily unprepared, and divided both geographically and ideologically, was in a position to dictate his terms. In conferences at Berchtesgaden and Godesberg with Mr Neville Chamberlain, and then at Munich, where M. Daladier and Mussolini, as well as Mr Chamberlain, were present, he put forward demands that France and Britain were not in a position to refuse. To save the peace of the world and to avoid their own destruction the Czechs were told that they must submit to the arrangements made by the four Great Powers at Munich, whereby all the German districts of Bohemia, together with the immense fortifications of the Erzgebirge, were handed over absolutely to Germany. In eight months Hitler had added 10,000,000 of Germans to the Third Reich, had broken the only formidable bastion to German expansion south-eastwards, and had made himself the most powerful individual in Europe since Napoleon I.

Czechoslovakia a 'protectorate'

In the course of his conversations with Mr Chamberlain Hitler had assured him that he had no more territorial claims to make in Europe – a phrase he had also used after the seizure of Austria. On March 15, 1939, the world was, however, startled to hear that the German Army was invading and overwhelming Bohemia, Moravia, and Slovakia, all that remained of the independent Republic. President Hacha, who under German pressure had succeeded Dr Benesh in the autumn, was summoned to Berlin and forced to accept terms which made his country a 'Protectorate' of the Reich. Hitler went to Prague to proclaim there another bloodless victory and then while the going was good travelled to Memel, which had been ceded under the Versailles Treaty to Lithuania, and announced its annexation on March 23.

Poland had profited from the dismemberment of Czechoslovakia by being allowed to annex the disputed region of Teschen. But she was marked down as the next victim. While German troops were still moving into Slovakia Hitler proposed to the Polish Government that Danzig should be returned to Germany and that Germany should build and own a road connecting East Prussia with the rest of the Reich, in return for which Germany would guarantee the Polish frontiers for 25 years – though a 10-year treaty of non-aggression already existed between the two countries, of which five years had still to run. Poland rejected the proposals and appealed to Great Britain and France for support. These countries at once gave Poland pledges to defend her independence, if necessary by war. The action of the Western Powers came as a shock to Hitler, who was further alarmed by negotiations shortly afterwards set on foot in Moscow by the French and British with the Soviet Government. The spectre of war on two fronts again arose to damp the German ardour for acquisition. Hitler, faced with the prospect of a check and a rebuff, fatal contingencies for an aspiring dictator, made his decision. Rather than give up his cherished, and indeed loudly proclaimed design of seizing Danzig and the Polish Corridor, he was prepared to eat every word he had uttered in condemnation, derision, and defiance of the Bolshevist regime, and to invite the Russians to agree to a non-aggression pact. Stalin on his side, finding the danger of a German attack suddenly exorcized, and distrusting the constancy of the Western Powers, was not unwilling to accept Hitler's overtures, and the Pact was signed on August 23.

Hitler Starts War

With the disappearance of any likelihood of Russian assistance being given to the western allies Hitler saw no further obstacle in the way of an immediate attack on Poland, and on August 31, 1939, he ordered the German Armies to cross the frontier. The Second World War had begun. With typical falsity Hitler and Ribbentrop – now his intimate and most pernicious adviser – had offered the Polish Ambassador terms of settlement, and broadcast them to the world, a few hours before the soldiers began the invasion, without, however, allowing the Ambassador time or means to convey them to his Government.

The attack on Poland gave the world its first taste of the horrors of a German *Blitzkrieg.* Hitler went East to superintend the slaughter in person. It was a swift and terrible war which he waged in bitter hatred and, when the issue was clear, with crude boastings and gross lies at the expense of a broken nation. In a speech at Danzig on September 19 he had the effrontery to declare that: 'Poland has worked for this war' and 'peace was prevented by a handful of (British) warmongers'. On the same occasion he took up what he called the British 'challenge' to a three years' conflict and announced that Germany possessed a new weapon. The grim business was over in a few weeks. Warsaw surrendered on September 24 and on October 5 Hitler visited it and swaggered among the ruins which were garlanded for the occasion.

The next day, speaking in the Reichstag, he made what he called his last offer to the allies. It was a remarkable rhetorical performance, though, obviously nervous, he hurried through the phrases in which he described his new friendship with the Russians. As a plea for peace it could, if only one of its premises had been sound and one of its promises could have been believed, scarcely have been bettered; but he had by that time to pay the price of his habitual contempt for truth. In early November he made a speech at Munich, on the anniversary of the *Putsch* of 1923, in which he said that he had given Göring orders to prepare for a five years' war. He ended earlier than had been expected and left the Burgerbräu beer cellar in which he made it for Berlin. Shortly afterwards there was an explosion in which six people were killed and over 60 injured. The official German News Agency claimed that the attempt had been inspired by foreign agents and offered a reward of half a million marks for the discovery of the instigators. One George Elsen was arrested. Official Germans were infuriated with *The Times* for suggesting that the explosion was no surprise to the Führer and that he had left early to avoid it.

France Crushed

On New Year's Day, 1940, Hitler declared that he was fighting for 'a new Europe'. On March 18 he met Mussolini on the Brenner, a presage, as it was later recognized to be, of great events. In April came the invasions of Norway and Denmark, and in early May he was congratulating his troops on their success and authorizing decorations for them. On May 10 his armies invaded Belgium, Holland, and Luxembourg, and on the same day he went to the Western Front. On the morrow he proclaimed that the hour for the decisive battle for the future of the German nation had come. In less than a month the bells were rung in Germany to celebrate the victorious conclusion of what he called 'the greatest battle of all time'. A few days later he congratulated Mussolini on the entry of Italy into the war. On June 22 the Armistice with France was signed. At that moment Hitler stood at the zenith of his success and power. Western Europe was his and there remained no one there to crush except Great Britain, weakened by her losses on the Continent and without an effective ally. As usual Goebbels was turned on to prepare the way.

Battle of Britain
Victory Promised for 1941

On July 19, speaking in the Reichstag, Hitler 'as a victor' made his final appeal to 'common sense' before proceeding with his campaign against her. He spoke with an unusual sobriety, but there was no mistaking his threats. He had his answer from a united and determined Empire. On September 4 he reiterated his menaces. Then he unleashed the *Luftwaffe* and the Battle of Britain began in earnest. On October 4 after a month of it he was back at the Brenner to talk things over with Mussolini. In a few days his troops entered Rumania. A little later he went to the Spanish frontier for a discussion with General Franco with a view, it was thought, to tightening the blockade of Great Britain. Before the end of the month he was back with Mussolini in Florence. He seemed about this time to understand that Great Britain could not be conquered from the air and to think increasingly in terms of U-boats. He described himself as the 'hardest man the German people have had for decades and, perhaps, for centuries'.

In his New Year's proclamation to the army Hitler promised victory over Great Britain in 1941 and added that every Power which ate of democracy should die of it. He continued, for he always seemed uneasy on this score, to place the blame for unrestricted air warfare on Mr Churchill, and he kept on expressing his confidence in the U-boat. All that spring, indeed, he seemed particularly eager to encourage his followers. In April he invaded Yugoslavia and Greece and went to join his advancing armies. And all the time he kept hammering at Great Britain from the air and striking under water at her supply lines.

On June 3, 1941, there was another meeting of the dictators on the Brenner Pass, and it was suggested that there would be an immediate start in the organization of a Continental peace; but on June 22 he cast aside his mask and struck at Russia. Once again the Soviet Government became the 'Jewish-Bolshevist clique', and once again he was free to indulge his inherent hatred of the Slav. There were the usual lengthy and disingenuous explanations; but they were not calculated to deceive close readers of *Mein Kampf*. For at least five years, indeed, he had contemplated this particular *volte face*, for in 1934 he had taken Dr Rauschning into his confidence in regard to his intention if necessary to employ a Russian alliance as a trump card.

In August he and Mussolini visited the Eastern Front. As a gage of affection he presented his brother-in-arms with a great astronomical observatory. After a long silence he spoke on October 4 at the opening meeting of the Winter Help Campaign and announced a 'gigantic operation' which would help to defeat Russia. A few days later he was boasting that he had smashed her.

The Supreme Command
Brauchitsch Dismissed

After the Japanese attack on Pearl Harbour of December 7 most of the world was in the conflict. In announcing his declaration of war on the United States to the Reichstag Hitler abused President Roosevelt and said that America had planned to attack Germany in 1943. Just before Christmas he dismissed Field Marshal von Brauchitsch, his Commander-in-Chief, and took supreme command himself. A promise which he had made two months before to capture Moscow had not been fulfilled, and his own troops were retiring before the Red Army. He felt, perhaps, that he had to find a culprit for the failure and also to put heart into his own troops. He spent Christmas at his headquarters in Eastern Europe, not as previously, among his front line troops.

Hitler's New Year message for 1942 was far less confident than that of 1941. 'Let us all,' he said, 'pray to God that the year 1942 will bring a decision.' There were rumours of disagreement with his generals and of pressure from the radicals within the Nazi ranks. In March he appointed Bormann to keep the party and the State authorities in close cooperation. He was making strenuous efforts to build up the home front, to increase the number of foreign workers in Germany, and to procure the forces for a spring offensive.

In April he received from the obedient Reichstag the title of 'Supreme War Lord' and measured the duration of the Reich by the mystical number of a thousand years. The tremendous eastward thrust of the summer of 1942 was delivered, reached the Volga, and went deep into the Caucasus. In September he claimed that Germany had vastly extended the living space of the people of Europe and called on his own to do their duty in the fourth winter of the war. On October 1, at the Sportspalast, he taunted, boasted, and promised the capture of Stalingrad. His effort to make good his word in the end cost Germany a tremendous loss of lives and material. He seemed, however, at this period to be more inclined to talk about the inability of the allies to defeat him than to prophesy a German victory. In November, after the allied landings in North Africa, his troops overran unoccupied France and seized Toulon.

A Chastened Man

In the New Year order of the day for 1943 he prophesied that the year would perhaps be difficult but not harder than the one before. He was certainly a much chastened Führer. The industrial effort of Germany was being seriously disrupted by air attack, and Russia was pressing perilously hard. On the tenth anniversary of his accession to power he did not speak, but entrusted Goebbels with a proclamation to read for him. His silence gave rise to rumours, some to the effect that he was giving up his command of the army, others that he was dead. On February 25, instead of speaking, he issued another proclamation to celebrate the birthday of the party. It added fresh fuel to the rumours.

On March 21 Hitler at last broke silence. The manner of his speech was lifeless and almost perfunctory. The matter, even for one as prone as he to endless reiteration, was all too familiar. His only news was that he had started to rearm not in 1936 but in 1933.

Mussolini's Fall

The Italian Capitulation

Hitler, in his appeal on the anniversary of the Winter Help scheme on May 20, told the German people that the army had faced a crisis during the winter in Russia – a crisis, he said, which would have broken any other army in the world. Soon another crisis faced the Germans. On July 25 Mussolini fell from power, four days after it had been announced that Hitler and Mussolini had met in northern Italy where it was believed Mussolini had demanded more help from Germany in the defence of Italy. But Italy was not to be kept at Germany's side, and on September 8 Marshal Badoglio, who had succeeded Mussolini, announced in a broadcast that his Government had requested an armistice from the allies. Hitler reacted in characteristic manner. He told the Germans that the collapse of Italy had been foreseen for a long time, not because Italy had not the necessary means of defending herself effectively, or because the necessary German support was not forthcoming but rather as a result of the failure or the absence of will of those elements in Italy who, to crown their systematic sabotage, had now brought about the capitulation. Though Hitler was able to claim this foreknowledge of events in Italy, it was clear from his speech, which was direct and effective, that he did not underestimate the seriousness of his new problem.

Hitler seemed still to have the collapse of Italy in mind when he emerged from his headquarters on November 8 to spend a few hours with the 'Old Comrades' of the National-Socialist Party at Munich. He spoke deliberately and forcefully. He was loudly cheered when he declared that the hour of retaliation would come. He said that everything was possible in the war but that he should lose his nerve, and he assured his audience that however long the war lasted Germany would never capitulate. She would not give in at the eleventh hour; she would go on fighting past 12 o'clock. At the beginning of his twelfth year in power – on January 20 – Hitler spoke of the danger from Russia. 'There will be only one victor in this war, and that will be either Germany or Soviet Russia.'

In the late afternoon of July 20 it was announced that an attempt had been made on Hitler's life. The attempt was a deep and well-laid plan by a group of generals and officers to end Hitler's regime and the military command. General Beck, who was Chief of the General Staff until November, 1938, when he was dismissed, was declared to have been the chief conspirator. It was added that he was 'no longer among the living'. On August 5 a purge of the Army was announced from Hitler's headquarters. 'At the request of the Army,' the announcement said, Hitler had set up a court of honour to inquire into the antecedents of field marshals and generals and to find out who took part in the attempt on his life. It was disclosed that several officers had already been executed. Further executions were announced on August 8.

In a proclamation issued on November 12 as part of the annual commemoration of the Nazis who fell in the *Putsch* of 1923, Hitler declared that Germany was fighting for her life. Throughout the proclamation there were references to his own life and to its unimportance compared with the achievement of German aims. 'If, in these days,' Hitler said, 'I have but few and rare words for you, the German people, that is only because I am working unremittingly towards the fulfilment of the tasks imposed upon me, tasks which must be fulfilled if we are to overcome fate.' In the spring the gravity of Germany's crisis became clear. The Russians reached the Oder; the British and Americans crossed the Rhine. On April 23 Marshal Stalin confirmed that the Russians had broken through the defences covering Berlin from the east. The battle for Berlin had begun, and Hitler, the man who brought ruin to so many of Europe's cities, was, according to Hamburg radio, facing the enemy in his own capital, and there he came to his end.

GENERAL G. S. PATTON

Brilliant American war leader

21 DECEMBER 1945

GENERAL GEORGE S. PATTON JUNIOR, commander of the United States Fifteenth Army, whose death is announced on another page, was one of the most brilliant and successful leaders whom the war produced. It was he who led the American attack on Casablanca, forged his way through to effect a juncture with the Eighth Army near Gafsa, commanded the Seventh Army in Sicily, and then swept at the head of the Third from Brittany to Metz and onwards.

George Smith Patton, a cavalryman by training and instinct, became a tank expert. Brave, thrustful, and determined in action, he was a remarkable personality, who taught his men both to fear and to admire him. At the same time he was a serious and thoughtful soldier. He was an early advocate of the employment of armour in swiftly moving masses to exploit the break-through, and was finally able, with the help of American methods of mass-production, to realize his theories in practice. A great athlete in his earlier days, he had also a taste for philosophy, literature, and poetry. He was the son of a California pioneer, and was born at San Gabriel, in that State, on November 11, 1885. Soldiering was in his blood for he was the great-grandson of General Hugh Mercer, who served under Washington, and his grandfather died in the Civil War. It was natural, therefore, that he should find his way to the United States Military Academy at West Point, where he graduated in 1909. After great achievements on the track at West Point he was to be placed fifth in the cross-country run of the Modern Pentathlon (in the main a military event) at the Olympic Games of 1912. He was also to be known as a fine horseman and show rider and a crack pistol shot. He developed a flamboyant and emotional character for which his men found expression in the sobriquet 'Old Blood-and-Guts', but he was a born military leader.

Commissioned in the cavalry, Patton served first at Fort Sheridan, Illinois. A little later he went to France to study the sabre there and after his return served as Master of the Sword at the Mounted Service School at Fort Riley, Kansas. In 1916 he was aide-de-camp to General Pershing on the punitive expedition into Mexico. Then, when America entered the 1914–18 war he, by that time a captain, went on Pershing's staff to France, where, in November, 1917, he was detailed to the Tank Corps and attended a course at the French Tank School and he was present when the British tanks were launched at Cambrai. After this he organized the American

General George S. Patton

Tank Centre at Langres and later the 304th Brigade of the Tank Corps, which he commanded with much distinction in the St Mihiel offensive of September, 1918. Having been transferred with his brigade to the Meuse-Argonne sector he was wounded on the first day of the offensive; for his services he was awarded the DSC and DSM and at the time of the Armistice was a temporary colonel.

Returning to the United States in early 1919, Patton in 1920 was given command as a permanent captain of a squadron of the 3rd Cavalry at Fort Myer. Then he was detailed to the general staff corps and served for four years at the headquarters of the First Corps area at Boston and in the Hawaiian Islands. After four more years at Washington he was ordered to Fort Myer, where, as a permanent lieutenant-colonel, he remained on duty with the 3rd Cavalry until 1935.

Patton received command of the 2nd Armoured Division in October, 1940, with the temporary rank of brigadier-general, becoming in the next year commanding general of the First Armoured Corps. While he was thus employed Patton learned that they might be required in North Africa. He therefore set up a large training centre in California, where he built up a coordinated striking force. At last his opportunity came and as commander of the Western Task Force he and his men succeeded in their swift descent in occupying Casablanca. He himself had a narrow escape, for the landing craft which was to take him ashore was shattered. Later, when the American Second Corps were it difficulties at Kasserine Pass, Patton was sent to retrieve the situation and, with timely British aid, not only did so but carried it on to Gafsa, near which it made contact with the Eighth Army. Thus it was that he was chosen to command the Seventh Army in the invasion of Sicily. It was while he was visiting a field hospital in that island that, suspecting a soldier of being a malingerer, he struck him. The incident was reported and General Eisenhower made it clear that such conduct could not be tolerated; but Patton, who made generous apology, was far too valuable a man to lose when hard fighting lay ahead, and a little later he was nominated to the permanent rank of major-general.

In April, 1944, he arrived in the European theatre of operations, and he took command of the Third Army, which went into action in France on August 1. With it he cut off the Brittany peninsula, played his part in the trapping of the Germans and drove on to Paris. In October he had another of his narrow escapes when a heavy shell landed near him but failed to explode. Driving on relentlessly towards the German frontier, it fell to Patton to reconquer Metz, and in recognition of this victory he received the Bronze Star. His next outstanding performance was in late December when the Third Army drove in to relieve the First and helped to hold Bastogne. He was famous for the speed of his operations, but surpassing himself on this occasion, he surprised the Germans, and slowed down and eventually checked the advance of Rundstedt's southern column. One of his most striking feats was when in the advance to the Rhine, he moved towards that river with his right flank on the Moselle. The Germans were apparently expecting him to force a crossing of the Rhine, but instead he suddenly crossed the Moselle near the confluence, taking the enemy 'on the wrong foot' and completely smashing up his array. In Germany his armoured divisions made the deepest advances of all, penetrating in the end into Czechoslovakia. A German staff officer, captured in the final stages, reported that his general had asked him each morning as a first question what was the latest news about Patton.

In April this year President Truman nominated Patton to be a full general. The Third Army occupied Bavaria last July, and in September Patton was ordered to appear before General Eisenhower to report on his stewardship of Bavaria. The summons was a result of Patton's statements to a Press conference that Nazi politics are just like a Republican and Democratic election in the United States, and that he saw no need for the de-Nazification programme in the occupation of Germany. In October General Eisenhower announced that General Patton had been removed from the command of the Third Army and had been transferred to the command of the Fifteenth Army, a skeleton force.

Patton, in spite of many idiosyncrasies, which included the free use of a cavalryman's tongue – 'You have never lived until you have been bawled out by General Patton' his men used to say – was a fundamentally serious soldier, offensively minded and bent on the single object of defeating his enemy. He affected a smart and sometimes striking turnout, and was insistent that those under him should also maintain a smart and soldierly appearance.

* * *

JOHN MAYNARD KEYNES

A great economist

21 APRIL 1946

LORD KEYNES, the great economist, died at Tilton, Firle, Sussex, yesterday from a heart attack.

By his death the country has lost a very great Englishman. He was a man of genius, who as a political economist had a worldwide influence on the thinking both of specialists and of the general public, and he was also master of a variety of other subjects which he pursued through life. He was a man of action, as well as of thought, who intervened on occasion with critical effect in the great affairs of state, and carried on efficiently a number of practical business activities which would have filled the life of an ordinary man. And he was not merely a prodigy of intellect; he had civic virtues – courage, steadfastness, and a humane outlook; he had private virtues – he was a good son, a devoted member of his college, a loyal and affectionate friend, and a lavish and unwearying helper of young men of promise.

The Right Hon. John Maynard Keynes, CB, Baron Keynes, of Tilton, Sussex, in the Peerage of the United Kingdom, was born on June 5, 1883, son of Dr John Neville Keynes, for many years Registrary of Cambridge University. His mother was Mayor of Cambridge as lately as 1932. He was brought up in the most intellectual society of Cambridge. He was in college at Eton, which he dearly loved, and he was proud of being nominated by the masters to be their representative governor later in life. He won a scholarship to King's College, Cambridge, in mathematics and classics, writing his essay on Héloïse and Abelard. He was President of the Cambridge Union, won the Members' English Essay Prize for an essay on the political opinions of Burke, and was twelfth wrangler in the mathematical tripos. Although he did not take another tripos, he studied deeply in philosophy and economics and was influenced by such men as Sidgwick, Whitehead, W. E. Johnson, G. E. Moore, and, of course, Alfred Marshall.

In 1906 he passed second into the Civil Service, getting his worst mark in economics – 'the examiners presumably knew less than I did' – and chose the India Office, partly out of regard for John Morley and partly because in those days of a smooth working gold standard, the Indian currency was the livest monetary issue and had been the subject of Royal Commissions and classic controversies. During his two years there he was working on his fellowship dissertation on 'Probability' which gained him a prize fellowship at King's. This did not oblige him to resign from the Civil Service, but Marshall was anxious to get him to Cambridge, and, as token, paid him £100 a year out of his private pocket to supplement the exiguous fellowship dividend – those were before the days of his bursarship of the college. Anyhow, his real heart lay in Cambridge. He lectured on money. He was a member of the Royal Commission on Indian Currency and Finance (1913–14). He served in the Treasury (1915–19), went with the first Lord Reading's mission to the United States, and was principal representative of the Treasury at the Paris Peace Conference and deputy for the Chancellor of the Exchequer on the Supreme Economic Council. After his resignation he returned to teaching and to his bursar's duties at King's, but he always spent part of his time in London. He was a member of the Macmillan Committee on Finance and Industry, and parts of its classic report bear the stamp of his mind.

In 1940 he was made a member of the Chancellor of the Exchequer's Consultative Council and played an important part in Treasury business. He was appointed a director of the Bank of England. In 1942 he was created Lord Keynes, of Tilton, and made some valuable contributions to debate in the Upper House. He became High Steward of Cambridge (Borough) in 1943. His continued interest in the arts was marked by his trusteeship of the National Gallery and chairmanship of the Council for the Encouragement of Music and the Arts (CEMA). In 1925 he married Lydia Lopokova, renowned star of the Russian Imperial Ballet – 'the best thing Maynard ever did', according to the aged Mrs Alfred Marshall. She made a delightful home for him, and in the years after his serious heart attack in 1937 was a tireless nurse and vigilant guardian against the pressures of the outside world.

Lord Keynes's genius was expressed in his important contributions to the fundamentals of economic science; in his power of winning public interest in the practical application of economics on critical occasions; in his English prose style – his description of the protagonists at the Versailles Conference, first fully published in his *Essays in Biography* (1933), is likely long to remain a classic – and, perhaps it should be added, in the brilliant wit, the wisdom, and the range of his private conversation, which would have made him a valued member of any intellectual salon or coterie in the great ages of polished discussion.

In practical affairs his activities in addition to his important public services were legion. As bursar of King's he administered the college finances with unflagging attention to detail. By segregating a fund which could be invested outside trustee securities he greatly enlarged the resources of the college, and, unlike most college bursars, he was continually urging the college to spend more money on current needs. From 1912 he was editor of the *Economic Journal*, which grew and flourished under his guidance, and from 1921 to 1938 he was chairman of the National Mutual Life Assurance Society. He ran an investment company. He organised the Camargo Ballet. He built and opened the Arts Theatre at Cambridge and, having himself supervised and financed it during its period of teething troubles, he handed it over, when it was established as a paying concern, as a gift to *ex-officio* trustees drawn from the university and city. He became chairman of CEMA in 1942 and of the Arts Council in 1945. He was chairman of the *Nation*, and later, when the merger took place, of the *New Statesman*; but he had too scrupulous a regard for editorial freedom for that paper to be in any sense a reflection of his own opinions. He also did duty as a teacher of undergraduates at King's College and played an important and inspiring part in the development of the Economics faculty at Cambridge. The better students saw him at his most brilliant in his Political Economy Club. He was interested in university business and his evidence before the Royal Commission (1919–22) was an important influence in causing it to recommend that the financial powers of the university should give it greater influence over the colleges.

To find an economist of comparable influence one would have to go back to Adam Smith. His early interest was primarily in money and foreign exchange, and there is an austere school of thought which regards his *Indian Currency and Finance* (1912) as his best book. After the 1914–18 war his interest in the relation between monetary deflation and trade depression led him on to reconsider the traditional theory about the broad economic forces which govern the total level of employment and activity in a society. He concluded that, to make a free system work at optimum capacity – and so provide 'full employment' – it would be necessary to have deliberate central control of the rate of interest and also, in certain cases, to stimulate capital development. These conclusions rest on a very subtle and intricate analysis of the working of the whole system, which is still being debated wherever economics is seriously studied.

Popularly he was supposed to have the vice of inconsistency. Serious students of his work are not inclined to endorse this estimate. His views changed in the sense that they developed. He would perceive that some particular theory had a wider application. He was always feeling his way to the larger synthesis. The new generalization grew out of the old. But he regarded words as private property which he would define and redefine. Unlike most professional theorists, he was very quick to adapt the application of theory to changes in the circumstances. Speed of thought was his characteristic in all things. In general conversation he loved to disturb complacency, and when, as so often, there were two sides to a question he would emphasize the one more disturbing to the company present.

His *Treatise on Probability* is a notable work of philosophy. Although using mathematical symbols freely, it does not seek to add to the mathematical theory of probability, but rather to explore the philosophical foundations on which that theory rests. Written clearly and without pedantry, it displays a vast erudition in the history of the subject which was reinforced by and reinforced his activities as a bibliophile.

Keynes had on certain occasions an appreciable influence on the course of history. His resignation from the British delegation to the Paris Peace Conference and his publication a few months later of *The Economic Consequences of the Peace* had immediate and lasting effects on world opinion about the peace treaty. The propriety of his action became a matter of controversy. Opinions still differ on the merits of the treaty, but about the point with which he was particularly concerned, reparations, there is now general agreement with his view that the settlement – or lack of settlement – was ill-conceived and likely to do injury to the fabric of the world economy. His subsequent polemic against the gold standard did not prevent a return to it in 1925, but largely added to the ill repute of that system in wide circles since. It was mainly through his personal influence some years later that the Liberal Party adopted as their platform in the election of 1929 the proposal to conquer unemployment by a policy of public works and monetary expansion.

In two wars he had a footing in the British Treasury. The idea of deferred credits was contained in the pamphlet entitled 'How to Pay for the War', which he published in 1940. From 1943 he played a principal part in the discussions and negotiations with the United States to effect a transition from war to peace conditions of trade and finance which avoided the errors of the last peace, and to establish international organization which would avoid both the disastrous fluctuations and the restrictions which characterized the inter-war period. He was the leader of the British experts in the preparatory discussions of 1943 and gave his name to the first British contribution – 'the Keynes Plan' – to the proposals for establishing an international monetary authority. In July, 1944, he led the British delegation at the Monetary Conference of the United and Associated Nations at Bretton Woods, where an agreed plan was worked out. He was the dominant figure in the British delegation which for three months, from September to December, 1945, hammered out the terms of the American Loan Agreement, which he defended brilliantly in the House of Lords. He was appointed in February Governor of the International Monetary Fund and the International Bank for Reconstruction and Development, and in these capacities had just paid a further visit to the United States, whence he returned only two weeks ago. These continuous exertions to advance the cause of liberality and freedom in commercial and financial policies as a means to expand world trade and employment imposed an exceptionally heavy and prolonged strain which, in view of his severe illness just before the war, Lord Keynes was physically ill-fitted to bear.

His life-long activities as a book-collector were not interrupted, even by war. His great haul of unpublished Newton manuscripts on alchemy calls for mention. He identified an anonymous pamphlet entitled 'An Abstract of a Treatise of Human Nature', acquired by his brother, Mr Geoffrey Keynes, as being the authentic work of David Hume himself. He had it reprinted in 1938, and it will no doubt hereafter be eagerly studied by generations of philosophers. During the second war his hobby was to buy and then, unlike many bibliophiles, to read rare Elizabethan works. His interest in and encouragement of the arts meant much to him. From undergraduate days he had great friendships with writers and painters and, while his activities brought him in touch with many distinguished people of the academic world and public life, he was probably happiest with artistic people. At one period he was at the centre of the literary circle which used to be known as 'Bloomsbury' – Lytton Strachey, Virginia Woolf, and their intimate friends. More than fame and worldly honours he valued the good esteem of this very cultivated and fastidious society.

And finally there was the man himself – radiant, brilliant, effervescent, gay, full of impish jokes. His entry into the room invariably raised the spirits of the company. He always seemed cheerful; his interests and projects were so many and his knowledge so deep that he gave the feeling that the world could not get seriously out of joint in the end while he was busy in it. He did not suffer fools gladly; he often put eminent persons to shame by making a devastating retort which left no loophole for face-saving. He could be rude. He did not expect others to bear malice and bore none himself in the little or great affairs of life. He had many rebuffs but did not recriminate. When his projects were rejected, often by mere obstructionists, he went straight ahead and produced some more projects. He was a shrewd judge of men and often plumbed the depths in his psychology. He was a humane man genuinely devoted to the cause of the common good.

HENRY FORD

Motor manufacturer and idealist

7 APRIL 1947

Mr Henry Ford, the motor-car manufacturer, who died suddenly at his home, Dearborn, near Detroit, on Monday night at the age of 83, was for many years one of the world's outstanding individuals.

In his own sphere as a maker of machines Ford effected the greatest revolution of his day. It was due largely to him that the motor-car, instead of continuing for years to be a luxury for the rich, was brought speedily within the reach of comparatively humble folk. In the course of this accomplishment the process of mass production was carried to new and unheard-of lengths and a novel conception of its possibilities was created. The industrial empire which Ford's imagination and drive established was in due course to yield him an immense fortune; but wealth was at no period his goal. He was in fact an emotional visionary, ignorant of much that quite ordinary people know, but with real good will for all and a power of handling the practical things of life which has never been surpassed. Thus for many years he was a continuing astonishment to his contemporaries, who, marvelling one day at his new designs for motor-cars or his new schemes for still vaster factories, would find him on the next with startling proposals for higher wages, shorter hours, or better methods of salesmanship, or, just as likely, attacking the bankers or preaching pacifism, bickering with his own Government, or at issue with organized labour. In all that he did or said moreover, he remained his independent and opinionative self, satisfied, as was indeed quite often true, that he was serving his age as successfully as he was supplying it with tractors, motor-cars, and aeroplanes.

Henry Ford was born on July 30, 1863, on a farm at Dearborn, Michigan, the son of William Ford, a prosperous farmer, who was of Irish stock. His mother was of mixed Dutch and Scandinavian origin and had been adopted by one Patrick O'Hearn. He went to the local school, where he seemed a normal boy, good but not exceptionally brilliant at his studies. At an early age, however, he disclosed a remarkable mechanical bent and an eager curiosity in regard to the working of machines. At 17 he became an apprentice in a machine shop in Detroit, but after nine months he felt he had learned all he could there and went on to another firm. After a time his employment failed to satisfy him and he returned to Dearborn, reconciled to it by the fact that Clara Bryant, whom he married in 1888, was a

Henry Ford and his son Edsel in a model 'F' Ford outside the Ford residence in Detroit in 1905.

neighbour. Years of happiness followed: but he nevertheless continued to be haunted by an early ideal of a machine which would do the heavy work of a farm. In the country he kept a machine shop of his own and worked in summer for a harvester company by repairing their portable farm engines. However, the promptings of his genius became too strong for him and eventually he decided to go back to Detroit where in 1890 he secured a post with the Detroit Edison Electric Company.

Ford had realized in his earlier Detroit days that the public were more interested in road vehicles than in tractors; but scheme as he would the weight of a steam engine had thwarted him. Then in an English paper, the *World of Science*, he had read of a 'silent gas engine' which used gas for fuel. A little later he had been asked to repair one of these Otto engines. Convinced by his study of it that its principles were sound, he had in 1887 built his first gas engine, and had kept on building more. After he returned to Detroit, however, he worked in his spare time on his first 'gasoline buggy', and in 1893 it was ready for public trial, at which it attained a speed of 25 miles an hour. In 1896 he began work on a second car. In 1899 he resigned his position and organized a local company in which, holding one sixth of the stock, he became chief engineer. The company made cars on the model of his first one. Ford, whose governing idea was to provide automobiles for the masses, was soon in disagreement with his associates, who thought chiefly of profits, and in 1902 he resigned, 'determined never again to put myself under orders'. At that time the public interest was centred on racing cars and Ford determined to enter the racing field. He proved astonishingly successful with some racing machines of his design and thus drew attention to his own car. In 1903, therefore, he was able to found the Ford Motor Company with 12 shareholders and a capital of $100,000, of which $20,000 was put into the company, the only cash investment in its long career which did not come from earnings. In 1908 Ford himself became the controlling owner and president, and in 1924 he and his son, Edsel, were to acquire all the stock. Ford had long had his own ideas about quantity production, and with control in his own hands was able to put them into effect. Sales began to rise and his products to enter foreign markets. His success in the Scottish Reliability Trials of 1905 had already helped him considerably in establishing himself in Great Britain. He also developed a new agency policy which included an agreement to maintain service stations. The car itself had, moreover, been steadily improving, and in 1908 and 1909 his famous model 'T' was put on sale. Standardization became thenceforward his settled policy, and the 'assembly line' was devised; but in this, as in all else, his ruling notion was service to the ordinary man.

In 1915 Ford was able to turn his attention to his first love, the farm tractor. The European war seemed to him to impose a delay in placing it on the market: but victory depended upon British agriculture making good the food shortage which the German submarines were causing, and Ford sent his Fordson tractor to the rescue. He also rendered notable service by fulfilling his undertaking to build Eagle submarine chasers by the same methods he employed in regard to his cars. From war, however, he refused to profit. At this period indeed the magician in production stood in strange contrast to the unrealistic pacifist who as leader of a group of cranks went in the Peace Ship to Scandinavia in order to have the 'boys out of the trenches by Christmas, never to return'. It was the foolishness of a child, but the intention was entirely sincere. Ford had his difficulties and in the slump of 1920 faced a serious financial situation: but he found his own way out and his vast undertaking went on from strength to strength. In 1924 its annual production reached the towering peak of 2,000,000 cars, trucks, and tractors. His achievements were, moreover, by no means in the material sphere alone. Of humble origin himself he had a deep feeling for his employees, and worked out rough and ready principles in regard to labour which he consistently applied. One was to pay the highest possible wages, and in this he was a true reformer; another to accept applicants for work without questions or references. Ex-prisoners were welcomed: but once a would-be employee was accepted he came under a rigid discipline which followed him even into his home. For years Ford would have nothing to do with unions. His passion for the perfect organization of production led him indeed into an effort to mechanize the human material he employed. It was, however, a deterrent to many independent-minded Americans and numbers of his workers were drawn from recent emigrants to the United States.

In 1918 Ford, who was a supporter of President Wilson, had run unsuccessfully for the Senate and in 1923 there was some talk – it caused alarm among the professional politicians – that he would run for the Presidency, and a movement to support him was started; but before long he himself announced his refusal to stand against Mr Coolidge. In the next year his acquisition of the Dagenham site in addition to his Trafford Park and Cork works was announced. It was part of a post-war policy of expansion, and between 1931 and 1946 over 1,000,000 vehicles were manufactured at the Dagenham factory alone. He then went into civil aviation, opened his company's private air service, and soon afterwards his all-metal monoplanes were on sale. It was the beginning of great developments. At this period the Press published many stories of his fabulous wealth, and his spectacular successes and good treatment of his workers were widely discussed, and Ford himself wrote three books concerning his own life's work and ideals – *My Life and Work*, *To-day and To-morrow*, and *Moving Forward*. In 1927 'Model T' was superseded and over 350,000 advance orders were received for his new car. In April, 1931, his 20,000,000th car came off the assembly line, but in that year also the company, suffering like all others from the depression, lost £10,000,000.

The years immediately before the 1939–45 war saw a revival in the Ford fortunes and fresh expansions of plant, and as the war developed his company did excellent work; but the production of his great plant at Willow Run scarcely lived up to his earlier estimates of his own capacity as a producer. In 1943 Ford lost his only child and close associate, Edsel Bryant Ford, who for many years had played a leading part in all his undertakings, and, although nearly 80, himself resumed the presidency of his company. He resigned, for the second time, in 1945, and on his nomination his grandson, Henry Ford II, was elected in his place. Henry Ford II, who was born in September, 1917, had been released from the United States Navy in 1943 to direct war production at the Ford Motor Company, of which he was appointed executive vice-president in 1944.

MAHATMA GANDHI

Apostle of independence

30 JANUARY 1948

Mr Gandhi, who was assassinated in Delhi yesterday afternoon, was the most influential figure India has produced for generations. He set out to promote national consciousness, and to defend the ancient Indian ideals of poverty and simplicity against the inroads of modern industrialism, though this part of his teaching was seldom heard in his later years. He judged all activities, whether of the State or of the individual, by their conformity to the doctrine of non-violence, which he held to be the panacea of all human ills, political, social, and economic. His day of triumph when British authority was voluntarily withdrawn was turned to profound sorrow, for communal strife and bloodshed, instead of ending as he had confidently hoped, were greatly intensified, and the two new Dominions of India and Pakistan were brought to the verge of war. To efforts to replace this fratricidal strife by Hindu, Muslim, and Sikh harmony and good will he devoted the last months of his long life.

In all parts of the world many regarded the 'Mahatma' ('great soul') as both a great moral teacher and a great Indian patriot. Others held him to be the victim of a naive self-delusion which blinded him to the race-hatred, disorder, and bloodshed which his 'non-violent' campaigns against British authority invariably provoked. But few critics have questioned the sincerity of his repudiation of force. A whole-hearted pacifist, he believed he had a mission not to India only but to all the world. To his own co-religionists he was certainly a 'saint'. His increasing asceticism, finally marked by a complete indifference to the comforts of life (though these were showered upon him by wealthy supporters), won him a reverence that bordered upon adoration; the popular mind long credited him with powers little short of miraculous; his gospel of the liberation of India from British rule early won the enthusiastic support of most of the younger school of Hindu politicians, and did much to wean them from the cult of anarchy; his defence of Hindu faith and culture against western 'materialism' gave him the adhesion of multitudes of the orthodox.

A convinced Hindu, but widely read in other faiths and a great admirer of the Christian ideal, he was a powerful advocate of social reform. The poverty of the masses and his desire for India to return to the simplicities of the past led him to proclaim the need for the people, rich and poor alike, to spin by hand their own cotton thread and to weave and wear their own hand-made cotton cloth. Wherever he went his *charka* (spinning wheel) went with him, and as he talked to those who sought him daily he spun his cloth.

Mohandas Karamchand Gandhi was born on October 2, 1869, at Porbandar, the capital of a small State in Kathiawar, Western India, where his father, though belonging only to the socially obscure Bania (moneylending) section of Hindus, was the Dewan. He was married when only 13 to a child of the same age, but from 1906 was a *Brahmacharya* – that is, a celibate within the marriage state for the purpose of realizing God. In early life he admired Western ways, and in this period he read law at the Inner Temple and was called to the Bar. He was meticulous in wearing the top hat and frock coat of the 'town kit' of the period. Some years later on, after conviction in India, he was disbarred. All his life he remained a strict vegetarian and total abstainer. In 1893 he went from Bombay to South Africa in connection with an Indian legal case of some complexity, and remained to oppose discriminatory legislation against Indians, and his stay lasted for 21 years. Gandhi was admitted an advocate of the Supreme Court. When the South African war broke out he organized an Indian Ambulance Corps, 1,000 strong, which often worked under heavy fire. Again, in 1906, on the outbreak of the Zulu rebellion, he formed a stretcher-bearer corps.

After the passage of an Act in 1913 restricting Indian migration between the different Provinces of the Union, some 3,000 Indians with Gandhi at their head, crossed the border from Natal into the Transvaal in order to court arrest. Many, including the leader, his wife, and one of his sons, were imprisoned. In 1914 Gandhi returned to India by way of London, and he landed here a few days before the outbreak of the 1914–18 War. He was instrumental in organizing from among the Indian students a volunteer ambulance corps, which rendered good service. In Western India he rapidly became the champion of all whom he regarded as weak and oppressed, and was associated with the whirlwind movement for Home Rule resulting from the activities of Annie Besant, but at the War Conference convened by the Viceroy at Delhi in the spring of 1918 he supported 'with all his heart' a resolution of support of the war effort.

In 1919, in pursuance of what he called *satyagraha*, or 'truth-seeking', he issued a pledge of refusal to obey the Rowlatt Acts, 'and such other laws as the committee to be hereafter appointed may think fit'. There followed the serious disturbances of April, 1919, both at Ahmedabad, Gandhi's home, and in the Punjab, notably at Amritsar. The loss of life thus caused led Gandhi to admit that he had made a blunder of 'Himalayan' dimensions. But from this time began his unquestioned mastery over the Congress Party organization. To him that party was India; and as its spokesman he was India's chosen mouthpiece.

In the spring of 1920 Gandhi considered that India was spiritually prepared to undertake a further campaign of passive resistance without risk of lapse into violence. He started a movement of 'non-violent non-cooperation', declaring it would be maintained until the claims of the Khilafat movement – started by Indian Muslims to obtain alleviation of the harsh peace terms imposed on Turkey after the 1914–18 war – were conceded, and until public servants alleged to be guilty of 'martial law excesses' in the Punjab were adequately punished. He promised *swaraj*, meaning complete self-government without the aid of the British, within a year. On paper at least he collected within a few months a crore of rupees (£750,000) for *swaraj*. Gandhi's open letter to the Viceroy (the first Lord Reading) dated February 9, 1922, giving him seven days in which to announce a change of policy, had scarcely been dispatched when at Chauri-Chaura, in the Gorakhpur district, United Provinces, a number of constables were attacked in their *thana* and burnt to death. He called a halt to the civil disobedience movement and imposed upon himself a five days' fast. On March 10, 1922, he was arrested, and was later tried for conspiracy. Gandhi pleaded guilty and was sentenced to six years' simple imprisonment, but was released in January, 1924, after an operation in gaol for appendicitis.

Early in 1929 Gandhi shared responsibility for a resolution of conditional acceptance of the proposed Round Table Conference passed at a meeting of political leaders. But on March 12, 1930, Gandhi, with 80 volunteers, began a march of 200 miles on foot from his *ashram*, near Ahmedabad, to Dandi, a village on the sea coast in the Surat district, for the purpose of collecting salt, and thereby defying the law. On May 5 he was arrested and interned at Yeravda Gaol, near Poona, under a Bombay Regulation of 1827. The economic effects of the second era of civil disobedience were much more serious than those of the first, owing in large measure to the intensity of the boycott.

The Round Table Conference met in London in the autumn of 1930. Lord Irwin (now Lord Halifax) released the Congress leaders to facilitate discussions and had a number of interviews with Gandhi. These led in March, 1931, to the signature of the famous Irwin–Gandhi Pact.

Gandhi came to London in the late summer as the sole delegate of the Congress at the Round Table Conference. The expectation formed in many quarters here of seeing a man of commanding gifts was not fulfilled. He had no mastery of detail: constitutional problems did not interest him. He was no orator; his speeches were made seated and delivered slowly in low, level tones, which did not vary whatever his theme might be. His interventions in discussion were mainly propagandist, and often had little real connection with the matter in hand. He made no real constructive contribution to the work of the Conference. Meantime the pact was breaking down, and on Gandhi's return to Bombay a renewed campaign of civil disobedience was initiated by the Congress under his chairmanship. Once more he was arrested, on January 4, 1932, and detained in Yeravda Gaol.

When the British Government's communal award was published he intimated

Mahatma Gandhi arriving at Folkestone in 1931.

to the Prime Minister (Mr Ramsay MacDonald) that he would starve himself to death unless the part of the award giving separate seats to the depressed classes (which in his view cut them off from the Hindu community) were withdrawn or suspended. The fast began on September 20, 1932, but some political leaders of the two communities negotiated a compromise, approved by the Mahatma and accepted by Government. Gandhi accordingly broke his fast on the seventh day. There was great diversity of opinion, in Hindu ranks particularly, on Gandhi's advocacy of legislation to secure admission of the depressed classes to the temples of higher caste folk. At the end of April, 1933, he announced his intention in this connection to fast for 21 days, and when the ordeal began on May 8 he was unconditionally released. Soon after Gandhi arranged to lead another civil disobedience 'march'. On the eve of the march, July 31, he was arrested, and a few days later was sentenced to a year's imprisonment.

Dissatisfied with the facilities given to him in prison to work for the Harijans (his name for the depressed classes), he decided once more to fast, and after a week of abstinence from food he was released purely for medical reasons on August 23. The civil disobedience movement was waning, and in April, 1934, Congress adopted his advice to suspend it. But his personal contact, and that of Congress leaders generally, with the Viceroy and the Governors was not resumed until, in the summer of 1937, the Viceroy (Lord Linlithgow) took the initiative in bringing the long estrangement to an end by inviting Gandhi to meet him at Delhi.

In the first general election for the Provincial Parliaments under the Act of 1935 the widespread Congress organization scored striking successes, and its candidates obtained majorities in six of the 11 Provinces of British India. When provincial autonomy was introduced in April, 1937, and the question of acceptance or non-acceptance of office by the Congress Party was under constant discussion, Gandhi casually admitted to a distinguished and sympathetic British public man that he had not read the India Act of 1935, for his entourage and advisers had assured him that it gave nothing of real worth to India. Persuaded by his visitor to repair the omission, he admitted when they next met that he had been mistaken and that the Act marked a very substantial advance. Thereupon he threw his immense weight against Pandit Nehru's policy of abstention and of course carried the day. Congress Ministries were formed, after a few months of the familiar attempts at bargaining with Government in which the Mahatma was such an adept. Gandhi then retired with his considerable entourage to a remote village near Wardha, in the Central Provinces, and it became known as Sevagram (the village of service). Gandhi showed an unexpected gift for realism by encouraging Ministers in paths of administrative orthodoxy, while pressing forward his ideals, such as a policy of prohibition by instalments, and what is known as the Wardha plan of primary education.

Though he had upheld for years a 'gentleman's agreement' that the Congress would not come between the Princes and their subjects, he did intervene early in March, 1939, in Rajkote, a small Kathiawar State, on the ground that the Thakore Saheb had gone back on his word as to constitutional advances. He issued a 24 hours' ultimatum, and as it was not accepted he began a 'fast unto death', but the Viceroy (Lord Linlithgow) suggested a solution of the immediate question, and Gandhi abandoned his fast at the beginning of the fifth day. The Mahatma's hold on Nationalist reverence was increased, rather than diminished, by his public apology and expression of contrition for having resorted to a coercive method not consistent with his non-violent principles. Yet he was to resort to it on future occasions. He was not free from 'the last infirmity of noble minds', and was skilful in exhibitionism.

When war broke out in September, 1939, it seemed for a short time that Gandhi would invite the Congress Party to give moral support to the nations seeking to prevent, though by armed force, the enslavement of the world by brutal aggressors. But he became convinced that only a 'free India' could give effective moral support to Britain; and his demand for 'complete independence' became more and more urgent. When Japan struck down Malaya and invaded Burma Gandhi became seriously perturbed at the defence measures which the Government of India initiated.

In the spring of 1942, when the discussions between Sir Stafford Cripps (then Lord Privy Seal in Mr Churchill's Government) and the party leaders had reached a hopeful stage, Gandhi advised against settlement and the negotiations with the Congress leaders broke down. The war situation was then unfavourable, and Gandhi was commonly alleged to have talked contemptuously of the draft Declaration whereby India was to secure complete self-government after the war as a 'post-dated cheque on a crashing bank'. He demanded that the British should 'quit India' (a slogan which had wide currency), that the Indian Army should be disbanded, and that Japan should be free to come to the country and arrange terms with a non-resisting people.

In August, 1942, he concurred in the decision to strike the blow of mass obstruction against the war effort – 'open rebellion', as he calmly called it. This led to his arrest and that of other Congress leaders and to widespread disorder and bloodshed. Gandhi was interned in the Aga Khan's palace at Poona and was barred from political contacts, though he was allowed the companionship of Mrs Gandhi, who died in February, 1944. Gandhi continued in detention until May 6, 1944, when he was released unconditionally on medical grounds. Later all the leaders were released to share in the prolonged discussions arising from attempts to bring an end to the increasing strife between Hindus and Muslims over the Pakistan issue.

A long prepared and carefully staged series of discussions between the Mahatma and Mr Jinnah, at the house of the latter in Bombay, yielded no tangible result, for Mr Gandhi stated that he spoke only for himself and had no commission from the working committee of the Congress. Indeed, for many years he had withdrawn from actual membership of the party, only to dominate it from without. The explosive possibilities of the situation developed with the end of the war. The historic Cabinet Mission, headed by Lord Pethick-Lawrence, went out in the spring of 1946 and spent three anxious months of incessant conference and negotiation in the heat at Delhi. The Mahatma took a large share in the negotiations chiefly behind the scenes, and in his inscrutable way was at times helpful and at times the reverse. When at long last and amid most serious outbreaks of communal violence the short-term and long-term plans of the Cabinet Mission led to the formation at Delhi of an interim National Government, with Mr Nehru as Vice-President of the Council, Gandhi remained outside the Cabinet, much to the relief of its members. But no major decision could be taken either at the Centre or in the Provincial Congress Governments without full consideration of the views and wishes of the Mahatma, the idol of the Hindu masses.

The announcement made by Mr Attlee in February, 1947, that complete British withdrawal would not be later than June, 1948, had the effect of accentuating the conflict between the two main parties, and the subsequent antedating of the time limit and decision to set up two Dominions, India and Pakistan, quickened savage outbreaks in the Punjab between Hindu and Sikh on the one side and Muslims on the other. Moreover, when Independence Day came the sanguinary unrest in Calcutta led to fears that the division of Bengal would have untoward consequences. 'Bapu', who had been travelling from place to place in Eastern Bengal and in Bihar preaching brotherhood, went to Calcutta, and at the beginning of September undertook another fast not to be ended until normal conditions were restored. The party leaders exerted themselves in exhortations to the people, and on the fourth day the Mahatma was able to end his ordeal. Thus he succeeded where armed force had failed. The miracle encouraged him to stage in Delhi early this month his fifteenth fast in the effort to bring harmony between India and Pakistan. He had shown himself acutely conscious that in the lust for communal reprisals his word did not carry the weight of former years. The fast began as the Security Council at Lake Success was considering the controversy on Kashmir and related problems between the two Dominions. One effect of the fast and leading to its cessation on the fifth day was the decision pressed on the Cabinet at New Delhi by the Mahatma no longer to withhold from the Karachi Government payment of the whole of the £41m, due from the undivided cash balances at the time of the British withdrawal.

GEORGE ORWELL

Criticism and allegory

21 JANUARY 1950

MR GEORGE ORWELL, a writer of acute and penetrating temper and of conspicuous honesty of mind, died on Friday in hospital in London at the age of 46. He had been a sick man for a considerable time.

Though he made his widest appeal in the form of fiction, Orwell had a critical rather than imaginative endowment of mind and he has left a large number of finely executed essays. In a less troubled, less revolutionary period of history he might perhaps have discovered within himself a richer and more creative power of imagination, a deeper philosophy of acceptance. As it was he was essentially the analyst, by turns indignant, satirical, and prophetic, of an order of life and society in rapid dissolution. The analysis is presented, to a large extent, in autobiographical terms; Orwell, it might fairly be said, lived his convictions. Much of his early work is a direct transcription of personal experience, while the later volumes record, in expository or allegorical form, the progressive phases of his disenchantment with current social and political ideals. The death of so searching and sincere a writer is a very real loss.

George Orwell, which was the name adopted by Eric Arthur Blair, was born in India in 1903 of a Scottish family, the son of Mr R. W. Blair, who served in the opium department of the Government of Bengal. He was a King's Scholar at Eton, which he left in 1921, and then, at the persuasion of his father, entered the Imperial Police in Burma, where he remained for five years. After that he was, by turns, dish-washer, schoolmaster, and book-seller's assistant. The name he adopted comes from the river Orwell – his parents were settled at Southwold, in Suffolk, at the time he decided upon it. Orwell preferred to suppress his earlier novels. *Down and Out in Paris and London*, his first book, published in 1933, is a plain, observant and, for the most part, dispassionate piece of reporting, which achieves without faltering precisely what it sets out to do. Orwell had strived in a Paris slum and in England had tramped from one casual ward to another, and the lessons of this first-hand acquaintance with poverty and destitution were never afterwards lost on him. Although in time he grew fearful of a theoretical egalitarianism, he made no bones about the primary need of securing social justice. In *The Road to Wigan Pier*, which appeared in 1937, he described the lives of those on unemployment pay or public assistance and made his own contribution to Socialist propaganda.

Next year he brought out his *Homage to Catalonia*, an outspoken and at times impassioned account of his experience and observation as a volunteer on the Republican side in the Spanish civil war. He had joined not the International Brigade but the militia organized by the small Catalan party predominantly syndicalist or anarcho-syndicalist in temper – known as POUM. He was wounded during the fighting round Huesca. With deepening anxiety and embitterment he had noted the fanaticism and ruthlessness of Communist attempts to secure at all costs – even at the cost of probable defeat – political ascendancy over the Republican forces. It was from this point that his left-wing convictions underwent the transformation that was eventually to be projected in *Animal Farm* and *Nineteen Eighty-Four*.

First, however, a few months before the outbreak of war in 1939, he published *Coming up for Air*, the book which is his nearest approach to a novel proper. It was not his first published essay in fiction. In *Burmese Days*, published five years earlier, he had written with notable insight and justice of the administrative problems of the British in Burma and of the conflict of the white and native peoples, though the personal story tacked on to this treatment of his subject was weak and rather lifeless. The book suggested clearly enough, indeed, that Orwell was something other than a novelist. Yet in *Coming up for Air*, for all that it sought to present, in a picture of the world before 1914, a warning of the totalitarian shape of things to come, he recaptures the atmosphere of childhood with a degree of truth and tenderness that is deeply affecting. Here was the creative touch one sought in vain in the later books.

Rejected for the Army on medical grounds, Orwell in 1940 became a sergeant in the Home Guard. He wrote spasmodically rather than steadily during the war years. His picture of Britain at war, published in 1941 under the title *The Lion and the Unicorn*, was a brave attempt to determine the relationship between Socialism and the English genius. A volume consisting of three long essays, *Inside the Whale*, one of which was the entertaining, if occasionally somewhat wrongheaded, study of boys' popular weeklies, preceded the appearance in 1945 of *Animal Farm*. In the guise of a fairy-tale Orwell here produced a blistering and most amusing satire on the totalitarian tyranny, as he saw it, that in Soviet Russia masqueraded as the classless society. The book won wide and deservedly admiring notice. In *Nineteen Eighty-Four*, published early last year, the premonition of the totalitarian wrath to come had developed into a sense of fatalistic horror. In Orwell's vision of a not too remote future in Airstrip One, the new name for Britain in a wholly totalitarian world, men had been conditioned to deny the possibility of human freedom and to will their subservience to an omnipotent ruling hierarchy. The book was a brave enough performance, though it fell a good way short of the highest achievement in its kind.

Orwell married in 1933 Miss Eileen O'Shaughnessy. She died in 1945 after an operation, and last year he married Miss Sonia Brownell, assistant editor of *Horizon*.

GEORGE BERNARD SHAW

A prophet in the theatre

2 NOVEMBER 1950

AFTER SIX DECADES of unsparing creative and controversial activity Mr Bernard Shaw, who died yesterday at the age of 94, still commanded an eager hearing on both sides of the Atlantic and in some European countries. He addressed himself habitually to the intellect, rarely to the heart; yet he was a master of comedy, and however acidly satirical or deliberately outrageous his opinions he was able to treat the driest or most delicate subject with a gaiety that disarmed and with a witty lucidity that entertained. Admiration he systematically courted and in abundant measure won, and for the sprightly patriarchal figure – a sort of intellectual Father Christmas – delightedly pulling important legs and pricking portentous bubbles with, on the whole, such stimulating and diverting effect, the public came also to feel affection.

Like so many of the most formidable critics of Victorianism, Shaw was himself a Victorian, and a fairly early one at that. He was born in the twentieth year of the Queen's reign and was in his middle forties when the reign ended. Before the Golden Jubilee he had written all his novels, he had been converted by Henry George to Socialism, and was making his mark as Fabian pamphleteer and orator. His art and music criticism were behind him, and he was 'G. B. S.' of the *Saturday Review*, the most dreaded and the most entertaining dramatic critic of the time, as well as the author of 10 plays, when the Diamond Jubilee was celebrated. In the following year he abandoned professional criticism for professional play writing, though he continued his Socialist crusading and gave up much time to platform work and national and local politics. But it was as an Edwardian that he entered the first of the three productive periods on which his reputation as a comic dramatist rests. From 1904 till 1907 he was the ruling creative spirit of the brilliant Vedrenne–Barker management at the old Court Theatre, and there some of his most exhilarating comedies were first seen. His second period was from 1911 until the outbreak of war in 1914, and with one of the plays of this period, *Pygmalion*, he introduced the Shavian comedy to the straitest sect of West End playgoers. The third began with *Heartbreak House*, written during the war; it continued with *Back to Methuselah*, and ended gloriously with *Saint Joan* in 1923. It was a height to which he never afterwards attained, but he continued to write plays of varying merit during the next quarter of a century, and before the end his dramatic compositions numbered nearly 60.

All this while he was the subject of a continually changing legend which, in each of its forms, he vigorously cultivated. In his days as a Fabian orator he was regarded as a saviour of society by his more enthusiastic disciples and as an emissary of the devil by his more frightened opponents; and he rejoiced in, and profited by, the extravagant alternative. During the time of his increasing fame as a dramatist before the 1914–18 war both the hopes and fears implicit in the alternative lost something of their edge, and his writings on the war were merely unpopular. They plunged him into relative obscurity; but within five years of the Armistice he had with *Saint Joan* become in the fullest sense a popular dramatist. Throughout the world the legend changed again and assumed gigantic proportions. Shaw became a benign major prophet, honoured in his own lifetime as Voltaire and Goethe in theirs.

George Bernard Shaw was born in Dublin on July 26, 1856, the third child and only son of George Carr Shaw, an impoverished and feckless Civil servant, and Lucinda Elizabeth, daughter of Walter Bagenal Gurly, the owner of land in County Carlow, which his grandson inherited. His early home was not happy. In it he learned three things: a hatred of the snobbishness by which he suffered; a dislike of Irish Protestantism, in which, as it seemed to him, hypocrisy and genteel pretensions were bound together; and, from his mother, whose consolation it was, a love and a knowledge of music. Such formal education as he received at the Wesleyan Connectional School, afterwards Wesley College, in Dublin, seems to have profited him less than the acquaintance with the works of great composers acquired at home. When still in his teens he entered the office of a land agent, in whose uncongenial service he remained four years.

At the age of 20, after some lonely dilettantism with a piano and amateur renderings of opera in 'Irish Italian', he threw up his employment and came to London to join his mother, who had attempted to become a singing teacher. In those days he thought of himself primarily as an evangelist rather than as an artist, and he appears, from contemporary accounts, to have been at that time not only a bad writer but, if the needs of the papers to which he sought to contribute are a standard of judgment, an unadaptable journalist. Consequently he failed in nine years to earn more than £6 by his pen. Afterwards the journalistic incompetence wholly disappeared; so soon as there began to be a Shavian legend, none knew better than Shaw how to feed it; but his preferring in himself the educationist to the artist never forsook him. Indeed, his letters to *The Times* on all sorts of subjects, their serious purpose hardly cloaked by characteristic sallies, were something of a feature of his last years; the last letter appeared only a few weeks ago.

There are in his works, in the plays no less conspicuously than the prefaces, superb pieces of writing, notably in *John Bull's Other Island* and in the last part of *Back to Methuselah*, the concluding speech of which must crown any anthology of

Anglo-Irish prose; but he was not primarily a man of letters; his mastery was as a salutary iconoclast. During his first nine years in London he wrote five novels: *Immaturity*, which was refused by Meredith for Chapman and Hall; *Cashel Byron's Profession*, of which Stevenson, who admired it, afterwards wrote: 'If Mr Shaw is below 25, let him go his path. It he is 30, he had best be told that he is a romantic, and pursue romance with his eyes open'; *The Irrational Knot*, later recognized by the proud author as 'an Ibsenite novel'; *Love Among the Artists*, a criticism of shallowness in art and in family relations; and *An Unsocial Socialist*, the first genuine blast of the Shavian gale.

At first no publisher could be found for Shaw's five books, but the result of his entry into the Socialistic arena of the eighties was the serialization of some of them in magazines of propaganda such as *To-day* and Mrs Besant's *Own Corner*. In time they became a rage in America, 'free of all royalty to the flattered author'. In 1884 he had joined the Fabian Society, one of whose leaders he became. He wrote and worked for them with an impassioned devotion, lecturing every Sunday on some subject that he was unconsciously storing up in his mind for subsequent use in the theatre. The strong and abiding influence on Shaw from his Fabian days was Sidney Webb, through whom he acquired that perhaps exaggerated veneration for blue-book method which was joined to the habit of iconoclasm he seemed to have taken over from Samuel Butler and to his own native love of paradox.

In 1885, thanks to William Archer, he became art critic of the *World*, and proved himself, in this and the other papers he served, one of the most sparkling contributors to contemporary journalism. He wrote on books for the *Pall Mall Gazette*, on music for the *Star* as 'Corno di Bassetto', on music for the *World* where the initials 'G. B. S.' first became famous, and on the theatre for the *Saturday Review*. He wrote also 'The Perfect Wagnerite', which appeared in 1898, and 'The Quintessence of Ibsenism', the most profound of all his essays in criticism. Meanwhile Bernard Shaw the dramatist had begun to displace the critic and the Socialist orator. His first play was *Widowers' Houses*, begun years earlier in collaboration with William Archer, but completed by Shaw himself for production by the Independent Theatre in 1892. It was a direct offspring of his Fabian activities. *The Philanderer*, a comment on Ibsenism, followed, but was not produced, and *Mrs Warren's Profession*, a discussion of prostitution, was withheld from public performance by the censorship and was not seen on the stage until given privately by the Stage Society in January, 1902. *Arms and the Man*, a derisive essay on the false romanticism of war, was, and remains, a remarkably good entertainment; *Candida*, *The Man of Destiny*, *You Never Can Tell*, *The Devil's Disciple*, *Caesar and Cleopatra*, and *Captain Brassbound's Conversion* occupied their author during the closing years of the century.

His marriage took place in 1898 to Miss Charlotte Frances Payne-Townshend, whose considerable wealth was of immediate assistance in helping him to consolidate his position as a dramatist and whose steady, clear-minded companionship was of the greatest value to him until her death in September, 1943. Important though his output had been it was not until the Vedrenne–Barker management began to produce a series of his plays at the Court Theatre that Shaw came into his own. *Man and Superman*, which had been published two years earlier, was produced there on May 23, 1905. It definitely established his fame and, together with a group of revivals, led to a collective reconsideration of his earlier work. *John Bull's Other Island* was performed at the Court Theatre at the end of 1904. *How He Lied to Her Husband*, after earlier production in New York, appeared a few months later; *Major Barbara* in November, 1905; and *The Doctor's Dilemma* in November, 1906. Shaw was now established. During the years that remained before the 1914–18 war he was continuously active, and, though *The Shewing Up of Blanco Posnet* fell beneath the ban of the censorship, *Getting Married* (1908), *Press Cuttings* (1909), *Fanny's First Play* (1911), *Overruled* (1912), *Androcles and the Lion* (1913), and *Pygmalion* (1914) regularly increased his fame.

It was with the production in this country, in 1921, of *Heartbreak House*, a play written during 1913–16 that was designed to illustrate 'cultured, leisured Europe before the war', that he began to acquire another and deeper reputation. Here was the unmistakable accent of prophecy, even of poetic prophecy. For the first time the visionary in Shaw stood revealed as he sought to bring contemporary history home to the conscience of the English middle classes. In the summer of 1921 *Back to Methuselah* was published, but had to wait two years for its first English production at Birmingham. This gigantic work, though parts of it were made tedious by the author's powerlessness to resist personal gibes and idiosyncratic divagations, revealed his increasing preoccupation with philosophy as distinct from contemporary social propaganda. Here the puritanism and the poetry in Shaw were fused in an austere vision of human destiny, a vision that drew something of majesty from Shaw's presiding sense of the purpose of the Life Force. From these remote heights he came out to the illuminated landscape of *Saint Joan*, which was produced by the Theatre Guild in New York in the last days of 1923 and at the New Theatre in London in the following March. This play was a summary of Shaw's strength and weakness. He was unable to resist his ancient quips at the expense of Englishmen, which had been good jokes once but now were a little hoary; he damaged an epilogue, not itself unjustifiable, by needless theatricalism; and he punctuated the most serious passages of the play with rather wanton farcical flourishes. But he did succeed in communicating the passion of insight with which he had dug for truth beneath the rigid crust of history.

In November, 1926, the Swedish Academy awarded to him the reserved Nobel Prize for Literature for 1925, with the proceeds of which he afterwards set up the Anglo-Swedish Literary Foundation. A long pause in his output followed,

George Bernard Shaw in the doorway of his garden shed in 1944.

explained in the summer of 1928 by the appearance of *The Intelligent Woman's Guide to Socialism and Capitalism.* What was virtually a new stage in his career began in 1929. *The Apple Cart, Too True to be Good,* and *On the Rocks* showed their author adroitly responding to the world's increasing distaste for Parliamentary forms – a distaste which he was the quicker to applaud because in England these forms had been preserved. In 1936 he was 80, as vigorous and as much himself as ever; but his greatest work was done. *The Simpleton of the Unexpected Isles, The Six of Calais, The Millionairess,* and *Farfetched Fables* were comparatively unimportant. Only in its third act did *Geneva,* produced in 1938, display the old arresting argument and a truly trenchant wit. His fiftieth play, *In Good King Charles's Golden Days,* was quietly entertaining and even seemed to possess an unfamiliar mellowness. And there were no new legends. In the decade before the war Malvern had become his shrine and lamps of his genius were lit there annually. Revivals of his plays here, there, and everywhere were endless. Broadcasting, the films, and even television united in exploiting him.

It was long a habit of Shaw's opponents to question his sincerity. The truth underlying this accusation was, simply, that, having something to say in which he sincerely believed, he allowed no scruple of good art or conventional good manners to influence the means he used to obtain an audience. There is also no doubt that it was his wit, good or bad, shrewd or knockabout, that won Shaw his audience. Thus, little by little, mixing wisdom with what was doubtful wisdom and relying always upon one device or other of merely arresting attention rather than upon the perfection of any work of art, Shaw imposed the reasoned contrarieties, or seeming contrarieties, of Erewhon upon generations younger than his own. Not himself an original thinker, since he drew his ideas from a miscellany of sources – from English Socialist tradition, from Bergson, from Nietzsche, from Butler and Butler's gloss upon Lamarck – he was nevertheless a leaven and stimulant of popular thought whose achievement is so large as to evade calculation. On his ninetieth birthday, an honorary freeman of the city of Dublin and a freeman of the borough of St Pancras, he was quite unmistakably acknowledged as a freeman of the world also.

There remains the comic dramatist who showed that it was possible to write comedies in which the dramatic tension should be sustained by the conflict, not of living men and women, but of ideas touched by genius into vivid theatrical life. For a while these stage discussions, stimulating and amusing as they were allowed to be, were not recognized for plays, but criticism came in course of time to realize that the excitement they produced was genuinely dramatic and that the apparently formless talk was in fact shaped by a firmly drawn logical line. It was when the logical line weakened, as it did in most of the plays written after *Saint Joan*, that the author's title to dramatist was once again called in question; but by that time the new comedy which Shaw had created rested on a solid basis.

In nearly all his plays he knew how to entertain for at least a part of the time. Some of the plays are already old enough to enable us to perceive that the seasoning of nonsense, which was a sop to their first audiences, is now the least acceptable part of them. So long as it remains serious the speech of Don Juan in Hell is of unswerving interest; the noblest part of Shaw's genius is in it. Together with *Candida*, the best of *The Devil's Disciple* and, at long range, *You Never Can Tell*, it forms an epitome of his claim to survive in the theatre as a comic dramatist who is also the author of *Saint Joan*; while survival, so far as the pleasures of reading are concerned, must surely extend to *John Bull's Other Island, Heartbreak House*, and – for all its imperfections – *Back to Methuselah*. If, indeed, the Shavian theatre as a whole lives on it will live as evidence of the influences that divided the twentieth century from the nineteenth, and of the saving poetic temper as well as the extraordinary vitality which enabled a man whose purpose was not consciously aesthetic to create a theatrical form suited to the needs of the artist driving him imperiously from within.

ARNOLD SCHOENBERG

Beyond chromaticism

13 JULY 1951

PROFESSOR ARNOLD SCHOENBERG, who died on Friday at his home at Los Angeles at the age of 76, was probably the most discussed musician of the twentieth century.

His system of atonality, or, as he preferred to call it, twelve-tone music, though reached by process of evolution from chromaticism, was the most revolutionary movement in musical history since Monteverde in the seventeenth century. It is so subversive of established ways of thought that its general adoption is improbable in the extreme, but it has provided a ferment of far-reaching influence on modern music. In this respect, as in some others, Schoenberg is like Stravinsky; between 1910 and 1930 these two men were the outstanding figures in the history of modern music. Curiously enough, both suffered the same fate. At the height of his fame each was forced to leave his country and to adjust himself to new conditions.

Schoenberg was born in Vienna on September 13, 1874. At the age of eight he learnt to play the violin and composed short violin duets for his lessons. Later on he taught himself the cello and composed a string quartet. For several years he worked without any outside help or supervision. Alexander von Zemlinsky (whose daughter he married in 1901), a composer of whom Brahms had a very high opinion, recognized his outstanding talent, gave him his first instruction in composition and brought him into the musical circles of Vienna. Schoenberg's earliest works were written in the style of Brahms, whose technique he admired, and later set as a model to his pupils when he was teaching composition himself.

The first work which Schoenberg made known to the musical world was a string sextet, *Verklärte Nacht*. It was an attempt to apply the symphonic form of a tone poem to chamber music. To the same period belong the *Gurrelieder*, a cantata for solo voices, chorus and orchestra written in 1900, a tone poem, *Pelleas and Melisande*, and a string quartet in D minor. A new development began with the Chamber-Symphony in E, opus 9, in 1906. Schoenberg's style became concise, his harmonies more daring. It was these works which first roused the opposition of conservative musicians and the admiration of a younger generation who were trying to find new ways of expression. This aim was achieved in the three piano pieces, opus 11, 1909, written in the so-called 'atonal style' which aroused much discussion among musicians all over the world. At this time Schoenberg left Vienna and settled in

Berlin. Here he wrote *Pierrot Lunaire*, a cycle of poems recited in a kind of song-speech accompanied by instruments. This work established Schoenberg's fame as one of the leading modern composers. In 1913 he returned to Vienna to teach composition, and, after the end of the 1914–18 war, he founded a society for the performance of modern music. He embodied his technical principles in the *Treatise on Harmony*, begun in the early years of the century and since revised, but it is only recently in a volume of essays, *Style and Idea*, that he has discussed their aesthetic basis.

The years between 1920 and 1925 were the most prosperous in Schoenberg's life. His works were performed regularly at the festivals of the International Music Society; his principal choral work, the *Gurrelieder*, aroused general admiration at a performance in his honour at the Vienna State Opera, and most conductors included his works in their programmes. He had now gained an international reputation. When Busoni died in 1924 in Berlin, Schoenberg succeeded him as a member of the Academy of the Arts, a position which should have given him financial independence for the rest of his life. After Hitler came to power, however, in 1933, he lost his position and accepted an offer from the Malkin Conservatory, Boston. He felt the change as a great shock. His health suffered from the eastern winter and he soon moved to Los Angeles, where he was appointed professor of music in the University of Southern California. Here he wrote a suite for string orchestra (1934), the fourth string quartet (1938), a violin concerto, a piano concerto, and the *Ode to Napoleon*. Schoenberg retired from his university post in 1944 at the age of 70, to spend the rest of his life in composing and teaching. He completed the opera *Moses and Aaron*, on which he had been working for many years, not long before he died. He had the satisfaction of seeing a revival of his works after the defeat of the Nazi regime and the re-establishment of his fame as one of the most inspiring innovators of contemporary music. His wife died in 1923 and he is survived by a son and a daughter.

JOSEPH STALIN

Dictator of Russia for 29 years

5 MARCH 1953

THE DEATH OF STALIN, like the death of Lenin 29 years ago, marks an epoch in Russian history. Rarely have two successive rulers of a great country responded so absolutely to its changing needs and piloted it so successfully through periods of crisis. Lenin was at the helm through five years of revolution, civil war, and precarious recovery. Stalin, coming to power in the aftermath of revolution, took up the task of organizing and disciplining the revolutionary state, and putting into execution the revolutionary programmes of planned industry and collectivized agriculture. He thus equipped the country to meet the gravest external peril which had threatened it since Napoleon, and brought it triumphantly through a four years' ordeal of invasion and devastation. The characters of the two men present a contrast which corresponds to the different tasks confronting them. Lenin was an original thinker, an idealist, a superb revolutionary agitator. Stalin neither possessed, nor required, these qualities. He was essentially an administrator, an organizer and a politician. Both were ruthless in the pursuit of policies which they regarded as vital to the cause they had at heart. But Stalin appeared to lack a certain element of humanity which Lenin generally maintained in personal relations, though allied statesmen who dealt with him during the war were unanimous in finding him approachable, sympathetic, and readily disposed to moderate the intransigence of his subordinates. As the war drew to its close Stalin, whether for reasons of health or for reasons of policy, became less and less accessible to representatives of the western Powers and so the rift began which was to widen in the counsels of the United Nations and in the policies towards the west of Russia's satellites, until the open warfare broke out in Korea which still festers and poisons the whole international scene.

A Man of Authority
Public Enthusiasm
In Russia and the adjacent Communist States Marshal Stalin at the time of his death occupied a position of personal eminence almost without parallel in the history of the world. His rare public appearances provoked scenes of tremendous enthusiasm; his speeches and writings on any subject – linguistics, the art of war,

biology and history, as well as on the theory of Communism – were treated as virtually inspired texts and analysed in meticulous detail by hundreds of commentators. A quotation from the works of Stalin was the irrefutable end to any argument. The mere mention of his name at a political conference in any of the satellite States was sufficient to bring all present to their feet by a prolonged ovation. The Stalin legend became an integral part of the chain which united orthodox Communists all over the world. In appearance Stalin was grey; his hair grey and stiff as a badger's; his nostrils and lower cheeks greyish white; his moustache, too, though in youth it had been richly brown and still showed some traces of that colour, was grey. He spoke softly, moved slowly, but his expression was quizzical, like a man enjoying a hidden joke, at times softening into a broad smile. Often as he spoke his look was oddly remote and withdrawn, the look of a man thinking through two or three processes at once. His expression was above all confident, without a trace of nerves; strong, calm or suddenly watchful in an amused kind of way. Tough, yet unathletic, dignified yet self-conscious, he dominated any group of which he formed a part for all his small stature.

Joseph Vissarionovich Dzhugashvili, known to the world as Stalin, one of his many revolutionary *noms de guerre*, was born at Gori, in Georgia, on December 21, 1879. His father, a cobbler of peasant origin, died when he was 11. Joseph was sent to the church school in his native town, where he remained until 1893. It was here that he learned to use Russian as an instrument of expression, since all ecclesiastical schools in Georgia at that time were the implements of the Tsarist policy of Russification. He emerged from the school at Gori sharply conscious of the suppression of Georgian nationalism and not unaware of the social inequalities and injustices prevailing in his native Georgia. Such feelings were never revealed however to the school staff, and in view of the fact that he was invariably the best pupil in his form, the head master and the local priest had no hesitation in recommending him for a scholarship at the seminary in Tiflis following upon his matriculation there in the autumn of 1894.

'A Model Pupil'; Clandestine Socialist

In his early period at the seminary Dzhugashvili was a model pupil, able and diligent at his work, but towards the end of his first year, unbeknown to his tutors, he was already in contact with opposition groups in Tiflis and published some patriotic radical verses in the Liberal newspaper *Iberya*. His contact with radical groups in Tiflis, headed by former seminarists, continued to develop until finally in August, 1898, he joined the clandestine Socialist organization known as Mesamé-Dasi. Thenceforward he began to lead a kind of dual existence. His few leisure hours were spent in lecturing on Socialism to small groups of working men in Tiflis; discussion in a secret debating society, formed by himself inside the seminary, and the reading of radical books. This state of affairs eventually came to the notice of the seminary authorities and in May, 1899, the 20-year-old Dzhugash-vili was expelled. He then embarked on a revolutionary career, but was faced with the immediate problem of employment. For a few months he made a little money giving lessons to the children of middle-class families and at the end of 1899 found a job as a clerk in the observatory at Tiflis – an occupation which seems to have afforded him much free time for political activity. He remained in this employ-ment until March, 1901, when his political activities forced him to go underground completely.

In November, 1901, he was elected to membership of the Social Democratic committee of Tiflis and a few weeks later was sent to Batum, where he proceeded with the establishment of a vigorous clandestine organization and an illegal print-ing press. The influence of this organization, under his leadership, on the oil workers of Batum was so remarkable in its manifestations that 'Koba' (as Dzhu-gashvili was then known) was arrested, and imprisoned in the spring of 1902 as a dangerous agitator. From his exile in Siberia he escaped a few weeks later and reappeared in Tiflis to find that the great schism which divided the Social Demo-cratic Party in 1903 had left the Mensheviks in virtual control of the Caucasian party. A few months after his return, with some hesitation, Koba took the side of Lenin and the Bolsheviks and proceeded to agitate energetically against the Mensheviks and other political groupings.

First Meeting with Lenin

Koba's role during the 'general rehearsal' of 1905 was a local rather than a national one. Apart from organizing the 'fighting squads' (later to be a subject of considerable controversy within the party) and the editing of the newspaper *Kavkaski Rabochi Listok* (Caucasian Workers' News-sheet), which enjoyed temporary legality, he continued to conduct a vigorous onslaught against the Mensheviks. When he attended the party conference in Tammerfors in December, 1905, as a delegate of the Caucasian Bolsheviks (a group of uncertain credentials, since most of the local leaders were Mensheviks), Koba emerged for the first time from the provincial arena of Caucasian politics into the atmosphere of a truly national gath-ering. Here, too, he first met Lenin. In the following year he attended the Stock-holm Congress and in 1907 the London Party Congress as a Caucasian delegate, where he encountered Trotsky.

Soon after his return from the London Congress he was elected to membership of the Baku Committee, and it was in the oil wells of Baku that Stalin, on his testimony, first learned to lead great masses of workers. He was arrested in Novem-ber, 1908, and deported to Vologda province. A few months later, however, he escaped and appeared again in the south, under the name of Melikyants. His period of freedom was brief, for he was re-arrested in March, 1910, and sent back to Vologda to complete his sentence of 1908. Released in June, 1911, he settled in Petersburg at the home of his future father-in-law, Alliluyev, although he had been forbidden to live in most large towns. In consequence, he was again arrested. Reaction was now at its height and the party fortunes at their lowest ebb. A small conference of Bolshevik stalwarts in Prague in January, 1912, coopted Stalin as a member of the central executive committee of the party; and on his escape a few weeks later he helped to found the new party journal *Pravda* in Petersburg.

A Turning-point
Lenin's 'Wonderful Georgian'

It was in the winter of 1912–13 that Stalin made his only extended visit abroad, spending some months with Lenin in Cracow and some time in Vienna. This was a turning-point in his career. Ten years earlier Lenin, in his famous pamphlet 'What is to be Done?' had first stated the case, on which he never ceased to insist, for a centrally directed party of professional revolutionaries, organized and disciplined in thought and deed, as the essential instrument of social revolution. Stalin had all the marks of Lenin's ideal professional revolutionary: he was intrepid, orderly and orthodox. It was a further asset that though born a Georgian and a member of one of the 'subject races' Stalin had had no truck with separatist or 'federalist' ideas within the party and was an out-and-out 'centralist'. Not for nothing therefore did Lenin at this time refer to Stalin in a letter to Maxim Gorky as 'a wonderful Georgian' who was writing an essay on the national question. The essay, eventually published under the title 'Marxism and the National Question' in a party journal, was an attack on the 'national' heresies of the Austrian Marxists Bauer and Renner and a statement of accepted Bolshevik doctrine, steering a cautious middle course between those who regarded any kind of nationalism as incompatible with international socialism and those who regarded nationalism as an essential element in it. It was the first of his writings to be signed by the name under which he was to become famous.

Back in Russia, Stalin underwent in February, 1913, his sixth and last imprisonment and exile. The revolution of February, 1917, released him, and he was probably the first member of the central committee of the party to reach Petersburg. In this capacity he temporarily took over the editorship of *Pravda*. This was the occasion of a short-lived deviation to which Stalin afterwards frankly confessed. In common with the other leading Bolsheviks then in the capital – excluding Molotov and Shlyapnikov – Stalin believed that the right tactics for the Bolsheviks were to support the provisional Government and rally to the defence of the fatherland; and this line, which would have assimilated the policy of the Bolsheviks to that of the

Social-Democratic parties of the Second International, was taken editorially in *Pravda*. Lenin, chafing inactively in Switzerland, denounced in his 'Letters from Afar' the weak-kneed Bolsheviks of the capital. When later he reached Petrograd in the sealed train and propounded his famous 'April theses' of no cooperation with the provisional Government or with any policy that would keep Russia in the war, he quickly rallied his faltering party, and geared it for the second revolution. Thereafter Stalin remained a faithful and undeviating disciple.

1917 Revolution

Enhanced Status in the Party

The difficulty for the biographer of this as of the earlier period of Stalin's life is to disentangle the authentic contemporary evidence from the mass of more recent and largely apocryphal accretions. It seems that he first became a figure familiar to party *cadres* at the time of his election to a new central committee of nine members in April, 1917, and after the difficult July days, when Lenin and Zinoviev were compelled to retreat to Finland and Kamenev, Trotsky and others were arrested, Stalin emerged to lead the party. On their return to the political scene, he retired again into the shadows. While there is but little information relating to any participation by him in the work of the Revolutionary Military Committee during the actual rising, he nevertheless undoubtedly performed an important function in the editorial office of *Pravda*. He supported Lenin against Zinoviev and Kamenev in the controversy over the preparation and timing of the October revolution and against Trotsky over Brest-Litovsk; and though his interventions recorded in the minutes of the central committee were on both occasions brief and inconspicuous, his fidelity to Lenin in these troubled times must have won the gratitude of the leader and greatly enhanced his status in the party. He was appointed People's Commissar for Nationalities in October, 1917, and in this capacity one of his first measures was to proclaim Finland's independence from Russia, at a conference in Helsinki. In spite of the opposition of elements within the party, who regarded this as an unwarranted concession to bourgeois nationalism, the decree was officially signed by Lenin and Stalin in December. He also played an active part in the drafting of the 1918 constitution of the Russian Socialist Federal Soviet Republic and he was still more closely concerned four years later in framing the federal constitution of the Union of Socialist Soviet Republics.

Breach with Trotsky

The civil war provided fresh scope for Stalin's unflagging energy and undoubted administrative talents. That the civil war provided the occasion of Stalin's first open breach with Trotsky; that Stalin and Voroshilov intrigued busily against Trotsky, criticizing both his disposition of his armies and his use of former Tsarist officers; that recriminations flared up to a dangerous point over the defence of Tsaritsin (renamed Stalingrad some years later) against Denikin; that Lenin tried to smooth over these animosities and to retain the services of two invaluable though quarrelsome lieutenants – so much is clear. But the historian of the future may well find it a superhuman task to extract the grain of truth from the chaff of subsequent controversy and the haystack of misrepresentation beneath which Trotsky's achievements have been hidden. For the rest Stalin's name figures little in the literature of the period. At any time up to 1922 the general impression which he made on his colleagues was apparently one of undistinguished competence; though admitted to the first rank of Bolshevik leaders he seemed the least remarkable of them, the most lacking in personality. But his capacity for hard and regular work more than balanced the more spectacular talents of his rivals, and indeed it could not have escaped the notice of a few that Stalin's influence in the state and his hold on the party machine had grown enormously. At the end of the civil war he filled three significant posts: membership of the Politburo, Commissar of Nationalities, and Commissar for Workers' and Peasants' Inspection (Rabkrin).

In March, 1922, he was appointed Secretary-General of the party – a newly created post obviously suited to his rather pedestrian gifts. Though not regarded by anyone as a potential stepping-stone to supreme power, nevertheless this post, considered in conjunction with his other spheres of influence, rendered his personal position most formidable. Although Lenin still held the reins, Stalin's influence was becoming comparable to that of Lenin. In May of the same year Lenin had a first stroke from which he recovered, temporarily and incompletely, to be finally stricken by a second in March, 1923. From this moment, though Lenin lingered on, totally incapacitated, till January, 1924, the succession was open. Had anyone seriously canvassed Stalin's chances, a letter from Lenin to the central committee of the party – commonly, though unwarrantably, known as Lenin's testament – might have seemed a decisive obstacle. Writing at the end of December, 1922, with a postscript of January 4, 1923, Lenin who evidently knew that his days were numbered, passed in review the principal party leaders. He noted that Stalin since he had become Secretary-General had 'concentrated in his hands an immense power', and expressed the fear that he might not always use it prudently. He described Stalin as 'too rough,' and proposed that he should be replaced by someone 'more patient, more loyal, more polite, more attentive to the comrades, less capricious, &c.' Fortunately for Stalin, the letter also treated Zinoviev, Kamenev, and Bukharin with scant respect, so that there was a powerful interest in limiting its circulation – though it was familiar to all members of the central committee, and its authenticity has never been contested. But Stalin must be credited with extraordinary skill in surmounting so formidable an obstacle. When the twelfth party congress met in

April, 1923, Lenin was known, though not yet publicly admitted, to be past recovery. The talk was of a group of three ('troika') to take over his authority; and the names of Zinoviev, Kamenev, and Stalin were freely mentioned. Stalin, with consummate tact, defended Zinoviev and Kamenev rather than himself from attacks made jointly on all three of them. Trotsky was gradually edged on one side. Attacks on him for undermining the unity of the party began in the autumn of that year.

The year 1924 was decisive for Stalin's ascent to power. During this year he for the first time exhibited to the full that amazing political dexterity which made all his rivals look like bunglers and amateurs. In the first place he brought about what may not unfairly be called the 'canonization' of Lenin. From the moment of Lenin's death, and almost entirely as the result of Stalin's initiative, every word that Lenin had uttered or written came to be treated as sacrosanct – as Lenin himself had treated the works of Marx and Engels; and everyone who had differed from him was now suspect not merely as a heretic in the past, but as a potential heretic in the future. This weapon was aimed primarily at Trotsky, whose impetuous character and long record of past bickerings with Lenin made him highly vulnerable. But it could also serve against Zinoviev and Kamenev, who had more than once been severely castigated by Lenin for their backslidings. Stalin had been too prudent or not conspicuous enough to come under the lash – except in the unofficial 'testament' now being gradually consigned to oblivion. This was a negative asset. But immense pains were taken, both at this time and afterwards, to build up a positive picture of Stalin as Lenin's ablest coadjutor, most faithful disciple, and chosen political executor.

Control of Party Machine Power Strengthened

Secondly, Stalin, well aware of the prestige attaching in the party to the master of Marxist theory, set out to establish his credentials in that field. In the spring of 1924 he delivered at the Sverdlov University in Moscow a course of lectures on 'The Foundations of Leninism' – a competent exposition of the development and application by Lenin of Marxist doctrine. He went on to take the offensive against Trotsky. In the lectures themselves he had followed the usual view that the ultimate success of the Russian revolution depended on the spread of revolution elsewhere in Europe. But the revolutionary failures of 1923 in Germany suggested that this consummation was remote; and the new international status of the Soviet Union, which had been recognized in 1924 by all the principal Powers except the United States, made the encouragement of world revolution an increasingly inconvenient policy. At the end of 1924 Stalin issued a revised edition of his lectures in which he proclaimed the doctrine of 'Socialism in one country'. Trotsky could thus be branded as an internationalist, a champion of the outmoded slogan of 'permanent revolution'.

Thirdly, Stalin strengthened his control of the party machine and discovered how to use it for the discomfiture of his enemies. As Secretary-General he was already master of all promotions and appointments to key positions in the party. Lenin's memory was now honoured by the admission of a large number of new members; and this admission, managed by Stalin and his supporters, brought a mass of recruits to the new orthodoxy. Whatever opinions were held among the leaders the weight of numbers must begin to tell. Before long Trotsky was being shouted down at party meetings by enthusiastic young Stalinists.

Trotsky's Expulsion

By January, 1925, the campaign against Trotsky had gathered sufficient momentum to permit of his deposition from his office as People's Commissar for War. Before the end of the year Zinoviev and Kamenev, taking fright at Stalin's growing power, were seeking a *rapprochement* with Trotsky. But the move came too late to save them. In 1926 Stalin secured a condemnation of Trotskyites and Zinovievites alike both by a party conference and by the Comintern; and in November, 1927, Trotsky, Zinoviev, and Kamenev were formally expelled from the party. Two months later Trotsky was forcibly removed from Moscow and sent to Alma-Ata in central Asia. He was finally expelled from Russia in January, 1929.

In the struggle thus concluded personal rivalries had been intertwined not only with the issue of foreign policy already referred to but with internal political controversies. Trotsky had always been an advocate of industrialization and planning. Stalin opened the campaign against him with the NEP slogans of conciliating the peasant and with the charge, repeated and illustrated *ad nauseam*, that Trotsky was guilty of 'underestimating the peasant'. But Stalin soon saw the dangers of going too far, and from the end of 1925 onwards cleverly steered a middle course between the 'left' opposition of Trotsky and Zinoviev, who were accused of ignoring the peasant, and the 'right' opposition of Rykov and Bukharin, who exaggerated the policy of appeasing the peasant.

After the rout of Trotsky, Zinoviev, and Kamenev, Stalin's position was not yet supreme in the Politburo. He still had to deal with the 'right' opposition of Bukharin, Rykov, and Tomsky. Contrary to the prophecies of the recently defeated opposition, the influence of the Bukharin group did not overshadow that of Stalin. The fifteenth Congress elected a new Politburo of nine and in the new line-up Stalin had a majority of votes, among them Kaganovich and Mikoyan. The flaring up of conflicting forces inside the Politburo did not come until 1928, when in view of the grain famine 'emergency measures' were instituted by the Politburo, resulting in Stalin's call for 'the elimination of the kulaks as a class'. Although in the councils of the Politburo these measures were opposed by Bukharin and his group, it was not until April, 1929, that Stalin openly denounced Bukharin as the leader of the 'right' opposition to his policy in the countryside. Soon after, Bukharin, Rykov, and Tomsky were excluded from the Politburo and other significant posts. Stalin's ascendancy in the Politburo was now complete, and from this moment he was recognized as the virtual ruler of the Soviet Union – a position consecrated by the unusual demonstrations with which his fiftieth birthday was celebrated in December, 1929. At the very moment of Trotsky's expulsion Stalin was preparing a powerful swing-over towards industrialization. The first Five-year Plan was launched by him in 1928. Its inevitable concomitant, the collectivization of agriculture, though not seriously taken in hand till 1931, had been on the party agenda since the end of 1927. Throughout this period, though mistakes were made (notably in the estimate of the pace at which collectivization could be carried out), Stalin's sense of timing was on the whole superb. Few, if any, of the policies which he applied were original to himself; but he was unique in his sense of when to act and when to wait.

In the middle thirties, with industrialization well on the way and collectivization a *fait accompli*, the Soviet Union may well have seemed to be sailing out into smoother waters. The second Five-year Plan promised an increased output of consumer goods. Stalin's public pronouncements assumed a more optimistic tone, and he may well have originally conceived the 'Stalin constitution', promulgated in 1936, as the crown of his work. Socialism had been achieved; the road to Communism, however distant the goal, lay open; increased material prosperity and broader constitutional liberties were a vision of the immediate future. These expectations, if they were entertained, were not fulfilled. In the middle thirties the Soviet Union entered a new period of storm and stress. The murder of Kirov at the end of 1934 was the symptom or starting-point of a grave internal crisis; and in international affairs Germany regained her power in a form particularly menacing to the Soviet Union. The internal crisis was obscure, the evidence relating to it contentious, and it was dealt with by methods which left a lasting cloud on Stalin's name. The growing-pains of collective farming, the liquidation of the kulaks, the need – in face of the Nazi menace – to increase the pace of industrialization had all imposed severe strains on the population and bred discontent, sometimes in high places. Stalin decided to strike hard. In the panic which followed old scores were paid off and new grudges indulged, and things probably went a good deal farther than Stalin or anyone else intended at the start.

Treason Trials

In 1935 and 1936 successive trials were held in which all those prominent Bolsheviks who had at one time or another been implicated in 'Trotskyism' or other forms of opposition to the regime – Zinoviev, Kamenev, and Bukharin among them – were condemned and shot for self-confessed treason. In 1937 a number of the leading generals were shot on similar charges without public trial. Of the leading Bolsheviks of the first generation hardly any survived except Stalin, Molotov, and Voroshilov. In 1938 the purge was at last stayed. Yagoda, long the head of the GPU and its successor the NKVD, who had been removed from office at the end of 1936, was now himself executed; and Yezhov, his successor, formerly an influential party leader, disappeared from the scene about the same time. Judgment on the purge will depend partly on the amount of credence given to reports and confessions of active treason on the part of the accused; and it has to be admitted that the Soviet polity afterwards survived the almost intolerable strains of war with fewer breaks and fissures than most observers had been prepared to predict. Nevertheless it is certain that the damage done by the purges to Soviet prestige in the west was a fatal handicap to the foreign policy of a common defensive front with the western Powers to which Soviet diplomacy was at that time committed. This was probably the gravest and most disastrous miscalculation of that period.

Munich and After

Treaty with the Nazis

Soviet foreign policy in the thirties, as much as Soviet domestic policy, was clearly Stalin's creation. He had long been by inclination a Soviet nationalist rather than an internationalist; and now that he was firmly established in the seat of power he was unlikely to shrink from any of the implications of 'Socialism in one country'. Faced by the German menace, he executed without embarrassment the ideological change of front necessary to bring the Soviet Union into the League of Nations and to conclude treaties of alliance with France and Czechoslovakia. In the end it was not lack of Soviet good will that defeated this project, but the weakness of France and what appeared to Soviet eyes as a dual policy on the part of Great Britain. So long as Great Britain could be suspected of hesitating between a deal with Germany and a common front against her, Stalin on his side would equally keep both doors open. Munich, though a severe shock to prospects of cooperation, was partly offset by British rearmament, and the riddle of British policy was unsolved throughout the winter. On March 10, 1939, at the eighteenth party congress Stalin gave what was doubtless intended as a note of warning that Soviet policy was 'not to allow our country to be drawn into conflicts by war-mongers'. But his speech was overtaken by the march of events.

It was Hitler's seizure of Prague in the middle of March which fired the train. Great Britain now prepared feverishly for war and sought for allies in the east. Two alternatives were still open to her. She could have an alliance with the Soviet Union at the price of accepting Soviet policy in Eastern Europe – in Poland, in Rumania, in the Baltic States; or she could have alliances with the anti-Soviet Governments of these countries at the price of driving the Soviet Union into the hostile camp. British diplomacy was too simple-minded, and too ignorant of eastern Europe, to understand the hard choice before it. It plunged impetuously into the pacts of guarantee with Poland and Rumania; and within a few days, on May 3, 1939, the resignation of Litvinov and his replacement by Molotov signalled a vital change in Soviet foreign policy. The British mission which had been sent to Moscow found itself unable to make any progress. Negotiations continued; but unless Great Britain was prepared to abandon the Polish alliance, or put severe pressure on her new ally, their eventual break-down was certain. When Hitler decided to wait no longer, Stalin for his part did not hesitate. Ribbentrop came to Moscow and the German-Soviet treaty was signed. It is fair to infer that Stalin regarded it as a *pis aller*. He would have preferred alliance with the western Powers, but could not have it on any terms which he would have found tolerable.

Uneasy Neutrality

Twenty-two months of most uneasy neutrality followed. The German advance in Poland was answered by a corresponding Soviet move to reoccupy the White Russian territories ceded to Poland by the treaty of Riga in 1921. Thus, by the autumn of 1939, Soviet and German power already confronted each other in Poland, on the Danube, and on the Baltic. The war against Finland in the winter of 1939–40 was designed to strengthen the defences of Leningrad by pushing forward the frontier in a westerly direction. It eventually achieved this object, but at the cost of much discredit to Soviet prestige and the formal expulsion of the Soviet Union from the League of Nations.

After the fall of France, Soviet fears of German victory and German predominance grew apace; and military and industrial preparations were pressed forward. Stalin now probably foresaw the inevitability of conflict, but was determined not to provoke or hasten it. In November, 1940, he sent Molotov on a visit to Berlin without being able to mitigate the palpable clash of interests. On the other hand, Japanese neutrality was assured when Matsuoka was effusively received in Moscow in April, 1941. In the following month Stalin, hitherto only Secretary-General of the party and without official rank, became President of the Council of People's Commissars – the Soviet Prime Minister. The appointment sounded a note of alarm at home and of warning abroad.

Russia at War
Heavy Burden of Responsibility

The German invasion of the Soviet Union on June 22, 1941, and the almost immediate threat to the capital placed on Stalin's shoulders an enormous weight of anxiety and responsibility. From the outset, the supreme direction of the war effort and defence organization became vested in the State Defence Committee consisting of five members – Stalin, Molotov, Voroshilov, Beria, and Malenkov, with Stalin as chairman, though it was not till March, 1943, that he assumed the rank of marshal, and later of generalissimo. During the war his customary public speeches on May 1 and on the eve of November 7 took the form of large-scale reviews of military operations and war policy. He was also active in a diplomatic role. Before the war Stalin had been almost entirely inaccessible to foreigners. Now, apart from regular conversations with the allied Ambassadors, he received a constant flow of distinguished visitors. Lord Beaverbrook and Mr Harriman were in Moscow in August, 1941, to organize supplies from the west; Mr Churchill came in August, 1942, and again, with Mr Eden, in October, 1944. In December, 1943, Stalin met President Roosevelt and Mr Churchill at Teheran, and in February, 1945, at Yalta. The last meeting of the Big Three, with Mr Truman succeeding Roosevelt and Mr Attlee replacing Mr Churchill in the middle of the proceedings, took place at Potsdam in July, 1945.

Among his diplomatic activities Stalin was particularly concerned with the perennial problem of Soviet-Polish relations. By dint of much patience he eventually secured the recognition of the new Polish Government by his allies, and the acceptance by them as the frontier, between the Soviet Union and Poland, of the so-called 'Curzon line' originally drawn by the Allied and Associated Powers at the Paris peace conference of 1919. He worked untiringly to secure for his country that place of undisputed equality with the other Great Powers to which its achievements and sacrifices in the war entitled it.

Domestic Policy
Comintern and Church

Two striking decisions of domestic policy during the war – the disbandment of Comintern and the renewed recognition of the Orthodox Church – were undoubtedly taken by Stalin out of deference for allied opinion; but they were in line with this long-standing inclination, accentuated by the war, to give precedence to national over ideological considerations. The reforms of 1944 which accorded separate armies and separate rights of diplomatic representation abroad to the major constituent republics of the Soviet Union were perhaps partly designed to secure to the Ukraine and White Russia independent membership and voting power in the United Nations. When the war ended Stalin was in his sixty-sixth year. A holiday of two-and-a-half months in the autumn of 1945 at Sochi on the Black Sea produced the usual crop of rumours, but was no more than a merited and necessary respite from the burden of public affairs. In December he was back in Moscow for the visit of Mr Bevin and Mr Byrnes. Thenceforward there were few personal contacts between Stalin and representatives of the western Powers. In February, 1946, he took part in the elections to the Supreme Soviet, making the principal campaign speech, in which he forecast an early end of bread rationing – a hope which was defeated by the bad harvest. He also declared that it was the intention of the Soviet Communist Party to organize a new effort in the economic field, the aim of which would be to treble pre-war production figures. Although advanced in years, Stalin still continued to hold the reins of power and in March, 1946, he was again confirmed as Secretary of the central committee of the party. In the same year the State Publishing House began publication of a collected edition of his works.

Growing Mistrust

The unparalleled popularity in the non-Communist world with which the Russian people in general, and Marshal Stalin in particular, had emerged from the war thus early gave place to mistrust. It had been hoped that the pre-war doctrine which was associated with Stalin's name, of 'socialism in one country', would provide the basis for peaceful coexistence in the post-war period. Stalin's own comments on international affairs sometimes tended to confirm, and sometimes to deny, this prospect. Thus in answer to questions put to him by the Moscow correspondent of the *Sunday Times* in September, 1946, Stalin declared that, in spite of ideological differences, he believed in the possibility of lasting cooperation between the Soviet Union and the western democracies, and that Communism in one country was perfectly possible. This provoked worldwide interest and was regarded as a welcome statement, contributing much to the easing of growing international tension. A month later, however, in reply to questions sent to him by the United Press of America, he asserted that in his opinion 'the incendiaries of a new war', naming several prominent British and American statesmen, constituted the most serious threat to world peace, and thus destroyed the earlier good impression.

Russia's post-war policy towards her neighbours did nothing to confirm Stalin's peaceful protestations. The independent Baltic States, Lithuania, Latvia, and Estonia, had already been incorporated in Russia in 1940. Finland and Bulgaria were compelled to surrender territory to Russia as the price of defeat, and Poland suffered even greater amputations as the reward of victory. In the Far East Russia claimed North Sakhalin and the Kurilles Islands as her price for taking part in the war against Japan. In all the countries which had been overrun by the Red Army it was only a question of time before a Communist regime had been set up and its opponents liquidated. By the middle of 1948 the borders of Communism stretched from the Elbe to the Adriatic. A year later Communism had triumphed in China. Stalin controlled the destinies of an empire far larger than any Tsar had ever dreamed of.

It was the *coup d'état* in Prague in February, 1948, which finally forced western Europe and North America into action for their common defence. The North-Atlantic Treaty was signed in April, 1949. But even before then the west had successfully met another outward thrust by Russia. It was in June, 1948, that the air-lift began which nullified the effects of the blockade of Berlin. Stalin remained, as always, in the background during this period of dynamic Russian expansion. It was only rarely that he received a foreign diplomat, though leaders of the satellite States naturally had readier access to him. From time to time the suggestion was made for a new conference between Stalin, the American President and the British Prime Minister, but none of them came to anything. It was in 1946 that President Truman disclosed that he had invited Stalin to Washington for a social visit, but that Stalin had found it necessary to decline for reasons of health. In the last interview which he gave to a foreign correspondent (to the representative of the *New York Times* in December last year) he indicated that he held a favourable view of proposals for talks between himself and the head of the new American Administration, President Eisenhower, and that he was interested in any new diplomatic move to end hostilities in Korea. President Eisenhower declared his willingness last month to hold a meeting with Stalin in certain circumstances, and Mr Churchill subsequently told the House of Commons that he did not rule out the possibility of three-cornered discussions.

Stalin's New Role: Economic Theorist

It was in the last year of his life that Stalin appeared in a role which would have surprised former colleagues, such as Lenin and Trotsky, but which therefore may well have given him most pride – as an economic theorist in the tradition of (and not less important than) Marx, Engels and Lenin. Shortly before the nineteenth congress of the Russian Communist Party, which was held in Moscow in October, 1952 – the first congress since 1939 – Stalin published his *Economic Problems of Socialism in the USSR*, which has since become the definitive text-book for Communists in all countries. In this work he warned his readers that, for all Russia's successes in building a new society, it was wrong to think that the natural economic laws did not apply as much in Russia as elsewhere. He also forecast a deepening crisis of capitalism, that west European countries would dissociate themselves from the United States, and that war between these capitalist countries was inevitable. He also outlined a programme of basic preliminary conditions necessary for the transition to Communism in the Soviet Union. At the Congress there was a reorganization of party organs – the Politburo and the Orgburo being brought together in a single body, the Praesidium of the Central Committee, of which Stalin became chairman.

On the occasion of his seventieth birthday in December, 1949, there were widespread celebrations throughout the Soviet Union and busts of Stalin were erected on 38 of the highest peaks in the Soviet Union. It marked, too, the inauguration of international Stalin peace prizes, to be awarded each year on his birthday. On March 3, 1953, it was announced by Moscow radio that Stalin was gravely ill as the result of a haemorrhage, that he had lost consciousness and speech, and that he would take no part in leading activity for a prolonged period.

Only a few details are known of Stalin's personal life. In 1903 he married Yekaterina Svanidze, a profoundly religious woman and the sister of a Georgian comrade, who left him a son, Yasha, when she died in 1907 of pneumonia. His second wife, whom he married in 1918 – Nadezhda Alliluyeva – was 20 years younger than himself and was the daughter of a Bolshevik worker, with whom Stalin had contacts in both the Caucasus and St Petersburg. She was formerly one of Lenin's secretaries and later studied at a technical college in Moscow. This marriage, too, ended with the death of his wife, in November, 1932. She left him two children – a daughter, Svetlana, and a son, Vassili, now a high ranking officer in the Soviet Air Force. Late in life he married Rosa Kaganovich, the sister of Lazar Kaganovich, a member of the Politburo.

ALAN TURING

17 JUNE 1954

DR ALAN MATHISON TURING, OBE, FRS, whose death at the age of 41 has already been reported, was born on June 23, 1912, the son of Julius Mathison Turing. He was educated at Sherborne School and at King's College, Cambridge, of which he was elected a Fellow in 1935. He was appointed OBE in 1941 for wartime services in the Foreign Office and was elected FRS in 1951. Until 1939 he was a pure mathematician and logician, but after the war most of his work was connected with the design and use of automatic computing machines, first at the National Physical Laboratory and then since 1948 at Manchester University, where he was a Reader at the time of his death.

The discovery which will give Turing a permanent place in mathematical logic was made not long after he had graduated. This was his proof that (contrary to the then prevailing view of Hilbert and his school at Göttingen) there are classes of mathematical problem which cannot be solved by any fixed and definite process. The crucial step in his proof was to clarify the notion of a 'definite process', which he interpreted as 'something that could be done by an automatic machine'. Although other proofs of insolubility were published at about the same time by other authors, the 'Turing machine' has remained the most vivid, and in many ways the most convincing, interpretation of these essentially equivalent theories. The description that he then gave of a 'universal' computing machine was entirely theoretical in purpose, but Turing's strong interest in all kinds of practical experiment made him even then interested in the possibility of actually constructing a machine on these lines.

It was natural at the end of the war for him to accept an invitation to work at the National Physical Laboratory on the development of the ACE, the first large computer to be begun in this country. He threw himself into the work with enthusiasm, thoroughly enjoying the rapid alternation of abstract questions of design with problems of practical engineering. Later at Manchester he devoted himself more particularly to problems arising out of the use of the machine. It was at this time that he became involved in discussions on the contrasts and similarities between machines and brains. Turing's view, expressed with great force and wit, was that it was for those who saw an unbridgeable gap between the two to say just where the difference lay.

The war interrupted Turing's mathematical career for the six critical years between the age of 27 and 33. A mathematical theory of the chemical basis of organic growth which he had lately started to develop has been tragically interrupted, and must remain a fragment. Important though his contributions to logic have been, few who have known him personally can doubt that, with his deep insight into the principles of mathematics and of natural science, and his brilliant originality, he would, but for these accidents, have made much greater discoveries.

* * *

HENRI MATISSE

A master of modern French painting

3 NOVEMBER 1954

M. HENRI MATISSE, one of the most outstanding representatives of the modern French school of painting, died on Wednesday at his home at Nice. He was 84, and had been in poor health for several years.

Partly, if not chiefly, because they were both subject to the same indiscriminate abuse from artistic 'diehards' in England, M. Henri Matisse and Señor Pablo Picasso were closely connected in the public mind. In reality they had not very much in common, though they were associated in their first departure from academic art. To some extent they were complementary, and Matisse was weak where Picasso is strong, and the other way about. Of the two Matisse was the less intellectual, and he had not the range and depth or the inventiveness and versatility of the Spaniard but it is questionable if he had not more of the special sensibility of the painter as distinct from other kinds of creative artist. His colour was enchanting and his handling of paint was masterly.

Henri Matisse, who is said to have had some Jewish blood, was a Norman, the son of a grain merchant in a small way, and was born at Le Cateau Nord, on December 31, 1869. His father wanted him to become a lawyer and put him into the office of a legal friend to pick up what knowledge he could before entering a law school. But after about a year the boy got appendicitis, and during his long convalescence at home he took up painting at the suggestion of a neighbour who had seen him sketching. The result was that when he was 20 Matisse went to Paris, where he entered the Ecole des Beaux Arts and studied under Bouguereau. When he was 24 he married Mlle Amelie Noellie Parayre, and before long he had a young family of a daughter and two sons. Times were hard, but besides being an excellent housewife Mme Matisse opened a small millinery shop to help out the family income.

Then Gustave Moreau, the 'mystical' painter, who may be said to have started the cult of 'Salome', saw Matisse working in the Louvre, making copies of pictures there, and invited him to study in his own studio at the Ecole des Beaux Arts which was destined to become a nursery of young rebels, the fellow pupils of Matisse including Rouault and Dufy. In 1897 Matisse met the veteran Camille Pissarro and for a time worked as successfully as an Impressionist as he had as a copyist of old masters in the Louvre. On the advice of Pissarro in 1898 Matisse visited London to study Turner. Matisse was not greatly impressed by Turner, which was not surprising, because the acute interest in Paris had shifted from Impressionism, but he heard about Whistler and his Japanese prints. On his return to Paris he began to study oriental art systematically, and after a visit to Corsica, where he stayed a year, he went to Munich to see an exhibition of Moslem art, which confirmed his impression of the decorative values of the East.

'Les Fauves'

Up to now, though he was experimenting, Matisse had not kicked over the traces. He was exhibiting regularly at the official Salon, and in 1904 the dealer Vollard, from whom he had bought Cézanne's 'Bathers' to hang in his studio, gave him a one-man show of nearly 50 pictures. The explosion came at the Autumn Salon of 1905. For this exhibition Matisse organized a collection of works by the more advanced painters, including himself, Derain, Braque, Rouault, and Vlaminck, and these were hung in a room by themselves. An indignant critic, Louis Vauxcelles, writing in *Gil Blas*, called the room a '*cage aux Fauves*' or 'cage of wild beasts', and the name stuck. Beyond distortion or deformation of natural appearance in the interests of design and vehemence in statement, the Fauves had no common doctrine. Fauvism, in fact, might be described as a violent wrenching away of the picture from literal representation.

A picture that came in for special abuse was Matisse's 'Woman with a Hat'. This, for which Mme Matisse was the model, was bought by the American writer Miss Gertrude Stein, who was doing useful propaganda for the rebels. In 1906 she introduced Matisse to Picasso, who was then painting her portrait. Matisse was now celebrated. The Galerie Druet gave him a big one-man show, and in 1908 he was introduced to the American public by Alfred Steiglitz.

Fauvism in Paris was followed by Cubism, which was originated by Picasso and Braque. Matisse is credited with the invention of the name, but he does not appear to have more than flirted with Cubism, though it was he who introduced Negro sculpture to Picasso. The truth seems to be that Matisse was too much of a painter in the special sense of the word to be greatly interested in geometrical abstraction. After 1908, when, refusing to take any fees, he taught for a short time at a school in Paris opened by his friends and supporters, Matisse did not greatly change his style. He spent two years in Morocco, stayed various times at Saint Tropez, Cassis and Collioure, and travelled in America, Tahiti, Italy, and Russia. In 1917 he took a villa at Nice, where he remained more or less for the rest of his life.

Visit to America

On his first visit to America Matisse was violently attacked and accused of obscenity in his work, so that he begged an interviewer, 'Oh please do tell the American people that I am a normal man; that I am a devoted husband and father; that I have three fine children; that I go to the theatre, ride horse-back, have a comfortable home, a fine garden that I love, flowers, &c., just like any man', and this self-description tallies with the impressions of an English observer who described Matisse as a quiet, sensible, bourgeois gentleman, without pose or affectation. America, too, revised its opinion, for in 1927 Matisse received a first prize at the Carnegie International, and a year or two later the Carnegie Institute invited him to be a judge in its competition.

Besides being a painter Matisse was an etcher, lithographer, and wood-engraver, and he produced a good many works of sculpture. He illustrated the poems of Mallarmé and an edition of James Joyce's *Ulysses*, published by the Limited Edition Club, New York, in 1935. His work is known all over the world, the largest collections being in the Moscow Museum of Western Art and the Barnes Foundation, Pennsylvania. Matisse, who is represented at the Tate Gallery by 'Le Forêt' and 'Nude', both bequeathed by Mr C. Frank Stoop in 1933, was included in both the Post-Impressionist exhibitions at the Grafton Galleries in 1910 and 1911, and in 1937 there was a very extensive exhibition of his work at the Rosenberg and Helft Gallery in London.

Though he was already well known in artistic circles in London, it was not until 1945 that Matisse really got 'into the news'. In the December of that year an exhibition of works by Picasso and Matisse, arranged by La Direction Générale des Relations Culturelles and the British Council, was opened by the French Ambassador at the Victoria and Albert Museum. Criticism began mildly enough with a letter to *The Times*, signed by Professor Thomas Bodkin and Dr D. S. MacColl, to the effect that the war-diminished space in our galleries and museums should be devoted to the exhibition of their own historical treasures rather than to the works of two contemporary foreign painters of highly disputable merit. There followed in *The Times* a spate of correspondence for and against, many of the blows aimed at Picasso falling upon Matisse. Red herrings were strewn, but the discussion as a whole ranged round the perennial question of the distortion of natural appearance under emotion and in the interests of pictorial design.

In 1947 Matisse offered to design and build a chapel for the Dominicans of Vence, and this was consecrated in 1951. An architect built it on a plan suggested by the artist and inside Matisse painted three large compositions in black on white ceramic tiles. Last year there was an exhibition of his sculptures at the Tate Gallery, and he was honoured by the National Arts Foundation in New York as an 'outstanding artist of 1953'. Matisse was a member of the French Communist Party, but his standing with the Communists in recent years was unclear. Criticism came from Russia of his chapel at Vence, and in 1952 the French Communist Party was reported to be considering his expulsion for not falling into line with Moscow's instructions that art must be 'realistic and depict Communist ideals'.

There can be no doubt about Matisse's technical competence as a painter, but graceful as they are, his innumerable 'Odalisques' in Mediterranean interiors may to some minds end by becoming rather boring. Matisse himself said: 'While working, I never try to think, only to feel.' That is enough to explain his distortions, perhaps also his defects. As a colourist he was something more than decorative, because he had in high degree the rare capacity to establish the position of objects in the depth of the picture by the relations between colours, without the aid of linear or atmospheric perspective.

SIR ALEXANDER FLEMING

Discoverer of penicillin

11 MARCH 1955

SIR ALEXANDER FLEMING, D.SC, MB, FRCP, FRCS, FRS, the discoverer of penicillin, died suddenly yesterday at his home in London of a heart attack at the age of 73.

Alexander Fleming, the son of a farmer, was born at Lochfield, near Darvel, in Ayrshire, on August 6, 1881. He received his early education at the village school and at Kilmarnock Academy. At 13 years of age he was sent to live with his brother in London, where, for the next two or three years, he continued his education by attending the Polytechnic Institute in Regent Street. At that time he displayed no particular scientific ability nor felt any urge to be a doctor. For some years he worked in a shipping office in Leadenhall Street, but he found office routine deadly dull and after four years in the City a small legacy enabled him to escape. The brother with whom he was living had already taken his medical degree and he encouraged his younger brother to take up medicine. Thus at the age of 20 he became a student at St Mary's Hospital Medical School, winning the senior entrance scholarship in natural science. He showed that he had found his true bent by winning almost every class prize and scholarship during his student career. He qualified in 1906 and at the MB, BS examination of London University in 1908 he obtained honours and was awarded a gold medal.

In 1909 he became a Fellow of the Royal College of Surgeons. In 1906 he had begun to assist Sir Almroth Wright in the inoculation department at St Mary's Hospital, and this association led to his taking up the study of bacteriology. Under the stimulating influence of Wright, who was at that time engaged in his researches on the opsonic theory, he acquired great experience and skill in bacteriological technique and in clinical pathology. For recreation he attended the drills and parades of the London Scottish, which he had joined as a private in the year before he resigned from his post with the shipping company. For some years he went to the annual camp and, being a fair shot, to the meetings at Bisley. On the outbreak of war in 1914 he resigned from the London Scottish so that he could go to France as a captain in the RAMC. He worked in Sir Almroth Wright's laboratory in the Casino at Boulogne and received a mention in dispatches. At the end of the war he returned to St Mary's as assistant to Sir Almroth Wright and was also appointed lecturer in bacteriology in the medical school. He subsequently became director of the department of systematic bacteriology and assistant director of the inoculation department. For some years he acted as pathologist to the venereal disease department at St Mary's and was also pathologist to the London Lock Hospital. In 1928 he was appointed Professor of Bacteriology in the University of London, the post being tenable at St Mary's. He retired with the title emeritus in 1948, but continued at St Mary's as head of the Wright-Fleming Institute of Micro-Biology. Though last year he formally handed over the reins to Professor R. Cruikshank, he continued his own research work there and only the day before yesterday was at the institute discussing plans for the lecture tour in the Middle East he had been asked to undertake by the British Council.

Fleming's first notable discovery, that of lysozyme, was made in 1922. He had for some time been interested in antiseptics and in naturally occurring antibacterial substances. In culturing nasal secretion from a patient with an acute cold he found a remarkable element that had the power of dissolving bacteria. This bacteriolyte element, which he also found in tears and other body fluids, he isolated and named lysozyme.

A Lucky Accident

Penicillin was discovered in 1928 when Fleming was engaged in bacteriological researches on staphylococci. For examination purposes he had to remove the covers of his culture plates and a mould spore drifted on to a plate. After a time it revealed itself by developing into a colony about half an inch across. It was no new thing for a bacteriologist to find that a mould had grown on a culture plate which had lain on the bench for a week, but the strange thing in this particular case was that the bacterial colonies in the neighbourhood of the mould appeared to be fading away. What had a week before been vigorous staphylococcus colonies were now faint shadows of their former selves. Fleming might have merely discarded the contaminated culture plate but fortunately his previous research work on antiseptics and on naturally occurring antibacterial substances caused him to take special note of the apparent anti-bacterial action of the mould.

He made sub-cultures of the mould and investigated the properties of the antibacterial substance. He found that while the crude culture fluid in which the mould had grown was strongly antibacterial it was non-toxic to animals and human beings. The crude penicillin was, however, very unstable and was too weak and too crude for injection. Early attempts at concentration were not very successful, and after a few tentative trials its clinical use was not pursued, although it continued to be used in Fleming's laboratory for differential culture. The position in 1929 was that Fleming had discovered and named penicillin, had investigated its antibacterial power, and had suggested that it might be useful as an antiseptic applied to infected lesions. Attempts to produce a concentrated extract capable of clinical application were not successful and had been abandoned. In the light of later knowledge Fleming's original paper of 1929 was remarkable. It covered nearly the whole field, realized most of the problems and made considerable progress in solving them. The resuscitation of penicillin as a chemotherapeutic agent was due to the brilliant work of Sir Howard Florey and his colleagues at Oxford, notably Dr E. B. Chain.

Overwhelmed with Honours

After the establishment of penicillin as a life-saving drug Fleming was overwhelmed with honours. He was knighted in 1944 and in the following year he shared the Nobel Prize for Medicine with Sir Howard Florey and Dr E. B. Chain. He was William Julius Mickle Fellow of London University in 1942, and received an award of merit from the American Pharmaceutical Manufacturers Association in 1943. He was elected FRS in 1943 and FRCP in 1944, under the special by-law. His other honours included the Moxon medal of the Royal College of Physicians (1945), the Charles Mickle Fellowship of Toronto University (1944), the John Scott medal of the City Guild of Philadelphia (1944), the Cameron prize of Edinburgh University (1945), the Albert Gold Medal of the Royal Society of Arts (1946), the honorary Gold Medal of the Royal College of Surgeons (1946), the Actonian Prize of the Royal Institution, and the honorary Freedom of the Boroughs of Paddington, Darvel, and Chelsea. He had innumerable honorary degrees from British and foreign universities, and in 1951 was elected Rector of Edinburgh University. Only last weekend thieves stole property from his flat in Chelsea worth about £1,000 and later an appeal was made to them to return a gold seal of great sentimental value.

Fleming was president of the London Ayrshire Society and of the Pathological and Comparative Medicine Sections of the Royal Society of Medicine. Apart from the papers describing his great discoveries, he contributed to the Medical Research Council *System of Bacteriology*, to the official Medical History of the 1914–18 War, and to many other publications. He was a keen amateur painter, and he had many friends among artists. He was also very fond of motoring and of gardening. He remained quite unspoiled by the publicity and acclaim that came to him and no one was more aware than he of the indispensable part played by other investigators in the development of penicillin. Animated by the spirit of the true scientist, he looked ever forward.

He was twice married, first to Sarah Marion, daughter of Mr John McElroy. She died in 1949, leaving a son. In 1953 he married Dr Amalia Coutsouris, of Athens, who had been a member of his staff at the Wright-Fleming Institute.

ALBERT EINSTEIN

Father of nuclear physics

18 APRIL 1955

PROFESSOR ALBERT EINSTEIN, the greatest scientist of modern times, died in hospital at Princeton, New Jersey, on April 18 at the age of 76. He had lived a secluded life for some years, though he had been a member of the staff of the Institute for Advanced Study in Princeton University.

Albert Einstein was born at Ulm, in Württemberg, on March 14, 1879. A year later his family moved to Munich, where they remained until he was 15. His parentage was Jewish, but few Jewish usages were observed in his home. He was slow in learning to talk and at the Catholic elementary school which he first attended was known as *Biedermeier* ('Honest John') from his ponderously accurate way of speaking. Both here and at the Luitpold Gymnasium, where the educational system was rigid, he saw little difference between school and barrack. His father, Hermann, had a small electro-chemical factory, but he had a greater genius for living than he had for success. Failing in Munich he moved to Milan and later to Pavia. The son, left unhappily at the gymnasium, was well on the way to manoeuvring his departure from it when he was unexpectedly asked to leave as being 'disruptive' of his class. Italy gave him as great an interest in art and music as he already had in Schiller, and the affairs of his father enforced him to seek a career. He had speculated at the age of five on the movement of a compass needle, and he knew that his mathematics, if not his other subjects, were well beyond the usual examination requirements. Combining interest and ability, he arrived at theoretical physics as the field that would most attract him but partly because of his father's work and partly from his own lack of formal attainment, he thought that technological training would be his best approach. He therefore proposed to study at the Swiss Federal Polytechnic School in Zürich, but was at first rejected. He had to qualify for the diploma in modern languages and biology at a cantonal school at Aarau. There he lost his dislike of schooling, and from the age of 17 until the age of 21 he conscientiously followed the course prescribed at Zürich for a teacher of physics and mathematics. In 1901 he became a Swiss citizen – a reflection of his dislike of authority.

Annus Mirabilis, 1905

Partly on account of his ancestry, he had difficulty in finding a teaching post, but by the influence of a fellow student he was appointed as a technical assistant in the Swiss Patent Office at Berne in 1902. This was the 'cobbler's job', which he maintained later was the way that scientists should earn their living. In the next year he married Mileva Maritsch, a fellow student at the Polytechnic. Two sons were born in quick succession, but there were differences of temperament and interest, and the marriage was dissolved after some years.

Einstein's first contribution to theoretical physics was made in the same year that he obtained his Patent Office job. Three years later was his *annus mirabilis*, 1905. Then he burst without warning into an extraordinary range of discovery and new ideas, of which the 'Special Theory of Relativity' was one part, not at the time the most comprehensible by his colleagues. In his earliest work he had simplified Boltzmann's theory of the random motions of the molecules of a gas, and in 1905 he applied this method to the 'Brownian movement' – the impetuous, irregular motion of microscopic particles, suspended in a fluid, that is produced by molecular bombardment. Einstein showed how the number of molecules per unit of volume could be inferred from measurements made of the distances travelled by the visible particles which they hit. Such measurements, made later by Perrin, verified Einstein's theory so well that the Brownian movement has ever since been regarded as one of the most direct – and impressive – pieces of evidence for the reality of molecules.

In the same year Einstein advanced a revolutionary theory of the photo-electric effect, which has exercised a decisive influence on the modern quantum theory of light. The essence of this effect is that the speed with which electrons are liberated from a metal surface illuminated by ultraviolet light depends only on the colour of the light and not on its brightness. Einstein suggested that the light (from which the escaping electrons must derive their energy) is not continuously distributed in space, but is like a gas with a discrete molecular structure – the 'molecules' being photons or units of radiant energy of amounts proportional to the frequency of the light. This assumption gave a concrete physical mechanism for the quantum theory of white light advanced by Planck in 1900, and it provided satisfactory estimates of the speed of photo-electrons. But the importance of Einstein's theory of photons far transcended the occasion of its suggestion. Its real significance is that it accustomed physicists to accept the dual character of light, which sometimes behaves like a continuous train of waves, and sometimes a hail of bullets, and that in 1924 it suggested to de Broglie that matter itself had a similar 'dual personality' and could behave either as a wave or a corpuscle. These conceptions have dominated all subsequent speculations about the ultimate elements of matter and light.

Special Theory of Relativity

Although Einstein's researches in the quantum theory were of vital significance and, in one direction, seemed to show a clearer grasp of its implications than was possessed by its originator, it is with the theories of relativity that his name will always be associated. The 'Special Theory of Relativity' was published in the same extraordinary year. It expressed in a simple and systematic form the effects produced on the basic instruments of physics – the 'rigid' scale and the perfect clock – by relative motion, and thus codified the earlier mathematical investigations of Voigt, the physical speculations of Larmor and the pioneer work of Lorentz. For the first time the optics of moving media received a satisfactory formulation, and Newtonian dynamics itself was generalized so as to express the effect of motion on apparent mass. In particular, Einstein's deduction that mass and energy are proportional became the basic law of atomic transformation. Apart from its spectacular demonstration in atomic energy, it is supported also by a host of experiments in nuclear physics, in which it is used daily as a tool with which nuclear physicists work. Equally, the design of large engineering machines, such as 'synchrotrons', in which nuclear particles are accelerated to high energies, depends directly on its use.

In this group of varied and important publications he showed at once qualities of imagination and insight which were even more vital to his work than mathematical ability, which indeed was a necessary qualification but was not (by the highest standards) exceptional. It was also well for his immediate career that he had more than one contribution to offer.

As soon as the remarkable researches published by Einstein in 1905 became known many attempts were made to secure for him a professorial post. As a result of these efforts he became a *Privatdozent* at Berne in 1908 and *Professor extraordinarius* at Zürich in 1909. In 1911 he became Professor of Theoretical Physics at Prague, but returned to Zürich to the corresponding post in 1912. During 1913 Planck and Nernst persuaded Einstein to go to Berlin as director of the projected research institute for physics, as a member of the Royal Prussian Academy of Science and as a professor in the University of Berlin – with no duties or obligations. He occupied this post until 1933.

General Theory of Relativity

The 'General Theory of Relativity', published in 1916, was the fruit of many years of speculation by Einstein on the questions: 'Can we distinguish the effects of gravitation and of acceleration?' and 'Are light rays bent by gravity?' To answer these questions he was led to build a great and complex theory, which needs for its systematic expression a new mathematical discipline invented by Ricci and

Levi-Civita. The divergences between the predictions of the planetary theory based on Einstein's theory and those based on the classical theory of Newton are all extremely small, but in one case (the slow changes in the orbit of Mercury) Einstein's theory provides an explanation which had never been found on Newtonian principles. Moreover, it successfully predicted the deflection of light from distant stars as it grazed the sun's disc – an effect subsequently verified by British astronomical expeditions in 1919 – and also the reddening of light from very massive stars – which was much later confirmed by observations on the dark companion of Sirius. The success with which 'general relativity' gave quantitative predictions of the new phenomena has created a presumption in its favour which has substantially survived.

The application of general relativity to cosmology was implicit in Einstein's original theory, but became explicit through a modification which he introduced into it in 1917. His contribution in this field was an attempt to provide an answer to an old and 'insoluble' problem: 'How can the universe of stars be uniform in density, fill all space and yet be of finite total mass?' The subsequent relation of observational evidence of 'the expanding universe' to the possible forms of theory that might be developed was done mainly by others, including Lemaître, de Sitter, and Eddington, to whom Einstein served as a stimulus.

During the 1914–18 war two other notable events occurred in his life – he refused to sign the 'Manifesto of Ninety-two German Intellectuals' which identified German culture and German militarism, and he contracted a second marriage, with his cousin Elsa. In 1921 he appeared publicly as a supporter of Zionism and he actively collaborated with Weizmann in the establishment of the University of Jerusalem. During the post-war years he travelled and lectured in Holland, Czechoslovakia, Austria, the United States (where he not only lectured on relativity but took part in Weizmann's campaign for the Jewish National Fund), and England (where he lectured at King's College, London, and calmed the fears of the Archbishop of Canterbury that relativity was a threat to theology). In 1922 he lectured in Paris, Shanghai, and Kobe, returning home via Palestine and Spain.

The Nobel Prize

In the same year he was awarded a Nobel prize, strangely enough, for his work in quantum theory, as the committee were not sure whether his theory of relativity was technically a 'discovery'! He was awarded a Copley Medal by the Royal Society in 1925. He visited South America in 1925 and lectured at Pasadena (California) during the winters of 1930–31, 1931–32, and 1932–33. In the summer of 1932 he lectured at Oxford, and was made an honorary Doctor of Science. The great purge of Jewish scientists began under Hitler in 1933 and Einstein decided not to return to Germany, where scientific freedom had ceased to exist. He lived for some months at La Cocque in Belgium and resigned from the Prussian Academy. In the winter of 1933, at the invitation of Flexner, he emigrated to America and became a Professor at the Institute for Advanced Study at Princeton, a post which he held until 1945. His second wife, Elsa, had died in 1936.

Indeterminacy Opposed

In his later years he was venerated – and loved – but became somewhat isolated in his work from the main stream of modern physics. Remembering his early contribution to the quantum theory, it might have been supposed that he would have accepted readily the principle of indeterminacy, which came to play so large a part in it, and that, in his quest for a further unification of the laws of Nature, he would have tried to weld together the discontinuous and indeterminate picture given by the quantum theory with the continuous and determinate picture of relativity. But for Einstein physics was firmly rooted in causality; God did not play at dice, and he would not admit the ultimate validity of any theory based on chance or indeterminacy. The quantum theory remained, therefore, for him as a passing phase, however important to working physicists. Instead, he attempted further generalizations of relativity, which should incorporate both gravitation and electromagnetism, together with the nuclear fields of force. This work, however, has received no better reception than have all other 'unified field theories'.

When we consider the basic character of the problems he attacked, the vast cosmical scale on which he worked, and his immense influence on physical cosmology as well as physics, we can only compare Einstein with Newton. If Newton's central achievement was to establish the reign of gravitation in its full simplicity and universality, the essence of Einstein's work was to reveal gravitation as a phenomenon expressible in terms of world geometry.

HUMPHREY BOGART

An actor of authority

14 JANUARY 1957

MR HUMPHREY BOGART, the American actor, died yesterday in Hollywood. He was 57. For over 20 years – since his playing of the Dillinger-like part of Duke Mantee in *The Petrified Forest*, which won him much praise – his seamed, sardonic cast of countenance and mordant tongue had been familiar to cinema audiences all over the world.

Bogart was born in New York on June 23, 1899, the son of Dr Belmont Bogart, a physician, and his wife, who as Maud Humphrey had made a name for herself as a watercolour artist and commercial illustrator. He was educated at Trinity School, New York, and at Phillips Academy, Andover, Massachusetts, whence he was destined to go to Yale, but this intention was not fulfilled. The United States had entered the First World War and Bogart joined the Navy. He had always been attracted to the theatre and as soon as the war ended he joined the staff of a promoter of theatrical ventures as manager of a travelling company. But he was determined to act and made his way to New York, where he made his first appearance in 1922 in *Drifting*.

Thereafter he appeared regularly in plays and it was not until 1930 that he went to Hollywood. Of his first efforts he himself later said they were 'a flop'. He returned to the stage and it was only after the success of the play *The Petrified Forest* that he again turned to the screen, to make an immediate impact with the film of the play with Leslie Howard and Miss Bette Davis.

There followed many other films, and notable among his earlier successes was *Dead End*, in which Bogart played the part of a gangster; and a gangster on the screen he often was, but a gangster with a difference. If Mr Clark Gable may be said to stand in the parts he plays for the uninhibited American male, the happy extrovert whom every college boy would wish to be, the lad for the girls and the lad for the liquor, Bogart represented a contrasting, yet allied, type of American hero.

He dwelt in the shadows and was on the other side, so far as the police and the law were concerned, but that was because the police and the law were themselves often shown as corrupt. He was the masculine counterpart of the girl of easy virtue who has a heart of gold. Typical was the role he played in *The Big Shot*. Here he was, of course, the 'big shot', the head of a gang which took beatings-up and murder in its stride, and yet at the end he gave himself up rather than see an innocent man, a

Humphrey Bogart pictured with his wife, the actress Lauren Bacall (left), and the actress Katharine Hepburn (right) as they arrived at Heathrow Airport after spending nine weeks in the Belgian Congo filming location footage for *The African Queen*, 1951.

man he did not even know, electrocuted. It is, of course, wildly improbable that the 'big shot' would do any such thing and, to make the climax convincing, some powerful acting would seem necessary. But that was not Bogart's way. 'He has charm and he doesn't waste energy pretending to act,' wrote James Agate. 'He has a sinister-rueful countenance which acts for him. He has an exciting personality and lets it do the work.'

Certainly Bogart seemed to do little more than project his film personality on to the screen and leave it at that, but it was astonishing how much he could convey with a suggestion of pathos in that husky voice of his, with a shadow of a smile wryly turned against himself, and in films which gave him a chance, a film, for instance, such as John Huston's *The Treasure of the Sierra Madre*, he showed that his acting could be positive even though it never moved far away from the essential Bogart.

Bogart appeared in a great number of films, among them *High Sierra*, *The Maltese Falcon*, *Across the Pacific*, *The African Queen*, *To Have and Have Not*, *Casablanca*, and *The Caine Mutiny*, and, while other reputations waxed and waned, he went on unchanged and unchangeable in calm, complete command of himself, the situation and the screen. He had what Kent found in Lear – authority.

* * *

ARTURO TOSCANINI

A legendary musical figure

15 JANUARY 1957

SIGNOR ARTURO TOSCANINI, who died in New York yesterday at the age of 89, was the most renowned of living conductors, since his reputation was internationally supreme. His pre-eminence was recognized in Italy, where he was born, in America, where he worked for the greater part of his career, and in German countries, where between the wars he conducted at the Bayreuth and Salzburg Festivals.

His quality as an interpreter was mainly known in this country from gramophone records, but his visits to London in the 1930s and in 1952 confirmed and amplified the judgment that for clarity of presentation and fidelity to the composer he had no peer. His tastes were catholic but his interpretations were always those of an Italian. Yet Siegfried Wagner made him the mainstay of the Bayreuth Festival in 1930 and 1931, and the connection was broken only by Toscanini's refusal to appear in Germany when Jewish musicians were maltreated by the Nazi Government. That he should thus be accepted by the leading institution which stands above all others for German music is certainly a remarkable testimony to the universality of his art. It was also a characteristic fulfilment of Toscanini's career. For he had been the first to introduce Wagner's *Götterdämmerung* to Italians; he had supervised the international repertory at the Metropolitan Opera in New York from 1898 to 1915; and it is on his performances of Beethoven's symphonies that his popular fame is founded.

In this country our opportunities of hearing him in the flesh were limited to a short series of concerts in each of the years 1930, 1935, 1937–39, and a last visit in 1952, and, though we heard no opera under his direction, his performances of choral works, including Beethoven's *Mass in D* and Choral Symphony, Brahms's *Requiem*, and Verdi's *Requiem* were memorable. It was widely claimed for him that his readings of these and other classics revealed them in their true character as their creators conceived them, if not for the first time, certainly in a definitive manner. The listener hearing some hitherto over-looked detail in a familiar symphony, noting some subtlety of tonal gradation or shaping of a phrase, was surprised to find that it was all marked in the score, which in point of fact the conductor never used either at rehearsal or at performances by virtue of his prodigious and, as it seems, photographic memory. Yet his interpretations were no more final than those of any other executant musician, and critics whose admiration was less idolatrous found the defects of his qualities in his reading of German music.

Beethoven's Symphonies

The Latin mind, like the Mediterranean sunshine which conditions it, views things with hard edges, clear outlines, and thorough-going logic. Toscanini's meticulous attention to detail in Beethoven's symphonies made them classical and brilliant but ultimately a little inhuman. The opening chords of the Eroica sounded, at any rate with the virtuoso orchestras of America, more like pistol shots than an announcement of the key of E flat, and his bourgeois German Mastersingers became a procession of Florentine nobles. This is only to say that he was true to himself, and no conductor of more single-minded integrity ever lived. This sterling honesty brought him into conflict with the Fascist Government, whose song 'Giovinezza' he refused to play, as it also caused him later to break with Nazi-dominated Germany. To show with an unmistakable gesture what he thought of their intolerance he went to Palestine and conducted the newly formed Jewish orchestra in its national home.

Born at Parma on March 25, 1867, he began his musical studies at the local conservatoire, where his principal subject was the cello. Attention was first called to his exceptional abilities by his remarkable memory, which enabled him after a few rehearsals to play his part in the orchestra without opening the copy on his desk. His opportunity came when, at Rio de Janeiro in 1886, he was called by a sudden emergency to leave his place among the cellos and conduct *Aida*, which he did by heart. From that beginning he went on to the Metropolitan in New York, where he was chief conductor from 1898 to 1915. In 1922 he returned to La Scala at Milan, where he had previously worked between 1898 and 1908, and when the theatre was reopened after alterations in 1922 he was appointed director and ruled it like the autocrat he was.

Arturo Toscanini (centre) at the Royal Festival Hall, Guido Cantelli (left) and Manoug Parikian (right).

Encores Abolished

Of new works, such as the eagerly expected performance of Boito's *Nerone* and the premiere of Puccini's last opera, *Turandot*, he refused to announce even the dates until he was satisfied that the productions were ready, in complete disregard of the convenience of those who were prepared to come long distances to attend them. Nor would he compromise on matters of artistic detail, still less on principle. Thus he abolished encores at La Scala in the face of long-standing Italian practice, and he demanded obedience from the singers and players whom he directed. Yehudi Menuhin, the violinist, who worked in happy association with him at concerts in New York, bears astonished testimony to his impulsiveness and to the general acceptance by others that his will was law. To stop a telephone bell ringing during a private rehearsal with Menuhin Toscanini pulled the instrument from the wall, plaster and all, and returned without a word to the piano. No one expressed any surprise, though Menuhin confesses that he had never before seen such an uninhibited obedience to impulse. There were therefore some qualms at the BBC when that body invited him to come and direct its orchestra, but he won the players' confidence, enthusiasm, and loyalty without any of the explosions with which he has been credited elsewhere. Indeed, Mr Bernard Shore, the violist who played under him, says in his book *The Orchestra Speaks* that playing under Toscanini becomes a different art. 'He stimulates his men, refreshes their minds; and music that has become stale is revived in all its pristine beauty.'

But his autocracy at Milan was bound to bring friction with those whose artistic concentration was less than his own, and after having taken the Scala Company abroad to Germany and Vienna and given performances, more particularly of Verdi's *Falstaff*, which entranced German-speaking audiences, he announced his intention of leaving Milan, and in the winter of 1929 accepted the post of conductor to the Philharmonic Society of New York. It was with the New York Orchestra that he first came to England and toured Europe. He remained with them until 1936.

Later Tours

He then formed his own orchestra, the National Broadcasting Company Orchestra, with which he gave concerts all through the Second World War, touring Latin America and making the gramophone records which preserve his interpretations for the rest of the world. In 1946 he returned for a while to Milan for a few months in order to contribute the proceeds of some concerts towards the rebuilding of La Scala in addition to a financial gift of a million lire. When the Festival Hall was being built in 1950 it was announced that he was willing to come to London and direct some of its inaugural concerts. This plan, however, had to be abandoned. Notwithstanding, he did conduct in the Festival Hall, when in

September, 1952, he came to London to give two concerts devoted mainly to the four symphonies of Brahms. In this connection it is worthy of remark that though he denounced other musicians for tampering with scores, he did himself play some tricks with the timpani of Brahms's C minor symphony.

This symphony also showed him sacrificing the brooding tragedy of the opening in favour of creating immediately a feeling of tremendous tension, a treatment which leaves him with a problem of what to do with the development section. In the milder Brahms of the St Anthony Variations and the D major symphony he showed a more ingratiating temper and in his interpretation of Debussy's *La Mer* sensuous tonal shading was not neglected. But in general it was the intensity, the urgency, the magnification of the life of a score, upon which he seized, and it was this remarkable dynamic drive which he preserved into extreme old age.

His last concert was given at Carnegie Hall in New York no longer ago than in April 1954, when he bade farewell to his orchestra and his public in a Wagner programme, at the end of which he dropped his baton and went out, not to return to face the plaudits of his audience, a symbolic gesture of retirement after 68 years of active music-making.

Signor Toscanini's wife predeceased him in 1951. There were a son and two daughters of the marriage, of whom one is married to Mr Vladimir Horowitz, the pianist.

CHRISTIAN DIOR

A master of couture design

24 OCTOBER 1957

M. CHRISTIAN DIOR, the famous French couture designer, died suddenly yesterday at Montecatini, Italy, at the age of 52, as announced in our late editions. Never strong, Dior had been in ill-health for some time and his death, although so sudden, was not entirely unexpected.

A master of his craft, a rare genius, Dior's name will stand high in the records of fine achievement in the field of couture design. Even more than this he will be honoured for the help that he, with the Marcel Boussac organisation, was able to give France just after the war when it was so greatly needed. Then, the great textile industry, the third most important in France, was nearly at a standstill, but following the tremendous success of his first collection in January, 1947, with its full-skirted styles each requiring many yards of fabric, orders began to flow into the French mills.

Today thousands of workers throughout the world owe their living directly to his inspiration, not only as a result of his couture showings, but also through the success of the wholesale houses and accessory businesses built up under the umbrella of the central organization in Paris, with offices in London, New York, and Caracas.

Born on January 21, 1905, at Granville, in Normandy, he was the only son of Maurice Dior, a wealthy chemical manufacturer. As a youth he enjoyed designing clothes for his sisters, and a costume representing Neptune, which he designed and wore at a fancy dress ball, won him the first prize. The Diplomatic Corps, however, not dress designing, was originally planned as a career for the intelligent, rather delicate, youth. He studied political science at the Sorbonne, but the French financial crisis of 1930–31, which crippled the family business, enabled him to escape from the prospect of a career which had never greatly attracted him. Always interested in art, with the collaboration of friends, he set up a small salon in the Rue la Boétie, in the centre of Paris, and helped to launch Christian Bérard among other young painters. Later Bérard was always to be seen sitting on the floor of the large salon at the première of Dior's collections, until the former's death in 1949.

Forced to give up his art gallery for reasons of ill-health Dior was sent to the mountains to recover. Returning eventually he took up couture designing in earnest, first of all with Agnes, for whom he designed hats, and later with Robert Piguet.

Shortly after the outbreak of war Dior retired to the country where he remained for some time with a sister who had a market garden business. On his return to Paris he became one of Lelong's designers, and remained with Lelong until the fortuitous meeting with a friend of his youth, Marcel Boussac. At this time Boussac was, in fact, looking for a designer in order to set up a couture house, and a partnership was arranged culminating in the widely publicized first collection in the spring of 1947.

Christian Dior's very real affection for England and things English stemmed from his first visit at the age of 19 when, to assist his recovery from a serious illness, his father gave him a sum of money and suggested it should be spent exploring Britain. He had, indeed, many English friends and always made a practice of having at least one English mannequin in the house on the Avenue Montaigne. And he always gave sympathetic attention to the products of British fabric manufacturers.

His feeling for line was allied to a wonderful appreciation of colour and texture, and whatever the 'line' the result was always feminine clothes designed to flatter the wearer. His early death at this moment is not only a tragedy for the house of Dior, but could have serious consequences for the French industry as a whole, following as it does the death or retirement of a number of other important French designers in the past few years.

DOROTHY L. SAYERS

Christian apologist and novelist

17 DECEMBER 1957

MISS DOROTHY L. SAYERS died at her home at Witham, Essex, on Tuesday night at the age of 64.

Sudden death would have had no terrors for her. She combined an adventurous curiosity about life with a religious faith based on natural piety, common sense, and hard reading. She made a name in several diverse fields of creative work. But the diversity of her success was founded on an inner unity of character. When she came down from Somerville with a First in Modern Languages she tried her hand at advertising. The directness and the grasp of facts that are needed by a copywriter stood her in good stead as a newcomer to the crowded ranks of authors of detective fiction. During the 1920s and 1930s, she established herself as one of the few who could give a new look to that hard-ridden kind of novel.

Her recipe was deftly to mix a plot that kept readers guessing with inside information, told without tears, about some fascinating subject – campanology, the backrooms of an advertising agency, life behind the discreet windows of a West End club. Lord Peter Wimsey came alive as a good companion to the few detectives into whom an engaging individuality has been breathed.

This was not done by chance; she had made a close, critical study of the craft. Lecturing, once, on Aristotle's Poetics she remarked that he was obviously hankering after a good detective novel because he had laid it down that the writer's business was to lead the reader up the garden, to make the murderer's villainy implicit in his character from the start, and to remember that the *dénouement* is the most difficult part of the story.

But it is some 20 years since Miss Sayers wrote a detective story, and, shortly before her death, she said: 'There will be no more Peter Wimseys.' The detective writer had been ousted by the Christian apologist. Miss Sayers approached her task of making religion real for the widest public with a zeal that sometimes shocked the conventionally orthodox (with whose protests she was well able to deal) and always held the ears of listeners and the eyes of the reading public. 'The Man Born to be King' became a BBC bestseller, attracting large audiences Christmas after Christmas.

Dante Translations

She carried what she regarded as the central purpose of her life on to the stage and into books. Dogma had no terrors for her. She did not believe in putting water into the pure spirit of her Church. Dante, with his colloquial idiom and unselfconscious piety, naturally attracted her. The translations she published of his *Inferno* and *Purgatorio* caught the directness of the original but failed, as Binyon did not, to catch the poetry. But her prose comments have done more than those of any other recent English author to quicken interest in Dante.

Dorothy Leigh Sayers was born in 1893, the daughter of the Rev. Henry Sayers and Helen Mary Leigh. She was in print before she was 21 with *Op I*, a book of verse, and followed it in 1919 by another, *Catholic Tales*. It was a medium in which she could be skilful, flexible, and effective, and readers of *The Times Literary Supplement* will, no doubt, remember her strong poem, 'The English War', which appeared in its issue of September 7, 1940. Lord Peter made his first appearance in 1923 in *Whose Body?* There followed *Clouds of Witness* (1926), *Unnatural Death* (1927), *The Unpleasantness at the Bellona Club* (1928) and *The Documents in the Case* (1930).

In 1930 Miss Sayers in addition to producing her *Strong Poison*, yet another detective book, made an interesting departure. Out of the fragments of its Anglo-Norman version she had constructed her *Tristan in Brittany*, in the form of a modern English story and produced it, partly in verse and partly in prose.

Have His Carcase (1932) introduced a companion for Lord Peter in the shape of Harriet Vane, a writer of detective stories. In *Hangman's Holiday* (1933), a book of short stories, she created another amateur detective, Mr Montague Egg, who was a simpler reasoner than Lord Peter, but almost as acute. In *The Nine Tailors*, though of the same *genre*, her theme was built round a noble church in Fenland, and possessed a majesty which disclosed powers the authoress had scarcely exerted until then. *Gaudy Night* (1935) took Lord Peter and Harriet Vane into the serene and serious life of a women's college at Oxford, and psychological problems deeper than those which belong to the detective convention arose.

Lord Peter on Stage

In 1936 her *Busman's Holiday*, a play which presented Lord Peter married – Miss Sayers called it 'a love story with detective interruptions' – was staged at the Comedy Theatre. She had a collaborator in M. St Clair Byrne, and between them they provided Lord Peter's public with an excellent entertainment. *The Zeal of Thy House* (1937), which was written for the Canterbury Festival and played there and in London, was set in the twelfth century and was a sincere and illuminating study of the purification of an artist, a kind of architectural Gerontius purged by heavenly fire of his last earthly infirmity. *The Devil to Pay* (1939) was also written for the

Canterbury Festival. It set the legend of Dr Faustus, one of the great stories of the world, at the kind of angle most likely to commend it to the modern stage. Later it was played at His Majesty's Theatre. By sheer alertness of invention and the power to fit her ideas into a dramatic narrative she accomplished an extremely difficult task with credit. *Love All* (1940) was an agreeable and amusing comedy.

In 1940 Miss Sayers published a calmly philosophic essay on the war, which she named 'Begin Here'. Then, in 1941, she followed it with her 'The Mind of the Maker', in which she analysed the metaphor of God as Creator and tested it in the light of creative activity as she knew it. *Unpopular Opinions*, a miscellaneous collection of essays, came out in 1946, *Creed or Chaos*, another series of essays, pungent and well reasoned, in 1947, and *The Lost Tools of Learning* in the following year. She began her translations of Dante for the Penguin Series with the *Inferno* which came out in November, 1949; *Purgatorio* followed in May, 1955. She found the third volume *Paradiso* the hardest and in August, 1956, her translation had reached Canto VII. Her commentary was one of the most valuable parts of her books. After she had finished her second volume, she slipped in, as a kind of relaxation, a translation of *Chanson de Roland*, published this year.

She was an honorary D.Litt. of Durham University. She married in 1926 Captain Atherton Fleming. He died in 1950.

FRANK LLOYD WRIGHT

One of the world's outstanding architects

9 APRIL 1959

MR FRANK LLOYD WRIGHT, the most celebrated American architect of his time, and one of the outstanding architects of the world since the early years of the century, died at Phoenix, Arizona, yesterday. He was 89. He exerted a very powerful influence on architects both in America and Europe. Indeed, during the second decade of the century, when his work was beginning to be known internationally, he was perhaps more readily appreciated in Europe than in his own country, where, in his early days, he met with a degree of opposition so often accorded to innovators.

His work, especially in the field of domestic building, represents the most important American contribution to modern architecture. Wright conceived building as an extension of the creative process of nature, and his work was actuated by the principles of organic growth and unity so that a building should appear as much as possible an integral part of its setting and surroundings. When speaking of the building of his own house in his autobiography he said that no house should ever be on a hill, but should be of the hill. He wanted, he said, a natural house, and he 'scanned the hills of the region where the rock came cropping out in strata to suggest buildings'. This indicates the essence of his domestic building.

He preached the ideas of organic architecture in his lectures and autobiography, and from these ideas formed a general philosophy of life. He was also responsible for many office buildings, a church, and the impressive Imperial Hotel in Tokyo, where trees and plants and pools of water are important elements in the composition of the exterior. When other buildings toppled and crashed during the earthquake of 1923, a year after its completion, the Imperial Hotel alone stood intact. That was due to an extensive use of the cantilever system which enabled him to rest each concrete slab on a central support, like a tray on a waiter's fingers. The hotel was made to float like a ship on a small area of mud poised on hundreds of slender, pointed eight-foot piles with its great weight evenly distributed, a system which was followed in some of Wright's later buildings.

Welsh Descent

Frank Lloyd Wright was a native of Wisconsin, where he was born on June 8, 1869, in a rural district near the town of Spring Green where his grandfather, an emigrant from Wales, settled 100 years ago.

After studying engineering at Madison, Wisconsin, for three years, Wright went to Chicago in 1887 and obtained employment as a draughtsman with J. L. Silsbee. A little later he entered the office of Dankmar Adler and Louis Sullivan, the latter of whom, with his ideas of organic building, exercised a considerable influence on the young Wright. Another important early influence was the domestic architecture of Japan, with its simplicity and its integration of house and garden. Wright designed several houses while in the office of Adler and Sullivan, but in 1893 he began to work independently, and during the next 20 years he built more than 100 houses throughout the Middle West quite unlike anything that had been seen before. They were mostly large and medium-sized houses and were all designed to integrate firmly with the earth and surrounding vegetation and were built with low pitched roofs and wide spreading eaves.

With the Husser House in Chicago, built in 1899, he developed the cruciform plan which became a distinctive feature of many houses of his middle and late periods. With this plan he often made the heating appliance the central feature of the dwelling. His method of design was generally from the interior outwards to the exterior, and the open plan, which he developed, was based on a logical sequence derived from living habits. The long horizontal masses are very pronounced in some of the large houses where the main accommodation spreads over a generous ground floor, and the merging of garden and house is often very marked as in the Darwin Martin house at Buffalo (1904) and the Robie House in Chicago (1909).

The habit of taking suggestions from the natural setting is exemplified in the house built over a waterfall at Bear Run, Pennsylvania, in 1939, where the concrete masses of the terraces above the waterfall are formalized repetitions of the horizontal mass of rock over which the water falls – one of the most dramatic houses in the world.

Wright's early non-domestic building is of a monumental massive character and frequently included valuable technical innovations. A well-known example is the Larkin building in Buffalo (1905), which was the first in America in which such devices were used as metal-bound plate glass doors and windows, all metal furniture, air conditioning, and magnesite as a building material.

Wright had married in 1890, but in 1909 he left his wife and family of six children and went to Europe. He returned in 1911 to his ancestral valley where his mother had bought some land, on which he built a house for himself. This house he named Taliesin after a druid-bard of Wales who had sung of the glories of fine art. In 1914 while Wright was away in Chicago attending to the building of the Midway pleasure gardens a mad Negro servant killed seven of the occupants of Taliesin and set the house on fire. Little remained of the house, which he set to work to rebuild. It came as a relief after this tragedy that he should spend the next five years in Tokyo building the Imperial Hotel.

In 1925 Taliesin II was burnt down and he built a house on the same spot for the third time. Additions have been made to this house over a long period; it is one of his most characteristic works and is justly famous. After building Taliesin III matrimonial difficulties and court proceedings ruined him and lost him his practice until a number of old clients and friends gathered round and set him up in 1929. He then embarked on a third career, building even more ambitiously than before, chiefly houses in suburbs and beyond. He had visions of homes all over the country each with an acre of ground, built to fit in with natural surroundings and for comfort and enjoyment. 'The future city,' he said, 'will be everywhere and nowhere.'

Time was on his side, and when the World's Fair opened in Chicago in 1933 there was everywhere to be seen modern buildings constructed on the lines Wright had followed many years before. At his house at Taliesin and in Arizona where he constructed the model of his idea of a modern city many students came to study with him and a fellowship was formed devoted to his ideals in building.

Among his later works should be mentioned the Johnson building at Racine (1936–39), noteworthy for its construction and method of lighting. The office hall ceiling is supported on tall mushroom pillars which taper towards the bottom. The spaces between the mushroom discs are filled with glass tubes through which the daylight percolates. This building evoked much discussion in architectural circles, some criticizing it as theatrical and others admiring it for the infusion of poetry into building.

The Johnson Building

In 1947–48 a new research laboratory was added to the Johnson building at Racine, and Wright's design is remarkable in many ways. The laboratory is a building of 15 storeys, the floors being cantilevered like tree branches from a central core as the sole support. This core rises 154ft high and is anchored in a foundation of concrete 54ft into the earth. From each alternate floor hangs a glass shell composed of tubes like those in the earlier administration building. This building is of considerable structural significance because it shows the multi-storey building erected in a manner completely different from the skeleton frame and the load bearing wall, while permitting great freedom of planning.

Wright's pursuit of expressive organic forms resulted, in several of his later buildings, in the considerable use of curved forms. Noteworthy examples are his design of the Guggenheim Museum, now almost complete, and the house he built for his son David in the Arizona desert in 1952. This house is constructed of concrete blocks very much in the form of a coiled rattlesnake. The entrance is approached by a semi-circular ramp rising from the ground and the house continues the circular rhythm with the kitchen, dining and living rooms and bedrooms in sequence. It is 'a plan that grows out of the earth and turns its face towards the sun'.

Wright visited England in 1939 when he delivered four lectures at the Royal Institute of British Architects. These lectures were afterwards published as a book entitled *An Organic Architecture, the Architecture of Democracy.* They are a discursive exposition of his philosophy of architecture. In 1941 he was awarded the Royal Gold Medal for architecture. In 1957 at the age of 88 Wright visited Iraq to design an opera house at Baghdad.

Wright was a powerful and picturesque personality, an assiduous propagandist with the style and appearance of a prophet. In spite of the fact that no younger architects of note have carried on his style of design the influence of his ideas has been very great, and indeed some recent developments in modern architecture have reached the same point that he seems to have reached by instinct many years ago.

ANEURIN BEVAN

A brilliant and controversial Labour leader

6 JULY 1960

MR ANEURIN BEVAN, whose death occurred yesterday at the age of 62, was one of the most prominent, vivid and controversial personalities in the Labour movement. He was a politician of brilliant if uneven talent, often at odds with the party leadership, a parliamentary performer whose wit, pugnacity and scintillating verbal imagery could dazzle and delight the House.

His unpredictability baffled and fascinated friend and foe; he could inspire the deepest affection and the liveliest enmity. The complexity of his character matched – and largely explained – the diversity of his political career. Within a few years of having launched, as Minister of Health, his National Health Service he had resigned from the office of Minister of Labour over differences with his Government on defence and social service expenditure. His leadership of the dissident group which became known as the Bevanites made him a storm centre of controversy within the Labour movement, and for a time in 1955 the party whip was denied him. Few could have predicted then that about four years hence he would become Deputy Leader of the Opposition.

The transformation from the fiery rebel to the more mellow statesmanlike figure he became may be said to date from his selection as party spokesman on foreign affairs. But it was not an easy process and it involved him in one of the most testing encounters of his career with those who had once been his most ardent followers. He risked forfeiting the esteem of many of them when at the party conference of 1957 he argued powerfully against a motion for the unilateral renunciation of nuclear weapons. It was not the only time he puzzled and disappointed his supporters.

Celtic Fervour

Bevan was in fact a much misunderstood figure. It was customary to compare him with David Lloyd George, but apart from their Celtic fervour the two had little in common. Bevan, surprisingly enough, was not a natural orator, and some would argue that there was ground for saying he was not an orator at all. Certainly he professed a contempt for oratory. He was a thinker, capable, while on his feet, of clothing in shimmering phrases the thoughts which darted through his lively mind. Although he was one of the most effective platform speakers of his day, he had a genuine distaste for large public meetings and, unlike Lloyd George, he was often at his worst in face of interruptions.

He was not a real demagogue because he continually asserted the necessity for basic principle. It was a favourite contention that while the expediencies of political life might enforce the modification of principle, it was impossible to construct a principle upon a series of modifications. His political outlook was undoubtedly influenced by bitter experiences in South Wales and in his work underground in the coalmines at the age of 13. Basically he was an anti-Conservative, believing profoundly in the class struggle, but he realized that a healthy democracy could function only if the citizens were educated to an adequate social conception. He foresaw a future in which the working classes would want to acquire a first-class copy of a Renoir as much as a Cup Final ticket.

Bevan was a dilettante in the best sense of the word. He had much in common with Charles James Fox, and in this respect one recalls Pitt's own appreciation of his lifelong adversary. When a distinguished Frenchman expressed surprise at Fox's dominance of Whig politics Pitt replied, 'Ah, but you have never been under the wand of a magician.'

Aneurin Bevan was born at Tredegar, Monmouthshire, in November, 1897, the son of a coal miner. He was educated at Serhowy Elementary School and after leaving it in 1910 went into the mines. After some years of employment there – it was eventually terminated by nystagmus – he went to the Central Labour College. Later he became increasingly prominent in the councils of the South Wales Miners Federation and was particularly active in connection with the great strike of 1926. In 1929 he was returned as Labour member for the Ebbw Vale division of Monmouthshire, a constituency which was to remain loyal to him throughout his political career.

In his early days in the House Bevan confined himself to speaking on mining matters. He had, however, a faculty for debate and a power for concentration in argument which were soon to impress his fellow members and to win him a reputation for forceful vitality. In 1934 he married Miss Jennie Lee, who until 1931 had been Labour member for North Lanark and was one of the Left wing of the Labour movement. She was returned for Cannock in 1945.

In March, 1939, Bevan, who had joined the 'United Front' movement of which Sir Stafford Cripps was the most prominent member, received a letter from the secretary of the Labour Party threatening his expulsion unless he dissociated himself from it. The expulsion was confirmed at the annual party conference at Whitsuntide, and it was not until December that Bevan was received back into the Labour Party.

In the war years Bevan was as frank a critic of Mr Churchill's as he had been of Mr Chamberlain's administrations. He was, moreover, prepared on occasion to indulge in what appeared to be a personal dislike for Mr Churchill, who once described him as a 'merchant of discourtesy'.

In May, 1944, Bevan led a challenge to the Government and to his own party, which very nearly resulted in a second expulsion, over Defence Regulation IAA which prescribed heavy penalties for the instigation of strikes in essential industries. The outcome was that the party organization decided that he should be expelled unless he would give written assurances of loyalty. This he promptly gave and later in the year he was elected to the National Executive of the Labour Party.

With characteristic self-confidence Bevan accepted the post of Minister of Health in the Labour Government of 1945. He carried through Parliament the Local Government Act of 1948, and with the Minister of National Insurance he was joint sponsor of the National Assistance Act of the same year, which wound up the Poor Law. Under his regime Britain, and principally British local authorities, produced far more new dwellings, temporary or permanent, than any comparable country in Europe, but at a cost which was almost certainly excessive.

Clash with BMA

Bevan's health scheme was one which he honestly believed, in spite of the opposition of the leaders of the British Medical Association, would be welcomed by the doctors themselves. He produced a Bill based on the Coalition scheme with certain daring changes, never before contemplated even by the Labour Party, such as the nationalization of hospitals, their management by 'mixed' regional boards, and the stopping of the sale of publicly remunerated general practices. The Health Act was a masterly attempt to cut the Gordian knot of contending interests by a bold compromise not wholly to the liking either of the Labour Party or of the doctors, but sufficiently imaginative to earn for Bevan the respect of all parties in Parliament and at least the respectful neutrality of the consultants and specialists.

These early hopes were soon dashed, partly by psychological blunders on the part of Bevan and some of his less responsible political supporters, no less by the attitude of the BMA leaders. When Bevan became Minister they gave him neither quarter nor credit for the many unpalatable changes he forced his own party to accept. In spite of his noticeably cynical realism and flexibility, Bevan was not free of doctrinaire ideas, which he betrayed in emotional remarks about the sale of practices and in his long insistence on a 'basic salary' for every general practitioner. The BMA made effective use of all this in its campaign. Even his self-imposed silence during most of 1947, when negotiations with the medical representatives were resumed after the passing of the Act, was turned against him.

The revulsion of feeling became general at the end of 1947, when the doctors' negotiating committee came back crestfallen from their talks with Bevan without a single one of the major concessions which the BMA was demanding. The doctors prepared themselves without enthusiasm for a boycott of the service due to start in July. Bevan was at first tempted to be equally stubborn. But by early April he was persuaded to make a final effort at reconciliation. He was wise enough and big enough to swallow his pride. The basic salary was made optional, he promised an amending Bill to make the introduction of a full-time medical service impossible without fresh legislation, and met the doctors' leaders once again to agree on a final settlement. This quarrel, so belatedly settled, hampered the smooth launching of the new health service, but the blame for it does not rest wholly on Bevan.

From the completion of the administrative and legislative measures necessary to implement the National Health Service, Bevan's Ministerial career reached its zenith. But he felt himself in a situation of increased isolation in the Cabinet. Many of his colleagues resented the constant advice and criticism they received from the *Tribune* newspaper which, if Bevan had no direct association with it, was edited by close and intimate associates and frequently gave expression to views identical with his. In particular Bevan was known to distrust a good deal of the foreign policy of the Labour Government.

In fact the Labour Cabinet had at times been an uneasy coalition and disputes in the Cabinet over nationalization of steel and over foreign policy had aggravated this division. In 1947 Sir Stafford Cripps attempted a palace revolution for the removal of Mr Attlee which Bevan emphatically refused to support. But though he worked on terms of apparent amity with Mr Attlee, the two men never established a mutual understanding.

In 1947 and again in 1950 a group of Labour backbenchers, many close associates of Bevan, published pamphlets under the title of 'Keep Left' and of 'Keeping Left', highly critical of Labour Government policy, and the second of these pamphlets appeared on the very eve of the election of 1950 and aroused considerable controversy. Bevan was already under attack. In 1948 in a speech on the inauguration of the National Health Service he was reported as describing Conservatives as 'lower than vermin', and though he declared that in the context it applied to the South Wales coal-owners of the last century the observation was criticized by a number of his parliamentary colleagues.

Immediately after the election of 1950 which returned the Labour Government with a bare majority of half a dozen, the presentation of supplementary estimates for the Health Service amounting to nearly £100m resulted in a motion of censure in which Bevan came under heavy attack. He was compelled to agree to a declaration by Sir Stafford Cripps imposing a ceiling upon National Health expenditure.

In October, 1950, Sir Stafford Cripps resigned the Chancellorship owing to ill health and was succeeded by Mr Hugh Gaitskell. During the Christmas recess of 1950 it became known that following discussions in Washington the Cabinet had agreed to a very large increase in defence expenditure which would inevitably involve anxiety among Labour members. There was considerable talk about ministerial resignations.

In January Bevan became Minister of Labour. He was aware that a resignation by him at such a moment would involve him in old and buried hostilities, and cause deep cleavage in the movement, and he was known to be genuinely reluctant to take this course. The proposals in the Budget involving charges amounting to some £12m in respect of certain National Health Services, and the reduction by £100m of the surplus standing to the credit of the National Insurance fund were the ultimate reasons which brought about in April the resignation from the Government of Bevan and of the President of the Board of Trade, Mr Harold Wilson, and of Mr John Freeman.

'Keep Left' Pamphlet

The resignations led to widespread controversy in the country and in the Labour Party. On the whole the trade unions, through their leaders and the official central organizations of the Labour Party, condemned Bevan, while he received increasing support from the constituency parties. He naturally became the leader of those Labour members who had been principally critical of Cabinet policy and the group of members who had been responsible for the publication of the 'Keep Left' pamphlet was rapidly enlarged until it numbered about 50 Labour members, and was responsible for the publication of two more pamphlets, the latter of which 'Going Our Way', published under the auspices of *Tribune* and critical of Government financial policy, appeared on the eve of the parliamentary election of 1951 which resulted in the return of a Conservative Government.

At the annual conference of the Labour Party preceding the election an effort had been made to close the ranks, but some bitterness was caused by the result of the election for constituency party representatives on the Labour Party National Executive in which the Minister of Defence, Mr Shinwell, lost his seat after a very long membership while Bevan headed the poll and three of his supporters obtained seats. From this period the word Bevanite was constantly used to denote those Labour members whose votes would usually be cast in support of the policies advocated by Bevan. But a number of well-known Labour members included among this number were never members of the Bevanite organization.

Standing Orders Reimposed

After the defeat of the Labour Government it was soon made clear that the Parliamentary Labour Party was not prepared to tolerate what was referred to as a 'party within a party' and there were early demands for the reimposition and enforcement of standing orders to be followed by strong disciplinary action. In March, 1952, on the defence debates a three-line whip was issued which took the unprecedented course of instructing Labour members to vote not only for the Opposition amendment but also in support of the Government White Paper. There was in fact a large abstention on the vote on the amendment and 57 members, including Bevan, voted against the Government on the main question. There was an immediate demand for an expulsion of these 57 members from the party and at the meeting of the Parliamentary Party Mr Attlee moved a resolution calling for the reimposition of standing orders and for written undertakings to be called for from the members concerned. Ultimately a more moderate amendment moved by Mr Strauss calling for party unity and the reimposition of standing orders was carried by a substantial majority.

When the results of the constituency party elections were announced it was found that both Mr Herbert Morrison and Mr Dalton had been defeated. Two more Bevanites had been added to the executive, Mr James Griffiths being the only supporter of official policy to retain his seat. The deep cleavage in the Parliamentary Labour Party continued and the pattern remained the same. Bevan could count on overwhelming support from the constituencies and gained no additional support in the Parliamentary Labour Party. Bevan was faced with the dilemma of either refusing to submit himself for election to the Shadow Cabinet or of offering himself for election and remaining there in a permanent minority and bound by minority decisions. In 1952 he offered himself for election and secured the last of the 12 seats. His position was a singularly uneasy one and in 1954 a scene in the House of Commons, in which in a supplementary question on the South East Asia Treaty Organization Bevan was regarded as having strongly dissociated himself from the view just expressed by Mr Attlee, resulted in a formal rebuke of Bevan and his resignation from the committee. The vacancy thus created was, under the rules filed by the runner-up at the preceding election, who was Mr Harold Wilson, Bevan's principal lieutenant, and it was believed that his acceptance of office resulted in a weakening of the understanding between them.

In March, 1955, the continued controversy within the Parliamentary Labour Party which had ranged over German rearmament, the use of the hydrogen bomb, and the necessity for discussions with the USSR seemed to have been brought to a head when, at a meeting of the Parliamentary Labour Party, Mr Attlee moved a resolution for withdrawal of the whip from Bevan. This was finally carried, after the narrow rejection of a compromise resolution, by a majority of 141 to 112.

Whip Restored

The National Executive of the Labour Party then discussed the expulsion of Bevan from the Labour Party. Mr Attlee, who had undoubtedly been surprised by the narrow majority in the Parliamentary Party, moved a resolution for postponement and for discussion with Bevan which was carried by one vote only and after Bevan had given assurances of his desire to conform to the constitution of the party, the Executive, again by one vote only, decided not to expel him though Mr Gaitskell and Mr Morrison were among those voting for expulsion. A week or two later, in face of a general election, the parliamentary whip was restored.

Bevan gave up his seat on the National Executive of the Labour Party to enter into a contest for the office of treasurer of the party left vacant by the death of Mr Greenwood. This brought him into direct conflict with Mr Gaitskell who had been nominated by the principal trade unions. Bevan had declared that while he knew immediate defeat was inevitable he would continue the contest for some years.

In December of 1955 Mr Attlee resigned his leadership of the party and a ballot resulted in 157 votes being cast for Mr Gaitskell, 70 for Bevan, and 40 for Mr Morrison, Bevan in fact retaining almost exactly the support he had had throughout the controversy.

Mellowed Style

Bevan made clear his intention to accept this decision and he did not contest the position in 1956. Mr Gaitskell and Bevan both made efforts to arrive at an understanding and in the course of the violently controversial debates on the Suez question they achieved a close association, cooperative if not cordial. Mr Gaitskell in assigning roles in the Shadow Cabinet first entrusted Bevan with colonial affairs in which he at once proceeded to take a very keen and active interest. In a later re-allocation of duties Bevan was trusted with the shadow role of foreign affairs, a position which he had always particularly desired.

During this period Bevan's parliamentary style noticeably mellowed and his speeches became less aggressive. He adopted a Parliamentary technique of offering thoughtful and constructive suggestions, but presented with the old artistry and inflection and in a manner which began to command increasing respect on both sides of the House.

But the new statesmanlike Bevan found himself in a sharp dilemma at the 1957 Party Conference when he had to oppose a composite motion demanding unilateral renunciation by Britain of nuclear weapons. One of the arguments he used in encompassing its defeat – with trade union help – was that its passage would mean sending a British Foreign Secretary naked into the conference room.

Some months later he angered some of his hearers when in a Commons debate he appeared to put a gloss on those words, and there were murmurs of 'over-diluted Bevanism'. Some of his former adherents gathered themselves into a 'ginger group' under the resuscitated title of 'Victory for Socialism', and their activities prompted a move to unite Labour forces behind an agreed policy on disarmament and nuclear tests. His championship at public meetings of the official line brought him under noisy protests from those who spurned it. In April,

1959, he startled the Commons by flinging into a Foreign Affairs debate a blunt declaration that a Labour Government would stop all hydrogen bomb and atomic tests at once.

At this time he was much preoccupied with the dangers of rearming Germany and in general his responsibilities as 'shadow' to the Foreign Secretary imbued his speeches at times with a certain melancholy foreboding about international events as evolving 'with all the inevitability of an ancient Greek drama'. Some of his speeches seemed to lack his former buoyancy and ebullience, though one he made in the early days of the new 1959 Parliament, advocating the televising of the House, recaptured the old brilliance in full.

Blackpool Inquest

Bevan had gone with Gaitskell to Moscow in the summer recess of 1959 but they came home immediately the date of the general election was announced. Bevan was returned by Ebbw Vale with a majority increased by more than 1,000, and soon after the new Parliament met he was elected Deputy Leader of the Opposition on the resignation of Mr James Griffiths. In all the heart-searching in which the Labour Party engaged after their decisive defeat, many of the rank and file who feared a retreat from essential Labour policies, particularly on public ownership, looked hopefully to Bevan. Whether, at the party's grand inquest at Blackpool, they got the reassurance they desired seemed to be left in some doubt. But they revelled in the sparkle of his wit and basked in the mellowness of his mood.

The bitterness which sometimes entered into Bevan's political utterances was completely absent from his private life. His marriage to Miss Lee was singularly happy and the visitor to his house in London or later to his farm in Buckinghamshire had the rare privilege of being entertained by two outstanding Parliamentary personalities of exceptional charm. Bevan loved the good things of life and there were few subjects on which he could not talk with considerable knowledge and none on which he could not talk attractively. He delighted in conversation for its own sake. A genuine appreciation of art and literature was reinforced by a remarkable memory. His philosophical outlook had moved from a Marxist foundation to an appreciation of the theories of Jose Rodo on the Protean nature and perfectibility of man. He might be found cheerfully, brilliantly, but without ostentation, discussing in painting the modernism of Braque or approving the exquisite drawing of Fragonard, quoting from such widely varied poetry as Chesterton and Crabbe or illustrating a musical disquisition with records of Stravinsky or of Negro spirituals. He was generous to a fault and kindly and considerate in adversity.

SIR THOMAS BEECHAM

Conductor, impresario and benefactor of music

8 MARCH 1961

THE DEATH yesterday of Sir Thomas Beecham, Bt., CH, removes one of the most remarkable figures in contemporary musical history. He was 81.

It is primarily as an orchestral conductor that he is celebrated. As an interpreter of a wide range of music he counts as one of the comparatively few executant geniuses this country has ever produced: continental Europe and America alike recognized him as such. In the last two decades of his life his stature was recognized as second to none among the great conductors of the world. But the work he did by shouldering the functions of the impresario, by his insistence on the highest standards of performance, can now be seen to have left a more enduring influence on the musical life of this country than was apparent in 1944, when he published what he described as 'leaves from an autobiography'. In *A Mingled Chime* he recounts in the form of an *apologia pro sua vita* his Sisyphean labours in the cause of opera and orchestral music. The years since the war have showed that the enterprises which seemed at the time to have foundered have proved to be foundations upon which, in changed circumstances, the remarkable vitality and vigour of our present institutions, alike in opera and in orchestral music, have been established.

Born on April 29, 1879, at St Helens, the eldest son of the late Sir Joseph Beecham, the wealthy manufacturer of pills, Thomas was endowed not only with riches but with a quite unusual degree of musical sensibility. An ordinary schooling at Rossall, followed by a brief residence at Wadham College, Oxford, provided him with no special musical training. Yet in 1899, at the age of 20, he had founded and conducted an amateur orchestra, and seven years later, after a brief experience with a touring opera company, he created the New Symphony Orchestra, with which he gave a remarkable series of concerts at the Queen's Hall. After two years with this orchestra, another was formed and called the Beecham Symphony Orchestra.

The most important work done by Beecham during these years was the production of the works of Delius, whom he persistently championed in the face of general opposition or apathy until the composer gradually took his proper place in the scheme of things. Twenty years later his faith in Delius was reaffirmed in a triumphant festival in London in the presence of the then stricken composer and again, after the 1939–45 War, in a Delius festival in 1946, and subsequently in gramophone recordings under the auspices of the Delius Trust. The biography of Delius published two years ago crowned his efforts in that it made public what no other person knew about the personality of the composer. The writing of it was the fulfilment of a pledge made to Mrs Zelka Delius many years ago, and though more concerned with Delius the man than with detailed technical analyses of the works themselves, yet it nevertheless proves that man and artist were very much one.

Eclectic Tastes

In 1909 Beecham started upon his career as an operatic impresario, when he produced Ethel Smyth's *The Wreckers* at His Majesty's Theatre. In the following year a more ambitious season was undertaken at Covent Garden, when Strauss's *Elektra* and Delius's *Village Romeo and Juliet* were presented for the first time in England. Other seasons followed in rapid succession and among the operas produced were *Cosi fan tutte*, which had not been given in England for many years, *Fidelio*, *Salome*, and Stanford's *Shamus O'Brien*. It will be seen from this selection of titles that Beecham's tastes were thoroughly eclectic and that he kept a corner warm for the British composer. In 1911 he was instrumental in bringing to England Serge Diaghilev's Russian Ballet, an event which has had profound effects upon almost every branch of art. This innovation was followed up two years later by the importation of a Russian opera company, Chaliapin being among the singers, and *Boris Godounov*, *Khovanshchina*, and *Ivan the Terrible* were introduced to the astonished musical public of England. He was knighted for his services to music in 1916 and that same year succeeded to the baronetcy which had been conferred on his father in 1914. No other honour was given him until 1957 when he was made a Companion of Honour.

During the 1914–18 War Beecham's musical activities were unceasing. He produced opera in English and the repertory of his company ranged from Leoncavallo and Puccini to Mozart, Wagner and Moussorgsky. In the orchestral sphere he undertook the conductorship of the Royal Philharmonic Orchestra in London and of the Hallé Orchestra in Manchester and kept these two societies above water both by his enthusiasm and by financial assistance in those difficult days.

After the war he continued to give opera in English, adding, among other works, *Parsifal* and *Falstaff* to his repertory. In 1920 he gave a 'grand' season at Covent Garden. His enthusiasm had, however, outrun his financial resources and possibly his discretion. For a time he had to retire from active musical work. The Beecham Opera Company was transformed into the British National Opera Company, which bravely attempted to maintain in the face of adversity the standard he had set.

Undiminished Vitality

A few years later he reappeared as an orchestral conductor, undiminished in vitality and deepened in musical understanding. He added Handel to the number of his especial favourites among the composers, and gave performances of *Messiah* and other oratorios, which astonished everyone by their vitality and their insight. In 1928 he became conductor of the Leeds Triennial Festival and in all festivals up to the outbreak of war in 1939 secured some remarkable performances – of Delius's *Mass of Life*, Verdi's *Requiem* and of the choral works of Berlioz as well as of more conventional masterpieces.

He continued his work for opera by association with various syndicates at Covent Garden and a renewal of his Russian enterprises at the Lyceum in 1931, but his attempt to found an Imperial League of Opera, which he launched in 1927, though promising well at first failed before it could begin the large scale operations projected for it throughout the country. Another project, the founding of an orchestra which should be moulded to his style of playing, was brilliantly successful while it lasted. This was the creation of the London Philharmonic Orchestra in 1932, which was in part a counterblast to the BBC, with whom Beecham sometimes found it difficult to work in harmony.

From this time until the outbreak of the second German war the LPO played regularly for the Royal Philharmonic Society for various serial concerts as well as for opera and ballet during the summer. Its characteristics were crisp ensemble and such an intensity of sheer singing tone that in Haydn and Mozart at any rate it sometimes seemed as though the ear was being lashed with thongs of silk. Beecham's style was essentially lyrical, though he was not always considerate to singers in his operatic performances. Wagner in his hands – he conducted *The Ring* annually at Convent Garden for a number of years – shrank a little from epic size but gained in mellifluousness, so that *Lohengrin*, for instance, became a singer's, almost an Italian, opera.

Prodigious Memory

It was part of Beecham's eclectic taste that though not fundamentally in sympathy with the heroic element in Wagner – nor indeed, with Beethoven – he could redress the balance of his sympathies with their other qualities, with all the elements that appealed to his acute sensibility, so that his readings of the German masters were unusual or individual, yet free from distortion. Mozart was his favourite above all others. Intellectual music made little appeal to him: the appearances of Bach or late Beethoven in his programmes were rare and his interpretation of Brahms (e.g. the C Minor Symphony) was not always convincing. His memory was extraordinary and he conducted everything, except concertos and operas, without a score, but with evident knowledge of its contents. Indeed, it was taken as a sign that he did not really know the work if a score was brought on of a purely orchestral composition. His dramatic gestures at one time gave offence – they were interpreted as an affectation and dubbed 'ballet dancing' – but careful observation showed that he rarely made an insignificant gesture, and the details of his exquisite phrasing were moulded by his hands.

In 1940 he went to Australia and to America on conducting engagements, and during the 1939–45 War remained in the United States, to which he had long threatened to emigrate in disgust at artistic conditions in this country. Beecham used to give expression to his ideas of what the nation and in particular, though he was no democrat, of what the wealthier members ought to do for music, in pungent terms. In speech he was often indiscreet and took pleasure in indiscretion. He allowed his very acute wit unrestrained play and there was an imp of mischief in his make-up. He had the gift of quick repartee and his quips and sallies gave rise to many stories, more true than fabulous.

Widely Read

There is little doubt that his wit, which is less congenial to his fellow countrymen than humour, his benevolent dictatorship in artistic matters, and a touch of aristocratic disdain in manner contrived during his middle life to create some distrust in the minds of the British public. It was to combat what had become a liability to all his schemes for his country's good that he portrayed himself in his autobiography as a conventionally educated man of the world, a musician who could read a balance-sheet as easily as a full score, a hard-headed Lancastrian with no Celtic nonsense about him.

He was no doubt all of these things and a well and widely read man into the bargain. But these qualities were overlaid by his extraordinary sensibility, his darting wit, his prodigious memory, his idiosyncrasies and above all by his genius, to make him a legendary figure in his lifetime. The legend, like the work he did for our musical life, will survive after the laurels of the dead conductor have, inevitably, withered.

The effervescence of Beecham's personality was such that at the time most people think of retiring he returned to the scene with a remarkable outburst of new musical vigour. His eightieth year was marked by a triumphant season at the Teatro Colon in Buenos Aires, during which he conducted *Otello, Carmen, Samson et Dalila, Die Zauberflöte,* and *Fidelio.* This followed hard on the heels of a concert tour which had taken him to Paris, Switzerland, Vienna, Spain, Portugal, Monte Carlo, and Rome (where he directed the soundtrack for a musical film). In the autumn of 1958 he returned to England, and after proving that his wit was unimpaired when unveiling a bronze of himself by David Wynne at a ceremony in the Festival Hall, proceeded to direct a series of concerts which were like a tonic to the orchestra and audience alike. Not only his energies but also his range of interests increased with the years. In the recording studio he was no less active than in the concert hall as a recent issue of Bizet's Symphony in C testifies. He was to have conducted 10 performances of Mozart's *Die Zauberflöte* at last year's Glyndebourne festival but his health did not allow him to fulfil the engagement. There had also been discussion of a possible visit to Russia with his orchestra, the Royal Philharmonic.

Sir Thomas married first in 1903 Utica, daughter of Dr Charles S. Welles, of New York, a descendant of Governor Thomas Welles, one of the Puritan Fathers and a member of an old Bedfordshire and Northamptonshire family, and secondly, in 1943, Betty Humby, the pianist. She died in 1958 and he married thirdly, in 1959, Shirley Hudson, who is connected with the Royal Philharmonic Orchestra on the administrative side. His eldest sister Emily (Madame Helena Dolli) is a teacher of operatic dancing. He is succeeded in the baronetcy by the elder of the two sons by his first marriage, Adrian Welles Beecham, who was born in 1904.

ERNEST HEMINGWAY

An outstanding creative writer

2 JULY 1961

THE ANNOUNCEMENT of Ernest Hemingway's death at the age of 61 can, in a sense, come as no surprise to his readers. Death was always one of his principal themes as a writer, and he had himself been confronting it directly ever since he had broken away from the suburban environment in which he had been raised to volunteer in 1918 for service on the Italian front as a driver with the Red Cross field ambulances. 'By my troth, I care not; a man can die but once; we owe God a death and let it go which way it will he that dies this year is quit for the next.' He was fond of the quotation and used it as a touchstone of conduct.

Ernest Miller Hemingway was born on July 21, 1899, the second of the six children of Clarence Edmonds Hemingway, a doctor with a reputation as a sportsman, practising in Oak Park, Chicago, Illinois, and Grace Hall Hemingway, a devout and musical woman. He was educated at the local High School and, after volunteering for active service in 1917 and being rejected on account of an eye injury, he became briefly a cub reporter on the Kansas City *Star*. He left for Italy in May, 1918, and was badly wounded in the course of duty in July; but by October he was serving, again as a volunteer, with the Italian infantry on the Austrian front. He was twice decorated by the Italian Government for his services.

His experience of war was his initiation into manhood and, like so many who underwent it, he spent his later life in trying to understand its significance, for the individual and for his generation. He wrote about the war itself most directly and fully in *A Farewell to Arms*, but in all his writings the moral and psychological problems he had been brought face to face with in action were explored, whether in the setting of later wars or civil violence, big game hunting, or bull fighting.

Roving Correspondent

He returned from Europe to North America in 1919 and resumed journalism, this time in Toronto with the *Star Weekly*, and, later, the *Daily Star*. He wrote for these papers until 1924 but spent the greater part of the time as a roving correspondent in Europe, covering, among much else of importance, the Greco-Turkish war of 1922. He had now the bitter opportunity of seeing how the general disillusionment that followed so speedily upon the Armistice was accompanied by political chicanery and the rise of fascism. He had married Hadley Richardson in 1921; a son was born in 1923.

He went back to Toronto in August, 1923, but upon deciding to withdraw from journalism and devote himself to fiction, he resigned from his newspaper in January, 1924, and returned immediately to Paris. Once he had begun to make a reputation, his domicile abroad was widely criticized at home as unpatriotic, but he himself knew that his experience of war had so essentially identified him with Europe that it was there alone that he could develop freely. And no matter how long he lived abroad he remained at heart and in the imagination thoroughly American.

He had earlier met in Paris, among other American expatriates, Ezra Pound and Gertrude Stein, and their encouragement and criticism of his early work were to influence him deeply, though he was later to quarrel publicly with Miss Stein. His first and second books, *Three Stories and Ten Poems*, and *in our time* (enlarged and published as *In Our Time*, New York, 1925), which appeared in Paris in 1923 and 1924, won him some praise from the critics; his third, *The Torrents of Spring* (1926), a hastily written satirical novel ridiculing Sherwood Anderson, a friend from his Chicago days, made him more widely known; and the novel, *The Sun Also Rises* (1927, published under the title of *Fiesta* in England), a collection of short stories *Men Without Women* (1927), and lastly, *A Farewell to Arms* (1928) brought him fame and fortune. His deliberate, skilful, economic prose, learnt under the discipline of his earlier journalism, the complex and symbolically wounded character of his typical hero, and the sharp contemporaneity of mood and action were at once recognized as highly original and promoted him to the front of living writers, a position of eminence which he never lost. 'Hemingway is the bronze god of the whole contemporary literary experience in America', Alfred Kazin wrote in 1942; but his influence was felt almost as deeply abroad in Britain and on the Continent, as at home.

At Key West

After his divorce in 1927 and his marriage to Pauline Pfeiffer, by whom he had two sons, he returned to America and made his headquarters at Key West, Florida, for the next 10 years. During this time he published another collection of short stories, *Winner Take Nothing* (1933), and an uneven novel, *To Have and Have Not* (1937); but more important works were *Death in the Afternoon* (1932), a remarkable, discursive study of bull-fighting, and *Green Hills of Africa* (1935), an equally discursive account of big game hunting. The character he offers of himself in both books so closely resembles and seems often to parody the hero of his own fiction, that Edmund Wilson remarked that this Hemingway 'is certainly the worst-invented character to be found in the author's work'. He rapidly became a legendary figure in the eyes of the public.

When civil war broke out in Spain, he actively supported the Republicans both by purchasing ambulances for them at his own expense and by going to Spain in 1936 to write a documentary film, *The Spanish Earth*. The most lasting result of his experience of the civil war was, however, *For Whom the Bell Tolls* (1940), often held to be his best novel. A play, *The Fifth Column*, had appeared earlier in 1938.

Pulitzer Prize

Shortly after his divorce in 1940 and his marriage to Martha Gellhorn, the novelist, he went to live at Finca Vigia, a farm outside Havana; and after America's entry into the war he kept up an anti-submarine patrol of Cuban waters in his motor-yacht, the Pilar. Tiring of this distant activity, he came to Europe as a war correspondent in 1944 and flew on several missions with the RAF. When the invasion of Europe started he was so hotly involved in the American advance that he was nearly court-martialled for violating the Geneva Convention on the conduct of war correspondents. He was awarded a Bronze Star. His third marriage ended in divorce in 1944, and after the war he returned to Havana with his fourth wife, Mary Welsh.

His renewed experience of war and a desire to sum up all he had learnt in his varied career inspired him to write *Across the River and into the Trees* (1950), an embarrassingly autobiographical and unsuccessful novel, in which the mannerisms and sentiment dangerously latent in some of his earlier writing rose destructively to the surface. His career as a writer seemed about to end in disgrace but he suddenly recovered himself in *The Old Man and the Sea* (1952), a noble and allegorical account of an old fisherman's lonely struggle in the Gulf of Mexico to land a huge marlin. The tale was awarded a Pulitzer Prize in 1953. The following year his international standing as a writer was recognized with the award of the Nobel Prize for Literature.

Hemingway said himself that he tried to write prose 'which would be as valid in a year or in 10 years or, with luck and if you stated it purely enough, always'. The remark illustrates the devoted artist concealed in the legendary figure, and whether or not his work will read freshly for 'always', no history of the literature of our time will be able to ignore his achievement or his far-reaching influence.

MARILYN MONROE

Hollywood legend

5 AUGUST 1962

MISS MARILYN MONROE died yesterday at the age of 36, as reported on another page.

Her career was not so much a Hollywood legend as *the* Hollywood legend: the poor orphan who became one of the most sought after (and highly paid) women in the world; the hopeful Hollywood unknown who became the most potent star attraction in the American cinema; the uneducated beauty who married one of America's leading intellectuals.

The story thus dramatically outlined was in all essentials true. Marilyn Monroe began life as Norma Jean Baker in Los Angeles, where she was born on June 1, 1926. She was brought up in an orphanage and a series of foster homes, married first at the age of 15, obtained a divorce four years later and began a career as a photographer's model. From this, in a few months, she graduated to a screen test with Twentieth-Century Fox, a contract and the name which she was to make famous. Nothing came of this contract immediately, however, and her first appearance in a film was for another studio in 1948, when she played second lead in a not very successful B picture called *Ladies of the Chorus*. There followed a number of small roles in films such as *Love Happy* (with the Marx Brothers), *The Asphalt Jungle*, directed by John Huston, in which she was first seriously noticed, Joseph Mankiewicz's *All About Eve*, Fritz Lang's *Clash by Night* and others, until in 1952 she was given her first starring role in a minor thriller, *Don't Bother to Knock*, in which she played (improbably) a homicidal baby-sitter.

This was where she began in earnest to become a legend: during the shooting of the film it came to light that some years before she had posed nude for a calendar picture, and her career, hanging in the balance, was saved by the simple avowal that she had needed the money for the rent and was not ashamed. From then on her name was constantly before the public, even if the parts she played were not always large or important, and the advertising for her next major role, in *Niagara*, which showed her reclining splendidly the length of the Niagara Falls established the image once and for all.

Marilyn Monroe with her husband, the playwright Arthur Miller, arriving at Heathrow Airport. Monroe was in London to star in the film *The Sleeping Prince* with Sir Laurence Olivier in 1956.

Gift for Comedy

At about this time she married the baseball star Joe di Maggio – the marriage was dissolved in 1954 – and began to show signs that she had talent as well as a dazzling physical presence. In *Gentlemen Prefer Blondes* and *How to Marry a Million-aire* startled critics noticed a real gift for comedy and by the arrival of *The Seven Year Itch* there was no doubt about it: she gave a performance in which personality and sheer acting ability (notably an infallible sense of comic timing) played as important a part as mere good looks. From then on she appeared in an unbroken string of personal successes: *Bus Stop*, of which as severe a judge as Jose Ferrer has said: 'I challenge any actress that ever lived to give a better performance in that role', *The Prince and the Showgirl*, in which many critics felt she outshone her director and co-star Sir Laurence Olivier, *Some Like It Hot*, and *Let's Make Love*.

In 1956 Marilyn Monroe was married again – to the playwright Arthur Miller (they were divorced in 1960) and his next work, the original screen play of *The Misfits*, was written for her. This was, in the event, her last film (the most recent, *Something's Got to Give*, being shelved after her failure to fulfil the terms of the contract) and in it under John Huston's direction she gave a performance which provoked its reviewer in *The Times* to a comment which might stand for her work as a whole: 'Considerations of whether she can really act seem as irrelevant as they were with Garbo; it is her rare gift just to be in front of the camera, and, to paraphrase the comment of her apologetic employer in an earlier, more frivolous film, "Well, anyone can act".'

* * *

JOHN F. KENNEDY

Courage and idealism at the White House

22 NOVEMBER 1963

PRESIDENT JOHN F. KENNEDY, whose assassination at the age of 46 is reported on another page, has died in the fullness of his fame. Whatever qualifications there may be about some of his detailed policies – and no man could hold that awesome office without receiving his measure of criticism – he will take his place in the roll of strong Presidents. Throughout his time in office he had major difficulties with Congress, but he was the master of his own Administration, a man of decision and nerve. Had he lived he would have remained a forceful influence on international affairs for many years to come. In that sense he was still a man of promise.

President Kennedy's years in office will always be marked with distinction, above all for his handling of the Cuban crisis. It was then that he took the supreme risk, told the American people, and indeed the free world, what had to be faced, and firmly blocked the advancing convoy which was bringing medium-range rockets to sites in Cuba, from which they would profoundly have altered the strategic balance of power. The decisiveness of United States policy at this time not only won President Kennedy an abiding place among the great Presidents of the United States but leading, as it has done, to an easing of the cold war, and last July to the nuclear test ban treaty, may well be regarded as one of the real turning-points in history.

Youngest Ever

He was the youngest man ever to be elected to the White House. He was the first President to be born in the twentieth century; the first Roman Catholic, and the first of purely Irish descent. He was the first since Harding to come to the Presidency directly from the Senate. But for the most part these were mere accidents of history. He happened to be a signpost to new trends in American life and politics.

He had many of the qualities necessary to achieve greatness in the White House – a cool and practical judgment; emotional detachment from the passions of the moment; a penetrating intellect; and a keen and ruthless political sense. All these gifts were combined with enormous driving energy. He had an appetite for his job.

It is sometimes said that an American President can be effective abroad or effective at home, but not both. The range of subjects that he had to deal with makes it impossible for him to follow through problems simultaneously as a foreign minister and a politician. Mr Kennedy from the first faced trouble in Congress. His first – the eighty-eighth – gave him a fair majority for anything but civil rights issues in the Senate, but only a dubious and paper majority in the House, even under skilled democratic leadership. In the first two years he was forced to water down his measures which were introduced in bold presidential messages; in his second Congress he encountered heavy defeats as the result of the strengthening of the opposition – normal in a mid-term election. Plans which the nation seemed to need most fared worst. His plans for federal aid to education, especially higher education, ran into the difficulties of state rights. His cherished scheme for medical care for the aged fell through because of fears of socialized medicine. In strengthening the economy he met the same Congressional suspicion that the aim was to increase federal power and that the Democrats were engaged in their usual 'spendthrift' finance. Unbalanced budgets are a congressional bogy, and Mr Kennedy's plan to cut taxes fell foul of it. He was held back by the difficulties of the balance of payments from a real cheap money policy, and though he was successful in getting the support of Congress for trade expansion, the Administration was perpetually hampered in its efforts to raise demand effectively enough to absorb unemployment, perpetually being increased by technological change. President Kennedy saw what was wanted – a selective public investment aimed at bringing work to the nation's underprivileged. America was affluent enough, and Wall Street soared with a considerable measure of expansion. But affluence did not reach down far enough or fast enough to prevent the brewing upsurge of discontent by the Negroes.

The Negro Protest

Mr Kennedy's period of office saw the full emergence of the Negro protest, which erupted in novel forms, in violence, in clashes with two southern governors, in the use of troops. He knew it was coming. He had had the Negro vote in the presidential elections and expected to hold it. From the first, the Administration's chances of getting a major civil rights bill through Congress, and its timing was discussed. He failed, however to gauge the impatience of the Negroes and the extent to which it was losing support for the conservative organizations, like the National Association for the Advancement of Coloured Peoples, and leaders devoted to constitutional methods like the Rev. Martin Luther King. Unemployment for the unskilled, the necessity of obtaining higher education and the difficulties for Negroes to get it, and the success of African and Asian countries in asserting their independence and dignity all combined to create an explosive racial situation. Mr Kennedy relied heavily on his brother, the Attorney-General, to set a rapid enough pace in the laborious procedure of winning Negroes the right to vote or be secured from discrimination in public places or amenities by legal action following from Supreme Court rulings. In his second and third years impatience boiled over, the freedom riders, the sit-in strikes, the determination of young Negroes to enrol in key southern universities, precipitated the riots which presented the United States in an embarrassing light. While doing everything to get his way without direct confrontation, the President had to fight when Federal power was defied. His civil rights Bill was prepared after the clash with Governor Barnett and the march on Washington, but by then the Negroes were unappeasable by gradualist measures – and he faced a hard fight in getting even a gradualist measure through – while there were ominous signs that white America was reacting adversely both in the Northern cities and in the South. The growing sentiment in the Republican party in favour of Senator Goldwater was a sign the President's sensitive political antennae could not miss, and he faced possible major party realignments as the result of the Negro question. Some observers thought that he faced some disasters for law and order in cities like Chicago and New York. In spite of legal and administrative measures to end discrimination against Negroes in the Federal field, Mr Kennedy ended three years of power with a worse race problem than he had inherited.

Kennedy took office with his Administration alleging negligence in defence matters against the Republicans (and with ex-President Eisenhower warning the nation against the 'technological military complex'). In three years the missile gap with which the country had started, at least in Democratic imagination, had become a vast lead in missiles over the Russians; the disadvantage which the west was felt to be in against the Russians had become a lead so great that the President and his Defence Secretary, Mr McNamara, were talking of cutting down manpower, and a tremendous reforming operation had swept through the Pentagon, though it had not wholly subjugated the generals and admirals, in spite of their heavy losses when in revolt against White House policy and discipline. Severe standardizing and reappraising of projects led to the scrapping of many Service favourites like the B 70 bomber and the 'Skybolt' missile, on which Britain had pinned its hopes. This military change led President Kennedy to press, in his third year, for more readiness by Europe to contribute to its own defence, with an eye to the use of American weapons like the multilateral force using Polaris submarines, and saving the much more intractable foreign exchange costs of American divisions and air force formations abroad.

One of the most important features of Kennedy's foreign policy was what became known as the Grand Design for the Atlantic Alliance, which was expounded most inspiringly though not for the first time, in his famous address to the conference of state governors delivered on the steps of Independence Hall, Philadelphia, in July, 1962. The essence of this policy was the concept of two major equal partners – the United States on the one hand, and an enlarged European Community on the other. This broad vision was temporarily shattered by President de Gaulle's exclusion of Britain from the Common Market, but in spite of the difficulties created by French intransigence Kennedy continued to devote all his endeavours to strengthening the Alliance.

On the economic side his concept of partnership was most strikingly revealed by the Trade Expansion Act passed by Congress in the autumn of 1962, which gave him greater power to negotiate mutual tariff cuts than any of his predecessors ever possessed. To some extent, of course, this was a practical defensive measure taken for the benefit of American industry, for in a world of high tariffs the European Common Market could pose a real threat to American exports. But the passing of the Act aroused the hope of wide-ranging tariff cuts on an international basis that would be of the greatest benefit to world trade. If the Kennedy Round, as the negotiations under Gatt have become popularly known, does succeed it will be a fitting posthumous reward for an imaginative initiative that was more politically bold at the time than it may seem in retrospect.

In the Far East, the President had to face the contradictions of American policy. Laos, which seemed to be threatening when he took office, became more stable when it was left to local personalities to settle, and the American military and C.I.A. ceased to think they could impose their own (contradictory) solutions. In Vietnam there seemed no alternative but to pour money into the Diem regime, even though the Americans were well aware that it spent more time, energy, and American money in securing itself than on prosecuting the war with the cooperation of the people. This frustrating situation continued until the generals, with covert American approval, and angered and emboldened by the repression of the Buddhists, overthrew Diem and his brother. If it removed one of the many foreign incubi from the President, it was hardly a success for American policy on the spot.

The 'Alliance for Progress' was first designed to be a model programme for American aid to the underdeveloped, and a scheme to promote the agrarian and social reform which so much aid failed to accomplish. Roughed out before the President took office it was designed to halt the deterioration in Latin American developments. But it proved much harder than was anticipated to get Latin American establishments to see the dangers of social revolution, and some governments, like Brazil, consumed aid simply as day to day subsidies, without reforming at all. After three years of planning and conference talk, it was charitable to say that the Alliance was still in its early stages: the Administration's critics said it had failed.

John Fitzgerald Kennedy was born in the Boston suburb of Brookline on May 29, 1917, into a remarkable family that was to have an exceptional influence on his development. It was an intensely political family of Irish Catholic stock on both sides. The Kennedys had settled in the United States about halfway through the last century. John Kennedy's father, Joseph P. Kennedy, was the son of Pat Kennedy, who kept a saloon and was one of the city's Democratic bosses. John's mother, Rose, was the daughter of the Mayor of Boston John F. Fitzgerald – or 'Honey Fitz', as he was known – whose speciality was a spirited rendering of 'Sweet Adeline' on political occasions. The future President was thus nurtured in the distinctive atmosphere of Boston Irish politics – with its zest, its love of intrigue, and its conception of politics as a contest to be won.

Patrician Influences

At the time of his birth the family were living in a comparatively modest neighbourhood, but his father's financial fortunes were rising rapidly. Through investment banking and a number of business enterprises, including an excursion into the film industry, he was becoming a multi-millionaire. The family moved from Boston to New York, with holiday homes at Palm Beach and Hyannisport. All the perquisites of wealth were theirs – foreign travel, expensive schooling, luxuries at home – although the family were still not accepted in some social circles where the father's business methods were disliked as much as his origins.

Nevertheless, patrician influences were mingled with those of the Boston Irish. Jack Kennedy attended only one Catholic school, and that for only one year. At the age of 14 he went to Choate, the exclusive private school in Connecticut, and then to Princeton – very briefly – and to Harvard. After leaving Choate he had studied for a short while at the London School of Economics, but his time there was interrupted by illness. A bright and able, though not a brilliant, student, keen on games, though again without exceptional prowess, he seems to have been generally and quietly popular.

Further opportunities to broaden his contacts overseas came with his father's appointment in 1938 as Ambassador in London. Out of this experience came Jack Kennedy's book, *Why England Slept*, originally written as a university thesis. As an examination of the British reaction to the Nazi threat it was thoughtful and showed a readiness to probe beyond the most obvious answers, but it was not a remarkable work. More important in the long run was that Mr Joseph Kennedy proved a most controversial diplomat. Believing that Britain was sure to be defeated, he became notorious as a vehement advocate of American isolationism and accordingly had to give up his post in 1940. As a result, his son, in his political career, while benefiting greatly from the family wealth found the father's political reputation a heavy liability.

Where the father's impact was most beneficial was at home. He inspired his nine children, of whom Jack Kennedy was the second son, with a vitality, a competitive instinct, and a cohesion which was to be of lasting significance. He wanted them to excel in their studies and at their games. He encouraged free and fierce discussion of public affairs. Yet his devotion to the gospel of success prevented any trend towards dreamy idealism.

In September, 1941, Kennedy enlisted in the Navy and after a spell of shore duty was appointed in March, 1943, to command a motor torpedo boat in the Solomons. The following August came the incident that was to make him one of the authentic American war heroes. Suddenly one night a Japanese destroyer bore down upon the boat, cut it in half, and left Kennedy to do the best he could for the survivors. After a series of adventures – which included towing a badly burned man on a three-mile swim to a neighbouring island with his teeth in the other's life jacket, and long and dangerous swims in search of assistance – they were finally rescued five days later. The ordeal, terrible as it was, demonstrated Kennedy's powers of leadership and endurance. He emerged with the greatest credit, and was awarded the Purple Heart and the Navy and Marine Corps Medal.

Family Support

While Jack was still recovering from his injuries – his back, which had earlier been hurt in a football match at Harvard, was badly damaged this time – news was received in August the following year of the death on a bombing raid over Europe of his elder brother, Joe, a dominant and able young man who might well have had a bright career ahead of him. This was an event of more than personal sorrow for Jack. It meant that he was now the focus of the family ambitions.

Whether this was the cause of his entry into politics, as so many stories tell, must be very doubtful. But it followed soon after. First, he had a brief flirtation with journalism. He was one of the correspondents who covered the inauguration of the United Nations at San Francisco and the British election of 1945 for the Hearst newspapers. He was, however, already looking about for some opportunity to run for political office, and when the Eleventh Massachusetts Congressional District fell vacant in November of that year he gave up whatever thoughts he may have had of a journalistic career.

It was a mixed and difficult constituency for a political newcomer, and it was a general surprise when he defeated the other candidates for the Democratic nomination the following June – which made it certain that he would win the seat in such a Democratic stronghold. But it was no fluke. Many of the features which were to mark later Kennedy campaigns were evident in this first one. He got into the contest early and spent months stumping the constituency with amazing energy and singleness of purpose. He made full use of his boyish charm and attractive appearance by meeting and letting himself be seen by as many people as possible. He built up his own political machine with great efficiency and largely independently of the official party organization. The family wealth and the active support of all the immediate members of the family were devoted to the cause. Moreover, whatever liability the family background was to be in later years, the name of Kennedy was still an asset in Boston.

Youthful Appearance

During his years in the House of Representatives Kennedy did not look an embryo President. His youthful appearance and nonchalant habits did not fit the conventional view of the dignity of a Congressman. For the most part his political activities were centred on the problems facing Massachusetts. He was assiduous in looking after the interests of any constituent who approached him for help. He was a 'bread-and-butter' liberal, concentrating on housing and other welfare programmes which directly and immediately affected the well-being of his constituents. Where these were concerned he could be forthright and courageous – as, for instance, when he denounced the attitude toward housing legislation of the American Legion, one of the awesome bodies of the American Way of Life. But in general he did not involve himself so much with the wider and less tangible issues of the day.

Admittedly, it was in these years that he began his keen interest in labour reform, and he was one of those to vote against the passing of the Taft–Hartley Bill – though that was not likely to weaken his position back home. Also, he dissociated himself from the blatantly isolationist views of his father and openly attacked the Far East policies of the Truman Administration on the floor of the House. But he was far from an unswerving supporter of foreign aid and other programmes whose value would seem self-evident to an orthodox liberal. The main importance of his period in the House is that the time was spent in building an impregnable base for himself in his own state.

He gained the benefit of this in 1952 when he ran for the Senate. He had been re-elected unopposed to the House in 1948 and on a very substantial margin in 1950. But two years later a further term did not attract him and he boldly challenged for the Senate seat held by the formidable Mr Henry Cabot Lodge, Jnr., then one of Mr Eisenhower's leading backers for the Presidency and later to be Ambassador to the United Nations and Mr Nixon's running mate in 1960. To oust a man of such standing and ability seemed an awesome proposition. But Kennedy set to with the same technique as before – he had in fact been virtually campaigning for years by accepting an incredibly intense programme of speaking engagements up and down the state. Kennedy won by some 70,000 votes at the same time as Mr Eisenhower was sweeping Massachusetts for the Republicans by more than 200,000. It was, therefore, a double triumph for Kennedy to have succeeded in such a contest when the tide was against his party.

In his early months in the Senate Kennedy still concentrated mostly on the regional needs of New England. But two other factors were soon to take more prominence in his life: one private and the other the issue that was to dog him for years. On September 12, 1953, he was married to Jacqueline Lee, daughter of John V. Bouvier III. Her charm, her good looks and her youth were to be an asset to him in his public as well as his private life. Of the three children born to them a son and daughter survive.

McCarthy Issue

The other development was not such a happy omen. Kennedy had remained on the sidelines as resentment and concern grew over the investigating techniques of Senator Joe McCarthy. His equivocal attitude to what became the most pressing issue in American politics raised a question mark over his integrity which took very long to obliterate in the eyes of a good number of people. How could a man of real principle, it was asked, remain as silent as Kennedy was at such a time?

It is important to note that he was never in the McCarthy camp. Although he voted for McCarthy a number of times he was not a party to McCarthy's methods and was to be found on the other side just as, if not more, frequently. But he delivered no root and branch condemnation, and when the Senate finally censured McCarthy in December, 1954, Kennedy was gravely ill in hospital and unable to vote.

There were plausible reasons why Kennedy never took an open stand against McCarthy. His father was a friend of the Wisconsin Senator and contributed to his fund. His brother Robert, whom he was later to make his Attorney-General, served for a while on McCarthy's staff in 1953. Apart from such personal inhibitions,

Kennedy also had to consider the warm favour in which so many of his Irish Catholic constituents held McCarthy. A vehement attack from Kennedy might have been an act of political suicide, and many a prudent man in his position would have manoeuvred with equal circumspection.

Perhaps such considerations would have convinced more people if Kennedy had not published his second book, *Profiles in Courage*, early in 1956 – for this study of a selection of eminent Senators who had risked their careers for some principle eulogized the very quality Kennedy had not shown in the McCarthy affair: the readiness to defy public opinion for a basic belief whatever the personal consequences. But then it would be hard to judge any author, and particularly a practising politician, by the standards of his heroes.

In general, however, the book was extremely well received – it received a Pulitzer award – and helped to strengthen a rising reputation. It was written while he was convalescing from his illness, a major spinal operation in October, 1954. So serious was his condition at one stage that his life was despaired of and the last rites were administered.

Hardening Views

Some commentators have compared the impact of this illness on Kennedy's development with Franklin Roosevelt's polio attack. Kennedy's emergence as a man of strongly liberal convictions, it has been suggested, was born of his suffering. But that would appear too emotional an interpretation for a man whose guarded liberalism was of a highly cerebral nature.

What his illness may well have done was to advance his maturity and quicken his ambition. At all events, soon after his return to Washington in May, 1955, his name was being mentioned as a possible Vice-Presidential candidate in the 1956 election. At the Chicago convention the Presidential nominee, Mr Adlai Stevenson, took the surprising course of throwing the selection of his running mate to a vote among the delegates rather than making the choice himself. At first it looked as if Kennedy would win but there was a final dramatic swing in the balloting to Senator Kefauver, who won by the narrowest of margins.

As it proved, this was a concealed blessing for Kennedy. He had been brought into national prominence without having to suffer the subsequent stigma of defeat at the hands of the country's voters. With this start he soon began his long and brilliantly organized campaign for the highest office. His speaking engagements now ranged over the country as a whole. No longer did he put the main emphasis on the problems of New England. His liberal views began to harden so that it became easier to judge exactly what he stood for – and much of what he stood for was likely to be politically advantageous. His attitude on civil rights became firmer and was to become more forthright still. On foreign policy he was an internationalist, with an enlightened appreciation of the forces of nationalism in Africa and Asia. In July, 1957, he provoked a minor international storm by his attack in the Senate on France's Algerian policy. Where the Eisenhower Administration dwelt on the need for a stable dollar Kennedy put the emphasis more on expansion. And, of course, he had long been a believer in 'bread-and-butter' liberalism – government-sponsored social welfare policies.

Labour Reform

Yet while his liberal commitments became more decided, he did not renounce his sense of the practical. This was particularly evident in his handling of labour reform legislation. Hearings before the Labour Rackets Committee revealed grave abuses in some union activities. Clearly there was a case for some tightening up of the law, but there were some who wanted to make this an excuse for draconian legislation. Kennedy decided on compromise and was the co-sponsor of such a measure which passed the Senate in 1958 but was lost in the House. The following session he successfully piloted another labour reform Bill which after further compromise became law.

This may not have made Kennedy many friends – there were people on both sides who intensely disliked the final outcome – but it confirmed his position as an accomplished legislator and one of the Senate's 'inner circle'.

That, however, was only a limited advantage to his Presidential ambitions. Only one man had moved straight from the Senate to the White House, and the precedent of Warren Harding was not a happy one. Added to the supposed disadvantage of being a Senator, Kennedy also had to face criticism of his youth and his Roman Catholicism. The only way to overcome these obstacles was to demonstrate to the party professionals that he had massive popular backing. In other words, he had to enter and win the primaries.

He won all seven primaries that he entered, and by the time the Democratic convention assembled at Los Angeles in July, 1960, his election on the first ballot was almost a foregone conclusion. The convention also provided him with the radical programme that he wanted – particularly on civil rights and social welfare questions such as education, health, care of the aged and housing. At the same time, he kept his shrewd political judgment by choosing the more conservative Mr Lyndon Johnson as his running mate with the special task of keeping the southern states loyal to the Democratic cause.

Throughout the months of electioneering Kennedy was always striving to catch up the lead naturally enjoyed by Mr Nixon through the years of publicity as Vice-President and the declared support of the incumbent President. Kennedy was helped by the historic innovation of the first televised debates between the candidates in which he showed to advantage. Yet so close was the voting that even days

President Kennedy, his wife Jackie, Vice President Johnson, Arthur Schlesinger, Special Assistant to the President, and Admiral Arleigh A. Burke watching the televised broadcast of the first US Astronaut Alan B. Shepard Jr's successful 15-minute suborbital space flight, May 5, 1961.

afterwards it still seemed possible that Mr Nixon might win. Finally Kennedy triumphed by one of the narrowest margins on record.

He had stumped the country so arduously for such a long period that many people were surprised that his health, which had remained subject to occasional breakdowns, had stood the strain. Soon after he assumed the Presidency the fears began to be realized. He injured his back again while planting a tree at a ceremony in Canada. After his return from Europe in the summer of 1961 he had to resort to crutches for a time, and although his back seemed to improve he continued whenever possible to use the rocking-chair which eased any discomfort.

Nuclear Tests

After the series of atmospheric nuclear tests by the Soviet Union in the autumn of 1961 President Kennedy was under military pressure to resume the testing of United States devices. He let it be known that he was ready to do so if necessary, but he deferred a decision for some months. On March 2 he declared that the United States would resume atmospheric testing in the latter part of April unless the Soviet Union agreed before then to sign and apply an effective treaty banning all nuclear tests. He expected the Russians to show their intentions at the disarmament conference which was about to meet at Geneva. He and Mr Macmillan would be prepared to meet Mr Khrushchev to sign an effective treaty, an essential condition of which was on-site inspection.

The offer was not accepted and on April 25 the United States began a new series of tests in the Pacific. Mr Macmillan was in Washington at that time for his fifth round of conversations with the President and he found that the failure to reach an understanding with Russia about nuclear tests had not changed President Kennedy's determination to seek accommodation with Russia by patient discussion and negotiation.

The American series of tests was completed on November 4, 1962, and efforts to reach a test-ban agreement were renewed in the very different atmosphere that followed the Cuban crisis. In June agreement was made to hold high-level test ban talks in Moscow, with at last a fair prospect of success, and in July these efforts were crowned by the signing of the treaty, limited in its terms, but of the greatest significance for the future of east–west relations.

Cuban Challenges

Cuba showed him at his weakest and at his best. There could be no excuse for the original catastrophe of Cuba in the spring of 1961. He was condemned from all sides – for conniving at an armed attack upon a neighbouring country, and for failing to give the rebels the assistance to make their assault successful.

The result was that he seemed to have the worst of both worlds. Castro remained in power, perhaps even more secure than before. The free world's confidence in Kennedy's judgment was gravely undermined. To the neutral nations he seemed to have infringed his own high principles. And there was the jolt to his own self-esteem.

The second crisis of October, 1962, sudden in its arrival and decisive in its outcome, was the central event in President Kennedy's handling of foreign policy. It measured his daring judgment and determination, and had a profound effect on Russo-American relations.

Russian military interest in Cuba and political pressures in the United States that it be terminated had been building up for months. But the crisis when it came, came suddenly. On October 20 Mr Kennedy broke off an election tour with a 'diplomatic cold'. On the 22nd he announced in a broadcast to the nation that he had ordered the blockade of Cuba to prevent all supplies of offensive military equipment from reaching the island. It had, he said, been established the previous week that offensive missile bases were being prepared on the island. The transformation of Cuba into an important strategic base constituted an explicit threat to the peace and security of all the Americas and contradicted the repeated assurances of Russian spokesmen that the arms build-up in Cuba would retain its original defensive character. 'It shall be the policy of this nation to regard any nuclear missile launched from Cuba against any nation in the western hemisphere as an attack by the Soviet Union on the United States requiring a full retaliatory response upon the Soviet Union.'

Emergency Meeting

He was asking, the message went on, for an emergency meeting of the Security Council of the United Nations, and would call for the prompt dismantling and withdrawal of all offensive weapons, under the supervision of UN observers. 'I call upon chairman Khrushchev to halt and eliminate his clandestine, reckless and provocative threat to world peace and to stabilize relations between our two nations.'

Clear notice had been given that the United States was not prepared to tolerate the disturbance to the strategic balance that missile bases on Cuba implied; effective military measures had been taken to check any further build-up; and the immediate objective of dismantlement of the bases had been defined. Mr Khrushchev could not proceed without engaging in a limited war in the Caribbean, which he was in no position to win, or precipitating a nuclear exchange.

By the clarity and boldness of his policy Kennedy had seized the advantage, but he was careful not to put the Russians in a position from which withdrawal would be virtually impossible and careful also to keep all diplomatic channels open especially at the United Nations. Four days later, after some initial blustering by Mr Khrushchev, both he and the President replied in conciliatory terms to an appeal by U Thant for the suspension of arms shipments and steps to search ships. Meanwhile ships from the eastern block were reported to have turned back on approaching the area of the blockade. Later Mr Khrushchev ordered Russian ships to stay out of the interception area, while the President assured U Thant that American vessels would do everything possible to avoid a clash. On October 28 Mr Khrushchev agreed to dismantle the missile bases under United Nations verification, a decision which Mr Kennedy at once greeted as a statesmanlike and constructive contribution to peace. Having come within sight of achieving the objective of his bold and carefully calculated policy, he showed no desire to extract humiliation from the Russian leader. By the beginning of November the offending bases were being dismantled. This direct confrontation between the two major nuclear powers was a turning point in post-war history; and from the insight the two leaders gained into each other's purposes and strength, they moved during the succeeding 12 months towards a less tense and insecure phase of east–west relations.

Riding Out Trouble

During his first Presidential visit to Europe he failed to establish either friendly personal relations or any deep respect in his first meeting with Mr Khrushchev at Vienna. Yet throughout these difficulties Kennedy's calmness stood him in good stead. In spite of a reported sensitiveness to criticism, he was never panicked into making a bad situation worse by desperate measures. In his conduct of the nerve-stretching Berlin crisis he was admirably resolute and moderate – at a time when such a happy combination of virtues was not always apparent in the pressure from his allies and from opinion at home.

He had demonstrated his ability to ride out trouble and, to some extent, to grow with his job as he had done throughout his career – both essential attributes for the White House. His last visit to Europe this summer, in the course of which he had talks with Mr Macmillan at Birch Grove, was particularly notable for the sentimental visit he made to Ireland, in the course of which he won many friends, and for his rousing reception by the people of Berlin.

LORD BEAVERBROOK

Quest for power in press and politics

9 JUNE 1964

THE DEATH OF Lord Beaverbrook yesterday at his home at Cherkley at the age of 85 removes a personality held in affection and vehemently criticized for more than 50 years. The young Max Aitken, fresh from Canada, puzzled Westminster before the First World War, winning a few friends, making some enemies and leaving many members of parliament suspicious of him. The brilliance he showed as a go-between in the crisis that led to the fall of the Asquith Government first taught those behind the scenes that he was more than a colonial adventurer who need not be taken seriously. Then he acquired the *Daily Express* and proved, in the twenties, that his finger on the pulse of mass-circulating journalism was more sensitive than those of Northcliffe's heirs. This turned him into a household figure. He helped in this process of building up by freely allowing himself to be caricatured. The little impish figure with the eyes sometimes twinkling and sometimes steely – the image of a gnome who would be jovial company at dinner for all those round the table who had armed themselves with long spoons – was irresistible.

When in the Second World War it became known that he had the friendship of Sir Winston Churchill, the image grew larger in public consciousness. Housewives cheerfully gave up their kettles to this persuasive salesman. Sober citizens, who shook their heads over his antics as a director of newspaper policies, relaxed into a chuckle at the latest story about him or against him – likely enough told by himself. He was a natural and disarming self-publicist. He once remarked:

> 'Just a few days ago Churchill asked me "What are you doing?" "Writing," I replied. "What do you write about?" he asked. "Me," I answered. "A good subject," he said, "I have been writing about me for fifty years, and with excellent results." '

Child of the Manse

Old age became him. He changed relatively little in appearance and not at all, except for a little mellowing, in his enthusiasm for causes, his relish for power, and his sense of fun. Time will be needed to get him in perspective. The child of the manse, on whom Christianity never lost its hold, the quickly rich player of markets for whom wealth was always delightful, the politician in the long run *manqué*, make

207

a complicated unity. But unity there was in Beaverbrook. It was his misfortune that he could not bring himself to accept that, fundamentally, he was a lightweight in public life. But lightweights so full of gaiety as he was are rare and he would not mind being mentioned with that fictional character who achieved great riches and remained unspoilt, Arnold Bennett's Card, and, so, identified 'with the great cause of cheering us up'.

William Maxwell Aitken was born on May 25, 1879, at Maple, a village 15 miles from Toronto. He was a son of the Rev. William Cuthbert Aitken, a Presbyterian minister at Newcastle, New Brunswick, and both his parents came of Scottish Lowland stock. He was educated at the village school, and at the age of 18 entered a solicitor's office. He had a hard struggle, but not for long. Success gave him a golden handshake while he was still in his early twenties. He became connected with successful enterprises in his own province and a prominent figure in the Canadian financial world. He engineered several 'mergers' which gave him a reputation for business acumen and power of organization. Before he was 30 he was the owner of a large fortune but in the process of making it he had failed to create the good will necessary to a successful career in Canadian public life.

Friend of Bonar Law

He therefore came to England, where he had a friend in Bonar Law. On his advice he stood for Parliament and won a sensational victory in what was regarded as the Liberal stronghold of Ashton-under-Lyne in the second election of 1910. He purchased a country house in Surrey, and for some years devoted himself to politics and to a certain amount of City business. He made no particular mark in Parliament, but acquired a circle of political friends. He was knighted in 1911.

On the outbreak of the War he volunteered at once for the Canadian Expeditionary Force and was appointed 'Eye-Witness' to the Canadians in 1915, and in 1916 representative at the front of the Canadian Government. He was also officer in charge of the Canadian War Records, and brought that department to a state of high efficiency. Towards the end of November, 1916, he took a leading part in the events which led to the fall of the Asquith Government. With a natural aptitude for political tactics and gifted with conspicuous powers of persuasion as well as audacious courage, it was largely to him that Lloyd George owed his accession to the post of Prime Minister. He has himself left an account of the part he played in those hectic days and of the silence which succeeded the constant ring of his telephone – an instrument of which he made the fullest use – when Lloyd George had received the King's commission and began to form his Government.

During 1917 he took little part in public life, contenting himself with his activities at the Canadian War Records and with organizing the cinema work of the British War Office. To him was due the admirable series of war films taken on the

Western front and their successful distribution throughout the world. In February, 1918, when Sir Edward Carson's resignation from the War Cabinet left the Department of Information without a ministerial head, Lord Beaverbrook was appointed Chancellor of the Duchy of Lancaster and Minister of Information. The two volumes of his *Canada in Flanders* had already appeared.

Minister of Information

His work as Minister of Information showed that he possessed unusual administrative gifts. Many of his actions were attended with great success, notably the visits which he organized of large parties of representative Americans to this country and to the front. In August his health broke down, and in October he resigned his post as Chancellor of the Duchy. The Ministry of Information was closed towards the end of the year. In 1917 he was created a baronet and in the same year a peer. He took his title from Beaverbrook, the name of a small stream near his early New Brunswick home.

In December, 1925, Beaverbrook published a revealing little book, *Politicians and the Press*, which is almost an autobiography of the years from the Armistice to that time. He followed this in 1928 with a much larger book, *Politicians and the War, 1914–16*, the chief object of which was to pay a whole-hearted tribute to his old friend and benefactor, Bonar Law. When he recovered his health he devoted himself to various business activities, among them the cinema industry in Britain. But his chief interests lay in the newspaper world. He had for some years controlled the *Daily Express*, and he soon made this paper, together with the *Sunday Express*, which he founded, a leader in popular journalism. A special Scottish issue began in the autumn of 1928, and he had previously purchased the control of the *Evening Standard* and greatly increased its size and circulation. On the advice of Sir Abe Bailey he had taken up racing as a hobby, and acquired a house at Newmarket, and horses from the stable, usually bearing Canadian names, had some success on various courses.

Early in 1929 his interest in politics suddenly revived. He started a campaign for Empire Free Trade, believing that the only line of economic salvation for Britain lay in making the Empire a single economic unit like the United States, with internal free trade, and tariff barriers against the rest of the world. This creed he preached not without inconsistencies but with conviction and fervour. He urged it in the House of Lords and on platforms throughout the land, and his earnestness, combined with effective journalistic support, gave him a hearing though he won few converts. He had never been a good speaker and had always disliked the duty, but now practice and enthusiasm made him a platform draw.

His attitude involved him in conflict with the party leaders, and his active part in the promotion of independent candidatures at by-elections led to a controversy with Baldwin marked by a vituperation commoner in politics a hundred years ago than in more recent times. The prominence given to these Eatanswill exchanges in the *Daily Express* exaggerated their real significance. Public opinion was diverted rather than impressed by his presentation of economic realities in crusading terms.

During subsequent years his interventions in politics were less open and personal, though his papers were inclined to be critical of the National Government until Neville Chamberlain became Prime Minister. Lord Beaverbrook found the views and policy of that statesman more congenial. He was one of Chamberlain's supporters and up to the very eve of the outbreak of war was convinced that war could and should be avoided. When it came he did not flinch. Eight months after its declaration, he readily accepted the new post of Minister of Aircraft Production, created, it is believed, at his own suggestion, in the administration formed by Mr Churchill. He was eminently fitted for the part of a new broom. His methods made critics, but they also impressed friends. His personality was felt everywhere. The situation called for speed and improvisation and Lord Beaverbrook's qualities exactly filled its requirements. The knowledge of British feeling which his journalistic experience had given him proved invaluable. He knew when to call on the men in the factories for a special effort and when to mobilize public sympathy for gifts of aluminium saucepans and support of Spitfire funds. But the scale of his new Ministry was such that he could also keep personal control over details and himself take steps to secure a particular worker for a particular factory. In the grim months of that autumn Lord Beaverbrook was faced with the duty of securing the utmost possible output of machines while at the same time dispersing the industry by way of protection against air attack, and his success in meeting this double emergency contributed materially to victory in the Battle of Britain.

By the spring of 1941 the crisis was past. In a broadcast delivered in March, notable for its warm tribute to a few named research workers, Beaverbrook was able to tell the nation that six new types of aircraft and five new engines had been brought into production. The department had acquired its own momentum and its head rightly felt that his best work in it had now been done. Just under a year after his appointment he vacated his office and became a Minister of State, a post created for him by the Prime Minister in order that he might bring his energies to bear upon the more general questions of policy coming before the War Cabinet. In his new post he became a member of the Defence Committee of the Cabinet and deputy chairman of its supply section.

Mission to Moscow

The new arrangement, with its divorce of responsibility for policy from executive control, proved unsatisfactory. At any rate it was abandoned within two months, and Beaverbrook, while remaining a member of the War Cabinet, took over the Ministry of Supply. Russia had just entered the war, and the new Minister threw himself into the congenial task of speeding up the production of tanks and guns. In September, after visits to the United States and Canada, he headed the British section of an Anglo-American mission to Moscow. Before he left he sent a telegram to all factories engaged in tank manufacture assuring them that the whole of their product for the following week would be sent to Russia. The mission undertook to satisfy, in the words of the communiqué, 'practically every requirement for which the Soviet military and civil authorities asked'. On his return he delivered a broadcast, rich in vivid detail, and calling for the production of 30,000 tanks.

On taking over the Ministry of Supply, he let it be known that he hoped to complete his work there in six months. As the year wore on the asthma from which he suffered gave him increasing trouble and it caused no surprise when in February, 1942, he was transferred to the newly created Ministry of War Production with general supervision over supplies. Within a fortnight, however, he had left the War Cabinet and, after carrying through yet another mission to the United States, he withdrew from the Government. Eighteen months later he returned to office as Lord Privy Seal with general duties which included the supervision of civil aviation policy. Circumstances called for a cautious approach hardly to his taste and he was probably thankful when the appointment of a Minister of Civil Aviation left him free for other duties. He had secured agreement at the Empire Air Conference in 1943 and had avoided a breakdown in his discussions with Mr Adolf Berle in the following year. Another matter to which he gave eager attention was an understanding with the United States on the difficult question of oil supplies. Here he negotiated an arrangement which it proved impossible to implement. He retained his office after the Coalition broke up and vacated it on the Government's resignation in July, 1945.

After the war he spent less time in his English homes in Arlington Street and in Surrey and more in the south of France and the Bahamas. But he never ceased to take a close and almost a daily interest in the newspapers from which he had nominally detached himself and he kept a critical eye on the performances of successive governments. The veteran crusader rode again at the challenge of the Common Market which to him was an infidel conception – a betrayal of the principles of Commonwealth unity. His delight in hospitality – he was happy alike as host and guest – remained with him.

In recent years his talents as a political historian of his times became more widely appreciated: telling his story from the inside his works were not only immensely readable but will prove valuable material for historians in the future. Some of his earlier books were republished and in 1956 came *Men and Power 1917–18*, a sequel to *Politicians and the War*. Last year *The Decline and Fall of Lloyd George* was published. Beaverbrook also wrote a number of a more various nature: *Don't Trust to Luck* (1954), *Three Keys to Success* (1956), *Friends* (1959), an account of his lifelong connection with Lord Bennett, the former Canadian Prime Minister, and *The Divine Propagandist* (1962).

A fortnight ago his eighty-fifth birthday was marked by a dinner given in his honour by Lord Thomson of Fleet at which more than 650 guests were present. In his speech on this occasion Beaverbrook gave convincing proof that his zest and mental energy were unimpaired.

In 1906 he married Gladys, daughter of the late General Drury, of Halifax, Nova Scotia. She died in December, 1927. They had one daughter and two sons, of whom the elder, the Hon. Max Aitken, DSO, DFC, chairman of Beaverbrook Newspapers Ltd., survives and now succeeds to the peerage. Last year Beaverbrook married secondly Marcia Anastasia, widow of Sir James Dunn, first baronet.

IAN FLEMING

The creator of James Bond

12 AUGUST 1964

MR IAN FLEMING, whose death at the age of 56 is announced on another page, was one of the most successful and controversial thriller writers in recent years.

Ian Lancaster Fleming was born in 1903, son of Major Valentine Fleming, MP, DSO. He was educated at Eton and Sandhurst, and then at Munich and Geneva universities. In 1929, having failed to secure a place in the Diplomatic Service, he joined Reuter's at a time when the international wire services were struggling for supremacy. 'Reuter's was great fun in those days,' Fleming said afterwards, 'a very good mill. The training there gives you a good straightforward style. Above all, I have to thank Reuter's for getting my facts right.' He covered the trial of the Vickers-Armstrong engineers in Moscow in 1933, and was offered the job of Reuter's assistant general manager in the Far East. He decided instead to seek his fortune in the City, an attempt which he continued, without much success, first as a banker, then as a stockbroker, until he joined the Navy in 1939. As personal assistant to the Director of Naval Intelligence, he found the war 'intensely exciting'. When it was over, Lord Kemsley offered him the foreign managership of Kemsley (now Thomson) newspapers. Fleming accepted on condition that he could have two months' holiday a year to spend at his house, Goldeneye, in Jamaica, where subsequently he did most of his writing.

If his war experiences and his post-war job provided the background for his thrillers, Fleming maintained that it was his marriage to Anne Viscountess Rothermere in 1952 which spurred him to start writing. 'I was in the process of getting married,' he said, 'which is a very painful thing to do at the age of 44; so to take my mind off the whole business, I sat down and wrote a novel.' The novel was a spy story, *Casino Royale* (1953), remotely derived from a real case in the history of Soviet espionage activities in France: it introduced the handsome, ruthless British agent, James Bond ('007 – licensed to kill'), and the various elements – a gambling scene, a torture scene, physical luxury and knowingness about the world's ways – which were to become the hallmarks of Fleming's style. It was well received and he soon followed it with other James Bond adventures, *Live and Let Die* (1954), *Moonraker* (1955), and *Diamonds Are Forever* (1956).

Soaring Popularity

His popularity soared: his books became fashionable and they roused fierce opposition. He was accused of trading in sex, snobbery, and sadism. Fleming replied by explaining his own attitude to James Bond: 'I wanted to show a hero without any characteristics, who was simply the blunt instrument in the hands of the government. Then he started eating a number of meals and dressing in a certain way so that he became encrusted with characteristics much against my will ... apart from the fact that he wears the same clothes that I wear, he and I really have very little in common. I do rather envy him his blondes and his efficiency, but I can't say I much like the chap.'

In 1959 Fleming left regular newspaper work to devote himself to his books and the management of what had become a very valuable literary property. By now there was already a slight flagging in his style, a tendency to repeat his effects. In *The Spy Who Loved Me* (1962) he tried the bizarre experiment of telling a James Bond story through the eyes of the heroine. He knew it was a failure, and the next book, *On Her Majesty's Secret Service* (1963), reverted to normal: but, like Holmes after the Reichenbach Falls, Bond never seemed quite the same man again. *You Only Live Twice* (1964) provoked discussion, not because it was shocking, but because it was not: two-thirds of it was mere travel writing about Japan. Fleming was finding the process of invention increasingly difficult.

The snowball of success, however, continued quite unchecked. Each book headed the bestseller list for weeks. Paperback editions proliferated: James Bond was imitated and parodied. President Kennedy and Mr Allen Dulles were numbered among his admirers. The fame and profitability of the books were spectacularly enhanced by a triumphant film debut. With Mr Sean Connery as Bond, *Dr No* maintained a delicate balance, hovering on the edge of farce; its successor, *From Russia With Love*, was outstandingly successful; a third, *Goldfinger*, will be released shortly.

In March of this year, Fleming struck a unique and ingenious bargain, under which he sold 51 per cent of all his future royalties, excluding film rights, to Booker Brothers, the sugar and investment company, for £100,000.

Fleming had completed, and was revising, a new novel, *The Man With the Golden Gun*, set in the West Indies, and there are several James Bond short stories which have not yet been published in book form.

He had one son.

T. S. ELIOT

The most influential English poet of his time

4 JANUARY 1965

MR T. S. ELIOT, OM, and Nobel Prizeman, died yesterday at his home at the age of 76.

He was the most influential English poet of his time. His work had won him a high reputation, not only throughout the English-speaking world but in all countries where the European tradition, which he himself so faithfully upheld, still flourishes. His works in verse and prose have been translated into almost every European language and have been the subject of more books and articles than have ever before been published about an author during his lifetime.

Thomas Stearns Eliot came of a New England family which had emigrated in the seventeenth century from the Somerset village of East Coker – a village which gave its name to one of his most famous poems and will now give the shelter of its church to his ashes. He was born on September 26, 1888, at St Louis, Missouri, United States, the younger son of Henry Ware Eliot and Charlotte Stearns. Apart from some schoolboy verses in the *Smith Academy Record*, the first of his poems to be printed appeared in the *Harvard Advocate* (May 24, 1907), a publication of which he was later an editor. At Harvard Eliot was a contemporary of Ezra Pound, to whose poetic example he acknowledged a debt in the dedication of *The Waste Land*. After taking his degree, Eliot studied in the Graduate School of Philosophy, where his rare intellectual gifts were recognized by his appointment as Assistant in Philosophy (1912–13) and by his election later to the Sheldon Travelling Fellowship in Philosophy, which enabled him to spend an academic year at Merton College, Oxford, working under Bradley and Joachim. A period of study at the Sorbonne confirmed what was to be a life-long interest in French literature. Eliot then made his home in England and lived in London for the rest of his life. He had been a naturalized British subject since 1928.

His literary gifts began to be noticed by a discerning few of the 'Bloomsbury Group' – among them Maynard Keynes and Virginia Woolf – during the 1914–18 War. At this period his activities included the assistant editorship of the *Egoist* (1917–19), teaching at Highgate Junior School, lecturing to LCC evening classes, and reviewing; from 1919 onwards he contributed to *The Times Literary Supplement* a memorable series of articles on the Elizabethan and Jacobean dramatists. These and some earlier reviews were collected in *The Sacred Wood* (1920), a volume which marked him out as a critic well equipped and perspicuous, provocative if something 'donnish' in manner. His position in the world of letters was thus assured. His first poems to appear in book form had been printed in Pound's *Catholic Anthology* (1915); *Prufrock* was issued separately in 1917, and in 1919 some 200 copies of *Poems* were hand-printed by Leonard and Virginia Woolf at the Hogarth Press.

In Lloyds Bank

After the war, which ended as he was about to be commissioned in the US Navy, he was employed at Lloyds Bank in Cornhill, where it was his business to prepare the bank's monthly report on foreign affairs. His City career came to an end in 1922, when he was appointed the first editor of the *Criterion*, which he directed until it ceased publication in 1939. In its first issue appeared *The Waste Land*, which announced the arrival of a major poet and, by the mingled enthusiasm and execration with which it was received, the impact of an original talent. Its presentation of disillusionment and the disintegration of values, catching the mood of the time, made it the poetic gospel of the post-war intelligentsia; at the time, however, few either of its detractors or its admirers saw through the surface innovations and the language of despair to the deep respect for tradition and the keen moral sense which underlay them.

In 1925 he joined the board of Faber's, where he was responsible during the next 40 years for the publication of much of the most important poetry of our time, and was a source of counsel and encouragement to many younger poets. His own later works included *Ash Wednesday* (1930), *Four Quartets* (1943), the poetic dramas *Murder in the Cathedral* (1935), *The Family Reunion* (1939), *The Cocktail Party* (1950), *The Confidential Clerk* (1954), and *The Elder Statesman* (1959), and several volumes of collected essays and addresses.

It was in one of these, *For Lancelot Andrewes* (1928), that Eliot had announced his allegiance to the Church of England. He at once became a leading and influential layman of the Anglo-Catholic persuasion, engaging in vigorous, but always closely reasoned, controversy upon matters of doctrine and ritual, especially after the Lambeth and Malvern conferences and during the contentions over Church Union in South India. Eliot's attitude in ecclesiastical affairs was dogmatically, even intransigently, conservative: there was perhaps a certain intolerance here in his zealous but uncompromising defence of tradition. He was a devoted church-warden, and an active but discreet propagandist. His most imposing work of a purely religious character appeared in 1939 as *The Idea of a Christian Society*.

Anglo-Catholic Tradition

Of the non-literary influences which most contributed to Eliot's poetic development his religion must be put first. The fastidiousness, the moral taste, and the intellectual severity, which were a legacy of his New England ancestors, merged with the Anglo-Catholic tradition to direct his poetry ever farther in the exploration of spiritual awareness, the search for spiritual values. From *The Waste Land* and *The Hollow Men*, through *Journey of the Magi* and *Ash Wednesday*, to the *Four Quartets* there ran a steady line of development towards the positive treatment of religious experience, so that he could say in the last-named work that 'the poetry does not matter' while leaving the reader in no doubt as to its strictly poetic integrity. At the same time, a long-drawn-out private tragedy which darkened his middle years left a deep impression on his poetry: the rawness, the shuddering distaste, the sense of contagion, the dry despair which emerge from certain passages of *Ash Wednesday*, for instance, and *The Family Reunion*, are traces of it. But for this emotional wound, so long unhealed, his poetry might well have been more genial, less ascetic; but, equally, it might well have been less intense.

Eliot's chief literary influences were the French Symbolists and, above all, Dante. But both as poet and critic he drew deep from the whole European tradition which, as editor of the *Criterion*, he had sought to preserve and reinvigorate. His poetry, each poem 'a raid on the inarticulate', strove incessantly towards greater purity of utterance and wider integration of experience, just as it displayed an increasing mastery of those personal rhythms, sometimes colloquial, sometimes hieratically formal, which he developed from the blank verse line. Technically, his influence over younger English poets was for many years marked and widespread. No English poet since Wordsworth had so constantly, so unequivocally, or so openly insisted upon absolute self-dedication to the art, or approached it with greater humility. A critic truly said of him: 'In struggling towards a discipline of spirit through a discipline of language, Eliot has reaffirmed in his own practice the value of poetry.'

The quality of his writing was inseparable, to those who knew him, from the integrity of his character. In public Eliot, a stooping, sombre-clad figure, appeared to be shy and retiring, formal in his manner, which was courtly and attentive, but detached. The impertinence of the curious, the sometimes intemperate attentions of admirers, he kept alike at arm's length by a playful, evasive wit. With his intimate friends he enjoyed banter and jokes – even, in earlier days, practical jokes. Although, in his earlier verse and prose, he often gave the impression of having been born middle-aged, he remained very youthful in some of his responses: children were devoted to 'Old Possum', and relished his elaborate and agreeably mystifying fun, which found such ingenious and rhythmically diverse expression in *Old*

Possum's Book of Practical Cats. He was, above all, a humble man; firm, even stubborn at times, but with no self-importance; quite unspoilt by fame; free from spiritual or intellectual pride.

Poetic Drama Revival

Eliot's chief preoccupation since the mid-1930s was the revival of poetic drama. By precept and example he strove to restore to the English stage a form of writing without which, he believed, drama could never express the full range of human sensibility. His entry into the theatre was made with characteristic deliberation, step by step, each preparing for the next. His first experiment, in *Sweeney Agonistes* (1932) – two brilliant 'Fragments' of an Aristophanic melodrama – was never fully exploited. Its dramatic possibilities were barely explored in *The Rock* (1934), a commissioned work, something between a conventional pageant and an ecclesiastical revue and chiefly distinguished for its liturgical choruses. *Murder in the Cathedral*, first performed in the Chapter House at Canterbury in 1935, explored these possibilities to some purpose and became a theatrical success both here and in America and later (in translation) on the Continent. The play's effectiveness as drama is attested by the number of times it has been revived, but Eliot himself considered that its verse had only the negative merit of avoiding any echo of Shakespeare.

The Family Reunion (1939), the most wholly poetic of his plays, was the first of four dramas of modern domestic life whose basic theme is derived from Greek tragedy. It was also the first in which he perfected by a masterly use of the stressed line, an instrument which successfully captured the cadence and rhythm of everyday conversation in verse and passed, without breaking its own texture, from small talk to the statement of profundities. With this instrument he fashioned *The Cocktail Party*, which in 1949 and the following year had a remarkable success on both sides of the Atlantic. *The Cocktail Party* chatter, light, easy, amusing, was gaily decorated with the sprightly extravagances that make in the theatre the effect of wit; and at the same time the play told the story of four people, emotionally interlocked, who discover their appropriate forms of salvation after the impact of a shaking experience.

Not all Eliot's followers shared the public's enthusiasm. They felt that he had adhered all too closely to his self-imposed rule to avoid poetry which could not stand the test of dramatic utility. And even those who appreciated the practical value of the rule in the existing state of the theatre still hoped that the next play might more boldly seize new ground for the poetic drama. But in *The Confidential Clerk*, which came in 1953, Eliot seemed to have relinquished some of the ground he had won at least for dramatic poetry. The poetic overtones this time were fainter, for the comedy sought to hold audiences through laughter and surprise and there were lesser demands on feeling. The falling off went unchecked in his last play, *The Elder Statesman* (1959), which failed to hold the stage.

Yet no dramatist of our time has come more firmly to grips with the conditions which the theatre imposes on poetry. Verse, and prose, he saw clearly, were but means to an end – the rendering whole of an imagined reality in terms of the stage. It may well be that *Murder in the Cathedral* will come in the end to have a longer life than the later experiments. But, in spite of their weaknesses of construction and characterization, there is the precision, the personal yet exquisite and unobtrusive rhythm, of the dialogue to keep them in mind and to offset the somewhat chill sense they give of moving in a kind of emotional twilight.

After the 1939–45 War Eliot's work outside the theatre was confined to the writing of lectures and addresses for various occasions at home and abroad, many of them in connection with the bestowal of honorary degrees, prizes, and other official tributes. He was never revisited in his later years by the inspiration that produced *Four Quartets*, his greatest poetic achievement.

He received many honours and awards: the Order of Merit and the Nobel Prize for Literature, both in 1948: the Légion d'Honneur; the Hanseatic Goethe Prize (1954); honorary doctorates from 16 universities in Great Britain, Europe, and the United States. He was an Honorary Fellow of Magdalene College, Cambridge, and of Merton College, Oxford.

Among his many appointments he was Clark Lecturer at Trinity College, Cambridge (1925), Charles Eliot Norton Visiting Professor at Harvard (1932–33); president of the Classical Association (1942); first president of the Virgil Society (1944); president of the London Library (1952). He married in 1917 Vivienne Haigh-Wood, who died after a long illness in 1947. In 1957, his seventieth year, he married secondly Miss E. V. Fletcher. There were no children of either marriage.

SIR WINSTON CHURCHILL

The greatest Englishman of his time. World leader in war and peace.

24 JANUARY 1965

SIR WINSTON CHURCHILL, whose death in London yesterday is reported on the centre page, led Great Britain from the peril of subjugation by the Nazi tyranny to victory; and during the last four years of his active political life he directed his country's efforts to maintain peace with honour, to resist another tyranny, and to avert a war more terrible than the last. In character, intellect, and talent he had the attributes of greatness.

An indifferent schoolboy, he was indifferent at nothing else which he attempted. Inheriting Lord Randolph Churchill's energy and political fearlessness, and being granted twice as many years, he carried to fulfilment a genius that in his father showed only brilliant promise. Leader of men and multitudes, strategist, statesman of high authority in the councils of nations, orator with a command of language that matched the grandeur of his themes, able parliamentary tactician, master of historical narrative, his renown is assured so long as the story of these lands is told.

The great war leader of his age, he lived through the fastest transformation of warfare the world has ever known, charging with the 21st Lancers at Omdurman in his youth, and in his old age arming his country with the hydrogen bomb.

He first entered Parliament in the sixty-fourth year of the reign of Queen Victoria. Sixty-four years later, in the thirteenth year of the reign of her great-great-granddaughter, he retired from it. Through more than half a century of British history there was not a year – barely a month – in which he was not actively and prominently engaged in public affairs.

Churchill's outstanding political virtue, which never deserted him, was his courage. There was the sheer physical courage which led him to seek more risks on active service before he was 25 than many professional soldiers know in a lifetime; and which gave him the will, when he was past 75, to overcome an affliction which would have laid other men low from the start. But there was moral and intellectual courage in equal degree. He served in Kitchener's Army in the Sudan – but attacked Kitchener publicly for his desecration of the Mahdi's tomb. He was returned as a Conservative in the 'Khaki Election' of 1900 – only to devote a passage in his maiden speech to a generous tribute to the Boers. No sooner was his maiden speech over than he shocked the Conservative front bench again by turning on one of his own party leaders, the Secretary of State for War, with a scorn which would have been startling even in a member of the Opposition.

Change of Party

He was still under 30 when, finding himself at odds with the tariff reform policy of Joseph Chamberlain, he crossed the floor of the House. So it continued all through his life – the habit of following his own judgment, his own intuition, and his own impulses. When he resigned from the Conservative 'Shadow Cabinet' in 1931, as a protest against its attitude to India, he was acting with the same courage and independence which – they were inherited from his father – he had displayed from the very beginning. His independence frequently baffled his contemporaries, who tended to conclude, as did Margot Asquith in 1908, that he was a man of 'transitory convictions'. But the point is not that they were transitory but that they were his own. His mind was always restlessly surveying the political scene. He was for ever testing, courting, encouraging new ideas. No politician of this century has been less conservative and less hidebound.

This adventurousness, of course, had its disadvantages, of which his colleagues were often painfully aware. His mind never stopped roaming, and Asquith's Cabinet was described by one of its members as 'very forbearing to his chatter'. During the 1939–45 War – as the famous memoranda published as appendices to his history of *The Second World War* show – any question however trivial or however far removed from the central direction of the war might gain his attention. He seized on new ideas so indiscriminately that it became necessary for some of those closest to him to act as a sieve, and so prevent valuable time from being wasted on the wilder schemes. Yet, when the dross had fallen through, there remained in the sieve one or two nuggets. There is in Printing House Square a letter written early in the 1914–18 War by a high personage accusing Churchill of madness because of some impracticable scheme which he was pressing through in the face of much opposition. The 'scheme' was the tank.

The independence of his ideas always made it difficult to define Churchill's political position. He was more of a Tory than a Conservative. The symbols of Toryism – Crown, Country, Empire – which might seem abstractions to some were to him realities. There was, indeed, always a personal element in the service he gave to his Sovereigns, which found quite different expressions in his attitude to the abdication of Edward VIII and in the tributes he paid when George VI died and Queen Elizabeth II was crowned. But it was a Toryism infused by another abstraction which to him was equally a reality: the People. He believed deeply that the People existed – not different and warring classes of people. In an earlier age he would have stood committed to the idea of the King and the People against the great Whig magnates – the cardinal principle of Disraelian Toryism. He was, in brief, a Tory Democrat, and in a speech to the Conservative conference in 1953 he proclaimed again the creed of his father, the first prophet of Tory Democracy.

Sense of History

Least of all was he a 'Little Englander'. No statesman has ever been more aware of his country's position in the world and its responsibility to the world. It was not merely his awareness of the facts of Germany's rearmament which made him speak so clearly from the beginning of the thirties: it was, even more (as befitted a descendant of Marlborough), his fundamental assumption that Britain was a part of Europe. He could no more have talked of Czechoslovakia as a far-away country than of Blenheim and Ramillies as far-away towns.

His politics were infused with a sense of history. It was a common gibe of his opponents that he lived in the past – that he was, in the words of Harold Laski, a 'gallant and romantic relic of eighteenth-century imperialism'. Nothing could be farther from the truth. He was as aware of the present, its opportunities and its challenges, as any of his contemporaries. But he drew from the past a profound conviction in the greatness of Britain, her people and her heritage. Romantic? It may be. But it was from this reserve that he drew the inspiration which he communicated to his fellow-countrymen in their and his finest hour. He was the symbol of British resistance, but of how much more as well. In his voice spoke the centuries which had made Britain as they had made him, and those who heard him in those days will never forget the echoes of Burghley, of Chatham, of Pitt, and countless more. 'The last of the great orators to reach the heights.'

The Right Honourable Sir Winston Leonard Spencer-Churchill, KG, OM, CH, FRS, was born on St Andrew's Day, 1874, at Blenheim Palace. He was the elder son of Lord Randolph Churchill and a grandson of the seventh Duke of Marlborough. His mother was the beautiful and talented daughter of Leonard Jerome, a New York businessman. Surviving her husband until 1921, she lived to see her son's fame firmly established.

Soldier and Journalist

The year had been an eventful one for Lord Randolph. Apart from his marriage and the birth of a son and heir, it had begun with his election as Conservative MP for Woodstock and included a maiden speech which drew from Disraeli, who had a good eye for a duke's son, a warm commendation. Lord Randolph's rise to power and influence was to be rapid, but his decline was even more rapid, and when he died in 1895 he left his son with memories of defeat and failure which carried a moral he was often to remember. Winston Churchill's education was conventional in its pattern; from a preparatory school at Ascot, to a small school at Brighton, to Harrow in 1888, and then, after twice failing to gain admission, to the Royal Military

College at Sandhurst. But his verdict on Harrow was individual, for he left there, as he later confessed, convinced that he was 'all for the public schools, but I do not want to go there again'.

In 1895, soon after his father's death, he entered the 4th Hussars at Aldershot, and immediately obtained leave to go to Cuba for the *Daily Graphic* to watch the Spanish Army at work. While he was there he participated in the repulse of the insurgents who tried to cross the Spanish line at Trocham. After enjoying the London Season in 1896 he embarked for India, where he relieved the monotony of morning parades and evening polo by indulging his delight in reading. He was back in London for the Season in 1897, and then left in September to join the Malakand Field Force on the North-West Frontier of India. After being mentioned in dispatches for 'making himself useful at a critical moment', he had to return to the 4th Hussars at Bangalore early in 1898, and there he occupied himself with the writing of his first history, *The Story of the Malakand Field Force*, which had considerable success at the time and is still consulted.

While he was at Bangalore he also wrote his only novel, *Savrola, a Tale of the Revolution in Laurania*, which he later urged his friends not to read. It contained, however, the sentence which seems to be as autobiographical as any he wrote: 'Under any circumstances, in any situation, Savrola knew himself a factor to be reckoned with; whatever the game, he would play it to his amusement, if not to his advantage.' During these early years Lieutenant Churchill, enjoying a liberty not likely to be granted nowadays to a serving officer, was able to combine the roles of a soldier and a newspaper correspondent, and it was as the representative of the *Morning Post* that at last, after three rebuffs from Kitchener, he joined the Sirdar's Army in Sudan. He reached Cairo in time to take part in the advance south into the Mahdi's country, and was present at the final victory at Omdurman.

Prisoner of the Boers

The strategy, tactics, and what a later generation has learnt to call the logistics of the campaign were set out by Churchill in *The River War, an Account of the Reconquest of the Sudan*, which was immediately successful when it was published in 1899. His early military writings showed a grasp, remarkable in a man of his years, of the operations of war, which was best revealed in the clear separation of the essential from the accidental. They were also distinguished by a dogmatic self-confidence which never hesitated in its criticism of senior officers. His outspokenness did not improve his prospects and he was doubtless wise to resign his commission after wearing the Queen's uniform for only four years. Moreover, his success as a journalist had enabled him to think of giving up the Army as a career, and he had even turned his attention to politics, addressing a Conservative garden party at Bath (his first political speech) and fighting a by-election (unsuccessfully) at Oldham.

It was as a correspondent, again for the *Morning Post*, that he left for South Africa within a fortnight of the outbreak of war in the autumn of 1899. There he met with sensational adventures very much to his taste. Taken prisoner on an armoured train expedition by a Boer by the name of Louis Botha he succeeded in escaping from the prison camp at Pretoria within three weeks, 'jumped' a train, and after an extraordinary journey reached Delagoa Bay. He saw the campaign out until he could re-enter Pretoria with the victorious Army, and when he returned to England he was received tumultuously at Oldham, where, in the 'Khaki Election' of 1900, he won the seat from Walter Runciman. He was not yet 26, and contemporary accounts record that Joseph Chamberlain sat up and nudged his neighbour on the front bench when, in his maiden speech. Churchill declared: 'If I were a Boer fighting in the field and if I were a Boer, I hope I should be fighting in the field ...'

Tariff Reform

Chamberlain was right to take notice: there was an ominous smack about the words, and in his first session in the House not only did Churchill speak vehemently against the Conservative Government's plans for Army reform – and their unfortunate advocate, Mr Brodrick – but he voted against them as well. His unorthodoxy had deep roots. He was at work on his life of his father, who had remained in a party with whose orthodox leaders he was at war and had suffered in the end only isolation and defeat. At the very beginning of his political career Churchill was in much the same position. He was as much a Tory Democrat as his father, in a party led by Balfour, who had always seemed to Lord Randolph to be the main opponent of Tory Democracy. Moreover, there was little intellectual adventure to be found in the Conservative Party of 1902, and Churchill, who always retained a great respect for the academic and cultured intellect, felt drawn to the company of Morley, Asquith, Haldane, and Grey.

Then, in the summer of 1903, Joseph Chamberlain made his great effort to revive protection – 'playing Old Harry with all party relations', as Campbell-Bannerman excitedly remarked. With the Duke of Devonshire and Lord Hugh Cecil, Churchill declared himself a Unionist Free Trader, and by September, when it became clear that the Protectionists in the Cabinet had won, he was publicly exclaiming to a meeting at Halifax, 'Thank God for the Liberal Party.' Not unreasonably, the Oldham Conservative Association took exception to this and disowned him, and in the following year he crossed the floor of the House. How many who were there on that May 31, 1904, could foresee the irony in the incident as Churchill took his seat by the side of none other than David Lloyd George?

Before the end of 1905 Churchill had completed the life of his father. It stands, over half a century later, as one of the most brilliant political biographies of all time. The prose was perhaps never excelled by Churchill – later in his life the influence of the platform and the House of Commons made his prose too rhetorical – and the bringing to life of the political scene is so vividly and precisely done that the reader never loses his interest.

No sooner was this work of filial vindication done than Balfour – after months of trying to pacify his party and the House by 'expressing no settled conviction where no settled conviction exists' – threw in his hand, and Campbell-Bannerman took office. Churchill accepted the office of Under-Secretary of State for the Colonies and was the spokesman of his department in the House of Commons. A month later, at the general election, Churchill was returned as a Liberal for North West Manchester – while Balfour was defeated in the adjacent seat. In the House it fell to him to maintain the Government's decision to grant full self-government to the annexed Boer Republics – a controversial issue – and he began to develop his parliamentary style in the thick of a major parliamentary battle. At the same time his mind was moving to a new outlook on home affairs. Before leaving the Conservative Party he had looked back to the time 'when it was not the sham it is now, and was not afraid to deal with the problem of the working classes'. Now he confidently declared that the Liberal Party's cause was 'the cause of the left-out millions'.

He was a Radical, describing the obstructive attitude of the House of Lords as 'something very like an incitement to violence'. In 1908, when Asquith succeeded Campbell-Bannerman, Churchill was promoted to the Cabinet as Lloyd George's successor at the Board of Trade, having turned down the Local Government Board on the ground that he refused 'to be shut up in a soup-kitchen with Mrs Sidney Webb'. Under the law then still in force his promotion forced him to submit himself for re-election and a tempestuous by-election ended in his defeat by Mr Joynson-Hicks. But he was found a seat at Dundee, and he returned to London, his official career uninterrupted, to marry Miss Clementine Hozier.

In the political field he became a less conspicuous figure in the House of Commons, but in the country was second only to Lloyd George in his advocacy of the new Liberalism. A natural association developed between these two dissimilar men. Side by side they tried to check the rising naval expenditure, for, war-leaders though they were both to be, in 1908–09 their whole interest was focused on the first experiments in the 'welfare state'.

Bitter Attack
Churchill hesitated for a moment when Lloyd George introduced his People's Budget in 1909, but then threw himself into the fight in the country. Bitterly he denounced the House of Lords – especially the backwoods peers 'all revolving the problems of Empire and Epson' – and as president of the Budget League he enthusiastically praised the social policies which had made the Budget necessary.

There were Conservatives who, though they could have overlooked his treason to his party in 1904, never could forgive his treason to his class, as they saw it, in 1909. They were later to have their revenge. He was now becoming – though still only 35 – one of the leading members of the Government. In Cabinet, where one of his colleagues thought him 'as long-winded as he was persistent', he distributed long memoranda to the rest of the members on all subjects – however far removed from the affairs of his own department. (In the Board of Trade he was teaching his subordinates the duties which now belong to the Ministry of Labour.) 'Winston,' recorded Grey, 'will very soon become incapable from sheer activity of mind of being anything in a Cabinet but a Prime Minister.'

After the bitter general election of 1910 Churchill was promoted to the Home Office, where his interest in the future welfare of prisoners helped to launch the movement for penal reform. But the most famous episode of his term at the Home Office was the Sidney Street 'siege', which he characteristically insisted on witnessing personally. Germany's intervention in Morocco had made it imperative to put a term to the controversy over the British naval programme which was dividing the Liberal Party, and Asquith took what proved to be the decisive step of inviting the First Lord of the Admiralty (Reginald McKenna) and the Home Secretary to exchange offices. Churchill went to the Admiralty, with a mandate to maintain the Fleet in constant readiness for war with Germany.

Preparing for War

Germany's threat had completely changed Churchill's attitude to naval and military armaments, and he became (as 25 years later) a powerful advocate of preparedness, so much losing his interest in party differences and social policies that Lloyd George said he was apt to approach him with 'Look here, David' and then 'declaim for the rest of the afternoon about his blasted ships'. In fact, the post exactly suited Churchill's temperament and gifts. His speeches in introduction of the Navy Estimates rank with Gladstone's Budgets as classical expositions of the relationship of policy to departmental practice. In the face of considerable service opposition he created a Naval War Staff. At weekends and when the House was in recess he familiarized himself with the work of the Navy, going everywhere, seeing everything, and exercising a magnificent judgment in his selection of officers.

When war came Churchill mobilized the Fleet on his own responsibility, forcing from Morley a sad reflection on 'the splendid *condottiere* at the Admiralty'. But two years later, when he was dismissed to satisfy the Conservative Party leaders, Kitchener took to him the personal message: 'Well there is one thing at any rate they cannot take from you. The Fleet was ready.' Heads were to fall in the 1914–18 War which never should have fallen, and Churchill's was one of them.

He had carefully prepared for the Navy's first task – the carrying of the British

Expeditionary Force to the Continent – and it was done well and without mishap. He had also foreseen the possibility of a German advance threatening the Channel ports, and in October it seemed that the way to them would be open unless Antwerp could be held – or, at least, not given up without a struggle. He himself organized and accompanied the expedition to Antwerp which not only delayed the fall of the city by five days, but by doing so saved the Channel ports and prevented the Germans from gaining a quick decision in the west.

Back in London Churchill took a decision which was eventually to involve him in misfortune. Although it was due to Prince Louis of Battenberg that the Fleet which was concentrated at Portland in the last fortnight of peace was not allowed to disperse, Churchill felt under the pressure of popular agitation that his name and origin deprived him of public confidence, and he suffered him to go into retirement.

The Dardanelles

In his place he recalled to active service Lord Fisher, a warrior after his own heart, dauntless and indefatigable, a master of every detail of the sea service. The Navy could confidently look for a direction equal to any emergency so long as these two men saw eye to eye. Together they brilliantly restored the British command of the sea, which had been compromised by the destruction of Cradock's squadron off the South American coast. But still there was no decisive victory over the main German fleet, and the shelling of Scarborough and Hartlepool brought public criticism of Churchill and the Admiralty to a focus.

He had, at the beginning of 1915, little public support – a relevant fact to keep in mind as one begins the confused story of the Dardanelles. The breach between Fisher and Churchill had come over a fundamental issue of the direction from which British sea power could make the most effective impact on the course of the war in Europe. Fisher favoured the Baltic, Churchill the Dardanelles. Few would now dispute the strategic insight underlying Churchill's conception of a swift, dramatic stroke at a vital point. Success might have been achieved by the employment of such a combination of sea and land forces as was eventually brought to bear – but only after the initial advantage of surprise had been lost.

The most important criticism of Churchill's role is that he persisted in the enterprise without securing the support of his own department and the co-operation of the War Office. The documents do not support the criticism. He was careful from the very beginning to seek and obtain the approval of those with whom he had to work, and when the idea of the operation was submitted to the War Council there was no expression of dissent. The Dardanelles did, in fact, become official policy, and the French and Russian Governments were informed of it. The two main causes of the failure were the late hour of the objections raised by the unpredictable Fisher and the War Council's inability to resolve the question of a divided command. The delays, hesitations, and postponements are in many cases directly traceable to Fisher's behaviour – he resigned shortly after the first military landings – and it was only at the very late stage of his resignation that the admirals turned against Churchill's plan.

Out of Office

Churchill took to heart the lessons of 1915. A notable feature of his direction during the 1939–45 War was his assumption of the post of Minister of Defence. In this capacity he was able to secure uninterrupted and effective liaison between the Chiefs of Staff themselves and between them and the Cabinet which he led. The 1939–45 War was singularly free of the disputes between commands, between the Services, and between the Services and the politicians which Lloyd George never succeeded in ending between 1916 and 1918.

The political consequences of the Dardanelles were immediate – so immediate that when Churchill crossed to Downing Street to inform the Prime Minister that Sir Arthur Wilson was ready to take Fisher's place he found that others had preceded him. Now was the hour of the Conservative Party's revenge. Bonar Law had informed Lloyd George that if Fisher had resigned Churchill must depart as well. Between them – and faced with a critical debate on the Dardanelles – Lloyd George and Asquith determined on their best way out: a Coalition Government formed at the cost of the resignation of Churchill. This was a hard political decision against which there could be no appeal, and in the new Government Churchill had to be satisfied with what the Conservatives were prepared to grant him – the Chancellorship of the Duchy of Lancaster. The public, then deeply suspicious of Churchill's talents, drew obvious conclusions. Six months of idleness and frustration were sufficient, and in November Churchill resigned his sinecure and rejoined the Army.

Not to Blame

Within a few days he was at the Front, attached to the 2nd Grenadier Guards. A month later, with the rank of colonel, he was given command of a battalion of the Royal Scots Fusiliers. But his thoughts remained fixed on the conduct of the war, and in the spring of 1916 he was home on leave delivering a weighty speech in which with the magnanimity which marked him all his life, he urged the recall of Fisher to the Admiralty. Later in the year his battalion was absorbed and he returned permanently to political life. Asquith had meanwhile refused all Lloyd George's attempts to place Churchill in the Ministry of Munitions, and even when Lloyd George replaced Asquith as Prime Minister the Conservatives were still firm that they would not admit him to the Cabinet. But, in February, 1917, in spite of all

Asquith's protests. Lloyd George published the report of the Dardanelles Commission, which Asquith himself had appointed.

Asquith's interest in the matter was soon apparent to the public, for it was Asquith who was severely condemned and Churchill who was exonerated. The commission could find no grounds on which to indict Churchill: his plan had been right and the delays and ill-organization had not been his fault. Churchill's stock rose immediately and, after a brilliant survey of the war situation during a secret session of May, 1917, Lloyd George (with Smuts's support) appointed Churchill Minister of Munitions. Established less than two years before, the Ministry had become the greatest directorate of industry in the country. No episode in the whole of Churchill's career is so eloquent of his exceptional capacity as a departmental head than the success with which he imposed unity and order on this vast organization and established himself as the source and controller of its multitudinous activities.

During these last months of the war Churchill became a close adviser of Lloyd George on its central direction. He was not in the War Cabinet, but Lloyd George consulted and used him frequently on matters far outside his departmental activities. Churchill's visits to the Continent, in fact, became so frequent that the backbench Conservative members, still harbouring their grudge, warned Lloyd George that he must not take the renegade into the War Cabinet. But Lloyd George still turned to Churchill and, after the German break-through in March, 1918, summoned him to a conference with Haig and Bonar Law: Haig found Churchill 'a real gun in a crisis', and as the situation worsened Churchill slept at his Ministry so that he might be more closely in touch with the Prime Minister. He was Lloyd George's emissary at a meeting with Clemenceau, Foch, and Rawlinson – the prelude to the appointment of Foch as Supreme Commander – and at the hour of victory could feel that he had been at the heart of things, playing his part.

Damaged Reputation

Churchill had entered the war as a Liberal with an enviable popular reputation. He emerged from it a Coalition Liberal with a damaged reputation. As long as Lloyd George's Coalition held together Churchill was certain of office and could hope for promotion. But after that? The immediate tasks were, however, pressing. Lloyd George (who had been impressed by his departmental ability) asked him to move to the War Office (with which he combined the Air Ministry) to smooth away the friction which had at first attended demobilization. This he did in a fortnight. In this dual office Churchill became prominently involved in the question of Bolshevist Russia – eager, as he was, to continue the resistance to the Bolshevists. His appeal for a volunteer force to cover the withdrawal of British troops from

Murmansk and Archangel – 8,000 men were raised – lent weight to the suspicion that he was anxious to provoke a war with Russia.

Early in 1921 the growing difficulties in framing a policy suited to Britain's new position in the Eastern Mediterranean led to his transfer to the Colonial Office. In this capacity he was a member of the Cabinet Committee which in 1921 negotiated with the Irish leaders, and he played the role of peace maker. 'Tell Winston,' said Collins afterwards 'we could never have done anything without him.' But the pugnacity which he had kept in restraint during the Irish negotiations found new and unfortunate expression in 1922. The new Turkish state which was constituting itself under Mustapha Kemal clashed with British power in the Dardanelles. Thanks largely to the tact of the British Commander, Sir Charles Harington, a conflict was avoided, but Churchill's attitude, and especially his premature appeal to the Dominions, contributed both to the fall of the Government and to his own defeat at the ensuing election.

The Conservatives had for some time been restless under their allegiance to Lloyd George, and at a meeting at the Carlton Club on October 19, 1922, decided to end their association with him. Lloyd George immediately dissolved Parliament, and a confused general election gave the Conservatives power for the first time since 1905. Churchill was defeated – and for the first time since 1900 was out of the House of Commons with no certain hope of returning. He was politically isolated. He had severed himself from the Asquithian Liberals. He distrusted the Labour Party. And there was still much to divide him from the Conservatives: indeed all the more when, in the autumn of 1923, Baldwin appealed to the country on the issue of Protection – the very issue on which Churchill had left the Conservative Party 20 years before. He fought and lost the election as a Coalition Liberal – a term which barely had meaning any longer.

During 1923 Churchill completed the earlier portions of *The World Crisis*, though the whole work, together with its sequel, *The Aftermath*, was not completed until 1931. The volumes were not entirely successful. The style was too rhetorical and there was not the breadth of vision that marked his history of *The Second World War*. Balfour was not far wrong when he wrote to a friend: 'I am immersed in Winston's brilliant autobiography, disguised as a history of the universe.' In the following year Churchill severed his last links with Liberalism, and when, in February, a by-election was pending in the Abbey Division of Westminster he stood as an Independent Anti-Socialist. There was an official Conservative candidate in the field, but Churchill had the support of many of the more independent Conservatives, including Austen Chamberlain and Birkenhead. He was defeated by only 47 votes.

Chancellor of Exchequer

He fought the general election of 1924 as a Constitutionalist – and since there was no Conservative opponent was in effect the official Conservative candidate. He was returned to the House of Commons and (greatly to his surprise) was appointed Chancellor of the Exchequer. Baldwin had, in fact, decided to go outside the ranks of the safe and the orthodox: Austen Chamberlain and Birkenhead were also brought in. Even so, Churchill, as Asquith said, 'towered like a Chimborazo or Everest among the sand hills of the Baldwin Cabinet'. His first Budget, brilliantly introduced, contained provisions for widows' pensions, but its most conspicuous feature was the decision to return to the gold standard. This act of policy, though roundly condemned in the light of after events, was generally approved at the time by almost all except Keynes, who contributed a lively polemic entitled *The Economic Consequences of Mr Churchill.*

Keynes's warnings proved right. The mine-owners decided that in order to retain their markets in the world they must cut down their costs and there followed the tragic course of events which led to the General Strike in 1926. Churchill's role was not a happy one. All the evidence suggests that he was not one of the more conciliatory members of the Cabinet, and his production of the *British Gazette* from the commandeered premises of the *Morning Post* – though the object was sound; the communication of information to the public – was marred by his eagerness to turn it into a partisan anti-strikers sheet, which could only inflame feelings still more on both sides. The remaining years of the Baldwin Government were quiet. In 1929 Baldwin appealed to the country and lost the general election. Churchill, however, was again returned at Epping. Two years later the National Government was formed, but Churchill was not a member, and he remained out of office until the outbreak of the 1939–45 War.

Rebel over India

In 1930 the Simon Commission on India published its report, and the Round Table Conference was summoned the following autumn. Churchill opposed this moderately liberal policy, refusing to cast away 'that most truly bright and precious jewel in the crown of the King' – an almost precise echo of a phrase used by his father, Lord Randolph. In January, 1931, he resigned from the Conservative 'Shadow Cabinet' as a protest against its support for the Labour Government's Indian policy. It was a courageous act whatever one may think of the merits of his views: Churchill's conduct of the opposition to the India Bill in the House of Commons – fighting it clause by clause in committee – was perhaps his most brilliant parliamentary performance. But even weightier issues were beginning to hold his attention. In 1932 there started his seven-year struggle to halt the drift to what he later called the unnecessary war.

His freedom from office did, however, give him time to write the biography of Marlborough, which his cousin, the Duke of Marlborough, had long urged him to do. Based on a mass of material in the muniment room at Blenheim, the work was planned and completed on an ample scale, the last of its four volumes appearing just before the Munich crisis. Never restrained in the expression of his dislikes, Churchill pursued Macaulay with a rancour excused rather than justified by family loyalty. But no one else could have so brilliantly attempted to vindicate the qualities of a man of genius from the reproaches cast by a master of invective.

The Nazi Menace

Wherever the balance of advantage for foresight lies between the Conservative, Liberal and Labour Parties during these years, Churchill's record is not open to even the smallest criticism. His views developed all the time – and consistently. As long as the Weimar Republic had endured he had urged the wisdom of encouraging Germany in a policy of peaceful cooperation with Europe through the revision of the Versailles clauses most obnoxious to German sentiment. Even after 1932 when he already saw that Hitler was 'the moving impulse behind the German Government and may be more than that soon', he still demanded an effort to remove 'the just grievances of the vanquished'. But after Hitler's confirmation in power Churchill's theme changed. He sought, first, British preparedness – especially in the air – and carried on a persistent cross-examination of the Government's intentions in this respect. His warnings seemed to be dramatically confirmed by Baldwin's 'confession' in 1936, and his influence in the country was steadily growing when an extraneous incident suddenly restored Baldwin's popularity and emphasized Churchill's isolation and unpredictable temperament. This was the abdication of Edward VIII.

During the crisis Churchill seemed sometimes on the verge of forming a 'King's Party', and his actions and public utterances stood in unhappy contrast to the steady and wise guidance offered by Baldwin. This was undoubtedly a setback, but Churchill continued his campaign for preparedness, seeking the cooperation of all who agreed with him. His views had now developed further. More and more he put the emphasis on the need for collective strength – collective security. He had never trusted the League of Nations as an instrument for general disarmament, but he looked to it now as the instrument of collective preparedness by all the non-aggressive Powers of Europe.

At the Admiralty Again

It was all in vain, and on September 3, 1939, Britain was again at war; Churchill returned to office as First Lord of the Admiralty – an appointment greeted with relief by the public which had for so long been heedless of his warnings – and from the first he established himself as the popular war leader. At the Admiralty he took the first steps to combat the submarine menace which later became so formidable, but the main episode of his term was the brilliant operation in which Commodore Harwood, in command of *Ajax*, *Achilles*, and *Exeter*, drove the *Graf von Spee* to its destruction. His voice meanwhile was strengthening the nerve of the British people – an invaluable task in the confusing days of the 'phoney war'. There was the characteristic cockiness with which he offered 'to engage the entire German Navy, using only the vessels which at one time or another they have declared they have destroyed'. Meanwhile he was still pursuing his concept of collective security, urging the small European neutrals to understand the danger. But they did not heed either, and in the spring of 1940 Norway, Denmark, Belgium, and the Netherlands were all invaded.

On Churchill, as First Lord, fell the responsibility for the dispatch and disembarkation of the forces sent to strengthen Norway. Once more, as in 1915, an improvised undertaking ended in failure. The debate which followed – in which Churchill manfully defended the Government – decided the fate of Chamberlain's Government, and, on May 10 Chamberlain resigned and advised the King to send for Churchill. The Labour and Liberal leaders agreed to serve with him, and so the great Coalition was formed which was to remain united until victory in Europe had been won.

In the first volume of his history of the war Churchill has described his feelings on that night in words which are as moving as they are simple: 'During these last crowded days of the political crisis my pulse had not quickened at any moment. I took it all as it came. But I cannot conceal from the reader of this truthful account that as I went to bed at about 3 a.m. I was conscious of a profound sense of relief. At last I had the authority to give directions over the whole scene. I felt as if I were walking with destiny and that all my past life had been but a preparation for this hour and for this trial ... I thought I knew a good deal about it all, and I was sure I should not fail.'

Undramatic Confidence

This undramatic confidence – recalling Chatham's 'I know that I can save this country and that no one else can' – was quickly communicated to the people of Britain. 'What is our aim?' he exclaimed when he first met the House of Commons as Prime Minister. 'I can answer in one word: Victory – victory at all costs, victory in spite of all terrors, victory, however long and hard, the road may be; for without victory there is no survival.' And then: 'I have nothing to offer but blood, toil, tears, and sweat.' Was ever language so matched to the occasion?

Meanwhile, attacking through country which before the days of mechanization had been regarded as unsuitable for large-scale operations, the Germans drove a wedge between the Franco-British armies advancing north-eastwards and the main French Army. Holland surrendered after five days, Belgium held out until the allied troops were cut off both from their support and from the sea. There followed the unexpected success of the evacuation from Dunkirk, which so lifted the hearts of the British people that Churchill had to warn them that 'Wars are not won by evacuations.' It was at this point that Churchill ended a survey of the campaign with the words: 'We shall not flag or fail. We shall go on to the end ... We shall defend our island whatever the cost may be. We shall fight on the beaches. We shall fight on the landing grounds. We shall fight in the fields and in the streets. We shall fight in the hills. We shall never surrender. And even if – which I do not for a moment believe – this island or a large part of it were subjugated and starving, then our Empire beyond the seas, armed and guarded by the British Fleet, would carry on the struggle until, in God's good time, the New World, with all its power and might, steps forth to the rescue and liberation of the old!'

Fall of France

The agony of France was now prolonged for another three weeks, heavy with disaster, during which Churchill himself carried the whole weight of the British effort to keep France in the war. He visited the French Ministers at Tours, and crossed the Channel again a few days later after he had already made his brave offer of a solemn Act of Union between the two countries. It was too brave for the Ministers at Bordeaux, and on June 21, 1940, France surrendered, without giving Churchill an undertaking not to allow the French fleet to fall into German hands. Churchill, bowing to the logic of necessity, then took what must have been one of the hardest decisions of his life: the French warships – constituting the flower of the French fleet – were fired on, with damage and destruction, by British vessels as they tried to make their way from a North African port to Toulon.

Britain was now alone and almost unarmed. For her immediate deliverance she relied upon the chosen band of her own young men flying a few machines. Churchill neither planned nor directed the Battle of Britain on which the future of human freedom depended; but it was he who had evoked and deployed the indomitable strength behind the British airmen which now inspired their unsleeping fight against enormous odds. It was fitting that he should stamp on men's minds the character and significance of this battle in the simplest of all his phrases: 'Never in the field of human conflict was so much owed by so many to so few.' The bombing of London followed in September – with Churchill cheerfully calculating that 'it would take 10 years at the present rate for half the houses of London to be demolished. After that, of course, progress would be much slower.'

Conduct of the War

The organization through which every department of Government consciously worked under Churchill's superintending eye and felt the drive of his personality was built up gradually in the light of experience. When first constructed his administration was modelled on Lloyd George's War Cabinet, and of the Prime Minister's four colleagues, Mr Chamberlain, Mr Attlee, Mr Greenwood, and Lord Halifax, only the last carried, as Foreign Secretary, the burden of heavy departmental responsibilities. But three months later the intimate relationship already apparent between the issue of the war and the activities of the Ministry of Aircraft Production – itself one of Churchill's creations – led to the inclusion in the War Cabinet of its head, Lord Beaverbrook. As the war developed the Prime Minister brought in the Ministers in charge of other departments most directly concerned with its conduct, so that in its later form the War Cabinet had a membership of eight or nine, and included the Chancellor of the Exchequer and the Ministers of Labour, Production, and Home Security. Gradually, too, Churchill worked out his functions as Minister of Defence, a title which he had assumed when he became Prime Minister. It was never his intention to create a full-blown Ministry such as has now been established. His purpose was to give definition and authority to his transactions not with the service Ministers who were members of his Government but with the Chiefs of Staff, and to this end he provided himself with a small technical staff headed by General (now Lord) Ismay.

The system which Churchill created was emphatically personal in principle and was devised to give full scope both to his military knowledge and to his vast departmental experience. It worked because he was able to handle a mass of details which would have overwhelmed any other man. It was equally personal in its method of operation. Its timetable was governed by the Prime Minister's habits. Churchill's practice was to go to bed and sleep soundly in the early afternoon. When he had dressed again he brought a refreshed mind to bear on the immediate business of the day. Exhilarated by his contact with practical difficulties, he went on to address himself to questions of policy, regularly called Cabinet meetings for 11 p.m., and, after they had ended, continued for some time to pour out comment and suggestion to those of his associates who could keep his hours. Nor was he merely equal to his self-imposed tasks; as Mr Attlee said later, he set the pace.

The war surveys for which his return from his journeys often provided the occasion rank among the outstanding events of his parliamentary career. Worldwide in range and profound in matter, they at once informed and inspired both the

House and the country. The richness of their content was enhanced by a delivery characteristic of their author. Churchill's voice was not impressive in volume. But it was wide in compass. In his loftiest moments its somewhat metallic tones vibrated with passion, the more combative passages were given colour by the effective use of the rising inflexion and the frequent assertions of high resolve were made resonant by the accompaniment, felt rather than heard, of a sort of bull-dog growl. Read over in the light of after events these speeches are notable for their masterly restraint. They revealed much but they concealed more; of the great plans which filled his mind and with the execution of which he must have been busy up to the moment when he rose in his place not a hint was allowed to transpire.

Campaign in Africa

Italy's entry into the war had exercised a decisive influence upon British strategy. Her geographical position combined with her armed strength in all three elements enabled her to close the Mediterranean to all except the most heavily convoyed traffic. The main line of Britain's Imperial communications was perforce diverted round Africa and the extension greatly added to the strain on the British mercantile marine. On all counts, therefore, it was essential to counter the Italian threat to the Suez Canal. It was with special satisfaction that Churchill informed the House of Commons of the 'crippling blow' struck at the Italian Fleet in harbour at Taranto and he threw all his energies into the task of building up an effective striking force in the Middle East. He realized that though the war could not be won in the Mediterranean it could be lost there, and his sensitiveness to any threat in this quarter as well as his eagerness to give aid to a small and very gallant ally induced him to move troops from Africa to Greece when Germany struck her blow in the Balkans. The wisdom of this decision may be questioned. The reduction of British strength in Africa and the necessity, which Churchill immediately recognized, of returning the Australian troops when Japan declared war, opened the way to the successes of Rommel's Afrika Corps, whose formidable military quality was not, and perhaps could not have been, foreseen. There was less excuse, however, for allowing the lesson of Norway, that an army could not maintain itself against hostile air supremacy, to be repeated in the Aegean. It was widely felt that Crete should either have been evacuated earlier or more effectively held and its capture, after a tremendous German effort which came within an ace of failure, provided the one occasion in the whole war when Churchill's strategic judgment was seriously criticized by Parliament or public.

In the summer of 1942, while Churchill was in Washington, Rommel launched the greatest of his attacks. The British front was driven in for hundreds of miles and the crowning shock came when Tobruk, which earlier had resisted a long siege, fell almost without a fight. The blow was softened by President Roosevelt's immediate offer of American tanks to help in retrieving the position, and West-minster echoed Washington by defeating a no-confidence motion by 475 to 25. Some two months later Churchill was himself in the desert, having taken a visit to Moscow in his stride, and there effected those changes in the higher command which launched both Lord Alexander and Lord Montgomery on their great careers.

The decision to deploy American military strength in Africa was thus sufficiently in line with Churchill's strategic thought for him to describe it as 'per-haps the end of the beginning', but he was also at pains to make it clear that the plan was Roosevelt's and that he had been no more than the President's lieutenant. The two met at Casablanca early in 1943 and there proclaimed 'unconditional sur-render' as their aim. They decided as a first step to attack what Churchill pungently described as 'the soft under-belly of the Axis', and by the following September unconditional surrender had been made by such governmental authority as was left in Italy. Churchill was again in Washington when he received the news of this complete turn of fortune's wheel. But the Germans continued to turn the country into a battlefield and as 'the rake of war' – the phrase is again Churchill's – was drawn throughout the length of the peninsula, he did not conceal his pity for the Italian people. Pneumonia attacked him on his return to London after the Casablanca conference and he suffered another attack towards the end of 1943, but his determined will to live pulled him through.

From the first Churchill had looked forward to the eventual participation of the United States in the war. Deeply appreciative of the support, material as well as moral, given by the American Government while nominally neutral and deter-mined that friction with Britain should not obstruct the evolution of American policy, he was sympathetic towards American plans for the more effective defence of the western hemisphere and was even prepared for some small cession of terri-tory. President Roosevelt, however, asked no more than 99-year leases of land for naval and air bases, and in September, 1940, an agreement was concluded. The bases in Newfoundland and Bermuda were leased 'freely and without consider-ation', Britain thus aligning herself with Canada in treating the defence of North America as a matter of partnership. Six bases in the Caribbean were also leased in exchange for 50 destroyers from the United States Navy.

Pearl Harbour

The Lend-Lease Act of March, 1941, and the Atlantic Charter of the following August carried the process further, and when in December Japan attacked at Pearl Harbour Churchill gave effect to his warning, uttered a month earlier, that a British declaration of war would follow 'within the hour'.

Six months before Pearl Harbour Churchill had triumphantly surmounted a severer test of his appreciation of the needs of war. No man had shown fiercer opposition to the Soviet Power in its revolutionary phase, and though time and the growth of the German menace had modified his judgment, he had been a party in 1939 to plans, happily found impracticable, for the dispatch of an Anglo-French expeditionary force to aid Finland in her war with Russia. Hitler's decision in June, 1941, thus confronted him with a difficult choice. He made it without hesitation, and in the most dramatic of his broadcasts announced that every possible aid would be given to the latest victim of German aggression. The declaration had prompt results. Early in July an Anglo-Soviet agreement was signed in Moscow, and in the following month the two Governments sent troops into Persia to eradicate German influence and to secure the use of the Trans-Persian railway for the conveyance of supplies to Russia. The operation led in September to the abdication of the Shah. Under his son and successor Persia signed a treaty with the allies. Meanwhile the American Government, which had followed these developments with sympathy, had in August itself signed an agreement with Russia, and on the joint suggestion of the President and Churchill a three-Power conference met in Moscow at the end of September. In the following May Mr Molotov came to London and Anglo-Russian cooperation was rounded off by the signature of a treaty of alliance. Meanwhile 26 allied nations had signed a declaration committing them to fight to a finish against the Axis. The Grand Alliance was in being.

Through Disaster to Victory

With Churchill's efforts from the middle of 1941 onwards to establish unity of policy and action between Britain, Russia, and the United States his war Premiership entered upon its second phase, the first, that of preparation for insular defence, having closed when Britain ceased to fight alone. At the beginning of 1942 this second phase was overlapped by the third in which British arms suffered what Churchill himself described as 'the greatest disaster which our history records'. The Prime Minister was under no illusions as to the probable consequences of Japan's entry into the war. The new enemy was a first-class Power whose might the British Commonwealth, already engaged in a fight to the death with Germany and Italy, could not hope to meet on equal terms. But the Japanese pressed home their advantage with a success whose rapidity and extent exceeded all expectations. In December, 1941, the *Prince of Wales* and the *Repulse* were sunk in Malayan waters. Their flanks thus safeguarded the Japanese land forces advanced and completed their conquest by the capture of Singapore at the end of February.

The tale of misfortune was not yet complete. Rangoon was occupied early in March, and with the evacuation of Mandalay the whole of Burma, which Churchill's father had added to the Empire, passed into enemy hands. Churchill firmly refused to allow any examination of the causes of these distressing events. The House of Commons endorsed this view by a vote of 464 to 1, but it is instructive for the estimate of Churchill's attitude towards public opinion to contrast his firmness in holding the veil drawn over the loss of an Empire in the Far East with his readiness to grant an inquiry into the successful escape of the *Scharnhorst, Gneisenau,* and *Prinz Eugen* from Brest into German waters which occurred a few days before the fall of Singapore. It is equally instructive to note his disregard of the cry for 'a second front now' which began to be raised in the spring and summer of 1942 as the Germans thrust ever more deeply into Russia. Dieppe was a final warning against operations on an inadequate scale and Churchill now flung himself into the elaborate preparations which occupied two full years and constitute the fourth phase of his Premiership.

With the victories of Stalingrad and El Alamein towards the close of 1942 the 'awful balance' of war began to incline towards the allies and another aspect – the fifth – of Churchill's activities became increasingly prominent. Issues of reconstruction began to thrust themselves forward, though it was not until late in 1943, the year which saw the establishment of UNRRA and the preliminaries to the creation of the Food and Agriculture Organization, that vital decisions were reached. After a conference of Foreign Secretaries at Moscow in October had cleared the ground and itself reached important conclusions as to the future organization of Europe, Churchill and Roosevelt met General Chiang Kai-shek at Cairo in November and there agreed to strip Japan of all her conquests during the past 50 years. President and Prime Minister then flew to Tehran, where they met Stalin. The three statesmen declared their resolve to conclude a peace which would banish the scourge and terror of war for many generations and their readiness to welcome all freedom loving peoples 'into a world family of democratic nations'.

There was no meeting of the Big Three in 1944, but Churchill's many journeys, apart from visits to the front, took him to Quebec in September to concert plans with Roosevelt, to Moscow in October to seek a solution of the Polish difficulty, and to Athens at Christmas in an effort to bring toleration and decency back into Greek public life. Churchill's ceaseless journeyings between 1941 and 1945 serve to emphasize that if the war was won by the collaboration of the three great Powers, he was the architect of their cooperation. He built the Grand Alliance and held it together. The most vital of all the great Power meetings came in February, 1945, at Yalta.

Seeds of Later Problems

At that conference the Allies concerted their plans for the final assault on Germany, settled the terms on which Russia should enter the war against Japan, and sought agreement about a defeated Germany and about the future of the United Nations Organisation. Many of the problems which later beset the world have been traced in their origins to Yalta. But references in published memoirs and the American version of the proceedings published 10 years later all bear witness to

Winston Churchill and Field Marshal Montgomery after the Battle of the Bulge, 1945.

the prescience and grasp of realities Churchill brought to the conference table. Roosevelt, enfeebled by the great strain of his office and within two months of his death, believed that he could 'handle' Stalin and took an optimistic view of his trustworthiness. Churchill had a juster appreciation of the uses Russia would make of the great power and opportunities she possessed. His ideas on the settlement of Europe displayed an altogether deeper sense of history. Deprived this time of the President's solid support in negotiation, and placing allied unity first among the objects to be achieved, he was obliged to acquiesce in decisions about which he expressed deep misgivings.

Berlin and Prague

In the final throes of Germany's defeat Churchill saw more clearly than ever the importance of thrusting as far eastwards as possible before the Russian armies should be drawn into the vacuum of central Europe. He pressed this view upon Roosevelt, Mr Truman who succeeded him in April, 1945, and General Eisenhower who commanded the allied armies on the western front. Particularly he urged that our troops should advance to Berlin and Prague when these capitals came within their grasp. As early as April 5 he warned Roosevelt that 'we should join hands with the Russian armies as far to the east as possible, and, if circumstances allow, enter Berlin'. But another policy prevailed in Washington.

Perhaps the best account of Churchill's part in the war was given in 1957 by

Lord Alanbrooke, who was Chief of the Imperial General Staff and chairman of the Chiefs of Staff committee from 1941 until the end of the war, in *The Turn of the Tide*, written by Sir Arthur Bryant and based on Alanbrooke's war diaries. Irritation at Churchill's incorrigible desire for action, which was seldom related to the resources available, is frequently expressed, and at his perpetual goadings of his staff – 'I sometimes think some of my Generals don't want to fight the Germans', Churchill once remarked when his plans for a landing at Trondheim were being opposed. This was taken by some at the time to be a denigration of the great man, but the book was in fact a truthful panegyric. Churchill's greatest single contribution in Alanbrooke's view was that he carried the Americans with him – he kept together the alliance that won the war.

At Potsdam

Soon after the German surrender the Coalition Government broke up. Churchill, after forming a 'care-taker' Government, was preoccupied for a while with final plans for the defeat of Japan. In June, accompanied by Mr Attlee as his 'friend and counsellor', he went to Potsdam to settle with Stalin the many matters which the end of the war had made ripe for decision and join with President Truman in a final warning to Japan. Then he returned to London to receive the election results which dismissed him from office. The conduct of Churchill during the campaign of the 1945 election will always seem one of the strangest episodes of his career. The swing against the Conservative Party, which had started before the war, was so strong that even his reputation as a national leader could be of no avail. But he could have emerged from the election with that reputation untarnished. Instead he indulged in accusations, imputations and even personal abuse against his wartime colleagues which shocked his hearers – even his friends – and embittered his opponents.

Churchill was undoubtedly dismayed and unsettled by the verdict of the election – and he had to lead a party which was just as disheartened and just as unsure of itself. In the House of Commons he was less assured than ever before, and his weekly brushes with the Leader of the House, Mr Herbert Morrison, which came to be known as 'Children's Hour', saddened many of his admirers. In his criticisms of the Labour Government's social and economic policies he never seemed able to strike the right note. He struck some of his old notes in his speeches opposing the Government's Indian policy. He was bitterly critical of the proposal to give independence to India, and when, towards the end of 1946, the Government announced their intention of granting self-government to Burma he denounced it fiercely as a policy of scuttle. In 1947 the Government fixed a date for the handing over of power to the Indians, and Churchill's opposition was even more violent.

However, he welcomed as a statesmanlike means of averting civil war the intention to confer immediate Dominion status on the two succession states likely to emerge in India and promised to facilitate the passage of the necessary legislation. For a man whose vision could be so wide Churchill appeared sometimes to close his eyes to the nature of the problems facing Britain in India. He had inherited from his father a romantic – Disraelian – attitude to India which warped his judgment. The story, nevertheless, ended on a happier note. When he again returned to office his own and his Government's relations with India were cordial, and it was his Government which supported Indian initiative on the Korean question at the United Nations.

He used the years out of office to make headway with his history of *The Second World War*. The first volume was published in 1948 and the sixth and last six years later. 'In War: Resolution. In Defeat: Defiance. In Victory: Magnanimity. In Peace: Goodwill' was the motto of the work; the greatest of the war leaders, he chose with perfect aptness these ancient, simple, and resonant virtues. The work, which puts forward his personal interpretation of events, varies considerably in quality, but at its best it matches the magnificence of its theme. Churchill had moved far from his early models, Macaulay and Gibbon, and had fashioned a less studied manner of his own. His account of the battle for Crete stands comparison with the finest passages of narrative prose, and the closing chapters of the work are charged with a tragic irony that Aeschylus would have acknowledged with applause.

Fulton Speech

His vision did not desert him in the post-war years when he addressed himself to the problems of foreign policy. Churchill's ideas on foreign policy developed so consistently after 1945 that it is impossible to draw a line at the point in 1951 when he was again returned to power, the Conservatives under his leadership winning a parliamentary majority, of 17. But it is worth noticing the precise nature of his achievement while he was in Opposition. He made a series of speeches which were as important as statements by a sovereign Government. They had a worldwide influence. They were creative. They helped to form the policies not only of Britain but of the whole free world. Yet when be made them he was out of office and speaking only for himself.

It was in March, 1946, when he visited the United States at the invitation of Mr Truman and was accompanied by the President to the town of Fulton, that he first addressed the world as its seer. The occasion, with the President of the United States present, was clearly chosen to give the speech the widest prominence – and Churchill began by offering openly his 'true and faithful counsel in these anxious and baffling times'. The first purpose of the speech was to present a clear picture of the change which had been wrought in the world since the end of the war. The 'splendid comradeship in arms' had not continued. Instead, 'from Stettin in the

Baltic to Trieste in the Adriatic, an iron curtain' had 'descended across the Continent'.

Here, in two words, was the crystallization. The phrase, the 'iron curtain', only summarized a cogent argument, but it vividly painted the background against which all thinking about foreign policy had to be done. From this followed Churchill's three important conclusions: that there should be a close association between Britain and the United States – providing 'no quivering, precarious balance of power to offer its temptation to ambition or adventure'; that 'the secret knowledge or experience of the atomic bomb' should remain largely in American hands; and that 'the safety of our world requires a new unity in Europe from which no nation should be permanently outcast'.

This last point was elaborated in a speech which he delivered at Zürich University on September 19, 1946. 'What is the sovereign remedy,' he asked, 'for the tragedy of Europe? It is to re-create the European family, or as much of it as we can. We must build a kind of United States of Europe.' There followed another forward-looking proposal. 'I am now going to say something that will astonish you. The first step in the re-creation of the European family must be a partnership between France and Germany. In this way only can France recover the moral leadership of Europe ... the structure of the United States of Europe, if well and truly built, will be such as to make the material strength of a single State less important.' A United States of Europe – 'or whatever name or form it may take' – to include 'a spiritually great Germany'; the seeds of future policy were being sown. The next time Churchill spoke in a foreign affairs debate in the House of Commons (October, 1946) he was able to say, with perfect truth, that 'what I said at Fulton has been outpaced and over-passed by the movement of events and by the movement of American opinion. If I were to make that speech at the present time and in the same place, it would attract no particular attention.'

Throughout 1947 and 1948 Churchill devoted much of his energy to the concept of a United Europe. He had no very clear idea of what he meant or intended. The differences between federation and confederation baffled and did not particularly interest him. But much of the criticism of his role in these years was misplaced. Churchill was not primarily concerned with building a political structure. He himself said at a United Europe meeting at the Albert Hall on May 14, 1947, 'We are not acting in the field of force, but in the domain of opinion.' And he went on: 'It is not for us at this stage to attempt to define or prescribe the structure of constitutions. We ourselves are content, in the first instance, to present the idea of United Europe ... as a moral, cultural and spiritual conception to which all can rally ... it is for us to lay the foundation, to create the atmosphere and give the driving impulsion.'

Negotiation from Strength

When, at the Congress of Europe in May, 1948, he noticed that '16 European States are now associated for economic purposes; five have entered into close economic and military relationship', he could not hide the implication that these achievements owed something to the general concept of a United Europe. They certainly owed much to his own initiative. At the back of Churchill's ideas from Fulton onwards was the belief in negotiation from a position of strength. It was possible to deal with the Russians he said in March of 1949, 'only by having superior force on your side on the matter in question; and they must be convinced that you will use – you will not hesitate to use – these forces, if necessary, in the most ruthless manner'. He found encouragement in the fact that 'our forces are getting stronger, actually and relatively, than they were a year ago'.

It was because of this slowly changing balance of power that in February, 1950, he threw out 'the idea of another talk with Soviet Russia upon the highest level'. The suggestion was made at the end of an election speech at Edinburgh and was immediately dismissed as a 'stunt'. At the time it seemed, even to the non-partisan, to offer few real hopes. But the idea was a natural development of his Fulton argument and not a contradiction of it.

At intervals throughout the next five years the idea of 'talks at the summit' recurred in Churchill's foreign policy speeches. It was taken up by the Opposition, and he was increasingly criticized for delay in bringing a meeting about. His explanation came at an unexpected moment. It was in the course of a debate on the White Paper on Defence in March, 1955. Churchill had opened the debate with a speech which can be rated among his great parliamentary orations. He held a packed House in silence while he expounded his appreciation of the world situation which had determined the Government to press forward with the manufacture of the hydrogen bomb and the means of its delivery. On its deterrent power he founded his hopes for peace. If the ability and determination to use the weapon in self-defence were well understood on both sides war might be averted. 'That is why,' he said, 'I have hoped for a long time for a top-level conference where these matters can be put plainly and bluntly ... then it might well be that, by a process of sublime irony, we shall have reached a stage in this story where safety will be the sturdy child of terror and survival the twin brother of annihilation.'

But later in the debate when Mr Bevan taunted him with being prevented from holding such a conference by the United States, Churchill rose to explain the reasons for delay. He would have liked, he said, to have seen a conference shortly after Malenkov took power and he had prepared to go over to see President Eisenhower to arrange for the invitation. 'However, I was struck down by a very sudden illness which paralysed me completely physically, and I had to put it all off, and it was not found possible to persuade President Eisenhower to join in that process.' He went on to speak of the hopes he had entertained of a dual meeting at Stockholm or some like neutral place. 'But then the Soviet Government began a very elaborate process of trying to stop the ratification of EDC, which I thought had been more or less accepted ... and so all this other matter has come up now and stood in the way of further general talks.'

Domestic Policy

Through all the diplomatic activity of the autumn of 1954 which followed the French Assembly's rejection of the European Defence Community treaty, Churchill remained in the background. It was his Foreign Secretary who described and executed British policy and who announced the Government's historic decision, reversing the policy of ages, to commit troops to the Continent for a period of some 50 years. And it was Sir Anthony Eden who went to Geneva the following summer for the long-awaited conference of heads of state.

Churchill's record in domestic affairs during the Parliament of 1951 is less impressive. This is partly accounted for by the policy of his Government, which was to repair the national economy and grant a respite from major legislation, and partly by his preoccupation with the great questions that lay unsettled between the nations. In the more controversial domestic debates it was not he but his subordinate Ministers who appeared in the front line. Churchill himself, in contrast to his tactics while in opposition after 1945, exerted his parliamentary talents in the mitigation of party strife. Yet it was while under his leadership that the Conservative Party revolutionized its policy, became a guarantor of the welfare state, and stole so many of its opponents' clothes; and it was while he was Prime Minister that the party gave proof of its new convictions in office. It was not too difficult a transformation for one who had been a member of the Liberal Government of 1906.

Shortly after the Coronation he became suddenly ill and was ordered a complete rest by his doctors. Though he was back at work in October rumours grew of his retirement and of incapacity brought on at last by age. His movements it was noticed were less vigorous, his uptake in the Commons less quick, but again and again he came to the dispatch box and reasserted his mastery.

His eightieth birthday on November 30, 1954, found him still in office and in full control. The occasion drew forth tributes from his countrymen and from abroad of such number and warmth as have never been accorded to any English statesman before. Both Houses of Parliament met in Westminster Hall to present him with gifts. It was an occasion with no parallel.

This was perhaps the climax of the public honour paid him during his lifetime. His resignation of the office of Prime Minister had long been preceded by rumour, and when it came on April 5, 1955, it unhappily coincided with a strike in offices of the London national newspapers which prevented their publication. Yet the public did not need to be reminded in order to be aware that the last page was turned on one of the greatest chapters of British statesmanship. Preferring to the highest honours which might have been bestowed upon him to remain a private member of the House of Commons, he presented himself again to the electors of Woodford, as he did once more in 1959. Though he was often to be seen in the chamber of the House during these last years, he took no further part in its debates. In the summer of 1962 he fell and fractured a thigh bone. About 12 months later he announced that he would not seek re-election in the next Parliament. On July 28, 1964, shortly before the dissolution of Parliament, the House of Commons accorded him the rare honour of passing a motion 'putting on record its unbounded admiration and gratitude for his services to Parliament, to the nation and to the world.' He did not take his seat in the Chamber that day. The motion was brought to him by the party leaders at his home at Hyde Park Gate. His ninetieth birthday last year was the occasion of widespread celebration.

A glowing loyalty to the Monarchy, which was fed by the romantic strain in Churchill's nature, was matched by a warm personal regard for the Sovereigns whom he served. His attachment to George VI was especially marked, and can be measured by the fact that he deferred to the King's wish that he should not, as he had planned and as he dearly wanted to, embark in a warship on D day to observe the bombardment of the Normandy coast. The panegyric which he broadcast the night after King George's death was deeply moving in its sincerity. For similar reasons the Knighthood of the Garter, conferred on him by Queen Elizabeth just before her coronation, was a source of particular gratification to him. He had declined the same honour at the hands of her father in 1945, before the restoration of the practice by which conferment of the Order is the sole prerogative of the Sovereign who does not act on the recommendation of the Prime Minister.

In the spring of 1956 he was awarded the Charlemagne Prize for services to Europe, at Aachen. That this should have gone to the man who was above all responsible for the overthrow of the German Reich was a sign of the rapidity with which the European scene had changed in 10 years. In his speech on that occasion he cast his last stone that was to ripple the surface of international waters. He spoke, as he had so often done before, of the grand design of a united Europe. Russia, he said, must play a part in the alliance that would guarantee the peace of Europe; if that position was first achieved, it might be that the reunification of Germany would be more easily effected. In Bonn the reaction was chilly to this strategy, which did not accord with the rigorous views there held about the steps by which reunification should be accomplished. During the Suez crisis Churchill, to the disappointment of many, was silent except for two letters to his constituents, in which he intimated that the Government's actions had his full support.

He used his leisure to work at the long-projected *History of the English Speaking Peoples* in four volumes. Professional historians found much to cavil at, in spite of the assistance Churchill had from some of their number. But the public recognized in it a master hand of historical narrative, a shrewd and appreciative judgment of magnanimity, and an endearing preference for the good old stories, however 'tiresome investigators' might have undermined them.

Two of his private pursuits in particular excited public interest – his horse-racing and his painting. He became a racehorse owner late in life. His racing colours were registered in 1949 and two months later he won his first race with Colonist II. It was a popular victory.

His taste for painting was of much longer standing. He began during enforced inactivity after his removal from the Admiralty in 1915. Four years later he exhibited a portrait at an exhibition of the Royal Society of Portrait Painters. But it was land-scapes that he grew to prefer. 'Audacity,' he wrote, 'is a very great part of the art of painting.' And his decisive, boldly coloured, impressionistic works became familiar at the Royal Academy. His election to that body as Royal Academician Extraordinary was an honour he particularly relished, and his speeches at the annual banquets added much to the gaiety of the occasion. An exhibition of 62 of his paintings held at Burlington House in the summer of 1959 brought more than 140,000 visitors.

The honours that crowded upon him towards the end of his life are far too numerous to list. First in esteem was his honorary citizenship of the United States of America, which was declared by proclamation at a ceremony at the White House on April 9, 1963 – an honour that has been bestowed on no one else in the history of the union. In 1958 he was decorated by General de Gaulle with the Cross of Libera-tion. He was made Grand Seigneur of the Company of Adventurers of England into Hudson's Bay; he was the first non-American to receive the Freedom Award; he was Lord Warden of the Cinque Ports and Grand Master of the Primrose League; he held honorary degrees at more than 20 universities and was a freeman of some 50 towns and cities from Thebes and Cap d'Ail to Harrow. Among the minor honours in which he took special delight was the annual invitation to song night at Harrow School.

He married, as recorded earlier, Clementine, daughter of Colonel Sir Henry M. Hozier and Lady Blanche Ogilvy, and granddaughter of the seventh Earl of Airlie. From then on, he wrote in *My Early Life*, they 'lived happily ever afterwards'. That judgment, given in 1930, was not to be disturbed by time. Lady Churchill added grace and harmony to innumerable occasions in Sir Winston's public life, and made for him a secure and happy home at Chartwell. Three children of the mar-riage survive: Mr Randolph Churchill; Miss Sarah Churchill, the actress; and Mary, wife of Mr Christopher Soames, M P. Diana, formerly wife of Mr Duncan Sandys, M P, died in 1963.

The proposal was made by Harold Laski in 1944 that a fund should be raised in token of the nation's gratitude to its Prime Minister. In thanking Laski, Churchill remarked that things of that kind were better left until a man is dead. 'If, however,' he added, 'when I am dead people think of commemorating my services, I should like to think that a park was made for the children of London's poor on the south bank of the Thames, where they have suffered so grimly from the Hun.'

*　*　*

LE CORBUSIER

The outstanding architectural figure of his time

27 AUGUST 1965

WITH THE DEATH of Le Corbusier (Charles-Edouard Jeanneret-Gris), the world has lost one of its greatest architects and certainly the most controversial architectural figure of our time.

Le Corbusier was both a major pioneer of the modern architectural movement and a visionary who saw in the revitalizing of urban planning and in a new architecture the one hope for the future well-being of western man. Broadly he was convinced that our towns should be built upward instead of outward and that we should separate our pedestrians from our motor traffic leaving the land for large open spaces laid out with trees and lawns. He advocated this vision with relentless propaganda and great, even poetic eloquence setting out his faith in his many writings of which the best known are perhaps *Vers une architecture* (1923) and *La Ville Radieuse* (1935): 'I have said that the materials of city planning are: sky, space, trees, steel and cement, in that order and that hierarchy.' Learning from earlier pioneers like Peter Behrens, Auguste Perret and Tony Garnier, and standing in line with such modern masters as Taut, Poelzig, Oud and Mallet Stevens, he outvied them all by the reach and freshness of his imagination and the variety and inventiveness of his resource.

Le Corbusier found in ferro-concrete a new material for the entire remaking of urban life which seemed to him to be dictated by the growth of towns and populations and permitted by modern developments in engineering in such fields as lighting and heating, air-conditioning, insulation against noise, lifts, ventilation and the manipulation of large surfaces of glass. He was a notable innovator in house construction and design, and developed a method whereby the structure hangs on concrete columns thus permitting complete freedom of planning on each floor. A common feature of much of his early domestic building is the open, or partially open, ground floor which he incorporated later in many larger buildings, and which has been widely copied throughout the world. He significantly described the house as 'a machine for living in', and in *Quand les Cathédrales étaient blanches* (1937) his argument was that mankind's nostalgia for the sky, trees, and the country had, in fact, had no other result than the annihilation of large spaces of real country, the cancerous spreading of the suburb, and all the waste and fatigue of the long daily journey to and from one's place of work.

Much of Le Corbusier's design, especially in his domestic buildings, was controlled by a scale based on human proportions which he called The Modulor. This resulted in designing according to geometric principles, and by the golden section, which determined the proportions of many of his famous houses, and influenced the design of buildings like the immense block of flats at Marseilles.

Virtues of Ferro-concrete

Jeanneret came of a Swiss watchmaking family and was born on 6 October, 1887, at La Chaux-de-Fonds, in the Canton of Neuchatel. His mother, whose name was Perret, passed on to him her musical tastes; but, on leaving school in 1900, he entered a local school of arts and crafts, where his teacher was Charles L'Epplatenier. At 18 he headed a group of 15 students who built a house for L'Epplatenier. There followed a period of study of early medieval art in Italy, and in 1908 Jeanneret entered the studio of Josef Hoffman, in Vienna. But he found the atmosphere uncongenial, and within a few months went to Paris to study under Auguste Perret, who taught him the virtues of ferro-concrete.

In 1910 his old school at La Chaux-de-Fonds financed a trip which began with a period of work in the studio of Peter Behrens, in Berlin, and then carried him on to Greece and Rome and the Middle East, whose 'architecture of masses brought together in the sun' came as a revelation and remained as an inspiration to him all his life. From 1911 to 1914 he was in Switzerland, working as an interior designer, but during that time he built a house for his father. From 1914 to 1921 he worked in Paris as a factory manager, but kept up a brisk sideline practice as architect, painter, and journalist. Being Swiss, he was a neutral in the war. In 1916 he held a big exhibition of his watercolours at the Kunsthaus, Zurich; the following year came some abattoirs in ferro-concrete at Bordeaux, and in 1920, with Dermée and Ozenfant, he launched a review called *L'Esprit Nouveau*, which lasted until 1925.

Meanwhile in 1922 he started an architectural practice in Paris with his cousin

Pierre, using his maternal grandfather's name, Le Corbusier, for architecture, and painting under his own name. Working always against ultra-conservative opposition, the cousins nevertheless soon made their way by sheer force of original thought and practice. As long before as 1914 Le Corbusier had evolved the 'Domino' framework for standard concrete houses. The cousins now pressed on with this device, but its use was held up by war and politics until the operation of the Loucheur Law in 1929. In their first year of partnership the Jeannerets produced for the Autumn Salon a plan and panorama for a City of Three Million Inhabitants, and at the same exhibition showed the 'Citrohan House', 'a house like a car, conceived and worked like a bus or a ship's cabin'. This scheme was first put into practical production in the Weissenhof Colony at Stuttgart in 1925–27.

Traffic and Planning

In this period from 1922 onwards Le Corbusier designed, with his cousin, those houses in concrete where the structure is suspended on concrete columns, and planned to give flexibility on each floor, and designed in conformity with geometric formulae like the golden section. The most famous of these houses, such as that at Garches, near Paris (1926), and the Villa Savoye at Poissy (1931) excited interest and discussion throughout the world, and it is doubtful if any houses of the century have won greater fame.

Le Corbusier had been profoundly struck by the advance in constructional engineering during the war and by the effect of the motor car on traffic circulation and the planning of cities. Coming to the conclusion that the car was responsible for muddle and mess, he reasoned that if this point of view were put to one of the big motor manufacturers, money might be forthcoming from that source to finance a thorough exploration of the possibilities of replanning the whole of central Paris. The Peugeot and Citroën companies showed no interest, but M. Mongmeron, of Voisin, agreed to support him. Thus there came into being the Voisin Plan for Paris, shown at the International Exhibition of Decorative Art in 1925. It comprised a system of skyscrapers, 'stepped' and set back, cruciform in shape, with no interior wells and occupying only five per cent of the total area.

This far-reaching and revolutionary plan, and others comparable to it, were held up because of the enormous expense involved and the difficulty of getting municipalities and vested interests to throw all current ideas of town planning on the scrap heap. But, apart from a healthy domestic practice, the Jeannerets, as the years went on, were entrusted with many ambitious schemes, like the Centrosoyus (Co-operative) building in Moscow, reorganization plans for Algiers, Nemours (North Africa), Antwerp, Barcelona, Stockholm, and the sixth *arrondissement* of Paris. During the thirties of the century much work was done in South America. They won first prize in 1927 for a design for the Palace of the League of Nations, at

Geneva, but the scheme was later rejected. Other setbacks were the rejection of the city plans at the Paris Exhibition of 1937 and the failure of the committee for the Swiss National Exhibition, Zurich, 1939, to invite the participation of the firm.

The year 1940, with its cataclysmic events, broke up the partnership. Pierre Jeanneret settled in Grenoble. Le Corbusier, after taking refuge in unoccupied France, returned to Paris in 1942, in which year he evolved a master plan for Algiers, based on earlier studies. From 1934 onwards he had been widening his scope, by consultation with sociologists and engineers. He had from the first conceived of architecture as one element in the integration of a modern civilization, and now, during the occupation period, he founded *Ascoral* (*L'Assembée de Constructeurs pour une Rénovation Architecturale*), which included architects, farmers, lawyers, economists, and craftsmen.

The Ronchamp Chapel

In 1945 he founded *Atbat* (*L'Atelier des Batisseurs*), in association with 25 engineers and architects, and the same year headed a cultural relations mission to the United States. This, indeed, was a fruitful year. It brought the completion of one of his most ambitious and forward-looking public buildings, the Ministry of National Education and Public Health at Rio de Janeiro, which embodied his distinctive feature, the use of *brise-soleils*, to temper excessive glare in summer and to catch as much sunshine as possible in winter. It brought also a commission to redesign the industrial town of La Pallice (heavily bombed by the RAF while it was in German occupation). His notion here was to preserve the undamaged old Gothic town of La Rochelle in a green belt separating it from a new linear design for the industrial and residential twin-town of La Pallice, to the west, on the sea-coast.

In October, 1952, there was completed, at Marseilles, a 'town for 1,600 people under one roof', built in the teeth of much virulent criticism and opposition, at a cost of some 350m francs. Based on concrete piles, it contained almost every conceivable facility on the premises – shops, laundry, hospital, club rooms, crèche, swimming pool, running track, gymnasium, roof garden, and had an external wall of sheer glass, with *brise-soleils*. The whole is placed in a park of eight acres.

The famous chapel at Ronchamp built in 1950–55 is a very different work from Le Corbusier's previous buildings and represents another side of the architect. It replaces a former chapel destroyed by bombing. The building is of concrete and stone with a very irregular plan with two towers and one wall of thick pyramidal section pierced by small irregularly placed windows admitting a small amount of light, the purpose of which is to give a religious atmosphere. Light is also admitted by a space of a few centimetres between the walls and the curved concrete roof, while the floor slopes with the natural slope of the hill. It is an organic conception yet controlled in design by the architect's 'Modulor' theory. Few modern buildings have been the subject of more enthusiastic study among architectural students.

Another notable ecclesiastical building is the monastery and church for 100 Dominican Friars at Eveux-sur-Arbreste, near Lyons, which was built in 1954–58. Constructed of reinforced concrete on the slope of a valley adjoining a forest it provides, on the upper floors, for individual human needs, 100 cells each with a balcony opening to the valley, and for the needs of the community on the ground floor in the church, refectory, chapter house and other smaller rooms.

New Punjab Capital

Perhaps Le Corbusier's greatest town planning and building achievement is to be seen at Chandigarh, the new capital of Punjab. The first stage of this city is for a population of 150,000, but it is to be designed ultimately for a population of half a million. Building began early in the fifties and will probably continue throughout the century. It is the product of team work, but Le Corbusier had a major role for as adviser to the Government he prepared the outline plan and directed the planning for the future growth of the city while he was appointed architect of the capital buildings and the surrounding park.

The site of Chandigarh lies at the foot of the Himalaya mountains on a vast plateau between two great rivers, which are dry for 10 months of the year. A lake was created by a dam about 66ft high by about 21 miles long to irrigate the area as a first stage in building the city. Le Corbusier's plan follows the classical formal system of rectangular division with the capitol in the centre, which consists of the Parliament building, the secretariat, the Governor's palace, law courts, and a symbolic sculpture of 'the open hand' all set among large pools of water in a spacious park.

Architect, engineer, mural painter, watercolourist, Le Corbusier was also a prolific author, beginning with *Vers une Architecture* in 1922, continuing with *Urbanisme* (1924), *Précisions* (1930), *La Ville Radieuse* (1935), *Destin de Paris* (1941), *Perspectives Humaines* (1946), *Propos d'Urbanisme* (1946), *Le Modulor* (1951), and *L'Unite d'Habitation de Marseille* (1952), most of which have been translated into the European languages and Japanese.

Analogies were drawn from the liner, the motor car, and the aeroplane. Standardization was insisted on in the interests of speed, cheapness, and order. Le Corbusier's prose was rhetorical, combative, and positive in statement, so that he often laid himself open to easy refutation. Yet in spite of all the criticism of Le Corbusier's ideas, there can be no question of the stimulating quality of his imagination, the bright, bold clarity of his mind, and the ingenuity, effectiveness, and beauty of many of his buildings.

Le Corbusier married Yvonne Gallis, who died in 1957. Though no seeker after national or academic distinctions he accepted the honorary degree of Ph.D. from Zurich in 1933 and the RIBA Gold Medal for architecture in 1953, but he refused the ribbon of Chevalier of the Legion of Honour. On the occasion of his seventieth birthday a comprehensive exhibition of his work was held in Switzerland, which subsequently travelled the western world. It was shown in London in 1959, the year Cambridge made him an honorary LLD.

* * *

EARL ATTLEE

Presiding figure over the post-war years of social revolution

8 OCTOBER 1967

EARL ATTLEE, KG, PC, OM, CH, FRS, was Prime Minister for six and a half years in the third Labour Administration, the first to hold office with an independent majority in the House of Commons. His Government carried through, with un-exampled speed, a comprehensive programme of nationalization and social reform. When the importance of that social revolution and the smoothness with which it was effected are set beside the surface qualities of the man who presided over it, there emerges the paradox that lurks in all assessments of his statesmanship.

Both his opponents and his more impatient colleagues were prone to underrate him as a political force. He was devoid of those external marks which Aristotle thought necessary for men of consequence – sincere and quietly impressive was the most that could be said of his public personality. More than any of his predecessors in the highest political office he was innocent of poses and deficient in the more popular arts of leadership. Much that he did was memorable: very little that he said.

The absence of these superficial qualities was a handicap in his exercise of democratic government. It contributed to the failure of his party to dispel the air of drabness that gathered over post-war socialism. But as a basis for judgment on Attlee's public life it is totally inadequate. Attlee came from a middle-class home and received a conventional education at public school and university. He was not an undergraduate socialist. His politics were grounded on his observation of life in the East End of London in the early 1900s, and were laced with local government and the 'gas and water' socialism of the Webbs. He came to the leadership of the

Labour Party not by the thrust of ambition but by virtue of his parliamentary competence and general acceptability. The party was still embittered by the events of 1931, its morale still shaken. Pacifists, theorists and social revolutionaries warred within it. Attlee's influence was steadying, but not steadying enough to transform it into a convincing Opposition in the years before the war.

Honesty of Approach

'For myself,' he once wrote, 'I have seldom, if ever, had such a high opinion of my own judgment as to esteem it above that of the consensus of views of my colleagues. The majority are more likely to be right than I am. As a democrat I accept that position.' This conceals the pertinacity with which he asserted his view when he had absolute confidence in it but it does explain his failure to conjure out of the Labour Party a consistent and acceptable alternative to the Government's policies in the period of dictatorial aggrandizement on the Continent.

By 1945 he had overcome this weakness. He had never shrunk from assuming responsibility; his post in the War Cabinet gave him experience in its exercise. He remained sensitively attuned to what his party could and could not be induced to accept. But the idea that his statesmanship began and ended in compliant chairmanship is completely wide of the mark. His role in the Labour Cabinet has often been misunderstood. He worked extremely closely with two or three senior colleagues, especially Bevin, and sometimes settled questions with them rather than with the full Cabinet. Many other Ministers in and outside the Cabinet went somewhat in awe of him, and his comments at ministerial meetings had on occasion a sharp and waspish note. Indeed, his language in private meetings and personal converse had a racy pointedness that was altogether lacking on the platform. In certain matters in which he felt confident of his own judgment – for instance, India and Abadan – he himself played a dominant part in the Cabinet. He was always ready to take upon himself clear and heavy responsibility, as in the remarkable decision that Britain should make an atom bomb in complete secrecy.

Sense of History

He was a guide rather than an imaginative leader, a pilot in charted waters rather than a pioneer. Yet his essentially practical mind did not exclude breadth of vision, most notably in his concept of the Commonwealth, which had occupied him from his early years in Parliament. He inspired respect more than devotion. He was a man who stood aloof and whose intimate friendship was rarely given. A steadiness of judgment, a matter-of-fact honesty of approach, and a quite uncommon degree of common sense mark him out as one of the least colourful and most effective of British Prime Ministers of this century.

He was born on January 3, 1883, the fourth of the eight children of Henry Attlee, a solicitor. He was educated at Haileybury and University College, Oxford, where he obtained second class honours in modern history. His shelves were filled with works of serious historical study, especially on the development of Parliament, many of which he managed to read even while Prime Minister. His sense of history was manifest in many of the larger political decisions that he had to make. He was called to the Bar by the Inner Temple in 1906.

Gallant War Record

His early Conservative opinions underwent a rapid change, the result partly of personal reasoning, partly of experience of life in the East End, and partly of association with Sidney and Beatrice Webb. He joined the Fabian Society and became a member of the London School Board. After the publication of the Ministry Report of the Poor Law Commission, he was appointed lecture-secretary of the organization the Webbs established for the furthering of the minority report's policy and later took the post of secretary of Toynbee Hall. In the meanwhile he and a younger brother had lived in Poplar in a workman's dwelling and also for a time he was manager of Haileybury House in Stepney. As an additional means of investigating working-class conditions of life Attlee took work at the docks. In 1911 he was lecturing at Ruskin College on trade unionism and trade union law. By now he had abandoned any intention of practising at the Bar and was giving himself to politics and social work. From 1913 to the outbreak of the First World War he was a lecturer at the London School of Economics in social science and administration and resumed the work after his return to civil life.

Attlee had a gallant record in the war. He was 31 years of age when, within a few weeks of the opening of hostilities, he joined the Inns of Court O.T.C. His first commission was in the 6th Battalion of the South Lancashire Regiment, with which in the following year he went to Gallipoli. Promotion came quickly and he was already a captain in command of a covering party at the Suvla Bay landing. Falling ill, he went to hospital in Malta. After the evacuation of Gallipoli in 1916 his battalion sailed for Mesopotamia and took part in the first and unsuccessful attempt to relieve the garrison in Kut. Severely wounded, he was invalided home. After recovery he served in the Tank Corps for a time but, returning to the infantry, and now a major, he was with the 5th South Lancashires in France in 1918. Sickness sent him home again in the autumn and upon recovery he was discharged from the service.

Entering Parliament

In 1919 Stepney Council invited him to become Mayor. Unemployment was already a severe affliction in the East End and when an association of Labour mayors was formed to strengthen the hands of men with little administrative experience it was to Attlee that they turned for a chairman. He led a deputation of mayors on foot to Downing Street to convince the Prime Minister of the gravity of unemployment in both its social and individual consequences.

Attlee's parliamentary career began in 1922, when he stood for Limehouse and won a seat which he continued to hold till it lost its identity in the redistribution of 1948. Thereafter he sat for West Walthamstow. In the 1922 general election Labour won more seats than the Liberals and attained the status of the official Opposition. The total Labour vote had risen in 16 years from 323,000 to 4,312,000. The composition of the party also showed a marked development. Whereas formerly the trade unions had provided nearly all the Labour members, there was now a considerable admixture of middle class and professional elements. Ramsay MacDonald, returning to the House after four years' exile, was elected leader in succession to J. R. Clynes, and chose Attlee to be one of his private secretaries. The Parliament was shortlived.

Seeking a mandate for tariff reform, Stanley Baldwin appealed to the country at the end of 1923 and lost heavily, though still the leader of the largest party in the House of Commons. A combination of Labour and Liberals overthrew him and the first minority Labour Government entered upon a short and uneasy tenure of office. Attlee held the post of Under-Secretary for War (the Secretary of State being Stephen Walsh).

In the Government

In the election of 1924 Labour lost 41 seats; but Attlee's own position was unshaken, and, in opposition, he took up the task of presenting the party's case in Parliament, notably on the Electricity Bill and the Rating and Valuation Bill introduced by Neville Chamberlain – so that two experts on local government worthily crossed swords – and of building up the party in the country. Attlee was soon too much absorbed in national affairs to have time for local government. The severance came in the autumn of 1927 when he was appointed a member of the Statutory Commission on India, of which Sir John Simon was chairman. A large part of the next two years was occupied with a study of the political problems of India and the preparatory steps for the development of Indian self-government. It was in these two years that he formed the conclusions that guided his later Indian policy. He was still engaged on the work of the commission at the time of the 1929 election and for this reason had no place for several months in MacDonald's second Government.

An opening came in the spring of 1930 when Oswald Mosley, at odds with the Government on the measures necessary to combat unemployment, resigned the office of Chancellor of the Duchy. Attlee succeeded him but was not directly concerned, as Mosley had been, in the preparation of an unemployment policy. He assisted the Prime Minister with the work of the Imperial Conference which met in London in 1930 and became familiar with the wide differences on tariff policy which separated Labour Ministers from other Commonwealth Governments. He was also associated with Addison in the preparation of an agricultural policy. All this was quiet, unostentatious work. Later he was transferred to the Post Office and, being immersed in the duties of a post which was not of Cabinet rank, the ministerial crisis of 1931 found him, as it did most Ministers, unprepared and suspicious of a needless surrender. He certainly did not realize the gravity of the economic crisis.

MacDonald's formation of a coalition Government was wholly unexpected by his colleagues. Confronted with the division of opinion in the Cabinet, Attlee had no doubt of his personal decision, which was to remain with the party and go into opposition to the new Government. He had had close association with MacDonald (both in and out of office) but had retained a firm independence of opinion. In the autumn, when the coalition Government went to the country, the judgment passed on the Labour Party by a panic-stricken electorate was severe, and Labour returned with only 52 members. The National Government had the unwieldy majority of 493.

George Lansbury, the one surviving Minister of Cabinet rank, was elected leader and Attlee outrode the hurricane to become deputy leader. It was an arduous time for him. The criticism of Government policy devolved on so few, and Attlee was required to speak on a wide range of subjects and to speak often.

Attlee led his party in the general election of 1935. Only three weeks before the opening of the campaign Lansbury resigned. Attlee's succession to the leadership was challenged by Morrison and Greenwood, but he was elected after a second ballot. He stepped quietly and confidently into the vacant place. He returned to Westminster with a following of 154, and his leadership was confirmed.

The war in Abyssinia moved to its inevitable end in the absence of effective intervention by the League of Nations, Germany denounced the Treaty of Locarno, and the civil war in Spain disclosed the ominous share which Italy, Germany, and Russia were taking in the conflict, and Attlee more vehemently attacked the weakness of British policy. But a new note was heard in his speeches; he began to doubt whether the system of collective security could survive the shocks it was suffering. Continuing to accuse the Government of betraying the League, he continued also to oppose the increase of the armed forces. He now began, however, to shift the emphasis to the argument that a vote for the defence estimates implied support for the Government's foreign policy. This precarious and equivocal position began to be attacked by some of the more realistic Labour members of Parliament in the privacy of the party meeting, but it carried the support of the still large pacifist wing of the party, whose views Attlee felt he could not ignore. In the summer of 1936 he refused to support the recruiting campaign of a Government whose foreign policy he did not trust and whose armaments policy he thought futile and inept. He began to feel his way towards a more realistic and logical position. Before long the cynical disregard by Germany and Italy of the agreement on non-intervention in Spain brought him to face the contingency of war.

Attitude to Hitler

He was soon to show acute alarm at the increasing Nazi aggression and to realize the danger and even the imminence of war. Such was the ironical development of events that he had to deny that the Labour Party wanted war. Eden resigned office as Foreign Secretary. Austria was helplessly over-run in the March of 1938. Attlee now redefined the attitude of the Labour Party thoroughly aroused to the menace of Hitler's territorial ambitions. He posed the anxious question of whether, if we allowed the fortresses of liberty to be captured one by one, this country could survive. A few days later Chamberlain outlined his foreign policy. The Government could not accept an unconditional, automatic liability to go to war to defend an area – Czechoslovakia – where British vital interests were not directly concerned, but should war break out it was unlikely to be confined to those who had assumed such automatic obligations. Attlee's vigorous rejoinder, showing unwonted passion, was a declaration that we could not barter our freedom for peace and we could not have a peace of slavery.

Then came the Nazi pressure on Czechoslovakia. Attlee read the portents clearly and wondered for how long the world could continue to live under a militarist menace and how – sooner or later – a war would break out. It was a new experience for him – a zealous supporter of the no-more-war movement after the First World War, a steadfast believer in collective security, and, almost to the end, an opposer of rearmament – to be confronted in his constituency with demonstrators who chanted in chorus 'we want peace: Attlee wants war'. His mind was made up and he declared that Britain and France could not in honour desert Czechoslovakia. He was not deceived by the Munich agreement; it was but a temporary armistice and Hitler had won a tremendous victory.

Outbreak of War

The military catastrophes of the spring and early summer of 1940 compelled the formation of a National Government. Chamberlain sounded the Labour leaders on their willingness to join a reconstructed Ministry. They refused to serve under him but welcomed the opportunity to join an administration led by Churchill. Attlee became Lord Privy Seal, deputy Prime Minister and a member of the small War Cabinet. Leadership had come to him as the due of service rather than the prize of ambition, but it had made him the unquestioned head of the second largest party in the state. Now he was to reveal an unaffected readiness to disregard personal assertion, and to accept and even to seek partial effacement. Attlee was no rival of Winston Churchill's supremacy. He was an assiduous and able member of the small group of Ministers forming the War Cabinet, informed and able in council and steady in judgment. The War Cabinet itself was remarkably harmonious, and this harmony, derived in large measure from the knowledge and temper of the Labour movement, both political and industrial, which Attlee and Bevin supplied, was a powerful influence in maintaining an undistracted determination throughout the nation.

Forming a Cabinet

In 1942 while Churchill was in Washington it fell to Attlee to make one of the periodical reviews of the state of the war which Churchill had inaugurated. Henceforward he took the Prime Minister's place, in this and other ways, with some regularity as military strategy and the invasion of Europe, first from the south and afterwards from the west, more and more engrossed Churchill's time and energy. The grave turn of events in the Far East in 1942 brought an added responsibility to Attlee. Japan's drive through Malaya, Singapore, and the Dutch East Indies had caused deep apprehension in Australia and New Zealand, and they needed confirmation of the active concern of the Cabinet in London. Attlee became Secretary of State for Dominion Affairs and thus Australia, along with the other Commonwealth nations, had direct and continuous representation in the War Cabinet as well as special representation by their own Ministers when any were in London. He held the appointment for 16 months and relinquished it knowing that the unity of the Commonwealth was inviolable. He returned to the office of Lord President of the Council and was responsible for the coordination of home policy. The tide of war had turned, and the Government was preparing a social programme for application after the war. Attlee was able to say at the reopening of Parliament in November, 1943, that part of the reconstruction programme was already in legislative form.

Attlee went to the San Francisco conference in 1945 for the foundation of the United Nations Organization in company with Anthony Eden, Foreign Secretary, Lord Cranborne (now Lord Salisbury), Secretary for the Dominions, and Lord Halifax, Ambassador at Washington. Victory in Europe was announced on May 8. Ten days later Churchill formally sent to Attlee a proposal that the coalition should continue until the end of the war with Japan. Churchill's letter was seen in draft by Attlee, who did not disapprove its purpose and indeed suggested an amendment likely to improve its chance of success. Churchill had proposed to say 'It would give me great relief if you and your friends were found resolved to carry on with us until a decisive victory had been gained over Japan.' Attlee's suggested interpolation, which Churchill embodied in his letter, was 'In the meantime we should do our utmost to implement the proposals for social security and full employment contained in the White Papers which we have laid before Parliament.' The Labour Party executive would not consider a prolongation of the coalition nor assent to a referendum on this single issue and the Labour members left the Government. Churchill formed a caretaker administration, Parliament was dissolved on June 15, and polling took place the following month. Labour's resounding triumph returned Attlee with 393 followers, an increase of 227, and a majority far greater than he had regarded as adequate for the socialization of the key industries and services. He became Prime Minister at the age of 62.

Out of India

Attlee's first Cabinet reflected the currents of opinion and even the various moods and tempers within the party and established a convenient balance between the distinctively trade unionist and the other elements in the party structure. The transfer of Ernest Bevin from the Ministry of Labour and National Service to the Foreign Office caused more surprise than it should have done. For the strategic posts in the van of the socialist revolution Attlee chose men of aggressive energy and debating skill. Mr Dalton was sent to the Treasury to take charge of the nationalization of the Bank of England and to control monetary and credit policy. To the salient post of Minister of Fuel and Power for the nationalization of the coalmining and electricity industries, Attlee appointed Mr Shinwell, while the drive and ruthless vitality of Aneurin Bevan were harnessed to the housing programme of the Ministry of Health and the inception of a national health service which was certain to encounter difficulties notwithstanding general assent to its essential principles. The development of relations between Britain and India and the consummation of Indian self-government were entrusted to the urbane, wise, and tactful Pethick-Lawrence. As the Government's policy unfolded and India was found to be unready to reconcile its major communal antagonisms, Attlee's Government added to the incentive of self-determination the constraint of a time limit for the continuance of the British occupation.

The Government launched its massive legislative programme, but these great plans alone did not absorb all Attlee's concern. He endeavoured to arouse the country to the imminent and grave dangers of inflation and to temper majority rule, as he would also temper the pride of victory, with regard for human qualities and rights. He strongly maintained that the one principle to save the world was the Christian principle that all men were brothers. In the autumn of the year he went to America to discuss with President Truman, and afterwards with Mr Mackenzie King, the problems of atomic energy. The result was a tripartite declaration of willingness to share basic scientific information for peaceful ends accompanied by a refusal to spread specialized knowledge concerning the application of atomic energy until effective safeguards against its use as a war weapon had been devised. The duty of establishing safeguards was referred to the United Nations.

US Loan Dwindling

His own and his Government's repudiation of imperialism was given practical expression in the withdrawal from Egypt and from India and from Burma and the surrender of the mandate for Palestine when it was found impossible to reconcile the conflicting claims of Jews and Arabs. Never did the nation's economic position allow him rest of mind or a happy assurance of the social security which from the first had been his political aim. When he moved the second reading of the National Insurance Bill, six months after the Government took office, he qualified his exultation with the warning that the country could afford the new service only if it employed all its resources of skill, organization, and labour, and reinvigorated its economic life. The American loan which followed the abrogation of lend-lease dwindled rapidly and in the autumn Attlee was appealing again to his supporters and the trade union leaders to face the economic facts. The outlook was darkened in the early months of 1947 by a severe fuel shortage, which deranged the year's production estimates: and time and again within the next two years Attlee was renewing his appeals for greater output. Further generous American financial help in the form of the Marshall plan staved off immediate drastic reductions in the standard of living. Marshall aid was no less significant in the field of foreign policy which increasingly became as pressing an anxiety for the Government as the economic situation. In facing the mounting gravity of international relations, Attlee and Bevin worked as one man. Bevin's staunch and unwavering support for the Prime Minister, whom he affectionately called 'the little man' became the main pillar of Attlee's personal position, safeguarding him against attacks in the Cabinet and the party. More than once his lack of the capacity to dramatize his leadership led to widespread criticism in the press and in the Parliamentary Labour Party. On one occasion one at least of his senior colleagues seriously considered challenging Attlee's tenure of the Prime Ministership. Bevin unhesitatingly scotched the attempt.

Middle East Setbacks

Towards the end of 1948 there came the Berlin airlift which was hastily improvised to counter Russia's attempt to cut off the city and starve it into surrender. In March, 1949, Attlee paid a visit to Berlin to see the airlift in full operation with a continuous stream of British and American aircraft landing at Templehof. Meanwhile the problem arose of the method by which western Europe was to be consolidated. A federalist movement came to the fore on the Continent that wished to merge the existing states of Europe into a new political unit with central organs of government. Attlee shared Bevin's instinctive determination to preserve Britain's national identity. The Government therefore resisted the blandishments of M. Schuman and M. Spaak and incurred the charge, which was echoed by the Opposition, of 'dragging its feet'. The desire for European integration was, however, sincere and Bevin put his energy into the creation of intergovernmental organizations of the type of ECE, OEEC, and the EPU. Neither Attlee nor Bevin had much patience with those who wished to set up the Council of Europe which they regarded as an important talking-shop that would get in the way of the real work to be done.

Another problem that soon pressed upon the Government was the rise of nationalism in the Middle East. Attlee attempted to come to terms with this force in the same manner as in India and Pakistan. But he became increasingly involved in intractable difficulties that dogged him to the end of his Prime Ministership and did much to bring about his ultimate defeat at the polls.

Against setbacks in the Middle East must be put the consolidation of the new and enlarged Commonwealth. This was a sphere of activity in which Attlee felt confident and at home and the progress made was largely his personal achievement. He quickly established relationships of trust and friendship with the other Prime Ministers of the Commonwealth and this stood him in good stead in the four Prime Ministers' meetings over which he presided with singular success. When India, Pakistan, and Ceylon attained independence it was by no means certain that they would remain in the Commonwealth; indeed to most observers the odds seemed the other way.

It was Attlee's simple and undogmatic approach to this question that largely settled it. As a matter of course he invited the Asian Prime Ministers to join their colleagues in conference before they had decided whether or not to continue in membership of the Commonwealth. Their inside view of the Commonwealth at work, their realization that it was truly an association of equal nations whose concern was to help one another, became an important factor in their decisions to remain in the Commonwealth.

Attlee's masterly handling of two crises in the Commonwealth smoothed over difficulties that might otherwise have split it asunder. Towards the end of 1948 it became clear that India would become a republic. For a time it seemed that the problem of fitting a republic into a Commonwealth whose basis was common allegiance to the Crown would be insuperable. Attlee set about the problem with care and vigour. He instituted a searching study of the question and in January resorted to the unusual device of sending personal envoys to talk the matter over with the other Prime Ministers. The Prime Ministers' meeting that assembled in April 1949 was the most thoroughly prepared that had ever been held. It confined its discussions to the single point of India's membership as a republic and the

declaration that it produced on this subject takes its place among the basic constitutional documents of the Commonwealth. The solution found was that India as a
republic recognized the King as Head of the Commonwealth and that all the other
members recognized India's continuing membership. All the Prime Ministers
went in a body to the Palace to report the outcome to the King, who had already
signified his acceptance of the formula.

Kashmir Question

The second Commonwealth crisis with which Attlee dealt occurred in January,
1951, when Mr Liaquat Ali Khan, Prime Minister of Pakistan, announced at the last
moment that he would not attend the meeting of Prime Ministers that was already
assembling in London unless the question of Kashmir were placed on their agenda.
Mr Nehru's refusal to agree to this course produced a deadlock. Attlee held firm to
the principle that the Prime Ministers could discuss only matters to which all
agreed; that the purpose of those meetings was not to air differences but to deal
with common problems. At the same time Attlee actively sought for a solution that
would satisfy Pakistan. All the Prime Ministers agreed that the problem of Kashmir
should be talked over in informal gatherings outside the formal and plenary
sessions. The Prime Ministers met in this manner in various combinations in
strenuous efforts to find an agreed solution, though without success. However, a
precedent had been created that might help Commonwealth disputes to be
handled more smoothly in future. Whatever other judgments may be formed on
Attlee's role as Prime Minister, his place is secure in history as one of the great
architects of the Commonwealth.

The economic and international problems of the country seemed to have eased
when Attlee decided in February, 1950, to go to the country. The Labour Party
entered the election with confidence on the assumption that its establishment of
the welfare state by means of the Health Service, family allowances and a comprehensive system of social insurance would win it a reduced but still considerable
mandate for a second term of office. It fought the election on a policy statement
entitled 'Labour Believes in Britain', which was in effect a justification of the
Government's policies and an appeal for their continuance.

Labour put up its vote by over 1,250,000 but saw its majority slashed to 10. This
came as a great shock to the party. But Attlee decided without hesitation to continue
in office. Few in the party or outside it thought that the Government could survive
for more than a matter of weeks. In the event it continued for 18 months. During its
course Attlee was subjected to great strain which affected his health. His judgment
and leadership became less sure.

Changing Relations

After the election he undertook a limited reconstruction of his Administration which considerably reduced its average age. Death soon struck the new Government heavy blows that deprived him of his two principal colleagues. In October, 1950, Cripps was forced under doctors' orders to resign and died 18 months later after a painful illness courageously borne. In March, 1951, Bevin, who had been kept for some time by ill-health from continuous discharge of his official duties, resigned from the Foreign Office, dying a few weeks afterwards. Bevin was the only one of Attlee's colleagues who succeeded in penetrating his reserve and getting onto terms of intimate friendship with him and Attlee was deeply affected by his loss. The whole balance of the Cabinet and the basis of Attlee's personal leadership was altered. He had managed to remain Prime Minister of a Government that contained greater and more dynamic men than himself because Bevin, Cripps, and Morrison formed a kind of triangle of forces that maintained a political equilibrium beneath Attlee's feet.

Support for Truman

The survivor of the triumvirate, Morrison, who succeeded Bevin as Foreign Secretary, never enjoyed good personal relations with Attlee. The incompatibility and lack of full confidence between the two now came to the fore in a Cabinet that had lost its previous internal poise. Gaitskell, who replaced Cripps as Chancellor, belonged to the younger generation in the Party. Throughout his second Administration Attlee failed to establish the relations of trust and understanding between a Prime Minister and his Foreign Secretary and Chancellor of the Exchequer that are necessary to a stable and harmonious Cabinet.

In July, 1950, North Korea suddenly invaded the South. Attlee at once supported President Truman's decisions to dispatch United States forces to Korea under the authority of the United Nations. Despite the heavy commitment of British forces in various parts of the world, a brigade was sent to Korea which became the nucleus of a Commonwealth Division. Considerable British naval strength was also put at the disposal of the United Nations Command. The open Communist aggression in Korea faced the Government with the crucial problem of a sharp increase in armaments expenditure. The economy was heavily overloaded when the world prices of raw materials rose very rapidly. Attlee failed to persuade the Americans of the seriousness for Britain of the rise in world prices. A number of international committees were set up to allocate raw materials, but they never worked effectively and in any case it was too late to shut the stable door; prices were already at war-scarcity levels.

The mounting economic crisis also brought strains and divisions in the

Cabinet. Gaitskell, now Chancellor of the Exchequer, stuck firmly by the decision to rearm and used his Budget to help close the inflationary 'gap' between the supply of, and the demands upon, national resources. This led him to impose a charge to meet part of the cost of false teeth and spectacles supplied under the National Health Service, making use of legislation earlier introduced by Bevan. Bevan strongly opposed these charges in the Cabinet, later widening the area of dispute to include the whole question of rearmament. In the midst of these discussions, which became bitter and personal, Attlee fell ill and had to go to hospital for treatment of duodenal ulcers. He tried from his bedside to compose the quarrel but without success. He returned to work in time to preside over the Cabinet held on the day before the Budget at which Bevan and Mr Wilson, President of the Board of Trade, resigned. This was in April, 1951. The following month a new crisis broke on a shaken Government, the product once again of Middle Eastern nationalism. In May, 1951, the Shah signed decrees nationalizing the Persian oil industry and taking over the refinery at Abadan. Between that date and October, 1951, when the Anglo-Iranian Company ceased operations in Persia – a period that coincided with the remaining term of office of the Government – the Cabinet was perplexed and embarrassed. Attlee had to face again the problem of Britain's relations with nationalist forces in areas in which previously British influence had been unquestioned. His instinctive reaction was the same as it had been towards Indian independence – namely, that Britain must come to terms with nationalism.

Run on Reserves

The ultimate closure of the Abadan refinery gravely increased the economic difficulties that were already pressing on the country. The run on the gold and dollar reserves began to gather perilous momentum. Attlee came to the conclusion that he needed a larger majority to face this situation. The King was due to visit Australia and New Zealand in the following year and Attlee did not want to subject him to the constant anxiety of a possible fall of Government during his absence from the country. This was characteristic of Attlee's personal consideration of others, even in matters of high party political moment and of the close and warm relations that grew up between him and King George VI. He gave some expression to these when he paid tribute to the King's memory in the House of Commons, a speech in which he displayed more emotion than was his wont.

Had Attlee gained victory in 1951 he would have been the first Prime Minister to win three consecutive elections. In fact the Labour vote increased by 700,000 and was larger in total than the Conservative poll; but Labour lost 19 seats and control of the Commons passed to Sir Winston Churchill. Attlee at once tendered his resignation to the King who conferred upon him the Order of Merit. After 11 continuous years of high office Attlee proved a less successful leader of the Opposition than in the years before the War. He seemed to miss the authority that a Prime Minister derives from the disposal of office and could not quite recapture his former touch in his relations with members of a Parliamentary Committee who owed their position to election by their fellows. The former divisions in his Cabinet had hardened into organized faction. For several years Bevan and his supporters in Parliament and the country formed a cohesive party within the party that on a number of occasions defied the authority of the leaders. Bitter and prolonged disputes broke out, all turning in reality on a struggle for the succession to the leadership of the party. Attlee assumed almost the attitude of a detached observer to the intrigues and manoeuvres that rent the party and brought it low in public esteem.

Morecambe 1952

The tensions reached their high point at the 1952 conference at Morecambe at which it was doubtful till the last moment whether or not the established leaders would succeed in carrying their policy of support for German rearmament. Attlee's part in this debate lacked the vigour and clarity with which he had opposed Lansbury's pacifism in 1935. He conveyed the impression that he was not greatly concerned with the outcome and left the main burden of the battle to Morrison. The policy of the leadership was endorsed by an extremely narrow majority.

In 1954 Attlee published his autobiography, *As it Happened*, in which he recounted with dry matter-of-factness the world-shaking events in which he had played so prominent a part. The book was spiced with occasional flashes of quiet wit and digs at Sir Winston Churchill. It was the unassuming self-portrait of a simple and contented man and its closing words would serve as a fitting epitaph on Attlee's life: 'Up to the present I have been a very happy and fortunate man in having lived so long in the greatest country in the world, in having a happy family life and in having been given the opportunity of serving in a state of life to which I had never expected to be called.'

It was a still divided party that Attlee led in the General Election of 1955 called by Sir Anthony Eden on his succession as Prime Minister to Sir Winston Churchill. For the fifth and last time Attlee made his customary wide-ranging tour, mainly through marginal seats, driven in a small car by his wife. The calls on him were as imperative as ever and he never flinched nor spared himself physically. As in the past he would make up to eight speeches in a single day and he spoke for the party over the air. But the old assurance and deftness of stroke were no longer in evidence. No election since 1935 had been fought by the Labour Party with so little confidence in victory. The Conservatives increased their majority to 60. When Attlee appeared on television after the results of the election were known he wore the air of a weary man, no longer looking forward.

Leadership Surrendered

Soon after, in August, he suffered a slight stroke from which he made, in due course, a complete recovery, and his relinquishment of his post as Leader of the Opposition became widely expected. Yet the occasion came as a surprise. He made a typically brief and modest speech to a regular meeting of the Parliamentary Labour Party and then slipped quietly out of a side door from the famous Committee Room No. 14 in which he had presided over uncounted similar gatherings. That was the way he chose to end his 20 years' unbroken leadership of a party that he had done more than any other of its leaders to bring to maturity and to shape as a permanent political power in the state. Next day, on December 7, 1955, the Queen conferred an Earldom upon him.

After he left office and particularly after laying down the leadership of the party Attlee travelled widely. The most notable of his visits was his leadership of a Labour Party delegation to Russia and China. But he also paid many visits to Europe, Asia, Africa, and North America, journeying privately, attending conferences, or lecturing with his habitual terseness and restraint.

As time went on he dwelt more and more upon the theme of world government. He also provided timely support for Hugh Gaitskell in the Labour Party conflict over unilateral nuclear disarmament, and in 1961 accepted the presidency of the Campaign of Democratic Socialism. The other issue which provoked him to vehement controversy in his later years was the Common Market: he was an outspoken critic of Britain's application for membership.

Attlee was a successful if not a great Prime Minister. He left his mark on the great office. One of his contributions to British constitutional development was that, as the first Labour Prime Minister with a majority, he quietly and unostentatiously fitted himself into the traditional descent. After the 'betrayal' by MacDonald there had been a persistent movement in the Labour Party to hamstring any future leader by subjecting his choice of Ministers, as in Australia, to the vote of the caucus or party meeting. Attlee did not hold with such notions and on taking office in 1945 he chose his own Ministers in the established manner. He also gave stable and regulated form to the Cabinet committees that had grown up during the war and thus made this system a permanent part of British Cabinet Government.

Family Life

Perhaps more than any other Prime Minister he brought the atmosphere of family life into the dignified abodes of office. He abandoned the attempt to live in the state apartments at 10 Downing Street and converted the previous servants' attics into a family flat in which he led the same domestic life as previously in Stanmore. His Boxing Day parties at Chequers for the children of his ministerial colleagues and private secretaries, which followed year by year exactly the same routine, ending always with the Prime Minister himself standing by the open front door handing every departing child a bag of sweets, were perhaps the occasions when he most unbent and felt most happy.

He was to an extraordinary degree impervious to public criticism and political abuse. Often he failed even to look at the 'popular' press and sometimes his main interest in *The Times* was the crossword puzzle, which he unfailingly solved. He delighted to pore over works of personal reference like *Who's Who*. His sturdiness of character, his unwavering resolution, his staunch but inarticulate love of British things were qualities of the highest worth in the silent revolution at home and in the Commonwealth over which he presided. His integrity was absolute.

He married in 1922 Violet Helen, daughter of the late H. E. Millar of Heath-down, Hampstead, and they had one son, upon whom the family honours now devolve, and three daughters. His wife died in June, 1964.

YURI GAGARIN

First man to fly in space

27 MARCH 1968

YURI GAGARIN, the first man to make a successful flight into space, died in an aircraft crash on Wednesday. He was 34.

One hundred and eight minutes on April 12, 1961, in the front of the Soviet multi-stage rocket, Vostok 1, turned an unknown 27-year-old Soviet Air Force officer into 'The Columbus of the Interplanetary Age' or, as Mr Khrushchev pointedly put it at the wildly enthusiastic reception given to Gagarin in Moscow, 'the first Soviet swallow in the cosmos'. Discarding their usual impersonal style the Soviet radio and news agency mentioned Gagarin's name in the 30 words or so of the historic announcement 'that the road to the planets was open'.

While honours and congratulations from statesmen showered in on Gagarin, painters and sculptors promised to portray him and a street and a new-born child were named after him, it was a young man with a typical Soviet *curriculum vitae* who was undergoing medical tests to ascertain the effects of his extraordinary journey. The son of a collective farmer, he was born on March 9, 1934, in the Gzhatsk district in the Smolensk region of the Russian Federation. The first two big events in his life occurred within two weeks of each other in 1941: he started school and the Germans invaded Russia. His hometown lay directly in the path of the Nazi invaders, and three months later the future spaceman and his parents joined the stream of refugees fleeing eastwards. His elder brother and sister were less fortunate. They were deported by the Germans – but eventually freed by Soviet troops.

When the war ended, Gagarin went back to secondary school, and later to a vocational school at Lyubertsy, near Moscow, where he graduated with honours as a foundryman in 1951. From early childhood he had shown a love of adventure and of flying in particular. One of his favourite authors was the nineteenth-century science fiction writer Jules Verne. As is often the case at technical schools he also attended evening classes in arts subjects. He then entered an industrial college at Saratov on the Volga, graduating with honours in 1955. He began his flying career while still a student, taking a course at the Saratov aero club. After he had finished this course in 1955 he entered the air school at Orenburg. He had been a pilot since 1957.

It was at 0758 (BST) on April 12, 1961, that Tass announced that the first man had been put into space. Moscow radio interrupted its programmes to give the news. The sequence of events and the reports from Gagarin quoted by the radio were:

0707. The spaceship weighing 4.725 kilograms (about 43/4 tons) was launched by rocket into an elliptical orbit with greatest height 187 miles and least 109 miles. The inclination of the orbit to the Equator was 65 deg. 4 mm. The period of revolution was 89min. 6sec.

0722. Gagarin reported by radio that he was over South America and said: 'Flight is proceeding normally. I feel well.'

0815. Gagarin reported over Africa. 'I am withstanding state of weightlessness well.' He also reported over Asia Minor.

0825. The spaceship's braking system was put into operation and Gagarin began his descent.

0855. The spaceship landed safely and Gagarin said on landing: 'Please report to the Party and Government and personally to Nikita Khrushchev that the flight was normal. I feel well. I have no injuries or bruises. The completion of the flight opens new perspectives in the conquering of the cosmos.'

While in flight Tass said that Gagarin carried out direct two-way 'cosmos–earth' radio communications for the first time in history by means of short and ultra-short waves. A special correspondent of *Izvestia*, who was at the landing place, reported that the landing had been an excellent one; Gagarin had not waited for a helicopter. Instead, he walked out to meet the people who had spotted him in the sky.

That he seemed in prime condition was clear from the historic press conference he gave in Moscow the day after his flight had been completed. There were the customary polite remarks about the party and the government, thoughts of whom apparently kept Gagarin from feeling lonely while in the upper airs, but there was also a vivid description of what it had felt like to go right round the great globe itself and what he had seen from his unique point of vantage.

Though much that he then said has since become common knowledge through succeeding space flights his impressions re-read have, even in translation, a certain magic about them that suggests that though a most un-Keats-like man he felt much as Keats felt (in a very different situation) '... like some watcher of the skies when a new planet swims into his ken'.

'The day side of the earth was clearly visible,' he said. 'The coasts of continents, islands, big rivers, big surfaces of water and structural features were clearly distinguishable.'

'During the flight I saw for the first time with my own eyes the earth's spherical shape, you can see its curvature when looking to the horizon. I must say that the view of the horizon is unique and very beautiful.'

'It is possible to see the remarkably colourful change from the light surface of the earth to the completely black sky in which one can see the stars. This dividing line is very thin, just like a belt of film surrounding the earth's sphere.'

'It is of a delicate blue colour and this transition from the blue to the dark is very gradual and lovely. When I emerged from the shadow of the earth, the horizon looked different,' Gagarin continued. 'There was a bright orange strip along it, which again passed into a blue hue and once again into a dense black colour.'

'Everything was easier to perform. Legs and arms weighed nothing.' Objects swam about inside Vostok's cabin and he sat suspended above his chair in mid air, gazing in admiration at the beauty of the earth while floating in a black sky.

'I ate and drank and everything was like on earth.' He said he had no feeling of loneliness, adding that he could have spent much longer in the spaceship but the duration of the flight had been fixed in advance. After the press conference came the full-scale hero's welcome in Moscow where there was a good deal of hugging and kissing with Mr Khrushchev and the bestowal of honours: Hero of the Soviet Union; Order of Lenin; Pilot Cosmonaut of the Soviet Union (newly minted); and Honoured Master of Sport.

Soon afterwards he visited Prague and Sofia and in July arrived in London to a rapturous welcome. Great crowds surrounded him wherever he went and everyone wanted to shake him by the hand. He took luncheon with the Queen, had a talk with the Prime Minister, Mr Macmillan, and flew to Manchester to be made an honorary member of the Foundryworkers Union who presented him, a former moulder, with a gold medal inscribed: 'Together moulding a better world.'

On all these public occasions Gagarin, without conscious effort, won friends; he was a nice-looking young man which was a good start, and he had an engaging manner, but at the long press conference which he held on his arrival in London and at later sessions he showed that he was no empty-pated handsome hero; he handled awkward questions skilfully and when asked about the difficulties of being a celebrity he spoke up with great feeling and sincerity: 'I am still an ordinary mortal,' he said, 'and have not changed in any way.'

The warmth of Gagarin's reception in London, the first western country he visited after his flight, caused a good deal of worried comment and criticism both at home and abroad. In America, Germany, and Switzerland it was interpreted in some circles as showing moral and intellectual softness, gullibility and possible lack of the fibre necessary to meet the approaching Berlin crisis.

Probably there were a number of elements behind the enthusiastic welcome. Foremost, was simple admiration for a brave pioneer; then there was his undoubted charm which went to the heart of crowds but which had not a jot of political significance. Undoubtedly there was also an element of longing which exists among ordinary people on either side of the iron curtain for opportunities to break through the rigidities of the cold war and make contact with the other side.

Gagarin visited many other countries in the years after his space flight including India, Egypt, Czechoslovakia, Canada, Argentina, Brazil and Cuba. It is thought that he never made a second flight, though he played a major role in preparing and training other cosmonauts. He was for several years commander of the Soviet Cosmonauts' Detachment but later handed this post over to Andriyan Nikolayev, who spent almost four days in space in August, 1963, aboard Vostok 3. Gagarin was last seen in public in Moscow in December when he attended the opening night of a Moscow season by the Royal Shakespeare Company.

It was while he was training at the air school at Orenburg that he met an attractive medical student, Valentina, who later became his wife. Their second daughter, Galya, was born shortly after his first space fight.

MARTIN LUTHER KING

Baptist minister who championed Negro rights

4 APRIL 1968

DR MARTIN LUTHER KING, vitriolic champion of Negro civil rights in the South, Nobel Peace Prize winner, and Baptist minister who never tired of turning the other cheek, died on Thursday after being shot. He was 39.

In the maelstrom of racialistic strife, King's strict adherence to non-violence struck a still point of respect for the Negro struggle among millions. The essential dignity of the Negro remained intact: King was 'a kind of modern Moses who has brought new self-respect to southern Negroes'. As regards the ultimate success of the civil rights movement, King's discipline proved that unlike white extremists, Negroes could fight for their rights in a civilized way.

King's non-violence tactics were based on Gandhi's thinking. They went further: he included the Christian element of love – realizing that the reconciliation of the Negroes to the whites was just as important for his cause as vice versa. Unlike Gandhi, King was fighting for the rights of a minority. Unlike the Indian leader, King had no easily defined opponent such as an imperial overlord – he had to conquer the confused racial prejudices and fears of a white, dominant race.

Though initially apolitical, King suddenly found himself the centre of party politics after Kennedy, then a presidential candidate, had rung Mrs King in 1960 at the height of his campaign to express sympathy for King, then imprisoned. For Kennedy the telephone call helped to swing the vital Negro vote.

For King, though he found his stature immediately one of nationwide significance, it meant inviting the contempt from militant Negroes who now had more cause to dub him a contemporary Uncle Tom. For his followers, however, King's youth and idealism appeared remarkably akin to Kennedy's. He was also a minister who no longer preached the comforting words of the more conservative Negro ministers to reconcile their brethren to their lot. King abandoned his political neutrality in 1964 – urging Negroes to shun Goldwater.

King was born on January 15, 1929, at Atlanta, where his father was a Baptist preacher, as was his maternal grandfather. Both had been involved in Negro protests against discrimination at one time or another. Twice before he was 13 King attempted suicide: in both cases jumping from a second storey window. The first time was after he thought his grandmother dead; the second after she actually died. In both instances he was unhurt.

Martin Luther King, with Canon Collins, at St Paul's Cathedral, where he preached in 1964.

King was a bright pupil: at the age of 15 he entered Atlanta's Negro Morehouse College, where his father had studied before him. He wanted to be a doctor or a lawyer, but two years later chose the ministry – always his father's wish. He was ordained and named assistant pastor in his father's church. After completing a degree in sociology he went to the Crozer Theological Seminary in Chester, Pennsylvania, where he was the most outstanding student of his year. There he realized the futility of protesting against racial discrimination using only the normal legal channels. There, too, Hegel, Kant, and Gandhi's thinking had their influence on him. In 1955 he was awarded a doctorate by Boston University. Meanwhile he had married a young soprano, Coretta Scott, and become the pastor of an upper-income church in Montgomery – the Dexter Avenue Baptist Church. His thinking on racial issues still tended towards the conservative approach of the NAACP, and the interracial Alabama Council on Human Relations of which he was vice-president.

Then, in December, 1955, he was suddenly thrust into the vortex of a struggle which had all the markings of violence. A Negro seamstress, Rosa Parks, had refused to give up her seat in a bus for a white as she was required to do under local ordinances. Her arrest triggered off a boycott of the bus service by the Negroes – which stretched out to 382 days. King presided over the boycott committee – later known as the Montgomery Improvement Association – which was at first modest in its demands to the authorities. Balked however by white organized opposition, the fight intensified, until finally – and ironically for King's demonstration tactics – a Supreme Court order imposed desegregation on the Alabama buses. Nevertheless, King emerged triumphant: despite bombing of his house, riot-thirsting followers, his own arrest, he had remained calm and courageous. More – he had managed to keep his followers under control. The fruits of victory were his – he became president of the newly founded SCLC; he was among the speakers who addressed the thousands who made the Prayer Pilgrimage to the Lincoln Monument in 1957; he was invited to the independence ceremonies of Ghana; he was Nehru's guest.

The Negro struggle however waned in its intensity. The emancipation of African colonies had its effect, but the eventual prod came from youth demonstrations in 1958 and 1959. King decided to hurl himself wholeheartedly into the civil rights movement – resigning his pastorship in 1960. He strove to channel the mounting student discontent in a Student Nonviolent Coordinating Committee.

In December, 1961, came a dismal turning point: King's attack on Albany, Georgia, fizzled out. He had vowed he would stay in gaol until the city agreed to desegregate public facilities. But after two days he was out – on bail. He was bitterly attacked for this fiasco. His next major attack on Birmingham – a centre of diehard segregationists – redeemed his reputation. He had carefully recruited non-violent demonstrators willing to be gaoled. Next he worked for the ultimate confrontation – or 'crisis' – so necessary to put his cause across. His initial sally was postponed more than once: just before Easter, 1963, he declared he would lead demonstrations in Birmingham until 'Pharaoh lets God's people go'.

Though certain Negro clergymen thought his timing bad, King was right in sensing the tension in the Negro community there. The mass demonstrations and sit-ins had their full backing. More than 3,300, including King himself, were gaoled. It seemed as if in 'Bull' Connor, the defeated mayor who had refused to relinquish office, the Negroes had met their match. Then, on May 7, the police, using dogs, fire hoses, and clubs, turned on the Negro crowds – children and all. Within hours this 'crisis' was making headline news throughout the world. King had triumphed. As Kennedy put it later to him: 'The civil rights movement owes Bull Connor as much as it owes Abraham Lincoln.'

When King's wife heard nothing from her husband after his arrest in Birmingham, she tried to reach the President. Once before in 1960, Kennedy, then a presidential candidate, had rung her to express his sympathy. Now he rang again to offer his reassurance. Kennedy did more – a Civil Rights Bill (eventually passed after his assassination) was quickly drawn up. King was released. In gaol he had written a

Letter from Birmingham Jail setting out his objects. Later that summer he delivered his 'I have a dream' oration, with its peroration of 'Let freedom ring' to the millions who marched to the Lincoln Monument.

Only a few years before, under Eisenhower, he had pleaded 'Give us the ballot' in the same place. Now there was quicker desegregation in schools, in swimming pools and restaurants. *Time* magazine named King its Man of the Year. He was awarded a Nobel Peace Prize in 1964, the youngest man ever to get it. He had now become a civil rights leader of international repute. But in the wake of the new-won rights, the ugly terrorism of the white backlash erupted.

In the centenary year of the Emancipation Proclamation which had freed the Negroes from physical slavery, King made an assault on St Augustine, Florida. For his purposes it was a good target: a totally segregated city celebrating its 400th anniversary, and it had a strong local SCLC following. King's group fought with stand-ins, swim-ins, night mass marches – only to meet with terrorism from white reactionaries and few gains. Nothing daunted, King made an attack on Selma, Alabama, in 1965, to register more voters.

Here he was assaulted by a white reactionary, and also arrested. But this time President Johnson called for the nation to exert moral pressure on behalf of the Negroes and threatened to send federal troops. King called for a national boycott of the state of Alabama. Segregation, he said, was on its deathbed – it was merely a matter of how expensive Mr George Wallace, the Governor of Alabama, and others were going to make the funeral. For the Negroes, however, with the failure of the southern courts to convict in cases involving race relations, matters were reaching stalemate. In 1966 King led a march into a Ku-Klux-Klan stronghold – Philadelphia, Mississippi – where three civil rights workers had been murdered two years before.

At the end of October last year he spent four days behind bars at Bessemer, Alabama, for taking part in an illegal demonstration four years earlier. In November, he received an honorary doctorate from Newcastle University.

King wrote several books: *Stride Towards Freedom*, which told the story of the Montgomery boycott, and *Why We Can't Wait*, which told of the 1963 protests; *Chaos and Community* appeared this year.

ENID BLYTON

Froebel teacher who became author of best-selling children's books

28 NOVEMBER 1968

MISS ENID BLYTON, who died yesterday, was perhaps the most successful and most controversial children's author of the post-war period. Certainly she was the most productive: at her death something like 400 titles stood to her name.

Inevitably, her name is linked with her creation (or, as those who disliked her work called him) her creature, Noddy. Noddy became a household name. Though a figure of fiction, fiction could not hold him; he became a hot commercial property. At different times you could find him on the West End stage, on the back of breakfast food packets, on the handles of toothbrushes, and in the form of an egg-cup. He was loathed by many adults – particularly librarians – and loved by many children. The antis found him odious, unwholesome, and wet – he was said to weep when confronted by some intractable Toyland problem. The case for the antis was crystallized some years ago in a witty article in *Encounter*. But it is probably true to say that those children who enjoyed Noddy were not much influenced by the knockers. They looked on the works of Miss Blyton and found them good. They could not see what all the fuss was about.

However, to judge the prolific Miss Blyton solely on the merits of the mini-adventures of Noddy, Big Ears and Mr Plod would be unfair. The enormous success of her Famous Five and Secret Seven series and the enduring popularity of such books as *The Island of Adventure*, *The Sea of Adventure*, and *The Valley of Adventure* was earned for she could write a readable tale, a tale with action in it, and a tale that children, shrewd critics, found credible.

The daughter of T. C. Blyton, her early years are not easy to chart exactly; she was not one to favour the publisher's practice of printing on the dust-jacket of a book a piece about its author. She was born in the late 1890s and brought up and educated in Beckenham; she was musical, taking her LRAM at an early age. Her father wished her to become a concert pianist but she had already decided that she would write for children and to prepare for this left home and took Froebel training. Subsequently she was governess to a family of boys in Surrey and this experience encouraged her to open a small school of her own.

By now she was writing stories, poems, and plays for her pupils, the themes and ideas for these often coming from the children, and contributing regularly to *Teacher's World*. Her first published book, *Child Whispers*, a collection of poems,

Enid Blyton at home with her husband, Kenneth Waters, and her two daughters, 1949.

appeared in 1922. Her first stories were published by George Newnes and she was intimately connected with the popular children's magazine *Sunny Stories*. It was at Newnes that she met and in 1924 married her first husband, Lieutenant-Colonel H. A. Pollock. After her marriage she spread her wings yet further editing books on teaching and a children's encyclopaedia.

Early in the 1940s it was suggested to her by a London publisher that she should emulate Angela Brazil and write school stories for girls. She took the advice and the tales she wrote went like hot cakes. So successful were they after the Second World War when there was a continuing shortage of paper and printing facilities that it was difficult to keep them in stock. At least three publishers were taking her work. Books of all kinds flowed from her pen; she produced an abridged edition of T. A. Coward's *Birds of the British Isles and their Eggs*, a children's life of Christ, some Old Testament tales, a version of *Pilgrim's Progress*, readers for class use, and books on botany and volumes of verse. These, of course, in addition to her immensely popular Secret Seven and Famous Five series. Her success was not loved by the public librarians who in some cases imposed sanctions against her books. Children asked for her books and were told they were not in stock. Cold war broke out. While the librarians were probably unwise to betray their prejudices so openly, Miss Blyton was perhaps wrong in contending that children should have what they liked no matter what other books were squeezed out. Whoever was in the right the fact remains that though Miss Blyton's writings were not great literature they were harmless, as any adult who has worked through a bout of Secret Seven or Famous Five knows.

There are many children who can read but do not read much; they find Miss Nesbitt or *The Lion, the Witch and the Wardrobe* just a little too much for them; Miss Blyton they pick up and they are away; they are better catered for now but it was not always so. Undoubtedly she helped many a child on the frontiers of book reading to take his first step.

She did not frequently get what is called a good press and over the years became as cagey as Marie Corelli about herself and her affairs. Yet her relations with children were of the best. Many years ago she reluctantly agreed to speak at a children's book week and arrived not noticeably well turned out. She was a huge success. On the spot it was arranged that she should appear each day. For many years after that she was a first choice at one famous book fair and always drew packed houses.

Her second husband, Kenneth Waters, FRCS, whom she married in 1943, died in 1967. She leaves two daughters by her first marriage.

WALTER GROPIUS

Influential modern architectural philosopher

5 JULY 1969

DR WALTER GROPIUS, the architect, who died in Boston at the age of 86, had been for many years one of the major world forces working towards an architecture that acknowledged and exploited modern technology. With his master, Peter Behrens, with Le Corbusier in France, Aalto in Finland, and Frank Lloyd Wright in the United States he may be classed as one of the most influential architects of modern times: and his influence was spread not only by example but by precept issuing from the Bauhaus at Dessau, that great institution which combined all the crafts in one philosophic unity and brought the work of the artist into the closest association with industry.

Gropius was nevertheless always on his guard against abstract terms like 'functionalism' (which he did not scruple to call 'catchwords'), and deprecated the propaganda which would make the new architecture a fashion 'as snobbish as any of the older academic fashions which it aims to displace'. His attitude was based not only on the frank acceptance and full exploitation of steel, glass, and reinforced concrete but on the realization that the day of the individual craftsman was done. He regarded the craftsman's role, in the modern industrial age, as that of creating well conceived and serviceable building components capable of being multiplied in quantity by mass production.

This great architectural philosopher and teacher was driven from his own country by the Nazi regime. Germany's loss might have been England's gain, for Gropius lived and worked among us for three years, but in the end it was America which offered him a post consonant with his status, the Chair of Architecture at Harvard.

Walter Gropius was born in Berlin on May 18, 1883, the son of an architect, Walter Adolf Gropius, and his wife Manon Scharnweber. From his formative years he determined to follow his father's profession; and after studying at the technical high-schools at Charlottenburg and Munich he worked as assistant to Peter Behrens, one of the fathers of modern architecture, and it was in this period that his originality and far sightedness began to emerge.

In 1910 Gropius set up his own office; and in the following year, working with Adolf Meyer, produced one of the most remarkable industrial buildings of pre-war years. This was the Fagus shoe-last factory at Alfeld-an-der-Leine, which had the forthright cubic outline and the huge areas of glass which were later to become associated with modern factory architecture. In 1914 he designed the Hall of Machinery for the Cologne exhibition of the Deutscher Werkbund, and (with Adolf Meyer) the Administrative Building at the same exhibition. From August, 1914, he served for some three years and a half as an air observer in the war, winning the Iron Cross of the first class and being shot down on one occasion by the French. Meanwhile, in 1915, he had been granted leave to discuss with the Grand Duke of Saxe-Weimar his taking control of the Saxon Academy of Arts and Crafts from the Belgian architect Henry van de Velde, who had himself suggested Gropius as his successor.

After the war Gropius took over two schools, the Grossherzogliche Sächsische Kunstgewerbeschule and the Grossherzogliche Sächsische Hochschule für Bild-ende Kunst, combining these institutions in 1919 as the Staatliches Bauhaus, at Weimar. Here he gathered round him a brilliant group of instructors and began to put into effect his theories about the relationship of design to industry. But he was severely hampered by the obscurantist attitude of the Government of Thuringia, and in April, 1925, left Weimar to start afresh in the smaller town of Dessau.

Now began a fruitful period of teaching, experimentation, craftwork, and build-ing that was to have incalculably beneficial effects on architecture in every civilized country. The Bauhaus at Dessau has been described as 'the one school in the world where modern problems of design were approached realistically in a modern atmosphere'. A distinguished team of professors included Johannes Itten, Oskar Schlemmer, Wassily Kandinsky, László Moholy-Nagy, and Paul Klee.

The Bauhaus building itself, begun in autumn, 1925, and finished in December 1926, was a triumphant vindication of the principles of its architect and of the lines on which he had educated the students who worked on it. The whole of its interior decorations and fittings were produced in its own workshops.

At Dessau, as at Weimar, Gropius encountered vigorous and often ill-informed criticism from official bodies, craft organizations and so forth, and the press was full of controversy. Though he had forbidden any kind of political activity in the school it was constantly urged by his enemies that the Bauhaus was a centre of 'bolshevism'; and in 1928 Gropius gave up the struggle.

Meanwhile Gropius had continued with his private practice. In 1926 he designed two houses for the Weissenhof permanent housing exhibition at Stutt-gart, to which several of the most famous European architects contributed designs. In 1929 he won first prize in the Spandau-Haselhorst housing competition, and although the design was never executed it exerted considerable influence.

His most noteworthy designs of this kind in Germany actually carried out were those for the large Siemensstadt estate near Berlin. Gropius was the supervising architect for the scheme in which several others collaborated, and he was responsible for two of the blocks. In this scheme he was able to put many of his theories into practice. Among the best in Europe at the time it was designed and served as a model for much subsequent work.

The rise of Nazi power brought with it hard times and hard words for modern-minded artists, and in 1934 Gropius left Germany for London, along with several other architects who had become refugees from Nazi persecution. These included the late Erich Mendelsohn and the Hungarian-born Marcel Breuer, who had taught under Gropius at the Bauhaus and was later to become Gropius's partner in America. Gropius set up in practice in London in partnership with Mr E. Maxwell Fry. He stayed for three years, and during that period he and Fry made several interesting projects, including an influential and prophetic one for high flats in a park-like setting at Windsor, and they were the architects of several buildings including Impington Village College, Cambridgeshire (1936), which was one of the four village colleges erected by the county council in support of the late Henry Morris's educational ideas with which Gropius found himself in close sympathy. A one-storey building with single depth classrooms, fan-shaped hall and club amen-ities, it serves the dual purpose of a secondary school, library and local community centre.

Early in 1937 Gropius was appointed Senior Professor of Architecture at Har-vard University, and the following year he became Chairman of the Department of Architecture. He quickly began work on a house for his own occupation. A modern version of the traditional New England house, it has much of the classic serenity of the houses that he had designed for himself and the Bauhaus teachers in 1926.

For the first four years after his arrival he entered into partnership with Marcel Breuer, who had followed him from England. Between 1943 and 1948 Gropius resumed his experiments with standardized building elements for mass-produced housing which he had begun in Germany in 1932. His new experiments, chiefly with houses composed of timber panels based on a module both horizontally and vertically of 40 inches, were made in collaboration with Konrad Wachsmann in Long Island, and examples were erected on a considerable scale in California.

In 1945 Gropius went into partnership with several architects of the younger generation forming a team of eight under the name of 'The Architects, Collabor-ative'. In this enterprise Gropius was the guide and leading spirit. That he was able to work enthusiastically with so large a group demonstrates his great belief in the value of team work, which he had always felt to be necessary in modern building. Buildings for which the team has been responsible include the Harvard University Graduate Centre, Cambridge, Massachusetts (1949–50), the McCormick office buildings in Chicago (1953), and the United States embassy building in Athens (1961). In recent years Gropius's name reappeared on English building sites as a result of his agreeing to become consulting architect for several big property developments, notably that of the (still vacant) Monico site in Piccadilly Circus.

Gropius's work as a designer of buildings however, though necessary to him as a means of keeping him in touch with the practical problems of a rapidly changing profession, was not as outstanding as his great reputation might suggest; only his Bauhaus building at Dessau can claim a place among the significant buildings of this century. His reputation was due to his vision as an architectural philosopher, his understanding – far in advance of his time – of the nature of architecture's place in the industrialized world of today and his dedication and integrity as a teacher. The whole essence of the challenge that the twentieth-century architect must face was contained in the ideas he spent his life expounding, and the reason why in the past few years, his name was less frequently than hitherto on the younger architects' lips was simply that those ideas – through Gropius's efforts – had become widely accepted and were no longer revolutionary. Nevertheless, the opportunities the younger generation of architects now enjoy owe to him more than to anyone else. Gropius was an honorary FRIBA, vice-president of the Congrès Internationaux de l'Architecture Moderne (at whose conferences he was a revered and influential figure) and an Honorary RDI. In 1956 he was awarded the Royal Gold Medal for Architecture. He presided over numerous international committees including those responsible for appointing and briefing the architects of the Uno building, New York, and the Unesco building, Paris. His writings include *Staatliches Bauhaus* (1923), *Internationale Architektur* (1924), *Bauhaus Bauten* (1933), *The New Architecture and the Bauhaus* (1935), and *Bauhaus 1919–28* (1939), this last edited with his wife, Ilse Frank, and Herbert Bayer.

BERTRAND RUSSELL

Philosopher who sought involvement with problems of the age

2 FEBRUARY 1970

EARL RUSSELL, OM, FRS, died last night at his home, Plas Penrhyn, Merioneth-shire. He was 97.

Bertrand Russell's claim to be remembered by history rests securely on his work in mathematical and symbolic logic and in philosophy, on which his influence was pervasive and profound. The story of symbolic logic and of the philosophy of mathematics in the twentieth century is the story of the expansion of the edifice which Russell and Frege founded. There have been major reconstructions, but they are reconstructions from within. In general philosophy, when we think of G. E. Moore and Ludwig Wittgenstein as shapers of the thought of our half-century, we are thinking of men who were fired by Russell and themselves gave Russell fire. There exist no disciples of Russell. Instead there exist scores of inquiring philos-ophers driven by questions which Russell was the first to ask. For Russell not only combined the hardihood of the extremist with the candour of the artist: he also had a lively sense of the ridiculous. So, if there were logical absurdities latent inside his own abstract constructions, he exposed them with cheerful callousness. The incongruities which he would not hide have become the cruces of philosophy.

Russell looked every inch a Russell and had all the 'crankiness' of a Russell. He spoke his mind with Olympian disregard of the censure he might incur from established persons or received opinions or for that matter the law, which twice committed him to prison. He was throughout his life an ornament and an acquisi-tion to a variety of public causes generally of an unpopular kind. Into the last and for him the greatest of these, unilateral nuclear disarmament, he threw himself, now in his mid-eighties, with unabated fervour, seized with the mission of rousing his fellow men to the peril in which they stood. He was obsessed by the enormity of the evil of which these weapons could be the instrument. In the intensity of his denunciation and the galvanic activity of his failing powers there came to be less and less room for sober assessment of the political means of deliverance from the doom so vividly before his mind.

He was the intellectual in the twentieth century who, perhaps, before all others in this country, solved the problem of communications. Russell found a way of communicating with ordinary men, and explored it to the full, especially, and deliberately, in his later life. There was nothing new in the method. He merely expressed lucid thoughts in a lucid style. But how few of the thinkers or artists who were contemporary with him could do half as much!

Equally important, he could use not just terms of language but terms of reference which were intelligible to ordinary men and women, because they were inside their experience. Here was a man of uncommon ancestry, uncommon intellectual brilliance, uncommon habits of mind and behaviour, who yet was at ease in addressing common men – and they were at ease in listening to him. The answer is to be found in the paradox that he yet shared with them a common ancestry. His thought was English to the core. He dallied with Hegelianism when he was at Cambridge, but no one with his roots as firmly in English thought and in England – Whig England at that – could have long remained an apostle of Hegel.

The Right Honourable Bertrand Arthur William Russell, third Earl Russell, was born at Ravenscroft, near Tintern, in Monmouthshire, on May 18, 1872. He was the second son of Viscount Amberley and grandson of Lord John Russell, who had been created Earl Russell at the end of his long political life. His mother was Katherine, daughter of the second Lord Stanley of Alderley. He was as much a Russell as his elder brother, the second Earl, was a Stanley. In his appearance, his artistic qualities, and his versatility the Russell genius found expression. Russell would have been the first to admit that much of his life was determined by his early years, which were not calculated to produce a conventional citizen. His father and mother had moved from orthodoxy to agnosticism before his birth. But his mother died when he was two, his father when he was three, and he was placed under the care of his grandmother, 'a Puritan with the moral rigidity of the Covenanters', as he called her, who maintained a gloomy theism at Pembroke Lodge. His father had directed that the two children should be brought up agnostics and had appointed two free-thinkers as guardians, but the direction was set aside in court and the children made wards in Chancery.

Until he went to Cambridge, Bertrand Russell lived (not very happily) and was educated by governesses and tutors, at home. Cambridge was his first release into the outside world, 'a new world,' as he said, 'of infinite delight', and of friends such as Lowes Dickinson, Dr Trevelyan, McTaggart, and G. E. Moore. The last two cast their spell over him. Under J. M. F. McTaggart's influence he became for some time a Hegelian, or, more precisely, a Bradleian, but Moore, whose influence on the whole of that Cambridge generation was so profound and so fortunate, broke Hegel's spell. Russell had gone to Trinity College as a scholar in 1890, but was only bracketed seventh Wrangler in 1893. His relatively low position may be explained by the fact that mathematics interested him not so much for its own sake as for being an example of certain knowledge; his interest was philosophical. The following year he took a First Class in the Moral Science Tripos with exceptional distinction. On going down from Cambridge he spent some months as honorary attaché at the British Embassy in Paris, and later made in Berlin a study of social and economic questions which bore fruit early in 1896 in six lectures on German Social Democracy for the London School of Economics. But the political career which seemed marked out for him by his heritage was abandoned – if he had ever seriously considered it – in favour of the greater interest of laying afresh the foundations of mathematics, and his later resumptions of political interest were always, until nearer the end of his life, rather desultory.

In 1895 he had been elected a lecturer at Trinity, and in 1896 he lectured in America on non-Euclidean geometry. He published an *Essay on the Foundations of Geometry*, and then his training in mathematics and philosophy led him to study the thinker in whom their union was most perfectly exemplified. His *Critical Exposition of the Philosophy of Leibniz*, a work of great distinction, was published in 1900 – his first major work. It set a higher estimate on Leibniz's thought than was usual at the time – an estimate he never altered, describing Leibniz, in his *History of Western Philosophy*, as 'one of the supreme intellects of all time'. Russell's judgment was, of course, founded on his recognition of Leibniz as 'a pioneer in mathematical logic, of which he perceived the importance when no one else did'. This was the field in which Russell was to do his most revolutionary work, and in outlook as well as in achievement he resembled Leibniz closely.

In 1900, at a mathematical congress in Paris, Russell drew attention to the works of Peano, and in 1903 to those of Frege – at the time the two most immediate influences on his thought. It was their explorations and those of Leibniz which led him in 1903 to give to the world his *Principles of Mathematics*, whose purpose was 'first, to show that all mathematics follows from symbolic logic, and, secondly, to discover, so far as possible, what are the principles of symbolic logic itself'. The *Principles of Mathematics* was intended to be a first volume to be followed by a second giving a deductive exposition of results. This task was in fact carried out in a separate work in collaboration with A. N. Whitehead. Their *Principia Mathematica* was begun in 1900 and completed 10 years later in three volumes, which were published in 1910, 1912, and 1913 respectively. It was republished, with a new introduction, in 1925 and in succeeding years. The Royal Society, into whose Fellowship Russell had been admitted in 1908, made a grant towards publication from the Government fund. Of its composition Russell later wrote: My intellect never quite recovered from the strain. I have been ever since definitely less capable of dealing with difficult abstractions than I was before.'

Principia Mathematica is one of the decisive books in the history both of mathematics and of logic. More completely and satisfactorily than in any previous work, the reduction of mathematics to a branch of logic was effected. In the course of the reduction a new symbolism, of great logical power in skilled hands, was developed. It was the use of this power which was Russell's most enduring contribution to philosophical thought and the most constant feature of all his philosophical writings. He himself termed his contribution 'Logical Atomism', and it is a term which does justice to his skill and perception in logical analysis – his attempt to break down complex ideas into, if not simple, at least irrefutable components.

The details of Russell's achievement, which allows one, without the least exaggeration – in terms of British thought at least – to talk of pre-Russell and post-Russell philosophy, are the concern of the student of philosophy. But even the layman can comprehend the value of freeing logical analysis from the tyranny of ordinary grammar or syntax. 'The utility of philosophical syntax in relation to traditional problems is very great' – such was his own modest estimate of his achievement late in his life.

The point is best illustrated by a summary of one of his most important discoveries, the theory of descriptions, first developed in *On Denoting*, published in *Mind* in 1905. Such phrases as 'The present President of the United States' have caused a lot of fruitless distress to philosophers trying to find the meaning of existence. 'Suppose I say "The golden mountain does not exist", and suppose you ask "What is the golden mountain?" It would seem that, if I say "It is the golden mountain", I am attributing some sort of existence to it.' In the two phrases 'The golden mountain does not exist' and 'The round square does not exist' the only difference lies in the words 'The golden mountain' and 'The round square', implying that the one is one thing and the other another, although neither exists. It was this problem which Russell sought to meet by the theory of descriptions. The statement 'Scott was the author of *Waverley*' is, by this theory, interpreted as saying: 'There is an entity c such that the statement "x wrote *Waverley*" is true if x is c and false otherwise: moreover c is Scott.' Thus 'The golden mountain does not exist' means: 'There is no entity c such that "x is golden and mountainous" is true when x is c, but not otherwise.' 'Existence' therefore, can only be asserted of descriptions. Russell was scarcely putting his claim too high when he said of the theory that it 'clears up two millennia of muddle-headedness about "existence", beginning with Plato's *Thætretus*'.

In 50 years of philosophical writing Russell used the destructive power of this logical technique to examine the traditional problems and traditional philosophies, and the mere use of the technique, however acceptable or unacceptable his conclusions, was a source of clarification and enlightenment, particularly in his analysis of relations, classes, continuity, infinity, and language forms. His progressive extension of methodological doubt into every field of philosophical inquiry is his most lasting monument. The incorporation of mathematics and the development of a powerful logical technique were, as he himself said, what distinguished his modern analytical empiricism from that of Locke, Berkeley, and Hume. Empirical knowledge and deductive knowledge were the only two kinds of knowledge which Russell was prepared to admit. He sought answers to the problems of philosophy which had 'the quality of science rather than philosophy'. He admitted that there might be problems to which science and the intellect could not find the answers, but he refused to admit that there was any other way, intuitive or otherwise, by which the answers could be found.

Russell's empiricism is perhaps the most valid quality in his erratic and usually 'popular' intrusions into political philosophy. He was no political philosopher. But a man born with the blood of the Russells in his veins could hardly avoid carrying the spirit of Locke in his head. 'The only philosophy,' he wrote in *Philosophy and Politics* in 1947, 'that affords a theoretical justification of democracy, and that accords with democracy in its temper of mind, is empiricism. Locke, who may be regarded as the founder of empiricism, makes it clear how closely this is connected with his views on liberty and toleration.' From this Russell argued that 'the essence of the Liberal out-look lies not in what opinions are held but in how they are held; instead of being held dogmatically, they are held tentatively'. It cannot be said that he himself followed this precept in all his public utterances.

In 1907 he stood unsuccessfully for Parliament as a woman suffrage candidate at Wimbledon. But it was the 1914–18 War which was to find an outlet for his unsatisfied impulse to do good. Without hesitation he flung himself wholeheartedly into the pacifist campaign. The unhappy results made him a national storm-centre and need be only summarily recalled. In *The Times* he avowed the authorship of a pamphlet for the No-Conscription Fellowship and was duly fined £100 at the Mansion House and removed, with petty illiberality, from his lectureship at Trinity College. His library there was seized to pay the fine. In the autumn of that year, 1916, he was due to lecture at Harvard, but it was made known to the Harvard authorities that the British Government did not consider it in the public interest to issue a passport enabling him to leave the country.

In September of the same year he was forbidden from entering any prohibited area and a little later a book, *Justice in Wartime*, in which he likened the warrings of nations to the fighting of dogs angered by each other's smell, caused great resentment. Finally, in February, 1918, he was sentenced at Bow Street to six months' imprisonment for having, in the organ of the No-Conscription Fellowship, made comments on the American Army 'intended and likely to prejudice his Majesty's relations with the United States'. On appeal the sentence was ordered to be served in the first instead of the second division. It was while he was in prison that he wrote his *Introduction to Mathematical Philosophy*.

After the war he allowed his mind to range over almost the whole gamut of human studies. A visit to Russia in 1920 with the British Labour delegation left him unimpressed by the 'military dictatorship' of the Bolsheviks. He immediately uttered his first warning of what Bolshevism really was – in his *Practice and Theory of Bolshevism* – and he remained a critic of Soviet Communism even during the 1939–45 War, when Russia's popularity was at its height. His *Analysis of Mind* was the book form of some lectures given in London, and was published in 1921. Meanwhile, in 1920, he went to China for a brief period as Professor of Philosophy at Peking. It led to the publication of *The Problem of China*, a peg on which he hung his animus against western and Japanese civilization. On returning from China he stood unsuccessfully, in 1922 and 1923, as Labour candidate for Chelsea. Between the *A.B.C. of Atoms* (1923) and the *A.B.C. of Relativity* (1925), both beautifully lucid expositions, was sandwiched *The Prospects of Industrial Civilisation*, written in collaboration with his second wife.

In 1927 their interest in education led them to establish near Petersfield a school where a great measure of licence was allowed to the children; in 1934 his wife removed it to Hertfordshire. He wrote two books on the subject, *On Education*, in 1926, and *Education and the Social Order*, in 1932; in them modern tendencies were carried to exaggerated lengths. Between these books appeared *The Analysis of Matter*, a magnificent review of modern physics, with more questionable metaphysical deductions. Other books followed: An *Outline of Philosophy*, *Sceptical Essays*, *Marriage and Morals*, and the *Conquest of Happiness*. In his books on social and ethical questions Russell mixed with his sometimes revolutionary ethic some wise advice. He could not write a chapter which, however unacceptable his conclusions, did not contain some provoking, stimulating, or penetrating observation. He certainly, in such offerings, often wrote trivially, on weighty matters, throwing away sense for the sake of a jest or a paradox. But they had a more serious intent and the perceptive reader could usually find and profit by it.

In 1934 he published his most considerable work outside the realms of logic and philosophy. *Freedom and Organisation* traced the main causes of political, economic, and social change in Europe and America during the nineteenth century. It foreshadowed his monumental *History of Western Philosophy* by its attempt to see ideas in the context of the age which gave them birth. But it was quite different in construction from the later work, being more of a synthesis than an analysis, and it contained some of his most sparkling writing.

Russell, during the thirties, was being profoundly influenced by the rise of Hitler, confessing to a Fabian gathering that it had almost persuaded him to become a Christian. But though the success of such an irrational force as Hitlerism shook, as with so many others, so many of his rationalist predispositions, and made him abandon pacifism, and although he sought (but failed) to analyze the nature of power in a popular book, he lacked the political equipment to reach a satisfactory statement of the twentieth century's political problem. This was apparent in the

Reith lectures which he delivered in 1948–49 on *Authority and the Individual*. He chose the wrong subject on which to speak, but he left no doubt of his ability to relate complex ideas to ordinary men's everyday experience.

During the later years of his life Russell was in some danger of becoming a popular, a revered, even a respectable figure. He was awarded the Nobel Prize for Literature in 1950, and the year before had been given the OM. In 1953 the man who had once been judicially pronounced unfit to hold an academic chair at a certain American university was elected an honorary associate of the New York National Institute of Arts and Letters. His could have been the serene old age of a tame philosopher, a domesticated sage, publicly honoured, listened to with affection and respect, vouchsafing the occasional quip often enough and sharp enough to keep alive the legend of the rebel.

He chose otherwise. There still echoes in the memory a broadcast he gave in 1954 after the explosion of the first hydrogen bomb, his thin, sing-song voice charged with the detached intensity of a prophet: 'Remember your humanity and forget the rest. If you can do so, the way lies open to a new paradise: if you cannot, nothing lies before you but universal death.' It was the warning he was to reiterate, with a rising pitch of stridency, until the end of his life.

He assisted at the birth of the Campaign for Nuclear Disarmament in February, 1958, and became its president. Before and after that he strove to mobilize the opinions of scientists in support of his views. In September 1960, impatient of the law-abiding methods of CND and finding its chairman, Canon Collins, 'impossible to work with', he branched out with the Committee of 100 'for civil disobedience against nuclear warfare'. The disobedience proved to be of a fairly orderly kind, and Russell, who was then 88, continued to speak for the campaign up and down the country, to issue urgent statements to the press, and to stage public demonstrations to the extent that his health allowed. He also made a practice of sending admonitory telegrams to world leaders, notably at the height of the Cuban crisis in October, 1962.

His defiance of authority again led to imprisonment. In September, 1961, he was summoned with others of the Committee of 100 for inciting members of the public to commit a breach of the peace – a forthcoming sit-down demonstration in Parliament Square. Having refused to be bound over to be of good behaviour, he was sentenced to two months' imprisonment, a term which the magistrates reduced to seven days after representations by Russell's counsel. He served the sentence in Brixton prison, with which he had become acquainted 43 years before.

At the beginning of 1963 Russell resigned the presidency of the Committee of 100, stating among his reasons that he had become occupied with work of a different kind, though directed towards the same end. And later in the year he announced the launching of two foundations, the Bertrand Russell Peace Foundation and the Atlantic Peace Foundation, whose purpose was to develop inter-national resistance to the threat of nuclear war. In his last years he lived in growing isolation at Plas Penrhyn, his country home in North Wales. His dealings with the outside world were conducted by his secretary Mr Ralph Shoenman; while his public undertakings to which he attached his name became increasingly bizarre – like his international war crimes tribunal, in which a bench of celebrated intellec-tuals were to try the United States in absentia on charges arising out of its policies in Vietnam. After some difficulty over a venue, the tribunal held its first session in Stockholm, and returned a unanimous verdict of Guilty.

These controversial activities, inspiring to some, misdirected or ridiculous to others, obscured in his final years the extraordinary achievements of his long life; his influence on philosophy and, something the general public had better reason to remember, his genius as a popularizer of unfamiliar or difficult ideas. He retained the style which puts him in the company of Berkeley and Hume, who adorned literature as well as philosophy. Whether he wrote in symbols or in words he was equally dextrous and equally happy. His clear-cut antitheses, his magnifi-cent self-assurance, his polished ruthlessness of argument, his dazzling paradoxes, his wit and gaiety are the envy of all others who try to write. When passion intruded, when the Whig possessed the philosopher, his writing must be ranked with the noblest in the language. He was equally a master of the microphone and gave several memorable series of broadcasts after the war. His vignettes of some of his eminent contemporaries, crisp, witty, half-mocking, half-sympathetic, recalled the succinct vivacity of John Aubrey's sketches. In 1967 the first part of his autobiogra-phy was published, 1872–1914. It had been delivered to the publishers 10 years before. Though rather sketchy in his provision of conventional biographical material Russell, taking relish in his candour, is unusually informative about his love affairs in and out of marriage.

Russell was four times married: first to Alys Whitall Pearsall, daughter of the late Robert Pearsall Smith. The marriage was dissolved in 1921, and in the same year he married Dora Winifred, daughter of the late Sir Frederick Black. The mar-riage was dissolved in 1935, and in 1936 he married Patricia Helen, daughter of Mr Harry Evelyn Spence. The marriage was dissolved in 1952, and in the same year he married Edith, daughter of Mr Edward Bronson Finch, of New York. By his second marriage Russell had two children, John Conrad, the Viscount Amberley, and Lady Katherine Jane Russell. By his third marriage he had a son, the Honourable Conrad Sebastian Robert Russell. He is succeeded in the peerage by Viscount Amberley, who was born in 1921 and married, in 1946, Susan Doninhan, daughter of the late Vachel Lindsay, by whom he has two daughters.

JIMI HENDRIX

A key figure in the development of pop music

18 SEPTEMBER 1970

JIMI HENDRIX, the pop musician, died in London yesterday, as reported elsewhere in this issue.

If Bob Dylan was the man who liberated pop music verbally, to the extent that, after him it could deal with subjects other than teenage affection, then Jimi Hendrix was largely responsible for whatever musical metamorphosis it has undergone in the past three years.

Born in Seattle, Washington, he was part Negro, part Cherokee Indian, part Mexican, and gave his date of birth as November 27, 1945. He left school early, picked up the guitar, and hitch-hiked around the southern States of America before arriving in New York, where he worked for a while with a vaudeville act before joining the Isley Brothers' backing band. He toured all over America with various singers, including Sam Cooke, Solomon Burke, Little Richard, and Ike and Tina Turner, until in August, 1966, he wound up in Greenwich Village, New York, playing with his own band for $15 a night. It was there that he was heard by Chas Chandler, former bass guitarist with the Animals, who became his manager and persuaded him to travel to England. Once in London he put together a trio with drummer Mitch Mitchell and bass guitarist Noel Redding, called the Jimi Hendrix Experience. The guitarist's wild clothes, long frizzy hair, and penchant for playing guitar solos with his teeth quickly made him a sensation.

His playing was rooted in the long-lined blues approach of B. B. King, but was brought up to date through the use of amplification as a musical device, and his solos were often composed of strings of feedback sound, looping above the free flowing bass and drums. The whole sound of the group, loose and improvisational and awesomely loud, was quite revolutionary and made an immediate impact on his guitar-playing contemporaries.

As a singer and composer he was one of the first black musicians to come to terms with the electronic facilities offered by rock music, and his songs and voice, influenced considerably by Dylan, created perhaps the first successful fusion of blues and white pop.

After his phenomenal success in Britain he returned to America, where he was banned from a concert tour by the Daughters of the American Revolution, who considered his onstage physical contortions obscene. That served only to increase interest in him and he rapidly became one of the world's top rock attractions. Then, at the beginning of 1969 and at the height of his fame, he disappeared and spent more than a year in virtual seclusion, playing at home with a few friends. Early in 1970 he unveiled a new trio, the Band of Gipsies, and returned to Britain last month to play at the Isle of Wight festival. In his last interview he was quoted as saying that he'd reached the end of the road with the trio format, and was planning to form a big band.

In direct contrast to the violence and seeming anarchy of his music, Hendrix was a gentle, peaceful man whose only real concern was music. His final public appearance was when he sat in with War, an American band, at Ronnie Scott's club in London last Wednesday, and it was typical of the man that it was he who felt honoured by being allowed to play.

* * *

PRESIDENT NASSER

Creator of modern Egypt

10 SEPTEMBER 1970

PRESIDENT GAMAL ABDEL NASSER, President of the Republic of Egypt since 1956, and of the United Arab Republic since 1958, died on Monday night in Cairo as reported in later editions of *The Times* yesterday. He was 52.

Whatever the ultimate verdict of history, he will be remembered as one of the outstanding rulers of Egypt. His most enduring memorial will be the diversion of the Nile and the High Dam, which has altered the geographical features of Egypt and northern Sudan.

His political achievements are no less notable, if more controversial, but he stands out as the man who was the driving force behind the Egyptian Revolution and the creator of the United Arab Republic and the Arab Socialist Union. Unpopular in Western Europe and America for his anti-imperialistic, anti-Israeli policies and his turning to Russia for support after the clash over the Suez Canal, he was by the same token admired by the Arabs as a whole as the great liberator and unifier, the man who was to restore their former greatness by overcoming the intrigues of the imperialists and the Israeli menace.

In Egypt he not only raised the country's prestige and the standard of living of the masses, but introduced social reforms that were long overdue. In his relations with other Arab countries he suffered from the defect of being unable to tolerate a rival in the Arab world, and he sometimes pursued antagonisms which were contrary to the interests he had at heart, actuated apparently by personal feelings rather than the general good of the Arab cause. He nurtured a particular animosity for kings but was prepared to come to terms with Arab monarchs and bury the hatchet at least temporarily for the sake of Arab unity.

In international affairs he followed a policy of non-alignment and was active in support of the Afro-Asian block. By many of his compatriots he will be judged by the measure of his success, but they cannot fail to recognize, as indeed must his bitterest foes abroad, that he was above all a sincere patriot working selflessly for a cause in which he believed and that compared with other dictators his methods were singularly mild.

Gamal Abdel Nasser was born in Alexandria on January 15, 1918, the son of a small post office official from Bani Murr, Asyut Province in Upper Egypt, and was educated at various schools in Cairo and other places in Egypt. From Ras-al-Tin Secondary School in Alexandria he went to the Military College, graduating in 1938. Born in the days of the British Protectorate and growing up at a time when Egypt was in a period of transition from partial to complete independence, he seems to have been imbued with a keen sense of patriotism and a passion for reform.

At that time the Egyptian Army was just about to be expanded from the small and largely ceremonial army it had been and made into a fighting force. The young Nasser embarked on a military career with enthusiasm and with equal gusto started to conspire with other like-minded junior officers to reform if not to overthrow the existing order. He proved himself a brave and efficient soldier, graduating from the Staff College in 1947 and distinguishing himself in the war against Israel in 1948, and was wounded at Faluja. The scandals of this war spread the discontent in the army and Nasser and his fellow conspirators formed the Free Officers Committee which planned the *coup d'état* of July 23, 1952.

When this took place it was an efficient, bloodless revolution; King Faruq abdicated in favour of his son and left Egypt for good. As the conspirators were fairly junior it was necessary to find a senior officer to act as a figurehead and their choice fell on Major-General Muhammad Neguib. Their original object seems to have been to enforce the necessary reforms and then withdraw from politics, so that to begin with they kept very much in the background. Neguib on the other hand became a popular figurehead and began to intrigue with the old politicians, or at any rate to show sympathy for the old ways Abdel Nasser and his friends sought to change. He was soon removed from the scene and played no further part in the drama which began to unfold.

Nasser now emerged into the limelight and replaced Neguib as the national hero. At first he was welcomed by the British Government as a more reasonable and amenable leader than Neguib and he successfully negotiated the Canal Zone agreement with Britain. But he now began to interest himself not only in domestic matters but in the Arab world. At home he introduced land reforms and suppressed the Muslim Brotherhood; abroad he opposed the Baghdad Pact of 1955 and began to look towards the Iron Curtain for arms against Israel. In spite of the violence of his radio attacks he still maintained good relations with the west, and relied on America and Great Britain to cooperate in financing the High Dam project. When the offer of help was suddenly withdrawn in July, 1956, Nasser retaliated by nationalizing the Suez Canal.

The fiasco of the subsequent invasion by Anglo-French forces and the withdrawal of the Israelis from Sinai which they occupied at the same time, left Nasser with enhanced prestige in the eyes of Egypt and the Arab world, and also with the Suez Canal, which was soon reopened to all shipping except that of Israel. He also took over the base and all British assets in Egypt. It was some years before relations with Britain were fully restored. He now seemed to be at the height of his success. He had arms and help with the High Dam from the Russians, while rigorously repressing Communism at home. He established the United Arab Republic of Egypt and Syria in February, 1958, which was confirmed by a plebiscite.

Six months later the revolution in Iraq overthrew his main rival, Nuri Salid, and broke up the rival Hashemite Union of Iraq and Jordan. But the new dictator of Iraq proved no more pro-Nasser or pro-Egyptian than the previous regime. Iraq left the Baghdad Pact but showed no sign of drawing any nearer to the UAR. In 1961 Syria seceded from the UAR and though there have been advances and retreats no other Arab state has joined the union.

The Yemen revolution, started with Egyptian help in September, 1962, was only partially successful and resulted in the tying down of an Egyptian force of 50,000 or more for several years. Relations with Saudi Arabia from which the Yemeni Royalists drew support became strained, as did those with Britain owing to the encouragement by the Egyptians of terrorism in the adjoining territory of South Arabia. He denounced the Tunisian President, Habib Bourghiba, for his attitude to Israel and the refugees.

His agreement with King Faisal of Saudi Arabia for a ceasefire and the eventual withdrawal of Egyptian forces from the Yemen in 1965 came to nothing, Egyptian forces remaining in the Yemen at about the same strength as before, until the virtual triumph of the Yemeni republicans rendered their presence unnecessary.

At home things went rather better in spite of the worsening state of the country's finances, and the drain of the Yemen war. Many socialist laws were introduced and the country was proclaimed an Arab Socialist Union. Contrary to western forebodings, Nasser avoided becoming a Soviet satellite, or being drawn into the Soviet camp, by keeping his bridges with the west open for the time being. He continued to draw on Russian help for the High Dam, which went according to plan, and for the South Arabian military venture, which did not. The Suez Canal worked well, contrary to the expectations of many people in the west, and this, with the money brought in by tourists, provided a welcome source of income. Khrushchev visited Egypt and Nasser was made a Hero of the Soviet Union when the Nile was diverted in 1964. All this friendliness with Russia, and later China, did not prevent his rigorously suppressing Egyptian Communists. In the matter of Israel he was intransigent and broke off relations with West Germany in 1964 because of support given to Israel, though he split the Arab world on the issue, and probably did more harm to his own country than to West Germany.

Israel's successful blitzkrieg in June 1967 was provoked by Nasser's request for the withdrawal of the United Nations Emergency Force from Egyptian territory, the subsequent reoccupation of Sharm al-Shaikh, and the threat to close the Gulf of Aqaba again to Israeli shipping. It seems unlikely that he expected the Israeli attack (though he said later that he was prepared for an attack on his airfields within 72 hours), but rather he may have hoped to regain his prestige in the Arab world by the gesture (and as he said relieve pressure on the Syrians) since all the Arab rulers, however hostile, would be compelled to support him against Israel, the common enemy, as in fact they did. He also counted on the backing of Russia and may have thought that Israel would hesitate to strike the first blow against such a formidable array.

The swift, decisive blow of the Israelis, might well have caused his downfall, but after a gesture of resignation he was acclaimed in Egypt and in the Arab world with apparently undiminished popularity. He invoked the spirit of Dunkirk and attributed the defeat to the hidden forces of Imperialism, to wit Britain and the USA, whose aid to the Israeli aggressors was skilfully camouflaged. The extent of the defeat was less obvious to the Egyptian public than to the unfortunate Jordanians, since the war scarcely touched the Nile Valley and losses of armament and equipment were rapidly replaced by the Russians. Memories of collusion with Israel in 1956 and the unsympathetic tone of the press in Britain and the USA. lent colour to the accusation of western support for Israel, which was for a time sustained by King Husain, though France, the principal supplier of Israeli arms, was absolved from blame. As a result of this false accusation the Suez Canal was closed and an oil embargo was imposed by the Arab countries on Britain and America. In his speech on the fifteenth anniversary of Egypt's revolution, Nasser accepted personally much of the blame for what had happened, but maintained an uncompromising attitude of hostility to Israel and repeated the charges of collusion, particularly against the United States.

His health deteriorated after the events of 1967 and he paid another visit to the

USSR for medical treatment. At the same time, the Russians replaced his losses in the June War and oil was discovered in some quantity in the Western Desert. He maintained his popularity with the masses and abortive *coups d'etat* found no support, the middle classes preferring 'the devil they knew' to any likely successor. His honesty, piety and happy domestic life appealed to many.

His recent agreement to a Middle East ceasefire and peace negotiations with Israel raised hopes for an end to the Arab-Israeli conflict which has flared into warfare three times in the past 22 years.

From the British point of view it is a pity that Nasser had so little contact with Britain in his early years. Both Egypt and Britain might have benefited by a closer association. He visited Russia and various Eastern countries, but never came to Britain. He was married with two daughters and three sons.

* * *

'COCO' CHANEL

Famous French fashion designer

6 JANUARY 1971

MLLE GABRIELLE CHANEL, 'Coco' Chanel, la grande couturière, died on Sunday night at the age of 87, as reported in later editions of *The Times* yesterday.

She reached a peak of fame and popularity in the 1920s when she succeeded in replacing the extravagant pre-war fashions with simple comfortable clothes. The same cardigan jackets and easy skirts that she popularized then were revived in her successful comeback in the late fifties and her famous Chanel No. 5 scent kept her name in the public eye throughout her long career.

She became something of a legend in the world of fashion and a Broadway musical, based on her career and starring Katharine Hepburn, was put on in 1968.

Most sources suggest that 'Coco' Chanel was born in 1883, although this fact, like so many others about her life, was a jealously guarded secret. Traditionally, her nickname 'Coco' was earned by her habit of riding in the Bois when the cocks were still crowing 'cocorico', but she later claimed that it was merely a respectable version of 'cocotte'.

Orphaned at an early age, she worked with her sister in a milliners in Deauville, where she finally opened a shop in 1912. After a brief spell of nursing in the war she founded a couture house in the Rue Cambon in Paris. There she worked, lived and entertained for much of the rest of her life, although she actually slept in the Ritz hotel on the other side of the road.

Chanel sensed the profound need for change, renewal, and emancipation that was sweeping the world in 1914 and set out to revolutionize women's clothing. It was her talent, drive, and inspiration that brought about a complete metamorphosis of fashion in post-war years. She began by liberating women from the bondage of the corset. In 1920 she made the first chemise dress and the 'poor girl look' in contrast to the rich woman of pre-war years was born. She succeeded in making women look casual but at the same time elegant by using the then revolutionary combinations of jersey, tweed, and pearls. Dior was to say of her later: 'with a black sweater and 10 rows of pearls Chanel revolutionized fashion'.

In 1925 she made fashion history again with the collarless cardigan jacket. Her bias-cut dress was labelled by one critic 'a Ford because everybody has one'. It was Chanel who introduced the shoe-string shoulder strap, the strapped sandal, the flower on the shoulder, the floating evening scarf, the wearing together of 'junk' and real jewels. Chanel launched the vogue for costume jewellery, particularly rows of fake pearls, bead and gold chains, and gee-gaw-hung bracelets.

At the height of her career, Chanel was said to be the wealthiest couturière in Paris. She was at that time controlling four businesses: the couture house, textile and costume jewellery factories, and perfume laboratories for her famous scent. At this time also her private life, particularly her friendship with the second Duke of Westminster, became a subject of constant public interest and speculation. But although Mademoiselle Chanel's engagement to Paul Iribe, a well-known artist and fashion sketcher, was reported in 1933, she never married.

In 1938, after a losing battle with the rising influence of Schiaparelli, Chanel retired from the couture scene. Sixteen years later she staged a spectacular comeback, roused into action it is said by the irritation of seeing Paris fashion taken over by men designers. Her first post-war collection in 1954 was ill received by fashion critics, for instead of launching a new fashion revolution, she went on from where she had left off – cardigan suits, short pleated skirts, crisp little blouses, short chiffon and lace dresses, masses of 'junk' jewellery. But her timing proved to have been perfect. Rich and famous women once again adopted the Chanel look and when the French magazine *Elle* ran a Chanel pattern they received a quarter of a million requests for it.

In 1957 Chanel won the American Nieman Marcus award for fashion, but even without this official recognition, her continuing influence was indisputable. Many different factors contributed to her success as a dress designer, but chiefly it was the result of immense flair coupled with ruthless good taste. In her own language she described all that she most disliked as *vulgaire*. Her clothes were the antithesis of that.

* * *

IGOR STRAVINSKY

The most influential composer of his time

6 APRIL 1971

MR IGOR STRAVINSKY, who died yesterday in New York at the age of 88, was for three generations and more than half a century the most influential and the most discussed composer of the day. His life was long – in his youth he met not only Tchaikovsky and Balakirev, but Ibsen, Monet, Petipa, Réjane, Sarah Bernhardt, Proust; he reached maturity as a composer just before Diaghilev launched his revolution in the Russian ballet, and he lived to keep pace with the most audacious musical explorers of the 1960s.

He seemed ageless in his music, because he never closed his mind to the evolution of the art, or to the creative musician's place as a reflector of current attitudes; in his younger days he led musical fashion, and in his old age he observed, translated, and revealed afresh whatever he found new and exciting and fruitful in the work of composers with a quarter of his years. He was too serious ever to count as an *enfant terrible*, and too lively (too determined) of mind ever to become an old master. He became the acknowledged GOM of music, but unwillingly for, as he wrote in 1960: 'All my life I have thought of myself as the "youngest one".'

Stravinsky's chief contribution to twentieth-century music was without doubt the new rhythmic possibilities, especially of asymmetrical pattern, that were suggested, and are still being suggested, in his ballet score *The Rite of Spring*, a work which, with *Tristan and Isolde* (though some would say *Parsifal*) is fundamental to modern music. Language, the manner of self-expression, was an inexhaustible preoccupation for Stravinsky in music, perhaps because also in words he declared himself a 'convinced etymologist', concerned with 'problems of language all my life'. He seems never to have been at a loss for something worthwhile to say – in age

299

Igor Stravinsky

as in youth his intellect was as clear, as radiant, and as sharp as a diamond; it was the choice between alternative methods of formulating the truth that perennially absorbed and stimulated him. When invited to contribute to an Old Testament symposial oratorio, Stravinsky typically chose *Babel*. Whatever the language, there was never any doubt about the identity of the speaker.

His linguistic inheritance and history are closely connected with the chameleonic versatility which he displayed in his music – particularly in the years between 1910 (when he left Russia) and 1952 (the beginning of his overt preoccupation with serial techniques). Stravinsky's father came of a Polish family, his mother from the Ukraine: he was brought up by a German nanny, speaking German as fluently as Russian. After leaving St Petersburg he sided linguistically with France, and eventually became a French citizen in 1934, but in 1939 destiny took him to America and in 1945 he adopted American nationality. His writings show an eloquence and feeling for niceties of language as remarkable in English and French as in the tongues with which he grew up, though he acknowledged Russian as his prime vehicle of thought to the end of his days, and musically, too, he never lost a trace of Russian accent; in the *Requiem Canticles* (1966) it is still strongly discernible.

Igor Stravinsky was born at Oranienbaum, near St Petersburg, in June, 1882. His father was principal bass-baritone at the St Petersburg Opera, his mother an amateur of music, but there was no strong family heritage of musicianship. Thanks to his father's post Igor (the third of four sons) was able to attend rehearsals and performances of opera and ballet whenever he wished; in his teens he took full advantage of this. Almost as important to his development was his father's extensive library; Igor Stravinsky was an omnivorous reader all his life, and enjoyed the retentive memory of a polymath. His father was sceptical of the son's musical gift, though Igor had, at two years old, correctly reproduced the songs of peasants in the neighbourhood. He began piano lessons at nine years, harmony and counterpoint a little later. He was already composing music when, in 1900, he stayed at the country home of his school-fellow Vladimir Rimsky-Korsakov, and from then onward he showed his compositions to Nicolai Rimsky-Korsakov until in 1902 he became that composer's pupil for orchestration and form. Stravinsky was destined for a legal career and during these years read jurisprudence at St Petersburg University, from which he graduated in 1905. But by this time music absorbed his whole interest, and there was no question of another career. His father had died in 1902; Stravinsky's first catalogued work, a piano sonata (now lost) dates from 1904. He was still Rimsky-Korsakov's pupil when, in 1906, he married his first cousin Catherine Nossenko, and began his symphony in E flat major, a rather Wagnerian piece still occasionally performed (it was with this symphony that he made his conducting debut in Montreux, at Ansermet's invitation, in 1914).

When Rimsky-Korsakov died in 1908 he had passed on to Stravinsky the serviceable, even virtuoso orchestral technique which can be found in two orchestral works of that year, the *Scherzo Fantastique* and *Fireworks*. It was a performance of this last which aroused the interest of Sergei Diaghilev, then preparing to launch his Russian Ballet company. Diaghilev gave Stravinsky some orchestration work (for *Les Sylphides*) and then asked him to write music for Fokine's ballet *The Firebird*, since Ladov, the original choice, was working too slowly. Stravinsky, now in revolt against the methods and ideals of Rimsky, did not care for the subject but accepted the commission. *The Firebird* (1910) made his name in Paris and subsequently all over Europe; the score does show Rimsky's influence, particularly in the full orchestral version which Stravinsky later reduced, and is strongly Russian in character, though Diaghilev's company found it perplexing and unmelodious. For Stravinsky it was an artistic necessity to abandon the voluptuous style to create hard, bright colours and lines, crisp and invigorating rhythms. He and his family had now left Russia (apart from a brief visit in 1914 he did not return to his native soil until 1962) and were living in Switzerland; Stravinsky began work on a piano concerto which Diaghilev soon persuaded him to transform into *Petrushka* (1911). These two ballets, and a third, *The Rite of Spring* – at its first performance in 1913 there was a riot – triumphantly proclaimed the viability of the one-act ballet as a medium of dance-drama and not merely more or less trivial *divertissement*; as such they are of first importance in the history of ballet. But in *Petrushka*, and still more in *The Rite of Spring*, Stravinsky was increasingly preoccupied with musical structure in terms of phrases and rhythmic shapes for their own non-associative shape; significantly he took exception to the work of his choreographers in these ballets, and significantly too they have been as successful in the concert hall as in the theatre.

Stravinsky's fortunes were now firmly involved with Diaghilev's enterprise; when Diaghilev had produced *The Nightingale* (1908–13), Stravinsky turned his back on Russian romantic nationalism, and when war broke out he was obliged to proceed without Diaghilev's support. During the war years in Switzerland he composed a succession of short works for small groups – the best known are the opera-ballet *Renard* (1917) and *The Soldier's Tale* (1918) – and these forced Stravinsky to sharpen and subtilize his invention, as well as allowing him to develop his rhythmic experiments. The *Ragtime* for 11 instruments (1918) signalled a new interest in jazz rhythms and tone-colours, and similarly, the study for pianola (1917), subsequently orchestrated as 'Madrid', inaugurated an extensive interest in the possibilities of the mechanical piano and eventually in the piano itself which the composer cultivated once more as the vehicle of his own performances.

His piano concerto was the first of these; later his second son, Soulima (an old Polish family name), became an exponent of his piano music, and the majestic, very difficult concerto for two solo pianos (1935) was composed for father and son together. From the mechanical piano to the gramophone was a single, logical step. Stravinsky welcomed every opportunity to record his own performances partly to fix tempi and phrasing for the aid of other performers, partly because he abominated the 'recreative' type of interpreter who labours to make another man's work his own (he compared the ideal conductor to a bellringer at the end of a rope).

After the armistice in 1919, Stravinsky worked occasionally for Diaghilev, notably in *Pulcinella* (1919), in which he rearranged Pergolesi to suit his own features;

The Wedding (1923), a tough, heavily stylized, and earthy evocation of Russian peasant life with an orchestra consisting of four pianos; and *Apollon Musagete* (1928)
which most strongly typifies the statuesque neo-classicism that was Stravinsky's
chief ideal at this time. The choreography of this ballet was by George Balanchine
with whom Stravinsky was to enjoy a further, very fruitful period of collaboration
in New York. In the same year Stravinsky and Diaghilev parted company after the
composer had accepted a commission from a 'rival', Mme Ida Rubinstein.

The ballet in question, *The Fairy's Kiss*, took its thematic material from Tchaikovsky, and showed that Stravinsky's command of his own style was sufficiently
assured to absorb features of romanticism without sounding like nineteenth-
century music. Traces of a Tchaikovskian texture could, however, have been
remarked already in the aria 'Non erubescite' from the sombre and monumental
opera oratorio *Oedipus Rex*, to a Latin text by Cocteau (of which Diaghilev mounted
a concert performance in 1927) though the predominating traits of the work derive
more obviously from Bach and Handel. The grandest and most granite-like of
these neo-classic works is the *Symphony of Psalms* composed in 1930 for the jubilee
of the Boston Symphony Orchestra; its noble, monolithic texture looks back to the
exalted *Symphonies of Wind Instruments* (1920, in memory of Debussy) and forward
to the gravelly hieratical *Threni* (1958), Stravinsky's first completely serial composition – all three are strongly 'Russian' in character, though the Russia of
Mussorgsky rather than Rimsky-Korsakov.

Stravinsky had indeed re-embraced the Russian orthodox faith in 1926, but his
cast of mind and way of life had become west European and, particularly, French.
His major works of the 1930s reflected the nationality which he adopted in this
decade; the melodrama *Perséphone*, text by Gide (1934), in which the composer took
deliberate liberties with the stress of the French language – believing that words
should no more limit the metre and phrasing than the musical themes should, and
the concerto for two pianos, *Jeu de Cartes* (1937), another ballet for Balanchine.

In 1939 Stravinsky was offered the chair of Poetics at Harvard University. Happiness in his Paris home had been broken by the deaths of his mother, his wife, and
his daughter Ludmilla, within the space of a year. When French friends advised
him to accept the chair he left his new homeland on the eve of war. He settled in
California, gave his lectures on *The Poetics of Music*, married the painter Vera de
Bosset in 1940, and in 1945 became an American citizen. Stravinsky plunged
enthusiastically into the musical life of America; he made an arrangement of the
Star-Spangled Banner in 1941 (forbidden as being too peculiar), wrote a *Circus Polka*
(1942) for Barnum and Bailey's elephants, a *Tango* (1941) for a 'pop' music publisher,
and the *Scènes de Ballet* (1944) for a Billy Rose revue; he flirted with film music, but
without becoming seriously involved – the *Norwegian Moods*, the slow movement
of the 1945 symphony, and the middle movement of *Ode*, all originated as film

music; and he returned to American jazz in the *Ebony Concerto* (1945) for Woody Herman's band. He also collaborated again with Balanchine, most notably in *Orpheus* (1947) and the outstanding *Agon* (1957). And he returned to the orchestral symphony with the works in C (1940) and in three movements (1945), the latter a masterpiece of argument and invention which sums up all Stravinsky's diverse explorations since *The Rite of Spring*. This immensely fruitful period closed in 1951 with *The Rake's Progress*, the three-act opera to an English text by W. H. Auden in which Stravinsky adopted the techniques of Viennese classical *opera buffa*. The remarkable beauties of this 'number-opera' cannot disguise the distinction between self-assertive *pastiche* and original composition: unlike the Tchaikovsky and Pergolesi transcriptions, or the neo-Baroque *Dumbarton Oaks* (1940), which are evocatively timeless and therefore modern, this opera represented a bid to take over the assets of another century, to compose not neo-classical but actually classical music.

For 30 years Stravinsky had been acclaimed the antipode of 12-note music, the high priest of diatonicism. From 1952 onwards his works moved steadily towards the 12-note principle, at first in the *Septet* (1953) only through diatonic serial construction, later with less overt dependence upon tonality, in the *Canticum Sacrum* (1955) to honour St Mark's cathedral in Venice, until in *Threni* (1958) he adopted the 12-note row entirely. A half-way house was the ballet *Agon* which begins and ends in C major but also includes strictly atonal and serial dance numbers. Stravinsky was undoubtedly attracted to serial methods by their application to his predilection for asymmetrical metres and rhythmic phraseology, but also by its non-associative 'pure' significance – Webern, rather than Schoenberg, was his starting-point in this new adventure, and it is of Webern that one is reminded, both in the exiguous but oddly moving *Epitaphium* for the *Prince of Fustenberg* (1959), and in the epigrammatic concentration of the Movements for piano and orchestra (1959) which cultivate and harvest a broad field of textures and moods within the confines of eight minutes.

In 1962 Stravinsky celebrated his eightieth birthday by revisiting Russia, and by composing three new works: a short, exquisite anthem 'The Dove Descending' to lines by T. S. Eliot; a miniature oratorio *A Sermon, a Narrative, and a Prayer*, which returned to a more direct style than that of *Movements* and included a splendid setting of St Stephen's last sermon; and a morality, *The Flood*, to be sung, spoken, acted, and danced on television.

He followed these with *Abraham and Isaac*, in 1963, a stern, rather hermetic setting of the Hebrew Bible text for baritone and orchestra; in 1964 the orchestral Variations in memory of Aldous Huxley and the tiny but marvellously concentrated *Elegy for J.F.K.* (to a haiku text by W. H. Auden); then in 1966 the *Requiem*

Canticles whose hieratic, deeply moving music seems to sum up the essence of all Stravinsky's religious composition.

Stravinsky's eighty-fifth birthday in 1967 was marked by worldwide celebrations. The composer had planned to take part in many of these, but age had begun to make inroads on his physical, if not mental, vitality, and his doctors would not let him travel.

In his late seventies Stravinsky was persuaded, by his young American disciple, Robert Craft, to talk at length about his early life, his recollections of his works, and his views on other music. The four conversation-books derived from these talks made stimulating reading, and provide invaluable source material for biographers and students of musical psychology alike. He regards them as more self-revealing and faithful than the *Chronicle of My Life* (1935) written with Walter Nouvel, or the *Poetics of Music* in which his collaborator was Roland-Manuel. The conversations revealed the broad range of his interests, and also his intolerance of many other musicians; there was an attractive streak of malice, including self-deflation, behind the eager bonhomie that his slight birdlike figure presented. One could identify the deep mysticism of the Slav, the debonair gaiety of the Frenchman, the affability and thirst for knowledge of the American; but these traits were personal rather than environmental, just as his music remained completely idiosyncratic whether Grieg, Bach, Machaut, or Boulez was his model. He may have hidden his face behind masks of other men, but his personality imprinted itself upon the whole face of music for over half a century, perhaps for the rest of time.

Less than a month ago, in a letter to *The Times*, he crossed swords with a critic on the subject of *The Firebird*. His letters are now being prepared for publication and he remarked that the one he was then writing might well be his last.

LOUIS ARMSTRONG

The greatest jazz trumpeter of his time

6 JULY 1971

LOUIS ARMSTRONG, the jazz musician, died in New York yesterday at the age of 71. He was the greatest trumpeter and one of the best singers in jazz.

He was born in New Orleans in 1900 and is said to have received his first musical training, on cornet, in the Waifs' Home where he was placed after being caught firing a revolver during the 1913 New Year festivities. Released two years later, he made a living working at odd jobs, selling papers and driving a coal cart, until in 1918 his increasing musical skill secured him a job in Kid Ory's band, replacing Joe 'King Oliver' who had just left for Chicago.

The next two years he spent playing on the Mississippi river boats, then two more years in New Orleans until in 1922 he was summoned by King Oliver to join his legendary Creole Jazz Band in Chicago. It was Armstrong's growing reputation which had made Oliver, hitherto the most renowned New Orleans cornettist, send for him to play alongside him and there was something neatly symbolic about the way in which it was soon realized that Oliver's second cornettist was now the greater player.

In 1924 Armstrong went his own way, meanwhile changing to trumpet from cornet, and the pattern of his life now reflected the spreading popularity of jazz, because after five years in Chicago playing in bands which he seldom led but always starred in, he followed his fame to New York, where he starred at a Harlem ballroom and in a top revue at the same time. He went to California, worked his way back across the United States and then followed his fame again across the Atlantic, visiting London in 1932 and virtually remaining in Europe until 1935. From now until the end of his life he was an international figure, travelling everywhere and welcome everywhere.

He led a big band from 1936 to 1947, then in response to the renewed interest in small groups formed a band which, whatever the future personnel, was always called his All Stars, although this was most accurate a title in the early days when Earl Hines and Jack Teagarden were with him. With his All Stars he toured widely, to Latin America for example in 1956, to London for the first time in two decades the same year, and in 1957 to Africa. But he also appeared in films (notably *Satchmo The Great*, *New Orleans*, and *High Society*), played with symphony orchestras, produced a book and even surprised everyone in the early sixties by making a best-selling record of *Hello Dolly*.

The Jack Parnell band featuring (L to R) Sid Phillips (clarinet), Bill Jones (piano), Lenny Bush (bass fiddle), Louis Armstrong and George Chisholm (trombone) and, at the drums, band leader Jack Parnell, 1956.

His achievement as a jazz trumpeter was to have come at a time when jazz musicians' short variations on a theme were starting to turn into sustained melodic lines; he seized instinctively on this development and carried it farther than anyone else. The recordings he made in the twenties display playing remarkable by any standards, but doubly so considering how recently jazz had begun to forge its own language. The way Armstrong soars up to a high note, peels off into a dive at exactly the right moment, alters the shading of a long note, separates notes crisply or slurs them together, steers a slow phrase into a sharp rhythmic figure, explores upper and lower register with equal mastery – this superb manipulation of a new language is staggering now, but in the twenties it created an effect on his fellow players which wholly identified him with jazz.

It would be unfair to contemporaries such as Jabbo Smith and Red Allen to present him entirely as a lone pioneer; what was significant about his playing was that the intuitive sense of logic and balance with which he welded phrase to phrase, and the sheer breadth, power and nobility of his style suddenly opened up vistas of what future jazz soloists might achieve and it is this liberating influence rather

307

than any specific technique that was his greatest legacy. His singing presented the same warmth and grandeur on a different plane – his slightly surrealistic abandonment of the lyrics, often halfway through a song, and his abrasive but appealing voice were a good deal more human and appealing than most popular singing but would hardly have brought him into a recording studio if he had not also been a great trumpeter.

It is of course by his achievements inside the recording studio that he will now have to be remembered and the greatest of these undoubtedly took place before 1930, but although he was never quite so good again and became a star of entertainment as much as a great jazz musician there is still some very good music to be found on his post-1930 records. And we should remember, as Humphrey Lyttelton once pointed out in some of the wisest words ever written about Armstrong, that to him jazz was his native form of entertainment, not a music apart, and that the show business routines to which some people objected were as much an essential part of him as the great music.

He was at once a jovial yet dignified father figure of entertainment, a considerable comedian in his own right, the man who led the way in transforming jazz from a folk music into an art and the thorough professional who would never interpret his own life in such terms.

DUKE OF WINDSOR

King who gave up a throne to marry the woman he loved

28 MAY 1972

THE RECENT HISTORY of British Monarchy presents no figure of stranger or more contrasted interest than that of the Duke of Windsor (whose death is announced elsewhere in this issue), the only British Sovereign who, of his own will, resigned the Crown. In early manhood he possessed – he held it all his life to a considerable degree – a magnetic quality which made him one of the most popular characters in the world. In his ways and tastes he was of his age, charming to those who met him, and impatient of all except the minimum of ceremonial. He was, too, a remarkable speaker and had many of a leader's gifts. In the years after the 1914–18 War he seemed the embodiment of a new era in which youth had come into its own. He became the hope of an Empire which, knowing him, was proud to possess him, and the envy of foreign peoples. When as King Edward VIII he succeeded to the Throne, his popularity had scarcely diminished, and his subjects throughout the Empire felt assured of a reign which would be both 'happy and glorious'. That it was not, and that there was much unhappiness and little surviving glory, is, sadly indeed, a matter of history. But the manner of his going should not be allowed to eclipse the preceding years of strenuous service to the Commonwealth and its peoples. His father's views on discipline allowed the young Prince but little freedom; and the Navy, with its strict code and proud tradition, reinforced an upbringing of stern imperatives. He was contented in it, worked hard, and although in some ways curiously immature, he was popular and well reported on. Then he was taken away and sent to Oxford. In his dismay at this course, which was by no means to his liking, and in his introduction there for the first time to a relaxed and tolerant society, may be traced the beginning of an impatience with older heads and with their counsels of prudence. Oxford brought out no latent aptitude for study in the Prince, and before war came in 1914 it had already been decided that he should go down and take a commission in the Grenadier Guards.

In France and Flanders he proved that he possessed courage in a high degree. So much so that his constant and often successful efforts to reach the front line were an embarrassment to his commanding officers. There he found, not for the last time, how irksome could be the restrictions imposed on him by his station in life. After the war came the triumphal series of Dominion tours and visits abroad, which, though raising him to a pinnacle of popularity, placed a heavy strain on his physically nervous constitution.

By the time of his accession he had become very much a man of his age. He was impatient of tradition for its own sake. He had developed a social conscience about urban squalor and the armies of unemployed; he was an ally of change. He had no taste for the solid domesticity and stately rhythm of his father's way of life, prefer-ring a less predictable programme and more stimulating company. His private life and his public routine had grown apart. These characteristics, applauded as modern in a Prince of Wales, were, in a profoundly conservative society, less readily accepted in a King. But Edward VIII was not a man to play a role in a way that was consistently false to his character. He had ideas about modernizing the monarchy, of adapting the tone of its constitutional functions to the changing conditions of society. He thought to dispense with some of the ceremonial, and if this was found impossible he suffered it with a not very good grace. He entered upon drastic economies in the royal estates, which hurt the feelings and the prospects of many faithful retainers. In his impatience of some of the business of state his former courtesy was known to desert him. These rather precipitous changes might have been tolerated and later approved, given time. But before the first painful impression had faded his mod-ernity in the matter of marriage and divorce had brought his reign to an end.

He was no doubt right in thinking that the movement of opinion was in the direction of his own views about the remarriage of divorced persons. But he failed altogether to distinguish between what people will approve of in themselves and among their acquaintances and what they will approve of in their Sovereign. Nor did he appear to understand the full consequences in this respect of his being the head of the Church of England. During the years after the 1914–18 War he had been greatly attracted by a succession of women, none of whom was free to marry him; finally, when he was 40, he fell deeply in love with a married woman who already had two husbands living. He was brought to see, though it seems to have been anything but clear to him at first, that he could not marry Mrs Simpson as King without precipitating a grave constitutional convulsion. So he took what he insisted in his last broadcast was necessarily his decision and his alone: for the sake of his love, he who had been born with the ability to sustain it at its highest, renounced the greatest of all crowns.

Thereafter his life presented in its public aspect the appearance of tragedy. The exception taken to his marriage, having lost him his Throne, continued so as to perpetuate his exile and, except for his term as Governor of the Bahamas, to deny him office in the service of the Commonwealth. The judgment that he brought these consequences on himself does not diminish the tragic contrast between the adulation in which he was once held and the long functionless years that followed. He bore with dignity and without bitterness the equivocal status of a royal duke with no public role to fill, and found in his fateful marriage much to compensate him for the sense of loss.

The Duke of Windsor was born Prince Edward of York at White Lodge, Richmond Park, on Saturday, June 23, 1894. Never before in the history of these islands had the reigning Sovereign seen three male descendants in the direct line of inheritance: and, during the remainder of her life, a deep affection united the aged Queen Victoria and the Boy Prince. Three days after his birth she drove from Windsor to see him. On July 16 he was christened by the Archbishop of Canterbury (Dr Benson) by the family names of Edward Albert Christian, to which were added those of the four patron saints of the British Isles, George Andrew Patrick David. Officially he used to sign himself 'Edward P', but to his family and close friends he was and remained David.

The chief landmarks of his early years were the departure of his parents on their world tour of 1901, when he and their other children were constantly with King Edward and Queen Alexandra; the death and funeral of Queen Victoria; and the Accession and Coronation of King Edward VII. Apart from his share in these public events, he lived the quiet, active, happy life of an ordinary English boy. He romped and played rounders with King Edward VII, who loved and understood him thoroughly, practised cricket with boys from Eton, and football with others from the Sandringham estate. He did his lessons with Mme Bricka, his mother's former governess, and with Mr H. P. Hansell, the Ludgrove and Rossall master, who was his tutor from 1902 until he went to the 1914–18 War.

Hansell, whose opinion it was that the Prince would have been better off at a boarding school, did what he could to reproduce the conditions of a school in the regimen of private tuition. He was, on the evidence of his pupil's recollection, a conscientious but uninspiring teacher. The task of grounding the Prince in the doctrines of the Church of England was entrusted to Canon J. N. Dalton (the father of Hugh Dalton), who some 30 years earlier had been selected by Queen Victoria to be tutor to his new pupil's father. The canon had only qualified success, though he did arouse in the Prince a certain dread of the society of Church dignitaries which was to accompany him throughout life.

He learnt to talk French and German, to recite long lists of poems, and he studied dancing, singing, and voice production. He worked too at his lathe at Sandringham and learnt the elements of seamanship in a model brig on Virginia Water. The more formal part of the curriculum was geared to the entrance examination at the Royal Naval College; and when his mathematics looked like letting him down they were brought on by special coaching. He was in some trepidation lest he fail the examination, for he stood at that time in considerable awe of his father, whose stern admonitions and insistence on punctilio and punctuality made, naturally enough, a deep impression on him.

In 1907, just before his thirteenth birthday, he went to Osborne to live the life of the ordinary cadet. In 1909 he passed on to Dartmouth. He worked hard and happily in the engineering shops, was whip to the beagles, had measles, and did his fair share of punishment drills. In 1910, while he was still there, King Edward VII died and he became Duke of Cornwall. On his sixteenth birthday he was created Prince of Wales. The next day he was confirmed by the Archbishop of Canterbury (Dr Davidson). In March, 1911, he left the College. On June 10 he was invested with the Garter and in July went to Caernarvon for his investiture, the first of 19 English Princes of Wales to be invested in the Principality. The ceremony in the ruined castle was picturesque and splendid. As its Constable Mr Lloyd George received him, and, thanks to his coaching, the Prince was able to introduce a phrase or two of Welsh into his speech. He was afterwards to use them with telling effect upon Welsh audiences.

In October, 1912, he went up to Magdalen College, Oxford, accompanied by his valet, Mr Hansell, and an equerry, Major the Hon. William Cadogan, to live (so far as this retinue allowed) the normal life of an undergraduate. During his vacations he paid two visits to Germany and one to Scandinavia, when he gave early expression in his diary to his impatience with ceremonial: 'What rot and a waste of time, money and energy all these state visits are!! This is my only remark on all this unreal show and ceremony!!'

At Oxford he played football with the Magdalen second XI, joined the University OTC, ran with the beagles, began to hunt, saw through Sir Herbert Warren, the head of his college, and read with Sir William Anson and other hand-picked tutors. No particular love of scholarship was kindled in him, and it was decided that he should leave at the end of the academic year in 1914 and go for a period of soldiering. When war came he was gazetted to the Grenadier Guards, but Lord Kitchener, to the Prince's deep distress, would not allow him to proceed to France. Seeking an interview with Lord Kitchener, he asked what it would matter if he were killed since he had four brothers. Kitchener replied that the line of battle was not then stabilized and he could not take the risk of his being captured. A little later, however, he had his way and in November he was posted to the staff of GHQ in France. He was next assigned to HQ, Guards Division, where he contrived to spend much of his time in or near the front and was occasionally under fire. He was not, however, allowed to return to regimental duties. After a visit to the Mediterranean theatre and Egypt he was appointed to HQ, 14 Corps, and in 1917 moved with the corps headquarters to Italy, to shore up the defences after Caporetto, and there made the acquaintance of the King of Italy. Throughout his service he was only too ready to endanger his life and he had the satisfaction of one narrow escape.

Less than a year after the Armistice he sailed for Canada in HMS *Renown*. He went with a war reputation which made him the comrade of every veteran. He had in addition 'the smile that conquered Canada', the appeal of his boyishness, and his own way of identifying himself with the peoples among whom he moved. His personal dignity when he asserted it required no accessories, his memory for faces was exceptional, and he could talk well. Moreover, his voice, memory, and resourcefulness as a public speaker, together with his command of French, gave him an immense additional advantage. Mr Lloyd George did not exaggerate his qualities in calling him our greatest Ambassador. On August 12, 1919, he struck at St John's, Newfoundland, the keynote of his tour. After the official reception the inhabitants, many of whom had served in the war, surged round him, an enthusiastic escort. They enjoyed themselves immensely. So did he. It was the same all over Canada and in Washington and New York as well. Right across the continent to Victoria and back again there was never a moment's slackening of the delirium of welcome. It was such that the newspaper correspondents were suspected of exaggerating it. To do so would have been well-nigh impossible. Before long he was saying that he was just a Canadian, and later he bought a ranch to prove it.

In Quebec he was a French Canadian, talking the language of the people. In the Eastern Provinces he became an Easterner; in the Western, a Westerner; to the farmers, a farmer; to all a sportsman and to the ex-Service men everywhere one of themselves. Above all, he never patronized. The task was heavy, but he made it seem easy by the pleasure which he so plainly took in it. In March, 1920, the *Renown* sailed with him again, by Barbados, the Mexican coast to San Diego and the Panama Canal, to Honolulu across the Line (he was ducked by Father Neptune) to Fiji and at last to Auckland, which was sighted on the morning of April 24. His tour of both the North and South Islands of New Zealand was triumphal. In Australia, too, he came, and smiled, and conquered.

He sailed away on August 19: but Australia had laid a spell on him never to be effaced.

He came home victorious but, it was felt, in need of rest. The claims upon him and his own active disposition would not, however, permit it. Public speeches, appeals for ex-Service men, printers' orphans, the Boy Scouts, and many other objects followed each other rapidly. The conferring of honorary degrees by Oxford and Cambridge, and of a Fellowship of the Royal College of Surgeons, created important occasions. It was only indeed in the late summer of 1921 that he took a holiday, and then he used it chiefly to prepare for the arduous undertaking of his Indian tour.

Since the days of the Indian Mutiny, disloyalty to the Crown had never been so widespread as in 1921, and to pit the personality of the Prince against the influence of the extremist agitators was a grave and anxious experiment. It was chiefly his individual charm and his real sympathy with his father's Indian subjects which carried it through. On October 26 he sailed again in the *Renown* from Portsmouth. After a long, exhaustive, and exhausting journey he returned in July.

Shortly afterwards he was elected Captain of the Royal and Ancient Golf Club at St Andrews and was invested as Senior Grand Warden of the United Grand Lodge of Ancient Free and Accepted Masons of England.

In March, 1925, he sailed in the *Repulse* to Africa.

It was a time of acute political division in South Africa; but, thanks to a loyal unanimity of welcome given by the respective leaders of the parties, General Hertzog and General Smuts, and to his own unfailing tact, the harmony of his tour was undisturbed by racial or party feeling. He travelled all through the Union area and on to Southern and Northern Rhodesia.

He was away for seven months and on reaching England received magnificent ovations both at Portsmouth and in London. Perhaps, however, the governing feeling of the public was that he needed the rest he had so richly earned. In the winter of 1925–26 he hunted, for the second time broke a collar-bone, and rode in one or two regimental point-to-points. He took much delight in the hunting field and in the company it provided, at Melton Mowbray in particular. His frequent falls, however, attracted the solicitous notice of the King, who requested him, and of the Prime Minister (Ramsay MacDonald), who appealed to him, to give up the sport. During the next four or five years the Prince's life was one of a perpetual round of visits to every part of Great Britain varied by occasional trips to France and Spain and rather longer stays in Africa and Canada. By 1930 he must have set foot in more British towns than even the hardiest of commercial travellers and delivered a greater number of speeches than any politician in the same length of time. Their range was as wide and varied as his travels.

In the autumn of 1928 he went to East Africa with the Duke of Gloucester. While there he learnt of his father's illness and sped home from Dar es Salaam in what was then the undreamed-of time of 10 days. During King George V's convalescence, which entailed extra work for him, he sold his stud of hunters, gave up point-to-point racing, and instead took to flying. Later he purchased a light Moth aeroplane of his own, the precursor of others. Thus he saved the time he always grudged.

The serious illness of King George V marked a change in the Prince's life. Before 1928 he was acquiring experience of the Empire and the outer world; after it he took an increasing interest in national affairs, particularly in trade and unemployment. In 1931 he undertook the most important of all his later visits abroad. Accompanied by Prince George (afterwards Duke of Kent) he went to open the British Exhibition at Buenos Aires. The Princes also travelled through Peru, Bolivia, Chile, and Brazil, spending their time almost exclusively with South Americans.

When in 1931 the economic crisis raised unemployment to an appalling level, the Prince felt that the efforts made by the State, the municipalities, and industry were not enough. He thought that through his experience of the British Legion, Toc H, the National Council of Social Service, and the Boy Scouts organization, which he had always been eager to assist, he had detected a remedy in voluntary service. At a meeting at the Albert Hall he said there was no central machinery which could provide a substitute for the good neighbour. He did not rest content with speech making. In April, 1932, he began a series of visits to unemployment clubs all over the country. In the year of his accession some 200,000 unemployed men and women were associated in occupational clubs as a result of the campaign he started. Yet he was often uncomfortably conscious of the contrast between the eminence of his position and the political importance it forced upon him.

The formal splendour of great houses never appealed to him. His favourite residence was Fort Belvedere, a country house near Virginia Water which his father assigned to him in 1930 with the words, 'What could you possibly want that old place for? Those damn weekends, I suppose.' In the Fort, as he called it, he enjoyed as nowhere else the pleasures of privacy and possession. There indeed he spent much more time with his own small circle than was generally known and latterly slept only now and then in London. Consequently, although he performed his public duties, he withdrew increasingly from London social life. This, and his preference for company which could not be admitted to his father's Court – a matter of general comment in London society – caused anxiety to the advisers of the Crown and, not least, to King George V himself.

He had, of course, his various hobbies, into which he threw himself with tremendous though sometimes transitory enthusiasm – music, hunting, flying, golf, angling, and gardening. He also began to take a keen interest in pictures, became at his own request a Trustee of the National Gallery, and although his knowledge was not deep, he was a first-class guide to the royal collections.

In 1930 the Prince's friendship with Mr and Mrs Simpson began. Mrs Simpson was born on June 19, 1896, the only child of Mr Teakle Walter Warfield, whose family has long settled in Maryland. Her mother was a Virginian. In 1915 she married Lieutenant Spencer, of the American Navy, but she divorced him in 1927, and in 1928 married in London Mr Ernest Simpson, a member of a shipping firm, who had served in the Coldstream Guards during the 1914–18 War. The Simpsons became known in some Anglo-American circles, and the Prince, who first met her casually at a party, became attracted by her amusing talk and gifts as a hostess. He began to entertain her and her husband frequently at Fort Belvedere. In 1934 she and her aunt, Mrs Merriman, were among his guests when he cruised in his chartered yacht *Rosaura* along the Riviera. In February, 1935, Mrs Simpson, with other guests of his, was with him at the winter sports at Kitzbuhel.

About this time he took enthusiastically to gardening at Fort Belvedere, and Mrs Simpson helped him. By 1934 he was deeply in love with her. In 1914 Queen Alexandra had done her best to engage him to a charming and suitable princess. He refused even to consider it and told his grandmother that he would in no circumstances marry any woman unless he loved her. The sincerity of his devotion to Mrs Simpson is beyond doubt. There is authority for believing that as early as 1935 he did not discount the possibility of renouncing his right to the Throne in order that he might marry Mrs Simpson, but he had not spoken to the King before the latter's illness and death removed the opportunity.

On January 20, 1936, the life of King George V closed in peace and the Prince of Wales ascended the Throne as King Edward VIII. The next day he flew to London in his Dragon aeroplane for his Accession Council. To it he pledged himself to follow in his father's footsteps; to the Empire he broadcast: 'I am better known to most of you as the Prince of Wales ... as a man who, during the war and since, has had the opportunity of getting to know the people of nearly every country in the world under all conditions and circumstances. And, although I speak to you as the King, I am still the same man who has had that experience and whose constant effort it will be to continue to promote the well-being of his fellow men.'

He had, he protested many years later, no intention of upsetting the proud traditions of the Court: 'All that I ever had in mind was to throw open the windows a little and to let into the venerable institution some of the fresh air that I had become accustomed to breathe as Prince of Wales.' However that may be, he managed to create a draught that chilled the warmth of his own reception. For instance, the 20 'privileged bodies' to whom custom accords the right of presenting singly their loyal addresses to a new Sovereign he decided to receive *en bloc* – 'a most unfortunate decision' as one of the disappointed parties said. In matters of ceremony and official business he was apt to question things which had long been immune from question. He shocked his advisers by asking if it was necessary to preface his Speech from the Throne at the opening of Parliament with a declaration maintaining the Protestant succession. It was necessary. Then in March he abolished the royal stud at Sandringham, which had been formed in 1877: an act which caused circles enjoying much influence to fear for the soundness of the King's judgment in matters of moment. He also set in train measures of economy in the royal estates which caused hard feelings among his father's old retainers. These innovations, which showed that he intended to be King after his own fashion, occasioned apprehension in those connected with the Court who believed his predecessors' methods to be right if not immutable.

On July 16, when returning to Buckingham Palace, after presenting new colours to six battalions of the Guards, a man threw a loaded revolver into the roadway on Constitution Hill. It fell between the King and the following troops. He saw what happened, reined his horse, and after a surprised look in the direction from which the missile came calmly proceeded to the centre gateway of the Palace and took the salute as had been arranged. The assailant was afterwards convicted at the Central Criminal Court of wilfully producing a pistol near the person of the King with the intention of alarming His Majesty. The judge who tried him was satisfied that there was no intention of harming the King, and sentenced him to 12 months' imprisonment with hard labour.

In July he unveiled the Canadian National Memorial at Vimy Ridge. He had intended to spend August at Cannes, but cancelled his arrangements as he did not wish to add to the responsibilities of the French authorities already much increased by the civil war in Spain. Instead he chartered Lady Yule's yacht *Nahlin*, and left in early August for a cruise along the Dalmatian coast. He travelled incognito as Duke of Lancaster, though a Cabinet Minister was in attendance for part of the time. Some friends accompanied him; among them was Mrs Simpson, whose society he had courted no less assiduously since his accession. He visited the Prince Regent of Yugoslavia and the King of the Hellenes, and went to Istanbul, where he established friendly relations with Mustapha Kemal. In September he returned overland, visiting President Miklas and Chancellor von Schuschnigg on his way.

Scarcely was he home before he had a house party at Balmoral for Mrs Simpson, and asked some prominent guests to it. The Duke and Duchess of York, and the Duke and Duchess of Kent, and other members of the Royal Family also either visited or stayed at the Castle. If it were intended for the social advantage of Mrs Simpson it was scarcely a success. Leaving Scotland, Mrs Simpson went to stay at Felixstowe and was therefore able to enter her action for divorce at the Assizes at Ipswich. Mr Simpson did not appear or contest the case and, after what is known as hotel evidence had been tendered, a decree *nisi* was granted on October 27.

In November King Edward VIII opened Parliament, and after a visit to the Home Fleet at Portland made a tour of the distressed areas in South Wales, showing deep sympathy with the personal histories he learnt from talks with unemployed men on the dole. The emotion aroused prompted him to declare that 'something will be done' which led to a comparison by certain newspapers of the King's personal concern with the supposed apathy of his Government.

For months American papers of a sensational kind had been enlarging on the King's friendship with Mrs Simpson with preposterous exaggeration and frequently sheer invention, and in November, 1936, had announced his forthcoming marriage. The most responsible American and Canadian journals began at the same time to publish statements which betrayed anxiety and bewilderment at the extraordinary campaign of publicity. Though enough of the facts were well known in every newspaper office in Britain, no public reference to it appeared in any reputable journal here until December 2. On the previous day the Bishop of Bradford (Dr Blunt), speaking at his diocesan conference on the Coronation Service, commended the King 'to God's grace, which he will so abundantly need as we all need it, if he is to do his duty faithfully. We hope he is aware of his need. Some of us wish that he gave more positive signs of his awareness.' The press, realizing that the American campaign of publicity had gone beyond that side of the King's life which might be regarded as private, broke, first in the North and then in London, its self-imposed ordinance of restraint. The Bishop said he was surprised at this.

Meanwhile by October 18 the Prime Minister (Stanley Baldwin) had become sufficiently perturbed to ask for an urgent audience of the King. It was principally the knowledge of the impending Simpson divorce case that caused the Prime Minister to break the studied inactivity with which he had been watching the approaching crisis. The audience took place at Fort Belvedere on the following Tuesday. Baldwin expressed his fears, explaining the peril he saw to the integrity of the British Monarchy. His immediate object was to see if Mrs Simpson could be persuaded to withdraw her divorce petition. In this he received no encouragement from the King. On November 16 the King sent for Baldwin again and, having been told that the marriage was not one that would receive the approbation of the country, he declared that he intended to marry Mrs Simpson as soon as she was free and that if the Government opposed the marriage he was 'prepared to go'. Baldwin answered, 'Sir, that is most grievous news, and it is impossible for me to make any comment on it today.' On November 25 there was a further audience at which the King mooted the possibility of a morganatic marriage. Baldwin said that his first reaction was that Parliament would not pass such a Bill, but at the King's request he agreed to consult the Cabinet and the Prime Ministers of the Dominions. At their next meeting on December 2 Baldwin assured the King that such a proposal was impracticable. The issue was therefore narrowed to one fateful choice. In all the conversations the King had repeated that if he went he would go with dignity and with as little disturbance of his Ministers and his people as possible.

In the course of the memorable speech in the House of Commons in which, after the King's final decision had been disclosed, Baldwin gave an account of the preceding events, he asserted that there had been no kind of conflict. The King's action had been dictated by a determination to avoid the gossip and rumours which would be dangerous not only at home but throughout the Empire to the moral force of the Crown. His own efforts had been directed in trying to help the King to make the choice which he had not made, and they failed. But Baldwin felt that he had left nothing undone which he could have done to move the King from his decision. He added that on December 9 the Cabinet had pleaded for reconsideration and had been told that the King was unable to alter his mind. The Bill of Abdication was passed on December 11 and at 1.52 p.m. on that day the Royal Assent was given; the reign of King Edward VIII ended, and that of King George VI began.

The same evening 'His Royal Highness Prince Edward' broadcast to the Empire from Windsor Castle. 'You all know,' he said, 'the reasons which have impelled me to renounce the throne … But you must believe me when I tell you that I have found it impossible to carry the heavy burden of responsibility and to discharge my duties as King as I would wish to do without the help and support of the woman I love. And I want you to know that the decision I have made has been mine and mine alone. This was a thing I had to judge entirely for myself, the other person concerned has tried up to the last to persuade me to take a different course.' There had never, he went on to say, been any constitutional difference between Ministers and himself or between himself and Parliament. 'Bred in the constitutional traditions by my father, I should never have allowed any such issue to arise.' In conclusion he added: 'I now quit altogether public affairs, and I lay down my burden. It may be some time before I return to my native land. But I shall always follow the fortunes of the British race and Empire with profound interest, and if at any time in the future I can be found of service to his Majesty in a private station I shall not fail.'

In his own account of the Abdication drama, published some 15 years afterwards in his memoirs, the Duke of Windsor did not disguise his feeling of resentment against Baldwin, whose part in the fateful proceedings he understood as that of a deep and relentless politician bent upon creating an alignment of forces – the Established Church, the Conservative Party organization, *The Times*, and the Opposition leaders included – sufficiently powerful to force the King's hand. The impression does not do justice to Baldwin, but it is easy to understand how it arose. As the strain of the crisis increased so did the King's isolation. At the climax he retired to Fort Belvedere – for the wholly creditable reason that he did not want to excite popular demonstrations by his appearance in London – and was there besieged by reporters and photographers. He chose, or was able, to consult chiefly those who wished him to keep both his intended marriage and his Throne; and he had, early in the proceedings, withdrawn his confidence in matters relating to his marriage from his private Secretary, Lord Hardinge of Penshurst. In these circumstances it was easy for him to imagine a vast and only partly discernible conspiracy working against him.

At a late stage, urged by some of his unofficial advisers and detecting signs of a popular movement in his favour, he entertained the idea of challenging his Ministers and appealing direct to his subjects. On reflection he put the project firmly aside in the belief that it would do irreparable damage to the institution of the monarchy. He believed, however, after the storm, as he had believed before it, that with a better disposed set of ministerial advisers it should have been possible for him both to have continued his reign with the full confidence of his peoples and to have taken Mrs Simpson for his wife.

The first act of the new King was to declare his brother Duke of Windsor. No minor title was added. Subsequently, since it had lapsed, he restored to the Duke the membership of all his orders of Knighthood and his ranks in the Royal Navy,

Army, and Royal Air Force. By letters patent of May, 1937, the King declared that his brother should be entitled to hold and enjoy for himself alone the title of Royal Highness, but that neither his wife nor descendants should possess it. It was a limitation that the Duke of Windsor deeply resented. Arms were recorded for the Duke. They were those he bore as King differenced by a label of three points charged with the Imperial Crown proper. All the Duke's official income had ceased; but no application was made to the Parliament for a grant since it was understood that adequate income would be provided for him by the other members of the Royal Family in concert. King George VI purchased outright the Sandringham and Balmoral estates which the Duke had inherited from his father.

On the early morning of December 12, having driven there through the night, the Duke of Windsor left Portsmouth in the destroyer *Fury*. He went to Baron Eugene de Rothschild's residence at Enzesfeld, near Vienna. His sister (the Princess Royal), the Earl of Harewood and the Duke of Kent visited him there. In May, 1937, Mrs Simpson's decree was made absolute, and in June, as Mrs Wallis Warfield, the Duke married her according to French Law at the Château de Candé, near Tours, the home of their friends, Mr and Mrs Charles Bedaux. No member of the Royal Family was present. There was a subsequent marriage service of the Church of England conducted by an incumbent from the diocese of Durham, who had volunteered without ecclesiastical permission or sanction to celebrate it. The honeymoon was spent in Carinthia.

The first three years after their marriage were spent in restless movement between hotels and hired houses in Paris, Versailles, and the Cote d'Azur. The Duke had no wish to become an expatriate; he missed moreover the ordered life of public service. In 1938 he sounded the Prime Minister (Neville Chamberlain), who happened to be in Paris, about the possibility of his return to England now that his brother was firmly established on the Throne. Chamberlain was non-committal but said he would explore the ground. The matter disappeared in the no-man's-land between Downing Street and Buckingham Palace and the Duke heard no more about it. The war, however, and its opportunities for service seemed to offer the chance the Duke awaited. In September he was summoned to England being given to understand that he would be offered a choice of employment with the Military Mission at French GHQ or as Commissioner for Wales in the civil defence organization. He leant towards the latter which contained the prospect of becoming established once again in his own country. He found, however, that that way was not open, and he accordingly went again to France with the rank of major-general. The role of a former monarch in a subordinate military post was not an easy one either for the Duke or for his fellow-soldiers.

When France was overrun the Duke and Duchess made their way, with some difficulty, to Spain. There he received a message that Sir Winston Churchill wanted him to return to England by way of Portugal. Much as this coincided with his own wishes, he insisted upon two conditions: that he should be given notice of the kind of job the Government had in mind for him, and that the Duchess should be accorded equality with the wives of the other royal dukes. The refusal of the Court to receive her when they were in England the year before had wounded him. The attitude was the cause of continuing estrangement between the Duke and other members of his family, and the continuing obstacle to his permanent return to England. Although his pride was touched, England's 'darkest hour' was an unfortunate moment at which to make an issue of this matter. His conditions remained unsatisfied, and he was offered instead the post of Governor of the Bahamas, which he immediately accepted.

While the Duke of Windsor was in Lisbon with his future still unsettled, the German Minister there got wind of the argument with Churchill and duly reported it to Ribbentrop. The latter wired to the German Embassy in Madrid that the Duke should be lured back to Spain, told that Germany wanted peace with England and that only the Churchill clique stood in the way, and further that Germany 'would be prepared to accommodate any desire expressed by the Duke, especially with a view to the assumption of the English throne by the Duke and Duchess'. There followed various farcical and half-hearted attempts by German agents to delay the Duke's departure for the Bahamas. This curious story was told in the official publication in 1957 of an instalment of *Documents on German Foreign Policy*. The British Government prefaced the volume with a note saying that the Duke of Windsor 'never wavered in his loyalty to the British cause or in his determination to take up his official post as Governor of the Bahamas'. That the Germans thought they could tamper with his loyalty is of value only as evidence of the grotesque unreality of German foreign intelligence of the period.

In mid-August, 1940, the Duke and Duchess arrived at Nassau. His four and a half years there were the most satisfying period he was granted after his abdication. The sphere of action was, it is true, narrow but it was not without its importance and its problems. The Bahamas were in the process of transformation into a major military base, and the Governor was also able to give a new impetus to the islands' commercial and industrial enterprise, as well as organize their war effort. His energy, habit of command, and long training for public service were given something to work on, and his life was once again afforded a round of ordered duties. From the point of view of colonial administration too the term was a success. Towards its close the Duke began to chafe at his isolation from the main theatres of the war, and when no prospect of a new appointment nearer to his wishes was held out to him, he resigned.

After the war the Duke and Duchess returned to Paris. In October, 1945, he made a short visit to England to see Queen Mary and the King, his first since the early days of the war. Fairly frequent though always short visits followed over the succeeding years. He attended the funeral of King George VI and that of Queen Mary. He did not attend the Coronation of Queen Elizabeth, having stated that it would not be in accordance with constitutional usage for the sovereign or former sovereign of a state to attend.

In 1964 the Duke underwent an operation in Texas for an aneurysm of the abdominal aorta and in the following year several operations were performed in London on his left eye. He was visited in hospital by the Queen, the Princess Royal, and other members of the Royal Family. In May Mr Jack Le Vien's film *A King's Story*, made with the Duke's cooperation, was shown in London. The Duke saw it in Paris at a private showing to some 300 of his friends. In the summer of 1967 both the Duke and the Duchess attended at the invitation of the Queen the unveiling of a plaque to Queen Mary at Marlborough House. This was the first time the Duchess had attended an official public ceremony with members of the Royal Family.

SIR NOEL COWARD

Playwright and actor who was a master of comedy

26 MARCH 1973

SIR NOEL COWARD has died in Jamaica, as announced on another page, at the age of 73. Playwright, composer, director, actor, singer, and dancer, he was also on occasion novelist, short-story writer and autobiographer, and he wrote fluent, entertaining light verse. None of the great figures of the English theatre has been more versatile than he. Whatever he had found to do was done with elegantly professional certainty of effect.

During his lifetime, his place in the theatre depended on no single vein of achievement but on his complete mastery of all the stage required for whatever work he had undertaken. One or two of his sentimental songs keep their place among the popular classics of light music; others, wittily mocking, are destined for a longer life. He had little voice; but no singer more naturally gifted could project the wit of these songs with half the effect of his own dry, *staccato* style. As an actor he carried naturalism to its farthest extremes, but in a number of roles like that of Lewis Dodd, the bohemian composer of Margaret Kennedy's *The Constant Nymph*, in the 1920s and Shaw's King Magnus, in *The Apple Cart*, which he played in the Coronation season of 1953, he made every necessary effect with a delightful simplicity and punctuality, adding often to their weight by understatement; he was too disciplined and conscientious an artist to essay what was beyond his capacity for effectiveness.

Posterity may reject his musicals as limited by the tastes and techniques of the 1920s and 1930s. His serious pieces – like *Cavalcade* among his musicals, *The Vortex* and *This Happy Breed* among his plays – may seem too easily sentimental to appeal to later ages, but they reflect the mood of their times with startling clarity. Of all his multifarious achievements, it is as a master of the comedy of manners that he is irreplaceable; his work in this special field is precisely written and, elegantly economical, it belongs to the classical tradition of Congreve, Sheridan, Wilde, and Shaw.

Noel Coward was born at Teddington on December 16, 1899, the son of Arthur Coward, who worked for a firm of music publishers. His formal education was limited, for he made his first public appearance when he was 10, in a children's play, *The Goldfish*, at the Little Theatre. This brought an offer of a page boy's part, in *The Great Name*, from Charles Hawtrey, by whose skill, professionalism, and

Noel Coward, in a cabaret rehearsal at the Cafe de Paris, London, 1951

disciplined craftsmanship Coward was permanently and beneficially influenced. Until 1915, when a mild attack of tuberculosis sent him for treatment to a sanatorium, he played a large number of juvenile parts. Because of his illness, when he reached military age in 1918 he was put into a labour battalion, but transferred from that to the Artists Rifles OTC.

After the war he joined Arthur Bourchier's company, but in 1920 he appeared in his own first play, a light and flimsy comedy, *I'll Leave It to You*, at the New Theatre; this was later followed by *The Young Idea*, and in 1923 he acted, sang, and danced in *London Calling*, a revue of which he was part-author and part-composer. Changing his tone, in 1925, he made his first great success with *The Vortex*, a somewhat melo-dramatic confrontation between a foolish, amorous, middle-aged woman and the drug-taking Hamlet who was her son. In it, Coward found an authentic desperation in the self-conscious gaiety of the first post-war period.

Hay Fever, written in a weekend in 1925, is a more dazzling achievement; like *The Importance of Being Earnest*, it is pure comedy with no mission but to delight, and it depends purely on the interplay of characters, not upon elaborate comic machin-ery. This was followed by a series of musicals produced by C. B. Cochran, which culminated in *Bitter Sweet*, probably the best of Coward's work for the musical stage, in 1929, and *Cavalcade*, a magnificently spectacular pageant of English history, from the death of Queen Victoria to the great slump, as it was seen through the eyes of an upper-middle-class family. *Cavalcade's* sincere, sentimental patriotism converted to Coward's cause many theatre-goers who had distrusted the flippancy, the facil-ity, and the witty light-heartedness of his earlier work. Between the two musicals came *Private Lives*, a comedy as beautifully and smoothly made as *Hay Fever*, and no less witty but with a closer relevance to the moral concerns of its day. It exploits with inventive delight its author's gift for the retort discourteous, the comic inflation of the obvious, the urgent pursuit of the wild irrelevancy, and his mastery of cleverly economical effect.

In the 1930s he was active in management in England and New York, in partner-ship with Alfred Lunt and Lynn Fontanne, and he continued to create plays and musicals with no less ease and effect, though for a time with less wit. In 1941, however, *Blithe Spirit* broke new ground, admitting the fantastic into his mocking picture of the age; it ran for nearly 2,000 performances. *Present Laughter*, written in the following year, displays moral perplexities like those of *Private Lives* against a theatrical background; the background is beautifully sketched and the problems are worked out with undiminished wit and hilarity. Between these two un-cloudedly sunny plays came *In Which We Serve*, Coward's film in tribute to the Royal Navy, which he wrote and directed himself and in which he played the leading role. *This Happy Breed* achieved a working-class *Cavalcade* of life between the two World Wars.

His later work, with occasional novels and short stories, a War Diary to link his pre-war autobiography *Present Indicative* to its post-war sequel, *Future Indefinite*, could not always recapture the wit and the tingling contemporaneity of his earlier plays. His musicals remained gracefully made and precise in effect, but they belong to the days before the war, and of his plays, only *Nude With Violin* and *Relative Values* seemed to awaken his sharp revelatory wit. Never idle, he made Feydeau's *Occupe-toi d'Amelie* into *Look after Lulu*, a typically Coward work even though it seemed unblushingly to allude to earlier effects and to earlier dialogue for effects he knew to be infallible. He appeared in small parts, beautifully observed, magnificently understated, and extremely wittily played in a variety of films in the later 1950s and the 1960s.

In 1964, a year in which Granada presented four of his plays on television under the omnibus title *A Choice of Coward*, he had the satisfaction of directing the National Theatre production of *Hay Fever* – the second modern play to be included in the National repertoire and the first play ever to be directed there by its author. This was followed by a musical version of *Blithe Spirit*, supervised but not written or composed by Coward, and by a revival of *Present Laughter*, with Mr Nigel Patrick playing Coward's old part and directing, which ran for close on 400 performances at the Queen's. Last year Coward attended the first night of *Cowardy Custard* in London – a revue of his revue material. A revival of *Private Lives* with Maggie Smith and Robert Stephens opened in London. He also received an honorary degree from Sussex University.

'If and when,' Coward had written in 1958, 'she [success] chooses to leave me I shall not repine, nor shall I mourn her any more than I mourn other loved ones who have gone away. I do not approve of mourning, I only approve of remembering, and her I shall always remember gratefully and with pride.'

By the time he reached his seventieth birthday in 1969, the year in which he was awarded a knighthood, it was possible to see how firmly the best of Coward's work was rooted in the English comic tradition. It is an attack in suitably comic terms on the insincere inflation of emotion, on the dishonesty of meaningless fine manners and unexamined conventions, and on the hypocrisy which masquerades as moral censoriousness; it rejects the easygoing, the undisciplined, and the unprofessional. Claiming no more than, in the words of one of his songs, 'a talent to amuse', Coward, his public had come to learn, amused them for their own good as well as their delight.

Coward was widely admired and loved in his own profession for his generosity and kindness to those who fell on hard times. Stories are told of the unobtrusive way in which he relieved the needs or paid the debts of old theatrical connections who had no claim on him.

OTTO KLEMPERER

A conductor of international renown

6 JULY 1973

DURING THE LAST years of his long and eventful life Dr Otto Klemperer, who died on Friday night in Zurich, was revered, in this country at least, as the greatest of living conductors. He was 88.

This renown was the reward of uncompromising honesty and limitless determination. The honesty drove him to seek only, in his performances, for a strictly truthful and just representation of the composer's instructions (not merely his intentions). The determination enabled him to survive and continue conducting after fate had struck him down again and again.

Klemperer was born in Breslau on May 14, 1885. He spent his schooldays in Hamburg, then studied music at the Hoch Conservatory in Frankfurt-am-Main and in Berlin, specializing in composition, under Pfitzner, and the piano. In 1905 he met Mahler in Berlin and, being passionately desirous of joining the great man's musical staff at the Vienna Court Opera, made a piano transcription of Mahler's second symphony; early in 1907, while visiting Vienna for a recital at which he was the accompanist, Klemperer called on Mahler, presented him with the transcription and played the scherzo from memory. Mahler advised him to continue as a pianist, but gave him an open letter of recommendation as a conductor.

An overheard remark led him to apply for a post at the German Opera in Prague; Angelo Neumann gave Klemperer the post simply on Mahler's recommendation, and in the autumn of 1907 Klemperer made his debut as a conductor; the opera was *Der Freischütz*. Three years later he was appointed chief conductor at Hamburg Municipal Opera (where Lotte Lehmann and Elisabeth Schumann made their joint debuts as Pages in *Lohengrin* under his baton), and he remained there until 1914; he conducted his first important symphony concerts during this period.

In 1917 he moved from Strasbourg to Cologne and made his name as a champion of modern music with a repertory, symphonic and operatic, that included the newest and most progressive works; soon after the First World War ended he was in demand internationally as an opera conductor. In 1924 he was offered a post at Berlin State Opera but he turned it down in favour of the musical directorship at Wiesbaden.

A Berlin musical directorship was forthcoming in 1927, at the Kroll Opera, which had been opened three years earlier. During Klemperer's four years in office there the Kroll Opera was rated the leading experimental opera house in Europe, some said in history. The repertory included Schoenberg's *Die glückliche Hand* and *Erwartung*, Stravinsky's *Maura* and *Oedipus Rex*, Janáček's *From the House of the Dead*, Hindemith's *Cardillac, Hin und zurück*, and *Neues vom Tage*. Productions and scenic designs, not only in these but in the whole repertory of 44 operas ranging from Gluck to Offenbach, were in the hands of the most brilliant progressive artists of the German theatre.

During these years too Klemperer's symphony concerts in Berlin included new works by Bartók, Webern, Krenek, and Weill, as well as by the composers already mentioned. In 1928 he re-formed and built up the Berlin Philharmonic Choir.

Klemperer's activities at the Kroll caused much displeasure to the more conservative music critics and politicians as well. In 1931 the Kroll Opera was closed down, but Klemperer continued to conduct in Berlin at the State Opera. In January, 1933, President Hindenburg presented him with the Goethe Medal for his services to German culture. Two months later German culture acquired other significance. Klemperer's contract was abruptly terminated (even if his artistic policies had been less controversial, he was by birth a Jew – though by faith a Roman Catholic convert) and he took refuge in Switzerland.

The New World claimed him, like many of his German colleagues. In the same year he was made musical director of the Los Angeles Symphony Orchestra and now his secondary career as a symphonic conductor became his principal activity. Honours were conferred upon him; in 1937 he formed the Pittsburgh Symphony Orchestra; he conducted frequently in New York. The new life seemed as promising as the old one. Then fate struck its first hard blow. Klemperer was found to be suffering from a brain tumour (caused, it was thought, by a fall from the rostrum in Leipzig in 1933) and the treatment for this, though successful, left him lame and partly paralyzed.

After some fruitful years at the Budapest Opera in the early post-war period he began once again to appear in concert halls all over Europe, and in 1951 contributed two splendid concerts to the Festival Hall's inaugural season. They were given with the Philharmonia Orchestra, a body with which he was henceforth to be particularly associated.

But not at once. At Montreal Airport, later in 1951, he fell and fractured the femur of his unparalyzed leg, and was obliged to walk on crutches and to conduct sitting down. Further operations retarded his recovery, but in May, 1955, during a broadcast performance of *Don Giovanni* at Cologne he involuntarily rose to his feet to bring in the trombones at the Commendatore's arrival in Don Juan's house. He remained standing.

Klemperer began a period of intense activity in London. His repertory was no longer the challenging progressive one of his younger days, but centred firmly on the German classics and romantics from Bach to Richard Strauss, with Beethoven as its centre and crown. Klemperer's fingers could not hold a baton but his arm movements were sure and expressive, his personality and willpower ample to communicate all that he wished to an orchestra.

The Philharmonia Orchestra's founder, Mr Walter Legge, was also artistic director of Columbia records, and Klemperer was able to prepare many of his performances in the unhurried calm of the recording studio, committing an interpretation to disc and then repeating the finished performance in the concert hall. So it was that London heard the superb, heaven-storming Beethoven cycles conducted by Klemperer in the 1950s, a series memorable particularly for spacious, perfectly proportioned architecture, strength, and intensity and inner radiance of sonority, majesty of line, qualities signally favourable to the Eroica and seventh symphonies, above all to the ninth symphony and the *Missa Solemnis*. In these, Klemperer had the collaboration of the magnificent Philharmonia Chorus, whose debut in a performance of the Choral Symphony under him was a musical high-point of the decade.

There were superb series of Brahms concerts, too, and Mozart cycles – Klemperer's reading of Mozart was idiosyncratic, too heavy and earnest for some tastes, but undeniably illuminating. For the season 1958–59 Legge had planned a series of 21 Klemperer concerts in London comprising a tremendous repertory. Yet a third time misfortune fell upon him: recuperating from bronchitis he fell asleep while smoking his pipe, woke to find the bedclothes alight, and seized the nearest liquid to douse the flames – it was spirits of camphor and he was grievously burned.

But Klemperer triumphed yet again to conduct. His concerts in the 1960s and after included further excursions outside the German classics and romantics: Bartók's Divertimento, Tchaikovsky, Dvořák and Berlioz (a glorious interpretation of the Fantastic Symphony). He conducted and recorded much of Bruckner, some Mahler (notably the Resurrection Symphony), and a deeply moving account of Bach's *St Matthew Passion*. In 1961 he turned once again to opera and made his Covent Garden debut in his own production of *Fidelio*, which was traditional, unfussy, grandly conceived, and profoundly revealing.

Klemperer had been appointed principal conductor for life of the Philharmonia Orchestra when he returned to conducting in 1959 after recovery from his burns. In 1964 Mr Legge dissolved his orchestra, and Klemperer's last appearances with it were in a recording of *The Messiah* and in two Mozart concerts for the City of London Festival. But the players had reconstituted themselves as the New Philharmonia Orchestra, and Klemperer at once accepted the honorary presidency.

His physical stature was huge, and he remained erect and unbowed by calamity. In this he was like his interpretations, as in his fearless honesty which often caused offence in his younger days. During the last days of romantic interpretation he was, as we have seen, a modernist. When he turned to the classics the trend of the times was favouring extreme virtuosity and high polish. Klemperer again swam against the tide; having established the balance he favoured, as the 'Klemperer sound', he concentrated entirely on the structure and inner content of the music, resisting any fashionable desire for glamour or high speed.

It was the plain truth alone that guided his work.

He married in 1919 Johanna Geissler. They had one son and one daughter. She died in 1956.

* * *

PABLO PICASSO

Most influential artist of his age

8 APRIL 1973

PABLO PICASSO, who died yesterday as announced on another page, was the most famous, the most controversial, in many ways the most influential, and undoubtedly the richest artist of his age.

He was a draughtsman of genius, and there is probably no single artist, except Giotto or Michelangelo, who can justly compare with him in being responsible for so radically altering the course of art in his time. It was natural to think of him in superlatives. Yet the most pertinent superlative of them all, only leads into a maze of, as yet, unanswerable questions. Was he, quite simply, the greatest artist of the first half of the century?

The question poses itself because Picasso bestrode the earlier decades of it with an indisputable authority. His art was always astounding for its diversity, the rate of its production, and its plain ability to surprise. For artists it held, for many years, a sort of bemusing and inescapable glamour. Yet, particularly towards the end of his life, it was seen to lie open to a number of grave charges.

Briefly, these hinged on the fact that Picasso fed, to a degree unprecedented in so eminent an artist, on the stylistic devices of other ages and of other artistic traditions, and that it was only by a peculiar legerdemain, the 'transformation' process that was the Picassian hallmark, that he was able to absorb them and, as it were, re-edit then as a personal manner. A museum-bred art of this sort, it was urged, had had all its really serious artistic problems solved for it before it began: Picasso, to whom disguises and transformations were a life-long passion, was in fact only engaged, though with startling brilliance of invention and improvisation, in icing somebody else's cake.

This charge led to the secondary but almost as damaging criticism that his skill was fatally facile and it is certainly true that after the 1930s only a handful of his paintings can, individually, be said to escape a certain feeling of triviality engendered by the reckless speed of their execution and a tendency to dissipate the pressures of an extreme emotionalism in a dazzling multiplication of pictures rather than concentrate them in the perfection of a few.

It may, however, be said that much of this is symptomatic of the exasperation, neurosis, and tragic despair of the age Picasso's art was reflecting. For as important as the strictures on his methods and achievements, and surely as relevant, are the claims that Picasso mirrored the emotional stresses of his times more compendiously than any of his contemporaries. His vein of savagery drew its power to shock from his Spanish blood, but it was as apt as Goya's and as timely for indicting the worst affronts to humanity of the modern age. For Picasso's art can be more easily interpreted in terms of Mediterranean humanism than most. It can be seen to have encompassed an exceptionally wide range of human emotional experience – horror, cruelty, and death on the one hand; fantasy and the love of art, domestic tenderness, and the gaiety of living on the other.

'Guernica', the terrible, apocalyptic picture recording the bombing of the little Basque town in 1937 and one of the few indisputable masterpieces of modern painting, is clearly the representative example of the first group. Picasso, indeed, seemed to give his *imprimatur* to this, the 'black' side of his work, when he made himself responsible for the selection of paintings shown in an important exhibition in Rome in 1953. It contained many of his most horrifying images, like the almost beastly 'Man Sucking a Lollipop' (1938) and the appalling 'Nude Dressing her Hair' of 1940, and played down other aspects.

This 'black' mood for obvious reasons aroused continuous controversy, and there was a notable outburst of pain and indignation, recorded in a memorable correspondence in *The Times* when a selection of Picasso's most bitter works, many of them painted during the German occupation of Paris, was exhibited at the Victoria and Albert Museum at the end of 1945.

But the vein of sentiment or of impish gaiety was quite as persistent an element of his art. It accounted for a number of occasions when he disconcertedly reverted, in the middle of some particularly perverse style of distortion, to a simple naturalism in order to record the face of a friend, a mistress, or a child. It became predominant in the period of his 'antique' arcadian manner after the Second World War, and it was seen in a particularly touching form in a sequence of drawings shown at the Marlborough Gallery in 1953, in which the artist played subtle psychological variations on the themes of the artist and his model, intelligence and sensuality, which had always attracted him.

Pablo Ruiz Picasso was born on October 25, 1881, at Malaga, where his father, Jose Ruiz Blasco, a competent painter in an academic tradition, was a teacher at the local School of Art and Crafts. Picasso was his mother's family name, and there has been some suggestion, as it is uncommon in Spain, that the family was of Italian origin; as far as both branches can be followed with any certainty, however, they were predominantly Andalusian.

The young artist soon gave evidence of the talents proper to prodigy. His father undertook to give him a sound academic training when he was seven, and when he was 13, handed over his paints and brushes to him in token of resignation to his superior powers. At 15, when his father had been promoted to the staff of the School of Fine Arts in Barcelona, he completed the competitive entry examination to the school, usually spread over a month, in one day; he was under age, but won first place over all the adult competitors. Two years later he repeated these examination feats for the Academy of San Fernando in Madrid.

While in Barcelona he had been drawn towards a small group of poets and painters who had founded a 'revolutionary tavern' called *Els Quarte Gats*, the Four Cats. The prevailing attitude among these young Catalan intellectuals was an anarchic, rebellious bohemianism not untinged with *fin-de-siècle* decadence. It was in the spirit of this group combined with first-hand observation of the miseries of poverty both in the slums of Barcelona and in the peasant communities of villages like Horta Da Ebro in Catalonia, where he was sent for a long convalescence after an attack of scarlatina, that he formed his first distinctively personal style, known as his 'Blue Period'.

It was with this style, nervous, highly charged with pathos and with a greater social consciousness even than he showed in his paintings of social outcasts, clowns, beggars, jugglers, and harlequins who were the subjects of the ensuing 'Rose Period', that Picasso finally arrived in Paris. He had made three unsuccessful attempts on the art citadel of Europe, during one of which he had been reduced to burning his own drawings to keep warm. In 1904 he came to stay, and found himself a studio in a battered Montmartre tenement derisively known as the Bateau Lavoir.

Here he worked for five years, the centre of a growing circle of writers and artists, among whom were his first patrons, Leo and Gertrude Stein, and the first champion of Cubism, Apollinaire. It was to this studio, too, that in the spring of 1907 he invited a few friends to see the large and astonishing canvas, now in the Museum of Modern Art, New York (and never, incidentally, finished) known as the 'Demoiselles d'Avignon'. It came as a shock even to his most devoted admirers, and no one (Braque, Derain, and Matisse were of the company) pretended to understand what Picasso thought he was doing.

It is nevertheless from this famous picture, with its brutally angular nudes and the savagely scarred faces which reflected Picasso's absorption at that time in Negro art, that Daniel-Henri Kahnweiler, who soon afterwards was to become Picasso's dealer, has dated the birth of Cubism. Cubism proper, however, is generally regarded nowadays as the joint invention of Picasso and Braque, arrived at independently by both artists while on holiday in the summer of 1908, and made public when the word 'cubist' as a term of derision was first used to describe Braque's landscapes in the Salon d'Automne of that year.

From now until 1914, when the outbreak of war permanently disrupted the early Cubist movement, Picasso and Braque worked together in an artistic partnership of extraordinary intimacy and concentration. The two artists submerged their individuality in a common style. The idiom they were working out was partly an excessive application of Cézanne's formulation of the geometry underlying natural appearances, partly an attempt to grasp pictorial space intellectually by presenting simultaneously the various views of an object which would contribute to a full knowledge of its shape and solidity. The first phase was appropriately known as 'analytical' cubism, and this style, in which Picasso even executed a few portraits, remains the hardest to 'read'. But a desire for less involved complexity, and also for a new way of grasping 'reality' by actually introducing 'real' textures, or *collage*, into the composition, led in 1911 to what is now known as 'synthetic' cubism.

In 1917 Jean Cocteau invited Picasso to go to Rome with him to design for Cocteau's new ballet *Parade*. In this way he was drawn into the creative circle of Diaghilev's Russian Ballet, and the discipline of cubism gave way to less cloistered delights both in his life and in his work. In 1918 he married a dancer from the troupe, Olga Koklova, and in 1919 his travels with the ballet brought him to London for the world premiere of *The Three-Cornered Hat* at the Alhambra, for which he produced perhaps the most celebrated of his stage designs.

Picasso's styles during the following two decades can only be briefly recorded with a comprehensive remark on their protean variety and their lack of any logic of development; 1920–21 saw the first massive, impassive goddesses of his 'neoclassic' period. Between 1923 and 1926 he executed a number of extraordinary, sumptuous, and complex still-life subjects which were the final, and, as it were, nostalgic flowering of synthetic cubism, but in 1923 there had already begun the series of disquieting disruptions of human anatomy which were to culminate in his most horrifying images.

The element of horror had entered his art with his interest in Surrealism and had broken out in a purely sensational form, in the so-called 'bone' styles of 1928–29. In 1935, owing to the disruption of his marriage, he stopped painting for 20 months. But it was in this year that he completed his most elaborate and haunting print, the large etching called the 'Minotauromachie'. Picasso's print-making was always an activity parallel and complementary to his painting, and it may even be said that it forms as a whole the most perfectly satisfying achievement of an artist whose talents were essentially linear rather than those of the colourist, and who was more at home with technical invention than with purely painterly sensitivity.

No artist in history lived more in the glare of publicity than Picasso and after the Second World War he became as good for a *bon mot* in the popular press as his work had ever been for an artistic furore. His uncompromising integrity during the occupation, and the publicity surrounding his attachment to the Communist Party the moment it was over, are the two factors which probably contributed most to the very personal form of attention which was now centred on him and continued till his death. On the other hand, his influence on contemporary art was suddenly seen to have declined, although his own artistic activity, which now branched out into sculpture and especially ceramics as well as painting, drawing, and print-making, remained as prolific as ever. It seemed natural that by 1957 a London gallery should mount an exhibition called 'Post-Picasso Paris'.

The result was a beginning of the embalming process. Documentary information surrounding him had never been in short demand, but now film-records were added to it. The most remarkable of these were one by Lucio Emmer and one by H. G. Clouzot. The first was of Picasso's days at Vallauris, in the south of France, with the artist working at his pottery or executing, clad only in shorts and sandals and perched on a pair of steps, a trial fresco in a matter of minutes across the vault of a deserted chapel. The second concentrated on the stages of development through which Picasso's designs were propelled. In these films a larger public than ever before was introduced not only to the artist's squat, simian, but muscular appearance, with the owlishly wise and humorous face and the piercing black eyes, but also to the turbulent inventiveness of his mind: the speed of hand and wit of line, the characteristic *horror vacui*, the creation based on destruction, and the endless process of transformation that made up the characteristic strengths and weaknesses of his art.

In 1960 the Tate mounted the most comprehensive exhibition of his work – and about 450,000 people saw it. Russia was persuaded to send several works from the Hermitage, and every important western gallery lent others to make it a more or less complete illustration of his artistic development.

By now, few weeks went by without news of Picasso works changing hands at high prices. In 1964 £90,000 was paid by the Bavarian Government for a single portrait – said to be the largest sum ever paid for a work by a living artist. And early in 1965, not without criticism, the Tate bought 'Les Trois Danseuses' for £60,000.

Exhibitions of a large scale giving a wide survey of Picasso's work early and late and accompanied by elaborate catalogues included 'Picasso and Man' (the Art Gallery of Toronto and Montreal Museum of Fine Art, 1964). A salient aspect of his astonishing versatility, his sculpture, was commemorated in the exhibition at the Museum of Modern Art, New York, 'The Sculpture of Picasso 1967', the published record containing an essay by Roland Penrose. His versatility in graphic art and graphic processes was a continuing feature of his later years, as witness a remarkable series of colour linocuts produced in the 1960s, exhibited in London at the Hanover Gallery in 1963.

Of special note among the many displays and tributes given throughout the world to mark his eighty-fifth anniversary was 'Hommage à Picasso 1966–67', Grand Palais, Paris, a comprehensive exhibition in the catalogue of which Jean Leymarie made the trenchant remark: 'Picasso dominates his age as Michelangelo dominated his own.'

His first wife, Olga Koklova, had died in 1955, and in 1961, at the age of 79, he married Jacqueline Roque, his model.

Probably the most intimate and in some ways the most unpleasant biographical work about Picasso appeared in 1965. It was written in collaboration with Mr Carlton Lake, by Françoise Gilot, whom he first met in 1943, who shared his life for seven years and mothered two of his children.

In a series of court actions, Picasso attempted, without success, to suppress editions of the book, and extracts of it in magazines.

SAMUEL GOLDWYN

One of the fathers of the American film industry

31 JANUARY 1974

MR SAMUEL GOLDWYN, one of the last survivors from the first generation of American movie magnates, and judged by his work by far the most distinguished of them, died yesterday in Los Angeles. He was 91.

In his lifetime he became something of a Hollywood legend, for his malapropisms and his exuberant but often immature enthusiasm for culture were often held up for ridicule. Yet he was a born showman, with all the showman's instinctive appreciation of what the public wanted, and his admiration for the classics was genuine, even though it was often naive. He entered the film industry when it was in its infancy, and became one of its pioneers, helping to transform it from a childish novelty into one of the most popular mediums of story-telling in the twentieth century. He also had a flair for discovering star players.

He was born in Poland on August 27, 1882; his real name was Samuel Goldfish. He emigrated early to the United States and entered the clothing business, where he achieved some success through his business acumen. His entry into the film business was largely accidental; he married Blanche Lasky, sister of Jesse L. Lasky, who was at that time a theatrical impresario. Lasky had become interested in the commercial potentialities of the film and, when he and an aspiring young actor and dramatist, Cecil B. de Mille, decided to try their hand at film-making, it was only natural that Goldwyn should be enlisted to take charge of the financial side of the venture. He became treasurer and general manager of the Jesse L. Lasky Motion Picture Company in 1913, was briefly associated with its successor, Famous Players-Lasky, and later the Goldwyn Company, formed in 1916 (the name was a composite of Goldfish and Selwyn, the name of the company's two vice-presidents; it was not 'till 1918 that Samuel Goldfish legally became Goldwyn). It was not long before Goldwyn realized that to make films the way he wanted he had to have complete control of them. His first personal production was *The Eternal City* (1923), a tale of the early days of fascism, but the fortune of his company was based for several years on the outstanding popularity of his *Potash and Perlmutter* and its two sequels.

From the first he persevered in his policy of hiring the leading talents of the time: among his stars were the Talmadge sisters, Constance Bennett, Vilma Banky, and, in film after film, Ronald Colman. Indeed, most of Ronald Colman's most notable films in the 1920s were made under Goldwyn's guidance: *Tarnish, A Thief in*

Paradise, His Supreme Moment, and a long series in which he starred with Vilma Banky, such as *The Dark Angel, The Winning of Barbara Worth* (which also marked the debut of Gary Cooper), *The Night of Love, The Magic Flame, Two Lovers,* and others. All of these were outstanding commercial successes, but it could not be claimed that any of them offered a notable contribution to creative film-making, with the possible exception of *Stella Dallas* (1926).

With the coming of sound, Goldwyn was able to show his full stature as a producer. At first, understandably, he played safe with Ronald Colman as an impeccably suave Bulldog Drummond (1929) and Raffles (1930), or musicals with Eddie Cantor (*Whoopee, Roman Scandals, The Kid from Spain*) or Evelyn Laye (*One Heavenly Night*). But in 1931 he produced *Street Scene,* adapted by Elmer Rice from his play, and directed by King Vidor with a realization, remarkable for its time, of how to convert a fairly talkative and static stage play into strong cinema.

This film first signalled Goldwyn's readiness to interest himself in current problems and serious social analysis within the framework of the commercial film. At this time also there appeared for the first time on the credits of his films some of the distinguished names associated with Goldwyn's greatest achievements: Gregg Toland, the brilliant photographer whose experiments he encouraged and exploited; writers such as Preston Sturges, Lillian Hellman, Ben Hecht, Robert Sherwood, and Maxwell Anderson; directors like Vidor, Ford, Hawks, Mamoulian, and above all Wyler.

Wyler's first film for Goldwyn was *Dodsworth* (1936), from another of Sinclair Lewis's novels – John Ford had made *Arrowsmith* in 1931. In 1936 also Toland joined the partnership for *These Three,* a neatly tailored version by Lillian Hellman of her play *The Children's Hour,* and in subsequent years the three talents were reunited on *Dead End, Wuthering Heights, The Westerner, The Little Foxes* (which contained one of Bette Davis's best performances and some of Toland's most masterly photography), and finally, after the war, on *The Best Years of Our Lives,* the best-loved of all Goldwyn films. Though these films represent the crown of Goldwyn's achievement during those years, they were not the only notable films he made by any means. In 1937 Ford's *Hurricane* included some of the finest storm scenes on film, and Vidor directed a new version of *Stella Dallas* with a striking performance by Barbara Stanwyck. In 1938 Goldwyn brought Balanchine to Hollywood to direct the ballet sequences in *The Goldwyn Follies,* otherwise, despite two of Gershwin's best songs, an interesting misfire; and in 1941 Howard Hawks directed for him one of the most intelligent films ever made about popular music, *Ball of Fire.*

During the war Goldwyn contributed to international understanding with Milestone's *North Star,* a rather rose-tinted view of Russian life with some fine battle-scenes, and to national morale with two good Bob Hope films, *They Got Me Covered* and *The Princess and the Pirate,* and several films starring a new discovery of his, Danny Kaye. His first post-war production was *The Best Years of Our Lives*, but unfortunately after this peak his films began to show a decided decline: *The Secret Life of Walter Mitty* provided Danny Kaye with one of his aptest vehicles, but the 'serious' films offered little of interest except *A Song is Born*, a diluted remake of *Ball of Fire*, and *Edge of Doom*, a dark but powerful film ruined by reshooting with an eye to general popularity (one of Goldwyn's very few remarkable concessions to public taste). In 1952 he imported Roland Petit to provide a ballet for Hans Christian Andersen, and from that time on produced only a small number of very expensive films, starting with *Guys and Dolls*, and a wide-screen version of the Gershwin opera *Porgy and Bess*.

Samuel Goldwyn made his mistakes, like any other film-maker – though fewer than any comparable figure – but his record is quite without parallel for its determined seeking of the best in all fields connected with film-making: the best writers, the best directors, the best actors, the best technicians. From his earliest days he sought to make films of style and intelligence, and along the way he acquired, as well as a formidable knowledge of the film medium, a wide and varied background of culture, which helped him to deal with collaborators of the greatest distinction in their own fields. His fractured English was legendary, although most of the famous examples were apocryphal, and the genuine ones, such as 'a verbal contract isn't worth the paper it's written on', contain a measure of shrewd comment. He once said 'I make my pictures to please myself' and that might serve as his most fitting epitaph.

CHARLES LINDBERGH

First non-stop solo flight from New York to Paris

26 AUGUST 1974

COLONEL CHARLES LINDBERGH, the American flier, who made the first solo transatlantic non-stop flight from New York to Paris in 1927, has died at the age of 72.

Lindbergh came of Scandinavian stock. He was born on February 4, 1902, in Detroit but, while he was a child, the family moved into Minnesota and his father was elected to the House of Representatives where he opposed the entry of the United States into the war in 1917. On his death Mrs Lindbergh returned to Detroit and Charles Augustus grew up in the developing world of motor engines. He soon turned to flying and ground his way forward from wing-walking and parachuting to piloting through a flying school at Lincoln, Nebraska, and into the struggling air line at St Louis.

One night, while ploughing through a storm, he decided he would try to win the $25,000 offered by a French hotel proprietor for a direct flight from New York to Paris. He planned his flight from the start, persuaded his backers in St Louis to support him, did his own negotiating with the Ryan company and almost his own designing, laid down in the most precise terms what he wanted, and lived on the construction job to make sure he got it, worked out his own navigation scheme, finally did his own interpreting of a dubious weather report, and at last asked permission of Admiral Byrd to make use of the runway he had prepared for himself. To all this meticulous planning he brought his own skill and peculiar accomplishment in estimating risks and playing them not foolhardily yet up to the limit. In his air mail days he had twice stepped out and used his parachute. This time he had no parachute.

On May 20, 1927, Spirit of St Louis with nearly one and a half tons of petrol on board staggered off the runway at Roosevelt Field, New York, narrowly missing some trees and telephone wires.

With a single engine, no radio aids and no forward view from his cockpit, he appears now as he did then to have been accepting ridiculous odds. His compatriots indeed promptly named him the 'flying fool' and nobody believed he could pull off so enormous a hazard. When he did, the achievement stood out so much the more brightly among the series of other and bigger projects he beat to the post, especially as his adventure in comparison had been financed on the proverbial shoestring.

Lindbergh's great flight lifted him at one spectacular stroke out of obscurity to a position of popular interest which shocked and embarrassed him then and was to lead him into difficult situations thereafter. He had a powerful sense of personal rectitude and no sense at all of the effects his fame, allied with his intense serious-ness and honesty, might have in the wider field of public affairs. He was a fine pilot and navigator and at least as able an engineer. His clear mind, thrusting initiative, love of achievement, persistence, and transparent honesty guaranteed him success in his chosen line but when, in a brief 33½ hours over the ocean, success came to him, it was of a nature and quality that were wholly outside his experience.

At the Paris airport, he was virtually mobbed. At Croydon later, his arrival was greeted by an enormous crowd. He shrank from these unbridled manifestations of public favour as something indecent and dangerously intemperate. He was almost as startled by the attention he received from the press and soon was as hard for a reporter to get hold of as a crowned head. Having been received and decorated by the heads of states, having been fêted and congratulated by important societies, he was so impressed by his new status that, like Agag, he trod delicately wherever he went and retired into the natural reserve which, hitherto, only his fellow-pilots had penetrated when they nicknamed him 'Slim' on his little air mail line centred on St Louis.

This betokened no lack of courage. It marked rather bemusement, distrust, fear, and distaste together with an obstinate resolution not to be made use of in projects he did not understand and could not fully control.

His feat, which blazed the trail for the massive air traffic of today, fired the imagination of the world. Lindbergh was an instant legend; babies, streets, even a town were named after him. In 1932 his child was taken from his crib at Lindbergh's New Jersey home and a note asking for a ransom of $50,000 left on the window sill. Although the ransom was paid the child was found murdered. Bruno Hauptman, tried and convicted of the crime, was not executed until 1936. The case attracted enormous publicity, and Lindbergh paid dearly for his fame both then and later when in 1940 he brought a hornet's nest about his ears by his intervention in world politics as an outspoken isolationist.

He was heavily handled by members of Roosevelt's Government, taunted by Harold Ickes, then Secretary of the Interior, with being 'a knight of the Golden Eagle' and having retorted that he had accepted his German decoration on the advice of the United States Ambassador in Berlin he resigned his commission in the United States Army Air Corps Reserve and stepped down from his isolationist platform and out of the limelight.

Yet, true to type again, he did not step out of his chosen profession or sidestep his duty as a citizen. Throughout the war he was engaged on work he could do well, on testing new aircraft, trying them on active service, sometimes in combat, advising on technical and tactical matters, all under his chosen shroud of deep secrecy. Not until long after the end of the war was he commissioned again. He published his autobiography (*The Spirit of St Louis*) in 1953. A film of his first epic flight called by the same name appeared in 1957 with James Stewart in the title role.

Many years before, on a flight to Mexico City, he had made the acquaintance of Dwight Morrow, the United States Ambassador and a former banker. In 1929 he married Morrow's daughter, Anne, and settled in New Jersey, not far from New York. After their domestic disaster the Lindberghs secretly left the United States and stayed first in South Wales and later in Kent, where they enjoyed a welcome freedom from the attentions of the press. Eventually they returned to the United States. Earlier in their married life they had flown on long journeys together. One of the first was to China by way of the Arctic. A number of other long flights was made after their return from England, most of them in a single-engined float seaplane. These trips yielded material for Mrs Lindbergh's books in which some of the best writing on flying is to be found.

P. G. WODEHOUSE

Creator of a timeless fairyland

14 FEBRUARY 1975

P. G. WODEHOUSE, who died on Friday in a Long Island hospital at the age of 93, was a comic genius recognized in his lifetime as a classic and an old master of farce. His span as an author was as long as the biblical span of man. His first fans were schoolboys at the turn of the century; seventy years later he had them in the whole English-speaking world and beyond – he was translated into many languages, including Chinese and Japanese. He was that rare literary phenomenon, a best-seller who became a cult among highbrows. Popularity did not inflate him any more than the burst of hostility provoked by his wartime broadcasts from Berlin upset his balance. He remained always a modest, retiring man avoiding the lime-light, absorbed in the technicalities of his craft and happy in his circle of friends to whom he was affectionately known as 'Plum'. To the surprise of some and to the pleasure of many he was created KBE in the last New Year Honours.

Pelham Grenville Wodehouse was born on October 15, 1881, at Guildford, the third son of Henry Ernest Wodehouse, CMG, a judge in Hong Kong. The family had its roots in Norfolk and had sent many members to Parliament. While his parents were in the Far East, Wodehouse stayed with aunts, several of whom were married to country clergymen. He spent part of his youth in Shropshire, a county he was to people with some of his happiest characters and in which he sited Bland-ings Castle. He went to school at Dulwich College, doing well as a classical scholar and playing in the first football and cricket teams. He remained loyal to Dulwich throughout his life. A career as a banker in the East was planned for him. But he soon discovered (as did his employers at the Hongkong and Shanghai Bank) that he was not cut out for a career in commerce. He left the bank to earn his living as a journalist and storywriter. For some years he wrote the 'By The Way' column in a London evening paper, the *Globe*, and he contributed a series of school stories, 'The Gold Bar', 'The White Feather', and others, to the *Captain*, a magazine for boys that was popular in the early years of this century. By 1910, still largely unknown to grown-ups, he had won an enthusiastic following of schoolboys. His stories, coming out in monthly parts, were more realistic and true to Public School life than most of their predecessors. He created in them two outstanding characters, one of whom was to keep in the foreground of his later popularity. Mike, the brilli-ant cricketer and solid citizen, was a pin-up for the average schoolboy, and a perfect foil to his friend, Psmith. It was with Psmith that Wodehouse tried his first experiment in fooling with English prose, an art that he subsequently carried to such dizzy heights.

Going to New York before the first war he quickly made it his second home and found there a market for other than school stories. At the same time he began his connection with the stage which was to make him part author and writer of lyrics of 18 musical comedies, including *Kissing Time, The Golden Moth*, and *The Cabaret Girl*. His recognition as a new star in the small constellation of really funny writers – those who can provoke spontaneous laughter in a reader as opposed to a smile – began before the First War was over and spread like wild fire in the twenties. This was his great creative period, which saw the births of Jeeves and Bertie Wooster. The books poured out and so did praise of them. The Earl of Emsworth, the Drones Club, and other names and places in the canon became household words. *Punch* said that to criticize their author was like taking a spade to a soufflé. VIPs were known to carry the latest Wodehouse to bed with them on day of publication. Among the admirers of this quickly maturing vintage comic were Asquith, Gilbert Murray, Kipling, Wells, and Montague James. Belloc called him the best living writer of English.

Correspondents, learned and facetious, argued in the columns of *The Times* about the evidence for and against Bertie having a receding chin. Wodehouse joined in with the official statement that the chin is 'undoubtedly opisthognathous'. The Public Orator at Oxford asked, when the Vice-Chancellor was admitting Mr Wodehouse to a D.Litt, 'Petroniumne dicam an Terentium nostrum?' Such of Bertie Wooster's old school chums as remembered their Latin might have told the Public Orator that Wodehouse was much funnier than Petronius and Terence put together. But the Public Orator deserved praise for the ingenuity with which he worked Bertie and Jeeves, Mulliner and Lord Emsworth, Psmith, the Hon. Augustus Fink-Nottle, and the Empress of Blandings into Latin verse. Thus Wodehouse was given the accolade of the Establishment in 1939. There had been nothing like it since the crazes for the *Diary of a Nobody* and the Sherlock Holmes stories.

Captured by the Germans at Le Touquet in 1940, Wodehouse was sent to an internment camp in Upper Silesia. As he turned 60 he was released, but not allowed to leave Germany, and in Berlin he was approached by the representative of an American broadcasting company who persuaded him to talk over the air to the United States. The broadcasts were attacked with savagery and Duff Cooper, then Minister of Information, ordered the BBC, against the wishes of its chairman, to allow William Connor, 'Cassandra' of the *Daily Mirror*, to broadcast a vulgar blackguarding onslaught on Wodehouse. This was in its turn attacked by correspondents in *The Times*, angrily protesting against the hounding down of a man without regard to what he had actually said. The words were indeed free from suspicion of favouring the Nazis. But anyone less naive than Wodehouse would have kept his mouth shut. He made his own confession in 1953 in *Performing Flea*, a self-portrait in letters to his old schoolfriend, W. Townend. 'Of course I ought to have had the sense to see that it was a loony thing to do to use the German radio for even the most harmless stuff, but I didn't. I suppose prison life saps the intellect.' He claimed without resentment that he had been falsely accused of having accepted favours from the enemy and denied having spoken over the air against his own country, expressed unpatriotic sentiments or been indifferent to the outcome of the war.

As a result of this sorry business Wodehouse could only have returned to England after the war at the risk of being the centre of a major row, involving a demand for his trial for treason. So he went from Paris to New York and, taking American citizenship in 1955, never came back. He would have liked to do so; but feelers put out on his behalf showed that the risk of trouble was too great and he remained in exile until he was too old to revisit his old haunts.

Exile was far from leading to sterility. Through the fifties and sixties Jeeves staged a comeback and there was a steady flow of books that pleased his old admirers and won him others in a new generation. The remarkable thing about the work of his old age was that it stayed true to the formula of earlier days without seeming to date. His mind as an artist had been set in his teens and, superb and accomplished craftsman though he was, he remained a teenager even in his eighties – and a late Victorian one at that. Boat Race night of Mafeking year may be said to be roughly the point at which he came to a standstill. Yet, paradoxically, he never took on a period flavour. His 'Eggs', 'Old Beans', and 'Crumpets' lived in a timeless fairyland in which it was irrelevant whether transport was by Hansom cab or jet aircraft. Theirs was a permissive society, only cramped in style by Aunt Agatha and that super-aunt, Jeeves; as with Saki, the memory of the aunts of his youth remained green with Wodehouse. The boundaries of this unfading, escapist fairyland were never crossed by serious sex or crime. Its inhabitants never grew up. A member of the Drones Club once lamented that he was 'twenty-bally-six and no getting away from it'. But that was an exaggeration. Like their creator, Bertie and his buddies were Peter Pans. They stayed adolescents.

Wodehouse knew what he was doing. He was a professional to the tips of his fingers. 'I believe,' he declared, 'there are two ways of writing novels. One is mine, making the thing a sort of musical comedy without music and ignoring real life altogether; the other is going right deep down into life and not caring a damn. The ones that fail are the ones where the writer loses his nerve and says: "My God! I can't write this, I must tone it down." ' He classed all his characters as if they were living salaried actors, being convinced that this was the right way of casting a novel. 'The one thing actors – important actors I mean,' he wrote, 'won't stand is being brought in to play a scene which is of no value to them in order that they may feed some less important character, and I believe this isn't vanity but is based on an instinctive knowledge of stage craft. They kick because they know the balance isn't right.' This discipline, which kept him consistently within chosen limits, is reflected in his hundred books and came through in the successful television versions of them. It guided, too, his excursions into drama and films. He collaborated with Ian Hay in farce writing in the thirties and gave British films *Summer Lightning* in which Ralph Lynn appeared. He told something of himself in *Bring on the Girls* with Guy Bolton (1954) and his autobiographical *Over Seventy* (1957). He continued to write until the last.

There was nothing of the literary man about Wodehouse. He might have been a retired master from Wrykyn, the public school of some of his best early stories. Dressed in blue blazer and grey flannel trousers, figure kept trim by golf, swimming, and leading the simple life, he made no attempt to shine in any company.

Wodehouse married in 1914 Ethel, widow of Leonard Rowley, of Dee Bank, Cheshire, whose daughter Leonora he adopted. She married Mr Peter Cazalet, the racehorse trainer, and died in 1944. There were no children of the Wodehouse marriage.

AGATHA CHRISTIE

A subtle narrative gift

12 JANUARY 1976

DAME AGATHA CHRISTIE, DBE, died yesterday at the age of 85. She belonged to the great period of English detective fiction. Her work typified the genre, and, after Dorothy Sayers died, she was recognized as the undoubted queen of her profession.

The popularity of her books not only survived into an era when other crime writers had abandoned detection and were trading in sex and violence, but continued to grow. According to a Unesco report, she was the most widely read British author in the world, with translations into 103 languages – 14 more than Shakespeare. Her principal detectives, Poirot and Miss Marple, hold a secure place on the roll of classic sleuths which is headed by Sherlock Holmes.

She was born in September, 1890, at Torquay, the youngest daughter of Frederick Alvah Miller, an American from New York. 'My father,' she recalled, 'was a gentleman of substance, and never did a handsturn in his life, and he was a most agreeable man.' She received little or no formal education, but was brought up in a house full of books and by a mother who encouraged her to read and tell stories. Further encouragement came from Eden Phillpotts, who was a neighbour. When she was 16, she went to Paris to be trained as a singer, but found her voice not strong enough for opera or the concert platform. She wrote some poems and 'rather gloomy stories of unrequited love'.

In 1914 she married Archibald Christie (later Colonel Archibald Christie, CMG, DSO). While he was in France, she did VAD work at a local hospital and qualified as a dispenser. Her first detective story, *The Mysterious Affair at Styles* (1920), not only utilized her knowledge of poisons but introduced Hercule Poirot, with his egg-shaped head, comically broken English, and his reliance on 'the little grey cells', who was based on Belgian refugees she had met. The book enjoyed a modest success, but it was her seventh novel, *The Murder of Roger Ackroyd* (1926), which brought fame. In that same year a curious episode occurred: she vanished from her Surrey home, and was found 10 days later, after a nationwide search, staying under a false name in an hotel at Harrogate, apparently suffering from amnesia.

She divorced Colonel Christie in 1928. Left with a daughter to educate, she began to write seriously, and to travel. Two years later, while visiting Sir Leonard Woolley in Iraq, she met another archaeologist, Max Mallowan, now Sir Max Mallowan, CBE, Emeritus Professor of Western Asiatic Archaeology in the University

Agatha Christie in 1968.

of London. They were married almost at once, and she subsequently accompanied him on many of his expeditions to the Middle East, learning to help with photography and the piecing together of shards. Several of her detective stories had a Middle Eastern background, and one, *Death Comes As The End* (1945), was set in Ancient Egypt.

Although she continued to write about Hercule Poirot – *Murder on the Orient Express* (1934) and *The ABC Murders* (1936) were *tours de force* to equal *Roger Ackroyd* – largely because her readers insisted, she came to think him too artificial a character and she totally discarded the Watson-figure of Captain Hastings. She preferred, and increasingly used, Miss Marple, the inquisitive spinster from *Murder at the Vicarage* (1930), who found the solution to all mysteries in her experience of human behaviour in an English village.

Mrs Christie (as she continued to call herself for professional purposes) also wrote, more or less for her own pleasure, a series of 'straight' novels under the strictly guarded pseudonym of 'Mary Westmacott', but year after year, throughout the Second World War and the decades which followed, her detective stories continued to be, and usually deserved to be, best-sellers. Her style scarcely changed and her inventiveness showed little decline: *Mrs McGinty's Dead* (1952), *4.50 from Paddington* (1957), and *At Bertram's Hotel* (1965) are every bit as good as *Cards on the Table* (1936) or *The Moving Finger* (1943). Her occasional experiments with different formulae, as in *Endless Night* (1967) and *Passenger to Frankfurt* (1970) were perhaps not altogether happy, but her public bought them as enthusiastically as ever and they did serve to demonstrate her continued alertness to social trends and quirks.

Meanwhile she continued, almost to the end, to publish prolifically with *Nemesis* (1971); *Elephants Can Remember* (1972); *Akhnaton* (1973), a play written in 1937 which had remained unpublished and which she did not intend to be staged; *Poems* (1973); *Postern of Fate* (1973); *Poirot's Early Cases* (1974); and a final salute to her detective hero Poirot entitled *Curtain*, which she had written during the Second World War intending it for posthumous publication, but in fact releasing it in 1975.

She had achieved spectacular success in another field. The stage adaptations of several of her early books (including one of *Roger Ackroyd* with Charles Laughton playing Poirot) had dissatisfied her; so, in 1943, she made her own dramatization of *Ten Little Niggers*, and followed it with a series of other plays, culminating in *The Mousetrap* (1952) with its fantastic London run (at her death it is at the St Martin's Theatre in the twenty-fourth year of its world record breaking course) and *Witness for the Prosecution* (1935), the film rights of which were bought by Hollywood for what was then the record price of £116,000.

She never cared much for the cinema, or for wireless and television (though *The Mousetrap* was originally a short radio play, written at the special request of Queen Mary). The famous stage play, *Love from a Stranger* (1936), taken from one of her short stories, was filmed twice, however, and there was a series of adaptations for the screen with Margaret Rutherford as Miss Marple, notably *4.50 from Paddington*; *Witness for the Prosecution* was also a notable box office success and, more recently, *Murder on the Orient Express* was launched with a host of stars including Ingrid Bergman, Lauren Bacall, and Albert Finney.

Dame Agatha's private pleasures were gardening – she won local prizes for horticulture – and buying furniture for her various houses. She was a shy person: she disliked public appearances, but she was friendly and sharp-witted to meet. By inclination as well as breeding she belonged to the English upper middle-class. She wrote about, and for, people like herself. That was an essential part of her charm. She was not, in fact, a particularly good writer, certainly not the quality of Dorothy Sayers. But she had a real and subtle narrative gift. Her stories could be gulped down as smoothly and pleasantly as cream. Her handling of the plot-structures, too, was very skilful. She brought a peculiarly English form to its perfect, and perfectly English, flowering. She was, beyond question, one of the half-dozen best detective story writers in the world. She was created CBE in 1956 and advanced to DBE in 1971.

HOWARD HUGHES

5 APRIL 1976

MR HOWARD HUGHES, the American millionaire businessman, film producer, pilot, aircraft designer, and formerly majority shareholder of Trans World Airlines, died on April 5 at the age of 70.

A man whose considerable talents, urge for novelty, and endless financial success kept him constantly in the public eye, Hughes considered himself accountable to no one for his conduct of his own business. When he climbed out of his aircraft after breaking an air speed record before the war he said to a reporter: 'Well, I said I'd do it and I've done it. What else would you expect me to say?' In his last years his deliberate avoidance of publicity became obsessive, and more was said and written about it than about the man himself.

Many theories were advanced for his being a recluse who had shunned all public appearances for nearly two decades. Some said that his bacteriophobia allowed him no contact with the 'diseased' outside world; others claimed that he was no longer alive or had been kidnapped and that only a mythical presence kept his empire going. Even the Nevada State Gaming Commission failed to provoke Hughes to prove his existence; he sent it a handwritten letter with fingerprints instead.

Born in Houston, Texas, on December 24, 1905, Hughes was the son of a Harvard lawyer, a flamboyant, pushful man who invented the Hughes oil drill and left his son an actual fortune of nearly a million dollars and a potential fortune infinitely greater. 'He never asked me whether I liked things, he just shoved them down my throat', the son said afterwards in a rare, expansive moment. 'But he was a terrifically loved man.'

Young Hughes had a conventionally expensive education and went to law to win control of his fortune while still a minor. He turned over the Hughes Tool Company to professional managers at once, ran away with an heiress in 1923, and went into the film business. In 1928 with *Hell's Angels* (starring Ben Lyon and Jean Harlow) he successfully married his twin interest in aviation and the cinema, in one of the most profitable films about flying ever made. At least two other pictures he produced achieved a good reputation: *The Front Page*, which was about newspapers and starred Adolphe Menjou and Pat O'Brien, and *Scarface*, a gangster tale in which Paul Muni had the leading part.

During the next 20 years he divorced his first wife, Ella Rice, in 1928, 'discovered' Jean Harlow and Jane Russell, broke the world air speed record, the California–New York transcontinental record, and the round-the-world record in successive

349

years from 1935 to 1937, and founded a pioneer electronics company (Hughes Aircraft). He bought himself into TWA with 600 shares in 1939. Jack Frye, then president of TWA, needed $15m to buy new aircraft and Hughes was persuaded to use the resources of his tool company to buy the aircraft and lease them to the airline. He designed several aircraft himself, including the celebrated plywood craft to carry 700 passengers and save metal which he and the Federal Government developed during the war. It flew once, in 1947, and has been laid up ever since.

He amassed a fortune of over $2,000m, and was involved in a series of spectacular incidents, like the plane crash in 1947 which nearly killed him while he was testing one of his own designs. The next day he was conducting business in his bed. Before he left hospital he had a working bed specially designed by himself. He was constantly reported in the company of rising young women in Hollywood but evaded all but the barest publicity about his affairs. Occasionally he made brief incursions into public affairs, like the Congressional hearing in 1946 which broke the career of Senator Owen Brewster, but more and more he avoided public accountability for his actions.

A perfectionist, he laboured endlessly to satisfy himself about the virtues of a course of action before following it. He delayed the use of jet aircraft by TWA until long after other airlines had adopted them. He is reported to have brought design managers of aircraft manufacturing concerns to the point of nervous collapse.

Those who had dealings with him in his later years reported his manner as relaxed but remote. Although he seldom wore a tie, the stories of his sloppy clothing were exaggerated. But he did like to conduct business in the informality of a car seat or on board a train or aircraft in a peripatetic life from one of his half-dozen establishments to another. He had a predilection for night work and considered his staff fair game for telephone calls at all hours. Outsiders he normally telephoned during the day. He was said on occasion to work for more than 24 hours continuously, and then go to bed no matter what time it was and sleep until he was rested.

He was stubborn and inordinately suspicious of business partners, never regarding a verbal discussion as anything more than an indication of what might eventually be hammered out in writing. For some 20 years before he died his affairs were protected from inquisition by a battery of confidential assistants and the negative services of a public relations company. He allowed the day-to-day conduct of his companies to go entirely to his managers, and vested a large part of his fortune in a medical foundation. When TWA eventually sued him in a squabble over company policy and control, he simply disappeared for weeks. After five years he eventually sold his majority interest for more than $500m. It was only many months later that a study of the markets in California indicated that he had put most of the money in short-term government bonds.

In a final step in his defence against publicity, Hughes vested all copyright in publications concerning himself in a company he controlled. But this measure did not protect him. In 1972, McGraw-Hill, a New York publishing company, announced it was about to publish his autobiography, based, so the claim went, on a series of interviews Hughes had given to the author Clifford Irving. Hughes broke a 13-year silence in a long distance telephone call from the Bahamas to deny the authenticity of the 'autobiography'. He said he had never met Clifford Irving. This led to a complicated series of court hearings both in the United States and Switzerland, and the disposal of $650,000 deposited by the publishers in a Swiss bank as advance payment for the book. Irving himself was later convicted of fraud and jailed, as was his wife Edith, who had used the name Helga Hughes to deposit the advances in Switzerland.

This was not the only legal action he was embroiled in. TWA's action against Hughes resulted in a judgment against him for $142m: TWA had alleged that Hughes had used his position as a 75 per cent stockholder to damage the airline by failing to buy jets for its fleet. His second wife, Jean Peters, whom he married in 1957, divorced him in 1971. He was sued by Los Angeles Airways; by Mr Robert Maheu (who formerly ran his gambling operations in Nevada), and by Dr Robert Buckley (his former personal physician).

In 1971 Hughes had moved to the Bahamas from Nevada where he had lived as a hermit since 1966 on the top floor of a Las Vegas hotel. From there he had bought other hotels, casinos, land and mining claims after he divested himself of his interest in TWA.

A tall, lanky man, 6ft 3in in height and for many years less than 10st, Hughes was curiously unanimated for a man with such a taste for violent novelty. He was said to be hard of hearing. In his later years he put on a couple of stone, but became more pinched and severe in the face. He had no children.

FIELD MARSHAL MONTGOMERY

Soldier who became victor of El Alamein
and a legend in his own lifetime

24 MARCH 1976

Field Marshal Viscount Montgomery of Alamein, KG, GCB, DSO, whose great victory in the Western Desert in 1942 made him famous throughout the world in the course of a few days, has died at the age of 88, as announced on another page. Later in the war he was British Commander-in-Chief in the final victory over Germany in north-west Europe in 1944 and 1945.

It has been said that Montgomery never lost a battle. In its most literal sense this judgment is valid, although there were two occasions, at Enfidaville in Tunisia and on the Sangro in Italy when offensives which he conducted were checked; and it is of course true that in the airborne landing at Arnhem he failed to crown with final success an otherwise well-conceived and skilfully conducted offensive. History will almost certainly judge Montgomery amongst the great British generals. Although there were notable deficiencies in his political and strategic armoury, his skill and judgment on the battlefield, together with his unique qualities of leadership were beyond question. His technical expertise and his capacity to inspire total confidence in his troops have been universally recognized. No one admired him more than the German soldiers and officers who were his enemies in battle.

After the campaign in the Western Desert he became a national figure. His stature grew throughout the Second World War and when it ended and he began to visit London from time to time from his post in Germany, crowds used to form in Whitehall and outside theatres in the hope of catching a glimpse of the great man. 'Monty' was one of the rare breed that become a legend in their own time.

It is no exaggeration to say that the British, not always disposed to love their generals, took Montgomery to their hearts in the heady atmosphere of *après-Alamein*. Those who lived through the Second World War will recall that whereas up to the autumn of 1942 it had seemed to be a series of strategic withdrawals, if not outright disasters, now, at long last, there was a resounding, incontestable battle victory that all had yearned for.

Winston Churchill, who not infrequently sensed what ordinary people felt, judged the mood rightly in Volume IV of his book *The Second World War*: '... the Battle of Alamein will ever make a glorious page in British military annals. There is another reason why it will survive. It marked in fact the turning of "the Hinge of Fate". It may almost be said "Before Alamein we never had a victory. After Alamein we never had a defeat." '

An Ulsterman, Bernard Law Montgomery was born on November 17, 1887, a son of the Rev. Henry Montgomery, who became Bishop of Tasmania in 1889. Montgomery's childhood holds the key to the complex and often abrasive character which he became in later life. The Montgomery family were worthy respectable stock, pillars of Victorian society, guardians of the high standards of unselfish devotion to public service in the Church and in the Empire. The personal philosophy of Montgomery's father is summed up in one of his remarks to his children: 'You come of a family of gentlemen. You know that word does not signify mere outward refinement. It tells of a refined and noble mind to which anything dishonourable or mean or impure is abhorrent and unworthy.'

Montgomery's mother was Maud, third daughter of Dean Farrar, sometime Dean of Canterbury and author of *Eric, or Little by Little*. She married Henry Montgomery when she was 16 and she was a strict and often harsh disciplinarian. Bernard suffered most from her rigid routine and lack of demonstrative affection perhaps because his character was so similar to that of his mother. At a very early age his stubborn and inflexible character began to emerge, and clashes between his mother and himself were inevitable.

He began to seek compensation for his mother's lack of affection in the satisfaction of authority and leadership. Even as a child he showed a strong desire to be the leader and the winner at all games. It was only in his relationship with his father that Montgomery displayed the normal childish qualities of affection and love. Henry Montgomery was a remote and intensely spiritual man and his turbulent son worshipped him almost as a saint; but fundamentally Montgomery's childhood was unhappy and emotionally deprived.

He was born at Kennington but he was only two years old when his father was consecrated Bishop of Tasmania. It was there that he spent the most formative years of his life. Bishop Montgomery's nature and the circumstances of his mission dictated that the head of the household and of all domestic arrangements was the mother. The regime was a fearsome one, sweets were forbidden, the children rose at dawn and began lessons at 7.30 in a schoolroom built outside the house.

It was therefore a strange, complicated, and unhappy child who returned to England in 1901, at the age of 13, when his father was appointed to the Society for the Propagation of the Gospel in London. The family went to live in a large house in Chiswick, and in January, 1902, Montgomery and his brother Donald entered St Paul's School as day boys.

Within three years Bernard Montgomery was Captain of Rugby and a member of the cricket xi and the swimming team. All his formidable qualities of concentration and determination were harnessed to the pursuit of athletic excellence – not for its own sake, but as an activity in which his intense desire for personal power could find expression. As an ordinary member of a team he was often a nuisance – argumentative, uncooperative, obstructive; as captain he was perfectly happy. His skill at games was not matched by his academic record. He was, indeed, described as backward for his age, and a 1905 report on his English sums up perceptively not only the schoolboy but the man he was to become: 'Tolerable; his essays are sensible, but he has no notion of style.'

Even in this field, however, his inflexible determination and unshakable self-confidence were not to be undermined by intellectual deficiency. He had chosen the Army class at school and intended to go to Sandhurst. He was told by his masters that to have any serious chance of getting there he must give more time to work. He therefore got down to work and passed into Sandhurst halfway down the list (or as he would prefer it, halfway up) at the age of 19. At the Royal Military College his career was distinguished only by his athletic preoccupations and a taste for the kind of rough horseplay that was characteristic of the Sandhurst of those days. This combination almost ended in disgrace. As a notable games player he could always command a following among the more hearty and impressionable of his fellow cadets; and he became something of a leader of a clique who did as little work as they could get away with, and who filled their leisure time in beating up people whose views or personal appearance displeased them.

After an episode in which a cadet suffered serious injury Montgomery, who was a lance-corporal, was reduced to the rank of gentleman cadet.

This was the first serious reverse in Montgomery's military career and, as at St Paul's, the effect upon him was sobering and decisive. He began to work, and although his graduation from the college had been put back by six months, when he eventually passed out he was 36th out of 150 cadets – a creditable if not exactly brilliant performance. The young officer who was gazetted to The Royal Warwickshire Regiment in 1908 was a strange and not altogether attractive figure. He lacked polish and personal charm; he was irritatingly self-confident and greedy for only one thing in life – success and the power that brings with it.

Bravery in the First World War

Almost at once Montgomery was posted to the 1st Battalion of his regiment on the North-West Frontier of India at Peshawar. Here he began to lose some of his rough edges. His obsessive desire to excel at sport led him to enter the local point-to-point, although he was an indifferent horseman. After falling off at the start Montgomery remounted and charged through the field like a demented Lord Chiltern. After winning the race he fell off again; but he had won, and the Army loves a winner. After two years of Frontier life, in the course of which he discovered, without losing an invincible belief in his own superiority, how to live harmoniously in an officers' mess – the most claustrophobically gregarious institution in the world – he emerged as the embryonic general, a dedicated, industrious soldier, with resilience, a certain Jack Russell pose and an ability to accept life in the same spirit as the celebrated lady who decided to accept God – because on the whole it was more prudent to do so.

At the end of 1912 the 1st Royal Warwickshire Regiment returned to England and Montgomery began to take the first small steps in his advance to the military summit. He passed out top of the musketry course at Hythe and played hockey for the Army. Until 1914 his life was well ordered, predictable, and dedicated. When the war came Montgomery fought with his regiment at the Marne and the Aisne; and at the first battle of Ypres, while leading his platoon in a bayonet charge, he was seriously wounded and came near to death. For his bravery in this action he was awarded the Distinguished Service Order and promoted to the rank of captain. The DSO for a subaltern is a rare decoration, regarded by most soldiers as a 'near miss' for a Victoria Cross. This was another of the decisive moments in Montgomery's life. He had faced danger and death and conquered both.

When he left hospital he returned to France and by the end of the war he had experience of staff work and operational command; he had reached the rank of lieutenant-colonel at the age of 30 – an impressive achievement in the Army of those days, even in war. He had also been awarded the French Croix de Guerre and been mentioned in dispatches six times. The revulsion against militarism which led the intellectuals of the 1920s towards pacifism predictably left Montgomery untouched. In 1920 he went to the Staff College at Camberley, an establishment at that time virtually innocent of any element of intellectual inquiry. He passed out successfully although he never knew whether he had earned a good report as, according to the custom of the day, no one ever told him. However he was posted as brigade major to the 17th Infantry Brigade stationed in Cork. In 1926, after a variety of staff appointments (including one at HQ, 29th West Riding Division, where he ran tactical courses for officers at which he was the sole lecturer and fount of all military wisdom), he returned to the Staff College as a member of the directing staff; his industry and single-minded preoccupation with the profession of arms was beginning to pay dividends.

It was at this time that another event took place that was to have a crucial impact on the character of Montgomery. He met Betty Carver, whose husband had been killed at Gallipoli in 1915. In July, 1927, they were married. Their son David was born in 1928 and in October, 1937, after being stung by an insect on the beach at Burnham-on-Sea, Betty Montgomery died of septicaemia after her leg had been amputated. Montgomery's short marriage had been successful and happy and his wife's death was a terrible blow. Although, with the help of close friends, he was able in time to return to the normal routine of his Army life, it is possible to say that in a very real sense, he never recovered from it.

In the meantime he had left Camberley again and succeeded to the command of the 1st Battalion of his own regiment – the first ambition of every infantry soldier of his generation. He took them to the Middle East, first to Palestine and then to the Suez Canal. Here he had a series of minor clashes of temperament with his colleagues and superiors, but won a reputation as 'an officer of great military ability who delights in responsibility ... definitely above average and should attain high rank in the Army. He can only fail to do so if a certain high-handedness, which occasionally overtakes him, becomes too pronounced.'

Appointed to the Eighth Army

From 1934, after his battalion had been moved to India, until 1937, Montgomery was Chief Instructor at the Staff College in Quetta with the rank of Colonel, and after three happy and busy years he returned to England to take over command of the 9th Brigade at Portsmouth. Here he maintained his reputation as a thorn in the side of the military establishment, by letting War Department land to a fairground proprietor and using the rent for garrison amenities. If the General Officer Commanding-in-Chief Southern Command had been a less urbane and tolerant soldier than Archibald Wavell, Montgomery's star might have waned from that moment, such is the sacred power of Army Regulations; but in spite of his crime, Montgomery was promoted to Major-General in 1938 to command a division formed to deal with the Palestine troubles. While there, he heard the news which was to open the door to all his future success; he had been selected to command the 3rd Division, one of the regular divisions of the Army and part of the British Expeditionary Force formed to go to Europe when war began. After a short but fierce illness which brought him back to England he was told plans had changed and that he was to go into a pool of temporarily unemployed major-generals. Characteristically he pestered the War Office into submission and on August 28, 1939, Montgomery assumed command of the 3rd Division.

The division was part of the II Corps, commanded by Lieutenant-General A. F. Brooke, later Field Marshal Lord Alanbrooke, who formed a high opinion of Montgomery and was to be his collaborator and occasionally his saviour in the years to come. Montgomery regarded 'Brookie' as the best soldier that any nation had produced for many years. Inevitably Montgomery got himself into trouble in the first winter of the war by writing a somewhat hair-raising confidential minute to his subordinate commanders on the subject, in those unpermissive days extremely delicate, of venereal disease. Like the masters at St Paul's, Gort, the Commander-in-Chief at GHQ, and Brooke, the Corps Commander, thought little of Montgomery's literary style and less of his tact. However, thanks largely to Brooke's sympathetic handling of the matter, the turbulent divisional commander escaped with a reprimand. After the evacuation from Dunkirk he commanded V and XII Corps and in late 1941 became General Officer Commanding-in-Chief South Eastern Command. It was during this period of his career in England that the Montgomery legend began to take root. From these years come most of the stories, of the lectures at which not only smoking but coughing was forbidden; of the contemptuous and icy reprimands; of the sudden, brutal dismissals – the endlessly repeated anecdotes that fused together over the years into the familiar picture of the austere, dedicated autocrat, monastic, Spartan, and single-minded. Yet it was also in these years that Montgomery began to take hold of the imagination of the British soldier, who liked his colourful eccentricities, his informality, his impatience with the more fatuous rituals of martial protocol. By the summer of 1942 Montgomery was ready for what lay ahead. In August, with disastrous news arriving from Egypt, General Gott, a Desert Corps Commander, was appointed to command the Eighth Army: at the moment of taking up his appointment he was killed when his aircraft was shot down by the Germans. Montgomery flew out to take over command of the Eighth Army, then holding the position at El Alamein to which it had been driven back by the Axis forces. He arrived on August 12, 1942.

At once he had to meet an attack by the German commander, Rommel, launched on August 31. The Germans were halted in front of the Alam el Halfa ridge where Auchinleck had stopped them dead the previous month. Rommel was compelled to break off the action on September 4. Montgomery permitted no major counter-attack because he did not wish to interrupt preparations for his own offensive or to use troops whose general standard of training was still not high. The defensive victory, however, raised the Army's spirit and gave it confidence in its new commander.

Churchill and the War Cabinet now began to press Montgomery to expedite his own offensive, but he firmly refused and was backed by his superior in the Middle East Command, General Alexander. The Battle of El Alamein began on the night of October 23. The enemy's strongly fortified position, covered by thick mine-fields, lay between the sea and the impassable Qatara Depression, so that only frontal assault was possible. Montgomery's skill and the determination of his newly inspired troops combined to open a gap in Rommel's defences through which the British armoured forces were to pass. With impressive flexibility Montgomery changed the direction of his thrusts whenever he met strong opposition. The breach was fully opened by November 2, and the enemy was then heavily defeated in an armoured battle. In the northern sector Rommel began a hasty retreat under air bombardment, which cost him thousands of vehicles. In the centre and south the greater number of his forces, here chiefly Italian, were captured.

A rapid pursuit followed in which the Eighth Army's progress was governed almost entirely by the factor of supply. It reached Tripoli on January 23, 1943, just in time to make use of the port; if it had failed to take the place within another two days it would probably have been compelled to draw back on its supplies. Meanwhile the enemy forces made their way back over the Tunisian frontier to join hands with the other Axis forces opposing the British and Americans in that theatre.

Montgomery fought four more battles in North Africa: Medinine, on March 6, when Rommel attacked his forward corps and was beaten off with serious loss in tanks; the Mareth Line, the old French frontier defences, which began on March 20; Wadi Akarit on April 6; and Enfidaville, where he was partially checked in the mountains. Troops were then withdrawn from the Eighth Army to aid the First in the area of Tunis where the terrain was easier. The victory which the First Army then gained completely crushed the German and Italian forces and brought about a general capitulation. Montgomery had been promoted to the substantive rank of lieutenant-general on October 17, 1942. A few weeks later, on November 11, he was promoted general for service in the field. On the same day he was created KCB.

His next task was the invasion of Sicily, in which the Eighth Army operated in concert with the United States Seventh. Indeed one of the features of the campaign was the personal rivalry between Montgomery and Patton. Although the American reached Messina first, Montgomery won the battle behind the scenes. Though he was only one of the Army commanders and had over his head a land force commander-in-chief in General Alexander and a supreme allied commander in General Eisenhower, he succeeded in getting the whole plan recast and in arranging that the Americans should land side by side with his own troops in the Gulf of Gela instead of at the north-west corner of the island. Though there was fierce fighting in the plain south and south-west of Etna and on both flanks of the mountain, the campaign lasted only 38 days after the landing on July 10.

The Allies Return to Europe

The Eighth Army began the Italian campaign by landing near Reggio in the early hours of September 3. An armistice with Italy was announced five days later, but the Germans had large forces in the country and were determined to fight for it. Having made contact with the United States Fifth Army, which had been heavily engaged on the Salerno beaches, Montgomery switched over to the Adriatic coast, where he took under his command other forces which had landed at Tarranto and Bari. He fought his way up the coast, exploiting small seaborne landings behind the enemy's flank with great skill, won a fierce and bloody battle on the Sangro, but was checked by the winter at the end of the year a short distance north of the river. Montgomery believed that the Allies had only themselves to blame for the delay – no master plan, no grip on operations, administrative muddle – the classic 'dog's breakfast' of Monty's colloquial vocabulary. He was not sorry to leave Italy on appointment to command the 21st Army Group for the invasion of north-west Europe from England.

Montgomery was placed in command of all British and American forces for the landing and the battle to secure the foothold, but it was understood that as soon as the allies broke out from their bridgehead the Supreme Commander, General Eisenhower, would assume direct command of the land forces and Montgomery would revert to the post of British Army Group Commander. Again he exercised influence in modifying the plan, which was considerably strengthened by his intervention. Establishing his headquarters in the High Master's room at St Paul's – which although an Old Pauline he entered for the first time as Commander-in-Chief – he began to impress his incisive mind and personality on the planning for the invasion. As one disenchanted general put it, the gentlemen were out and the players were coming in. Although he had mellowed and expanded during his triumphant days with the Eighth Army, Montgomery was still determined that the European campaign should be a Montgomery campaign – cold, clinical, and meticulously thought-out. One of his outstanding characteristics was that no commands, no persuasion, no pressure would induce him to act upon a plan in which he did not believe or with resources he did not consider adequate.

Though the landing on June 6 was bitterly opposed by the enemy under the command of Montgomery's old adversary Rommel, and though there were anxious moments at the outset, the operation was a full success. It was the intention of Montgomery to contain the largest possible numbers of the enemy, especially the German armour, in front of the British Army group on the left, while the Americans broke through from the Cotentin peninsula. The whole front, pivoting on Caen, was then to make a great right wheel and drive the enemy up against the Seine.

This programme was in its broad lines adhered to, though some of the individual British attacks were disappointing and costly. The long-drawn-out fighting aroused anxiety at home and even among some senior officers in the field. Many believed, and said, that Montgomery had failed; but he never lost his nerve. The American break-out duly took place on July 25, and was completely successful. The Germans then launched a desperate counter-offensive on August 7 at Mortain in the direction of the coast at Avranches, with the object of cutting the American forces in two. It played into the hands of Montgomery who mounted what was probably the last of the great classic land battles ever to be seen in Europe. He at once ordered the American right to wheel north and the Canadian Army to accentuate its thrusts southward in order to envelop the enemy force in a sack. After a fierce struggle this was achieved, and the Germans in the 'Falaise pocket' were largely destroyed.

This operation had not held up the allied advance on the Seine. Eisenhower now decided that the moment had come for him to take over operational command of the land forces and for Montgomery to step down. This would in any case have been demanded by American public opinion in view of American strength now in the theatre, but it was disappointing to Montgomery, who had confidence in his ability to continue the rout of the enemy. It was all the more disappointing because the strategic ideas of the two differed, Eisenhower proposing a general advance on a broad front, whereas Montgomery believed that he could end this war with one bold, decisive stroke. He wanted to mass a striking force of a million men on the narrowest front possible on the left Wing, provide it with the maximum transport and fuel, and drive it forward to the Rhine in the region of the Ruhr.

After long and bitter controversy, ending in a meeting between Eisenhower and Montgomery in Monty's caravan, the supreme Commander had his way. The armies dashed forward from the Seine, Montgomery's armour penetrating within a few days into Holland through Belgium. But an airborne operation conducted by him with American and British forces to cross the great rivers of Holland failed to secure the passage of the third, the Lower Rhine. The armies were now at the end of their tether, and Montgomery was directed to devote his energies to opening the port of Antwerp, captured intact, but useless while the Germans clung to its approaches from the sea. Meanwhile American progress to the Rhine had been almost halted though it continued by slow steps through the worsening November weather.

In December the enemy struck back. His thrust cut deep into the Ardennes, and a very awkward situation arose. Montgomery was given command of the American forces north of the German-made salient, though many senior American officers strongly objected. Monty's bearing was not, to say the least, tactful. This was the culmination of a long period of friction and controversy of which Montgomery was, inevitably, the centre. There were those who believed that he had failed in the Normandy fighting – and it is true that when Eisenhower took over the supreme command, Monty lost much of his élan and dash. Now he returned to his finest form and utterly destroyed the German offensive. His public relations operation, however, was less successful and a festering Anglo-American quarrel began which ended in another showdown between Montgomery and Eisenhower. Eisenhower, of course, won; but he was as magnanimous in his victory as Monty was gracious in accepting it. As soon as the German offensive had been routed, the salient smoothed out and, the 'misunderstandings' with the Americans removed, Montgomery returned to his own efforts to reach the Rhine.

This led to some of the hardest fighting of the campaign, but once it was achieved the rest proved relatively easy. For the second time the Germans had fought their battle with a great river behind them and could not renew the struggle on the far bank. The passage of the Rhine was not difficult, except as a problem of engineering and administration. Once it had been accomplished the 21st Army Group headed north-east towards the Baltic.

On May 2 troops of the 21st Army Group reached Wismar, on the Baltic, and made contact with the Russians the next day. On the 4th, on Luneburg Heath, all the German forces in north-west Germany, Holland, and Denmark surrendered to Field Marshal Montgomery. His own account of his campaigns has appeared in his two books *El Alamein to the Sangro* and *Normandy to the Baltic*.

British C-in-C in Post-war Germany

Montgomery was appointed Commander-in-Chief of the British Forces of Occupation, Military Governor of the British Zone, and British Member of the Allied Control Council of Germany, which held its meetings in Berlin. He met the Russians on friendly terms and got on particularly well with the genial Soviet Marshal Rokossovsky. He threw himself energetically into the task of restoring communications, reopening the Ruhr mines, and demobilizing German land workers to get in the harvest. He was a capable Military Governor, leaving, in his customary style, the administration to able subordinates under broad directives. His chief interest was in the armed forces, now being rapidly demobilized and going through the difficulties, material and moral, which such a situation inevitably entails.

He remained in Germany for about a year, and in June 1946 entered the War Office as Chief of the Imperial General Staff in succession to Alanbrooke.

Many doubted the wisdom of the choice, believing that he was not as well fitted for this appointment as for high command in the field. They disliked his mannerisms; they found his eccentricities undignified; they feared that he would be at loggerheads with the other two services and that he would seek personal glorification. Alanbrooke remarked to a friend: 'People seem to think that dreadful things will happen if Monty becomes CIGS; I am perfectly sure they will not.'

A peerage had been conferred on Montgomery in the New Year Honours of 1946. He had taken the title of Viscount Montgomery of Alamein, of Hindhead in the County of Surrey. In 1945 he had been advanced from KCB to GCB. In December 1946 he received a distinctive mark of royal favour when he was installed a Knight of the Garter.

The Controversial Autobiography

Montgomery was indeed far from being as good a CIGS as he had been a commander, but his qualities were such that they enabled him to do valuable work in spite of his inability to act as a member of a team instead of as its captain. He came under criticism about the number and length of his tours abroad, but he felt that in those years of confusion he ought to see all he could on the spot. His relations with the Minister of Defence, the then Mr A. V. Alexander, were appalling, and Montgomery later savaged the unfortunate politician in his memoirs.

Alexander, for his part, distrusted and disliked Montgomery, who, late in 1948, was 'released' to take up the international appointment of Military Chairman of the Western Union Commanders-in-Chief. In face of the threatening attitude of Soviet Russia, he had fought a hard battle in favour of a 'continental' strategy in which the British Army should take the maximum part, and won it. Thus, in the formation of the Western Union his role had been almost as vital as that of his ally, Mr Ernest Bevin.

The start was good. Nations which had appeared to be thoroughly disheartened and without defence policies, still less a united policy, became more confident. Coordination of ideas and information, frequent inspections, and exchanges of visits, tactical study on the ground – all these proved invaluable. The organization was, however, at best a stoppage, and an insecure one at that.

In a lecture in 1949 Montgomery said significantly that the real difficulties of such an organization began when generalities were left behind and the hour for decisions arrived. He hinted that the machinery of western defence needed fresh fuel. What actually happened was that it was absorbed into a system far more powerful and dynamic and with far stronger powers of command, in the initiation of which Montgomery again played a big part. In March, 1951, he became Deputy Supreme Commander to General Eisenhower, commander of the allied forces of NATO in Europe.

In this new role Montgomery accomplished some of his best peacetime work. The role was not, however, precisely that which its title implied. It was what Montgomery decided it should be. He was more inspector-general than deputy. He made constant visits to member states, and his reputation was such that he could make comments which from anyone else would have been unthinkable.

In 1958, shortly after his retirement, his autobiography, *The Memoirs of Field Marshal the Viscount Montgomery of Alamein, KG*, aroused even more controversy. Though it was touched by his old weakness of egotism tinctured with arrogance; and though it contained passages marked by prejudice and at least one (that referring to A. V. Alexander) which could only be considered grossly unfair, it was a remarkable work, making up in clarity of thought what it lacked in distinction of style. The most violent reactions came not from his own country but from allies. They bore witness to resentment in the United States and still more in Italy, though in the latter case he was writing of a country which had been an enemy under a Fascist dictatorship in war. The memoirs will occupy a permanent place in the records of the Second World War.

Montgomery's time was now his own and it was not to be expected that he would withdraw into a hermit's cell in Hampshire. Hardly had the cheers and counter-cheers over the autobiography subsided when his acceptance of an invitation to visit Russia created more excitement; this time, however, condemnation was more prevalent than approval – not because he was visiting Russia but because of the circumstances and some of his comments on them. The visit was labelled 'private', but it was a visit to the Government and the General Staff. It coincided with preparations for a conference designed to lessen tension between the western and the Communist worlds. It caused the British Government a certain embarrassment at a time when the United States, France, and the German Federal Republic were inclined to think that the British Prime Minister was going too far in the direction of appeasement.

The Field Marshal's own views had become distinctly more inclined to compromise. It was a curious turn of the wheel which led some unbalanced and strident American commentators to picture him as 'a stooge of Macmillan's' for selling the pass to the Reds, an accusation that reveals a good deal more about American political psychology than it does about Montgomery's character. His visit to the Soviet Union in 1959 was followed by visits to India in January, 1960; to China in May, 1960, and September, 1961; to Africa in November, 1959, and January, 1962; and to Central America in December, 1961. His account of these travels was contained in his *Three Continents*, published in 1962. Two of the more significant judgments of this book were that the key to the peace of the world lies in China; and that Britain should not become entangled in the political systems of Europe by joining the Common Market.

At the beginning of 1963 Montgomery saw the beginning of a military reform which he had consistently advocated for many years, and which is now virtually complete – the reorganization of defence planning under a single central Ministry, and the abolition of the three separate service Ministries. In a speech in the House of Lords he remarked characteristically that it had come too late. By this time Montgomery was deeply involved in preparing his *History of Warfare*. This was a monumental work of research – understandably not all Montgomery's own. Indeed, he was in the habit of telling friends to concentrate on the first two chapters and the last – 'I wrote those myself.' The book was published in 1968 and although its critical reception was mixed it sold well. Meanwhile, in 1967, Montgomery returned to the battlefields of the Western Desert to celebrate the twenty-fifth anniversary of Alamein. He was warmly received by the Egyptians and his week-long tour ended with a lecture to about 150 generals and senior officials at the Nasser Higher Military Academy in Cairo.

Montgomery spent the last years of his life quietly in his converted mill at Islington in Hampshire, tending his garden, which he loved, and ruling his small household and his visitors with a firm military hand. From time to time he emerged for some engagement which he considered important enough to disturb the routine of his evening years. Although he had to refuse on medical advice an invitation to be a pall-bearer at Sir Winston Churchill's state funeral in 1965, he was present in 1969 at St George's Chapel, Windsor, at the funeral of his old chief, Field Marshal Lord Alexander. In the same year, at the age of 82, he carried the Sword of State at the State Opening of Parliament and no defence debate in the House of Lords was complete without his trenchant contributions, delivered from somewhere near the exact centre of the Conservative benches, but often turning his own front bench colleagues pale with apprehension.

A Great Battlefield Commander

By the most exacting standards, Montgomery was an outstanding general. Asked once to name the three greatest generals in history he answered with impish precision: 'The other two were Alexander the Great and Napoleon.' It will be for military historians and biographers to judge the validity of this half-serious, half-mocking remark. Certainly he was unique in the parade of great commanders. His military thinking combined immense conviction with clarity of expression and great simplicity. His method was to reduce a problem to its bare essentials – indeed he often over-simplified in a manner alien to the more sophisticated academic mind; but he went straight to the heart of the matter, and if in doing so he sometimes missed the subtleties of emphasis that might have avoided personal friction, just as often he reached by intuition solutions which his staff officers had failed to reach after hours of study. They were solutions of the sort which, once reached, appeared obvious to everyone.

He made some enemies along the way – and they were not all Germans and Italians. Many of his colleagues – political and military – found his flamboyant personality distasteful. They thought his eccentricities of dress, his preoccupation with personal publicity, and his florid, evangelical messages to his troops exaggerated and contrived. But Montgomery knew what he was about. He had grasped the importance to the soldier in the ranks of good public relations, and he exploited it coldly and deliberately. Few troops who served under his command were not inspired by 'Monty', who knew what he wanted and went all out to get it.

In his mature years he was obsessively neat and punctual himself and deplored untidiness or unpunctuality in others. His unhappy childhood, his early lack of *rapport* with his mother, and the tragedy of his wife's death made him a difficult, lonely, and complicated man. But he was, above everything, a soldier. It was in the mud, the snow, or the dust, in the fear, the pain, and the blood that he was at his greatest. He killed the enemy coldly and efficiently; but for the lives of his own soldiers he cared intensely. He was meticulous in preparation, in administration, and in execution. He knew his dark trade better than anyone else in his time. Perhaps his greatest single virtue as a soldier was his sense of 'balance'. Like the great athlete he would have liked to be, he was always poised in battle, able to work out his plans however the enemy reacted; and if afterwards he was ready too often to say that everything had gone *exactly* as he had planned, there was more truth in the boast than literal-minded critics have been ready to admit. The essence of his personal philosophy was that true freedom was having the liberty to do what you ought, not what you want. History will in time deliver its verdict on Montgomery the soldier; until it does, he will be mourned not only as a national figure, but, even by those far removed in spirit or in sympathy from the profession of arms, as the last of the great battlefield commanders.

* * *

MAO TSE-TUNG

Revolutionary leader who inspired the regeneration of China

9 SEPTEMBER 1976

MAO TSE-TUNG, whose death is announced on another page, was 82. His great service to China was to give his country what it longed for after a century of chaos and indecision – the revolutionary leadership, the strategy, and the doctrine that could inspire its regeneration. Mao could never have done this simply as an importer of Marxism, as so many other Asians did, sitting at the feet of western revolutionaries. His pride would not have allowed any such thing: Marxism had to be remade in a Chinese image before it could serve China's cause and it was Mao who did it.

At the core of his highly complex and contradictory personality was an intense nationalism. All that he did for China he did as a nationalist. He had grown up in a China set adrift by the collapse of the old imperial system and the undermining of Confucianism; a China in which the national aims of wealth and power meant China's equality with the West as an industrial power and the restoration of China's rule over those territories lost to her in a century of weakness.

These were Chinese aims and they were Mao's aims. He led no revolution against an established order as Communists did in Russia and sought to do in Europe; that order had disappeared with the fall of the imperial court and the bureaucracy that supported it in 1911. What had remained for Mao to attack in China was a social and economic order in which the hated class were not the capitalists who enraged the European revolutionary but the landlords whose oppression of the peasants had fired Mao's earliest sense of injustice. What Mao did in China was to build on Chinese traditions of peasant revolt and to reinvigorate dormant ideals of frugality, dedication, and service to the people fired anew by a messianic Marxism. He succeeded because his manner and his methods were Chinese. In 1949 China got a government that united the country as it had not been united for centuries.

But Mao the nationalist was also Mao the revolutionary who believed that revolution should be continuous since any weakening of revolutionary resolve brought decay and corruption. The Chinese people should put revolution first, above mother and child, husband and wife, or any other human relationship.

This meant a life of struggle. Mao had relished struggle in his youth, was absorbed by the guerrilla warfare so brilliantly controlled from Yenan, triumphed in the civil war, and thereafter could conceive of no life but one founded on the same constancy of endeavour against the enemies of revolution. Neither his colleagues nor, it may be said with confidence, the Chinese people could share this absolute dedication to eternal struggle in pursuit of a myth. Indeed, a people whose most powerful traditions were those of compromise in pursuit of harmony found Mao's revolutionary tenacity could hold their loyalty in the early years but thereafter exacted only an increasingly hollow and conformist obedience.

In many other ways Mao's ambitions far outran his achievements. He wanted more change than could be brought about in any man's lifetime. He wanted to implant his belief in the will to revolution to those activists whose unflagging cooperation would give birth to a new man and a new society. To many outside China the ideals offered in the Hundred Flowers movement of 1957 (which at least revealed how strong even then was the resentment in cultural circles at the conformism imposed by Mao), the Great Leap Forward, and the enormous upheaval of the Cultural Revolution were marks of Mao's creative imagination and dedication to revolutionary purity.

The means to bring about these changes were persuasive, not violent. Mao clung to a socialist legality. But the psychological pressures could be intense and the techniques employed were brutally abusive of Chinese sensibilities. The toll of suicides among the urban middle class was considerable. Nor was Mao's own vision of himself as pre-eminently a teacher one that many of his colleagues would have endorsed by the end of the Cultural Revolution.

By then the divisions that had begun to open up within the party and army leadership in earlier campaigns had become critical. In building up an inordinate personality cult of Mao during the Cultural Revolution Lin Piao had furthered his own ambition to succeed Mao, thanks to an army ascendancy established at the ninth party congress of April, 1969, when Mao's wife Chiang Ching and Lin's wife,

Yeh Chun, were both elevated to the political bureau along with Lin's military backers.

When that plot had been laid low – it was directed also against Chou En-lai who foiled it – China seemed ready in 1971 to revert to an ordered progress. But in fact the party conflict between radical newcomers raised to power by the Cultural Revolution and the majority surviving who deplored the damage done to China by that upheaval was unabated. From then onwards Chou En-lai, as leader of the pragmatists, found himself directly opposed to the radicals whose channel to Mao through his wife Chiang Ching was always used to impose the imperial fiat.

The tenth party congress in 1973 was followed by campaigns that absurdly linked Lin Piao and Confucius. In January, 1975, the much-delayed meeting of the National People's Congress led to the return to office and respectability of many dethroned during the Cultural Revolution. Such swings back and forth were all evidence of the unresolved and bitter battle carried on behind a screen of increasing secrecy. Chou's plan to ensure an ordered succession was foiled after his death by a fresh campaign against his chosen successor, Teng Hsiao-ping. Massive demonstrations in favour of the deceased Chou in Peking and all over China in April, 1976, were an unmistakable rejection of Mao throughout most ranks of the country's bureaucracy.

In contrast to his internal difficulties, Mao relished during his last decade in power the recognition given to China. There had been difficult times when America's war in Vietnam threatened to engulf China as Korea had done. The Russian action against Czechoslovakia in 1968 alerted China to some similar action on China's borders where 'mutual' hostility had built up large forces.

American Withdrawal from Vietnam

But signs of an American withdrawal from Vietnam promised a change in American policy towards China which Mao encouraged following Richard Nixon's election to the presidency. In 1971 Dr Kissinger's secret visit to Peking prepared the way for President Nixon's much applauded trip in February, 1972. Mao's wish as far back as 1945 to win for the Chinese Communists some recognition from President Roosevelt that might in time serve to balance China's inevitable relations with the USSR, was now at last rewarded.

Japan followed suit with recognition of Peking later that year and almost all other countries in the world were now ready to open embassies in Peking. Somewhat to their surprise the Chinese found their claim to the United Nations seat at last acknowledged with the expulsion of Taiwan in 1971.

Mao's view of world strategy now led him to cultivate relations with the European Community as a bulwark of firm resistance to the Soviet Union, in the west. The result was a succession of western visitors to Peking from Britain (now at last able to exchange ambassadors), France, Germany, Australia, New Zealand, Canada.

Relations with the United States did not bear as much fruit as Mao had hoped; nor did the western ministers share his outright hostility to détente with the Soviet Union. Mao himself was also ready to flout protocol by inviting Mr Nixon on a return visit after his resignation, Mr Heath as leader of the Opposition, and others such as Herr Strauss from Germany.

When compared with other Asian leaders of his day – Nehru, for example – it is often forgotten how important Mao's origins were within Chinese tradition and within the peasant life of the provinces. Born in the village of Shao Shan in Hunan on December 26, 1893, he was the son of a peasant who, by the son's later grading of class status, was a rich peasant, developing a rice distribution business besides his ordinary tillage. Mao was the eldest of four sons and a daughter, much attached to his illiterate mother, but disliking his father's avarice and tyrannical attitudes. He even led his mother and brothers in a family revolt against the father. After five years at the village school he was brought home to help his father but broke away to enter a school where 'western learning' formed part of the curriculum and where he was fascinated by the lives of such as Washington, Napoleon, Peter the Great, and Wellington. After a few months as a volunteer in the new republic army after the 1911 revolution he went to the middle school at Changsha, the provincial capital, and won a scholarship to the first normal school, from which he graduated in 1918, aged 25. He was unable to gain admission to Peking University but through the aid of his teacher in Changsha, now a professor there, he was employed as an assistant in the library.

At this time Mao's political ideas were still formless. He had joined a political study group in 1917 and his first published essay introduced the voluntarism that was to be characteristic of his whole career, the belief in human will conquering all obstacles. He had returned to Hunan in the spring of 1919 after a short stay in Shanghai bidding farewell to friends who left to study in France. Mao himself had been active in supporting this scheme of foreign study yet when it came to the point he hesitated and made no effort to go himself. An instinct for China? A fear of strange countries? Instead Mao plunged into the battle for change, editing a review, founding another when this was suppressed. Overcome by a particular case of ill-treatment Mao took up another of the themes that was to mark his life – the emancipation of women.

Indeed, at this time his political ideas were still a mixture of anarchism and liberalism, with as yet very little, and that at second hand, that could be ascribed to Marxism. The May 4 movement aroused Mao to greater efforts. He organized a student movement but the repressive cruelty of the provincial governor forced him to flee back to Peking. Mao dated his own Marxist beliefs from this time when the first Chinese translation of the *Communist Manifesto* was published; certainly it was the first moment at which Marxist ideas began to take shape in his mind.

In a brief stay in Shanghai working as a laundryman Mao contacted a Marxist study group set up by the Comintern agent Voitinsky and he soon became secretary of a similar group, in his own province Hunan. Thus, when 13 men met secretly during the summer holidays in a girls' school in Shanghai in 1921, Mao was one of the founding members of the Chinese Communist Party and went back to Hunan as secretary of the party group there.

On Comintern advice the Chinese Communists joined the Kuomintang, advice that Mao eagerly accepted. His zeal in cooperating with the Kuomintang at this time even earned him some suspicion among his fellow Communists, but Mao found his organizational ability was much appreciated in the KMT propaganda department and at the head of the Kuomintang peasant training bureau. For two years until 1927 he moved between Hunan and the KMT headquarters in Canton, missing the fourth Communist Party Congress and apparently unconcerned at the moves some members made to break the link with the KMT.

He remained a member of the central executive committee of the KMT even after he had lost his place on the central committee of the CCP. His high hopes of the planned northern expedition of 1926 even allowed him to disregard the obviously repressive measures against Communists that Chiang Kai-shek – now in control after Sun Yat-sen's death – had initiated. Needless to say, these years in Mao's career were obliterated from any subsequent published accounts.

The next turning-point in his career came with his report on the revolutionary potential of the peasants of Hunan. After April, 1927, when Chiang Kai-shek's massacre of Communists in Shanghai made the split final, the Communists gradually turned to violence, as in the Nanchang uprising and Mao's own autumn harvest uprising in Hunan. The outcome of these failures provided a nucleus, in the Chingkang mountains of Kiangsi province, of a liberated area under the partnership of Mao and the experienced military leader Chu Teh. A new Red army prospered as the area expanded and Chiang Kai-shek's attempt to eliminate the Communists failed. The circumstances brought out all Mao's brilliance as an organizer, as a tactician of conflict, and a political leader. His personal confidence and his ambition both flourished.

Other areas followed but the Kiangsi one offered the best security to the hunted members of the central committee living underground in Shanghai. Eventually Chiang Kai-shek's attacks on the base forced its evacuation. The 'Long March' that followed became the epic of the revolution and the turning point of Mao's career in the party. During its course, at Tsunyi, in Kweichow province, Mao's primacy in the party was established in circumstances never made clear, though it seems today that Mao owed his election as chairman of the military committee to the support of Chou En-lai, his senior in the party.

Arrived in the north-west, Mao set about giving the party his own stamp and offering to the Chinese people as a whole the leadership against an aggressive Japan over which Chiang Kai-shek still hesitated. In 1942 he began a movement to renovate the party known as the Cheng-Feng movement. The war ended with the Communists in a commanding position in the countryside of North China.

In 1945 the Communists held their seventh Party Congress, the first Congress for 17 years and the first to be held since Mao had totally refashioned the party. He was now formally elected as leader.

Civil war – interrupted by the wartime truce and coalition – was soon resumed and by 1948 the Communist victory was near. The party headquarters moved to Peking in March, 1949, and preparations began for the obvious task which then faced Communists of ruling all China. It was during this phase that one of Mao's valuable characteristics was made manifest. He was a Nationalist as much as a Communist, and his aim was to win over to the acceptance of Communist rule as many Chinese as possible. On the other hand, his bitter experiences in agrarian revolution had led him to see the landlord as the villain much more than the capitalist. In the land reform which began in north China many landlords suffered, not always justly, whereas in the preparatory period before the assumption of power in October 1949, a series of conferences were held in Peking which gave every opportunity for the educated, and even the capitalist, classes to show their sympathy for the new regime. In July, addressing the preparatory meeting of the Chinese People's Preparatory Consultative Conference, Mao set forth in *On the People's Democratic Dictatorship* the policies the new Government would follow. It was in this speech that he declared the Communist intention of 'leaving to one side' a decision to join with the Communist block which may not have been considered or decided until a few months before. On October 1, the new Government was proclaimed, with Mao as chairman of the People's Government Council and the capital reverted to Peking.

Earthy Sense of Humour

To have brought order out of the chaos of half a century was a tribute to a party that had been moulded and led by Mao. To have set China on a path that restored its confidence and done it by uniting as many as possible of its population behind him was an astonishing achievement. 'We have stood up,' he cried triumphantly when the new government took charge in 1949, and to the world at large it was the belligerence of China's new ruler that seemed most blatant in the years of his rule. This was to mistake his character entirely. There was more than the poetry to set against the strategist of world revolution or the bitter polemicist of the Sino-Soviet dispute. More than one acquaintance has testified to an almost feminine sensibility; to an earthy sense of humour; to a complexity of mind that may never have moved much outside a Chinese cast of thought but within that range was as subtle as any leader in the country's long history.

His personality as a revolutionary leader was far more complex than the Communist world he then joined could comprehend or a western world still ignorant of modern Chinese thought could assess. The strain running through his whole life was struggle; struggle was a law of society in which he saw himself as the supreme strategist. Hence his admiration for virtues such as resolution, dedication, patience, courage, self-sacrifice. In the world of 1949, bludgeoned by the Russian record, it was only too easy to translate this into Stalinist terms. On the contrary, Mao was no Stalinist. He could be flamboyant, quizzical, humorous – at heart perhaps a romantic individualist who struggled as a youth against the family and the Confucian ties that fettered him. It was only one of many paradoxes of his rule that he would have seen membership of the Communist party as an individualist gesture of personal salvation which others must be persuaded to take.

Mao the revolutionary leader was nevertheless a complete product of Chinese culture. His education never took him outside of it; whatever new wine had gone in, the man who stood on the south gate of the Forbidden City to watch the annual march past had nothing alien about him; the formation and furnishing of his mind was Chinese.

Tremendous Force of Persuasion

One of the myths that impelled him was his belief in the masses as the recipients of revolutionary leadership and as the supplicants for revolutionary change: 'from the masses to the masses' was his slogan. The revolutionaries got their energy from the masses and in return interpreted mass wishes. Though this may have been an illusion, easily fostered in the days of guerrilla warfare, but steadily less supportable after years of rule from Peking, Mao nevertheless retained his faith in the voluntary principle. He had rejected violence, he told Edgar Snow in Yenan in 1937, and he always thought of his methods as calling forth a voluntary response: the force of the revolution as it spread throughout China in the years after 1949 was the force – and it was a tremendous force – of persuasion.

Mao's career in power in Peking after 1949 was very different from the life he had known as a revolutionary leader in Yenan. In many ways he regretted this. At all times he harked back to the dedicated and simple life of those days. The man who turned from his political study to the plough and then to the rifle or the factory bench – the simple all-rounder – was Mao's ideal; in so far as any goal could be perceived to which his revolutionary path led, it was communities of such an all-embracing character. In the continual battle between the 'red' and the 'expert' his emphasis constantly returned to the political starting point from which all else followed: 'redness' meant the thoughts of Mao Tse-tung and no kind of progress for China was possible if these thoughts were not followed.

In his first years in power Mao concentrated on ideological purity and on accelerating the pace towards cooperative agriculture. The party, the administration, and the economy were shared between men like Liu Shao-chi and Chou En-lai. Thus, in its eighth Party Congress of 1956 a recognizable Chinese Communist establishment was in being – later to be attacked bitterly by Mao and the Red Guards in the Cultural Revolution.

In this year Mao's attention was alerted by the secret speech of Khrushchev dethroning Stalin and by ructions in Poland and Hungary which set going a stream of advice to the Russians at the way they were mishandling their east European neighbours and becoming revisionist in their approach to Communist theory. In his second visit to Moscow in 1957 on the occasion of the Soviet fortieth anniversary Mao was forthright in his criticism. By 1958, over the Taiwan straits crisis, and in 1959, when Khrushchev came to Peking after visiting Eisenhower at Camp David, Mao's resentment as a nationalist was added to his growing contempt as a theorist for post-Stalinist Russia. In 1960 an open attack on Russian revisionism was relentlessly pursued at party congresses in eastern Europe. The world Communist Congress at the end of that year made the Sino-Soviet split worldwide and beyond resolution.

The dispute might never have gone as far as it did if it had not caught up every one of Mao's qualities and personal dedication and absorbed him utterly. The nationalist who believed in the glory of China could expose Russian faithlessness; the revolutionary strategist could show up Russian cowardice and backsliding; the acute Marxist thinker could quote all the authorities to pin down Moscow's revisionism; the simple, incorruptible exponent of struggle could chastise a Russia sinking into bourgeois vulgarity and moral decline. Many of the polemics of the later period evidently came from Mao's hand alone; certainly the bitterness of the dispute might have been far less if Mao's own commitment to it had not been so great.

In thus transferring to the world's revolutionary 'countryside' of Asia, Africa, and Latin America the revolutionary strategy he had evolved in the Chinese countryside Mao may have seen himself as the universal leader of peasants, soon to surround and reduce the world's capitalist cities. In the sixties Mao became much more accessible to revolutionaries visiting Peking. Latin Americans and Africans especially were received in the world's new temple of revolution. In 1963 and subsequently Mao even issued statements in his own name on such pressing matters as the colour question in the United States. The evolution of the world revolutionary leader was complete.

Mao's concern with Russian revisionism in the late 1950s impelled him to hurry on the process of collectivism in the countryside lest the capitalist instincts of the peasant should reassert themselves. The Hundred Flowers movement of 1957 was an attempt to expose the party to criticism and in the process win over sceptical intellectuals to a real appreciation of Marxism. In the event the depth of intellectual distaste was only the more revealed and the party hierarchy called a halt to a movement that was undermining its own authority.

In the Great Leap Forward of 1958 Mao attempted to set up communes as wholly collectivist large units in the countryside with collective mess halls and a regimented life in the service of revolution. These were soon radically altered in face of confusion and opposition followed by three years of disastrous harvests from 1960–62. But Mao persisted with the commune idea coupled with his aim of breaking down the differences between town and countryside.

Eventually a system emerged in the late 1960s where self-supporting communes running small-scale industry not only met their own material needs and generated a surplus for running health and education but also linked many of the factories to larger industry in the cities. The result was not only an end to the famines that had been endemic in some parts of China for centuries but to bring variety and encourage initiative in a self-supporting rural life a – mode of economic development that was to attract visitors from many other Asian and African countries.

Mao was three times married. Disregarding a traditional family betrothal in his youth, he married first Yang Kai-hui, daughter of Yang Chang-chi, his teacher and later a professor of Peking University. She was arrested as a revolutionary by the Kuomintang in 1928 and executed in 1930. Not long after her arrest Mao had begun to live with Ho Tzu-chen, a landlord's daughter of 18 whom he later married as his second wife. She accompanied him on the Long March, in which she suffered injury and ill-health and was sent for treatment in 1937 to the Soviet Union not long after the Red Army had arrived in Yenan.

In 1938 Chiang Ching (before then an actress in Shanghai under the stage name Lan Ping) arrived in Yenan with Huang Ching, a party member with whom she had been living. Soon after they had met Mao proposed to marry her but Ho Tzu-chen protested to senior party members, all of whom sympathized with her case. But Mao insisted and in return his colleagues exacted from him a promise Chiang Ching would play no part in politics.

Little information about Mao's children has ever been divulged. Some children by Ho Tzu-chen were farmed out to peasants on the Long March. One son (by Yang Kai-hui) was killed in the Korean war; another is an engineer. There are two daughters by the marriage with Chiang Ching.

BENJAMIN BRITTEN

A major contribution to English music

4 DECEMBER 1976

LORD BRITTEN, OM, CH, who died on December 4 at the age of 63, was much more than the leading English composer of his time.

He was the first British composer to capture and hold the attention of musicians and their audiences the world over, as well as at home; he was the first British composer to centre his mature work prolifically on the musical theatre – grand opera, chamber opera, sacred music-drama. Brought up in a generation that still regarded music as a diversion for amateurs, he made himself a completely professional musician and, by example as well as precept, successfully preached the gospel of scrupulous, thorough, professional musicianship to his contemporaries, so that nobody with whom he ever worked could ever again regard music-making as a good job worth doing less than perfectly. In so doing he nurtured a musical (particularly a vocal) style that has become valid and acceptable in this country for past as well as present music – this facet of his influence is still underestimated. It is significant, too, that he preached professionalism to the amateurs and young people for whom he composed much of his music, as well as to his professional colleagues.

Musicianship was, for Britten, a comprehensive art. Like Boulez and Bernstein, but like no other major composers of our day, Britten presented himself to the world as a general practitioner of music, not only composer but conductor and pianist (in his own and other composers' music); his own Aldeburgh Festival would find him organizing, turning pages for other pianists, playing the recorder and singing madrigals and moving furniture. He did not naturally express himself in words – music was his chosen medium – but he could write well, as his Aspen Award speech of 1964 showed, and as some of his other occasional writings attested, and he was a lucid, vivid speaker – memorable in this connection were the declaration of faith with which he responded to the presentation of honorary membership of the Worshipful Company of Musicians in 1965, and his wartime broadcast reading of Mozart's letters. As a composer Britten emerged much more Continentally orientated than his senior compatriots; the composers who influenced him, and whom he continued to admire, and champion, included Verdi, Mahler, Berg, Schoenberg, and the pre-serial Stravinsky, as well as Shostakovich and Henze among younger men.

In his songs he set French, Italian, German, and Russian poetry – his liaison with Russian musicians was a major contribution to creative international friendship in the 1960s, not to be underestimated. But he was naturally rooted in England (to be precise, in East Anglia), as he found when he emigrated to the New World just before the Second World War, and among his abiding musical influences were the Elizabethan madrigalists, Dowland and Purcell, as well as Holst and Frank Bridge, with whom he had close connections. Britten's Englishness as a musician was a necessary part of his musical internationalism, just as his strong, thoughtful personality combined forthright political, social, and religious opinions which found more or less powerful reflection in his music.

From the moment of his return to England in 1942 he worked continually for the status and development of British music, finding performances for other composers, including the youngest generations, and helping talented British executant musicians to achieve their full potentiality. The famous dictum, 'Only connect', of E. M. Forster (whose article on East Anglia brought Britten home in 1942 and inspired *Peter Grimes*, who collaborated with Britten in *Billy Budd*, and who was a potent influence as well as a close friend) finds an outstanding example in the personality and work of Britten; everything that he did, whether playing the piano for Yehudi Menuhin in concentration camps, or composing music for children's percussion bands, or writing pacifist marches and documentary film music, or bird-watching, or playing piano duets with Sviatoslav Richter, or writing *Gloriana* for the Queen's coronation, had some intelligible, logical relevance to his personal faith and idealism.

Edward Benjamin Britten was born at Lowestoft on November 22, 1913 (the feastday of St Cecilia, music's patron saint appropriately enough). His father was a dental surgeon, his mother the secretary of Lowestoft Choral Society. Britten was raised in a musical atmosphere, and began to make music from his sixth year, composing as well as playing. He wrote a great deal of music in his childhood (he re-worked some of the themes in the *Simple Symphony* of 1934) and was fortunate, when he was 12, to become the protégé and pupil of Frank Bridge, an exceptionally adventurous British composer of his day. Britten continued to study with Bridge during schooldays at Gresham's and even after he had entered the Royal College of Music (when his professors were John Ireland and Arthur Benjamin) at 16. He used a theme by Bridge for the string orchestral variations which first brought him to international attention at the 1936 Salzburg Festival. From Bridge Britten learnt his predilection for 'clear, clean sound', for economy of means, and for adventures in texture and sonority. To these the RCM added contact with other colleagues, a part of life which always meant much to this apparently introspective self-contained musician.

It was symptomatic of the period that when Britten won a bursary for further study and elected Alban Berg as teacher, the RCM authorities, suspicious of Viennese dodecaphony, persuaded the boy's parents that the saintly Berg would be an undesirable influence on their son: Britten never forgot, and did not quickly forgive, this underhand blow to his progress – 'it might have taught me how to unlock gates; I did in fact have to climb over,' he later wrote. His devotion to the second Viennese school never faltered, and in later works he made use of some Schoenbergian technical procedures, particularly for thematic integration; but he remained content with invention in major and minor keys, for his own creative purposes, not out of dogmatic conviction (as with Shostakovich), but simply because he found keys viable for his invention.

After leaving the RCM Britten worked with the GPO Film Unit, writing incidental music for documentary films, among others by Cavalcanti and Lotte Reiniger, and including the now classic *Coal Face* and *Night Mail* which had scripts by W. H. Auden, already a friend of Britten, and an influence on his political thinking. Auden provided the texts for *Our Hunting Fathers*, a brave and brilliant satirical cantata which scandalized audiences at the Norwich Festival, which had commissioned it, for the precociously masterful song-cycle *On This Island*, and in part for the socialist *Ballad for Heroes*, as well as the plays *The Ascent of F6* and *On the Frontier*, for which Britten wrote incidental music. It was Auden whose example encouraged Britten to emigrate to America. Britten had found a publisher in Ralph Hawkes, and his works were reaching performance notably through the Macnaghten–Lemare concerts; but the English climate was unwelcoming to a progressive young composer, and Britten needed the stimulus of wider experience. The Continent seemed politically unfavourable; his gaze followed Auden's to the United States, and he went there.

The artistic climate in America helped Britten's brilliant talent to come of age; here he wrote the exploratory and deeply felt *Sinfonia da Requiem*, his only major work for symphony orchestra alone; the first string quartet; and the two fine song-cycles, *Les Illuminations* and *Michelangelo Sonnets*, the latter for Peter Pears, who had travelled with him to America, with whom he formed a non pareil recital partnership, and for whom he composed a procession of superb vocal works and operatic roles – artistically they were the making of each other, just as socially they proved ideally attuned when they came to share their home in Aldeburgh, a favourite resort of their innumerable friends of both sexes, many nationalities, and all ages.

Britten wrote his first opera, *Paul Bunyan*, to a text by Auden, while he was in America. It came to performance but was soon withdrawn: Britten claimed to have lost the score but close friends told of having heard him play and sing it at late-night parties. It was to be 35 years before Britten chose to lift the curtain on this mystery and *Paul Bunyan* reappeared to be performed on BBC radio in January, and at the Aldeburgh Festival in June this year. The most important moment of his stay in America was surely when Sergei Koussevitsky commissioned him to write his planned opera about fishing-folk in Suffolk, *Peter Grimes*. Britten knew that if he came home during wartime he would have to face a tribunal for his pacifist convictions (embraced and publicized by his music, as early as 1937). He returned to England, obtained unconditional exemption (he had volunteered alternatively for work with Friends' Relief Service) and divided his time between composition and concert tours for CEMA with Peter Pears. Among the many works he found time to write were the exquisite *Hymn to St Cecilia* (text by Auden, composed on the voyage home) and *A Ceremony of Carols*, written at the same time, the 18-part string Prelude and Fugue written for the tenth anniversary of the Boyd Neel Orchestra, which had commissioned his Bridge Variations, and the touchingly tender *Serenade* for tenor, horn, and strings, a consummation of Britten's fascination for the Mahlerian song-cycle with orchestra, and a work that equally challenged the virtuosity and expressive powers of Pears and Dennis Brain, for whom it was composed.

This was probably the work that set the seal on Britten's reputation in Britain, as near great music as makes no difference. But it was *Peter Grimes* which conquered the world with its close-packed compassionate drama, searing yet heady atmosphere, and magnificently characterized expansive vocal music. *Grimes* marked the beginning of worldwide fame for Britten and it is a certain masterpiece; but for Britten it was an end-product, an opera of the old-fashioned sort that offered him no immediate scope for further development. The necessary scope was soon forthcoming.

In the autumn of 1945 two concerts were given to commemorate the two hundred and fiftieth anniversary of Purcell's death. Britten contributed two new works, the *Holy Sonnets of John Donne*, written for Peter Pears, and the second string quartet, which has a Purcell-style *Chacony* (including several solo cadenzas) as finale and a scherzo which makes a point of fortissimi for muted strings; for these concerts Britten also made highly controversial realizations of Purcell songs, full of imaginative invention in an idiom more of the twentieth than the seventeenth century. Musicologists deplored the deliberate flouting of historical style, and Britten later found a happy compromise for his keyboard realizations of old music. But the exercise did alert untutored audiences to the drama and lyrical eloquence of Purcell's lesser known vocal works.

The spur to further operatic activity came when Britten, impatient of the established operatic scene in Britain, formed his own English Opera Group, a compact organization designed for travel. The orchestra had to be small and so Britten turned to chamber opera, with *The Rape of Lucretia* (1946) and *Albert Herring* (1947) (both first presented at Glyndebourne, then taken on tour in Europe). It took Britten these two chamber operas to discover how most effectively to use his modest instrumental force, not as an orchestra but as a chamber ensemble of solo instrumentalists blended with the voices on stage (and with the words, particularly the consonants, being sung). The experience had a decisive effect on all his subsequent music not only in chamber opera, above all in the terrible and magnificent *Turn of the Screw,* but in Britten's subsequent grand operas, notably *Billy Budd* (1951) and *Gloriana* (1953), and in his next symphonic work the *Spring Symphony* (1949), written for the Holland Festival, a rich, and vivid musical tapestry in the Mahler tradition, using three soloists, chorus, boys' choir, and a big orchestra; its four parts comprise 12 movements.

While touring Switzerland with the English Opera Group Britten and a few colleagues determined to give their work a home, centre, and shop-window in the form of an annual arts festival at Aldeburgh where Britten had recently bought a house. The aims were at once selfish and propagandist: to perform the music, exhibit the pictures, promote other artistic events that Britten and his friends liked best, in the manner they thought most fitting, for the pleasure of those who thought as they did. Britten was not conceited, even about his most cherished beliefs, and he was prepared to cater for very small audiences at his miniature festival. Aldeburgh Festival flourished and attracted ever larger audiences from far and near. Its atmosphere owes much to the intimacy of the available halls and churches, but space had soon to be found for a larger public, and recourse was had to country houses and larger churches in the vicinity, finally to a new large hall at Snape, the Maltings, which the Queen opened in 1967. It burnt down in 1969 but arose, Phoenix-like, in time for the 1970 festival.

Britten's delight in writing music for children can be traced back to the songs *Friday Afternoons* (1934), but it came to the forefront in the late 1940s, first with the excellent Purcell variations called *The Young Person's Guide to the Orchestra* (1946, originally designed as music for a film, *Instruments of the Orchestra*) then with the cantata *St Nicolas* (1948, written for Lancing College), the *Spring Symphony* (1949), and the entertainment for young people *Let's Make an Opera* (1949). In *The Turn of the Screw* (1954), arguably the masterpiece among Britten's chamber operas, he took full advantage of the importance of the roles of Flora and Miles in Henry James's ghost story, and there are important solo parts, and an ingeniously devised children's orchestra in the church opera *Noyes Fludde* (1957). Ever since hearing the Dutch boys in the premiere of the *Spring Symphony* Britten had expressed a preference for natural unsophisticated training of children's voices (the Continental, as opposed to the English Cathedral sound), as at Westminster Cathedral, for whose choir the *Missa Brevis* (1959) was composed, and among the London Boy Singers in whose formation Britten had a hand. In 1967 he brought the Vienna Boys Choir (*Wienersangerknaben*) to Aldeburgh and provided them with the short and characteristically poignant vaudeville opera, *The Golden Vanity.*

The Aldeburgh Festival, the English Opera Group, recitals with Peter Pears, and concert tours – these occupied Britten's energies quite fully, and provided occasion for most of his subsequent works. For the Royal Opera House he wrote *Billy Budd* (1951), *Gloriana* (1953), and the ballet *The Prince of the Pagodas* (1956). None of these was initially successful, although the merits of the operas were recognized when they were revived after 10 years' lapse. But *A Midsunmmer Night's Dream* (1960), written for Aldeburgh, was instantly and continually successful at Covent Garden and abroad. Leeds Centenary Festival in 1958 elicited the Nocturne cycle of songs for tenor, obbligato instruments (a different one for each song), and strings. The quincentenary of Basle University in 1960 produced the *Cantata Academica*, a work full of erudite and witty scholarly compositional procedures. The appearance of Mstislav Rostropovich at an Aldeburgh Festival in 1961 prompted the brilliant cello sonata and initiated a series of compositions for this superb Russian cellist, as well as a procession of eminent Russian musicians to Aldeburgh.

By far the most important work of these years was the *War Requiem* (1961) which, after many years' brooding, Britten wrote for the Coventry Festival when the new cathedral there was consecrated. His bold innovation of contrasting the Latin words of the *Mass for the Dead* (sung by solo soprano, and choirs with full orchestra) with English poems by Wilfred Owen (set for solo tenor and baritone with chamber orchestra) created a directly suggestible, subtly interwoven, image of church and state, God and man, faith and works, a contrast further conveyed in the thematic material of the music. Britten also used the occasion, a solemn atonement to God for man's folly in waging war, to write specifically for a Russian soprano (Rostropovich's wife, Galina Vishnevskaya, who was, however, refused official permission by her country to take part in the first performance, though allowed to sing it in later performances and in the best-selling records of the work), a British tenor (Pears), and a German baritone (Dietrich Fischer-Dieskau). The elaborate construction of the *War Requiem* is an enhancement to close study of the work, and adds a spectacular visual quality that audiences readily appreciated in performance. But it is the intense conviction, the completely direct yet original utterance of the music that has made this the most popular serious composition of the mid-twentieth century, admired and much performed the world over.

Britten's fiftieth birthday was celebrated in November, 1963, with loud demonstrations of love and esteem for the man as well as the musician, and the publication of a distinguished and elegant *Festschrift*. One contribution was a travel diary, by Prince Ludwig of Hesse (who translated many of Britten's vocal texts into German, and for whom the *Hölderlin Fragments* were written) of a trip to the East with Britten in 1956. They had seen a Japanese Noh drama, *Sumidagawa*, and in 1964 Britten produced his own, superficially anglicized, treatment of it, under the title *Curlew River*. As a sacred music-drama to be performed in church, it followed the lead of

Noye's Fludde and the locale of Orford church as an adjunct of Aldeburgh Festival. But the free, hardly metrical, melodically exotic manner of the music showed a new departure for Britten, which was confirmed in such subsequent works as the two *Cello Suites* (1965 and 1968) for Rostropovich and the grimly magniloquent *Songs and Proverbs of William Blake*, written for Fischer-Dieskau (1965). Britten was moving into a new period of freely flowing, unregimented yet still tautly organized music that was his own personal response to the world of Boulez and Stockhausen. To *Curlew River* Britten added *The Burning Fiery Furnace* (1966) and *The Prodigal Son* (1968), thus making a triptych of sacred music-dramas.

In 1971 he wrote *Owen Wingrave*, based on a short story by Henry James, specially for television, and it was given a simultaneous premiere on BBC-TV and American television. Although even Britten could not make the medium entirely acceptable for opera, he managed to combine the intimate directness of the home screen with the strengths of large-scale opera. The theme was once again one of the sensitive non-conformist up against a hostile society. The work was slightly altered for its first stage performance, at Covent Garden in 1973. That year also saw the premiere of his most recent opera, *Death in Venice*, based on the Thomas Mann novel, at the Aldeburgh Festival with Peter Pears as Aschenbach.

After Britten fell seriously ill in 1973, he confined himself to small-scale works, among them songs for Peter Pears and Osian Ellis, and a string quartet, but for last year's Aldeburgh Festival he wrote a dramatic cantata, *Phaedra*, for Janet Baker, a major work showing no lessening of his powers.

It will be seen that Britten always composed for specific occasions, places, or people, never differentiating between the grand and the humble circumstance. He was a high-minded and high-principled person, impatient of pomp or hypocrisy (a commission, unremunerated, from two Hungarian schoolboys was for him as serious as one from the Duke of Edinburgh). His absolute artistic honesty was dictated by his faith, as was his contempt for power and violence. His early left-wing socialism remained with him as a moral and social, rather than dogmatically political, belief. He gave homage to the monarchy in *Gloriana* and his widely performed arrangement of the National Anthem (significantly omitting the bellicose second verse), and accepted the Order of Merit and the Companion of Honour. He was made a Life Peer in the birthday honours list in June this year, taking the title of Baron Britten, of Aldeburgh, in the County of Suffolk.

His general musicianship was of the highest order. As a pianist he was unsurpassed in Lieder; he was also a fine interpreter of concerted chamber music and an eloquent harpsichord continuo player. From the time of *Albert Herring* until *Death in Venice* (when he was too ill) he conducted the first performances of his works himself; orchestras found him an inspiring as well as practical and proficient conductor, and gradually he began to conduct other men's music, excelling particularly in Mozart, Mahler, and J. S. Bach (he was the presiding genius of the annual weekend Bach Festival at Long Melford). In the early 1950s he began a recording contract with Decca for whom he conducted, played, or supervised recordings of a great quantity of his works, and these are of the greatest historical importance. Rarely have such artistic endowments been matched with such a sense of human responsibility for their best use.

* * *

ELVIS PRESLEY

'The king' of rock and roll music

16 AUGUST 1977

ELVIS PRESLEY, who died yesterday at the age of 42, will be remembered as one of the earliest and greatest exponents of rock and roll music, whose recordings of 'Blue Suede Shoes', 'Hound Dog', and 'Heartbreak Hotel' establish the music's otherwise fitful claim to be a twentieth-century art form. Presley was not the first to play rock and roll, nor can he be numbered among its faithful adherents, but such details have long become irrelevant in the immensity of his legend. To his own generation and to others born after his career began, to the uninformed as well as the aficionado, Elvis Presley remained 'The King'.

A new art form, a youth revolution, were not among the objectives of Presley or his promoters. He was launched in the middle fifties as a money-making confection with a life, possibly, of six months. It was inconceivable that the catch-penny excesses of the moment, the slicked hair and shaking torso, the guitar, flashed and flourished and spun, would create a style to fascinate millions of young people for 20 years. As a symbol, Presley dominates rock music, pop art, and unnumbered private ways of life; as a person he was largely untroubled by mortality. That he himself never did or said anything remotely outrageous, significant, or even interesting has only added to the purity of his myth.

Elvis Aron Presley was born in January 1935 in the small town of Tupelo, East Mississippi. His parents were poor, eking out a precarious sharecropper living as factory workers or farm hands. Elvis was one of identical twin boys; his brother Aron died at birth. Throughout his childhood, a doting affection was lavished on him, especially by his mother Gladys. Elvis, in return, became devoted to his mother, and was deeply affected by her death in 1958.

It was propitious that he should have grown up in that region of the American South. The lands around the Mississippi River, for all their outward dreariness, have fostered two distinct and vital musical cultures. From the Negro came slave and work songs, later formalized into the blues. The white man, too, evolved music to express his superior caste, with fine clothes and sentimentality and rapid banjo and guitar-picking. The two styles met, but did not coalesce, at the city of Memphis with its rich merchants and its depressed hinterland, nurturing the blues tradition of the famous, and infamous, Beale Street.

The Presley family moved to Memphis when Elvis was 10, living first in one room, then in an apartment-house for poor whites. Elvis had received a musical education no greater than any Southern boy, picking up the rudiments of guitar-playing, singing in church or at county fairs. When he left school, it was to work as a truck driver.

At the age of 19, he was signed to the local Sun record label by its proprietor, Sam Phillips, who had heard him singing in a record-your-voice machine. Phillips was the first to see the possibilities in a white boy who could sing black music: it was Phillips who encouraged Presley to develop a style unlike anything ever heard in Country and Western music. The result was 'That's All Right Mama', released on the Sun label in 1954.

Presley might none the less have enjoyed a merely regional popularity but for the intervention of 'Colonel' Tom Parker. A man in his forties, of doubtful fair-ground antecedents, Parker had already gauged what convulsions were threatening American popular music. In a market hitherto dominated by crooners and ballad singers, new and violent noises could be heard, compounded partly from boogie and bebop, partly of rhythm and blues and other Negro styles traditionally stigmatized as 'race' music.

Already, the appearances of a former dance band called Bill Haley and the Comets were providing scenes of hysteria among young people. With masterly timing, Parker wrested Presley away from Sun and signed him to the wealthy RCA label: under Parker's personal and exclusive management, the young man from Tupelo was launched upon the world.

From 1956 to 1958 Presley's music and his appearance became the scandal of America. He was universally denounced as an immoral influence on the mobs of girls who shrieked for him at his concerts, who tore at his clothes and covered his cars with lipstick. A new species, the 'teen-ager', became the preoccupation of the American establishment, and Elvis was condemned as the embodiment of its rebellion and uncleanliness. Every record that Presley made generated fortunes: 'Heartbreak Hotel' alone stayed for eight weeks at number one in the American hit parade. Merchandising empires were built up around his name. Films followed: *Love Me Tender*, *Jailhouse Rock*, *King Creole*. The sale of guitars rose to unprecedented figures. And all proceeded under the skilful tutelage of Colonel Parker, orchestrating 'Elvis the Pelvis', his gold suits, his pink suits, and gold Cadillac cars, together with intriguing glimpses of a quiet, religious, and respectful Southern boy. His fame grew subsequently in England but Parker, cautious of the fate of other teen-idols, saw to it that he played no concerts here. Rumours of his coming were to recur, however, throughout his career.

It was Parker's most adroit piece of management which brought about the end of the Presley golden age. In 1958 Elvis entered the army for two years' service. That potential disaster was converted, with the aid of the military authorities, into a commercial transfiguration. The film *GI Blues* signified the birth of a new Elvis: rebel and outcast no longer, but an all-American hero, clean-cut and close-cropped and dutiful.

The years that followed his discharge were devoted to the playing of this anodyne part. Throughout the early and middle sixties, Presley was cast in a series of second-rate musical films. His recording output, with such notable exceptions as 'Return to Sender' or 'His Latest Flame', entered the same decline. His public grew accustomed to his remoteness. Inordinately rich, he lived as a recluse in the mansions he had built for himself, maintaining a squad of his former army friends to be his aides and to allay the boredom of his wealth. In 1967 he married Patricia Beaulieu, an army officer's daughter whom he had met in Germany. They had one child, Lisa Marie. The marriage was dissolved in 1972.

Although the influence of rock and roll appeared to wane during the sixties, it was to provide the stimulus for most of the next generation of young musicians, including the Beatles. Inevitably the commercial 'rock revival' brought Presley out of retirement, first on a television show, then by personal appearances in the Las Vegas clubs. Overweight, self-conscious, self-mocking, he seemed astonished by the ovation which he received. The standard of his records improved, though inclining to middle-of-the-road-pop. As he passed the age of 40, surrounded by countless youthful imitators, his command of the hit parade had been restored.

His private life remained largely a matter of speculation. There were rumours concerning his erratic temper, his indifference to beautiful women, his diffidence, his preoccupation with his mother and with religion.

That he never visited England was felt by many to be a betrayal of his most faithful audience; to others it was part of his incalculable fascination. His total record sales are estimated at 150 million copies. He leaves behind clubs and associations dedicated to impersonating his voice and appearance. What lay behind the music was never clear, if indeed, there was anything at all. But merely by innuendo, he is assured of his place in history.

* * *

MARIA CALLAS

Operatic star of genius

16 SEPTEMBER 1977

MISS MARIA CALLAS, the most colourful, exciting, and traditionally powerful *prima donna* of the mid-twentieth century, whose career showed the hallmarks of genius, died yesterday at the age of 53.

Ever since 1948 she has added something intensely flamboyant and vividly personal to the world of international opera, for in the age of the common man, when even sopranos, whatever their quality, are expected to be rather like everybody else, she insisted upon being entirely herself.

Maria Meneghini Callas was born in New York, of Greek parents, on December 3, 1923; her second name she took from her Italian husband, Giovanni Meneghini, whom she married in 1947, but she took Greek citizenship in 1966 to facilitate a lengthy divorce suit which ended the marriage. She had returned to Greece with her family in 1936, and studied at the Athens Conservatoire. She was seen several times at the Athens Opera during and immediately after the Second World War – her first role was that of Martha, in d'Albert's *Tiefland* – before marriage took her to Italy and the beginning of the most spectacular career in modern operatic history. After an initial appearance in the Verona amphitheatre in Ponchielli's *La Gioconda*, she was at once accepted as a brilliant exponent of the 'heavy' soprano roles: Aida, Turandot, Isolde, Brünnhilde, and Kundry fell to her advance without a struggle, but the note of the incredible was sounded when within a single week in 1949 she not only sang Brünnhilde in *Die Walküre* but also deputized for an indisposed coloratura as Elvira in Bellini's *I Puritani*, dealing accurately and spectacularly with the elaborate vocal gymnastics of the role.

From then onwards she began to drop the great heroic roles from her repertoire and to specialize in the *bel canto* heroines of Rossini, Bellini, and Donizetti, to which she added those of the early and middle period Verdi operas. The unhappy Lucia of Lammermoor, Verdi's Violetta and Gilda, Bellini's Norma, and Cherubini's Medea were roles in which she spectacularly succeeded, and she found herself in demand, with audiences at her feet, wherever such works were sung. Rossini's *Il Turco in Italia* provided her with a great success as Fiorilla; she sang Euridice in the first modern performance of Haydn's *Orfeo ed Euridice* in Florence in 1951. The change in her repertoire was no more startling than the change in her appearance; her Brünnhilde had been an imposingly Wagnerian figure, but the new Callas of the great Italian operas was slim, elegant, 'glamorous' in the sense that Hollywood has applied to that adjective, and as fiery in her dealings with conductors and impresarios as was her Tosca – a role she never relinquished – in dealing with Baron Scarpia. Like any of the great sopranos of the past she knew her work and expected to dominate conductors and colleagues as well as her audiences. Unlike most singers of the twentieth century, she never moved outside opera, although her versatility within that wide field suggests that she might have sung other things no less memorably. When asked why she never gave a song recital, the story goes, she replied that she had never found time from operatic engagements to learn the songs that she might sing.

The effectiveness of her style and the magnetism of her personality made her one of the most powerfully effective instruments in the revival of interest in *bel canto* opera after 1945. There have been, and are, voices more sensuously beautiful in themselves than was that of Maria Callas, capable of a more moving pathos and equally attractive throughout as wide a register: in vertiginous regions towards the high E flat that was her upper limit, Callas's voice was usually thin and, when she was in less than her best form, it could be shrill. It was, however, remarkably athletic and accurate, so that Norma's *Casta Diva*, an aria published and usually sung in F, was, in her performances, put up to the G that is supposed to have been Bellini's original key for the aria. Her florid singing, especially in her lower register, was always brilliant and exciting.

It was, however, the dramatic truth of her performances which conquered the operatic world. Her greatest days coincided with those of Joan Sutherland, and whilst the Australian *prima donna* seemed incapable of singing a note which sounded less than perfectly and fully moulded, Maria Callas held her own against the tremendous opposition of Miss Sutherland's well nigh perfect voice because she was, in reality, an actress of genius whose field of action was opera and not spoken drama. She developed to an unusual degree the power of timing action and gesture along the line of the music in a way which seemed always dramatically true and could, by the force of her personality and the exactitude of her characterization, convince any audience that the speed or slowness of such actions and gestures was

Maria Callas pictured at her London hotel before appearing in *La Traviata*, 1958.

that natural to the character at the moment in question. Not only, as she played them, were Isolde and Aida real personalities whose tragedies referred to the depths of human experience; the harassed heroines of Bellini and Donizetti too became equally real personages of heightened intensity. The music of the closing scene of *La Traviata* may itself suggest that Violetta is weak and mortally ill, but Callas's interpretation went beyond that; it had the somewhat frenetic gaiety which can be associated with tuberculosis and it added to the halting pathos of the last act a voice made husky and veiled by the progress of the disease.

For many years Maria Callas's relationship with the late Aristotle Onassis, the shipowner, was the most widely publicized *affaire* in the world. She denied, however, that after Onassis married Mrs Jacqueline Kennedy, widow of the American President, she attempted suicide.

Almost as well publicized was the action which, in the late 1960s, Onassis and

Callas brought alleging non-fulfilment of an agreement made with their former friend, Mr Panaghis Vergottis, another Greek shipowner. The case went finally to the House of Lords, with Vergottis seeking a retrial, but the Lords upheld Mr Justice Roskill's earlier decision that Callas was entitled to receive shipping shares in return for an advance of £60,000, the venture having been made to provide for her on her eventual retirement.

By 1965, when she last appeared at Covent Garden, she had no more operatic worlds to conquer, and her dramatic genius seemed to express itself powerfully in these domestic fields. Her withdrawal from the opera stage was not, however, a complete retirement. In Autumn 1973, with the tenor Giuseppe di Stefano and the pianist Ivor Newton, she undertook a series of recitals – her first with piano accompaniment – in Europe, ending with two performances in the Royal Festival Hall. Her programmes consisted mainly of arias and duets from Italian opera, sung with her accustomed dramatic intensity. Though, in other respects, her personality seems to have mellowed into a new cooperativeness and warmth, she generated in the calm surroundings of the Festival Hall the intensity of feeling that had belonged to her stage performances. Her audiences, refusing to leave the hall, or to end their tumultuous homage, will remember her as a splendidly elegant, slim, and gracious personality at whose command they sorrowed, rejoiced, feared, and adored.

The greatness of Maria Callas was that of an actress able to impress on the improbably romantic heroines with whom she was associated, or upon the melo-dramatics of Tosca, a passionate reality which she had found, earlier in her career, in the more profound and exalted works of late Verdi and Wagner. Singing was not, for her, an end in itself through which she could express all there was to say about a character; it was another instrument in the hands of a powerful, vivid, and exciting romantic actress.

CHARLIE CHAPLIN

Comic genius of the cinema screen

25 DECEMBER 1977

SIR CHARLES CHAPLIN, KBE, Charlie Chaplin, the comedian, died on Christmas Day. He was 88.

He was the last survivor from among the founding fathers of the American cinema, one of the greatest comic creators in film, and achieved greater, more widespread fame in his own lifetime than perhaps anyone else in the history of mankind. He was the darling of the intellectuals, who loved to theorize on the significance of his comedy, its social responsibility, its relation to the great tradition of commedia dell'arte and circus clowning, its anarchic force and vigour. But he also had to a unique degree the common touch – people of virtually any culture were able to respond with laughter to his screen antics, and for generation after generation of children he was the first introduction to the magic world of the cinema.

During the latter part of his long life Chaplin, though loaded with honours and universally regarded as one of the unshakable monuments of the cinema (whatever controversy his political attitudes might arouse), did begin to suffer from a certain reaction to the excesses of his early admirers. This had something to do with a grudging but progressive disenchantment with his later films, and something to do with the rediscovery and revaluation of the work of his many rivals in silent comedy. As we moved into the 1950s it became permissible to prefer the refined and unsentimental art of Buster Keaton, who was certainly a far more subtle and imaginative film-maker than Chaplin could ever claim to be, or even the totally unpretentious humour of Laurel and Hardy. The time was coming, in fact, for a thorough reassessment of Chaplin's own work, concentrating on aspects of it which would be more congenial to modern sensibilities: the elements of childlike ruthlessness which had endeared it to the Surrealists, perhaps, rather than the sentimentalizing elevation of the 'little man' which had made him a hero to liberal humanists.

As with Chaplin's performances, so with his career as a whole; the secret of his success lay in his immaculate timing. His genius was essentially pantomimic, and so ideally suited to the silent cinema. He came into films at a period when the various functions of film-making were undefined, so that anyone with a strong idea of what he wanted to do (which Chaplin certainly had, almost from the outset) was free to go ahead and do it. Having got in on the ground floor, he was able, with the aid of extraordinary business acumen, to build at once on his great success with the public in order to become rich and powerful as well as famous – even in these early days Chaplin off-screen, the budding tycoon and central figure in many an over-publicized romantic drama, was sharply differentiated from the somewhat pathetic underdog he played in films, with his cane and baggy pants, his slum-bred cunning, and his understandable tendency to be overlooked by the girl of his dreams. By the beginning of the 1920s he was his own master in films, able to do exactly what he wanted, in exactly the way he wanted – and in his own time.

And with the coming of sound he alone was able to fight a long rearguard action, making what were in effect silent films with the addition of music and sound-effects, and in *The Great Dictator* a little localized speech, until right into the 1940s. He had had the foresight to own outright and control all his mature works, and to withhold them from general release for years at a time, so that each reappearance of a Chaplin film had a sense of occasion all its own. And even his later contretemps with the American authorities over his flirtations with Marxism and his staunchly preserved British nationality, which resulted in some years of exile from America, was eventually resolved to the complete satisfaction of both sides.

The central figure of this almost totally satisfactory and successful life, Charles Spencer Chaplin, was born on April 16, 1889, at East Lane, Walworth, and his childhood was spent at 3 Parnell Terrace, Kennington Road. His father was of mixed French and Irish descent, and his mother had gypsy blood in her veins. Both were well known in the music halls of their day.

His childhood was an unhappy one, and when Charles was five his mother, who was never strong, found that the problems of looking after the family in the face of poverty and adversity had become too much for her. Charles and his half-brother Sydney were therefore sent to an orphanage. This was a great shock to the sensitive child and it gave him a sense of insecurity which was to haunt him throughout his life.

He emerged from the orphanage in March, 1896, and became a waif of the London slums. His first stage appearance was made soon after at the age of seven, when he performed a clog dance: three years later he was appearing in music-halls all over the country as one of 'The Eight Lancashire Lads'. Then for a short time he became a legitimate actor, and played Billy, the office boy, in *Sherlock Holmes*, and was also seen as one of the wolves in the first production of *Peter Pan*.

When he was 17 Charles Chaplin joined Fred Karno's pantomime group, and in 1910 was taken as first comedian on the company's tour of the United States. In 1913 he was seen in New York by Mack Sennett, America's foremost producer of comedy films, playing a drunk in a sketch called *A Night in an English Music Hall*, and was taken on as a film comedian to replace Ford Sterling.

Chaplin was reluctant to leave Karno, and his early days in Hollywood only confirmed these doubts. His first film, in which he appeared in a frock coat and top hat, was a failure. Later he adopted the tramp costume of the baggy trousers and ill-fitting suit, but it was not until the making of *Tillie's Punctured Romance* in 1914, with Marie Dressler and Mabel Normand, that he became famous.

Chaplin made about 40 comedies for Sennett, then made 14 for Essanay, and in 1916 he went over to the Mutual Company after signing a contract for what was, in those days, an unheard-of salary. But by now he was world-famous, and was writing and directing his own films. More important still was the fact that the character of 'the little fellow', as the tramp was always known to his creator, had become firmly established in his mind.

For Mutual Chaplin made some of his best short comedies, including *The Floor Walker*, *The Rink*, and *Easy Street*. In 1918 he joined First National, and for them made eight films, including *A Dog's Life* and *Shoulder Arms*. Then he built his own film studios and formed his own company, and in 1919 he joined with the other leading film-makers of the period – D. W. Griffith, Douglas Fairbanks, and Mary Pickford – in forming the United Artists Corporation.

The 1920s were the golden age of the silent cinema, and Chaplin entered this golden age with wealth, power, authority, and complete freedom as an independent producer of his own work. To this period belongs *The Kid* (1920) with Jackie Coogan, *The Gold Rush* (1925) with Mack Swain, and *The Circus* (1928) with Merna Kennedy. During this period he also startled the film world by writing and directing a picture in which he did not himself appear. This was *A Woman of Paris* (1923), with Adolphe Memo and Edna Purviance – an interesting and original work, but one that attempted a sophisticated elegance which was not really within Chaplin's province and which Lubitsch was shortly to undertake with much more success in *The Marriage Circle*.

Up to this point in his career there was little room for controversy of any kind: his popularity was unchallenged, and even *A Woman of Paris* enjoyed considerable success, on its own merits rather than as a Chaplin film. It seems likely now that his lasting reputation will rest most securely on the films he made between 1916 and 1928: later reissues of *The Gold Rush*, *The Kid*, *Shoulder Arms*, *Easy Street*, and other films of this era in sparkling new prints with musical soundtracks composed by Chaplin himself confirmed their power over new generations of film-goers, while *The Circus*, which Chaplin had never considered one of his better films, came as a revelation when shown again in this new form. But from the beginning of the sound era things become more arguable. There were many, and are still, who regard *City Lights* (1931) as his finest film. But for others the sentiment in the 'little fellow's' love for a blind flower girl becomes cloying and for the first time a deathly self-consciousness about the character's symbolism and message for the world seems to intrude. In this film Chaplin resolutely turned his back on the talkie, making a silent film with the musical accompaniment on the soundtrack instead of live in the theatre. He used the same approach in *Modern Times* (1936), a would-be satire on the mechanization of man which leaned heavily on René Clair's *A Nous la Liberté* and despite funny moments demonstrated rather clearly that satire and explicit messages were not Chaplin's forte.

It was no doubt inevitable that eventually Chaplin would have to talk on the screen, and he took the plunge at the end of *The Great Dictator* (1940), with a six-minute speech driving home the point of his satire at the expense of Hitler and Mussolini. Most of the film remained speechless, however; it was the swansong of Chaplin's little man character, in the shape of the humble Jewish barber with an uncanny resemblance to a Hitler-like dictator also played by Chaplin. *Monsieur Verdoux* (1947) marked a complete break with the past: a talkative 'comedy of murders' suggested by the life and career of Landru, it gave us a suave, middle-aged Chaplin very different from anything we had seen before. For the first time it is unavoidable to see the limitations of Chaplin's skill as a film director rather than as a performer – the film is stiff and stagy in the extreme, and not too well written either, in a context where high style is a necessity. *Limelight* (1952) was something of a return to form, however: unashamedly Victorian and sentimental in its tale of an ageing clown's love for a waiflike ballet dancer, it took on an indefinable quality from Chaplin's own nostalgic re-creation of his early days in the London theatre, and at least it did not even try for most of its length to be funny.

Its appearance marked the beginning of an unhappy period in Chaplin's life. When he left America for the European premiere the State Department banned his re-entry (which they could do as he had never become an American citizen), and Chaplin took up residence, at first resentfully, in Switzerland. His next film, *The King in New York* (1957), made in Britain and for long unseen in America, was a bitter but ineffectual satire on America and the American way of life, notable chiefly for Chaplin's succumbing to what is supposed to be the classic comic's temptation, that of playing *Hamlet*, with an unfortunate rendition of 'To be or not to be' during a New York dinner party. But the anger on both sides, product of those witch-hunting days, gradually subsided as Chaplin moved into an honoured old age.

His last film, *A Countess from Hong Kong* (1966), was a light romantic comedy starring Marlon Brando and Sophia Loren, based on a script he had written for himself and his then wife Paulette Goddard in 1938 and showing signs of its age; for the first time since his earliest days he was working for someone else (the film was completely financed by Universal), and for the first time since *A Woman of Paris* he himself made only a token appearance. The film was kindly received, if with many reservations, and was an almost total disaster at the box office. Nevertheless Chaplin made definite plans to direct yet another film, *The Freak*, starring one of his younger daughters, but the increasingly delicate state of his health precluded him from doing so. In 1973 he was at last received back with open arms into the American film establishment, given a special Oscar in recognition of his lifetime contribution to film art, and commemorated with a statue at the historic corner of Hollywood and Vine. In 1975 he was made KBE in the New Year Honours.

During the intervals of film-making Chaplin wrote *My Autobiography* (1964), a fascinating if in certain respects disingenuous document which is of particular value for its vivid evocation of the London of his childhood and his early struggles in the theatre; the latter parts become heavy with dropped names and grievances rehearsed. In fact his off-screen life was considerably more eventful than the book gives one to suppose, and his three earliest marriages, to Mildred Harris, Lita Gray, and Paulette Goddard (who had starred opposite him in *Modern Times* and *The Great Dictator*) were stormy, plagued by scandal, and ended in divorce. His last marriage, to Oona O'Neill, daughter of Eugene O'Neill, brought him happiness, repose, and several children, one of whom, Geraldine, achieved considerable success in her own right acting in films, as had Sydney, the older of his two sons by Lita Gray. His old age was a satisfying crown to a life of activity and creative endeavour, bringing honours and reconciliation and universal reverence for the man and his work. Whatever the ups and downs of taste in the years to come, his greatness as a clown and his crucial role in the history and serious acceptance of the cinema as an art form are certain to stand the tests of time.

JESSE OWENS

Memorable performance at the Berlin Olympics

30 MARCH 1980

JESSE OWENS, the great black American sprinter who won four gold medals at the Olympic Games in Berlin in 1936, died yesterday in Tucson, Arizona. He was 66 and had been ill for some time. Not only did Owens win four medals in athletics events in Berlin, an individual medal haul that was to stand as a record for many years, but his performance will be remembered as being particularly galling to Hitler who had intended the games as a showpiece for Nazi Germany and as a propaganda exercise for his repugnant philosophy of Aryan supremacy.

Jesse Owens was born in Alabama on September 12, 1913, one of 11 children of a poor share cropper. Later, when disaster struck local cotton crops, his family was forced to move north to Cleveland, Ohio. At school he became a shoe-shine boy in his spare time and his ambitions might well have been circumscribed by the aim of having a shoe shop of his own when he grew up, if he had not attracted the attention of a sports school coach named Charles Riley, who persuaded him to take training seriously.

This move soon bore fruit when in 1933 he equalled the world record 9.4 seconds for the 100 yards at an interschool athletics meeting in Chicago. Owens attended Ohio State University and broke his first world record in 1935 when, while representing the university, he ran the 220 yards low hurdles in 22.9 seconds.

In the following week at the college championships in Ann Arbor, Michigan, he performed the astonishing feat that first signalled his immense potential to the athletics world when he broke five world records and equalled a sixth. He opened the meeting with a time of 9.4 seconds for the 100 yards, which equalled the world record. In the second event he broke the long jump record with a jump of over 26 feet. Next to fall was the 220 yard mark (and with it the 200 metre record) and he went on to break his own 220 yards low hurdles record, rounding off the meeting by breaking the 220 yards high hurdles.

These performances assured him a place in the United States Olympic team of 1936 where he won gold medals in the 100 metres, 200 metres, long jump, and the 4 x 100 metres relay. This success enraged Hitler, who snubbed Owens by refusing to shake hands with him. Owens, however, bore no grudges and was delighted to be invited to the Munich Olympics of 1972. After retiring from the track he had a variety of jobs in what was at first a somewhat chequered career, but eventually he settled down to operate a public relations firm in Chicago where he lived.

Jesse Owens pictured with his grandson Stewart Owen Rankin, 1972.

JEAN-PAUL SARTRE

A leading original thinker of the twentieth century

14 APRIL 1980

A LEADING ORIGINAL THINKER of the twentieth century, M. Jean-Paul Sartre, the French philosopher, novelist, playwright, critic, and political journalist, died last night at the age of 74.

His death removes from the world literary, philosophical, and political scene one of the most brilliant and versatile writers as well as one of the most original thinkers of the twentieth century. He stood alone among Western writers in his attempt to combine the thinking of Marx, Freud, Husserl, Heidegger, Mao, and Marcuse into a coherent world view that would enable men to understand and influence the intellectual life and social organization of their time. Truly French in his passion for ideas, he was also European by the range of his philosophical interest, and a figure of worldwide importance by the extent of his literary concerns and his general influence. From the moment in the early 1940s that his books and plays began to be widely read, no novelist, playwright, philosopher, psychologist, or political thinker could hope to grasp anything of the complexity of the modern world without taking Sartre's views into account.

He was born in Paris on June 21, 1905. His father, the son of a country doctor from Périgord, was a naval officer who died in 1907. His mother, Anne-Marie Schweitzer, cousin to Dr Albert Schweitzer of Lamberéné, remarried in 1916 the Comptroller of the shipyards at La Rochelle, and Sartre was educated at the local lycée and then at Louis-le-Grand and Henri IV in Paris. The first 10 years of his life, described with brilliant and destructive malice in the autobiographical fragment *Les Mots* (1964), were dominated by the figure of his maternal grandfather.

In 1925, Sartre gained entry to the Ecole Normale Supérieure of the rue d'Ulm, and in 1929 succeeded in his second attempt at the Agrégation de Philosophie. His closest friends at that time were Paul Nizan, later a well-known Communist journalist, Maurice Merleau-Ponty, Raymond Aron, and Simone de Beauvoir. The latter became his mistress and life-long political, philosophical, and literary ally. The two never married and had no children, but in 1965 Sartre legally adopted Arlette El-Kaïm, then 28, as his daughter.

From October, 1929, to January, 1931, Sartre did his military service at Tours, in the Meteorological Branch, and after teaching for two years at Le Havre spent the academic year 1933–34 at the Maison Française in Berlin. A fluent German speaker, he rapidly gained a thorough knowledge of the existentialist doctrines of Heidegger and Jaspers and the phenomenology of Husserl. It was the combination of these ideas with his own views on liberty and responsibility that was to make him one of the most significant and widely read authors of the 1940s and 1950s. He expounded them in formal philosophical treatises such as *L'Imaginaire* (1939) and *L'Etre et le Néant* (1943) as well as in novels and short stories (*La Nausée*, 1938; *Le Mur*, 1939), plays (*Les Mouches*, 1943; *Huis Clos*, 1944; *Les Mains Sales*, 1948), literary criticism (*Baudelaire*, 1946; *Saint Genet Comédien et Martyr*, 1952), filmscripts (*Les Jeux sont faits*, 1947), popularizing essays ('L'Existentialisme est un Humanisme', 1946) and through the articles that he selected for the monthly review, *Les Temps Modernes*, which he founded in 1945.

Certainly the most versatile and fluent of mid-twentieth century French writers – his collected essays on his personal and political acquaintanceships and on literature, painting, and politics make up the nine volumes of *Situations* (1947–72) – Sartre developed an essentially didactic approach to literature. He wrote in order to bring people, through a realization of their own contingency, to an awareness of their freedom and responsibility. Each human being, in his view, was both free to create new values, and inevitably condemned, by his situation, to bring values into being by every action which he performed. Those who failed or refused to recognize this – Baudelaire, the majority of the characters in the unfinished four-volume novel, *Les Chemins de la Liberté* (1945–49) – were condemned in terms that at times recalled the moral strictures of the nineteenth century, but no member of the middle-classes was ever presented in a favourable light in Sartre's fiction or plays. He was unremitting in his condemnation of the French bourgeoisie, which he saw as a major enemy of political freedom and moral honesty, and was, perhaps partly as a result of this, highly sympathetic to Marxism. Indeed, the second phase of his career as a writer and thinker was almost completely dominated by political problems, and marked a distinct movement away from the concern with individuals which had characterized his initial preoccupation with the philosophy of mind and private ethics.

The turning point came in the early nineteen-fifties when he published the highly revolutionary play *Le Diable et le Bon Dieu* (1951), broke with his erstwhile friend and ally Albert Camus because of the latter's attack on Communism in *L'Homme révolté* (1951), and quarrelled, again for political reasons, with Maurice Merleau-Ponty. From 1952 onwards he devoted much time and energy to an attempt at liberalizing the French Communist Party, and violently denounced the Russian intervention in Hungary in 1956. He was later to show comparable hostility to the Russian invasion of Czechoslovakia in 1968. The major philosophical work of this period, *La Critique de la raison dialectique* (1960), aimed at liberalizing classical Marxism by incorporating into it the existentialist concepts of freedom and intentionality, but also put forward a fundamentally pessimistic view of man that is highly at variance with normal Marxist thought. The outbreak of the Algerian war in 1954 made Sartre the spokesman in France for the whole cause of liberating colonial territories, and also led to some of his sharpest and most violent attacks on successive French governments. He had been politically active both in the Resistance movement during the Second World War – he was taken prisoner in 1940 and liberated in 1941 – and in the late nineteen-forties, when he attempted to rally the non-Communist Left in his *Rassemblement Democratique Revolutionnaire*, but it was only with the Algerian war that he became a major political propagandist. The use of torture by the French army to repress FLN terrorism inspired both his preface, *Une Victoire*, to Henri Alleg's book *La Question* (1958), and what many critics consider his best play, *Les Séquestrés d'Altona* in 1959. It was in this play that he most clearly put into practice his own views on the need for literature to take sides which had caused so much controversy when *Qu'est ce que la littérature?* was published in 1947.

The 1960s did indeed witness a considerable increase both in the interest which Sartre took in politics and in the violence with which he responded to political events both in France and elsewhere. In 1965, he registered one of his first protests against American policy in Vietnam by spectacularly cancelling his acceptance of an invitation to go and lecture at Cornell University, and the Vietnam problem took up much of his time in the following three years. In 1966, he accepted membership of the 'Russell Tribunal' on American war crimes in Vietnam, and protested violently against American policy. In May, 1968, he expressed strong support for the student rebellion, and addressed a number of open meetings. Both in 1968 and in subsequent years, his review *Les Temps Modernes* expressed violent opposition both to French policy at home and to American policy abroad, and with the resignation of several leading members of the editorial board Sartre appeared to be increasingly isolated. This isolation was something of which he became more and more conscious, especially after his condemnation in 1968 of the Russian repression of the Czechoslovak attempt to liberalize Communism. This cut him off from the orthodox wing of the French Communist Party, and he seemed to find an acceptable alternative only in the extreme Maoist faction.

It is perhaps in the extreme nature of his later views that Sartre, like Pascal, unconsciously bore out the accuracy of those critics who maintained that existentialism was always doomed to espouse the outer extremes of the most idiosyncratic positions. The length of the first three volumes of his long-promised book on Flaubert, *L'Idiot de la famille*, eventually published in 1971 and in 1973, after Sartre had worked on it some 15 years, nevertheless showed that his preoccupation with literary and philosophical matters had not entirely left him. His determination to follow his own line of thought also marks him out as a true descendant of his

Alsatian Protestant forebears, and his insistence on never following a multitude to do evil likewise expressed itself in his attitude towards those official honours normally accepted by more conventional men of letters in France. After the liberation of France in 1944, he refused the Légion d'Honneur and consistently opposed all attempts to present any of his works for one of the many literary prizes traditional in French society.

He travelled extensively and wrote approvingly of the social revolutions in China (1955) and in Cuba (1959). However, he later viewed subsequent developments in Cuba with greater scepticism, and showed an even greater disillusionment with the failure of the Algerian revolutionaries to develop a genuinely socialistic society after the liberation of their country in 1962. In company with Simone de Beauvoir, he became extremely fond of Italy, where he was in the habit of spending every summer vacation. He was strongly attracted by the more liberal policy of the Italian Communist Party, and even went so far as to say that he would be a member of it if he lived permanently in Italy. His interest in the visual arts, visible both in his fiction and philosophical works, also profited from his love of Italy, and inspired one of the best and most intriguing of his works, the essay on Tintoretto entitled *Le Séquestré de Venise* (1957). He was a very generous man, and gave away much of the large amount of money that he earned from his books. The most openly political of great French writers, his sometimes intolerant and always violent passion for freedom and justice made him as hated and as loved in his own day as Rousseau, Voltaire, and Zola were in theirs. His death marks the end of a period in French literary history in which writers sought, often with great success, to merge literature, politics, and art in order to become full witnesses of the many-sided dramas of their day.

SIR ALFRED HITCHCOCK

Master of screen suspense

29 APRIL 1980

SIR ALFRED HITCHCOCK, who died yesterday in Los Angeles at the age of 80, was perhaps the greatest single contribution of Britain to world cinema. He had the longest active career of any first-rate film-maker, over 80 films in 50 years, and several of these are to be found in even the severest critics' lists of all-time master-pieces. And this despite Hitchcock's persistence in working entirely within the framework of unashamedly popular, commercial cinema and his devotion to the conventions of a not very seriously regarded genre, the thriller.

Hitchcock's preoccupation with the thriller form began early in his career. He was born in London on August 12, 1899, into a Roman Catholic family, and had a Jesuit education. He began work in his teens as a commercial artist in the advertis-ing department of a telegraph company, and it was a natural extension of this to design the titles for the silent films then being made locally at the long-defunct Islington Studios.

Being a young man of ideas, he rapidly found himself not only designing the titles, but writing them as well. He was even sufficiently fascinated by film-making to set in train an independent production, modest enough in its scope, in 1921: *Number Thirteen*, which he began to direct himself and produced in cooperation with Ernest Thesiger and Clare Greet, who were to star in it. The project foundered for lack of finance, but the next year Hitchcock was called in to finish another film, *Always Tell Your Wife*, when the director fell ill, and from then on he worked full-time in the cinema, first as designer, assistant director, script collaborator, and jack-of-all-trades on five films directed by Graham Cutts, then in 1925 as full director on *The Pleasure Garden*, a Michael Balcon production made, like his second film, *The Mountain Eagle*, in Germany.

It would be fanciful to see any clear signs of Hitchcock's individuality in either of these films, but with his third, *The Lodger* (1926), he became unmistakably the Hitchcock the world came to know. The story was a psychological mystery based on the arrival of a strange young man in an ordinary London household at the time of the Jack-the-Ripper killings, and Hitchcock made brilliant use of the London fogs and the claustrophobic atmosphere of the beleaguered family.

From then on everything Hitchcock did was awaited with eager interest; he had become a name to conjure with, and the nearest thing Britain then had to a director of international importance. The rest of his silent films were varied in their subject-matter, including adaptations of Noel Coward's play *Easy Virtue*, Eden Philpotts' *The Farmer's Wife*, and Hall Caine's *The Manxman*, as well as, most interestingly, an original prize-fighting story, *The Ring*, in scripting which Hitchcock collaborated for the first time with his wife, Alma Reville. He did not have the chance to explore further the territory of the thriller until what was to turn into his first sound film, *Blackmail* (1929), which was begun silent and then transformed hurriedly into a talkie to meet the sudden demand for them in Britain.

Blackmail, though in certain respects it now looks naive and uncomfortable, established Hitchcock at the time as one of the first complete masters of the sound medium. He was compelled from the outset to experiment in various ways; since he had already shot most of the film with a leading lady who could hardly speak English playing an ordinary girl from the London suburbs, he had to devise a way of dubbing her with another actress's voice, and was also led to a non-realistic use of sound (in a medium then largely vowed to heavy literalness) in order to cover up the sudden, largely improvised reworking of something conceived in silent terms. *Blackmail* confirmed Hitchcock's reputation in Britain and abroad. Hitchcock himself established the habit of making a token appearance in each of his films, the moment being led up to and often disguised with considerable ingenuity so that it added to the sport of the film to try to spot him.

The succession of Hitchcock's famous films of the 1930s, six of them all made during the four years 1934–38, remains a monument to his technical genius and to his perfection of an irresistibly enjoyable but ultimately limited genre. *The Man Who Knew Too Much, The Thirty-Nine Steps, The Secret Agent, Sabotage, Young and Innocent, The Lady Vanishes* – they summon up a combined picture of an England gone for ever, and quite possibly invented by Hitchcock to begin with. A land of spies behind the scenes in local fleapit cinemas, sinister goings-on in the mission-halls of strange sects, bodies slumped over the keyboards of organs, nuns in high heels and silk stockings.

Of this world Hitchcock was the undisputed master. But by the end of the 1930s he was evidently beginning to chafe at the limitations of the kind of film he was making. Inevitably overtures came to him from Hollywood, and after completing work on a Daphne Du Maurier adaptation, *Jamaica Inn* (itself an unusual excursion for him into costume drama), he went to America under contract to David O. Selznick, with his first assignment the much-heralded film version of Daphne Du Maurier's best-seller, *Rebecca*. Though it has become fashionable to regard Hitchcock's arrival in Hollywood as the consecration of his talents, it must be said that for the first few years of his sojourn there he did not seem to be entirely at his ease.

Rebecca, and other of his early American films, suffered from studio intervention. In 1943, however, he made a return to form in the first of his films to show a direct reaction to the American scene, *Shadow of a Doubt*, made largely on location in California.

He made a quick visit to Britain to direct a couple of short propaganda films for the Ministry of Information, and then became involved in a series of big productions, like *Spellbound* and *Notorious*, in which potentially interesting subjects tended to get overlaid, if not overwhelmed, with Hollywood gloss.

The spectacular rebirth of Hitchcock's talents came with *Strangers on a Train*, made in America in 1951. This film, an adaptation of the Patricia Highsmith novel on which Raymond Chandler collaborated, is a masterly piece of plot manipulation which has a density, and moral ambiguity, about it which were to become the hallmark of Hitchcock's mature work – the thriller philosophized and psychologized without being therefore any the less a thriller. It was the model for a succession of brilliant films directed by Hitchcock throughout the 1950s.

In 1957 an eccentric but influential book by the French film-makers Claude Chabrol and Eric Rohmer revolutionized critical attitudes to Hitchcock by proposing a new view of him as a Roman Catholic moralist with a consistent subject matter and a consistently developing viewpoint throughout his entire oeuvre.

In 1954 came *Rear Window*, which explores with great virtuosity the possibility that a seemingly dispassionate observer can become a moral accomplice in what he observes; *The Trouble with Harry*, a charmingly wide-eyed comedy about an inconvenient body which remains the most 'English' of Hitchcock's American films; *Vertigo*, a dreamlike drama of obsession and shifting identity; *North by Northwest*, a picaresque adventure featuring some of Hitchcock's most spectacular set-pieces; and *Psycho*, which showed Hitchcock entering his seventh decade with a film of such cool and shattering modernity that it left members of the various 'new waves' around the world, often 30 or 40 years his junior, looking ultra-conservative by comparison.

In his sixties, at an age when most film-makers are thinking about, or forced into, retirement, Hitchcock continued with almost undiminished vigour to make films. Two of them, *Torn Curtain* and *Topaz*, tended to confirm that he was correct in his oft-expressed mistrust of the spy drama, at least as a subject for himself. But on the other hand *The Birds*, a terrifying piece of science fiction, and especially *Marnie* and *Frenzy*, two studies of crime and sexual obsession, clearly demonstrated that his powers were still at their height and that, in his own field, he had no rivals.

It has often been suggested that Hitchcock's subject-matter had something of the morbid about it. But this is by no means the impression his films give. There is, it is true, an element of cheery ruthlessness about many of the films, a black humour which is as far removed from the sick as Harry Graham's *Ruthless Rhymes for Heartless Homes*. But the strength of Hitchcock's work throughout his career resides in its constant sense of health and normality as the context within which his most monstrous and extraordinary characters move and have their being: it is precisely because they are presented as bizarre and extraordinary yet still within the bounds of the possible that they affect us so powerfully.

Hitchcock was also one of the cinema's great psychologists, not so much in his handling of character within his films, but in his handling of his audiences' responses; he seemed, in effect, to direct his audiences far more than he directed his films. He was the great master of shock effects, of lulling audiences into a sense of security before hitting them hardest, or building artfully to a calculated letdown. He also had the most detailed practical knowledge of exactly how the star system worked, and the ambiguity of our responses to the character within the drama.

He thus became the ultimate Hollywood director while remaining throughout his life defiantly British, a Billy Bunter who had somehow turned out to be a great artist. If the thriller is a minor genre, he contrived by sheer intensity of vision, allied with unchallenged technical skills, to make within that genre at least a dozen films which seem as likely to survive, still able to delight and amaze future generations, as any in the history of the cinema.

Hitchcock was created KBE in the New Year Honours this year.

He married, in 1926, Alma Reville. They had one daughter.

MAE WEST

Film humorist who made sex a shared joke

22 NOVEMBER 1980

MAE WEST, the only important female humorist in films and for more than half a century a universal sex symbol in the proper sense of that much abused term, died in Hollywood on Saturday, three months after suffering a serious stroke.

As a star she enjoyed unparalleled longevity: she played her first leading role on Broadway in 1913, and even in what may well have been her ninetieth year was a continuing star attraction, well able to command top billing for any appearance she made.

She was born in Brooklyn on August 17 some year between 1885 and 1893, and seems to have taken instantly to the greasepaint: she began at the age of five doing imitations at church socials, then went into stock theatre playing child roles like Little Eva and Little Lord Fauntleroy.

By the age of 15 she was doing her own song-and-dance act in Vaudeville, and in 1911 she got married, for the first and only time, to Frank Wallace, with whom she formed a vaudeville team. They soon separated and were divorced in 1943; he died in 1966.

In 1911, too, she achieved her first real public notice in a show called *A la Broadway*, and from then alternated vaudeville tours and appearances in New York musicals and revues. By 1913 and the Rudolf Friml show *Sometime* she was a top liner; in 1926 with the opening (and eventually the legally enforced closing) of her play *Sex* Mae West definitively became Mae West

From then on she was the writer and creator of her own material on stage and screen, as well as a prolific author of books and plays and a successful recorded singer. The raw material of all her work was sex; her approach was always comic. In play after play and film after film she embodied voluptuously proportioned sirens who took a frank sexual interest in the physique of the men in their lives, chose for themselves (the classic invitation 'Come up and see me some time' was offered at and for the lady's pleasure only) and found much comic relish in the advantages of being a fallen woman. By making sex a shared joke, she defused the subject of much of its offensive power – though clearly not enough for many people in the 1920s and 1930s, when she was constantly the target of outraged moralists even while she fortunately remained the darling of the public.

Sex was followed on stage by *The Drag*, a homosexual comedy she wrote but did

403

Mae West on her first visit to England, arriving at Southampton in the *Queen Mary*.

not appear in, and by two of her most famous vehicles, *Diamond Lil* (1928) and *The Constant Sinner* (1931), both of them also turned into novels and later filmed. It was inevitable that Hollywood, now eagerly on the lookout for talent from the stage that could handle the new talkie medium, and still relatively unrestricted by the self-censorship of the famous Hays Code, should beckon, and in 1932 she heeded the invitation, going out to play a subordinate role in a George Raft vehicle, *Night after Night*. At least, that was the intention, but from the moment that Mae West entered, about halfway through, to deliver the immortal response to a hatcheck girl who says wonderingly 'Goodness, what beautiful diamonds' 'Goodness had nothing to do with it, dearie', no one was in much doubt that this was Mae West's movie.

Though she still had to fight to do things her own way in films, the enormous earnings of her films were a powerful persuader, and she turned out in rapid succession *She Done Him Wrong, I'm No Angel, Belle of the Nineties, Goin' to Town* (in which she showed an unsuspected talent by singing for herself a scene from *Samson and Delilah*) and the less inspired (or more censored) *Klondike Annie* and *Go West Young Man*. In all of them the formula was much the same, the presence though much imitated, ultimately inimitable.

Her fame became inescapable: she was painted by Dali, parodied by Disney, and a little later entered the dictionary when, during the war, an inflatable lifejacket was named after her. With the puritanical backlash against her kind of humour on screen she became, paradoxically, one of the biggest stars of that family medium par excellence, radio, and continued to make occasional films, of which the most enjoyable, *My Little Chickadee*, teamed her with another eccentric, self-fulfilling monstre sacré, W. C. Fields. Without actually being sexy (she was after all, as the cameras made obvious, a lady of mature years by this time) she had become the world's shorthand for the idea of sex, a living embodiment of the dangerous truths that sex could be profitable and sex could be fun.

In the 1940s Mae West returned to the stage with a new vehicle, an historical parody *Catherine was Great* (1944), and revived *Diamond Lil* for a European tour. In 1954 she opened in cabaret in Las Vegas with her famous retinue of loin-clothed muscle-men. The 1960s brought her back to the screen, lending her disruptive presence to the film version of Gore Vidal's *Myra Breckinridge* (though not, unfortunately, in the title role), and found her singing a Beatles song to heavy rock accompaniment on record.

Her autobiography, *Goodness Had Nothing to Do with It*, came out in 1959 and she continued to write novels, plays, advice on life, love and diet, and even a biography of her favourite psychic, right up to the last. In 1976, when she may quite well have been 90, she was still active and energetic, planning a new starring film, *Sextette*, making a spirited appearance on a Dick Cavett television special, and blandly observing of a projected television remake of *Diamond Lil*: 'I could still do it; I still look like Mae West.' It was a great part of her charm, and perhaps the main reason for the durability of her legend, that she alone in the world steadfastly refused to be taken in by it.

JOHN LENNON

Dominant role in a pop music revolution

8 DECEMBER 1980

JOHN LENNON, who, as a dominating member of the Beatles, played an important part in a pop music success extraordinary even by the standards of that extraordinary genre, died after being shot outside his New York home on December 8. He was 40.

The Beatles dominated the pop music of the 1960s, creating in the 'Beatlemania' which struck their audiences and young followers wherever they went, paroxysms of enthusiasm which rivalled and even surpassed anything that had gone before them in the short history of rock and roll. Hairstyles, styles of dress, even styles of speaking – for the first time a transatlantic twang ceased to be a *sine qua non* for pop performers – followed in their wake. Indeed, not only were they an astonishing success in America but they completely wrested the palm from the country where rock and roll had been born and bred, and which in those days seemed to have a prescriptive right to adjudicate on what was feasible and what was not in pop music. After the Beatles it was never again possible for British groups to think of themselves as the poor relations in pop music. The Beatles paved the way for the American successes of the Rolling Stones and many others. They encompassed the change of heart which could lead an American rock writer to remark in the later 1960s – 'Everyone's just wild to see an English rock band.'

But this success was not merely a matter of finding a new formula to succeed the langorous balladeering into which rock and roll seemed largely to have sunk after the initial drive of Bill Haley, Elvis Presley, and Buddy Holly ran into the sands in the early 1960s. The Beatles brought a new musicality to pop music which succeeded in giving it a much wider appeal than it had had previously. In their genial, at any rate seldom less than pleasing, melodies and enticing, attractive harmonies, they somehow gave an impression of being more musically literate than any of their predecessors though in fact none of the four could either read or write music.

And this impression, coupled with their 'cleanlooking' appearance, gave pop music a sudden entrée into quarters where it had previously been virtually a proscribed subject. The mothers of their besotted fans liked the Beatles too – could contemplate in them, perhaps, future sons-in-law; while in the most severely critical musicological circles immoderate rhapsodies were to be heard on their musicianly attainments. With the pronouncement from one distinguished critic that the Beatles were the 'greatest song-writers since Schubert' they appeared, as ambassadors for pop music, to have secured an accolade for their genre that would have seemed impossible a few years previously.

Of this success John Lennon was an important – perhaps the most important – component. It was he who had started the group. With Paul McCartney he composed the songs which first projected the Beatles to fame. His caustic wit, his intellectual sharpness, and perhaps his sense of what was likely to be good for the mental health of a group of young men caught up in the kind of success which overtook the Beatles, were formative influences on the way the Beatles behaved. It was he who in particular disliked the fact that the Beatles appeared to have become the property of their more respectable fans. And when first the distancing from, and then the alienation of, those fans began with the retreat into kaftans, joss sticks, and drugs it bore the hallmarks of Lennon's cast of mind and intellectual preoccupations.

John Winston Lennon was born in Liverpool on October 9, 1940. His father, Fred Lennon, a ship's steward, and his mother, Julia, separated when he was a small child and John was brought up by his aunt Mimi. He was educated at Dovedale Primary School, Quarry Bank High School, and the Liverpool College of Art. A rebel in an era before child rebellion was officially subsidized by adult indulgence, he took little interest in the formal side of his schooling and in consequence made little formal progress. However, his head master at Quarry Bank did take an interest and it was this interest which enabled him to get into Liverpool College of Art in spite of the fact that he had none of the necessary certificates.

At art college he followed the prevailing mode of dress and behaviour, that of the Teddy Boy, and under the tutelage of his mother, who had reappeared in his life when he was in his early teens, learnt the banjo. The skiffle craze was then sweeping through Britain and this species of music which required little or no formal musical knowledge was enabling thousands of teenagers to participate in music making.

In particular hundreds of groups sprang up all over Liverpool, among them the Quarrymen, the group Lennon had formed at school. This group was joined in 1956 by a boy from another Liverpool school, Paul McCartney. George Harrison joined in the following year, and later, Ringo Starr replaced Pete Best as the drummer, to give the group the final form in which it was to take the world by storm. Lennon's mother died in a road accident in 1958, an event which affected him deeply.

Between 1956 and 1960, the name of Lennon's group was to undergo several metamorphoses – from the Quarrymen it was successively the Moondogs, Rainbows, Silver Beatles, and finally Beatles. None of these transformations brought much success however; the group came close to being discovered at talent shows and auditions on a couple of occasions, but a full career launch evaded it. For several years the group played, in common with its many rivals, the round of coffee bars, parties, small teenage clubs and dances, often for slender remuneration.

Lennon had however found that his meeting with McCartney enabled him to compose songs and the confidence this gave both men enabled them to persist. As these songs and their performance took on a more distinctive quality they began to become known especially in the Cavern club in Liverpool, one of the foci of the new Merseyside sound.

From 1960 onwards they also played at a nightclub in Hamburg's Reeperbahn – their first formal professional engagement to that date and one which had an important effect on their development. In the next two years they were to play at this and other Hamburg night clubs, and it was a song recorded in Germany which brought them to the attention of Brian Epstein, who was then running a record department in Liverpool. More discouragement was to follow – they were turned down by almost every major recording company in Britain – but it was Epstein's persistence which finally saw them to a recording contract with Parlophone in 1962.

Their first single, 'Love Me Do', was released in October of that year and entered the charts drawing considerable attention; 'Please Please Me' was at Number One in the January of 1963. These records were merely the first of a stream of singles which had by the summer of 1963 established a rhythmical style which took the music business, and the young, by storm. 'Twist and Shout', 'She Loves You', 'I Want to Hold Your Hand' – these and countless others invaded the dancefloors and discotheques with their fresh, insistent rhythms and boisterous – almost healthy – message, and drove the outmoded sentiment of the earlier 1960s before them.

This was the zenith of Beatlemania. On tour in this country they were mobbed wherever they went. America succumbed, audiences even outdoing the scenes of frenzy registered in Britain. With their triumphant return from the United States the Beatles seemed almost to become a piece of national property. They appeared to advertise abroad an English way of life – dynamic, creative, progressive, forward looking – that was pleasantly at odds with the received image of a country suffering economic, political, and foreign policy problems, with only a past to find pleasure in. And in 1966 the group's joint appointment as Members of the Order of the British Empire echoed a general feeling that the Beatles had been at the spearhead of the formation of a new role for Britain in the world.

The Swinging Sixties were suddenly launched. The lead in progressive music had been plucked from America's grasp; that in fashion was wrested from Paris. In design, architecture, motor engineering, lifestyle, the national mood was suddenly buoyant and the Beatles seemed to be the apostles of this buoyancy.

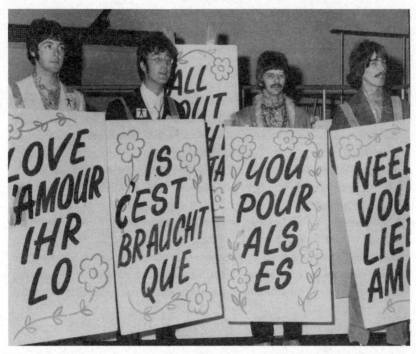

John Lennon with the Beatles, rehearsing in June 1967 for *Our World*, the first global satellite TV show.

Lennon himself had, in fact, had to acquiesce somewhat reluctantly in this species of popularity. It was not in his iconoclastic nature to relish, for example, an invitation to a formal banquet from a grateful local council. Journalists, too, found that his barbed ripostes went some way beyond the characteristic Beatles jollity and candour.

This individuality became more and more marked after 1966 when the group had ceased to tour and largely lived as individuals, coming together for recording sessions. Lennon embraced transcendental meditation, drugs, and religion, especially that of a mystical kind.

This did not stop the production of music. A flow of albums continued, culminating in the brilliant *Sergeant Pepper*, but Lennon now composed his own songs instead of working jointly with McCartney. Lennon's own contribution to these became, too, more surreal and enigmatic with songs like 'Lucy in the Sky with Diamonds' and 'Strawberry Fields'. In 1968, too, he divorced his first wife Cynthia, whom he had married in Liverpool in 1962, and became associated with the Japanese film producer Yoko Ono, who later became his wife. This seemed to increase his distance not only from the other Beatles but from the rest of the world. His returning the insignia of MBE in what he described as a protest against British involvement in Vietnam, Biafra, and Nigeria, appeared to signal his final renunciation of what the Beatles had stood for in their early days.

The end of the Beatles eventually came in 1971 when the partnership was finally wound up in the High Court. The Beatles Fan Club was disbanded in the following year and it was left to the millions of followers merely to dream of that chimaerical event, a reunion in the recording studio, of the four members of the group.

Lennon then began a long seclusion with his wife, Yoko Ono, surfacing only occasionally to make headlines with news that he was struggling against drugs, was resisting the attempts of the United States authorities to deport him, or that he had exchanged roles with his wife and was now devoting his entire energies to bringing up the son of their marriage.

Only recently had he shown signs of ending this seclusion. A new single 'Starting Over', recently released, seemed to mark the end of a virtual five-year retirement and this record was merely a precursor to a new album, *Double Fantasy*. At the time of his death Lennon's fortune was estimated at £100 million.

Lennon had a son, Julian, of his first marriage and a son, Sean, of his second.

BOB MARLEY

11 MAY 1981

BOB MARLEY, the singer and composer of reggae music who died on May 11, was the figure most responsible for disseminating the popular music of Jamaica around the world during the 1970s.

His uncompromising songs, style, and attitudes provided a rare and powerful example for young West Indians, particularly those living in Britain, to whom he presented the elements of a cultural identity. It was a position he never abused, and last week he was awarded the Jamaican Order of Merit by his country's Prime Minister, Mr Edward Seaga.

Robert Nesta Marley was born on April 6, 1945, in the parish of St Ann, near Kingston; his mother was a Jamaican woman, his father, whom he remembered meeting only twice, a serving captain in the British Army. During his adolescence, Marley gravitated quickly towards music and made his first record at the age of 19.

In 1965 Marley formed a group, the Wailers, with his fellow singers and composers Bunny Livingstone and Peter Tosh; they became popular within the Jamaican market, singing a light, lilting variation of the local idiom known as *ska* music. They became the first Jamaican artists to achieve fame abroad when, in 1972, they signed a recording contract with Island Records, the London-based company. Careful promotion, modern recording facilities, and the energetic proselytizing efforts of famous English musicians like Mick Jagger and Eric Clapton brought their music, and reggae in general, into fashion with the rock audience.

Although Livingstone and Tosh left the group, Marley reconstituted it and went on to even greater success, touring around the world and achieving enormous record sales in America, Africa, and Europe. At home, he exerted such a hold on the popular imagination that politicians habitually attempted to elicit his endorsement, which he resolutely withheld. Nevertheless, in 1977 he was wounded by gunshots on his house in an attack which was said to have been politically motivated. He considered his finest hour to have been his appearance at the Zimbabwe independence celebrations, to which he was expressly invited by Dr Robert Mugabe.

Whether on stage or on record Marley conveyed a vivid intensity, heightened by his use of the fiery biblical texts appropriated by the Jamaican cult of Rastafarianism, of which he was a prominent disciple. He was a deeply expressive singer and a composer whose range extended from the melodic lament of 'No Woman No Cry' to inspiriting and politically loaded dance tunes like 'Exodus' and 'Zimbabwe'.

He came to be seen as the embodiment of reggae, but possessed an originality which would have ensured his pre-eminence in any type of popular music. Reggae will survive the loss of his unique vision, but it may never have another spokesman of such eloquence and broad appeal.

* * *

GLENN GOULD

4 OCTOBER 1982

GLENN GOULD, the Canadian pianist and composer whose musical tastes were inquiring and eclectic, died on October 4 in Toronto at the age of 50.

Something of an eccentric, he virtually never played in public during the last 18 years of his life, preferring to devote himself to study, recording and producing for the radio.

Gould was born in Toronto on Sept 25, 1932, and studied at the Toronto Conservatory, winning its gold medal at the age of 12. At 14 he made his debut with the Toronto Symphony Orchestra and soon began touring throughout Canada with a wide repertory while starting to compose. In the 1950s he undertook his first tours abroad, making his European debut with the Berlin Philharmonic under Karajan in 1957 and playing in London for the first time the following year.

On the platform, Gould's manner was distinctly unorthodox. He often sat with his legs crossed and sometimes conducted an imaginary orchestra with whichever hand he was not using at that moment. His strange behaviour, however, did not inhibit vast interest in his perceptive and subtle interpretations of his repertory.

His Bach was renowned for rapid and precise fingerwork and clarity of parts, so that his account of the Goldberg Variations became something of a classic for those prepared to accept Bach on the piano rather than on the harpsichord.

However, his repertory was far from being confined to the Baroque. He recorded works by Byrd and Gibbons and, at the other end of the spectrum, all Schoenberg's piano music. He also took a special interest in jazz, and even arranged a score from Bach's music for a film on the bombing of Dresden.

As a radio producer for CBC he experimented with new techniques in documentaries, and as a writer he could be both perceptive and funny: he once wrote an appreciation of Petula Clark in mainly classical music terms.

As a pianist he will be remembered for making the listener think again about music that he thought he knew inside out. Although his sometimes outlandish ideas shocked the critics, they ensured that his interpretations revealed novel facets of rhythm and construction. Only one thing was anathema to him: that was academic boredom.

* * *

GROUP CAPTAIN SIR DOUGLAS BADER

Showing the way to the disabled

5 SEPTEMBER 1982

GROUP CAPTAIN SIR DOUGLAS BADER, CBE, DSO, DFC, who died on September 5, became a legend at first as the personification of RAF heroism and determination during the Second World War and in the years that followed, right up to his death, as a shining example of that defiant courage that overcomes disablement and refuses to accept that anything is impossible. The loss of both legs in a flying accident in 1931 seemed to have finished his career as a highly promising airman, but his iron determination and high degree of physical fitness enabled him to resume flying once war had broken out in 1939.

His subsequent career in the RAF, in the course of which he added a bar to both his DSO and DFC, has been told in two biographies, *Reach for the Sky* and *Flying Colours*, the second appearing last year to mark the fiftieth anniversary of his first artificial legs. A film was also made in which the late Kenneth More played the part of Bader. All this helped to enlarge the legend, so that his became a household name for triumph over adversity, delivering a message of hope to all those in peace time who have suffered from amputation or from other forms of disability.

The example he set in showing that the gravest form of disablement need not deprive a person of his independence or his ability to play a full part in society has been followed by other examples, but 50 years ago Bader's fight back to a fuller life than many of sound limb achieve stood out as a beacon whose light has since shone increasingly brightly.

Such self-discipline could not have been achieved without a stubbornness and hardness of character that sometimes upset those who stood between him and what he wanted. His aggressive attitude to authority in prison camps might not always be appreciated by his fellow prisoners, but without some such cutting edge and drive he could not have left behind the example that he has. In the same way he had the reputation of being something of a showman, but this trait developed later when he realized what his example could achieve in giving hope to those in all walks of life who were beginning the uphill struggle to some kind of normality. The touch of vanity that made him refuse to the end to use spectacles, and in consequence get some of his engagements confused, springs from the same quality of defiance that made him refuse ever to use a stick.

He had a clear mind in making decisions and he was insistent in getting what he wanted, cutting though red tape and going straight to the top if necessary in order to get it. Together with it went great charm and meticulous attention to dress which helped him to give the appearance of making light of his handicap. His willingness to help the disabled caused him to answer, often at short notice, many calls on his time. One of his last undertakings in the cause of limbless ex-Service men, whose association, BLESMA, he helped particularly in raising money, was a visit last year to a corporal who had lost both legs in a terrorist attack in Northern Ireland. Within four months of his amputation the corporal was driving himself and family to Germany for a holiday.

Douglas Robert Stewart Bader was born on February 21, 1910, in London after his parents had returned home from India. He was educated at Colet Court and Temple Grove, Eastbourne, where he excelled at games and from where he won a scholarship to St Edward's School, Oxford. In 1928 he won a cadetship to the RAF College, Cranwell, where his gift of leadership and his athletic prowess soon became obvious. He played rugby for Harlequins and was in due course picked to play cricket and rugby for the RAF.

In 1930 he graduated, coming second in his year, and was posted to No. 23 Squadron, equipped with Gloster Gamecocks at Kenley, and a year later he was a member of that squadron's team at the RAF Hendon air display.

No. 23 Squadron was re-equipped with Bristol Bulldogs, and it was in one of these at Woodley aerodrome on December 14, 1931, that he had a disastrous accident when he rolled his aircraft at a very low altitude and its port wing struck the ground. As a result, in an operation to save his life, his right leg was amputated just above the knee; in a subsequent operation his left leg was amputated below the knee.

He began, with a determination that was to become famous, to remake his life, both physically and mentally. He took up driving again. Then, through the agency of the Under-Secretary of State for Air, Sir Philip Sassoon, he got back into flying. He was given a medical examination at the Central Medical Establishment, found fit, and sent to the Central Flying School. But he was not allowed to fly solo and was given a ground posting to RAF Duxford. In April, 1933, he was placed on the retired list and given a disability pension.

In civilian life, and morally at a low ebb, he found a job with the Asiatic Petroleum company. His defiant spirit found expression in a return to sport. He took up tennis and squash again. He began to take a serious interest in golf; years later he reduced his handicap to two, and his frequent appearances in pro-ams and at St Andrews helped to keep fresh in people's minds the remembrance that courage did not end with the war.

In 1935 his application to rejoin the RAF was refused, but with the advent of war in 1939 he was re-employed in the RAF General Duties Branch, and having passed a test at the Central Flying School, flew solo again for the first time since 1931. In February 1940 he was posted to a Spitfire squadron – No. 19 at Duxford – at the age of 29, and two months later to another Spitfire squadron, No. 222, as a flight commander with the rank of flight lieutenant.

During the evacuation from Dunkirk his squadron operated over the beaches. Subsequently he was given command of a Canadian Hurricane Squadron, No. 242, which had suffered heavily in France. Promoted to squadron leader, he raised its low morale by his formidable personality and leadership and made it into an efficient fighting unit. While at Duxford during the Battle of Britain he evolved the 'big wing' theory which was supported by his AOC, Air Vice-Marshal Trafford Leigh-Mallory, but was later to cause controversy in Fighter Command.

In October, 1940, he was awarded the DSO for 'gallantry and leadership of the highest order'. He was given command of No. 12 Group Wing (three squadrons) at Duxford, and during the Battle of Britain became a famous figure among 'the Few'. In the course of it his wing shot down 152 enemy aircraft, losing 30 pilots. About that time he was called to a meeting at the Air Ministry to discuss day fighter tactics, and put forward his own experience of leading the Duxford wing in support of the idea of big formations of fighters. Later, when his AOC was posted to command No. 11 Group, No. 242 squadron moved to Martlesham.

A new phase in the war began for Bader in March, 1941, when he was posted to Tangmere as a wing commander leading three Spitfire squadrons – Nos. 145, 610, and 616. This was a crucial posting for him, not only because he became the first

Douglas Bader climbing into a Spitfire for a thanksgiving flight over London, 1945.

RAF 'wing leader' but also because of its consequences. With Fighter Command taking the offensive, 'sweeps' over France became routine, Bader leading the Tangmere wing. In July, 1941, he was awarded a Bar to his DSO, recognition that his high qualities of leadership and courage had been an inspiration to all.

This dazzling wartime career changed abruptly when he had to abandon his Spitfire over German-occupied France after colliding with an Me 109F near St Omer. There he was entertained by the Luftwaffe, who were anxious to meet their distinguished opponent, and made the acquaintance of Oberstleutnant Adolf

Galland, his 'opposite number'. One of his artificial legs was recovered from his crashed aircraft; it was damaged and the RAF flew him out a replacement.

Bader escaped from the hospital where he was being treated, thanks to the French Resistance, but was betrayed and recaptured. There followed a succession of removals from one prisoner-of-war camp to another caused by his unflagging determination to escape and his intractable and aggressive attitude towards his captors. This led inevitably to Colditz, the notorious camp for difficult and important prisoners. There, in spite of the arduous conditions, his vigour and initiative never wilted.

After returning home he began to fly again, and in June 1945, was appointed to command the Central Fighter Establishment at Tangmere, his old station, as a group captain. Then later that year he took command of the Essex Sector in No. 11 Group, Fighter Command, with headquarters at North Weald. This was to be his last post in the RAF, from which he retired in July 1946, retaining the rank of group captain. While at North Weald he had flown a jet fighter (a Meteor) for the first time, and had organized and led the victory fly-past over London on September 15, 1945. He also flew over to St Omer to see the French people who had aided his first escape.

On his return to civilian life he rejoined his former company, now Shell, who provided him with an aircraft for business flying. During 1946 he made an air trip through Europe and Africa and in 1947 was invited to the United States, where he met and helped by his example many people who had lost limbs. At the beginning of that year he had been thrice honoured: he was mentioned in dispatches, made a Chevalier of the Legion of Honour, and awarded the Croix de Guerre with Palm. When the Shell group's aircraft operations expanded a new department was formed in 1952 to look after them and he was appointed manager, subsequently, in 1958, becoming managing director of Shell Aircraft Ltd, a post from which he retired in 1969.

In the 1956 New Year Honours he was made CBE for services to the disabled; from 1972 to 1978 he was a member of the Civil Aviation Authority; he was a director of Trafalgar Offshore Ltd; and in June 1976 he was knighted 'for services to disabled people', so many of whom he had helped and inspired by his example and character.

He married in 1933 Thelma Edwards, a devoted partner until her death in 1971. Her sister, Jill, married another distinguished fighter pilot, P. B. Lucas. Bader married secondly, in 1973, Mrs Joan Eileen Murray, with whom he worked on a scheme for helping disabled children to ride.

ORSON WELLES

Formidable and inventive actor and producer

10 OCTOBER 1985

ORSON WELLES, the actor, producer, and film director, and one of the most formidable talents of his age, died in Hollywood on October 10 at the age of 70.

Physically and intellectually imposing, he brought an original and inventive mind to bear on radio, the cinema, the stage, and television. His work, though erratic, was never predictable or dull. His career suffered from the enormous critical acclaim for his first film, *Citizen Kane*, made when he was only 26. Its reputation dogged him for the rest of his life, constantly raising expectations that he could not match.

After *Citizen Kane* there was a sense of anti-climax, partly brought on by Welles himself. The freedom granted to him to make that film rarely came his way again. He gained a reputation (which he always refuted) for being extravagant and unreliable. His life was littered with unfinished projects and projects that were announced and never got started. By the end dozens of cameo parts in other people's bad films, and his voice-overs for sherry and lager commercials, came near to extinguishing the memory of a brilliant artist: an actor of power and charm, a film maker responsible for some of the finest work in that medium.

With his fine, rich voice and gift for anecdote he was, too, an outstanding raconteur; and he was a more than usually gifted painter. On everything he did, from the sublime to the dreadful, he left his mark; a huge talent that too often wasted itself and became frustrated.

George Orson Welles was born at Kenosha, Wisconsin, on the shore of Lake Michigan, on May 6, 1915. He was the younger son of Richard Head Welles, a prosperous businessman, and his wife, Beatrice Ives, a concert pianist and a woman of exceptional beauty and high intelligence. She treated her two sons as her intellectual equals, and as a result both reached intellectual maturity very early in life. At 10 Orson was being examined with interest by medical and psychological experts as an infant phenomenon, and by then he had already written a comprehensive thesis on *The Universal History of Drama*.

At 16 he had already travelled extensively, but had an unfulfilled ambition to visit Ireland. Within a few weeks of arriving there, in the autumn of 1931, he made his professional debut as an actor at the Gate Theatre in Dublin, having introduced himself to its directors as 'Orson Welles, star of the New York Theatre Guild'. He was given the part of the Duke of Württemberg in *Jew Süss* after one of the most remarkable auditions ever held in the theatre.

He played at both the Gate and Abbey theatres for a year, and then returned to America where he toured with Katherine Cornell. He made his debut on the New York stage as Chorus and Tybalt in *Romeo and Juliet* in December, 1934; in 1936 he became director of the Negro People's Theatre and directed a Negro version of *Macbeth*, and in 1937 was appointed a director of the Federal Theatre Project in New York. In the same year he founded and opened the Mercury Theatre with *Julius Caesar*, played in modern dress and without scenery.

By this time he had also made a name for himself on radio, where he earned huge sums in the part of 'The Shadow', but it was in October, 1938, that he achieved his radio *tour de force* by producing H. G. Wells's *The War of the Worlds*, which he presented with such reality that he terrified half America into believing that their country was being invaded by Martians.

Inevitably, after this, he was invited to go to Hollywood, where RKO signed a contract which gave him virtual *carte blanche* as producer, director, writer, and actor. His first production was to have been *Heart of Darkness*, from the novel by Conrad, but the outbreak of war in Europe caused a change in plan. Instead he made *Citizen Kane*, a far from flattering biography of a newspaper magnate with obvious similarities to William Randolph Hearst. The Hearst newspapers retaliated by either attacking the film or ignoring it. Kane was played by Welles himself, who described the character as 'a great lover, a great American citizen, and a dirty dog'. Technically dazzling with its wide-angle and deep-focus photography, intricate flashback structures, and such felicities as a devastatingly accurate parody of *The March of Time* newsreel, *Citizen Kane* was a critical sensation. It was hailed then as one of the best films ever made and time has not reversed that judgment. For a man in his twenties with no previous cinema experience it was an extraordinary achievement.

His second film, *The Magnificent Ambersons*, from Booth Tarkington's novel about the decline and fall of a late 19th century aristocratic family, was no less stylish and compelling; but it was severely cut against Welles's wishes and the final sequence, which threw the film out of balance, was shot by another director. Already Welles's disenchantment with Hollywood had started.

For the time being, however, he stayed, portraying a brooding Rochester in *Jane Eyre* and directing himself, as a former Nazi at large in a small American town, in *The Stranger*. He was director and leading man again for *The Lady From Shanghai*, a baroque and at times impenetrable thriller with a famous climax in a hall of mirrors. The female lead was Rita Hayworth, Welles's estranged second wife.

In the same year, 1948, he made a low budget version of *Macbeth*, shot in only three weeks with himself in the title role. Marred by a poor sound-track, the film nevertheless had a barbaric splendour. After this Welles came to Europe and played his most popular and enduring role, as the racketeer Harry Lime in Graham Greene's atmospheric thriller set in Vienna, *The Third Man*. Welles himself wrote in the picture's best remembered line, that 500 years of Swiss democracy had produced only the cuckoo clock.

While *Macbeth* was shot in three weeks, his *Othello*, released in 1955, took three years. His performance, passionate and deeply tragic, was modelled on that of the stage production with which he had made his London debut in 1951. Other notable stage appearances during the 1950s were in his own adaptation of *Moby Dick* and as *King Lear*. Breaking his ankle on the first night, he played the king on the second night from a wheelchair.

In the cinema he directed in two thrillers. One, *Confidential Report*, was taken from his own novel; the other, and more successful, *Touch of Evil*, was a triumph of style over plot with Welles at his most flamboyant as the corrupt police chief. His most striking performance outside his own films in the 1950s was as the defence attorney in *Compulsion*, based on the Leopold/Loeb murder trial.

In 1963 he directed his own adaption of Kafka's nightmarish novel, *The Trial*, making dramatic use of a disused Paris railway station. But though the film was often visually stunning, it did not quite cohere. *Chimes at Midnight*, a portrait of Shakespeare's Falstaff and his relationship with Prince Hal, was, on the other hand, a film to rank with Welles's best, not only for the central performance but an imaginative use of slender resources.

It was Welles's last completed feature. A film of *Don Quixote*, begun in Spain in the 1950s, came eventually to nothing, though much footage was shot; and a long-cherished *Lear* was also aborted. Welles's final two films as director were *The Immortal Story*, made for French television, and an impish semi-documentary about the art world, *F for Fake*.

Of his acting roles outside his films, the less said, on the whole, the better. Among the exceptions were his Cardinal Wolsey in *A Man for All Seasons*. When he celebrated his 70th birthday in May this year, he was in bullish mood. His *Lear* seemed at last to be getting off the ground; two other films, one started back in 1970 and taking the cinema industry as its theme, were announced as firm commitments. But as so often with Welles, the promise was unfulfilled.

He was married three times: to Virginia Nicholson, whom he divorced in 1940; to Rita Hayworth, from 1943 to 1947; and, in 1955, to Paola Mori. Each marriage produced one daughter.

HENRY MOORE

Sculptor of international reputation

31 AUGUST 1986

MR HENRY MOORE, OM, CH, FBA, who died yesterday, aged 88, was an outstanding figure among modern British sculptors and an artist of international reputation, whose works are to be found in public places and galleries throughout Western Europe and North America.

Like Brancusi, Gaudier-Brzeska, and Epstein, Moore turned away from the Greco-Renaissance tradition of sculpture. His earliest influences were archaic forms, the non-European, particularly Mexican work he had seen in the British Museum. In the 1930s, too, he had a period of geometrical abstraction.

But though he rejected the classical mode he did not turn his back on humanism. Instead he evolved a highly personal style, always returning to the organic and human forms which dominate his best work. To these he imparted a telluric character, liking to see human figures in relation to their surroundings, particularly landscape, and the art of the sculptor as a social one.

Moore was pre-eminently a carver, and it was his mode of expression which gave his images their immense vitality.

After the Second World War the increase in his international reputation led to a large number of public commissions, especially overseas, and he found himself occasionally led into grandiose statements or blandness of expression. Yet these changes were more apparent than real. His enormous inventiveness never flagged and the best of his public work continues to speak of his insight into the condition of humanity in the modern world.

Henry Spencer Moore was born on July 30, 1898, at Castleford, Yorkshire, the seventh child of a miner, Raymond Spencer Moore, and his wife, Mary. He won a scholarship to Castleford Grammar School, where his interest in art was fostered by the art mistress, Alice Gostick. He was also introduced to the Gothic carvings in neighbouring churches by his headmaster, Mr T. R. Dawes.

After qualifying as an elementary school teacher in 1916, he joined the 15th London Regiment (Civil Service Rifles) in 1917 and was gassed at the Battle of Cambrai later that year. Demobilized in 1919, he resumed teaching before obtaining an ex-servicemen's education grant to study at Leeds School of Art for two years.

He won a Royal Exhibition Scholarship in sculpture to the Royal College of Art in 1921. Sir William Rothenstein had just become principal and was to introduce more liberal curricula.

At Leeds, he had read Roger Fry's *Vision and Design* and visited Sir Michael Sadler's collection of modern art; in London, he was particularly interested by Egyptian, Etruscan, Mexican, and African sculpture in the British Museum. Thus began the conflict between what he ought to study for his teacher's diploma and what really appealed to him as a sculptor.

In 1922, away from the RCA, he began his first direct carvings in wood and stone, influenced by primitive and archaic sculpture and by Epstein and Gaudier-Brzeska.

Awarded an RCA travelling scholarship in 1924, Moore postponed going abroad on his appointment as an instructor in the RCA's Sculpture School on a seven-year contract; but early in 1925 he left for a six-month tour in France and Italy where he was particularly impressed by Giotto and Masaccio, early Renaissance busts, late Michelangelo, and the Indian sculpture in the Musée Guimet, Paris.

In 1928 Moore held his first one-man exhibition of drawings and stone carvings at Dorothy Warren's gallery in Maddox Street. The latter were noted for their architectural quality and adherence to the natural form of the stone. This truth to materials was to be a strongly held ideal for Moore and his circle in the 1930s and 1940s.

In 1928, too, Moore met an art student, Irina Radetzky. They married the following year and set up house in the avant-garde colony of artists and writers in Hampstead. Among them was Herbert Read, a fellow Yorkshireman, who became one of his earliest and staunchest champions.

That same year, Moore was given his first public commission, a relief, 'West Wind', for the tower of the new London Underground headquarters above St James's Park Station. This was notable for its monumental simplicity and exploitation of the rectangular stone block from which it was carved. By now, Moore had begun to attract the admiration of older artists, especially Epstein and Augustus John, who bought his drawings.

There was also some intense hostility from traditionalists, notably after the first of his Leicester Galleries one-man shows in 1931, and when his RCA teaching contract expired, rather than seek renewal as Rothenstein urged, Moore took a lower-paid post to start a sculpture department at Chelsea School of Art.

Apart from the later Time/Life Building sculptured screen (1952–53), he generally avoided architectural sculpture commissions, believing that sculpture should either be free-standing or set in relationship to a building on equal, not subordinate, terms.

During the 1930s Moore developed the reclining female figure theme, first tackled in 1926, and later transformed into the monumental figure pieces of

1929–30, inspired by the Toltec-Mayan sculptures of the rain god Chacmool. These were years of intense and varied experiment, and many later large-scale works were developed from ideas first explored in this period, such as the two- and three-piece reclining figures.

In the fierce debate between the abstractionists and surrealists, which reached its height in 1936, the year of the International Surrealist Exhibition in London, he took a typically commonsensical attitude, saying that both these elements were present in varying degrees in all good art.

Moore produced his first abstract biomorphic compositions and reliefs in the early 1930s as well as work which was surrealist in intention.

Yet other work of this period was essentially humanist, such as the Green Hornton stone 'Reclining Figure' (1938). In this sculpture the upper torso and thighs were hollowed out and pierced, emphasising the interplay between its chief elements. This was followed by the third of Moore's large elmwood carvings, 'Reclining Figure' (1939), where the interplay of voids and solids is carried much further. Other variations on this formal problem were the sculptures generically entitled internal and external forms, and the helmet heads of the 1950s.

On the outbreak of war, Moore gave up teaching and worked at his studio at Kingston, near Canterbury (which he had occupied since 1934), returning to London in 1940. Bombed out of his London studio, he bought Hoglands at Perry Green, Much Hadham, Hertfordshire, which was to be his home for the rest of his life. After the war, he bought several adjoining fields and made a landscaped sculpture park with additional large studios.

The famous series of shelter drawings, inspired by the sight of sleeping figures on the platforms of the underground stations, where they had sought refuge from German air raids, began as sketches in his notebooks, and Sir Kenneth Clark subsequently commissioned him to produce ten for the War Artists Advisory Committee; Moore did over one hundred drawings and two Shelter Sketchbooks. He also produced a series of drawings of miners at work for the WAAC in 1942.

The shelter drawings undoubtedly helped to bridge the gap between public taste and the modern movement, as represented by Moore, Ben Nicholson, Hepworth, John Piper, and others.

A commission from Walter Hussey (later Dean of Chichester) to carve a 'Madonna and Child' for St Matthew's, Northampton, in 1943, was a significant act of ecclesiastical patronage, and also demonstrated that a sculptor working in an uncompromisingly modern style could tackle successfully a traditional subject. The mother and child theme had preoccupied Moore and he was to return to it often in his later work, sometimes encompassing the male figure to form a family group.

Moore emerged in the 1950s as a public sculptor, a process begun with the stone

'Three Standing Figures' (1947–48), not perhaps one of his most satisfying works, shown at the first Battersea Park Open-Air Sculpture exhibition. As more public commissions flowed in, he employed studio assistants, but always supervised every stage of a major commission and put the finishing touches to the bronze or carving himself.

The massive interlocking pieces of the early 1960s, the arch torsos and sheep pieces of the 1970s, are, with the recurring reclining figure theme, falling warriors, mirror knife edges, and upright motifs, all explorations on a grander scale of ideas which had been germinating since the 1930s. Only occasionally did the inflation of scale produce grandiose, rhetorical statements.

Public honours and prizes were bestowed on him from all over the world. The first of many honorary degrees was conferred on him by Leeds University in 1945; in 1955 he became a Companion of Honour, and in 1963 was admitted to the Order of Merit. He was a member of many British and foreign academies and learned societies. He established the Henry Moore Foundation in 1977 to promote the study and teaching of sculpture, and during his lifetime generously supported many enterprises which would otherwise not have flourished.

Of medium height and sturdily built, he might have been mistaken by the unwary for a bluff Yorkshire farmer. Moore's natural courtesy and unaffected articulateness charmed his listeners.

He is survived by his widow and a daughter, Mary.

ANDY WARHOL

Art for publicity's sake

22 FEBRUARY 1987

MR ANDY WARHOL, a key face in the visual arts in the 1960s, who, paradoxically, achieved more fame by what he refrained from doing than by what he did, died yesterday in New York. He is believed to have been 59.

Wherever his most famous works may ultimately stand in critical estimation, his place as a 'superstar' of the arts during the 1960s will always rate a footnote in art history. If the term 'superstar' suggests a certain talent for publicity, scandal, and self-advertisement, that is not far wide of the mark. But even at the time of his greatest fame, his private personality remained mysterious and elusive.

It appears, however, that his real name was Andrew Warhola, and that he was born at Pittsburgh, Pennsylvania, of working-class Czech immigrant parents. Certain it is that he graduated from Carnegie Institute of Technology in 1949, and almost without a pause became one of the most successful and sought-after commercial artists in New York.

At this period in his career, he was still drawing, in a rather camp, fussy sort of style, and he became best known for his playfully accurate drawings of cats and shoes, real and fantastic.

He was much employed in advertising; designed a number of influential book-jackets; and deployed his brilliant if rather precious gifts as a draughtsman in a number of mostly humorous, privately printed books.

This phase lasted for about ten years. But by the beginning of the 1960s he had begun to change direction, becoming first a painter (his first important one-man show was in 1962), then by giving up painting proper for silk-screen printing, sometimes touched up by hand.

It was at this point that he first gained widespread fame as the painter of Campbell soup tins, and consequently a rallying point for those interested, either as creators or connoisseurs, in the new Pop Art movement. There was a certain internal logic in this transition – having made a living from drawing for advertisements, Warhol might seem to be carrying over the same sort of subject-matter into the fine arts.

But this was hardly apparent from the works themselves, for whereas his drawings had been highly personal and, in the series of shoes for instance, whimsical and fantastic, his paintings often seemed to originate in photographs and to aim at a harsh, precise, and mechanical finish.

After painting meticulously detailed pictures of Campbell's soup tins and Coca-Cola bottles, it was somehow natural that Warhol's next step should be to eliminate as far as possible the unreliable hand of the painter.

The works could be that much more efficient, precise, and mechanical if, instead of being laboriously painted from a photograph, it was silk-screened directly on to the canvas or paper, so that it could be multiplied *ad infinitum* (it is, after all, a considerable job to paint by hand hundreds of virtually identical canvases).

The role of the artist's personal intervention in his work would then be reduced to the choice of photographic material at the start and to the way it was tinted in reproduction or touched up with additional colour after reproduction.

One aspect of Warhol's artwork at this time seems to have some significance in relation to his coming involvement in the cinema: his interest in repetition as an artistic effect.

In many of his graphics a number of images, generally the same, would be placed in relation to one another, carefully sized and toned and grouped within an overall multiple image. 'Stars' like Monroe and Presley, or photographs of death and disaster, were treated in this way to produce some of Warhol's most famous works; occasionally also, as in his 'Robert Rauschenberg' (1963), a variety of different images might be pressed into service.

Because of the nature of the silk-screen process, no two images would be exactly alike in texture, colour, and so on, and Warhol was fascinated by the accidental variations which resulted. Images within the same frame might also be deliberately varied by the application of extra colour, as in the Elizabeth Taylor and Monroe pictures, or the 'Flowers' of 1965.

This kind of serial art might seem a logical step towards film-making, but since they were nearly all rigorously non-narrative, non-progressive, and turned for their effect on simultaneity of vision, they were surely bound to lead to a rather peculiar sort of cinema.

In 1963 Warhol made his first film, on a trip to Los Angeles, something called *Tarzan and Jane Regained, Sort of ...* , but later the same year he made the first famous film of his early period, *Sleep*. It is a six-hour, silent picture of a man sleeping, actually made, according to Warhol (though it would be impossible to recognize this in the finished film), by a carefully arranged pattern of ten-minute segments shot over a couple of weeks and cunningly repeated to make a satisfactory design.

All the same, the effect of *Sleep*, and of others like *Kiss*, *Couch*, and *Empire* (this last an eight-hour study of the Empire State Building from one fixed position), is

Warhol at the opening of his 1978 ICA exhibition

one of unblinking scrutiny of an object which remains uniform through a small cycle of change.

Boredom of a certain controlled sort, drugging the first levels of consciousness, seems to be a part of the films' psychological design, and though inevitably they exist in time, they are always working against it, dulling our awareness of it.

These films immediately became a talking point, even for those who had not seen them, and exerted a considerable influence (largely baleful) on the experimental cinema of the 1960s.

But through the sequence of them, Warhol himself as a personality became consistently more elusive. The nature of the films carried further his apparent design of reducing the personal participation of the artist to the minimum – they could be made, like many of his graphics, without the artist's being there at all.

And indeed, having progressively withdrawn from painting and then even from graphics, he began also to withdraw from active participation in film-making. Though hundreds of films were made under the blanket label of 'Warhol', different personalities around the Factory, his centre of operations, played the dominant role in their creation at different times.

Warhol became the still centre of activities, surrounded by an ever-changing entourage of junkies, transvestites, and freaks of all kinds who would be elevated for a few weeks to the status of 'superstars' in sketchily improvized films, then drift away again. His influence was pervasive, and yet impossible to pin down precisely; frequently he seemed to be a catalyst more than an inventor.

And curiously, for the leading figure in a society of this sort, he continued to lead a very quiet life, of which one could glean only that he lived with his mother in circumstances of solid middle-class respectability, was still quite devoutly religious, and himself disapproved of a lot of the drug-taking and drop-out life-styles of many of those around him (though never really of the inner circle).

His films during the later 1960s moved away from the abstraction and, after a brief flirtation with extravagant camp, lonesome cowboys and some more formal experimentation, settled on the classic Warhol style, turning a cool, detached gaze on a lot of really weird people and so allowing them to preserve their dignity as they lived out their fantasies before the camera.

It is typical of the Warhol paradox that the first major success in this style, *Flesh* (1968), was actually made by his most important associate, Paul Morrissey, while Warhol himself was in hospital recovering from being shot, in a much publicized incident, by a lady from SCUM (the Society for Cutting Up Men).

Whatever position Warhol may ultimately come to hold in the artistic pantheon of the 1960s and 1970s, there is no doubt that he will be remembered at least as the artist who most surely got the measure of art as a show-business during this period, the role of publicity and scandal in the making of art, the permanence (or anyway the chances for permanence) of the most resolutely disposable and momentary in art. 'In the future, everybody will be famous for fifteen minutes,' he once said.

It is hard to tell whether he made it all happen, or in some mysterious way it all just happened to and around him. But through the tangled art scene of his time he moved with the certainty of a sleep-walker, and left behind him some of the most memorable and characteristic images of a confused and possibly shallow and superficial era.

He was a slight man who wore a white wig.

JACQUELINE DU PRÉ

19 OCTOBER 1987

MISS JACQUELINE DU PRÉ, OBE, who died on October 19, at the age of 42, was regarded as one of the cello's most brilliant exponents, when her playing career was tragically cut short by multiple sclerosis.

Though she had her critics among the sterner sort of purist, her wealth of natural talent, which expressed itself in a warm-blooded, romantic approach to her material, made her a favourite on the concert platform, and made the sound of the cello popular with lay audiences.

Over the last few years she had established an enviable reputation as an interpreter of the solo cello repertory. Her name was particularly linked with the Elgar cello concerto, which she had played on many occasions all over the country and abroad.

Jacqueline du Pré was born on January 26, 1945. After being inspired by her mother, who, she once said, 'guided my first steps, wrote tunes for me to play, and drew pictorial descriptions of the melodies', she went to the London Cello School at the age of six. When she was 10, she went to William Pleeth, whom she always described as 'my cello Daddy'. She felt that she owed almost everything to him.

Her first public success came when she gave a Wigmore Hall recital at the age of 16. Then she went to study with Tortelier in Paris and Rostropovich in Moscow. At the same time she began a concert career which took her all over the world.

At the end of 1966 she met the pianist and conductor Daniel Barenboim, and they were married in the following year. He exerted a strong influence on her (as Barbirolli previously had done), particularly in the realm of chamber music. She became one of several players, soloists in their own right, who came together at fairly frequent intervals to tackle the chamber-music repertory. The most common combination was Zukerman, Barenboim, and du Pré.

Du Pré's style could, perhaps, be most aptly described as impassioned and grainy. She threw herself into the classical and more modern repertory with her whole body and soul. Some even found her wholehearted approach too subjective, too emotional. If that was a fault, it was one on the right side. In any case, it is inconceivable that one of her natural gifts would not, as she grew older, have developed a riper, more rounded approach to the cello's repertory.

But it was not to be. During a performance of the Brahms Double Concerto at the Lincoln Centre, New York, in 1971, she began to experience extreme difficulty fingering and bowing her cello. She was found to have contracted multiple

Jacqueline du Pré with Daniel Barenboim, at home, 1967.

sclerosis, and her concert career was over. The rest of her life was a brave battle against the ravages of the disease, and she was an example and inspiration to other sufferers.

With her husband she set up the Jacqueline du Pré MS Society Research Fund, which has been administered by the Multiple Sclerosis Society of Great Britain, since 1977.

She was appointed OBE in 1976, and had honorary doctorates from numerous universities.

Besides the memory of her concert performances Miss du Pré also leaves a considerable legacy of recordings to console her admirers for her cruelly early death. Among these, her playing of the Elgar will inevitably take first place, but her interpretations of the Delius and Dvorak concertos and of various sonatas are equally rewarding memorials.

Alexander Goehr wrote his evocative *Romanze* for her.

As a person, she was as outgoing and lively as she was as an artist, and her friends in the musical world were legion.

SIR FREDERICK ASHTON

Great choreographer and founder-figure of British ballet

18 AUGUST 1988

SIR FREDERICK ASHTON, OM, CH, one of the founders of British ballet, died on August 18 at the age of 83.

First as dancer, then as director, he played a distinguished part in the creation and growth of a national company and a native tradition. His unique contribution, however, was in his choreography. As a creative artist he was recognized to have been equalled by few and excelled by none in the whole history of the art he served.

There would, thanks to the determination and effort of others, have been some kind of British ballet today even without Ashton. It is impossible to imagine that it would have achieved the immense international reputation it enjoys had he not been there to create a repertory and a style. His public gifts brought him universal respect, and his private qualities ensured also that he enjoyed the love of those who knew him.

Frederick William Mallandaine Ashton was born of English parents at Guayaquil, Ecuador, on September 17, 1904. He was brought up in Lima, Peru, where he had two experiences crucial to his future career. The first was acting as acolyte to the Archbishop and thus acquiring a love of ritual; the second was being taken to see Anna Pavlova dance.

This gave him the urge to become a dancer himself, but such a career was unheard of in a respectable middle-class family at that time. 'My father was horrified,' Ashton once recalled. 'You can imagine the middle-class attitude. My mother would say: "He wants to go on the stage." She could not bring herself to say "into the ballet".'

Before he could follow his vocation he was sent to a minor English public school, where he was miserably unhappy, and put to work with an import–export firm in the City. Only then could he begin to take classes in secret and eventually, when frustrated ambition was harming his health, he was allowed to work full time and openly at what he wanted.

Luck had it that he began his studies with Massine, who happened to advertise for pupils. Massine in turn sent him to Marie Rambert, who quickly discovered his talent for choreography. So it came about that Ashton created his first ballet, *A Tragedy of Fashion*, in 1926 while still a pupil. This was a chic, amusing little work added to the revue *Riverside Nights*.

During the next few years Ashton danced in variety concerts, spent a year with Ida Rubinstein's company (where he enjoyed the chance to work under Bronislava Nijinska, a big influence on his own choreography), and performed with the small company Marie Rambert gathered together whenever possible. For them he created a series of ballets including *Capriol Suite* which long remained in the repertory.

Ashton's first big hit, however, was *Façade*, first given in 1931 by the Camargo Society with a cast including Lydia Lopokova and Alicia Markova. Its insouciant parodies of popular dances have remained a source of amusement ever since and it has been performed repeatedly all over the world.

His first work for Ninette de Valois's young Vic-Wells Ballet was *Regatta* in 1932. The following year he composed for these same dancers, with Stanislas Idzikowsky as guest, the light but brilliant *Les Rendezvous*, which also remains to this day in the international repertory.

He joined the Vic-Wells permanently in 1935 and began a richly productive period. His *Apparitions* in 1936 was by many compared favourably with Massine's *Symphonie Fantastique* on a similar theme, and that year saw also the touching *Nocturne* to Delius's *Paris*. These works have vanished, but the following year's witty *A Wedding Bouquet* and *Les Patineurs* are still with us.

Meanwhile, his fame was spreading abroad. Already in 1934 he had created dances for the Gertrude Stein–Virgil Thomson opera *Four Saints in Three Acts*, and in 1939 he made his first ballet for a foreign company: *Devil's Holiday* for Ballet Russe de Monte Carlo.

The outbreak of war inspired Ashton to the tragic, intense *Dante Sonata*; later he served in the Royal Air Force but was occasionally given special leave to create a new ballet. His next outstanding production, however, was *Symphonic Variations*, with which he greeted the company's transfer to Covent Garden in 1946: an outpouring of pure dance which shows his lyrical gifts at their finest. This began a series of beautiful plotless ballets, notably *Valses Nobles et Sentimentales*, *Scènes de Ballet*, and *Monotones*. But he also began a series of large-scale dramatic works adapting the formula of 19th century classical ballet into a contemporary idiom.

The first of these was *Cinderella*, in 1948, for which he drew ingeniously on the English pantomime tradition. There followed *Sylvia*, *Romeo and Juliet* (for the Royal Danish Ballet), *Ondine*, *La Fille mal gardée*, and *The Two Pigeons*.

Of these, *Fille* has proved his most popular ballet, reproduced with success all over the world, but all of them illustrated the multiplicity of his gifts: for the invention of always attractive, pure dances, for the vivid expression of character, and for a lively sense of comedy.

Nobody could better shape a role to the abilities of a dancer, often revealing qualities beyond those of which the dancer was aware. Margot Fonteyn, in particular, was developed by Ashton in a long series of roles from *Rio Grande* in 1935 to

Sir Frederick Ashton at the Royal Opera House, Covent Garden, to supervise rehearsals for his ballet *Ondine*, 1988.

Marguerite and Armand three decades later, and including, besides many of the works already mentioned, the sublime *Daphnis and Chloe*.

Ashton was also greatly adroit at turning a *pièce d'occasion* into something which long outlived the occasion which gave it birth. Examples were his coronation ballet *Homage to the Queen*; *Birthday Offering*, which celebrated the Royal Ballet's 25th anniversary in 1956, and the immensely amusing *The Dream*, which he mounted for the 400th anniversary of Shakespeare's birth.

He turned his hand successfully to opera production (*Manon*, *Albert Herring*, and a memorable *Orpheus* with Kathleen Ferrier) and also provided dances for films and plays. The list of his productions runs well into three figures. His position as one of the Royal Ballet's artistic directors was first officially recognized in 1948, although it had long been apparent in practice. He succeeded Dame Ninette as director of the company in 1963 and held the position until 1970, when he officially retired although actually remaining active as choreographer and performer.

The measure of Ashton's greatness can be seen in both the quality and the variety of his work. He had a gift which might, without immodest comparison, be called Shakespearean, for moving within a single work from the most tender expression of love to wild knockabout comedy or delicately barbed wit. Besides, it was the experience of dancing his ballets which helped to mould the whole style of dancing associated with the Royal Ballet. The freshness, purity, and poise of the English style at its best are in fact Ashton's style.

Ashton was created CBE in 1950, knighted in 1962, made a Companion of Honour in 1970, and received the Order of Merit seven years later. For his work he was also admitted to the Légion d'Honneur, made a Commander of the Danish Order of Dannebrog, and awarded the Swedish Carina Ari gold medal. In 1959 his own profession honoured him with the Royal Academy of Dancing Queen Elizabeth II Coronation Award.

The tribute of which he was perhaps most proud, however, was one entirely unique to him. On the occasion of his retirement from the Royal Ballet, the dancers planned, prepared, and rehearsed, in secret, a complete programme commemorating Ashton's achievements. Dances from old works, which everyone thought long-forgotten, were painstakingly remembered and restored.

No such retrospective display of a choreographer's career had ever been attempted before; nor is it easy to imagine it happening again, since the motive was the love which Ashton had the rare gift of inspiring in those who worked with him. Even those who knew him only through his work could share some part of this affection, since it was there alone that this shy, modest man revealed himself.

After he retired from the directorship Ashton continued to create new works, but naturally with less frequency and usually on a small scale, often for favourite dancers to perform on special occasions.

More important was the fact that, thanks to the enthusiasm and determination of Peter Schaufuss, Ashton's long-lost *Romeo and Juliet* was revived in a new production, supervised by the choreographer for London Festival Ballet, and that Anthony Dowell, as director of the Royal Ballet, later accomplished a similar salvation for another of Ashton's biggest works, *Ondine*.

Thanks to these acts of homage, the achievement of Ashton in his prime was shown to a new generation and will be available also for posterity as the ballets have now been recorded in a system of notation invented only since their creation.

He will be sadly missed, but his ballets will be an enduring memorial.

LAURENCE OLIVIER

Player of spellbinding power and versatility

11 JULY 1989

LORD OLIVIER, probably the greatest actor of his generation and certainly the most handsome, the producer who became the first director of the National Theatre, died peacefully in his sleep at Steyning in West Sussex yesterday. He was 82.

Lord Olivier had been ill for some time, suffering from diseases that would have killed earlier a less resilient man. One of his last public messages was as a co-signatory of a letter to *The Times* last May arguing for the preservation of the Rose Theatre.

One of the great triumvirate Olivier, Gielgud, and Richardson who dominated the British classical stage from the 1930s to the 1980s, Olivier was the only one to achieve a comparable film career. To a vast international audience who never set foot in the theatre, he was known as a film-maker and an actor of spell-binding power and versatility. Too much his own man, and too aware of the dangers of being devoured by the film-making system, he rarely aspired to the superstar rank after such popular successes as *Wuthering Heights*, *Rebecca*, and *Lady Hamilton*.

The films he directed himself, starting with *Henry V*, originated in the theatre. But from Heathcliff in the 1930s to Andrew Wyke (in *Sleuth*) in the 1970s, he left a gallery of electrifying performances; he revolutionized the art of filming Shakespeare; and in his wartime films, which included *49th Parallel* as well as *Henry V*, his voice carried over from Agincourt to far more contemporary battles.

He was uniquely empowered to speak for his own times through the mouth of a classical hero; and when, in 1970, he became the first actor to be granted a life peerage, it was partly in acknowledgment of those occasions when he assumed the identity of the British hero.

With so many of his major performances on record, his immortality is better guaranteed than that of any other classical star. Leading actors of the future will still have to escape the shadow of his *Richard III* and *Othello*. But however posterity judges Olivier, the judgment will be made on incomplete evidence. To feel the full charge he gave off at the height of his powers, it was necessary to be in his physical presence.

After *Henry V*, his best film was *Richard III*, which fully preserved his astonishing reptilian transformation and satanic comedy. But there is nothing in it to match the first sight of Olivier on stage, coming down to the audience to deliver the opening soliloquy, and then retreating upstage to lock the door so as to speak in conspiratorial privacy with 1,000 listeners.

A man of middle height with the off-stage appearance of a go-ahead bank manager, he had the imaginative authority to dwarf any surrounding company, and the animal magnetism to sweep the audience along to wherever he wished them to go. When asked to list his most valuable attributes he chose his eyes. Dark and commanding, they were a conspicuous natural gift. The rest of his equipment – his athleticism, his powers of mimicry, his voice – was largely self-created.

In his early years, his delivery was considered raw, and it never became an instrument in the strictly musical sense. Speech for Olivier was another form of action. Metallic in timbre, it never fell into the liquid cadences of Gielgud. Its music was the product of a struggle to extract every ounce of dramatic meaning from the text; often driven into harsh sardonic resonance and surprise inflections, and pouncing on isolated words with volcanic emphasis. 'The Lord said Let there be Light, and there was light.' As he spoke that line there was a full-stop after 'was', and the final word exploded like the miracle of the first sunrise. His playing disdained veiled nuances in favour of unambiguous clarity, with every decision fearlessly exposed and pushed to the limit.

'Danger' is an overworked word when applied to actors; but the sense of risk was integral to his work. Sometimes it took the form of direct physical courage, as in his precipitous 12-foot fall, caught dangling upside down by his ankles, as the slaughtered Coriolanus. Sometimes it was a matter of sensational trickery, like the gruesomely realistic self-amputation in *Titus Andronicus*. Significantly, when he spoke in praise of the old music-hall artists, the particular quality he singled out was their 'gallantry'. The sense of risk was no illusion. When Olivier did fail, as in his performance as Fred Midway, the Birmingham social climber in David Turner's *Semi-Detached* (1962), he failed on a scale that obliterated the surrounding play. That such occasions were few was due partly to his lifelong habit of observing human characteristics and storing them up for use on stage.

Even his legendary howl of anguish as the blinded Oedipus, a sound which Kenneth Tynan said would echo under the boards of the New Theatre for ever, had an external source. 'In the Arctic,' he once explained, 'they put down salt and the ermine comes to lick it, and his tongue freezes to the ice. I thought of that when I screamed as Oedipus.'

With some stars it seems that the finished performance happens by magic on the train from Brighton to London; but in Olivier's case it came from assembling innumerable details into a master pattern. However elevated the result there was always the sense that it had started close to the ground. In the thirties he said that he was 'carrying a torch for realism in Shakespeare'; and when in 1935 he and

Gielgud alternated as Romeo and Mercutio, Olivier described their partnership as one between earth and air.

He was too much a worker ever to pass as a gentleman player, though, of course, he could play gentlemen. He was at home in all the ranks, and as capable of making theatre history in supporting parts like Justice Shallow or Farquhar's Captain Brazen, as in the ultimate tragic roles.

Wary of expressing any political commitment, he achieved greatness in the theatre through his alertness to life outside it. From *Henry V* at the Old Vic in the mid-1930s to his farewell National Theatre performance as John Tagg, old gold Glaswegian Trotskyite, in Trevor Griffiths's *The Party* (1973), his playing reflected the spirit of the age. Patriotism, Realpolitik, cynical apathy, and the sense of national decline, Third World racial pride, and the new militancy of the 1968 generation were embodied one after another in what could be seen as a continuous commentary on the twentieth century.

Laurence Olivier was born on May 22, 1907, at Dorking, where his father, the Rev. Gerald Olivier, was an assistant priest at St Martin's Church. He showed precocious acting ability and made his stage debut at the age of 15 as Kate in a boys' performance of *The Taming of the Shrew* at the Shakespeare Memorial Theatre, Stratford-upon-Avon. On leaving St Edward's School, Oxford, he won a scholarship to Elsie Fogerty's Central School of Speech Training and Dramatic Art, and went on to join the Birmingham Repertory Company (1926–28).

As a young actor at a time that set a premium on romantic good looks, he was in some danger of falling into the matinee idol trap, and he made some short-sighted choices turning down the role of Stanhope in *Journey's End* for the sake of Beau Geste.

The turning point came in 1934 when, together with other rising talents of his generation, he joined Gielgud's crusading company, first as Bothwell in *Queen of Scots* (the origin of several long-lasting professional friendships, despite its commercial failure), followed by the 1935 *Romeo and Juliet*, which launched him as a heroic leading actor and (shortly afterwards) a Hollywood property.

A wartime commission in the Fleet Air Arm did not prevent him from making the film of *Henry V*, but it took him away from the stage until, in 1943, he became co-director with Ralph Richardson and John Burrell of the Old Vic company at the New Theatre. These were the years of Olivier's Richard III, Hotspur, and Lear; and the inspired double bill of Oedipus and Sheridan's *The Critic* in which Olivier, as Puff, was whisked off, still talking, up to the flies. Coupled with Richardson's Falstaff and *Peer Gynt* (to which Olivier, in a supreme stroke of luxury casting, played the tiny part of the Button Moulder), these seasons formed the most glorious chapter in the Old Vic's history.

However, neither that nor the knighthood he received in 1947 dissuaded the Governors, headed by Lord Esher, from picking a moment in 1948, while Olivier was leading the company on a triumphant Australian tour, from informing him that the directors' joint contract would not be renewed.

In 1940, following his divorce from Jill Esmond, he had married Vivien Leigh; and after his expulsion from the Old Vic ('the ruin of our house' as he called it), he set up his own management at the St James's Theatre for a mixed classical and modern repertory in which he directed or co-starred with his wife. These seasons included Fry and Rattigan premieres, important new work from Thornton Wilder and Tennessee Williams, and two Cleopatras from Miss Leigh, with Olivier paying successive court to her as Shakespeare's Antony and Shaw's Caesar.

In comparison with what had led up to it, the St James's episode marked a retreat into conventional stardom. The lull came to an end in 1957 when, to the distaste of some admirers, he took the plunge into the new wave and appeared as Archie Rice, the seedy bottomline comedian in John Osborne's *The Entertainer*, one of his favourite parts. You could sense the zest with which he discarded his regal West End wardrobe to swagger on leering in a loud check suit; exchanging the imprisoning refinements of eminence for the free speech of the dregs of the profession. Once again, he was touching the earth.

At the Royal Court (where he also played in Ionesco's *Rhinoceros*) he met the actress Joan Plowright, whom he married after divorcing Vivien Leigh. And his attachment to the Court became crucial in 1963 when he reached the summit of his career as director of the National Theatre.

Olivier had prepared for this task by directing the Chichester Festival Theatre from the turn of the 1960s: a trial-run that demonstrated his Henry V-like qualities as a leader of towering authority who could still learn from the young.

As an actor–manager he made himself at home in the new world of subsidy and permanent companies; as a prince of the classical stage, he opened his sympathies to the demotic upheaval. In particular, he engaged the two leading young Royal Court directors, John Dexter and William Gaskill, and took them with him from Chichester to the Waterloo Road.

Olivier's greatest strength as an artistic director was that, as an actor, he had nothing more to prove. After scaling his last Shakespearean peak in *Othello* (1963) he generally avoided great roles and gave his main energy to building a great company.

Legislated into existence, the National Theatre had the initial task of establishing its identity. Under Olivier and his associates, it wisely entered into no collisions of policy with the Royal Shakespeare Company, but settled instead for the role of a living museum: a place housing the best in world drama. The essential prerequisite for such an organization was a company that could play anything. And in its first charmed years the company presented Chekhov, Harold Brighouse, Noël

Coward, Ibsen, and Feydeau – a list with nothing in common beyond the fact that almost every one of them brought the theatre another success and redefined the reputation of the playwright.

With the exception of Sir Michael Redgrave, no leading actor approaching Olivier's own rank became a member of the team; and there were complaints (from Tyrone Guthrie and others) that any place calling itself a National Theatre should have found room for Gielgud, Richardson, and Scofield. However, after his inaugural production of *Hamlet,* for which Olivier imported Peter O'Toole over the heads of his regular troupe, he remained wedded to the ideal of the company actor and the ensemble; and (perhaps with memories of the Old Vic debacle) to defending his associates' judgment against the Governors as in the case of *Spring Awakening* and Hochhuth's *Soldiers.*

Edgar in *The Dance of Death* (1967) and Shylock in Jonathan Miller's production of *The Merchant of Venice* (1970) were two of his last major performances; much outnumbered by the supporting roles he played. But any doubts as to his indispensability were silenced by the difficulties the theatre encountered during a spell of illness which kept him away from it in 1970; and by his return, against medical advice, to avert the looming crisis with his performance in *Long Day's Journey into Night* playing James Tyrone, the embittered old actor who had sacrificed his talent to long-running stardom, it was as if he were facing the wreck he might have made of his own career.

Olivier, who handed over the artistic directorship to Sir Peter Hall in 1973, did not achieve his ambition of leading the company into the new South Bank building. In his last years, ill-health restricted him to film and television roles, including *Love among the Ruins* and an acclaimed performance as Lord Marchmain in *Brideshead Revisited.* His autobiography, *Confessions of an Actor,* appeared in 1982. It was followed by a second book, *On Acting,* in 1986.

He leaves one son by his first marriage, and, by his third to Joan Plowright, a son and two daughters.

'SUGAR' RAY ROBINSON

Supreme exponent of pugilistic skills

12 APRIL 1989

'SUGAR' RAY ROBINSON, generally regarded among boxing aficionados as one of the greatest if not the greatest fighter, pound-for-pound, who ever graced the ring, died yesterday at the age of 67.

In days like these when some fighters hold slices of several different titles at different weights, to state of Robinson that he held world titles at two weights, welter- and middle-, might seem to be a modest claim. But there was nothing ordinary about the talents of Ray Robinson, and to add to superlative pugilistic skill he had indomitable courage.

This was never better demonstrated than the torrid night in 1952, in New York's Yankee Stadium, on which he attempted to emulate Bob Fitzsimmons and Henry Armstrong to become a triple title holder. With an air temperature of 40 degrees C (104 degrees F) outside the ring, Robinson fought his heart out against Joey Maxim, the light-heavyweight title holder. But it was the heat, and not the defending champion's punches which got to him in the end, as he collapsed at the end of the thirteenth, and was unable to come out for the fourteenth, though ahead on points at the time.

Robinson's professional record speaks for itself. He boxed for 25 years and fought a prodigious 22 world championship contests. Out of 201 paid bouts he lost only 19, and no man ever knocked him out.

But the statistics scarcely conjure up the remarkable skills and graces with which Robinson was able to bemuse, torment, and overwhelm opponent after opponent. His hand and foot speed were breathtaking. He could move like a dancer, but hit like a pile driver. And although his famous 'bolo' punch might be looked at askance by some modern referees as an outright swing to the kidneys, it was merely one item in an arsenal of fistic equipment which put contest after contest in which he engaged beyond the judgment of the scorecard.

Robinson was as great a character out of the ring as he was in it. In an era before fighters received the kind of media exposure they do now, he was one of the ring's indisputable stars.

Glamour and Sugar Ray were indivisible. Flamingo-pink Cadillacs, scores of flunkeys, pretty women, were his natural milieu, and he loved the adoration. Occasionally it threatened his ring professionalism. He had been swanning around in a carefree manner in Paris before coming to London and being rudely relieved of his middleweight title by Britain's Randolph Turpin in July 1951. But he was not a man to toss away a title permanently.

The return, in New York, in September of that year saw a finely-honed Robinson finally end the Englishman's brave defence with a flurry of punches which almost challenged the eye to count them as they were thrown.

Robinson was born Walker Smith on May 3, 1921. He was an impressionable teenager when Joe Louis was beginning to make his mark, and he made the emerging heavyweight his idol. He won the Golden Gloves title in 1939, fighting 85 amateur bouts in all, winning 40 of them in the opening round.

He turned pro in 1940 and in the same year acquired his legendary name, almost by accident. Watching a small promotion from ringside one day he was suddenly asked to substitute for a fighter called Ray Robinson, who had failed to turn up for one of the bouts. Winning in style, he assumed that boxer's name. Later, an observer remarked to George Gainsford whose stable Robinson was in, that Gainsford had a 'sweet' fighter – the trainer replied: 'Yes, he's as sweet as sugar.' Thus, the legend was born.

Robinson progressed rapidly, moving up from lightweight to welterweight, winning the world title in 1946 and defending it successfully five times. He reluctantly abandoned it when he won the world middleweight title from Jake LaMotta in 1951. He was almost immediately to lose it to Turpin, but he had it back within 64 days.

Many were the battles he fought in its defence, or to get it back; particularly blood-stirring were a series of gruelling struggles with Carmen Basilio. Robinson did not win them all but he generally bounced back. Only the hurdle of light-heavyweight proved insurmountable, but Robinson never won more fans than on the occasion of his heroic attempt to win his third world title.

Even after that he continued boxing, regaining his middleweight title, and holding it until 1960, fighting a whole new generation of fighters such as Gene Fullmer and Paul Pender, when he was in his latter-thirties. Robinson went on fighting until he was 44, boxing his last bout in 1965, in which year he fought an incredible 15 contests.

But unlike so many, Robinson lived on with health intact, to enjoy the rewards of his ring career, and bask in his fame and prosperity. Whenever and wherever boxing is discussed, the name of Ray Robinson is inseparable from any consideration of the most richly rewarding moments in the sport.

Robinson leaves his widow, Eda-Mae Holly, by whom he had a son, Ray junior.

AYATOLLAH KHOMEINI

Cleric who led Iran to the past

3 JUNE 1989

AYATOLLAH KHOMEINI, who died in Tehran on June 3 aged 86, led Iran into a decade of revolutionary turmoil and economic mismanagement which has set back its development by many years. His Islamic Revolution, rejecting secular government and promising Iranians to bring them to the 'City of God', exercised influence far beyond Iran's borders.

Khomeini's brand of Islamic fundamentalism changed the political chemistry of the Muslim world. The destabilizing influence of his rhetoric on other Islamic regimes may prove his most lasting testimony.

To many Muslims, particularly among the poor, his rejection of modernization and its attendant disruption of Islamic traditions was initially seductive. His doctrine of simultaneous rejection of Communism and capitalism summarized in the slogan 'neither East nor West', seemed to promise, even to the majority Sunni Muslims, a return to familiar cultural roots. But to others, whose numbers increased as the fruits of the 'Islamic revolution' were tasted, Khomeini's rule seemed a hideous distortion of Islam. Iran's influence was diminished by internal injustice and arbitrary executions, by hostage-taking and international terrorism, and by failure in a war with Iraq which united much of the Arab world against the traditional Persian enemy.

About three million Iranians emigrated or fled their country after he took over, and the purges during his rule are thought to have resulted in the execution of at least 40,000 men and women, most of them former supporters of the revolution which then destroyed them. More than a million died in battle.

Sayyed Ruhollah Khomeini was little known in the non-Muslim world until 1978, when he used exile in France to capture international headlines with his calls for the overthrow of Shah Reza Pahlavi. His physical appearance – black turban, bushy eyebrows, severe expression – were in the following two years to make him more widely recognized than any other leader of a Third World country. His name probably inspired more intense and varied emotions than any figure since Stalin.

Sayyed Ruhollah was born in 1902 into a family of strong religious traditions in Khomein, a village some 60 miles south-west of Tehran, from which he took his clerical name. Both his grandfather and father were mullahs. The latter, Sayyed Mustafa, was murdered by bandits only five months after Ruhollah's birth, so that his mother and an aunt were responsible for his early upbringing. At the age of 16, he lost both mother and aunt within a year, and the task of supervising his education fell to his elder brother, Sayyed Morteza, later to be known as Ayatollah Passandideh, who now survives him.

He studied in the shrine city of Qom, now the spiritual capital of Shiite Iran, and, although his work in ethics and philosophy was not highly regarded, attracted attention for his xenophobia and overtly political preachings. He drew hundreds of students to his classes, where he exhorted them to regard the solution of problems of the day as part of their religious duties. Indeed, religion was not a politically neutral topic in Iran in the 1920s and 1930s. The then Shah, an admirer of Ataturk, was attempting to transform the Iranian monarchy into a modern centralized state, and saw the power of the mullahs as one of the principal obstacles he had to overcome. He drastically reduced their role in law and education, offended them by imposing Western dress on men and prohibiting the veil to women, and resorted to violence against those of them who opposed him.

In 1941 Reza Shah abdicated in favour of the Crown Prince Mohammad Reza, the Shah whom Khomeini was eventually to oust. The conflict between the two men started in 1941, and by the 1960s Khomeini was taking an uncompromising stand against the 'un-Islamic' innovations, including land reform, with which the Shah was trying to modernize his country, and attacking the corruption of the Shah's regime.

Matters came to a head when the Shah held a snap plebiscite on his 'White Revolution', which included women's suffrage. The mullahs were almost unanimously opposed to women's rights, but Khomeini moved the argument on to a different plane by denouncing the reforms as part of a plot to consolidate American dominance of Iran, and he now sought to identify himself with the 'oppressed masses'.

In March 1963 the seminary in Qom was attacked by the Shah's paratroopers and the secret police. A few months later Khomeini was arrested, and the resultant protests were suppressed with the death of hundreds of people. Khomeini was exiled, and spent the next 13 years in the shrine city of Najaf in Iraq. From there his periodic proclamations about developments in Iran were smuggled into the country and circulated clandestinely. By now he was convinced that monarchy was an intrinsically anti-Islamic institution, and he declared any form of cooperation with monarchs illegitimate.

But this did not mean that temporal government had to be given up as a corrupting occupation. Islam, according to Khomeini, was indeed political or it was nothing.

In November 1977, Khomeini's elder son, Sayyed Mostafa, died suddenly in Najaf. This was widely assumed by the Ayatollah's followers to be the work of the

Shah's secret police. Many went to pay their condolences to him and came back with taped denunciations of the Shah in Khomeini's own voice.

Two other factors were now destabilizing Iran. One was a severe dislocation of the economy by the reckless spending which had followed the rises in the price of oil. The other was that the Shah, prompted by President Carter's human rights campaign, was relaxing political repression.

On January 1, 1978, however, President Carter on a visit to Tehran gave a strong reaffirmation of American support for the Shah. Emboldened by this, the government launched a counter-attack on the religious opposition, denouncing Khomeini as an agent of foreign powers.

This proved to be a disastrous miscalculation. It provoked demonstrations that set off a cycle of death; each public mourning of one set of martyrs created a new set. By September, the Shah, who was now suffering from cancer, was no longer in charge of his own capital as thousands of people, shouting Khomeini's name, thronged the streets and burnt down banks and businesses.

Another disastrous miscalculation was the pressure from Tehran to expel Khomeini from Iraq. He flew to Paris, where he found easy access to the world's media and where he was aided and counselled by Western-educated Iranians.

The Shah finally quit on January 16, 1979, leaving power nominally in the hands of the liberal Dr Bakhtiar, who disbanded the secret police and promised free elections. But Khomeini was able to return to Iran to a massive and tumultuous welcome and announced the appointment of one of his supporters, Mehdi Bazargan, as provisional Prime Minister.

Fighting broke out between opponents and supporters of the Ayatollah within the armed forces, the latter receiving vigorous support from left-wing guerrilla groups. After two days the army declared itself neutral and Khomeini's supporters swept into power.

Bazargan, a liberal though devout Muslim, set out to reconstruct the economy, but he was denied decisive support from Khomeini against Islamic radicals, who now virtually ruled the country through a network of local committees and their own militia. Khomeini caused consternation among many women supporters of the revolution by ordering them to resume the veil.

In August he denounced the Kurdish autonomists as 'unbelievers', and sent the army and the new Revolutionary Guards against them. Persecutions of other minorities, including the Baha'i religious community, were to follow.

Meanwhile, the 'Assembly of Experts', comprising 83 clerics elected to draft a constitution for the Islamic Republic, was packed with hard-line fundamentalists who proceeded to give sweeping powers to Khomeini as so-called Guardian Jurist. The formation of the Islamic Republic was accorded virtually unanimous popular support in a national referendum.

On November 4, 1979, a group which proclaimed itself 'The Students of the Line of the Imam' occupied the American Embassy and seized its staff as hostages, demanding that the Shah, who had lately entered the United States for medical treatment, be extradited to Iran. Whether or not Khomeini had approved this action in advance remains unclear. In any case, he refused to disavow it and the Bazargan cabinet resigned.

Anti-American feeling now gripped the land. The Supreme Council of the Revolution, a body in which his former pupils predominated, assumed direct responsibility for the government. Hundreds of former officials were executed.

In September, 1980, by which time the Islamic Republican Party (IRP) had effectively won the power struggle, Khomeini at last gave explicit authority for serious negotiations on the release of the 52 American hostages. (They were finally released on January 20, 1981, the day of President Reagan's inauguration, 444 days after their capture.)

National unity against America did not, however, preclude fierce and bloody disagreements. Abolhassan Bani-Sadr, a radical economist who had spent many years in France, was elected the first President of the Islamic Republic, but Khomeini did not give him any firm support against the intrigues of ambitious mullahs. When the IRP scored a resounding victory in the Republic's first parliamentary elections, Bani-Sadr allied with the Mujahedin.

In June, 1981, when Bani-Sadr's formal dismissal by parliament was imminent, the left-wing Mujahedin guerrillas organized a mass demonstration in his support, and Iran entered on something close to civil war. Hundreds of the regime's opponents were executed every week. Bani-Sadr, deposed as President, fled to France.

Khomeini and his regime survived the crisis, but only at the price of a savage reign of terror involving executions on a scale the Shah had never contemplated. Yet this bitter struggle had proved not to be incompatible with a massive and organized effort of national defence.

For, in the meantime, the whole situation had been transformed in September 1980 by the invasion of Iran by the massed armour of Iraq. A series of offensives in the first half of 1982, all of them very costly in human life, drove Iraqi forces out of Iranian territory and enabled Iran to carry the war into Iraq.

The remainder of Khomeini's rule was marked by rapid economic decline as a consequence of the continuation of the war with Iraq and incompetence by the mullahs, whose rivalries for power at times broke into the open.

For most of the war Iranian prospects looked better than those of its enemy but, in early 1988, Iran received several military blows at the hands of the American Navy and the Iraqi army. Widespread use of chemical weapons by Iraq, which forced the expulsion of Iranian troops from the Fao Peninsula and other Iraqi territories, gradually made the war's continuation untenable.

In July 1988, the Ayatollah announced that he had ordered compliance with United Nations resolutions and a negotiated end to the eight-year conflict with Iraq. It had cost Iran the lives of an estimated one million troops. In February 1989, Khomeini issued a fatwa, or religious edict, ordering Muslims to kill the British writer, Salman Rushdie, on account of the latter's alleged blasphemy against Islam in his novel, *The Satanic Verses*. The decision led to a severing of diplomatic ties with Britain and the increased isolation for Iran in the world.

Khomeini also set a much more radical line for his government and dismissed his designated successor, Ayatollah Hosain-Ali Montazeri, who had become a bold and open critic of his leader's extremism. Khomeini's last decision was to order a review of the 1979 constitution to concentrate power in the hands of an executive president and draft new rules for the selection of a new supreme leader or a leadership council composed of junior clerics.

Khomeini's rule was, in all significant respects, a disaster. For Iran it was comparable to the Mongolian invasion of the 13th century. For neighbouring Islamic nations his effect was to frighten moderate leadership and paralyze reform. For the rest of the world he bears, in addition, a disastrous responsibility for inspiring and sanctioning state terrorism. All three legacies will be hard to erase.

HERBERT VON KARAJAN

Master conductor of opera, orchestra, and recordings

16 JULY 1989

HERBERT VON KARAJAN, the most celebrated and widely discussed conductor of the last four decades, died yesterday at Anif in his home outside Salzburg at the age of 81.

No conductor since Toscanini set higher standards of orchestral playing and no conductor has left a recorded legacy as extensive, as various and as generally distinguished as that which Karajan now leaves.

Admired by a huge public in Europe, Japan, and the United States, Karajan's qualities did not always meet with universal critical acclaim. His superstar status alienated many, whilst his unostentatious command of the orchestra and his belief in beauty of sound as a pre-condition of any successful musical performance were often mistaken for coldness or veneer.

There was often controversy in his life. Last April indeed Karajan's famous association with the Berlin Philharmonic Orchestra, stretching over more than 30 years, came abruptly to an end when he resigned the post he held as their conductor for life.

A somewhat rancorous note of resignation addressed by him to the Berlin Senate's cultural authorities had been preceded by months of political manoeuvring and, in the end, the conductor's departure was one of the consequences of the replacement of the Berlin Christian Democrats in power by a Socialist and Green coalition.

But the Berliner Philharmoniker, after years of extreme loyalty to their inspired director, had come to suffer divisions in their ranks owing to the ageing Karajan's arbitrary acts, while the authorities had grown restive as the heavily-subsidized orchestra was increasingly absent from Berlin as Karajan took them on extended tours of the Far East.

Even the souring disputes, however, of the 1980s cannot cloud the memory of what must be accounted one of the finest conductor–orchestra relationships in the history of music.

Born in Salzburg on April 5, 1908, Karajan was the younger son of a distinguished surgeon and his Slovenian wife. Originally called Karajannis, the Karajan family were Macedonian Greeks who had moved first to Saxony and later to Vienna where they held important academic, medical, and administrative posts.

Exceptional musical talent and relentless ambition were precociously evident in the young Karajan. He received piano lessons from the distinguished Czech teacher, Franz Ledwinka, at the age of five and gave his first public recital at the age of nine. As a choirboy he took part in the first Salzburg Festivals and was soon to come under the influence of the musicologist and conductor, Bernhard Paumgartner, who developed the boy's musical talents as well as instilling in him a love of Italian culture and an enthusiasm for motorcycles, thus starting Karajan's life-long interest in fast locomotion.

At the age of 18 Karajan was enrolled, at his father's behest, as a student of engineering at Vienna's Technical High School, but his continuing musical studies quickly superseded his technical ones. After a brief period studying the piano, Karajan joined the conducting class at the Vienna Akademie. During this period he learned more from observing the work of Krauss, Schalk, Richard Strauss, and, above all, Toscanini; but the classes gave Karajan his first conducting opportunities and in January 1929 he hired the Salzburg Mozarteum Orchestra to make his professional debut in a programme which included Strauss's *Don Juan* and Tchaikovsky's *Fifth Symphony*. The concert was heard by the Director of the Ulm Opera, who engaged Karajan as Kapellmeister on a salary of £10 a month.

At that time, Ulm occupied the lowest rung on the German operatic ladder with a permanent orchestra of 24 for opera, and a chorus of 16. With a resourcefulness characteristic of his whole career, Karajan used amateur singers and wind players from local military bands to swell his forces and supervised everything.

He made his operatic debut conducting Mozart's *Figaro* in March 1929 and during the next five years was bold enough to stage such works as *Fidelio*, *Lohengrin*, *Meistersinger*, *Salome*, and *Der Rosenkavalier*, teaching his Baron Ochs the role note by note in 120 piano rehearsals. Karajan's love of the operas of Mozart and Verdi, two composers whose music sounds well even with diminished forces, dated from this time, as did his loathing of small theatres – a prejudice which led him in later years to produce Mozart operas and Bizet's *Carmen* on a scale not always well-suited to their musico-dramatic content.

In 1933 Karajan conducted the off-stage music for Max Reinhardt's Salzburg Festival production of Goethe's *Faust*; the following year he was dismissed from the Ulm Opera in a harsh but well-intentioned gesture by the Intendant who saw Karajan's reluctance to move from Ulm as a barrier to a potentially brilliant career elsewhere. Desperate for work, Karajan had the good fortune to be auditioned for the post of Kapellmeister in Aachen. He was engaged and within a year had become Germany's youngest Generalmusikdirector. In Aachen he had a 70-strong orchestra and the resources to engage leading soloists.

The price that the ambitious young Karajan paid for these luxuries was a continuing involvement with the Nazi Party which he had joined in 1933.

In fact, Karajan's involvement with the Nazi Government proved to be a very mixed blessing. In post-war Europe and America, his reputation, in some people's eyes, was irreversibly tainted. At the time, the Nazis both advanced Karajan's career (in the late 1930s) and hindered it (from 1942). Karajan's fall from grace in 1942 came about after representations made by the conductor Wilhelm Furtwängler to Goebbels about the undue adulation of Karajan by the German musical press. Hitler was also said to be antagonistic to Karajan; according to Goebbels' own papers, negotiations begun privately by Karajan with the Dresden Opera were brought to an end on Hitler's instructions.

From 1937 Karajan's rise to fame in Germany had been meteoric. On the strength of a single performance of *Tristan* he was offered a post in Vienna, which he declined because he had more authority and better discipline in Aachen. In 1938 he was invited to conduct *Fidelio* and *Tristan und Isolde* at the Berlin State Opera, where Heinz Tietjen was looking for a conductor of sufficient ability to compete with the politically 'obstinate' Furtwängler. A newspaper headline, 'The Miracle Karajan', sparked the animosity towards Karajan which ended only with Furtwängler's death in 1954.

Saddened by the hostility towards him of a conductor he greatly admired, Karajan later determined that 'the only way to enjoy eminence is to encourage and help one's colleagues'. Karajan's generosity to younger colleagues, men like Abbado, Carlos Kleiber, Mehta, Muti, and Ozawa, appears to have been part of a consciously-formulated response to the Furtwängler experience.

Karajan's first Berlin period (1938–42), during which time he made his first recordings with the Berlin Philharmonic and the Concertgebouw Orchestra of Amsterdam, established him as the most able and exciting conductor of his generation in Europe. The admiration and friendship of Victor de Sabata also enabled him to work in Italy after his fall from favour in Berlin in 1942.

When the German theatres closed in 1944, Karajan was already in Italy. Penniless, he was bailed out by discreet financial help from the pianist Edwin Fischer.

His reinstatement was slow and painful. In 1946 he conducted one concert with the Vienna Philharmonic, but a further engagement was cancelled by the Soviet authorities. Despite a ban on all recording activities, imposed by the French and American authorities, Karajan was signed by Walter Legge in 1946 to make a series of recordings with the Vienna Philharmonic for EMI. Famous recordings of Beethoven's Ninth Symphony, Brahms's *German Requiem*, and Richard Strauss's *Metamorphosen* date from this period. In October 1947 Karajan celebrated his denazification with a memorable performance of Bruckner's Eighth Symphony, the first tangible demonstration of his profound feeling for Bruckner's music.

Karajan made his London debut at the Royal Albert Hall in 1948 with Dinu

Lipatti and the newly-founded Philharmonia Orchestra, whose principal conductor he was shortly to become. With the arrival of long-playing records imminent, Legge and Karajan embarked on the systematic recording of large areas of the standard and not-so-standard repertoire with the orchestra. The first recording, of Balakirev's First Symphony, established Karajan's outstanding skills as an orchestral trainer and manager, exacting but practical, with an acute awareness of his players' needs and capacities both in rehearsal and in performance.

His concert programmes were, and remained, less adventurous than his recording schedules but the Karajan/Philharmonia concerts were a highlight of the European musical scene in the 1950s. Toscanini's agreement to conduct the orchestra in London in 1952 was a token of Karajan's and Legge's achievement at this time.

Karajan's association with Legge and EMI produced a mass of fine recordings, including operatic recordings which probably remain unmatched: *Cosi fan tutte*, *Hansel and Gretel*, *Falstaff*, *Ariadne auf Naxos*, and *Der Rosenkavalier*. Karajan's unique skills as an accompanist and his innate sympathy with the human voice helped him to develop the careers of such singers as Elisabeth Schwarzkopf, Irmgard Seefried, and Christa Ludwig. Karajan, who worked closely with La Scala, Milan, in the 1950s and early 1960s, also enjoyed a productive artistic collaboration with Maria Callas. Their La Scala *Lucia di Lammermoor*, later seen in Berlin, was a sensation, as were their gramophone recordings of *Il Trovatore* and *Madama Butterfly*.

In 1954 Karajan succeeded Furtwängler as principal conductor for life of the Berlin Philharmonic; and in 1956 he succeeded the demoralized Karl Bohm as Director of the Vienna State Opera. He transformed the overstaffed and laxly run company from a local institution into one of the world's most notable houses. He introduced a variant of the Italian *stagione* system, had all Italian and French operas, except *Don Carlos*, sung in the original languages, and engaged the most distinguished singers, irrespective of nationality or cost. As a producer his work was not universally admired but his conducting of the music of Verdi, Wagner, Puccini, Debussy, and Johann and Richard Strauss won unbounded admiration. His departure in 1964 was a black day for the Vienna Opera.

During his Vienna years Karajan concentrated on the rebuilding of the Berlin Philharmonic, which had suffered badly in the post-war period. Recruiting the finest young players from Germany and elsewhere, he brought all the riches of his experiences in orchestral training to mould the orchestra into an audible manifestation of his own musical personality. He gave the orchestra a new delicacy and power, precision matched with flexibility, and tone that could be as transparent in Mendelssohn, Debussy, or Ravel as it was brilliant and deep in the later romantic repertoire. Under Karajan, the Berlin Philharmonic became the best and, by some distance, the best-paid and best-equipped orchestra in the world.

Karajan's relationship with his home city of Salzburg had an embattled history. In 1948 he conducted Gluck's *Orfeo* and Mozart's *Figaro* but a pact worked out between Egon Hilbert and Furtwängler barred Karajan from working there.

During a seven-year exile, Karajan conducted at Bayreuth, including memorable accounts of *Tristan* and *Meistersinger*, though a clash between his own and Wieland Wagner's conceptions and egocentricities ruled out further collaboration. Karajan concentrated his operatic work in Milan until his return to Salzburg in 1957.

From then on, under varying titles, he was the autocrat of the Salzburg Summer Festivals. In collaboration with the architect Clemens Holzmeister, Karajan determined the cinerama-like proportions of the stage of the new Grosses Festspielhaus which he inaugurated in 1960. In retrospect, it seems that Karajan had already planned his next move in Salzburg when he insisted on the 33-metre proscenium opening. During 1965 he announced that he would establish and personally finance Easter Festivals in Salzburg from 1967 onwards, beginning with a four-year *Ring* cycle. The scheme was a masterpiece of ruseful paramilitary planning and organization, which enabled him in one operation to surpass Bayreuth's standards, employ his own Berlin Philharmonic, and record the festival repertoire with musical rehearsals paid for by the record companies.

Karajan's scenic collaborator in Salzburg was Gunther Schneider-Siemssen. Though Karajan was probably at his most effective working with established producers, for instance the wonderful production of *La Bohème* with Zeffirelli at La Scala, his own productions, though often dimly lit, were never inept. At times, the massive Salzburg stage gave to the drama a strangely marmoreal feel but something like his 1964 *Elektra* achieved a musical and dramatic *terribilità* not easily forgotten.

In the 1970s Karajan continued to expand his repertoire and became increasingly preoccupied with the music of Mahler, which he had known, often ineptly performed, since his student days. The Sixth and Ninth symphonies and *Das Lied von der Erde* clearly meant a great deal to Karajan, the more so in the wake of his illnesses of the 1970s.

Like all great conductors, Karajan was a splendid conductor of lighter music of the Strauss family, Lehar, Offenbach, or German military marches, and he was a selectively gifted conductor of key works by Nielsen, Prokofiev, Honneger, and Shostakovich. His first record of *The Rite of Spring* was judged by Stravinsky to be too polished. Piqued, perhaps, by the criticisms, Karajan produced, at great expenditure of time and care, a set of readings of the music of Schoenberg, Berg, and Webern which revealed new aspects of both the music and his own musical perceptions.

Karajan's conducting technique was the prolongation of his musical will, the distillation of a lifetime's study in getting what he wanted with the minimum of fuss and physical effort. His power of communication to orchestras, performers, and audiences who flocked to his concerts in states of unusual anticipation was hypnotic. 'The real art of conducting,' he once stated, 'is to realize that the music comes implicity, by itself.' But this understates his painstaking attention to detail and his mastery of large forms which were so much a part of his success.

Karajan was a born teacher. He had endless patience, first clearly explaining and slowly demonstrating, then gently correcting. A first-rate mimic, he could parody or exaggerate faults in a way that made artists laugh at him and at themselves.

No one who had to deal with it much enjoyed the Karajan entourage or Karajan when surrounded by his entourage; but privately he was a man of great directness and simplicity with a quick, mordant wit and total recall of events and personalities spanning back over 60 years of European music-making.

In appearance he was spruce and distinguished, with hard, light eyes like fissures in a block of ice. Vulgarity was anathema to him. Obsessed with physical fitness and a need for inner quiet and concentration, he ate and drank sparingly, and practised yoga for two hours a day.

He delighted in acquiring new skills and curbed his natural impatience patiently to achieve expertise in sailing and piloting fast aircraft. Thrifty and prudent, he wasted neither time, energy, nor money, alternating periods of intensive work with concentrated relaxation in sport where he took every calculated risk except that of losing.

A major spinal operation in 1975 and a further operation in 1978 left him with a limp and in severe pain.

At his final London concert in October 1988 his advance to the rostrum was painful to watch; yet once installed there he conducted performances of Schoenberg and Brahms of towering splendour.

He was married three times, first to Elmy Holgerloef, second to Anita Gutermann, and third to Eliette Mouret, who survives him along with two daughters born when he was in his middle fifties.

SAMUEL BECKETT

Unassuming genius who probed the quandary of human existence

22 DECEMBER 1989

SAMUEL BECKETT, who died in Paris on December 22, aged 83, was one of the truly great literary figures of this century and his writings for the theatre in particular brought him universal acclaim. His plays, especially *Waiting for Godot, Endgame,* and *Krapp's Last Tape,* are part of the standard repertoire in theatres round the world.

These and his novels are considered classics of modern literature, as naturally a part of an educated person's experience as the works of Ibsen, Kafka, or James Joyce.

Although he once declared that 'the artist who gambles his being is from nowhere, and has no brothers', Samuel Barclay Beckett did possess a biography which he was characteristically modest and discreet about. His Schopenhauerian pessimism caused him to consider his birth (at Foxrock, near Dublin, on Good Friday, April 13, 1906) a calamity, and yet his early years were happy enough. His father, William Frank Beckett, a respected and well-to-do quantity surveyor, and his mother, Mary (née Roe), were very fond of their second son, and he of them: their deaths, in 1933 and 1950 respectively, grieved him deeply.

'Willie' Beckett was a cheerful, plump man, who much enjoyed taking long walks and sharing jokes with his son, whose outstanding sporting and academic record at school and university made him, an early school-leaver himself, immensely proud. Though like all the family a practising Protestant, Beckett senior was less passionate in his belief than his wife or his elder son Frank, who succeeded him at the head of the family firm. As for Samuel's faith, this did not survive his student years, but Christian mythology was to remain a haunting motif behind his writing until the end.

He was sent first to Miss Ida Elsner's Academy, a Stillorgan kindergarten, and then commuted on the old 'Dublin Slow and Easy' to Earlsfort House prep school. After that he went to Portora Royal School in Ulster and Trinity College Dublin, first as pensioner and then as Foundation Scholar.

He had an active extra-curricular life, notably in the Modern Languages Society and in the chess, golf, and cricket clubs. He is, in fact, one of the very few great writers to have played in first-class cricket: *Wisden* records his participation in the Northamptonshire versus Dublin University match in July, 1927. His first visit to France, a cycle tour of the Loire chateaux, took place in the summer of 1926.

Samuel Beckett

In the BA finals examinations in Modern Literature (French and Italian) held at the end of 1927 he was placed first in the first class, winning, like Oscar Wilde before him, the distinction of a medal. He was chosen to represent Trinity in the regular scheme for exchanging *Lecteurs* with the École Normale Supérieure in Paris; he filled the two-term interval by accepting a temporary teaching post at Campbell College, Belfast, and then took up his French appointment in October, 1928.

Jean-Paul Sartre was a near-contemporary at the École Normale, but the two men had little contact. On the other hand, Beckett formed a close friendship with Alfred Peron, who had been *Lecteur* at Trinity and whose death later at the hands of the Germans affected him deeply.

The major event of these years was the meeting with James Joyce. In spite of the fact that the two Irishmen differed in background (Joyce's of course was Catholic and lower-class) as well as in temperament, Joyce having an exuberance his more sombre junior lacked, their acquaintance grew into friendship based on mutual admiration and respect. Although never his secretary, Beckett helped Joyce in many ways and was at first influenced by him. He was particularly impressed by Joyce's dedication to his art, and came to share it, although his path as a writer soon diverged from his friend's.

On the expiration of his Paris contract in 1930 he returned to Dublin to take up a post as assistant in French to Professor Thomas B. Rudmose-Brown, a cultivated and widely read man who had had a decisive role in forming his literary tastes as an undergraduate. When the short critical study of Proust (commissioned by Chatto and Windus on Richard Aldington's recommendation) appeared in 1931, Beckett seemed well launched on the academic career which his ability naturally destined him for, and which his father very much hoped he would make a success of.

But he soon found he had no vocation for, and little skill at, university teaching. The crisis came during the Christmas vacation of 1931 when he was visiting friends in Germany, and he telegraphed his resignation. Irresponsible as the act appeared at the time, it was decisive in cutting the umbilical cord with Trinity and the Dublin circles in which a lesser man might have been content to accept the pre-eminent place his talents granted him. Not that Beckett ever denied his Irishness, or lost his respect for those Irish painters and poets, such as Jack B. Yeats, Denis Devlin, and Thomas McGreevy, whose work he praised in print whenever he was given the opportunity.

The years that followed were lonely and unhappy, but they were not wasted. Beckett travelled widely in Europe, making himself an expert in the visual arts (he later used his connoisseurship to champion neglected artists like Henri Hayden and Bram van Velde), and in the major European languages and literatures. He even lived for a time in Chelsea, but Paris was the only place where he felt truly at home, and in 1937 he settled permanently in Montparnasse.

In the following year the novel *Murphy* was published in London. Although he tried subsequently to repudiate most of his early work, Beckett still considered this book the foundation stone of his oeuvre. Its publication was hardly a triumph, but a few were affected by it, notably Iris Murdoch, who read it as an undergraduate at Oxford, and who later paid homage to it in *Under the Net*.

Throughout these years Beckett eked out the annuity which his father had left him by doing literary translations, his skill in this art being highly valued by editors. The outbreak of war found him vacationing with his family in Dublin; he got back to France just in time, preferring, as he later put it, 'France in war to Ireland at peace'.

His Eire citizenship would have protected him from molestation in occupied Paris, but influenced by Peron and his own distaste for Nazism he chose to join the Resistance. When the group was betrayed to the Gestapo, Beckett narrowly missed arrest and eventually found his way to Roussillon (Vaucluse), where he wrote his last novel in English, *Watt*. He went into hiding, bravely taking on the job of *agent de liaison*, classifying information about German troop movements and translating it into English for transmission across the Channel; traces of this dangerous occupation survive in the anxiety his heroes feel about 'writing their report'.

The liberation of France enabled Beckett to continue his annual summer visits to his family (ended only by his mother's death). It was, incidentally, a very musical family, the harpsichordist John Beckett being a younger cousin. After a harrowing spell as interpreter and store-keeper at the Irish Red Cross hospital in Saint-Lô

(Normandy), Beckett resumed his Paris existence. There he wrote, almost in an inspired trance, those works in French (later self-translated into English) on which his reputation will permanently rest: the trilogy of novels *Molloy*, *Malone Dies*, and *The Unnamable*, and the play *Waiting for Godot*. Nothing he composed later, not even *Endgame* or the BBC play *All that Fall* (1957), nor the novel *How it is* (1961), was quite to equal these earlier works in profundity, originality, and imaginative power. In profundity, because the trilogy and *Waiting for Godot* probe the big questions of human existence: who are we and why are we here? In originality, because Beckett evolved a style which succeeds in balancing comedy and tragedy, the grotesque and the sublime; in fiction it made him the greatest experimenter since Joyce, in drama an innovator more radical even than Pirandello. In imaginative power, finally, because his finest work, like Kafka's, attains almost effortlessly the status of universal myth: the outcast heroes of his novels, like his two clowns waiting by a country roadside for Godot, the elusive benefactor who never arrives, are to the literature of the post-war period what Joseph K was to the world which emerged from Passchendaele and Verdun.

His masterpiece is probably *Molloy*, written in 1947, a complex novel in two parts about the psychological odyssey of a man sent to look for another and undergoing in the process a painful transformation into the social reject whom he seeks but fails to unearth anywhere except in the depths of his own soul.

In later years, while still continuing to write new drama and prose, Beckett took an increasing interest in the direction of his own plays. His productions of *Krapp's Last Tape* and *Waiting for Godot* at the Schiller-Theater in Berlin and of *Happy Days* at the Royal Court in London, were the first of many which offered fresh, authoritative readings of works which he simplified and stylized in ways other directors would not have dared.

He 'loosened up' in other ways, too: his prose became increasingly autobiographical and even nostalgic in tone. In *Company*, published in 1980, he probed with candour his own complex motivations in creating so many 'wearish' old men 'for company', and wrote affectionately about his childhood and especially of his father, walking the hills armed with a packet of his favourite sandwiches and a flask of Scotch whisky as he waited for Mary Beckett's protracted labour to end and young Samuel to be born.

The Paris creation of *Godot* by Roger Blin in January, 1953, made Beckett world famous. The influence he exerted over the theatre, in terms both of writing and direction, was particularly important. Figures as pre-eminent as Harold Pinter and Peter Hall (director of the first British *Godot* in 1955) owe him an immense debt.

But, though universally admired and much written about (Beckett studies quickly became an academic growth industry), he accepted surprisingly few honours and then (the 1969 Nobel Prize especially) only with reluctance. A modest and unassuming man, he was courteous and generous with people he trusted and intransigent only about standards of production and translation of his writings. He refused steadfastly to don the mantle of the 'great man of letters' that he undoubtedly was, and, at least as far as the press was concerned, remained a recluse to the end, because in his view literature was too serious a matter to be trifled with: he felt it grotesque to receive personal attention for giving expression to what he called 'the issueless predicament of existence'. He wondered in his finest poem:

'Who may tell the tale
of the old man?
weigh absence in a scale?
mete want with a span?
the sum assess
of the world's woes?
nothingness
in words enclose?'

The answer is that Samuel Beckett did, with a wit, a humility, and a compassion which will ensure his immortality.

He married Suzanne Dumesnil, a musician and teacher; they had no children. She died earlier this year.

MARGOT FONTEYN

21 FEBRUARY 1991

MARGOT FONTEYN was one of the great dancers not just of her own time but of all time; her name will live as surely in the history of ballet as those of Taglioni and Pavlova.

She was also one of the rare artists whose names mean as much to the ordinary man and woman as to the devotees of their own particular art. Many dancers have excelled her in virtuosity or in the theatrical intensity they brought to dramatic roles. Fonteyn's special gift was for grasping completely the intention and balance of the dance and the music and bringing them to life for the audience. She never lost the enthusiasm which marked her dancing from childhood, and the ability to communicate her own enjoyment was perhaps the supreme secret of her art.

During the course of an extraordinarily long career she brought that gift to ever wider audiences in many parts of the world where she performed on stage; millions more saw her on television or in films. Consequently, even more than Anna Pavlova in the early years of this century, Fonteyn awakened a love of dance in untold thousands of spectators.

She was born Margaret Hookham, the child of an English father and a mother half Irish, half Brazilian. She claimed to have inherited her enthusiasm and response to rhythm and music from her mother; and from her father the tenacity and perfectionism to put those qualities to use. From the age of four she attended dancing classes with a local teacher, and continued them in various places abroad where her father's work as an engineer took the family. The liveliness of character dancing attracted her more than the pure classicism which was later to bring her fame.

It was not until she saw Alicia Markova dance *Les Sylphides* during a visit home in 1931 that Peggy Hookham became really ambitious to be a dancer herself. Her father was then working in China and the child was lucky in finding an exceptionally gifted teacher, George Goncharov, in Shanghai. After two years with him she returned to England and studied with Seraphine Astafieva (Markova's teacher) before joining the Vic-Wells Ballet School in 1934. Within a few weeks she was performing with the Vic-Wells Ballet, and before the year was out she had her first solo role as the child in Ninette de Valois's *The Haunted Ballroom*, under an interim version of her stage name, Margot Fontes.

Before her sixteenth birthday Frederick Ashton gave Fonteyn the leading part in a new production of *Rio Grande*, and when Markova left the company soon afterwards, Fonteyn was one of the dancers who shared the ballerina's roles among them. It did not take long for her to emerge as the front runner, and by the time she was 20 Fonteyn had danced the lead in three of the great classics, *Giselle*, *Swan Lake*, and *The Sleeping Beauty*, besides creating roles in a series of ballets by Ashton: *Le Baiser de la fée*, *Apparitions*, *Nocturne*, *Les Patineurs*, *A Wedding Bouquet*, and *Horoscope*.

Fonteyn was fortunate in the colleagues under whose professional influence she found herself at this time. De Valois, directing the young company, had a far-sighted grasp of strategy in repertoire and casting. Ashton, choosing Fonteyn as his new muse in the flush of his youthful creative energy, developed her interpretative gifts and also advised her on how to dress and behave off stage. She had Robert Helpmann as her most frequent partner, a man with a keen theatrical flair, and the company's music director, Constant Lambert, a man of wide culture, took her particularly under his wing.

The outbreak of war in 1939 brought a more urgent tempo to the company's work. Instead of only two or three performances a week, they began dancing nightly, with matinees besides, to provide entertainment for war workers and troops on leave; long gruelling tours were undertaken between short London seasons. The company was in Holland at the time of the German invasion and escaped with nothing more than what the dancers stood up in. Fonteyn by now was the company's undisputed ballerina, with a consequent demand for her to appear as often as possible. And there were still new roles to add, most notably two by Ashton which extended her range with the passion of *Dante Sonata* and the glitter of *The Wanderer*.

This experience must have helped develop the stamina that made her later career possible, but at the time it did more to consolidate her talent than to advance her artistry. The performances she gave in *The Sleeping Beauty* when the ballet moved to Covent Garden in 1946 seemed impressive at the time but would be only promising by today's standards. Luckily Ashton created in *Symphonic Variations* a work that showed Fonteyn's lyrical gifts to supreme advantage.

A turning point in her career came in 1948 when she went as guest artist to Paris to create the role of Agathe, the cat-woman, in Roland Petit's *Les Demoiselles de la Nuit*. The frank admiration of this glamorous young choreographer, and being treated as a star, seemed to add a new assurance and crispness to everything she did on returning to London. The acclaim she received in New York the next year, opening the Sadler's Wells Ballet's first season there with *The Sleeping Beauty*, completed the transformation into a ballerina of international quality.

Before the American tour, an injury during the first night of Ashton's *Don Juan* had kept her from the stage for several months and prevented her from dancing the premiere of his first three-act ballet, *Cinderella*. When she took over the role later, however, she made it peculiarly her own, showing new qualities of humour and romance.

Fonteyn's career was subsequently interrupted more than once by serious injury or illness, setbacks that might have precipitated early retirement in other dancers. Each time, however, she returned apparently stronger than before, and went on dancing long past the age when a dancer's powers usually decline. In Fonteyn's case the physical loss was compensated by continually developing expressiveness and artistic maturity. The initial impetus to extending her career came, however, when, in her early forties, she first danced with Rudolf Nureyev in 1962. He was, as she remarked, young enough to be her son, but there was such immediate rapport between them, such a chemistry between them on stage, and such unanimity of purpose in their preparation that they became a partnership of uniquely satisfying quality. Both learned much from the other, enriching their performances with other partners as well as their joint appearances.

Fonteyn's long career on stage was made easier because her performances had never depended primarily on virtuosity, although in fact her technique was stronger than was often said. It was she who introduced the long sustained balances now expected of Aurora in the *Rose Adagio*; and when younger dancers took over some of her created roles they revealed unexpected difficulties, probably for lack of her gift of phrasing steps to the music. It can be said that Fonteyn never lacked the technique needed for any role she was cast in.

These covered a wide range. Among the many leading parts created for her with the Royal Ballet were *Scènes de ballet, Daphnis and Chloë, Tiresias, Sylvia, Homage to the Queen, La Feri, Birthday Offering*, and *Marguerite and Armand*, all by Ashton; de Valois's *Don Quixote*, Helpmann's *Hamlet*, Petit's *Paradise Lost*, and *Pelléas et Mélisande*. As guest elsewhere, John Cranko created *Poème de l'extase* for her in Stuttgart, Martha Graham mounted *Lucifer* for Nureyev and her, and Peter Darrell presented her as a Beardsley seductress in *Scarlet Pastorale* with the Scottish Ballet.

She was (against the choreographer's wish but at the insistence of the Royal Ballet's American impresario Sol Hurok) the first Juliet in Kenneth MacMillan's production, and danced also in revivals of Massine's *Three Cornered Hat* with the choreographer, Balanchine's *Ballet Imperial* and *Night Shadow*, Fokine's *Firebird* and *Petrushka*, and Limon's *The Moor's Pavane* among others, also Nureyev's productions of the *Corsair pas de deux, La Bayadère, Raymonda*, and the Grand Pas from *Paquita*.

With the Royal Ballet, Fonteyn occupied a position of complete supremacy. It has sometimes been said that her presence held back the advancement of other dancers, but there was never any among her contemporaries or juniors to equal her. By 1959 the demand for seats when she appeared was such that special prices were charged, and in that same year she began to be billed as a guest artist so that she should be free to accept more of the engagements she was offered all over the world. Nevertheless the Royal Ballet remained her base until after Ashton's retirement in 1970, although she also danced with more than 30 other companies and specially assembled groups.

She continued dancing until after her sixtieth birthday, which was marked by Covent Garden with a special gala including a *Salut d'amour* by Ashton, which they danced together. Even after that she took on a new role as the leading nymph in Nijinsky's *L'Après-midi d'un faune* during Nureyev's 1979 summer season, and was persuaded by him to dance also two final performances of *Le Spectre de la Rose*. Occasionally thereafter she appeared on special occasions but only in roles that required no dancing.

In 1955 Fonteyn married Dr Roberto de Arias, a sweetheart of her girlhood who had meanwhile married and had a family before re-entering her life. Immediately after their wedding he was appointed Panamanian ambassador to the Court of St James's. Fonteyn managed to combine the duties of an ambassador's wife with her already demanding career, and when her husband fell from political favour she supported his attempts to regain power in his own country. This led at one point to her arrest. She also found herself in police custody once after attending a party in the hippie district of Los Angeles. The dignity with which she endured such incidents showed one aspect of her character. Another was revealed by the devotion with which she personally nursed her husband for 25 years until his death after he had been shot and crippled by an associate with a personal grudge.

Two careers, as ballerina and as politician's wife, would have been enough for most women, but Fonteyn also became in 1954 president of the Royal Academy of Dancing and committed herself wholeheartedly to its wellbeing.

In later years, Fonteyn developed a great interest in her husband's farm in Panama, and she continued to live there even after his death with few creature comforts because she had spent most of her money on caring for her husband and then incurred considerable costs having treatment in Texas when she developed cancer.

In spite of her illness she undertook some teaching and coaching, and also visited England each year for the Assembly of the RAD and for the degree ceremony at Durham University, which had elected her chancellor. She wrote and introduced a six-part television series *The Magic of Dance*. This was also the subject of one of several books she wrote; they included an autobiography, a study of Pavlova, and an account of *A Dancer's World*.

Fonteyn was created CBE in 1951 and DBE in 1956. She had honorary degrees from many universities and the Order of the Finnish Lion. A greater tribute however was the affection she inspired all over the world. The purity and musicality of her work won admiration; its liveliness and dedication inspired much warmer and deeper feelings, manifested in a special tribute performance at Covent Garden last May for which Nureyev danced and Placido Domingo sang.

Dame Margot Fonteyn, the ballerina, died February 21, 1991, in Panama City aged 71. She was born at Reigate, Surrey, on May 18, 1919.

* * *

PEGGY ASHCROFT

14 JUNE 1991

SINCE THE DEATH of Edith Evans, Peggy Ashcroft had held the undisputed place of first lady of the English stage. Her performances were among the Shakespearean peaks of the past 60 years, but she is no less vividly remembered for her work in the modern repertory and for the television and film roles that won her a huge audience during her final decade. She also had a larger vision of the theatre than can be conveyed by summarizing her acting career.

From her girlhood reading of Stanislavsky she was, from the start, an actress in search of a company. She briefly glimpsed her goal during the 1930s and finally achieved it after the war with the foundation of the English Stage Company, the Royal Shakespeare Company, and the National Theatre. To each she gave whole-hearted support at a crucial time in its fortunes. What they gained from her was not only the services of a great classical star but a moral force which was as visible in her performances as it was in her personal life. She was seen as an embodiment of British integrity, a factor that was turned against her by such critics as James Agate and Kenneth Tynan who persisted in regarding her as a class-bound home counties lady who had no business to be essaying Cleopatra or the Duchess of Malfi. In fact these parts were fully within her range and if one point emerges from the roll-call of her most successful performances it is that there was no such thing as a typical Ashcroft role.

What did set her apart from actors who simply disappear into whatever they are playing was the presence of a central moral intelligence authorizing whatever imaginative leap the character demanded. When she became the first establishment actress to play Brecht, or when she first hurled a four-letter word at a West End audience, she left a landmark behind. To recount her life is to tell the story of the English theatrical renaissance.

Edith Margaret Emily Ashcroft was born in Croydon, the second child of a land-agent father and a Danish-German mother herself an amateur actress who had taken lessons from the poetic speech pioneer Elsie Fogerty, at whose Central School of Speech and Drama the 16-year-old Peggy Ashcroft enrolled on leaving Woodford School. 'I learned very little about acting there,' she later declared, being as resistant as her fellow student Laurence Olivier to the school's stress on the Voice Beautiful. Her theatrical education began with her reading of Stanislavsky's *My Life in Art* and her discovery of his émigré compatriot Theodore Komisarjevsky who was then revolutionizing the English stage from his tiny theatre in Barnes. She made her professional debut in 1926, playing opposite Ralph Richardson in a Birmingham Repertory revival of Barrie's *Dear Brutus*, after which except for illness or personal choice she was seldom out of work.

In the early years, like any newcomer, she took what was going, though even then she was more at home in London's adventurous little theatres than in the commercial machine. Critics of the time were struck by her freedom from any kind of stage trickery and by the transparent honesty which remained one of her sovereign qualities.

One conspicuous early event was her 1930 performance of Desdemona to Paul Robeson's Othello, which also marked her political awakening (a star in the Savoy Theatre, Robeson was unwelcome upstairs in the hotel). The turning point came not on the professional stage but in the 1932 OUDS production of *Romeo and Juliet*, which brought her into contact with undergraduate George Devine and his guest director, John Gielgud, her two closest allies over the next 25 years.

The alliance was delayed by her marriage to Komisarjevsky and a season with the Old Vic where she piled up a succession of Shakespearean leads at breakneck speed under the direction of Harcourt Williams. By then a member of the unofficial 'family' that grew up in the Motleys' Studio (Gielgud's designers), hatching theatrical revolution over endless cups of tea, she came into her own as Gielgud's leading actress when he embarked on the untried adventure of setting up a classical company in the West End.

Beginning as Juliet in the legendary 1935 New Theatre production, she returned for Gielgud's subsequent seasons at the Queen's and the Haymarket, playing Nina in Komisarjevsky's *The Seagull*, Irina in Michel Saint-Denis's *Three Sisters*, and the *Duchess of Malfi* (then a controversial novelty) for George Rylands: productions that left an indelible mark on theatrical memory. True to her company loyalties, she also joined in Saint-Denis's ill-fated 1938 Phoenix season before the 'family' was dispersed by the war.

Had Gielgud's companies not kept breaking up, she would gladly have stayed inside them. As it was, she rebuilt her career at the Stratford Memorial Theatre (under Anthony Quayle) and in the West End. She often undertook parts with severe misgivings but then turned them to triumph: as with the alcoholic wife in Robert Morley's *Edward, My Son*, the victim-turned-avenger in *The Heiress*, and (originally her prime *bête noire*) the suicidal Hester Collyer in Rattigan's *The Deep Blue Sea*.

The pattern of her career underwent its second great change in the 1950s with the dawning of the age of subsidy. First she resumed her alliance with Devine in the 1954 *Hedda Gabler* and when Devine launched the English Stage Company two years later, Ashcroft at the height of her commercial success in Enid Bagnold's *The Chalk Garden* forsook the Haymarket for the wilderness of Sloane Square to double as Shen Te/Shui Ta in his production of Brecht's *The Good Woman of Setzuan*. The ESC, however, did not maintain a permanent troupe so, although she subsequently joined Devine in revivals of Chekhov and Ibsen, her main allegiance went to Peter Hall's newly-formed Royal Shakespeare Company. She began by reclaiming two shrews, Kate and Paulina in *A War of the Roses*, in which (then in her late fifties) she began as a young girl and aged into a demonic septuagenarian in *Richard III*. This was a woman, Philip Hope-Wallace wrote, 'kept alive by sheer passion of inner hate'. With Hall, she also became an incomparable advocate of Pinter, Albee, and (when Hall moved on to the National Theatre) Beckett. Just as she had championed the young Peter Hall at the start of the RSC, so she supported his younger successor, Trevor Nunn, with whom she achieved her crowning stage performance as the Countess of Rousillon in the 1981 *All's Well That Ends Well*, in which she lent something Chekhovian to Shakespearean comedy.

Nunn once made the point that actors achieve greatness only in old age when 'life has tested them and they've come through'. This was clearly true of Ashcroft, both on stage and in her final creative breakthrough on film.

Three times married, CND supporter, and veteran campaigner against social injustice (so much so that when she was created DBE in 1956 Hugh Beaumont nicknamed her 'the Red Dame'), she was not short of living experience. In her youth an epitome of the intelligent ingénue, in middle-age a radical actress exploring the desperation of women of violently contrasted classes and cultures, she finally took on a quality in which acting became wisdom.

Nunn again: 'You simply lose yourself in the largeness of her spirit.' In her film and television work she was able to take the spectator straight to the heart of character. One of her most remarkable small screen roles was Barbie Batchelor in Paul Scott's *The Jewel in the Crown* (1984), where she showed the development of character from robust decency to ferocious despair with minimal reliance on external effects. This performance won her a BAFTA award. She had acted in films from *The Wandering Jew* of 1933 and had a role in Hitchcock's *The Thirty-Nine Steps* of 1935. But she picked her film parts. She had a success as the Mother Superior in *The Nun's Story* (1958) and won an Oscar as the best supporting actress for her portrayal of Mrs Moore in David Lean's film version of E. M. Forster's *A Passage to India* (1984). At 81, in 1989, she shared the best actress award, the Coppa Volpi Prize, with Geraldine James at the Venice Film Festival for her performance in Sir Peter Hall's film *She's Been Away*. It was a remarkable achievement for an actress who had made her debut 60 years before. Her most recent public appearance was at the Olivier Awards in London in April when she was given a special award to mark her life's service to the theatre.

Her work was always hard to describe. She herself called it a process of arriving at psychological truth by means of tonal accuracy. Externally it was made up of innumerable small details of gesture and facial expression; but what she was clearly mattered more than what she did, with the result that any attempt to express it in words was liable to turn into gush.

Colleagues habitually summed her up by contrasts: 'English containment and wild passion', 'fearlessness and vulnerability', 'ferocity and tenderness'. Anthony Quayle put it more simply: 'She's a crusader, she's *Pilgrim's Progress* to the end.'

Besides Komisarjevsky, she was married to Sir Rupert Hart-Davis and to Jeremy Hutchinson (now Lord Hutchinson of Lullington), by whom she leaves a son and a daughter.

Dame Peggy Ashcroft, DBE, actress, died June 14, 1991,
aged 83. She was born on December 22, 1907.

MILES DAVIS

MILES DAVIS was an enigmatic and restless artist who continually re-shaped his style and his career – if not his individual sound – over four decades. Most of the greatest jazz musicians have developed one distinctive approach; Davis fashioned three or four including a controversial blend of jazz-rock. Along the way he cultivated a brooding persona which earned him the sobriquet 'Prince of Darkness'. The image was compounded by the sound of his voice, an eerie whisper which he acquired in the late 1950s after trying to shout while recovering from an operation on his vocal cords. Whether or not his rock-influenced recordings will endure, he secured his place in history with a series of hugely influential albums in the 1950s and early 1960s.

Miles Dewey Davis III was born in Alton, Illinois, and raised in East St Louis, about 25 miles south along the Mississippi. Unlike most black musicians of his generation, Davis came from a well-to-do family. His grandfather had been a book-keeper and land-owner in Arkansas, his father an affluent dentist who, after moving to Illinois, purchased a 200-acre ranch. Given his first trumpet for his thirteenth birthday, Davis received private tuition and played in his high school band. In 1944 he enrolled at the Juilliard School in New York. Studying by day, he spent the evenings in the jazz venues of 52nd Street, where Charlie Parker and his circle were setting out the rudiments of bebop.

Within months Davis had abandoned his studies and entered the studios as a member of Parker's quintet. The results show that he was no virtuoso. The rapid-fire trumpet cadenza which opens 'Koko', for instance, had to be played by Dizzy Gillespie, who had been 'sitting in' on the piano. However, Davis was later to turn his technical limitations to his own advantage; in contrast to the ultimately self-defeating pyrotechnics of the beboppers, he evolved a smoother, burnished sound rooted in the middle register.

The first real blossoming of his own talents took place in 1948, after he had set out to form his own band. Mixing with a circle of musicians who met in the flat of the arranger Gil Evans, Davis led a nonet which featured the saxophonists Gerry Mulligan and Lee Konitz. With its unorthodox instrumentation, including French horn and tuba, the group was too sophisticated for most audiences, and was a commercial flop. However Capitol Records were persuaded to stage recording sessions in 1949 and 1950. Years later the tracks were released on an album with the apt title *The Birth of the Cool*.

Davis was in no position to capitalize on his achievement. Once exceptionally clean-living, he had fallen into heroin addiction. At one point he scraped together money for drugs by pimping. It was not until 1954 that he returned to full health. The following year saw a string of outstanding tracks for the Prestige label, among them 'Walkin'' and 'Blue 'n' Boogie'. Perhaps the best of all came on a Christmas Eve session with a line-up featuring the eccentric pianist Thelonious Monk and the vibraphonist Milt Jackson. Davis's languid improvisations on 'Bag's Groove' and 'Bemsha Swing' made telling use of space and silence. During this period he also introduced the metallic harmon mute which, placed close to the microphone, produced the wistful tone that was to become his trademark.

In 1955 he formed his first great quintet, with John Coltrane (tenor saxophone), Red Garland (piano), Paul Chambers (bass), and Philly Joe Jones (drums). The group's finest recordings were made in unusual circumstances. Though Davis had been offered a lucrative contract with Columbia, he was under an obligation to make four more albums for Prestige. He solved the problem by recording all the required material in the space of just two sessions. A mixture of Broadway tunes and bop and blues themes, the music was released on four exceptional albums: *Cookin'*, *Relaxin'*, *Workin'*, and *Steamin'*. His relationship with CBS was to last for 30 years. Highlights included the three ambitious orchestral collaborations with Gil Evans, *Miles Ahead*, *Porgy and Bess*, and *Sketches of Spain*.

In 1959 came his masterpiece, *Kind of Blue*, a set based partly on modal patterns which freed the musicians from the constraints of the conventional song structure. Davis's terse solos were balanced against the effusive tenor saxophone of Coltrane, the bluesier alto of Julian 'Cannonball' Adderley and the impressionistic chords of the pianist Bill Evans. While not the first album to explore modes, it did much to popularize the concept.

By this time magazine features were portraying Davis as a high-earning, debonair man-about-town, complete with expensively appointed home and Ferrari sports car. For all his wealth, he was not free from racial pressures. In the summer of 1959 he was savagely beaten by two New York policemen following an altercation outside the Birdland jazz club. After a night in jail, he was later cleared of all charges against him. The experience left a residue of bitterness.

Another blow came with Coltrane's departure from the quintet. Davis, however, was in scintillating form on his first ever live album, taped in 1961 in the unglamorous setting of the Blackhawk club in San Francisco. Often overlooked in favour of later recordings at Carnegie Hall and the Lincoln Center, the Blackhawk double album contains Davis's most expressive live work.

The rest of the sixties found him searching for a new direction. With the advent of Free Form jazz and, above all, the rise of the rock superstars, he was being edged out of the limelight. Though he had recruited promising young players such as

Miles Davis in concert at the Apollo Theatre, Manchester, 1989.

Herbie Hancock, his concerts were locked into ever more complex chromatic forms, with the old standards being played over and over at a frenetic tempo. The studio albums also seemed to lose the balance between abstraction and emotion. Though these were performances of enormous technical assurance, they seemed almost a private dialogue between the musicians.

By 1968 Davis's audience was beginning to dwindle. His response was to tackle the rock movement head on. There were already hints of the change on *Miles in the Sky*, *Filles de Kilimanjaro*, and the ethereal *In a Silent Way* (arguably his last classic album).

With the release of *Bitches Brew* in 1970, Davis went all the way in an extravagant cocktail of jazz psychedelia. The venture had the desired effect: Davis was back in fashion and attracting a huge new audience and increased royalties. Soon he was appearing at rock stadia on the same bill as the likes of Neil Young and Steve Miller. The move ultimately proved a creative dead-end, apart from isolated flashes of excitement on *Live-Evil* and the soundtrack to the boxing documentary *Jack Johnson*.

While Davis had acquired cult status amongst the young and a suitably flamboyant wardrobe, the distinctive sound of his trumpet was soon submerged by the heavy rock ostinati of his musicians, who stayed rooted to one chord for minutes on end. With the release of the would-be street music of *On the Corner* in 1973 (perhaps the most monotonous album ever to bear his name), he was filtering his solos through an electronic 'wah-wah' pedal. The world's greatest trumpeter now sounded like a middling guitarist playing on an inadequate PA system. On stage he began to appear increasingly remote and apathetic. His health had been poor, and in 1972 he had suffered fractures after crashing his Lamborghini.

In 1975, after further bouts of serious illness, he withdrew into what turned out to be a five-year retirement. Speculation about his activities intensified: the truth, as later depicted in his autobiography, was that he descended into a squalid, semi-reclusive existence dominated by cocaine, heroin, and alcohol.

After repeated rumours of a comeback, he finally returned, in 1981, with *The Man with the Horn*, a moderate amalgam of jazz and pop. Still looking extremely frail, Davis resumed touring, winning a well-deserved standing ovation in London in 1983. There were hopes that he was about to embark on a new phase of creativity. *Decoy*, released in 1984, contained some of his strongest playing for 20 years. But the next album, *You're Under Arrest*, set the pattern for the rest of the decade, with Davis content to mark time by playing brief phrases on undemanding pop themes. The Cyndi Lauper hit 'Time After Time' hardly stood comparison with 'My Funny Valentine'. The standard of his sidemen also declined; musicians of the calibre of the guitarist John Scofield were replaced by anonymous apprentices.

Davis, meanwhile, masked his fluctuations in tone and pitch by making ever-increasing use of his mute. By the time he released *Tutu* in 1986 he had left Columbia for WEA. Assiduously crafted by the producer and multi-instrumentalist Marcus Miller, the synthesizer-based tunes required the minimum of involvement by Davis, who had only to add his trumpet solos over the pre-recorded tracks. A similar process was used on the subsequent albums *Siesta* and *Amandla*.

Uninterested in celebrating the past, Davis preferred to discuss his enthusiasm for Prince and Michael Jackson. When not touring he devoted much of his time to drawing and painting; his abstract sketches adorned the sleeves of a number of his records. In 1986 he made an appearance on the TV detective series *Miami Vice*, playing a pimp.

1989 saw the appearance of his long-awaited memoirs, *Miles: the Autobiography*. It was marked by a monotonous flow of profanities and a tendency to settle scores with old enemies including former wives but it was also an unflinching self-portrait which emphasized Davis's single-minded pursuit of his craft.

'To be a great musician,' he wrote, 'you've got to always be open to what's new, what's happening at the moment. You have to be able to absorb it if you're going to continue to grow and communicate your music.' In his continual search for something new, Davis was always alive to young talent in jazz, hiring Herbie Hancock when the keyboard player was 23 and the drummer Tony Williams as an 18-year-old. Among the experimentalist musicians he used were Chick Corea, Joe Zawinul, Dave Holland, John McLaughlin, Keith Jarrett, Airto Moreira, Billy Cobham, and Jack de Johnette.

His irascible temper and seeming indifference to audiences in the early years made Miles Davis a controversial figure, while his refusal to rest upon his laurels won him new admirers as it alienated others. More importantly, his elegant and lyrical musicality added anger, pain, and deep sadness to the emotional lexicon of jazz, ensuring that his stature as an innovative influence on jazz trumpet playing alongside Louis Armstrong, Bix Beiderbecke, and Dizzie Gillespie is unquestioned.

He was married at least three times, to dancer Frances Taylor, singer Betty Mabry, and actress Cicely Tyson. He is survived by a daughter and three sons.

Miles Davis, jazz trumpeter, bandleader, and composer,
died of pneumonia and a stroke in Santa Monica,
California, on September 28, 1991, aged 65.
He was born on May 25, 1926.

ROBERT MAXWELL

5 NOVEMBER 1991

ROBERT MAXWELL was one of the most turbulent and controversial entrepreneurs of his day. He never owned a pair of shoes until he was seven. When he died he owned newspapers, magazines, printing works, private jets, helicopters, and the 190-ft yacht, *Lady Ghislaine*, from which he disappeared. He had owned two football clubs, Derby County and Oxford United, and just failed to own another, Tottenham Hotspur. Though there were emerging doubts about the fragility of his enterprises in view of the great debts he had accumulated, there was no doubt about the scale of his success. A socialist who publicly admired Mrs Thatcher, he was often a guest at Downing Street as well as being the host at the most expensive parties of Labour party conferences.

In eastern Europe, where he was born in extremely poor circumstances to an Orthodox Jewish family in what was once Czechoslovakia and then Hungary, he was regarded as one of the most powerful Englishmen of his time. The neo-Stalinist leaders, from Zhivkov to Honecker, welcomed him and he published their books at inordinate and flattering length. Later, as the new men took over, he claimed to be the trusted adviser of Gorbachev. A recent article in *Playboy* described him as one of the biggest 'lords of the global village, that elite handful of individuals who control most of the world's media'.

Maxwell always wanted to be a media baron. He failed to buy the *News of the World* and later the old *Sun*. In both cases he lost to Rupert Murdoch. Later he tried unsuccessfully for the London *Evening Standard*, *The Observer*, and *The Times*. But his chance came at last in July 1984 when Reed International accepted his bid for the Mirror Group after saying that it would not be sold to a single bidder. On the night of the deal, Maxwell strode into the Mirror building after being warned that his arrival would start a strike by journalists or printers or both. 'If one copy is lost tonight I shall close the paper,' he announced. Not a copy was lost. And he went on as he began, dominating executives, interfering with specialists, rewriting copy. Joe Haines, the former Wilson press secretary who had told a union meeting that he would lead a walk-out if Maxwell arrived, became his leader-writer and biographer. Editors were changed, numbers of journalists and print workers were slimmed down, colour was introduced with remarkable success. Maxwell became one of the leading public figures of the 1980s.

His latter years were consumed by his desire to maintain control of his business interests until two of his sons, Ian and Kevin, were old enough to succeed him. But his attempts to establish himself beyond the narrow but highly profitable sector of scientific publishing were dogged by controversy.

Ian Robert Maxwell was the last of several names acquired during his wartime career. The facts of his early life are obscure but it appears that when he was born, in Slatinske Doly, a village in the Carpathian mountains on the Czech-Romanian border, he was named Abraham Lajbi Hoch. Those forenames were unacceptable to the Czech authorities and he was renamed Jan Ludvik. As the Nazis advanced eastward in 1939 he was sent to Budapest to evade anti-semitic restrictions. He arrived in France as part of the Czech Legion early the following year, sailing to Liverpool a few months later.

Arriving there with, as he was later to say: 'a rifle in my hand and a desire to fight the Germans', in 1941 he volunteered for the Pioneer Corps. He claimed to have learned English in six weeks, adding to the several other languages he had collected at the European crossroads where he grew up. Throughout his life he demonstrated a remarkable fluency in languages, and this was a considerable asset in his international business dealings.

After two years he was accepted as a private into the North Staffordshire Regiment and his command of languages earned him recruitment to the battalion's intelligence section. His Czech name was changed to Leslie du Maurier, after the cigarette brand. Once he landed in France after D-Day, du Maurier's name was rapidly changed to Jones and finally became Maxwell. Equally quickly, he was promoted to second lieutenant and met Elisabeth Meynard, his future wife, in Paris. Maxwell was transferred to the Queen's Royal Regiment (West Surrey), stationed in Brussels. On January 29, 1945, he led his platoon against a German defensive position, for which he was awarded the Military Cross. The medal was pinned on his chest by Montgomery and he married Elisabeth in Paris on March 15.

In the immediate aftermath of war, Maxwell was employed interrogating Germans. In what became a turning point in his career, he was then appointed to the Public Relations and Information Services Control in Berlin, the branch of the Allied Control Commission responsible for licensing films, plays, books, and newspapers. Maxwell's duties, which covered arranging paper supplies, editing, and distribution, gave him a taste for publishing which was the foundation of his subsequent business empire. He was by this time a captain and had admitted to colleagues an ambition to become a millionaire.

In August 1945 the US dropped atom bombs on Japan, events which Maxwell subsequently claimed demonstrated to him the power of scientific knowledge, which he realized he could tap by publishing that knowledge. The next month a fellow Czech, Arnos Lobl, went to London and formed a £100 company called Low-Bell, an import–export company in which Maxwell took a controlling interest shortly before he resigned from the Control Commission in March 1947. Once

established in London, he began distributing German newspapers to German pris-
oners-of-war in Britain, as well as laying hands on any goods in short supply to
resell them abroad.

In October 1947 Maxwell returned to Berlin to renew an acquaintance he had
formed with Ferdinand Springer, a scientific publisher to whom he had supplied
paper in his army days. He became Springer's foreign agent, making his own fortune and reviving that of the German. The bureaucratic controls applied by the
Allies to exports of publications from Germany were tailor-made for Maxwell to
exploit. Springer had a British company, jointly owned with Butterworth, the UK
publisher. When the arrangements with Maxwell dissolved in acrimony in 1951,
Maxwell borrowed from the banks to buy the company for £13,000. Renamed Pergamon Press, it was to become his master company.

At this stage he was keen to ingratiate himself with the British book-publishing
establishment. So he agreed to take a headache off their hands, a loss-making
wholesaler called Simpkin Marshall. But within four years it failed, owing £556,000,
and the Official Receiver criticized the directors including Maxwell for not closing
it sooner. Maxwell was gaining a reputation as a brash, arrogant showman, the
obverse of the typically restrained 1950s British publisher. But meanwhile he was
developing a powerful strategy for Pergamon. He realized that he could create
narrow but unshakable monopolies by launching scientific journals on precisely
defined topics which would be the accepted medium for the experts in that
discipline.

While academics would compete to write in the journals for no payment, or
even pay for the privilege, universities and science-based companies would pay a
high premium for the journals by advance subscription. Newcomers would have to
buy back-numbers from Pergamon at updated prices.

By 1964 Pergamon was publishing 600 book titles a year and 70 journals. It was
floated on the Stock Exchange with a value of over £4 million. That year Maxwell
was also elected Labour MP for Buckingham. He presented himself as a bridge
between business and socialism, a theme that fitted well with Harold Wilson's
commitment to a 'white-hot technological revolution'.

But this was to be Maxwell's zenith for the next 17 years. In 1968 he was rebuffed
by shareholders in the *News of the World* in a takeover bid where he was defeated,
not for the last time, by Rupert Murdoch. The newspaper's editor, Stafford Somer-
field, ran a notorious editorial comparing Maxwell's foreign origins unfavourably
with the *News of the World* which, he wrote, 'I know is as British as roast beef and
Yorkshire pudding'. But that defeat was a trifle set against the following year's
disastrous attempt to merge Pergamon with Leasco, an American computer company headed by the equally sharp-witted and brash fellow Jew, Saul Steinberg.
The idea was that Pergamon's scientific database could be loaded into Leasco's

Robert Maxwell at home, 1964.

computers. But while Leasco's accountants were having difficulty obtaining information from Maxwell, it emerged that two of Maxwell's family trusts had been selling Pergamon shares bought by Leasco at inflated prices. Then Leasco discovered that a large proportion of Pergamon's recent profits were derived from dealings with private Maxwell companies, thus casting doubt on their true value. Leasco withdrew its £25 million bid, but by then the American firm held 38 per cent of Pergamon's shares. Leasco banded together with institutional investors to vote Maxwell off the board, which did not please the academics who wrote for Pergamon's journals. Profits suffered accordingly.

The Department of Trade and Industry ordered an investigation into Pergamon in which the inspectors stated: 'We regret having to conclude that, notwithstanding Mr Maxwell's acknowledged abilities and energy, he is not in our opinion a person who can be relied on to exercise proper stewardship of a publicly quoted company.'

It was a verdict which was to dog Maxwell for the rest of his life, and would have broken a lesser man. He attempted to have the DTI report set aside by the courts. Although Lord Denning decided that the inspectors had behaved fairly, the rules were modified to give those criticized in such reports the explicit right of reply.

In 1970 Maxwell lost his parliamentary seat. Although he contested Buckingham twice more in 1974, he never again became an MP. But 1974 was also the year when he regained control of Pergamon, taking it private through an offer of 12p a share against Leasco's 185p bid six years previously. By that time Leasco and the institutional investors were glad to be rid of what they regarded as a troublesome investment. For Maxwell, of course, it was the return of his commercial base. He kept out of the spotlight and cultivated relationships with the City of London.

In 1980 National Westminster Bank turned to Maxwell to rescue the country's leading printing concern, British Printing Corporation, from financial difficulties. Notwithstanding the fact that it was a publicly quoted company, he gained control and turned the business round in the teeth of union opposition. The DTI slur was set aside, although not forgotten. In 1984, during an unsuccessful takeover bid for John Waddington, it emerged that control of Maxwell's business interests had been vested in Pergamon Holding Foundation, a trust incorporated in Liechtenstein. Although Maxwell claimed that the trust gave substantial sums to charity, the device had tax advantages and was understood to cede ultimate ownership to members of his family resident overseas.

Under Maxwell, BPC was soon strong enough to buy the Odhams printing operation from Reed International. In 1984 Reed decided to float Mirror Group Newspapers on the stock market, but Maxwell pre-empted that with a private offer of £80 million which Reed accepted. The Holborn head office was believed to be worth that much alone. He had fulfilled his dream of owning a national newspaper. Indeed, in addition to the *Daily Mirror, Sunday Mirror,* and *The People,* in 1987 he attempted to launch a 24-hour paper, *The London Daily News,* but had to close it within five months in the face of a relentless defensive campaign by Associated Newspapers, the owners of the *Evening Standard.*

Through BPC, renamed Maxwell Communication Corporation, he achieved the aim of the abortive merger with Leasco, to publish electronically on a global scale. But in 1987 he decided to abandon printing in favour of publishing, selling the BPC operations to their management. Two years later he tilted the balance of MCC firmly towards the United States by buying the Berlitz language-teaching business, the American Macmillan book-publishers, and Official Airline Guides. In 1990, after several delays, Maxwell launched *The European,* a London-produced English-language weekly designed to appeal to a current affairs readership throughout Europe.

During the past year, he was beset by the double impact of the transatlantic recession and high interest rates. In an effort to generate cash he floated Mirror Group Newspapers on the London stock market. He also sold part of his beloved Pergamon to Elsevier of the Netherlands but he shrewdly kept Pergamon's electronic publishing operations in America. Cash problems did not prevent him from buying the *New York Daily News,* which he did in characteristically dramatic manner, sailing up the East River in the *Lady Ghislaine* and announcing the deal just three days before the title would have closed forever. In remarkably trouble-free negotiations with the print unions he obtained savings equal to more than $80 million, including the shedding of 800 jobs. But the *Daily News* and *The European* were kept within his private interests. He was unable to resist the temptation to return to the habit which had attracted criticism during the Pergamon–Leasco battle, his tendency to shuffle businesses between his public companies and his private empire.

One ambition which he never realized was the ownership of a glamorous British football club. His name was linked at different times with Manchester United and Tottenham Hotspur, but he had to content himself with Oxford United and Derby County. Maxwell created a substantial business empire which will live on in various forms after his death, although it will be run on very different lines by his sons. His success owed everything to his boundless energy, despite a continual fight against overweight. But his achievements were overshadowed by his bullying and arrogant style of management, which seemed to be driven by the insecurity of his impoverished beginnings.

Maxwell had nine children, seven of whom survive him and at least three of whom are employed in his businesses. He also leaves his widow, Elisabeth.

Robert Maxwell, MC, newspaper proprietor, has been found dead,
after apparently falling overboard from his motor yacht in the
Canaries, aged 68. He was born on June 10, 1923.

MENACHEM BEGIN

9 MARCH 1992

FROM SOVIET labour-camp inmate, militant Zionist whose men blew up the King David Hotel in Jerusalem in July 1946, to Nobel Peace Prize winner for the peace treaty he signed between Israel and Egypt in 1979, Menachem Begin played a definitive role in the formative years of the Jewish state and in the world events of his time. The massacre of 250 Arabs by his Irgun forces at the village of Deir Yassin in 1948 changed the demography of the newly partitioned Holy Land and the hanging by his men of two British sergeants was credited with doing more than anything else to break British determination to continue its role in Mandated Palestine. Later, he averted a civil war between rival Jewish forces by belatedly accepting the authority of Israel's first prime minister, David Ben-Gurion, after the Irgun arms ship, *Altalena*, was blown-up by Israeli artillery off Tel Aviv (while he was aboard). He subsequently bowed to the democratic process; and after nearly 30 years running a tiny political grouping on the extreme right of the political spectrum won reward for his patience, gaining power in 1977 as prime minister.

It was his unquestioned commitment to the widest perception of *Eretz Yisrael* (the land of Israel) that enabled Begin to carry all but the most uncompromising of his followers with him when in 1979 he relinquished Israel's vast tracts of conquered land in the Sinai and signed the Jewish state's first, and so far only, peacetreaty with a neighbouring country. But it was his lack of vision and weakening command that was primarily responsible for Israel's failure to develop and build upon that first peace. And then, in what proved to be the evening of his political career, he proved unable to restrain the adventurist policies of Ariel Sharon, his defence minister, and General Rafael Eitan, his chief of staff, in launching the full-scale invasion of Lebanon in 1982. This aggressive war led to the massacre by extremist Christians of hundreds of unarmed Palestinian refugees trapped in the camps at Sabra and Chatila, cost 650 Israeli lives and thousands of Lebanese ones, divided Israelis, and lost the Jewish state much of the international sympathy it had gained over the previous 30 years.

Menachem Begin, who lost his parents and a brother in the Nazi holocaust, was driven by twin forces: an unswerving determination never again to see Jews betrayed to slaughter and a cast-iron belief in their destiny to reclaim all their ancient homeland. 'The world does not pity the slaughtered,' he said. 'It only respects those who fight.'

As unfailingly courteous in private as he could be vituperative in public, Begin was a slight, fastidious individual with angular features and poor eyesight. He was also a stickler for protocol and, in contrast to most of his casually dressed countrymen, was seldom seen unless smartly dressed in a dark suit and tie. He came to symbolize for much of the world the hard and uncompromising face of Zionism, determined to ensure the security of the Jewish state in its historic or biblical frontiers and seemingly indifferent to any suffering that this might cause to non-Jews.

Begin was always a controversial figure both at home and abroad. Yet he had the statesmanship to make the necessary concessions for the peace treaty with Egypt and at the end of his career, in spite of the disarray in which he left the country, he was revered by many Israelis almost as a father figure. Even some of his opponents came to regard him as a restraining influence on the more violent nationalist elements in Israeli society, though many argued that those elements had received fatal encouragement from his policies and speeches.

Menachem Wolfovitch Begin was the son of a convinced Zionist and grew up in the turbulent and often anti-semitic atmosphere of inter-war Poland. He was educated first at a *Mizrachi* (religious Zionist) elementary school, later at a Polish government high school, and finally at Warsaw University where he took a degree in law, although he never practised it.

Throughout his life he was an Orthodox, though not strictly observant, Jew in the religious sense. He insisted on kosher food and refused to write or to use wheeled transport on Saturdays, but did not attend synagogue every day, or even every sabbath, and made no secret of the fact that he listened to the radio on the sabbath.

At the age of 15 he joined Betar, the Zionist youth movement founded by the 'Revisionist' leader, Vladimir Zeev Jabotinsky (1880–1940), who insisted on the necessity of a Jewish state embracing both banks of the Jordan and on force as the only credible means to achieve this end. Begin became his most passionate disciple and this led to his first clash with the British in 1937, when he was imprisoned for leading a demonstration against the British embassy in Warsaw to protest at British policy in Palestine. Two years later he was appointed by Jabotinsky as head of Polish Betar, the largest section of the world movement.

After Nazi Germany and Soviet Russia had divided Poland between them in 1939, Begin was arrested by the Russians and sentenced to eight years' correctional labour as 'an element dangerous to society'. However, after three months in a labour-camp in the far north of Russia, an experience he later described in the book *White Nights*, he was released under the Stalin–Sikorski agreement of 1941 and allowed to join the Polish army formed under General Anders and sent by the Allies to the Near East. In 1942 his unit was posted to Transjordan, in Begin's eyes part of Eretz Yisrael. 'The military convoy stopped,' he wrote later in his book *The Revolt*.

'We rested, I left the automobile, waded a little way into the grass, and drank in the odour of my homeland.'

Begin's sense of honour would not allow him to desert even the strongly anti-semitic Polish army. Although working in Jerusalem from May 1942, he was released from the army ostensibly for propaganda work in America in late 1943. Soon afterwards he assumed command of the Irgun Zvai Leumi (National Military Organization), the Revisionist underground, and on February 1, 1944, proclaimed its revolt against British rule.

As long as the world war lasted, the Irgun did not attack British military instal-lations, only police stations and government offices. To minimize British casual-ties, advance warnings were given wherever possible so that civilians could be evacuated. Even so, the revolt was very unpopular within the Jewish community, and for a time the recognized Zionist leadership under Ben-Gurion cooperated with the British against it.

Once the war in Europe ended, things changed. The Haganah, the mainstream Jewish defence force, proposed a joint resistance campaign against British rule, and Begin accepted. This lasted until July 1946, when the Irgun blew up the King David Hotel in Jerusalem, the headquarters of British administration, killing 91 people, including 28 British, 41 Arabs, and 17 Jews. The intention had apparently been to humiliate the British rather than to cause so many casualties, but a tele-phoned warning did not reach the British in time. The Jewish Agency, which through the Haganah command had tried to get the operation postponed, promptly denounced it and ended the united resistance, concentrating thereafter on diplomatic methods to hasten the end of British rule.

From then on the Revisionists fought a lone and increasingly vicious battle with the British, retaliating for the flogging and execution of their own members by responding in kind. After a British military court sentenced two 17-year-old Irgun members to 15 years imprisonment and 18 lashes with a heavy cane, a British major and three NCOs were captured and flogged; and on July 30, 1947, two British ser-geants were formally hanged. The British put a £10,000 price on Begin's head, describing him as an 'irresponsible fanatic thirsting for personal power'.

After the hanging of the British sergeants Begin turned his attention to the danger of Arab resistance to the creation of the Jewish state. His greatest 'achieve-ment' on this front was the massacre of Arab villagers at Deir Yassin, on the out-skirts of Jerusalem, on April 9, 1948. Although he always denied that such a massacre had taken place (in spite of detailed eye-witness accounts, mostly from Jews), Begin did not scruple to claim the credit for its effect: the panic flight of most of the Arab population from what was to become Israeli territory. On the proclamation of the state of Israel in May 1948 Begin emerged from the under-ground and signed an agreement with the provisional government, providing for the merger of the Irgun into the national army. However, Begin regarded this agreement as valid only within the existing boundaries of the state. He thus considered himself free to continue fighting independently 'to put the nation in command of the whole country'.

In June the *Altalena*, a former US tank transport, arrived off the Israeli coast with a cargo of arms for the Irgun, violating a UN-monitored truce between Israel and the Arabs. Ben-Gurion, as prime minister, took this as a direct challenge to the new state's authority. The ship, with Begin on board, was shelled by the Israeli army on June 22 in full view of Tel Aviv beach. Fourteen Irgun fighters, including Begin's boyhood friend Avraham Stavsky, had been killed and 69 wounded before the ship surrendered. Begin said later there had been only two occasions he had wept. On the night the state was proclaimed and the night the *Altalena* was fired upon by fellow Jews. Not surprisingly the incident left a legacy of irreconcilable bitterness between the two men, and so between the two main branches of Zionism, Labour and Revisionist.

Thereafter Begin was a politician. He quickly transformed the Irgun into a political party, the Herut (freedom) movement, and emerged as a formidable speaker both in parliament and at public meetings. Yet to begin with he spoke only for a small minority of Israelis – 11.5 per cent in the 1949 elections, falling to 6.6 per cent two years later. His party was to lose eight consecutive elections before coming to power in 1977.

In the early years his style was much more that of a mob orator than a responsible parliamentarian, and in 1952 he came close to the brink of insurrection in his violent denunciations of the government's decision to accept reparations from West Germany. In 1955 he fought the general election from an open-topped Cadillac with an escort of young leather-clad motorcycle outriders – an image which uncomfortably recalled the fascist movements of the 1930s. Ben-Gurion even went so far as to compare him with Hitler.

But as the 1950s and 1960s wore on, Begin began to acquire respectability. In 1965 his party formed Gahal, an electoral block with the Liberal Party, as a united opposition; and on the eve of the Six Day War in 1967 he joined the national unity government formed by Levi Eshkol, becoming deputy prime minister. After Eshkol's death he remained in office under Golda Meir, but resigned in August 1970 when Israel first formally accepted the principle of a negotiated peace involving withdrawal 'from territories occupied in the 1967 conflict'.

In the election held just after the Yom Kippur war, a broader right-wing group, the Likud, still led by Begin, gained eight seats.

Golda Meir retired exhausted in the spring of 1974. In the three years that followed it became apparent that the Labour Party, after a quarter of a century in power, had lost both its grip and its sense of direction. Plagued by a succession of corruption scandals, it appeared to more and more Israelis, especially those of North African or Asian origin (by now roughly half the population), as the vehicle of a smug and patronizing aristocracy, almost exclusively European and based on the kibbutzim and the nationalized industries. Begin, although European himself, never talked down to the 'oriental' Jews and so came to be seen by many of them as a champion of the underdog against the self-serving governing clique. His intransigent nationalism also appealed to most of them.

In the elections of 1977, Yitzhak Rabin was forced to renounce the leadership of the Labour Party after the disclosure of financial irregularities involving his wife, and the Likud campaign, ably organized by the former air force hero Ezer Weizmann, swept Begin to victory.

Begin swiftly made it clear that he was determined to establish permanent Israeli control of 'Judaea and Samaria' (the West Bank of Jordan) by lifting restrictions on Jewish settlement there. His arrival in power effectively doomed President Carter's efforts to reconvene the Geneva peace conference of 1973, with a view to obtaining a peace involving a Palestinian 'homeland' on the West Bank. In July 1977 in Washington Begin had the first of many clashes with Carter on the settlement issue, and refused to budge.

Yet Begin was aware of the need to keep the door open for peace, and to make a good impression on foreign leaders. For that reason he chose Moshe Dayan, the former war hero and Labour defence minister, as his foreign minister, and in deference to him refrained from outright annexation of the West Bank. And when President Sadat of Egypt, after sending a special envoy to sound out Dayan at a secret meeting in Morocco, astonished the world by announcing his willingness to come to Jerusalem, Begin knew how to respond. He promptly declared that the Egyptian president would be welcome, and clearly relished every minute of his role as host in what must have been the most intensively publicized state visit in world history.

His response to Sadat's gesture was, however, one of courtesy rather than warmth. He took a month to formulate his substantive counter-proposals, which he put to Sadat at a second meeting, at Ismailia in Egypt, on Christmas Day 1977: Israel would withdraw from Sinai by stages, but the Jewish settlements in the Rafah salient would stay and would still be defended by the Israeli army. In the West Bank and Gaza the Arab population would have 'administrative autonomy' but Israel would keep control of security and public order and Israeli citizens would retain the right to settle. Sadat on his side continued to insist on complete Israeli withdrawal from all the territory occupied in 1967, and self-determination for the Palestinians.

Begin had accepted President Carter's invitation to a summit conference with Sadat at Camp David in September 1977, but went there fully prepared to resist

American pressure. He and the Egyptian leader never established an easy personal relationship and virtually all the negotiating at Camp David was done indirectly, through the Americans. It took Carter 12 days of patient, often extremely tense, argument to get Begin to agree to put the withdrawal of Israeli settlements from Sinai to the Knesset, since it was clear that this was a *sine qua non* for peace with Egypt, though even then Begin was not prepared to recommend the withdrawal of settlements, in one of which he had actually promised to make his home after retirement.

Sadat on his side accepted the proposal for autonomy in the West Bank and Gaza, but only as a five-year transitional solution. This left the door theoretically open for ultimate Israeli withdrawal, but also enabled Begin to avoid waiving Israel's claim to sovereignty. The form of autonomy was to be negotiated between Israel, Egypt, and Jordan, with possible Palestinian participation in the Egyptian and Jordanian delegations (but Jordan had not been consulted about this, and in fact refused to take part). Carter believed that he had secured Begin's agreement to freeze Israeli settlement activity during the transitional period. It turned out that Begin had only promised a moratorium of three months while the Egyptian-Israeli peace treaty was being finalized.

Despite an atmosphere soured by this misunderstanding, the Camp David accords were widely hailed as a major breakthrough (or, among Arab nationalists, as a sell-out) and the following month Begin and Sadat were jointly awarded the Nobel Peace Prize.

The haggling continued throughout the first eight months of 1978, while the atmosphere was envenomed in the spring by the invasion by Israel of southern Lebanon, which Begin ordered after Palestinian terrorists hijacked a tour-bus on the coastal road between Tel Aviv and Haifa and massacred 32 civilians. The invasion did not succeed in its objective of destroying the PLO guerrilla forces: it simply drove them a few miles further away from the frontier. Under American pressure Israeli forces withdrew, handing over part of the territory seized to a UN buffer force and part to a Lebanese auxiliary militia.

The peace treaty between Egypt and Israel was signed, after much further haggling and a personal shuttle between Egypt and Israel by President Carter, in Washington on March 26, 1979. Begin faced some fierce opposition to it within his own party but his authority, combined with the support of a large majority in the country, was sufficient to force it through and to enable the final, most controversial phase of withdrawal from Sinai three years later, after the assassination of President Sadat.

The West Bank autonomy plan, by contrast, was left to wither on the vine, despite sporadic and desultory negotiations between Israel and Egypt in which neither Jordan nor any representative Palestinians were prepared to join. For its outcome Begin must take much of the responsibility since he insisted on defining autonomy as restrictively as possible; allowed Jewish settlement in the West Bank and Gaza to proceed, with government funds, at an accelerated pace; and made it clear that Israel had no intention of withdrawing at the end of the five-year period.

By mid-1980 Begin had lost both his foreign and his defence ministers Dayan and Weizman, the two most independent-minded members of the government and the most committed to the idea of broadening the peace by giving real auton- omy to the inhabitants of the West Bank and Gaza. Begin gave the foreign ministry to Yitzhak Shamir, the former leader of the Stern Gang, an extremist off-shoot of the Irgun and by that time a hardline Herut member who had refused to support the Camp David accords. He kept the defence portfolio in his own hands. The 'peace process' marked time and public attention was diverted to economic policy where things were not going well as Begin failed to back the finance minister, Yigal Hurvitz, against other members of the cabinet.

To many observers the prime minister appeared to be heading for certain defeat in the 1981 general election. But the approach of another election campaign seemed to stimulate a new flow of adrenalin. In January 1980 Hurvitz resigned and was replaced by Yoram Aridor, whose extravagant reflationary policies brought real, if shortlived, benefits to many Israelis. Begin for his part rallied support with a furiously nationalistic campaign in the course of which he publicly abused the leaders of France and West Germany, talked himself to the brink of war with Syria over the deployment of missiles in Lebanon's Bekaa valley, and sent Israeli bombers to destroy a nuclear reactor in Iraq.

The government was only just re-elected: in alliance with the religious parties, Likud had an overall majority of two. But it was enough. Ariel Sharon, who as agriculture minister had been the driving force of Jewish settlement in the occu- pied territories, now became defence minister and, with the chief of staff, General Rafael Eitan, began planning a new war in Lebanon aimed at demolishing the Palestine Liberation Organization, the main focus of resistance in the occupied territories and, they supposed, ensuring Israel's lasting strategic supremacy in the area by humiliating Syria and wresting Lebanon from her control.

Begin, it seems, was an enthusiastic supporter of this project. For him the struggle with Syria coincided with a struggle to regain his own health and vigour after a fall in November 1981 which broke his hip and condemned him to some months of pain and discomfort, using first a wheelchair and later a stick. As soon as he was out of hospital he surprised the world with a bill to annexe the Golan Heights (Syrian territory occupied since 1967), which he rushed through the cabi- net, three parliamentary readings, and a committee stage in the course of a single day. This provoked a serious but temporary crisis in Israeli-American relations.

It took Begin and Sharon some months to convince their colleagues that the moment had come for a full-scale invasion of Lebanon: on four occasions in the first five months of 1982 they were dissuaded by American pressure. On the last occasion, in May, the cabinet agreed that the next attack on Jews or Israelis anywhere in the world would be treated as a *casus belli*. Accordingly when the Israeli ambassador in London was shot on June 3 (in fact by a Palestinian splinter group violently hostile to the PLO leadership), the Israeli air force was sent to bomb Palestinian targets in southern Lebanon and in Beirut. The PLO, which had observed a ceasefire on the Israeli-Lebanese frontier since the previous July, reacted by renewed shelling of northern Israel. On June 5 Israel's ground forces poured into Lebanon.

Begin wrote to President Reagan that the object of the operation was 'to push back the terrorists to a distance of 40 kilometres to the north'. It is not entirely clear whether he believed this, as a majority of his cabinet colleagues apparently did, or whether he was consciously a party to Sharon's deception. Certainly he did little to check the successive stages of the operation as it unfolded, except again under strong American pressure to halt the intensive bombing of Beirut in mid-August. Apparently Sharon and Eitan took many key decisions without consulting him, including the fateful one to send Phalangist irregulars into the disarmed Palestinian camps of Sabra and Chatila on September 16, which resulted in the massacre of hundreds of Palestinian refugees, but he was always ready to defend their actions after the event.

Begin never expressed any public remorse for what had happened to non-Jewish civilians as a result of his actions and policies. 'Goyim kill goyim and they blame the Jew' was his comment on the international outcry after the Sabra–Chatila massacre. Only under extreme pressure from the entire Israeli establishment did he consent to the appointment of a commission of inquiry into Israeli responsibility for the affair. When it reported the following February he took the minimum action required of him: he would not take the initiative in dismissing Sharon, but left the decision to the cabinet; and when Sharon very reluctantly agreed to relinquish the defence ministry, Begin allowed him to continue as minister without portfolio.

Yet during the summer of 1983 Begin sank into a deep depression which eventually made it impossible for him to continue as prime minister. This was no doubt partly the result of his wife Aliza's death but above all because of the lengthening list of Israeli casualties caused by the war in Lebanon, which his government had begun but seemed unable to finish.

Begin announced his intention to resign on August 28, a few weeks after his 70th birthday. He remained officially prime minister, though refusing to speak to anyone but close relatives and personal staff, until October 10 when Yitzak Shamir finally took over. So deep was Begin's melancholia that it was not until December

10, after a skin complaint which had prevented him shaving responded to a new treatment, that he felt able to move out of his official residence.

It was a sad end to his premiership. The qualities of leadership which had marked his command of the Irgun and, initially, his peace settlement with Egypt, finally deserted him. He had inherited a relatively prosperous, optimistic country proud of the prowess of its defence forces. He left a nation uncertain and divided, with fewer friends and more enemies. The invasion of Lebanon had divided the country, Israeli troops were stuck deep in hostile territory, and some 60 Israelis were in jail for refusing to serve there. The economy was in disarray and the hopes engendered by the peace with Egypt had evaporated.

In his supporters' eyes Menachem Begin had proved a doughty fighter for his cause, helped re-instil Jewish pride, and won the support of the 'oriental' Jews and others who felt excluded from the western-inclined society created by Ben-Gurion and his Labour successors.

From an international perspective he had responded with some courage to Anwar Sadat's risky peace initiative by inviting him to Jerusalem and grasping the nettle of relinquishing the Sinai and entering into an honorable peace with Egypt. In spite of his shortcomings he remained a towering cult figure held high in public esteem in Israel and continued to epitomize Jewish pride as well as stubbornness.

He always rejected the accusations that he had been a terrorist, saying that the Irgun had not attacked civilians. Arab civilians, however, were undoubtedly among Irgun's victims as were non-military personnel, including Jews, at the King David Hotel.

For a year after his resignation Begin remained in almost total seclusion. Last year, in a full interview given to mark the 40th anniversary of the founding of the Irgun Zevai Leumi, he recalled with pride his decision to launch the Israeli air-raid against Iraq's nuclear reactor, which he said had been vindicated by the events in the Gulf. The hardest decision of his career, he said, had been to order the hanging of the British sergeants. 'But after that cruel act there were no more hangings of Jews in the land of Israel.'

Menachem Begin leaves a son, Binyamin, a Herut member of the Knesset, and two daughters, Hassia (named after his mother who was murdered by the Nazis) and Leah.

Menachem Begin, leader of the militant Zionist movement Irgun Zvai Leumi (1943–1948), founder of the Herut party, prime minister of Israel (1977–1983) and Nobel Peace Prize winner (1978), died in Jerusalem March 9, 1992, aged 78. He was born in Brest-Litovsk, Poland, on August 16, 1913.

FRANCIS BACON

28 APRIL 1992

NO OTHER POST-WAR PAINTER transformed British art with as much energy, flair, and obsessive conviction as Francis Bacon. After a surprisingly tentative beginning, when he wavered between painting and designing furniture and rugs, the self-taught Bacon vision arrived fully formed in 1944. And it already had the ability to unnerve. In a searing orange triptych, he painted three alarmingly distorted figures at the base of the crucifix. Half-human and half-animal, they writhe, push their distended necks forward, and open their mouths in desolate howls.

When this excoriating triptych was exhibited at the Lefevre Gallery, it announced a new post-war mood of uncompromising anxiety. The advent of the cold war, combined with the horror of Hiroshima, confirmed Bacon's preoccupations. He returned, time and again, to the image of a solitary male figure enclosed in a bare interior.

During the 1950s this anguished presence often gave vent to his disquiet with a scream, nowhere more vehemently than in an extended series of paintings based on Velazquez's celebrated portrait of *Pope Innocent X*. In the original canvas, which Bacon never went to inspect in Rome, the Pope looks masterful and shrewd. But Bacon transforms him into a screaming grotesque, trapped like a prisoner in an electric chair, rather than on a Pontiff's throne.

In later life, Bacon himself came to regret spending so much time on the Pope images. He thought they were too sensational, and went on too long. But they were certainly instrumental in establishing him with a formidable international reputation. Another series, smaller in number and on the whole more powerful, took as its inspiration a Van Gogh painting of the artist walking through the French countryside on his way to work. Once again, Bacon changed the original image into a turbulent, troubled expression of his own ominous vision.

On the whole, though, Bacon's figures remain indoors rather than out in the open. Landscapes were rare in his work, and the paintings of recent decades concentrate, with remarkable consistency, on clothed or naked figures in the archetypal Bacon room. As if to stress how little his art had changed, he embarked in 1988 on a second, larger version of his 1944 triptych. The lacerating orange became a more sumptuous red, and the three figures are surrounded by more space than in the earlier version. But they twist and yell as hideously as before, and Bacon demonstrated his regard for the new triptych by presenting it to the Tate Gallery.

Francis Bacon was born of English parents. His father trained horses in Ireland. Bacon had little formal education except for a brief period at a boarding school in Cheltenham. He left home early and spent some years in Paris and Berlin. By 1930 he was in London earning a precarious living as a designer of furniture and rugs.

He had already begun to paint, but of his first experiments very little remains. There were some abstract paintings: they are seen in a picture of the corner of his studio painted by a great friend of that time, Roy de Maistre. There are one or two pictures which found their way into private collections: the best known is a Crucifixion which was reproduced in Herbert Read's *Art Now* (1933), but everything else Bacon destroyed. After 1936 he abandoned painting completely for eight years.

There was nothing tentative about his reappearance in the closing years of the war. From 1945 onwards he began to show pictures of great technical assurance and startling originality. The crucial moment was his first one-man exhibition at the Hanover Gallery in 1949, which thrust him to the forefront of contemporary painting.

Just as the name Kafka has passed into the language as evocative of a certain kind of anxiety-ridden impasse, so Bacon's name now began to be used descriptively. This is an indication of the way in which these pictures reflected a recognizable range of feelings. They were of men's heads set against thick curtains or enclosed in glass boxes, their eyes often obliterated and their mouths stretched open as if to scream. Melodramatic, they were also contemplative and the mood of extreme, yet stoical, despair seemed of a piece with the mood of Sartre's *Huis Clos* and the early Beckett novels.

It was perhaps this literary side to them which first captured the imagination of the public. Not since Fuseli had the horrific been the overt subject-matter of painting, and the novelty was both shocking and absorbing. There were other equally disturbing features. His painting was, for instance, the very antithesis of abstract at a moment when the general drift of painting seemed to be inexorably in an abstract direction. It was illusionistic, although in a novel and non-academic way; it drew upon the Old Masters, on Velasquez in particular, and equally on photography, not only for its imagery but for its surface appearance too. It was impossible to place him comfortably within any existing framework. Certain critics, notably Robert Melville and David Sylvester, wrote about him brilliantly and with deep partisanship. Others tended to dismiss him as a morbid sensationalist and a light-weight, a view in which they were strengthened when in 1953, on the occasion of a retrospective exhibition of Matthew Smith at the Tate, Bacon contributed a short tribute to the catalogue in which he said: 'I think that painting today is pure intuition and luck and taking advantage of what happens when you splash the stuff down ...' However, within a year or two, London was to become familiar with the achieve-

Francis Bacon in May 1985 at the Tate Gallery exhibition of his work, with *Self Portrait 1973*.

ments of the American painters of Bacon's generation. Chance and intuition with paint had begun to take on wider meanings and Bacon looked less isolated, more profound, and even more original than before.

His painting was shown in the British Pavilion at the Venice Biennale in 1954, and from then onwards his reputation rose steadily in Europe and America; indeed it could be said that as far as the international standing of British art went, Bacon did for painting what Henry Moore had done for sculpture a few years earlier. There was a major retrospective exhibition at the Tate Gallery in 1962, which later toured Europe, and from this point onwards hardly a year passed without some important showing somewhere in the world. He was the first English painter of this century to be taken seriously in Paris, where queues formed to see his retrospective at the Grand Palais in 1971–72. He was shown at the Metropolitan in New York in 1975.

In one of his first statements about his work Bacon had said: 'Painting is the pattern of one's nervous system being projected on the canvas.' It was always to have for him this quality of naked attack. It was able, as nothing else, to convey feeling directly, to 'come immediately on to the nervous system'. Above all it was able to do so through the mysterious equivalence of paint and flesh. He saw this power as an unbroken inheritance from the past, continually to be revivified by the risks and intuitions of the present. He had little regard for abstract art, which in his view avoided the challenge that made painting worthwhile.

For him the proper subject for art was the human figure, and specifically the portrait. As his work matured he dropped much of the menacing *mise en scène* of the earlier pictures, and his figures became more particular portraits. He painted the same close friends over and over, working from photographs and memory, placing them in simple modern interiors, naked or clothed, and concentrating on their faces with what to many observers seemed to be sadistic violence. Bacon would always deny this reading.

Neither his international reputation nor the success that went with it made Bacon a conformist figure. He sat on no committees and accepted no honours. He was indifferent to officialdom. Robert Melville once wrote of him: 'He is at home in the complicated night life of big cities, interested in the exhibitionism and instability of the people he chooses to mix with and absorbed by extreme situations.' His art was very close indeed to his life, and his life was lived on the very fringes of normality.

He was a man of infinite charm and generosity with a great gift for friendship. A prodigious host, his life was uncluttered by possessions. His appearance was ageless. His influence on younger artists during the 1950s and 1960s was very considerable not stylistically, for he had few imitators, but through his attitude to his work and the sense he gave of the ultimate seriousness of art.

Bacon's outstanding reputation was recognized, in 1985, by a second retrospective exhibition at the Tate Gallery. Until then, no living British artist had been granted such an honour, and in his foreword to the catalogue the then director, Sir Alan Bowness, categorically declared that Bacon's 'work sets the standard for our time, for he is surely the greatest living painter; no artist in our century has presented the human predicament with such insight and feeling. The paintings have the inescapable mark of the present; I am tempted to add the word alas, but for Bacon the virtues of truth and honesty transcend the tasteful. They give to his paintings a terrible beauty that has placed them among the most memorable images in the entire history of art. And these paintings have a timeless quality that allows them to hang naturally in our museums beside those of Rembrandt and Van Gogh.'

Francis Bacon, the internationally renowned British
painter, died April 28, 1992, in Madrid, aged 82. He
was born in Dublin on October 28, 1909.

ELIZABETH DAVID

22 MAY 1992

ELIZABETH DAVID was the doyenne of English cookery writers. She influenced the generations who came after her, whether they, too, were intending to be culinary experts or merely taking a well-thumbed Elizabeth David Penguin from the kitchen shelf for the next day's dinner party. 'Elizabeth David says ...' was the regular way of resolving how much spice and which spices should be added to a stew and how much garlic should be put in a dressing.

At its best, her prose was as precise as her instructions, unlike that of some of her predecessors, who sometimes wrapped up advice on what to do in the kitchen with impenetrable sentences. She was a pleasure to read, a stylist of true distinction. Perhaps only in Britain would she have been classified as a 'food writer', too often rather a damning phrase. Elizabeth David combined a scholar's feeling for history with the traveller–aesthete's gift of conveying a sense of place.

Elizabeth David's father was the Conservative Member of Parliament for Eastbourne; her mother the daughter of the 1st Viscount Ridley. At the impressionable age of 16 she was sent from her English boarding school to study French literature and history at the Sorbonne, living for 18 months with a family in Passy. It was then that she first became aware of food, the daily fare of the French bourgeoisie coming as a startling contrast to the bland food to which she had been accustomed.

On her return to London she worked briefly as an actress, then as a *vendeuse* for Worth, where her striking looks stood her in good stead. She was living in Greece at the outbreak of war and was evacuated to Egypt, where she lived first in Alexandria and later in Cairo. There she worked as a librarian for the ministry of information. In 1944 she married an English officer, Anthony David, and went to live in India, where he was stationed. The marriage was not a success, and she rarely referred to it. There were no children.

In the winter of 1946 she returned to England alone and went to live in a small hotel in Ross-on-Wye. Here, amid the gloom and deprivation of post-war England, she began to write about the food of the Eastern Mediterranean. In 1950 *A Book of Mediterranean Food* was published by John Lehmann, with drawings by John Minton, another expert on the eastern reaches of that sea. Its impact was colossal, both on those who were too young to remember the pre-war years, and on an older generation. Other books followed in rapid succession: *French Country Cooking* (1951), *Italian Food* (1954), and *Summer Cooking* (1955). The following year she started writing regularly for *The Sunday Times*, *Vogue*, and *House & Garden*. In 1960 *French Provincial*

Cooking was published, based on a series commissioned by *Vogue*. The next year she gave up working for Condé Nast and *The Sunday Times*, and began writing for *The Spectator*, which freed her from the chore of writing recipes.

In 1965 she opened her kitchenware shop in Elizabeth Street in Belgravia. This involved her in annual trips to France searching for merchandise, a distinct pleasure and rarely a chore. Over the next years she published a series of pamphlets for sale in the shop, one of which was the basis for her next book, *Spices, Salt and Aromatics in the English Kitchen*, which came out in 1970. Three years later she fell out with her partners and severed all connection with the shop, although it continued to trade under her name. In 1976 she was appointed OBE, in 1986 CBE, and in 1977 *English Bread and Yeast Cookery* had been published, destined to be her last original work.

The same year she was made Chevalier du Mérite Agricole, and two years later she received an honorary degree from Essex University. In 1982 she was made a fellow of the Royal Society of Literature, but despite repeated efforts on the part of her friends and colleagues she was never given the accolade she merited. Her last published work, *An Omelette and a Glass of Wine*, came out in 1984.

As the years passed she became more and more obsessed with research, and the *joie de vivre*, which had filled so much of her earlier writing, became muted. Her very first books shared an infectious enthusiasm for the joys of eating and living well, while the recipes were often sketchy, probably written from memory. With *Italian Food*, however, the first book written *in situ*, her tone became more scholarly, the recipes more precise. After a return to her former style in a short book, *Summer Cooking*, she resumed her research with *French Provincial Cooking*, probably her greatest book and the one no amateur or professional chef is likely to be without.

Ten years passed before her next book, originally intended as the first in a series on English food. The title alone of *Spices, Salt and Aromatics in the English Kitchen* shows the change in attitude, as it defines with typical accuracy its range of contents. This interesting book proved a watershed in her career, for after it her passion for research seemed to get out of control.

Seven years later her long-awaited *English Bread and Yeast Cookery* finally appeared, a disappointment to many of her admirers. A heavy tome, over-filled with intricate variations on the same theme, this was a work of reference rather than a pleasure to read. The following years were spent researching a book on sorbets and ices which was never completed. But the academic period towards the end of her life was balanced by the publication of *An Omelette and a Glass of Wine*, a collection of pieces written mostly between 1955 and 1965. These provided a timely reminder of her powers to amuse and entertain, as well as to instruct. Her wit was devastating, often caustic, usually at someone's expense.

She was highly critical, but fair, giving praise rarely, for her standards were very high. She did not suffer incompetents and the dimwitted gladly, if at all, as customers in her Elizabeth Street shop often found, to their discomfiture. This may have been a family trait, for her sister Felicité could be equally crushing with foolish enquiries in Sandoe Books, just off the King's Road, where she worked. Many people found Elizabeth David intimidating, yet she could be friendly and encouraging to younger writers. She had beautiful manners and was an accomplished letter writer. She was shy, unwilling to talk in public, or even to give interviews. In latter years she refused to be photographed, preferring to re-use earlier pictures by Cecil Beaton or the painter Derek Hill on her dust jackets. She became more and more reclusive and rarely went out except to see close friends. These had always been important to her, and included such figures as Norman Douglas, almost 50 years her senior, Derek Hill, and her publisher and editor, Jill Norman.

But even friends were kept at a distance. One, returning from abroad, tried to get her telephone number from directory enquiries, only to be told they were under strict orders not to divulge it under any circumstances, even in case of death.

For more than 34 years she shared a house in Chelsea with her younger unmarried sister Felicité, who died in 1986. Despite mutual regard and affection they lived quite separately. Elizabeth David was a solitary figure in old age, living alone with her books and memories of a warmer, more enchanting past, as in 1939, when she 'fell under the spell of the Levant, the warm flat bread, the freshly pressed tomato juice, the charcoal-grilled lamb, the oniony salads, the mint and yoghurt sauces, the sesame seed paste, the pistachios and the pomegranates and the apricots, the rosewater and the scented sweetmeats, and everywhere the warm spicy smell of cumin'.

Elizabeth David, CBE, cookery writer and expert on the cuisine of the
Mediterranean, died May 22, 1992, at her home in London, aged 78.
She was born on December 26, 1913.

WILLY BRANDT

8 OCTOBER 1992

WILLY BRANDT was one of the outstanding German statesmen of the post-war years, who played a leading role in re-establishing links between West Germany and the countries of the Soviet bloc. He had first come to prominence as mayor of West Berlin, which he came to symbolize at a time when it was under threat. He then turned to national politics, led the Social Democrats to power in Bonn and, through his *Ostpolitik*, transformed West Germany's external relations.

He was also a man who stirred the imagination of people both in Germany and abroad. He was the only German statesman of his time who could lay a wreath at the concentration camp at Buchenwald, and fall to his knees in the Warsaw ghetto, without striking a false note. When he went to Erfurt for his first meeting with the East German leadership he was all but mobbed by crowds of East Germans. He was cheered to the echo by the Norwegians when he went to Oslo to try to persuade them to join the European Economic Community (though they later rejected his advice).

The reason for this appeal lay in his warm and idealistic temperament and in the fact that, as a man who had resisted the Nazis and been forced to flee for his life, he had clean hands. It meant that as well as building bridges to the East through his policy of detente he did his country another great service. He was able to persuade those West European countries, like Norway, which had the greatest grounds for mistrusting all things German, to accept West Germany as an ally and a friend.

In West Germany itself his anti-Nazi record brought him the hatred of many older Germans who somehow confused his activities with a kind of treason. But he retained throughout his life the ability to appeal to young people, along with the thin skin which meant that, even after years in the Bundestag, he was easily hurt. Towards the end of his life, his ideals were reflected in the work of the Brandt Commission on relations between the industrialized countries of the 'North' and the developing ones of the 'South'. Brandt was an active chairman of the commission and was disappointed when its report, which called for a massive transfer of resources from 'North' to 'South' had so little effect. Brandt was awarded the Nobel Peace prize for his *Ostpolitik* in 1971.

Willy Brandt was born in Lübeck on the Baltic to Martha Frahm, a 19-year-old salesgirl. He was christened Herbert Ernst Karl Frahm and never knew his father, who did not marry his mother. His illegitimacy never troubled him and certainly did not hold him back, but Adenauer's unworthy gibe in the 1961 election campaign about 'Herr Brandt, alias Frahm' drew from its victim a display of seething contempt which it richly deserved.

The main influence in his early life was his maternal grandfather, a farm worker and casual labourer and committed SPD (Sozialdemokratische Partei Deutschlands) supporter who imbued him with political ideals almost from the cradle. He won a scholarship to the distinguished Johanneum Gymnasium (grammar school) at 13 and it was not long before his teachers noticed his political dedication. One told his mother: 'Keep your son away from politics. The boy is gifted ... politics will ruin him.' But he joined the SPD Arbeiterjugend (workers' youths) at 16 and the party proper a year later.

His sponsor on the latter occasion was Julius Leber, the local SPD leader and a newspaper editor who became the second surrogate father in the life of Herbert Frahm. From this moderate but committed socialist, the young man learned to recognize the magnitude of the threat Hitler and his Nazis represented to Germany and her neighbours.

The robust young Frahm was soon embroiled in the brawls between the brownshirts and the forces of the left. One of the fracas in which he was involved led to him and a number of others being charged with manslaughter, but it was established to the satisfaction of the court that he had not been close to the scene of the death of a demonstrator and he was therefore acquitted.

Frahm remained active and in 1931, impatient with the excessively, in his view, moderate policies being pursued by the SPD, he joined a revolutionary Marxist breakaway group called the Socialist Workers' Party. He and Leber fell out over this, but a year later Frahm returned to the fold and he began to write articles for his rediscovered mentor. The name 'Willy Brandt' first appeared at this time as a *nom de plume*.

Adolf Hitler became chancellor in January 1933. The following month saw a massive protest demonstration in Lübeck in which his friend Leber, on bail after having been arrested and beaten up by the Nazis and banned from taking an active part, delivered a statement: 'Freedom'. Brandt never saw him again as he found it expedient soon after the rally to flee for his life to Norway. Brandt fled again, from occupied Norway to neutral Sweden, soon after the German invasion and spent the rest of the war in Stockholm.

Discarding the name Frahm altogether now for that of Brandt, the exiled socialist took up full-time journalism. During the war, he ran a small Norwegian-Swedish news agency, having become by this time fluent in Norwegian and a Norwegian citizen. He had also married his first wife, Carlotta, a Norwegian (they parted in 1944 and were subsequently divorced). He had contact with such German resistance to Hitler as existed within the Reich.

After the war he went to Berlin as press attaché to the Norwegian military mission with his temporary major's commission in 1946. A year later, he took out German citizenship again in his native city and re-joined the SPD. The party very soon made him the representative in Berlin of its executive early in 1948, and that is where he stayed and rose to national fame.

The world first sat up and took notice of him in the wake of the Soviet intervention in Hungary late in 1956, when Brandt, by then president of the Berlin House of Representatives, personally defused dangerous scenes in which enraged mobs of West Berliners seemed set to storm into the Soviet sector of the divided city. In 1957 he was elected mayor and his calm in the face of the Khrushchev ultimatum at the end of 1958, when the Soviet Union demanded that all Berlin was made a 'free city', consolidated his reputation. He became a symbol of his divided city and a world figure.

In 1961 Brandt was adopted by the SPD, desperate for someone of stature to put up against the commanding figure of Konrad Adenauer as its candidate for chancellor in the West German federal election. On August 13, 1961, while Brandt was campaigning in Lower Saxony, his adopted city was physically divided and sealed off overnight by the Berlin Wall. Returning home to rally his fellow-citizens, Brandt was acutely disappointed at the low-key response, as he felt it to be, of the West in general and the Americans in particular. But President Kennedy's dramatic visit to the city in 1963, when he identified himself with the beleaguered half-city, reconciled Brandt to the United States.

The 1961 election campaign was an unscrupulous one, with frequent use being made of 'bastard mayor' gibes and the like. But the SPD improved its percentage of the poll by almost five per cent over 1957. So Brandt was the only conceivable choice as candidate for 1965, by which time he was chairman of the SPD as well, a position he was to hold for a good 20 years. A second failure in that hard campaign disappointed him, however, and made him ill with heart trouble. He swore he would never stand again.

But in 1966 the coalition of Christian Democrats (CDU) and Free Democrats (FDP), which had supported the brief chancellorship of Dr Ludwig Erhard, fell apart. After long negotiations, the 'Grand Coalition' of CDU and SPD was formed, with Dr Kurt-Georg Kissinger (CDU) as chancellor and Willy Brandt as vice-chancellor and foreign minister. The SPD had a share in power for the first time since the Second World War.

With the help of his éminence grise, Egon Bahr, Brandt lost no time in launching his *Ostpolitik* of reconciliation with the Soviet Union and the Soviet-dominated countries of Eastern Europe, all of which had suffered at the hands of the Nazis. The first step was to establish diplomatic relations with Romania at the beginning of 1967. This was the first move in this direction since relations had been formalized with the Soviet Union in 1955, and showed the pragmatism which Brandt was to adopt.

Brandt stood for the chancellorship again in 1969 in an election in which the SPD once more narrowed the gap between itself and the CDU. The CDU fell short of an absolute majority, and Brandt persuaded the new, left-liberal leader of the FDP, Walter Scheel, to join him in coalition. The shift of partner by the small liberal party brought the SPD leadership of a government in Germany for the first time since before the Second World War. Brandt became chancellor.

Strongly supported by Scheel, who became foreign minister, Brandt proceeded to give a strong new impetus to his *Ostpolitik*. There were three main areas of activity: the establishment of a *modus vivendi* with East Germany, the normalization of relations with Poland, and the negotiation of a treaty with the Soviet Union on the renunciation of force. As far as East Germany was concerned, the first results were seen on March 19, 1970, when Brandt went to Erfurt in East Germany for a summit meeting with Herr Willi Stoph, the East German prime minister, the first meeting of its sort since the foundation of the two states. Brandt received an ecstatic welcome from thousands of East Germans and laid a wreath at Buchenwald.

On December 7, 1970, Brandt went to Warsaw to sign a treaty with Poland. This declared that the Oder–Neisse line constituted the western frontier of Poland and affirmed 'the inviolability of their existing frontiers now and in the future'. On this occasion, too, there were emotional scenes when Brandt laid wreaths at the tomb of the Polish Unknown Soldier and at the monument commemorating the Jewish uprising in the Warsaw ghetto. The image of the West German chancellor on his knees in atonement for the Holocaust caught the world's imagination.

Brandt's most significant change of course, however, had been in negotiations with the Soviet Union. In August 1970 he and Scheel had visited Moscow and signed a treaty agreeing that both sides would 'refrain from the threat of force or use of force in any matters affecting security in Europe and international security, as well as in their mutual relations'. In the new climate created by this success, Brandt again visited the Soviet Union in September 1971 for talks at Yalta with Brezhnev.

All this and the accompanying Berlin Agreement between the three Western allies and Russia set the seal on West Germany's emergence as a political power. Brandt had been fond of saying that his country was 'an economic giant but a political pygmy'. By embedding West Germany in NATO and the EEC, Adenauer had provided half the political equation; Brandt completed it by normalizing relations with the Soviet bloc as far as it was possible to do so in his time. West Germany might occupy only half the pre-War Reich, but it was no longer half a state. The two Germanies entered the United Nations simultaneously but separately in 1973.

Not the least of Brandt's contributions to peace had been his decision to sign the Nuclear Non-Proliferation Treaty. When he became chancellor, this had been a controversial issue in West Germany for three years, with strong opposition from the right. But in November, 1969, he signed the treaty, expressing the hope that it would lead to further arms control and disarmament.

During those years, he also maintained his strong belief in the importance of the Atlantic Alliance, despite the fact that much of his attention was given to West Germany's eastern neighbours. He continued to support the concept of a unified Europe and helped to ease Britain's difficulties as it made its way to membership of the European Community.

He ran into stiff opposition to his *Ostpolitik*, however, from within West Germany, particularly from the Christian Democrats and their Bavarian allies, the CSU. In 1972 Brandt was forced to contrive the first premature election in West Germany's brief history because of opposition to the treaties with the Soviet Union and Poland. He made detente with the Soviet bloc the central issue of the campaign, and led the SPD to its most resounding victory in more than a century.

Despite this famous victory, however, and the crowning of his detente programme thereafter, Brandt's customary post-electoral depression took longer than ever to lift. Within six months, observers were writing him off, and within a year and a half he had resigned. It was a poignantly brief lapse of time between the zenith and the nadir of his career. The occasion of Brandt's resignation was the discovery that one of his closest advisers, Gunther Guillaume, had been an East German 'plant', itself an unfortunate and ironic development.

His resignation prevented another far more trivial scandal coming to light at the time, arising from Brandt's lifelong weakness for attractive young women. Brandt considered braving a vote of confidence over Guillaume, for whose treachery he did not feel morally responsible. But his old rival Herbert Wehner, then SPD floorleader, insisted that he should quit. It was also the last straw for a man who had lost the will to rule. Those closest to him, including his second wife, Rut, also a Norwegian, whom he had married in Berlin in 1948, knew that he had wanted to go long before it happened, and that it would have come about in any case.

Brandt remained chairman of the SPD, serving as a useful shield for his successor, Helmut Schmidt, whose pragmatic policies as chancellor always tended to irritate the party's increasingly volatile left wing. Brandt's contribution to Schmidt's electoral victories in 1976 and 1980 was crucial, although even the long-serving chairman's appeals for unity began to lose their impact soon after the latter poll. World recession, the stagnation of the West German economy and consequent social strains paralysed and divided the coalition with the FDP and exhausted the SPD, which was clearly tired of office, devoid of ideas, and divided against itself by 1982, when it was abandoned by the FDP.

If the party that had been his life-long cause proved disappointing to him in his declining years, Willy Brandt went on campaigning for peace and working for democratic socialism worldwide as chairman of the Socialist International, despite a heart attack in 1978 and a second divorce and his third marriage, to the much younger Brigitte, a year later. He was a changed man with a new lease of life, acquired in time for the 1980 campaign.

The Brandt Commission published its report in the same year. It was widely debated and generally welcomed. But its critics said that the result of implementing the report would be to perpetuate the industrial and economic dominance of the north, whose workers and capitalists would benefit from the proposed recycling and the concomitant increase in economic activity. But the debate ran out of steam when the world recession threatened to become a catastrophe, and this was a profound disappointment for Brandt.

Acknowledging the practical consequences of the report had been nil, the Brandt Commission in 1983 got out another more urgent appeal entitled 'Common Crisis, North–South Co-operation for World Recovery', but to no greater avail.

At home, Brandt used his continued holding of the SPD party chairmanship in a bid to restore the party's fortunes by espousing causes close to its left wing or the emerging Green party. This policy of appeasing the Greens, which alienated the FDP, proved to be a disastrous mistake: Helmut Kohl won three elections in a row in 1983, 1987, and 1990 against an SPD which had marooned itself on the left. Chief of the causes espoused proved to be the fierce controversy generated in Germany during 1983 over NATO's decision to deploy intermediate-range nuclear missiles. Brandt addressed the monster Bonn rally of that year, organized by peace groups (he had already committed the party against the missiles). But when he insisted he had not become anti-American or anti-NATO he was booed.

Brandt's final stepping down from his SPD post, after holding it for 23 years, was painful. Not due to do so until 1988, he made a surprise announcement that he would quit in March, 1987, carried out the following June after the party had revolted over his decision to name a young Greek as the SPD's first press spokeswoman, who was not even a party member. The appointment looked like a self-willed gesture from an old man losing his grip.

The dramatic events of the autumn of 1989, particularly the end of the Berlin Wall, brought the former governing mayor of Berlin back, however, once again into the national limelight. Even there, though, the role he naturally assumed as 'Patriarch of German Unity', proved to be only short-lived. It was the right-wing Alliance for Germany, driven by Chancellor Kohl, which resoundingly won the East German elections in the following March.

Like many others, Brandt had been overtaken by the swift-moving results of Gorbachev's decision to relinquish the Soviet Union's military hold over Eastern Europe. He had believed progress could only be gained by small steps and increased contacts between Germans. In 1988 Brandt had described the pledge on reunification in the Federal German Constitution as 'a living lie'. He was proved wrong, and his words came back to haunt him.

True as always to his *Ostpolitik*, Brandt, during East Germany's 1990 election campaign, made a moving gesture by going personally up to the Oder–Neisse frontier with Poland and publicly declaring: 'I came here to tell you that this frontier is final.' His role in the first all-German federal election in December 1990 was less prominent. With typical good grace Brandt did all he could to avoid overshadowing the ill-fated SPD chancellor candidate Oskar Lafontaine, who survived an attempt on his life but suffered a crushing defeat at the polls. Despite himself, however, Brandt loomed larger in the minds of eastern Germans than Herr Lafontaine. But for his reassuring presence the SPD might have fared even worse.

Brandt's was a complex character. An emotional and sensual man, he was easily hurt. He was also prone to lengthy bouts of melancholia. But he could display vitality and stamina when his mood was right, working well into the small hours day after day. In later life, he became a genial and philosophical figure.

Brandt is survived by his third wife, Brigitte, whom he married in December, 1983. He had a daughter from his first marriage, and three sons from his second.

Willy Brandt, chancellor of West Germany from 1969 to 1974 and before that governing mayor of West Berlin from 1957 to 1966, died on October 8, 1992, aged 78.
He was born on December 18, 1913.

RUDOLF NUREYEV

6 JANUARY 1993

WITH HIS GRACE and athletic prowess, Rudolf Nureyev was one of 20th century ballet's most extraordinary and charismatic figures. He dominated the world of ballet, by a force of personality and an eagerness, a greed even, to perform that has been rivalled only by Anna Pavlova in her great pilgrimage of dance around the world. Like Pavlova, Nureyev could and did dance unceasingly, more indeed than any dancer except Pavlova in this century. And like Pavlova's, his name became synonymous for the general public far removed from the closed world of the theatre with the art he served with such passion.

Rudolf Hametovich Nureyev was a Tatar, born on a train travelling round Lake Baikal near Irkutsk. A difficult childhood spent in the town of Ufa during and just after the war was enlightened by his scholastic ability and then by a first sight of professional dancing which determined him that this must be his career. By the age of 11 he had the good fortune to be taken under the wing of a former member of the Diaghilev corps de ballet, Anna Udeltsova: she it was who confirmed that the boy should become a dancer. Despite family opposition, the young Nureyev persisted in seeking training, basic though it was, and even then his determination was finally to bring him after setbacks and battles into which his temperament led him to his ultimate goal, the Vaganova School in Leningrad. Here, in the cradle of Russian ballet, he had the immense good fortune to enter the class directed by a master pedagogue, Aleksandr Pushkin, who saw that in this raw, difficult, gifted 17-year-old there was the potential for greatness.

In his student years with Pushkin, Nureyev's talent was shaped, his temperament focused upon work, his insatiable need for information slaked by the opportunities to learn repertory. On graduation into the Kirov Ballet, a fact that had seemed wholly unlikely to his contemporaries when he joined the school, Nureyev was given the extraordinary accolade of appearing with Natalya Dudinskaya, the reigning prima ballerina of the company, as his first professional engagement. In the next three years he danced principal roles in much of the repertory with a series of leading ballerinas, his performances in Leningrad already surrounded with a theatrical magic that his every interpretation would generate thereafter. But the young man was already a stormy petrel. He queried official decisions, sought extra occasions to dance. During the Kirov Ballet's first major visit to the West, in 1961, Nureyev's performances in Paris had been greatly admired; his nonconformist behaviour off-stage, meeting and moving freely with French friends, had excited official disapproval. As the Kirov Ballet prepared to leave for its first Covent Garden season, Nureyev was told that he would have to return to the Soviet Union to dance at a Kremlin gala. The message seemed clear to Nureyev: he would return to Russia, never to leave again. His decision was brave and immediate. He sought and was granted asylum in France, and thereby opted to leave all the security of the Soviet state ballet system behind him, and rely upon his talent.

The international fuss attendant upon this decision projected Nureyev into a limelight which was not thereafter to desert him. Never seeking publicity, Nureyev nonetheless attracted it at every turn throughout his career. He became the first male superstar in ballet since Nijinsky, his features recognized worldwide, his every least action chronicled, the larger dramas of his career charted and discussed interminably in the press.

He found his first role in the West in an over-decorated staging of *The Sleeping Beauty* presented by the de Cuevas Ballet, in which he was at last to dance with an outstanding ballerina, Nina Vyrubova. He was also soon to meet the great Danish danseur Erik Bruhn, whose Apollonian style he admired without qualification, and who was to become a close friend. And he was to make his London debut at a gala in aid of the Royal Academy of Dancing whose president was Margot Fonteyn. On this occasion, Frederick Ashton was to compose a brief, ardent solo *Poème Tragique* to Scriabin music which seemed to typify the fire and passion of Nureyev as he launched himself upon the Western world. A consequence of this performance was an invitation to appear as Albrecht to Fonteyn's Giselle with the Royal Ballet at Covent Garden, the initiation of a partnership which was to enrapture audiences wherever the couple danced during the next decade.

The partnership between the classically elegant Fonteyn, whose every dance quality seemed to celebrate the virtues of lyricism and dramatic sensitivity, and the flaring romanticism of Nureyev, was unlikely. Aged 24, Nureyev was 19 years Fonteyn's junior, and temperament, as well as artistic background, seemed to separate them. But as their first appearance together in *Giselle* got under way, the Covent Garden audience was to be profoundly moved by the emotional power, the intuitive responsiveness, of their interpretation. Thereafter, their joint appearances generated a massive public response to everything they performed in every theatre.

From this performance onwards Nureyev was to have a profound influence upon British ballet as he was, indeed, to have with many other companies worldwide. His reassertion of the importance of the male dancer; the bravura and intensity of his dancing, and his interpretations, far less conventional than had been known previously in British ballet, all led to a sense of controversy as well as stellar glamour about his appearances. There also became current at this time reports of bad temper, bad manners, intolerance of inadequacy from associates. Certainly

Rudolf Nureyev rehearsing for the ballet *Romeo and Juliet* at the London Coliseum, 1980.

Nureyev's hair-trigger temperament led to explosions of anger when, as a highly concentrated and highly conscientious worker, he found that other people did not respond to his own sense of urgency in getting work as perfect as was humanly possible. Arrogant he might also seem, but it was an arrogance based upon his own awareness of his value, of his achievement, and of his dedication to an art he served with extreme intelligence as well as passion.

The career in the West, thus launched in the 1960s, was to seem insatiable for new experience, new roles, new challenges. For a decade the partnership with Fonteyn, immortalized in the portraits of each performer drawn by Frederick Ashton in *Marguerite and Armand*, held every audience enthralled, and gave the Royal Ballet exceptional cachet. Nureyev also began producing and staging for the company, notably the 'Kingdom of Shades' scene from *La Bayadère*, and set about reviving and revising works from his Russian inheritance for ballet companies throughout the world. His versions of *The Sleeping Beauty, Raymonda, The Nutcracker, Don Quixote, Swan Lake* were to enter the repertories of many troupes, with Nureyev's presence as director and star a galvanic influence upon the company, and the box-office.

Films of these stagings ensued, and inevitably were followed by others featuring Nureyev (*I am a Dancer, Valentino* among them) which further helped to promote his image. There seemed no company with which Nureyev was not prepared to appear if new repertory, new incentives, to his artistry were available. He was the ultimate 'bankable' name for impresarios.

Seasons took place in London, New York, and on international tours, in which ballet companies were engaged as backing for his stellar figure, the posters announcing that 'Rudolf Nureyev will dance at every performance'. And not just once during the evening: he thought it right that his public should see him in three contrasted roles during a programme of short ballets. A prodigious routine of performance, a tireless immolation of himself in front of a public every night, seemed the ideal for which Nureyev strove year after year. He could and did accept every challenge, even, as the years progressed, the challenge of his own younger self.

Where once the jumps had seemed tigerish, broadly soaring, the inevitable depredations of the years brought a sad diminution of physical powers. Nevertheless, Nureyev still strode the stage as ballet's youthful princes and heroes, still excited his public to ardent applause, still offered what was becoming almost a caricature of his old manner.

He choreographed ballets, without lasting success, sought further new roles and fresh areas to conquer; he appeared with modern dance troupes, dancing with Martha Graham's company, with Paul Taylor, and in 1983 was appointed as director of the Ballet at the Paris Opera. With the departure of Serge Lifar in 1958 as director of the Opera Ballet, which he had dominated and revivified during nearly 30 years, France's national troupe had seemed ungovernable. A series of directors had been little more than caretakers of a technically superb but unfocused organization. Nureyev, possessed of an identity as commanding and demanding of respect as Lifar's, took charge and revitalized the company, providing a fascinating repertory made up of his own stagings and imaginative acquisitions and commissions.

He dominated the Byzantine organization of the Palais Garnier, promoting young dancers, restoring to the ensemble a sense of international significance that it had long lacked, and dividing critical opinion, as always throughout his career.

For six years, sharing his time between the demands of the Opera and his own urgent need to continue performing worldwide, Nureyev brought back to the company a lustre it had not known for many years. But changes in the organization of the Paris lyric theatres, the creation of the Bastille opera house and the decisions of Pierre Berge as supremo for both opera houses, brought a conflict of ideals. Nureyev did not renew his contract, and what had been one of the most stimulating periods for the Paris Opera Ballet came to an end.

Nureyev, meanwhile, had found a new theatrical vehicle in an extended North American tour of the musical *The King and I*, in which he played the role of the King of Siam. He also made his return to Russia in 1989 as a dancer (he had two years previously been allowed a brief visit to see his grievously ill mother). Arriving back in Leningrad in November 1989, he was to dance the role of James in *Les Sylphides* at the Kirov, his home theatre, for two performances (characteristically, he insisted upon dancing even though he was suffering from an injury). And among the audience was the centenarian Anna Udeltsova, who had been his first teacher 40 years before.

On his return to Europe, Nureyev once again embarked upon a series of tours, as punishing in their demands as any he had undertaken as a younger man. The saddening fact for his long-time admirers was that Nureyev's indomitable will to perform was now being eroded by his declining physical powers, and by illness. But nothing, neither the limitations of his health nor adverse comment, could deflect him from his mission to dance. The circumstances of his last tour in Britain, when he chose two roles that suited his powers – the insane teacher in Flemming Flindt's *The Lesson* and Othello in Jose Limon's *The Moor's Pavane* – were less than happy as he drove himself through performances under conditions that were far from flattering or worthy of his name.

It was at this time that Nureyev made a move as bold as any in his career, by deciding to train as an orchestral conductor. With the intelligence and intense application that marked all his work, he set about learning conducting technique in Vienna, and within months he had made his debut directing the Vienna Residenz Orchestra in works by Haydn, Mozart, Stravinsky, and Tchaikovsky.

Further conducting engagements, and a last sad tour of Australia as a dancer, were constrained by ill health, but in April 1992 he was in New York to conduct *Romeo and Juliet* for American Ballet Theatre. His final contact with the ballet was to come in October, when he realized a long-held ambition to stage *La Bayadère* at the Paris Opera. His ill health was now causing great concern, but he made a last appearance upon the stage on which he had first set foot during the visit of the Kirov Ballet to Paris in 1960. He looked exhausted, and stood supported by the principal dancers to whom he had made this last and splendid gift. The audience rose, cheering, and Nureyev seemed to take strength from their adulation as he had done throughout his professional life. It was a heartbreaking farewell.

Writing about Nureyev in the 1970s, the critic 'Alexander Bland' (the husband and wife team of Nigel Gosling and Maude Lloyd) assessed his character as 'burning with curiosity, energy and adventure, in which an almost academic professionalism (he is a much valued coach) is always imbued with passion. He has been self-propelled and self-sufficient all his life, a lone-ranger of the dance. A constellation rather than a star, he has excelled in many fields. To each he brings the whole of himself, and it is that self which has made him a legend.' This view was acutely true at that time, and remained so throughout Nureyev's career.

Nureyev dominated the consciousness of the ballet world from the moment he leapt to freedom in Paris. His devotion to the art of ballet was total, and used his every gift. Few performers have so bravely spoken of dedication to their art in every aspect of their lives. To stellar presence, Nureyev added a brilliant intelligence. He understood the art he served, and why he served it, and his performances touched and excited his public because they responded to his own passion for dancing.

Rudolf Nureyev, ballet dancer, died in Paris January 6, 1993, of cardiac complications, resulting from Aids, aged 54. He was born on a train in Siberia on March 17, 1938.

* * *

RICHARD NIXON

22 APRIL 1994

RICHARD NIXON was the only President in the history of the United States to be forced to resign in order to avoid impeachment. To the end of his life he remained a divisive figure whose demeaning of his office was never forgiven by at least half his fellow countrymen.

Yet the disgrace of Watergate masked some real and lasting achievements as a statesman. He had a sure touch in foreign affairs, something which most recent American Presidents have lacked. He achieved, for instance, a realistic Far East policy as only an acknowledged right-wing President could have done by reaching an understanding with Communist China. And he extracted his country, with as much dignity as was possible, from the quagmire of the Vietnam War.

To some extent he contrived to rehabilitate his image in the last years of his life. But then, as he had proved in crisis after crisis in his political career, Richard Nixon was nothing if not a dogged fighter with an amazing ability to bounce back after defeat. The phrase 'the greatest comeback since Lazarus' was applied to him by James Reston of *The New York Times* in 1968 and by the time he opened his presidential library at Yorba Linda in 1990 there were those prepared to say the same of his fight to restore his reputation.

Nevertheless, the damage the sheer sleaze of his methods inflicted on standards of American public life was enormous, and the modern presidency was never to be looked upon in quite the same reverent light again. It was Nixon who opened the floodgates for the spirit of public cynicism, spilling over into prurience, that today appears to characterize the American political process.

His original offence, the decision to cover up an unlawful but scarcely unique piece of political burglary on the part of over-zealous Republican apparatchiks, would have been bad enough if he had confessed to it when the stormclouds first gathered. But the damage came in the way the Watergate saga unfolded a long tale of evasion, lies, and, most distasteful of all, Nixon's tactic of allowing his underlings, one by one, to be thrown to the wolves while he denied responsibility.

The incidentals of the story were no less unprepossessing. It was painful for Americans, and their friends abroad, to watch the calibre being revealed of the men Nixon had assembled as his staff within the White House. And when the famous 'White House tapes' were finally published, even in expurgated form, eyebrows were raised at the coarseness of language that was evidently commonplace in the corridors of power: the phrase 'expletive deleted' entered the vocabulary of the black humour of the seventies.

But hackles rose, too, at the arrogance of some of those who hounded Nixon to his fate. The media inevitably played a big part in his downfall. (The phrase 'Deep Throat', codename of the informant who kept Bob Woodward and Carl Bernstein of the *Washington Post* on the President's trail, also passed into seventies' vocabulary.) The sense of power, the consciousness of an ability to bring down Presidents and presidential candidates, became itself one of the less attractive features of American democracy.

Even without Watergate, Nixon would have been one of the United States's most controversial politicians. His political style was in a robust tradition, a no-holds-barred approach that had characterized other Americans who had clawed their way to the top, but it was not a style for the squeamish. Nor, for that matter, was his frequent resort to unctuousness, as in his promise during his 1960 TV debates with Senator Jack Kennedy to restore decent language to the White House.

His lack of popular appeal was summed up by yet another piece of Nixon folklore. His opponents devised a poster to exploit an unfortunate physical characteristic: the heavy-jowled Nixon face, unless freshly shaved, could suggest a gangster-like quality. Its caption 'Would you buy a used car from this man?' was another catchphrase of the day.

It was all too easy to deduce that there were two Nixons: the one who could occasionally aspire to heights of political genius, the statesman who could put his finger on great issues of his times; the other, to use the nickname of which he never managed to rid himself, 'Tricky Dicky'. But the truth, as even so celebrated a chronicler as Theodore White eventually discovered to his cost, was that there never was 'a new' or 'an old' Nixon. There was just one insecure personality whose character, with its equally striking strengths and weaknesses, was always all of one piece.

Richard Nixon

A classic example of an autodidact, Richard Milhous Nixon was born into a modest Quaker family, within which he adored his devout, placid mother and barely tolerated his irascible, argumentative father. His boyhood was clouded by the death from tuberculosis of two of his brothers. But, inspired by the idea that if you start without advantages you need to try harder, the young Nixon soon made his own way up the educational ladder, eventually ending up at the law school of Duke University, North Carolina. He practised law first privately and then in government service until slightly belatedly and at the behest of his wife, Pat, whom he had married in 1940, he volunteered for the Navy in April 1942. He had an undistinguished war with none of the derring-do exploits that both J. F. Kennedy and George Bush were later able to exploit for campaign purposes.

At least, however, he had been in uniform and at the end of the war he answered a famous advertisement which invited applications for nomination as a candidate for California's twelfth congressional district. The local Republicans were looking for a vigorous candidate to oust the left-wing incumbent Democrat, Jerry Voorhis.

Nixon, against predictions, pulled it off, after a campaign more notable for his attacks on his opponent than his policies. He denounced Voorhis as 'a front for un-American elements'. It was a phrase that carried an unfortunate overtone in view of what was soon to be done in the name of extirpating 'un-American elements'.

So, almost straight from war service, Nixon entered the House of Representatives. He was young (33) and, a point that was to bring its own problems before long, he was not a rich man.

He was active from the outset on a sub-committee drafting the Taft–Hartley legislation, imposing restrictions on unions and strikes. This did not help his future relations with organized labour. His rapid rise to prominence really arose, however, from his membership of the House Committee on Un-American Activities, partner to the more famous Senate investigating committee where the egregious Senator Joe McCarthy was to make his mark.

The House Committee heard evidence from a self-confessed Communist, Whittaker Chambers, about the range of people who had been his comrades in Washington in the 1930s. Among the people he mentioned was Alger Hiss, who promptly demanded to be allowed to clear his name. Hiss was a distinguished diplomat who had held a key position under Roosevelt, and had recently been appointed to the impeccably respectable post of president of the Carnegie Foundation. By setting his sights on Hiss, Nixon was taking on the liberal establishment, which never forgave him.

But Nixon, with the instincts of a sharp lawyer, sensed that Hiss was lying: he was simply, Nixon wrote later, 'much too smooth'. Nixon was pilloried, accused of playing the politics of innuendo and smears. But he stuck to it and was vindicated.

Although he always protested his innocence, Hiss eventually went to prison for perjury.

The Hiss case made Nixon's name and his reward was to be chosen as candidate for one of California's two Senate seats in 1950. That election, in which his unfortunate Democratic opponent was a fellow member of Congress, Helen Gahagan Douglas, was widely held to have made even the campaign against Voorhis seem like a game of pat-ball. In terms of red-baiting, Nixon stopped at nothing and picked up his electoral prize in winning by a staggering margin of 680,000 votes.

Yet Nixon's reputation in California as a fierce rightwinger was not always borne out by his congressional record on Capitol Hill. If it had been, he would never have been acceptable to the liberal Republicans who secured the Republican nomination for General Eisenhower in 1952 in preference to Senator Robert Taft. Of course, presidential tickets are generally a matter of balance but it was Nixon's youth that was intended to balance Ike's age, not his political convictions. (It may also have been felt that Eisenhower's famous amiability could do with being offset by someone more aggressive.)

In any event, the Eisenhower–Nixon partnership very nearly came to grief. Once the campaign of 1952 was underway, a newspaper unearthed the story of a 'secret slush fund', financed by Californian businessmen with possibly suspect motives, without which Nixon would not have been able to lead such an active political life. The pressure on him to withdraw from the race was intense, not least from Eisenhower, who spoke of his needing to prove that he was 'as clean as a hound's tooth'.

Characteristically, Nixon decided to fight back. He took his case direct to the voters with a television broadcast which was a triumph but which nauseated his critics with its shameless sentimentality.

Yet he calculated correctly that the ordinary American would identify with a small-town boy struggling to the top in competition with men born with silver spoons in their mouths. For instance, his wife, he told the viewers, didn't have a mink coat, that classic symbol of political corruption 'but she does have a respectable Republican cloth coat. And I always tell her that she'd look good in anything.'

But, he went on, as his more sophisticated viewers cringed in front of their TV sets, he had to plead guilty to accepting one gift during the campaign. A well-wisher had sent a little cocker spaniel in a crate. His children had fallen in love with that little dog. His six-year-old, Tricia, had decided to call it Checkers, 'and you know, I just want to say this right now, that regardless of what they say, we're going to keep it.'

Nixon, with some help from Checkers, had pulled it off again. It must have been a testing episode for Pat Nixon, who was in the studio throughout. It needs to be said, however, that she and their two daughters provided one of the forces for decency and stability in a stormy political life.

Nixon remained Vice-President, that notoriously unsatisfying office (once said to be not worth 'a pitcher of warm spit') for the full eight years of Eisenhower's term, although there was some attempt by the President himself, who held out to him the prospect of Cabinet office, to replace him as vice-presidential candidate in the 1956 election. His slightly vulnerable position as a young man 'a heartbeat from the presidency' had been highlighted when Eisenhower had a heart attack in 1955, an episode which exposed the inadequacy of the rules relating to the constitutional procedure when a President is incapacitated.

In the second term he prevailed on Ike to allow him a more active role. In 1958 he made a sensational tour of Latin America, displaying courage in the face of violent demonstrations. In the following year he visited Moscow, engaging Khrushchev in the much publicized 'kitchen debate' (a reference to the exhibition stand venue in which it took place). Early in 1960 he also took a prominent part in settling a national steel strike.

He was now ready to bid for the presidency when Eisenhower, by law, was required to stand down. Not since 1835 had an incumbent Vice-President been selected for the top slot on the ticket, but Nixon's tight hold on Republican grassroots loyalty, the product of years spent on 'the chicken and peas circuit', now paid off. Easily deflecting an incipient challenge from the Republican Governor of New York, Nelson Rockefeller, although he had to make some policy concessions in the so-called Treaty of Fifth Avenue, he swept to the Republican nomination at the 1960 Chicago convention. The choice for the voters that year lay between Richard Nixon and John F. Kennedy. They were two of the toughest operators in the political business: but for many Americans it was not a choice that filled them with enthusiasm. Kennedy won but only by 112,000 votes out of 68 million and Nixon, in a statesmanlike decision, refused to challenge the nation's verdict, even though there was ample suspicion of ballot-rigging, particularly in Mayor Daley's Cook County.

Two years later the defeated Nixon unwisely made a bid for the governorship of California. He failed to dislodge a popular Democratic incumbent (Pat Brown, the father of Jerry Brown) and at a meandering press conference afterwards seemed to signal that his political career was at an end. 'Gentlemen,' he finally announced, 'you won't have Dick Nixon to kick around any more.'

Political failure, however, was to be followed by financial success. Nixon moved to New York and set up in a highly successful law practice. He was in demand as a speaker – he was an effective Republican fundraiser – and as a newspaper colum- nist. He published an interim, typically introspective, biography, *The Six Crises of Richard Nixon* (1962). He took to travelling the world, winning headlines with his pronouncements on international affairs.

Thus, skilfully leaving Barry Goldwater to be annihilated by Lyndon Johnson in the 1964 presidential election, he passed the seven years after his defeat at the hands of Kennedy. They were not proud years for America. Kennedy was assassinated; the Vietnam War became a disastrous running sore; at home, especially following the shooting of Martin Luther King in April 1968, there was an apparent breakdown in law and order.

As for Nixon, the end of those years saw him emerge as apparently a more mature, relaxed, self-confident figure or, as the slogan of his image-makers of the time had it, as 'the new Nixon'. He recognized a need to broaden the base of his support. He claimed to represent 'the forgotten people of America, the silent majority'. By promising to end the Vietnam War he sought also to mend his fences with the liberal wing of the Republican Party, from which, for obvious reasons, he had long been estranged. In order to repulse a late challenge from Ronald Reagan he also wooed the Southern conservative vote; it was for this reason that he made the choice – an unfortunate one as events proved – of Governor Spiro Agnew of Maryland as his running-mate.

The 1968 contest against Hubert Humphrey was, though, a close-run thing, although not as close as 1960. Nixon won, but it was clear that he had failed to command the instinctive loyalty of any outstandingly large segment of the electorate. His first Administration was an interesting mix of the orthodox and the unorthodox, the latter including the maverick intellectual Henry Kissinger, who was to become in some ways a bigger international figure than the President himself. The mix symbolized the 'new Nixon'.

Unfortunately, there was still that other, darker side to his character – the suspicious, some would have said paranoiac, side. It was that side which manifested itself in his choice of personal staff, almost exclusively young men who had been with him in his California campaign in 1962. Like their master, they had the small-towner's resentment at the influence of the great and powerful of American society. They were not unwilling to harness the machinery of government to destroy what they saw as the enemy. Most were in their own way corruptible; and, all too soon, they were to be corrupted.

Nevertheless, the President had started out by declaring that he saw his task as one of healing the divisions and hatreds which were tearing America apart and which were so dramatically symbolized by the anti-Vietnam demonstrations on the campuses, although feelings of disillusionment went far beyond Vietnam. Part of the trouble, Nixon calculated, was that his predecessors, Kennedy and then Lyndon Johnson, had antagonized ordinary people in Main Street, USA, with their undue haste to remedy social ills: the reformers had been moving too far, too fast. This may have been true, but the reformers still had powerful allies in Congress and in the media. So what Nixon saw as healing policies sometimes merely set up new bitterness. And the seeds were sown for Nixon's conviction, not wholly without reason, that there was a conspiracy against him in the liberal establishment.

His continuing poor relations with Congress hampered him, for instance, in trying to effect a much-needed overhaul of the welfare system, even though his plans included providing substantially more funds from the federal government. He hoped he could change the face of Congress in the mid-term elections of 1970, when he unleashed Vice-President Agnew to carry out a virulent campaign against the liberals in the media. But the new Congress was not very much friendlier.

Meanwhile, he harmed himself by failure to control his tongue. After the tragedy when panicking National Guardsmen shot and killed four students at a demonstration at Kent State University in Ohio, he talked about 'campus bums'. Following that incident evidence began to emerge of how he had lost touch with members of his Cabinet because the young men in his private entourage were restricting access to his office. The President's main interest and activity, however, lay in foreign affairs, where he had the extraordinary talents of Henry Kissinger to help him. In Vietnam, he was confronted in effect with a military defeat, the first in the history of the United States. The military aim was to withdraw, but there was the parallel political need to do so without a public admission which could have been disastrous to American sensibilities. Nixon gradually brought home the maximum number of American troops (about whose morale there were alarming stories) while backing the South Vietnamese to fight their own war. The US backing included bombing support, sometimes on a massive scale, which outraged the liberals at home. The war would be lost, so it was often said, not on the ground of Vietnam but on the campuses of America.

The other vital foreign policy area, where Nixon showed that he had a wise and clear head, lay in relations with the Soviet Union. Although Nixon often offended his European allies by failure to discuss his strategy with them, at least he demonstrated, by a number of European tours (the first in the second month of his presidency), that America had abandoned its preoccupation with South-East Asia. Meanwhile he gave a fair wind to the negotiations, the 'Salt' talks, on limitation of strategic arms. In contrast to earlier disarmament talks, where the two sides tabled effectively non-negotiable demands, the emphasis was now to establish how each side perceived the threats presented by the other to its strategic position.

In 1971 came the greatest coup of the Nixon foreign policy. In April the normally very visible Kissinger had disappeared from view in Pakistan, ostensibly into hospital. It emerged that he had, in fact, been to Peking – the city that for years had represented, to the gut feelings of millions of Americans, the seat of so much that was evil in the world Communist conspiracy.

Kissinger had arranged nothing less than a Nixon visit to China. The Russians, on hearing what their Chinese rivals were up to, invited him too. The two visits to the Communist capitals took place in May and June 1972, which happened to be the year when Nixon would be coming up for re-election. Agreements were signed in Moscow on cooperation in space and on trade, including the supply of American wheat to the Russians. There was also an agreed halt to further deployment of ballistic missiles. More important, there was a general fostering of detente, which was to help in extracting America from Vietnam, when the North Vietnamese saw the way the thoughts of their Communist allies were moving.

When the presidential election arrived in the autumn of 1972, although the fighting was still going on in Vietnam, Nixon was seen by most Americans as being a realistic man of peace. The successful extrication of the United States from Vietnam, which came soon afterwards (if in the humiliating final form of helicopters taking off from the roof of the US Embassy in Saigon), reflected credit on his political judgment and nerve, even if the original recipe for it had been supplied years earlier by a Republican senator from Vermont who publicly asked: 'Why don't we just pull out and announce we have won?'

Meanwhile his standing at home represented yet another remarkable comeback. Nixon, marginally defeated in 1960 and only marginally a winner in 1968, was re-elected in 1972 in one of the greatest landslides in presidential history, his opponent, George McGovern, carrying only Massachusetts and the District of Columbia.

Ironically, the basic strength of his position had not been appreciated by some of his backers who decided to use any device, fair or foul, to foil his enemies and get him back to the White House. As only one of many dirty tricks, agents of the sinisterly labelled CREEP (Committee to Re-elect the President) illicitly installed listening devices in Washington's Watergate Building while it was being used by the Democratic National Committee. The burglars were caught and eventually severely sentenced by a celebrated District judge, John Sirica. But a Senate committee set up to investigate the affair scented blood. The trail led to the White House, where the decision had been taken, with Nixon's approval, to cover up all traces of the trail. The man entrusted with the cover-up was the President's Counsel, John Dean, who now realized that he was being made – the language of the Hollywood gangster movies was to become all-too-appropriate – the fall-guy. Dean named others, and in due course Nixon was obliged to get rid of his most important courtiers, John Ehrlichman and H. R. Haldeman, two men already hated, long before Watergate, for their arrogance.

Watched by a wide-eyed world, the story was now moving to its climax and the various corpses seemed to be appearing on the stage as in the final scene of a Jacobean revenge tragedy. It emerged that Vice-President Agnew, as Governor of Maryland, had been involved in corrupt practices: he resigned. Then came John Mitchell, the Attorney-General; he was alleged to have granted immunity from prosecution to a notorious financial manipulator in return for a contribution to the President's election expenses and was forced to resign before being sent to jail. Further evidence of the 'us against them' mentality in the White House came from stories of pressure on the Internal Revenue to hound liberal opponents of the President. Meanwhile discrepancies came to light in Nixon's own tax affairs: he agreed to pay back a quarter of a million dollars.

The substance of all this unsavoury news rendered hopeless the one seeming chance he had of retrieving the situation: by pleading presidential privilege for the tapes on which, as was now well known, every word spoken in the President's presence had been recorded. The fact that he insisted on recording everything itself hinted at a siege mentality.

The tapes were grudgingly released by stages. Their contents provided fresh grist to the liberal mill, but shocked respectable conservative opinion too, not only with the coarseness of their language but with the cynicism and ruthlessness of the tone when the President got together with his closest associates.

Eventually the Supreme Court ruled that the needs of justice overrode any presidential privilege. On August 5, 1974, Nixon conceded that a tape existed showing his personal direction of the cover-up only five days after the Watergate break-in. A few days later he announced his resignation in a TV broadcast notable for its failure to admit any wrongdoing (his only admission of shame was to come almost three years afterwards in his marathon TV interviews with David Frost). In August 1974, however, he still faced indictment for interfering with the course of justice, a threat lifted only when his successor, Gerald Ford (who had stepped in to replace Agnew), decided on September 8 to grant him a pardon.

Ironically, the last six months of Nixon's Administration, while the world had had eyes for nothing but Watergate, had brought further foreign policy successes. Kissinger had secured an Arab-Israeli settlement. The boycott on oil deliveries to the United States had been ended. Soviet influence in the Middle East had been reduced. But as he left the White House with a defiant wave on August 9, 1974, all those achievements appeared to have gone for nothing.

At first, in exile at San Clemente, Nixon simply brooded. After his presidential pardon, which he initially resisted accepting since it implied an admission of guilt, he fell ill in October 1974 with phlebitis and very nearly died. Two years later his wife, Pat, suffered a stroke, reputedly as a result of reading *The Final Days* by Woodward and Bernstein, in which she is portrayed as a drunken recluse. Only very gradually did Nixon himself start emerging again into the world – the first sign of his sustained effort at rehabilitation being his visit to China in 1976. Two years later he played for even higher stakes with a visit to Britain, of which the highlight was probably his address to a packed house at the Oxford Union in November 1978.

Another indication of his growing confidence was his move from California to

New York in 1980, although an equal motive here was probably his wife's desire to be near her grandchildren (their younger daughter, Julie, had married Eisenhower's grandson, David, and their elder daughter, Tricia, a New York lawyer called Edward Cox).

Eventually, after getting something of the cold shoulder in Manhattan, the Nixons moved from New York to New Jersey, where the ex-President took to giving dinner parties for selected influential journalists. His wife seldom appeared at these functions and her last great act of self-sacrifice was to deliver a speech at the opening of the Nixon presidential library.

Pat Nixon died of lung cancer in 1993. Her husband's main consolation continued to be foreign travel, though, ironically, his last trip to Russia earlier this year was one of his most controversial. His visits to Aleksandr Rutskoi and Vladimir Zhirinovsky caused great offence to President Yeltsin.

As a man, Nixon himself was always reserved and inward-looking. He was driven by deep inner compulsions towards power and towards self-vindication: in the pursuit of his aims he spared neither himself nor those around him. The greatest successes in his long career came when he gave his undoubted gifts free play, unencumbered by the hostility he harboured towards so many of those who set the tone of American society. The saddest aspect of the White House tapes, by no means all of which have yet been revealed, threatens to be the evidence that, within himself, he never escaped from his hidden demons.

Richard Nixon is survived by his two daughters.

Richard Nixon, thirty-seventh President of the United States, died in a New York hospital on April 22, 1994, aged 81. He was born in Yorba Linda, California, on January 9, 1913.

JACQUELINE KENNEDY ONASSIS

19 MAY 1994

JACQUELINE KENNEDY ONASSIS, widow of President John F. Kennedy and the Greek shipping millionaire Aristotle Onassis, died from lymphatic cancer in New York on May 19, aged 64. She was born in Southampton, Long Island, on July 28, 1929.

For the two years, ten months, and two days that her husband was President of the United States, Jacqueline Bouvier Kennedy brought an unprecedented degree of youthful glamour to the role of First Lady. Unlike those staid matrons in whose paths she trod, the young and always exquisitely turned-out Jacqueline Kennedy proved to be her husband's best political asset during the primary campaign of 1960 (she sat out most of the actual election through being pregnant) and very rapidly became a celebrity in her own right. This despite the fact that John F. Kennedy had feared that she would be something of an embarrassment to his career possessing, as he put it, 'too much status and not enough quo' to appeal to the average voter.

Her family was the American equivalent of aristocracy, rich, Republican, and Catholic. Their ancestry could be traced back much further than the more boisterous Kennedy clan, on whom she tended to look down at first in consequence: 24 of them had come over from France to fight in the American War of Independence, returning with Lafayette to France, but a younger cousin, inspired by tales of frontier life, came back to Philadelphia in 1814, and subsequently made a fortune through importing and real-estate transactions in West Virginia.

If the initial response to Jacqueline Kennedy as First Lady was rather cool, what really swung not just Seventh Avenue but the grassroots American public behind her was the extraordinary reception she received from the people of France on the Kennedys' state visit there in May 1961. She completely stole the show from her husband, charming not only President de Gaulle but the entire French nation with her fluent French and her famous pill-box hats. On the final day of the visit, her husband began his farewell speech, not entirely without justification: 'I do not think it altogether inappropriate to introduce myself. I am the man who accompanied Jacqueline Kennedy to Paris.'

For the next two years she was taken unconditionally to the nation's heart and idolized by press and public alike. She became Washington's premier hostess, not just in name, as previous Presidents' wives had been, but in fact, holding fashionably informal parties at a White House which she had restored to its former elegance. But the idyll ended abruptly on November 22, 1963, when Lee Harvey Oswald assassinated Kennedy in Dallas.

Her extraordinary show of courage and dignity in the days immediately following his death, especially as displayed at the President's funeral, endeared her to the world. For the next few years, she was still prominent in high society, still consistently voted one of the most admired women in America. But in October 1968 the announcement of her engagement to Aristotle Onassis profoundly shocked the American people, not because her remarriage was unexpected, but for her choice of a man more than 20 years her senior, a rough-mannered, jet-setting Greek shipping tycoon.

Jacqueline Bouvier was the daughter of John Vernou 'Black Jack' Bouvier III, a wealthy Wall Street stockbroker. He was a hard-drinking man and a philanderer, but she adored him and it was perhaps for this reason that she tolerated her husband's later infidelities. Her father and her mother, Janet Lee Bouvier, an attractive society woman, separated when she was eight, divorcing in 1938. Her mother went on to marry Hugh D. Auchincloss, a wealthy lawyer and stockbroker from Washington. From then on Jacqueline played the two men off against each other, enjoying holidays both with her father and her horses in East Hampton, Long Island, and at her stepfather's estates.

It was her stepfather's third marriage. His second had been to Nina Gore Vidal, the mother of the writer, and for this reason, Jacqueline saw a good deal of the young Gore Vidal as a child. Her other early companion was her younger sister Lee, who was to marry an ex-Polish nobleman, and later London businessman, Prince Stanislas 'Stas' Radziwill.

Jacqueline was educated at the fashionable Chapin School in New York, where her mischievousness earned her the label of 'the very worst girl in school', and at Holton-Arms, a blue-chip girls' school in Washington. She was soon displaying an unusual degree of social poise. When she came out in New York at the age of 17, the society columnist, Igor Cassini, described her as the 'Queen Deb of the Year ... a regal brunette who has classic features and the daintiness of Dresden porcelain'. But she had no intention of being married off too soon to any of the young men she had grown up with. After two years at Vassar, she spent a year in Paris at the Sorbonne, an experience which gave her a lasting love for the country and put the final polish on her fluent French. Her education was completed at George Washington University.

Afterwards she won the first prize in a *Vogue* talent contest, with essays on Diaghilev, Baudelaire, and Oscar Wilde. Her prize consisted of spending six months working in the New York office of the magazine and six months in Paris, and, because of the latter period away from home, she decided to turn the offer down. But she was sufficiently interested in journalism to approach Arthur Krock, a friend on *The New York Times,* who found her a job on the *Washington Times-Herald* in 1952. This lasted for 18 months and led to interviews as a photojournalist. Jacqueline had her difficulties with the job: 'I always forgot to pull out the slide,' she admitted, but pulled off some minor coups, interviewing Pat and Richard Nixon, and the junior senator from Massachusetts, John F. Kennedy.

It was not the first time they had met. Indeed, by the time of her interview, they had known each other for a year or so, having been brought together by a matchmaking friend at a dinner party in Washington. Their relationship began to intensify after Kennedy had launched his bid for the Senate in 1952. He was beginning to realize that marriage to the right woman would enhance his political prospects, though even then he never played the devoted lover. He once sent her a rather perfunctory postcard from Bermuda saying 'Wish you were here. Cheers, Jack', which Jacqueline held up to friends as her sole piece of courtship correspondence.

That was not entirely true, for the following year, when she was sent to England to cover the Coronation in 1953, he sent her a telegram: 'ARTICLES EXCELLENT. BUT YOU ARE MISSED.' The day after she returned they were engaged, and married in September that year in an extravagant wedding attended by 1,700 friends and family, and officiated over by Archbishop Richard Cushing of Boston, who brought with him the blessing of Pope Pius XII. Not everything went smoothly: Jacqueline's father, who had planned to walk his daughter down the aisle, had started celebrating a little too early in his hotel room before the ceremony, and, being deemed unfit for the task by Jacqueline's mother, was replaced by Hugh Auchincloss.

Jacqueline devoted her early years of marriage to her husband, grooming his appearance, teaching him about art, and encouraging him to mend his occasionally abrupt social manners. Already there were early signs of strain: Jacqueline was not particularly interested in politics and saw her role as being primarily one of supporter. She was happy enough to switch from Republican, her family's party, to Democrat for her husband, though there was no evidence that she ever really understood the politics involved: 'She breathes all the political gases that flow around us, but she never seems to inhale them,' Jack once complained. She was also, even at this point, notoriously extravagant with her personal expenditure, particularly on clothes.

For her part, though she had had no illusions about his cavalier attitude to women before the wedding, she was hurt by her husband's frequent infidelities. But what rocked the marriage most was Jack's reaction in 1956 following the ending of her second pregnancy (the first had resulted in a miscarriage in 1955) in a premature and stillborn birth. Jack was then enjoying a Mediterranean cruise and, on being told the news, was reluctant to return home and comfort his wife. It was only when a friend bluntly put it to him: 'You better haul your ass back to your wife if you ever want to run for President' that he caught the next plane out. His behaviour was bad enough to prompt a rumour, never denied, that she had been offered $1 million by her father-in-law, Joe Kennedy, to stay with his son.

Eventually they did have three children – Caroline in 1957, John in 1960, and later Patrick in 1963, though the latter died almost immediately after his birth. Jacqueline became pregnant with John early in 1960, just after her husband had declared his candidacy for the Democratic nomination. Kennedy at first rebuffed his wife's offer to help him with his campaign: 'The American people just aren't ready for someone like you,' he told her, 'I guess we'll just have to run you through subliminally in one of those quick flash TV spots so no one will notice.'

This rather unflattering appraisal of her usefulness was not borne out by events. Jacqueline grew, over the next few months, into a very effective campaign wife, holding fund-raising teas and the occasional press conference, even delivering a couple of pretty speeches in her famously whisper-soft voice, and providing her husband with an endless source of campaign jokes on the subject of her heavily pregnant condition. Above all, she was visually pleasing to the electorate and the prospect of a young family in the White House at the dawn of a hopeful new decade was an invigorating one.

Her husband was sworn in as thirty-fifth President of the United States on January 20, 1961. At first Jacqueline found it more difficult than she had foreseen to accustom herself to the loss of privacy that went with being First Lady. She complained of feeling like a fish in a fishbowl, or a moth on a windowpane. But she adapted by trying to define her own areas of responsibility. Typically for the period, these centred around the First Lady's traditional domain, the home, although in her case they went far beyond a little light redecoration.

She decided to take on the complete restoration of the White House which, she complained, looked as though it had been furnished from 'discount stores', launching a campaign to restore it to its former glory and to make it a 'national historical object' which would reveal something of the history of the Presidency, back to Lincoln's day, through its furnishings, paintings, and sculpture. To this end, she persuaded Congress to designate the building a national museum and enlisted the help of museum directors and historians, forming committees to supervise and fund the project. Finally she published an *Historic Guide to the White House*, and appeared on television in 1962, watched by 48 million viewers, giving a guided tour through the newly restored rooms. The success of the project produced an enormous increase in the numbers of visitors to the White House, and proved to be another breakthrough in the public's growing estimation of her.

She became a successful political hostess, bringing together in informal dinner parties a stimulating mixture of artists, musicians, businessmen, and politicians. But it was perhaps abroad that she was most appreciated. The sort of adulation she received in France set a pattern for future foreign visits, where her poise, charm, and effortless linguistic skills endeared her also to the Canadians, to Nikita Khrushchev, who was then holding talks with her husband in Vienna, to the Queen in London, and to the peoples of India and Pakistan, which she toured in 1962. She became, for the American public, the nearest thing they had ever had to a queen.

For all the adulation she was receiving, she could still insist at times on withdrawing from the public gaze, much to her husband's annoyance. Once she even refused to appear at a Distinguished Ladies' Reception held in her honour (Jack eventually went in her place). And as rumours about her husband's infidelities continued to circulate around Washington, Jacqueline and her children, perhaps in retaliation, began to spend more time away from the White House, visiting friends and relatives, hunting from her country estate in Middleburg, Virginia, and spending holidays in Greece and Italy. But the death of her third child, Patrick, in August 1963, less than two days after his birth drew the family close again, though Jacqueline became depressed.

To try to raise her spirits, her sister, Lee Radziwill, invited her in October to join a group for a short break in the Mediterranean on the yacht belonging to the Greek shipping tycoon, Aristotle Onassis. She accepted, travelling without her husband again, but chaperoned this time by Franklin Roosevelt Jr, then under secretary for commerce, and his wife Suzanne. It was not the first time she had been on board *Christina*. That had been in 1957 in Monte Carlo, when the Kennedys had been invited to meet Winston Churchill, Onassis's guest. The meeting had not been a success. Churchill, then very old, was not on his best form, and Jacqueline later teased her husband 'Maybe he thought you were a waiter.' Nor did Kennedy approve of his sister-in-law's infatuation with Onassis (who was invited to stay at the White House during Kennedy's funeral).

Jacqueline returned from the trip restored and eager to give the world a most ostentatious show of marital happiness for the President's final public appearance, in Dallas in November that year. The full horror of the scene in Dallas after the shooting – Jacqueline's suit being drenched with the blood of her dying husband – was captured by television cameras and relayed around the world. Afterwards the fact that she was still wearing the suit during President Lyndon B. Johnson's swearing-in on Air Force One was seen by a grieving nation as an extraordinarily poignant and fitting tribute to her husband, as too was her quiet dignity at his funeral, when she stood fraily by his graveside supported only by their two small children. In those days immediately following the president's death and after her very statesman-like television performance when she thanked the American nation for their words of support, she became fixed in the mind of a traumatized nation as the necessary symbol of chief mourner.

Even after it was all over, it remained difficult for her to escape the attentions of the press, who were now more than ever intent on examining her private conduct, eager for proof of some indiscretion. She decided to move to a New York apartment with her children, and set to work on building up the memorial to her husband. She persuaded President Johnson to change the name of Cape Canaveral to Cape Kennedy (it was changed back in 1973), and launched the project of a John F. Kennedy Memorial Library in Boston.

She found it hard to escape completely the possessive attentions of the Kennedy clan. She became particularly close to Jack's brother, Bobby Kennedy, supporting him in his 1968 campaign for the Democratic presidential nomination. His murder in June that year, which shook her badly, may well have precipitated her rush into marriage with Aristotle Onassis, a man of whom Bobby strongly disapproved. The fact that she managed to keep their romance a secret for so long was partly because of the physical and social incongruities between them it seemed impossible to outsiders and partly because she had been seen very publicly with other men – the widowed Lord Harlech, a former ambassador to the United States, and Roswell Gilpatric, under-secretary of defense in the Kennedy administration.

They were married, after some hard bargaining on Jacqueline's part over the fine print of a marriage contract, on October 20, 1968, less than a week after word of their engagement had been broken on the front page of the *Boston Herald-Traveler*. The uproar with which the news was greeted was not the only complication. Onassis was a divorced man, whose first wife was still living, and a member of the Greek Orthodox Church. The Vatican was extremely critical of the match, announcing that Jacqueline Kennedy would be living in a state of mortal sin, despite a refusal to condemn the marriage by Cardinal Cushing, who had officiated at her first wedding. Maria Callas, the opera singer, with whom Onassis had been conducting a very open affair for years, was also enraged.

Ignoring the outcry, the couple were married on Onassis's private Greek island of Skorpios, ejecting some 90 passengers from a scheduled flight of the bridegroom's Olympic Airways in order to make the trip.

It was a measure of the public disapproval of the marriage that stories now began to circulate, indicating that Jacqueline Kennedy Onassis had been something less than perfect, even as First Lady. Her former personal secretary, Mary Barelli Gallagher, published a book, *My Life with Jacqueline Kennedy* (1969), in which Jacqueline was portrayed as both extravagant and tight-fisted; a woman who spent more than her husband's entire salary on herself, yet insisted that her staff shop at stores that gave trading stamps. The book was serialized worldwide.

The marriage to Onassis, meanwhile, was not going well and before he died, in March 1975, he was reported by *The New York Times* to be intending to sue for divorce. His bequest to Jacqueline of an income of $250,000 a year was considerably less than the lump sum of $250 million she had expected, and the will contained a clause that would stop the allowance if she tried to lay claim to the estate. Instead, Onassis left the bulk of his fortune to his daughter Christina, who had never been on friendly terms with her stepmother.

It was not until September 1977 that the legal wrangle between Jacqueline Kennedy Onassis and her stepdaughter over the provisions of Aristotle Onassis's will was finally resolved when Christina, who had reportedly inherited about $250 million, agreed to pay Jacqueline $20 million to settle the matter. This virtually doubled her inheritance, and was considerably more than the $3 million which Onassis had reportedly told friends he was offering for a divorce settlement.

In her own way, she continued to support the Kennedy clan, turning out for Ted Kennedy in his 1980 bid to win the Democratic nomination from Jimmy Carter, and putting in an appearance with the family in Florida in 1991 when William Kennedy Smith was charged with rape, although she always refused to allow her children to be exploited politically. She had never been like any of the other Kennedy women – she was too dignified to join in with the rough family games of touch football, but beneath the elegant, slightly vulnerable facade she shared their survivor instincts.

She returned, after her second husband's death, to New York and found her niche there in the last two decades of her life as a publisher, first as an editor at Viking – a connection she severed after a disagreement – and later as an associate editor at Doubleday, where she worked up to her death.

Her companion in later years was Maurice Templesman, whom she had first met in the late 1950s when he had arranged a meeting between Jack Kennedy and Harry Oppenheimer. She tried to protect their privacy and that of her family to the end, although even the smallest appearance or public comment was considered worthy of intense press speculation. Gradually she retired from public view as, in the last few months, she succumbed to the cancer that killed her. One of her last public appearances was hosting a party on board a yacht in Martha's Vineyard for one of Jack Kennedy's greatest admirers, Bill Clinton.

Jacqueline Kennedy Onassis is survived by her
daughter Caroline and her son John.

FRED PERRY

2 FEBRUARY 1995

FRED PERRY, lawn and table tennis player, and three times Wimbledon men's singles champion, died in Melbourne yesterday, aged 85. He was born in Stockport, Cheshire, on May 18, 1909.

Fred Perry was the last Englishman to win the men's singles title at Wimbledon and the first man this century to win it three years running (1934, 1935, and 1936). In a four-year reign in which he was pre-eminent in world tennis he also captured the US title in 1933, 1934, and 1936, the Australian title in 1934, and the French title in 1935. These are feats unexampled in modern British tennis.

Yet Perry's lawn tennis career followed an equally remarkable one at the table tennis table. By the age of 19 he had already reached the top, winning the world championship in Budapest to crown the 1928–29 season. Perry gave up table tennis in 1930 to concentrate on tennis, yet only two years after that he accomplished a unique double. In Paris, playing tennis in the daytime, he went through successive rounds of the Coupe Noel, to beat Jean Borotra, the 'Bounding Basque', in the final; while in the evenings he was participating in a Paris table tennis tournament, eventually beating Szabados, then world champion, in the final of that competition.

Perry's success in lawn tennis was built on qualities which did not always recommend themselves to the socially-conscious ethos of the All England Club as it was in the 1930s and for long afterwards. He was not, in the committee's perception, 'a gentleman'. As a player there was little reticence about him. He exuded confidence and was a swashbuckling competitor. None of these assets would have availed him if they had not been allied to a brilliant match-playing brain, speed of foot about the court and great strength of arm and shoulder. His running forehand was full of menace, and there were few opponents throughout the world who did not fear it.

Frederick John Perry was the son of Samuel Frederick Perry, who was a cotton spinner, leader of the local Co-operative movement and Labour MP for Kettering, 1923–24, and again, 1929–31. He went to elementary school in Stockport and started playing table tennis after joining the YMCA. Later, when the family moved to Ealing, he learnt his lawn tennis at the Herga Club, Harrow. His father, recognizing his talent, let him stop his office job and supported him for a year while he developed his game.

It was at the Herga club that his potential was first spotted, in particular his fleetness of foot and his ability to hit a rising ball early on both flanks with his immensely strong wrists. He early developed the passion for fitness which, if not then fashionable in the 'Corinthian Casuals' ethos of the day, was to stand him in good stead. He had an uncanny instinct for the first hint of wilting in the opposition and the stamina to exploit it, no matter how fast and furious the foregoing sets had been. In later years he would humorously recall that he was regarded as the first Englishman who hated to lose – a recollection which is probably faulty as applying to a game as competitive as lawn tennis has always been. More likely, Perry was the first to admit openly his dislike of losing.

Perry first announced himself as a force in world tennis when he won the US Open in 1933, beating the Australian J. H. Crawford 6–3, 11–13, 4–6, 6–0, 6–1. This made him the first British player to win the title since H. L. Doherty in 1903. Perry reinforced the impression that he was about to become the world's best when, in the following year at Wimbledon, he again beat Crawford, then reigning champion, in straight sets, 6–3, 6–0, 7–5. The brash newcomer did not go down well with Wimbledon officialdom.

After the match Perry overheard a committee member telling Crawford that the best man did not always win. Perry exploded when, in addition, he found his presentation tie merely draped over his seat instead of being given to him personally. He extracted an apology and in the following year, grudging approval of his qualities.

In the 1935 Wimbledon final his opponent was the German Gottfried von Cramm. Perry overwhelmed him 6–4, 6–4, 6–4, in a match which was only less one-sided than the 1936 final. Here again Cramm was the opponent. In his first service game the German pulled a muscle in his right thigh and, although he carried the injury as best he could, the match turned into a rout, Perry running out the winner, 6–1, 6–1, 6–0.

Perry had himself had a similar affliction in the US Open final in 1934, playing with a bandaged ankle as he won against the American W. Allison, 6–4, 6–3, 3–6, 1–6, 8–6, a gruelling marathon in which he was forced to husband his resources and take things as easily as he dared against such a top-class opponent. Allison was to avenge the defeat in the following year, knocking out Perry in the semi-final round at Forest Hills.

In the meantime Perry had become one of the most successful British Davis Cup players. Perry, Austin, Hughes, and H. G. N. Lee were the regular members of a British team which ruled the game until Perry eventually turned professional in 1936 after he had beaten Donald Budge for the US Open title in five sets. Earlier Perry had led Britain to her fourth successive triumph in the Davis Cup.

After turning professional Perry played a series of classic matches against Ellsworth Vines and Donald Budge. He played for several more years as a professional until an injury forced him to retire in 1942.

Settling in the United States, he was for some years a professional tennis coach in Florida and he also regularly wrote and broadcast on tennis. In 1950, with Theodore Wegner, he opened what was to become a highly profitable business in sports clothing, Fred Perry Sportswear.

Always a strict teetotaller, Perry seldom joined in post-tennis gatherings, preferring the company of one or two of his closer friends with whom, in a slight American accent, he loved to recall times past. To honour the fiftieth anniversary of his achievements, the All England committee erected a statue of him on the lawns in January 1984. On the same occasion the club's new gates were also dedicated to him.

Perry did not esteem the achievements of today's exponents of lawn tennis, supposedly so much fitter and better equipped technically than their predecessors, and did not hesitate to say so. In his autobiography, *Fred Perry*, published in 1984, he computed that with the time allowed between each point and for changing ends, in today's game, such an 'epic' as the four and a half hour 1980 Wimbledon final between McEnroe and Borg would, in his day, have lasted only an hour and three quarters, since the players were actually in repose between play for two and three quarter hours. He described his perception of the modern game with amusing irascibility: 'I don't know whether to laugh or cry when I watch the start of a tennis match these days. There they are, two young sportsmen trained to the limit. And what do they do? They play one game – just one game then they sit down for a rest. They'll be providing armchairs and Lilos next.'

Perry was four times married: to the film star Helen Vinson; to the fashion model Sandra Breaux; to Lorraine Pigeon, sister of the film actor Walter Pidgeon; and to Barbara Friedman, former wife of the Hollywood director Seymour Friedman. There was a daughter of his fourth marriage.

HAROLD WILSON

24 MAY 1995

LORD WILSON OF RIEVAULX, KG, OBE, PC, FRS, who served as Prime Minister, 1964–70 and 1974–76, died yesterday, aged 79. He was born on March 11, 1916.

Harold Wilson always liked to remind people, and be reminded, that he had been Prime Minister of the United Kingdom more times – four times – than anyone since Gladstone. He dominated British politics between 1963, when he became Leader of the Opposition, and 1976, when in a stunning *coup de théâtre* he announced his resignation from No. 10. But his overall achievement was much harder to pin down. He may have stripped his party of an outdated ideology but he put nothing in its place, leaving to his immediate successors a bankrupt political estate.

He once said that 'a week is a long time in politics', a saying that was to be turned against him when his voluminous published accounts of his various administrations proved to be not reflections on policy, still less a measured assessment of national or party objectives, but rather a remorselessly detailed celebration of his own skill in dealing with day-to-day crises and jealous threats to his leadership – sometimes real, often imagined.

Yet he succeeded brilliantly in his 20 months as Leader of the Opposition and during his first administration, 1964–66, in establishing the Labour Party as a plausible alternative to the Conservatives. He stole many old Tory clothes, including patriotism, for Labour's use. Eventually, however, keeping his party in office had too transparently become an end in itself. Few of the great economic or industrial policies promised in Labour's manifestos came anywhere near fulfilment. Perhaps his most enduring and characteristic achievement since he remained a bit of a don manqué (his last ambition, in which he was disappointed, was to become Master of University College, Oxford) was the founding of the Open University.

In office he became more and more given to nautical or military metaphors, talking often of 'being blown off course' or of how narrow were 'the limits of manoeuvre'. This was a tendency that developed early. In his *Diaries* Richard Crossman recalls his leader as remarking in a conscious echo of the Duke of Wellington's Peninsular Campaign that he was about to 'retreat to my lines at Torres Vedras' within a month of becoming Prime Minister.

He read military and political biographies but had few, if any, other intellectual or cultural interests except for a love of Gilbert and Sullivan. Politics was his only passion. He married a quiet, private and retiring person at a time when his own ambitions, and Mary Wilson's hopes for him, were both set on academic life. She was loyal to him, but found the exposure of public life hard to endure, especially when her modest but genuine talent as a popular poet was noticed and mocked because of his fame. A remarkable incident took place when, after Wilson's resignation, James Callaghan paid a tribute to his predecessor at his first conference as party leader. There was utter silence. But loud applause followed when he offered a conventional compliment to Mary Wilson.

James Harold Wilson was born in Milnsbridge, near Huddersfield, the only son and second child of Herbert and Ethel Wilson. His father was an industrial chemist and he was brought up in a comfortable section of the lower middle class. He did not take long to show signs of political precocity. When his parents visited him in hospital, where he had just undergone an appendicitis operation at the age of seven, he promptly urged them not to linger lest they miss the chance of voting for Philip Snowden in the 1923 general election; and there was also the much-reproduced photograph of him as an eight-year-old standing outside No. 10 on a visit to London. He came from a chapel-going, Congregational home and soon acquired a keen interest in Scouting, becoming a King's Scout – something which, no doubt, motivated him as a prefect to put down 'an outbreak of smuttiness' at his school by instituting compulsory lunchtime games.

But, as his teachers spotted, he was predominantly academic-minded. From the Wirral Grammar School, where he went from Royds Hall School, Huddersfield, after his family's move from Yorkshire to Cheshire, he won an exhibition in history to Jesus College, Oxford. Once there, he read PPE and in 1937 got the best first in the subject that year, also winning the Gladstone Memorial Prize and the Webb Medley Scholarship. He was awarded a lectureship at New College and, a year later, a research fellowship at University College, where before the war he began to work under the supervision of the Master, Sir William Beveridge, on the problems of unemployment.

On the outbreak of war, he did not volunteer for the Forces – something the Tories were to make something of in later years – but instead joined the Civil Service, where he rose quickly. This was partly thanks to his own characteristic energy, assiduity and efficiency but also owed something to patronage from Beveridge, about which he was engagingly candid. In 1943 he became director of economics and statistics at the Ministry of Fuel and Power and secretary of the British side of the important Combined Production Resources Board and the Combined Raw Materials Board. No Prime Minister has ever had such a thorough knowledge of the working of 'the machine'.

His great abilities had been noticed by several Labour ministers in the wartime coalition and he received a number of approaches to stand for Parliament, finally settling on the then marginal Lancashire seat of Ormskirk. He was elected in 1945 and Clement Attlee at once appointed him Under-Secretary at the Ministry of Works. Early in 1947 he was promoted to be Secretary for Overseas Trade at the Board of Trade. He led a trade mission to the Soviet Union which, though unsuccessful, revealed his self-confidence and toughness as a negotiator. When, in September 1947, Sir Stafford Cripps became Minister for Economic Affairs, Wilson succeeded him as President of the Board of Trade, entering the Cabinet at the remarkably early age of 31.

Yet Wilson had no real standing at this time within his party. His speeches were thoroughly researched but drily delivered, with no emotion and few debating skills. So some surprise was caused when he resigned from the Cabinet with Aneurin Bevan in April 1951 over priorities for expenditure, reflected in Bevan's case by his protest against the introduction of prescription charges into the National Health Service (Wilson himself gave much greater emphasis to the defence budget). Some thought he was a raw young man swept away by the power of Bevan's personality. Others, for tempers were high, denounced him as a rat deserting a sinking ship. He claimed merely that Hugh Gaitskell's proposed cuts as Chancellor in the social services, to pay for the rearmament programme, were damaging both to the poor and to the Labour Party's electoral prospects.

In 1952 he attained his reward by being elected at the party conference to the constituency section of the National Executive. But he was never of the doctrinaire or ideological Left. In 1954 Bevan suddenly resigned from the Shadow Cabinet, alleging that party policy over South-East Asia was too pro-American. Wilson was next-in-line for his seat, having been the runner-up in the PLP elections the previous year. He allowed himself to be co-opted, causing great fury to Bevan but retaining the support of some on the Left such as Crossman. With so many older men exhausted or retiring, Wilson, along with Gaitskell, had suddenly become a major figure within the party.

He saw himself as a conciliator, with better political antennae than Gaitskell, always trying to find the point of balance in the party. At this time he also broadened his knowledge and influence in the Labour movement by accepting nearly every invitation to address constituency or trade union meetings. Nor did he neglect contacts with industry and the universities. The intelligent, friendly, but enigmatic face behind the pipe became familiar. His personal closeness to talented publicists, such as Crossman and Barbara Castle (who had been his PPS), his talks around the country and, once Gaitskell had become leader, his constant exposure as Shadow Chancellor all improved his debating style. He worked on it methodically, equipping himself with 'impromptu repartee' and set jokes, which the Commons began to enjoy, and his stature started to grow.

But soon there came a hiccup. After Labour's defeat in the 1959 general election, Gaitskell – like Tony Blair 35 years later – sought to modernize his party by abolishing the notorious Clause Four of its constitution (which appeared to commit it to public ownership of nearly everything) and to assert his leadership by fighting back against the unilateralist resolutions passed at the 1960 party conference. Wilson disagreed with, and distrusted, both the nationalizers and the disarmers. Yet he felt that Gaitskell should not have forced a showdown. The Left was strong in the constituency parties and was determined that Gaitskell should be challenged. After Bevan's death in July 1960 they regarded Wilson as their candidate and, with some reluctance, he ran for the leadership in November 1960, being defeated by 166 votes to 81 in the Parliamentary Labour Party.

The episode earned him many enemies. But his attacks on Tory ministers – particularly on Lord Home once he became Shadow Foreign Secretary in 1961 – earned him a growing, if grudging, respect. So, on Gaitskell's sudden death in January 1963, he was the most generally acceptable leader, defeating George Brown (who had handily beaten him three months earlier for the deputy leadership) by 144 votes to 103. Again, there was some luck involved. The party had not shifted suddenly to the Left. The volatile Brown, with his love of drink, scenes, and quarrels, was simply regarded as too high a risk.

At the general election of October 1964 Wilson took personal command, making all the major decisions, holding all the press conferences, dominating Labour's campaign. The voters were encouraged to focus on Wilson, the 'new man', as against Home, the symbol of a tired and effete Britain. Even so, Labour won an overall majority of only four seats.

Once he got to No. 10, some of his own closest economic advisers urged immediate devaluation upon him. But Wilson – fearing the political consequences – stood out firmly against it. He sought salvation instead through domestic institutional changes. A Department of Economic Affairs was set up under George Brown, who persuaded both the CBI and the TUC to agree that prices and incomes should not rise faster than productivity, and that claims for increases should be put before a new Prices and Incomes Board. What some had long been calling 'corporatism' had been given institutional recognition.

In the spring of 1966, Wilson called the expected general election. His timing was excellent. A majority of 97 was secured and, again, he ran and dominated the whole campaign. The word went out that all issues were to be played down but one: himself or the new Tory leader, Edward Heath. With what Jews call chutzpah, he campaigned on his record, after 18 months, and pictured Labour as the new natural party of government. He radiated to the public an impression both of competent power and of humane concern. Even those who were a little sceptical admired his political adroitness.

Winning so decisively brought all the underlying economic problems home to roost. The targets of the much-vaunted National Plan had become a joke, for the balance of payments was massively adverse, wages and prices were rising, and production stagnant. The Cabinet was deeply divided about the merits of devaluation. Roy Jenkins, Anthony Crosland and George Brown led the devaluers and briefly (in July 1966) converted the Chancellor, James Callaghan, but Wilson swiftly reconverted him, believing deeply that it could only be to Labour's discredit and that bright skies were around the corner.

When the inevitable cuts in public expenditure were announced, George Brown resigned from the DEA but accepted the Foreign Office. The voluntary prices and incomes restraint became statutory and, to their astonishment and anger, the middle classes found their salaries frozen. Wilson proved unexpectedly tough in his defence of what soon turned out to be an undefendable position. No amount of austerity could stop Britain's reserves being eaten up in support of an historic rather than a realistic pound–dollar ratio. When 26 Labour MPs abstained in a crucial division, he first made his famous remark about 'being blown off course'. At last, in November 1967, a run on the pound forced him into a drastic 14.3 per cent devaluation, after seeing most of the Bank of England's reserves wiped out in a hopeless, stubborn defence.

His reputation went into a tailspin, for his personal responsibility was obvious. His relationship with the press had been excellent in his first Government. But from 1966 onwards it had turned sour on both sides. Many journalists had gone overboard for him in 1964 and now tried to make up for it. He felt betrayed, and mutual dislike and distrust grew rapidly.

The old Central Africa, now the Rhodesia, problem had been a constant thorn in the flesh to British governments. Wilson set out to solve it. He had a dramatic meeting with Ian Smith in December, 1966, at sea on HMS *Tiger*. But when Smith returned to Salisbury, he abandoned the agreement completely. Wilson had made the uncharacteristic mistake of announcing in advance that he would not use force against UDI (the unilateral declaration of independence). He later claimed that he was advised in the first days of UDI that military intervention was impossible. But retired defence chiefs and civil servants were to deny angrily that such advice had been either asked for or given.

He was bolder in grasping the nettle of Europe, over which, with the 1966 election safely won, he decided to make a new application for membership despite strong opposition, and not only from the Left of the party. In the spring of 1967 he and Brown toured the capitals of 'the Six'. The move was concerted with Ireland, Norway, and Denmark. No fewer than 62 Labour MPs voted against the bid. But it was all for nothing. General de Gaulle delivered the final French veto in November 1967.

With that ball on the ground, Wilson badly needed to throw a new one up in the air. He had gradually become convinced of the need, both for the sake of the economy and for the popularity of his Government, to bring in a reform of industrial relations, for stronger laws to regulate trade union organization, especially on how strikes were called. In the spring of 1968 Barbara Castle had become First Secretary of State in charge of the freshly created Department of Employment and Productivity. She was already thinking on the same lines.

In January 1969 a new policy was set out in a White Paper, 'In Place of Strife'. Opinion polls showed its popularity in the country but it was bitterly opposed by the trade unions and most of the activists in the Labour Party. Again, as with the prices and incomes policy (which had simply proved unworkable), there had been no real preparation. Wilson seemed to place his trust in his own hold on the party machine, the authority of his office and in Barbara Castle's great popularity with the Left. But more than 60 Labour MPs voted against the White Paper and the Chief Whip, Robert Mellish, and the chairman of the Parliamentary Labour Party, Douglas Houghton, had to tell the Prime Minister that it was unlikely that a Bill would find a majority. In the worst climbdown of his career he was forced by his own Cabinet – whom he characteristically accused of 'turning yellow' – to announce the withdrawal of the Bill. The TUC patched up appearances by offering 'a solemn and binding undertaking' – an expression of its own willingness in future to take action against unofficial strikes.

Paradoxically, Wilson's own standing in the opinion polls was temporarily enhanced. Perhaps the public thought that the Conservatives should have supported him, not quibbled. Certainly, the balance of payments had improved after devaluation, so a relatively neutral Budget from Roy Jenkins in 1970 offered £200 million of tax relief especially to the lower paid. Wilson was certainly confident when he went to the country in June 1970. This time, the campaign was positively monarchical in tone. The public, however, had had enough. A 4.7 per cent national swing gave Edward Heath an overall majority of 30.

For the first year of Opposition, Wilson neglected the Commons to an extraordinary extent. Like Winston Churchill before him, he devoted himself almost entirely to his memoirs, publishing in 1971 *The Labour Government, 1964–70*, a massive work which was remarkable for its complete lack both of any radical thrust and of any analysis of basic national problems. The book did not enthuse his party nor impress his critics. It did, however, make him a lot of money from a *Sunday Times* serialization, which was just as well since in those days a Leader of the Opposition was expected to run his office on a shoe-string.

The campaign against Heath's Industrial Relations Act gave Wilson the chance to mend his fences with the Left of the party, which now included some of the leaders of the largest unions. But grass-roots opposition to Heath's abortive attempts to apply market principles to the welfare state brought into an ageing party structure many of the student Marxists or 'New Left', who had become disillusioned with the Soviet Union itself after 1956. Typically, Wilson at first took a conciliatory rather than a combative tone towards them, though privately he groaned at this new cross he had to bear. This may partly explain his most spectacular 'U-turn'. Europe had always been unpopular with the Left of the party. After de Gaulle's death, Heath made a direct approach to President Pompidou. Britain's entry to the Community was assured. At first, Wilson had reserved his position but at a special conference of the Labour Party in July 1971 he announced that the terms were not acceptable, although in fact they were very much those he had been prepared to contemplate in his own wooing of Europe in 1967. This bouleversement severely damaged his own reputation, though his supporters were later to argue that he deliberately sacrificed it in order to preserve the unity of the party.

When Heath, incensed by the celebrated confrontation with the miners, went to the country in February 1974 the two parties emerged almost equal, with just four seats between them and with fourteen Liberals, ten Ulster Unionists, and nine Scottish and Welsh Nationalists holding the balance of power. Heath was unable to come to terms with the Liberals and, after three days' delay, resigned. During the election campaign, Wilson had often appeared tired, edgy, and dispirited. But delivered, as he had been, from an enforced retirement, all his old energy and political skill initially came back.

He promised the unions repeal of the hated Conservative Industrial Relations Act and appointed Michael Foot, the darling of the old Left, to be Secretary of State for Employment. Denis Healey as Chancellor promised higher pensions and higher taxes on the rich. James Callaghan, as Foreign Secretary, was sent around Europe to demand renegotiation in the loudest and most truculent manner possible. But, despite the much-promoted 'social contract' with the unions, wages continued to rise and the overseas spending account was in record deficit. Luckily, in the late summer, prices were still just behind wages. So Wilson boldly called a second general election for October 1974. The gamble did not work nearly as well as in 1966: this time Labour emerged with an overall majority, not of 97, but of just three.

Yet the parliamentary margin looked more precarious than it actually was. The narrowness of the majority gave Wilson a strong hold on his party. The Scottish Nationalists, who now had 11 MPs elected to the Commons, were kept in check by a Royal Commission on the Constitution to consider 'devolution' – a term he used to obscure any clear distinction between local government and federalism. But Wilson himself was tired and in his fourth administration he came more and more to rely on a 'kitchen cabinet' (which tended to vary as individuals went in and out of favour) and on his long-suffering Downing Street private office.

His devoted political secretary Marcia Williams (who served him from 1956 onwards and whom in 1974 he created a life peer as Lady Falkender) was widely felt to exercise too much influence. But she was an able and strong-minded woman whose political astuteness he rightly admired. He could also be a man of great personal consideration and kindness. When, in 1968, Marcia Williams found herself pregnant with the first of her two sons by the political correspondent Walter Terry, it was Wilson who advised her against having an abortion despite the inevitable risk of rumour and scandal to his own reputation. Deliberately posing as tough-minded in public, he was seldom anything but soft-hearted in private.

In his fourth administration he left more and more decisions to senior colleagues. But he kept the European question in his own hands. The renegotiations, not unexpectedly, yielded few concessions. Wilson was thus on the horns of a dilemma: the party was overwhelmingly against staying in, industrial and financial opinion (and the entire Civil Service machine) were not merely for staying but for playing a positive role, and the Cabinet was divided. Although by sixteen to seven they favoured remaining inside the Community, resignations were threatened from both camps. So Wilson, in putting the matter to the British people in a referendum, decided to waive the convention of collective responsibility. Cabinet members could, and did, campaign on rival sides. He got off the hook when the public in June 1975 voted by 67 to 33 per cent for the new terms.

With this humiliating defeat of the Left in the European referendum, Wilson felt able to move back towards the old panacea of an incomes policy. A joint statement with the TUC was made in July 1975. Compulsion had been dropped by the Cabinet and Foot secured the formidable backing of Jack Jones, the leader of the TGWU.

But in the autumn industrial strategy shifted towards greater support for the private sector and a major economic review heralded a sharp cutback in the growth of public expenditure. All this led to much protest on the back benches of the PLP and early in March 1976 there was a Government defeat, thanks to the abstention of 37 left-wing MPs. Wilson denounced them with unusual bluntness and bitterness, though he did not make the mistake of referring (as he had in his 1966–70 Government) to Labour MPs as having 'dog licences'. Nevertheless, his spell over his party was largely broken. He celebrated his sixtieth birthday and then took the political world utterly by surprise by announcing his resignation as Prime Minister on March 16, 1976.

There was wild press speculation about 'real' and 'hidden' reasons. But the reasons, for once, were almost certainly those he himself gave: his age, his length of service, his desire for some private life, and his reluctance to imperil his record of victories by leading the party into another election. (His claim that he had fulfilled his programme was more questionable.)

He accepted the Garter and awarded 42 honours to members of his entourage or friends (the latter overwhelmingly in showbusiness or financial undertakings) and retired to the back benches. Five years later none of the peers announced in the notorious 'lavender' Honours List still took the Labour whip. Though nominally impartial, such influence as he retained went towards the election of James Callaghan as his successor.

Several 'now-it-can-be-told' books followed from his old staff at No. 10, and there were some angry recriminations. But he would not be drawn into any of this. His silence on party issues was almost total. Old colleagues were first impressed by his tact and then depressed to realize that he had lost interest in national affairs and even in the Labour Party itself. Private life was authorship and, before Alzheimer's disease took a cruel toll on his memory, a childlike pleasure in accepting invitations to preside at public occasions, especially educational ones. Delighted school heads in Yorkshire and elsewhere discovered, while they still believed in giving prizes, that he gladly handed them out and delivered a long speech into the bargain.

He wrote, with some assistance, a surprisingly conventional book on *The Governance of Britain* (1976), an unsatisfactory effort at an academic treatment rather than a realistic account of high politics. He presented a 13-part television series on former Prime Ministers, which was turned into a book, *A Prime Minister on Prime Ministers* (1977). The tone was omniscient but benign, forgiving and congratulatory all round. A second volume of memoirs, covering his Government of 1974–76, was published in 1979. It was exactly like the first. His best book was devoted to a subject that had always been close to his heart, Israel. Published under the title *The Chariot of Israel* in 1981, it demonstrated that at that stage he still had his wits about him. His final effort at autobiography, covering his life up to the moment he became Prime Minister, came out in 1986 and was greeted with a general chorus of disbelief as to its inaccuracy.

The only public service he took on after leaving office was to chair a committee set up to review the functioning of financial institutions. It was established by Callaghan in 1977 as a rather Wilsonian device to buy time against backbench demands for investigations into City scandals and left-wing demands to nationalize the banks and insurance companies. After three years of deliberations its recommendations turned out to be minor, if not trivial.

In 1981 Wilson was the centre of attention for the last time when he said that there had been a high-level plot in 1968 and an effort at bugging in 1974 against him. Questions were asked in the House, but Margaret Thatcher declined to appoint a committee of inquiry. She was not alone in believing that all this amounted to paranoia on Wilson's part.

However, some real fire, as well as dense smoke, was revealed when Peter Wright's book, *Spycatcher*, was eventually published in 1988. He claimed that he and some rogue colleagues in MI5 had kept watch on the Prime Minister, being concerned at some of Wilson's social contacts and the frequency of his earlier visits to the Soviet Union. Nothing actually happened in either 1968 or in 1974, and the flurry of publicity did far more harm to MI5's reputation than to Wilson's.

He remained Labour MP for Huyton until 1983, when he decided not to stand again in the general election and was made a life peer. After his somewhat rambling maiden speech he took little active part in the proceedings of the Upper House, still less after 1983 in public life. An increasingly frail and forlorn figure, almost air-brushed out of the Labour Party's history, he would impinge on the public consciousness only once a year – though he did not attend last June – at the annual Garter ceremony at Windsor.

He is survived by his wife Mary and their two sons.

* * *

JACQUES COUSTEAU

25 JUNE 1997

A GENERATION WELL-NIGH glutted on multi-part television ecological spectaculars will inevitably find it hard to imagine the immense impact made by Jacques-Yves Cousteau's film *The Silent World* when it burst on astonished cinema audiences in 1955. In it, Cousteau led a magical adventure into an unknown world. The shimmering forms of leaping dolphins filmed from the hollow glass dome under the bow of his converted minesweeper *Calypso* are vivid in the memories of those who first saw them, even after 40 years. The book of the same title which had spawned the film became a runaway world best-seller, to date selling more than five million copies in 20 languages.

It may justly be said of Cousteau that he single-handedly converted marine science from a dark backroom minority interest into a popular science. He also recognized its political appeal. In the later years of his life he changed his stance from that of the effective 'father' of underwater hunting (through his development of the aqualung) to that of the articulate conscience of environmental concern.

This did not always go down well with his fellow marine scientists, many of whom felt that his activities were closer to those of Walt Disney than to the work of men like Harald Sverdrup or Richard Fleming. Many scientists heartily resented his impact on the media, and on politicians and public attitudes. It seemed to some of his contemporaries that, while physical oceanographers strove to understand the circulation of the oceans, and marine geophysicists unravelled plate tectonics, the spotlight was always on a French diver in a tropical lagoon.

Jacques-Yves Cousteau was born at St André de Cubzac, a small town not far from the Gironde. Conventional schooling bored him, and he was expelled for breaking 17 of his school's windows. He entered the Ecole Navale at Brest in 1930. His training and early cruises as a young officer took him to China, French Indo-China, and the Soviet Union, including work off the coast of Siberia.

He served in a number of warships up to 1942, and was trained as an air observer for the French Navy. He had intended to make naval aviation his career but a near-fatal car crash put paid to that ambition and set him on a new course. Swimming vigorously, as therapy for badly damaged and wasted arms, he discovered the element of water which was to dominate his life.

In 1937 Cousteau learnt to dive with closed-circuit oxygen equipment of the type used for escaping from submarines. This equipment was later developed by the principal navies in the Second World War to form a diver attack breathing set for sabotage, mine clearance, and beach surveillance. The equipment was limited to a safe maximum depth of 10–15 metres, because pure oxygen becomes poisonous at this pressure. Cousteau was familiar with the work done by Gilpatric, Taillez, Yves le Prieur, Dumas, Corlieu, and others, and gradually perfected the mask and fins which were used by spear-fishermen on the French Riviera during the 1930s.

In 1939 Taillez, Dumas, and Cousteau were already experimenting with an underwater cine-camera and Yves Le Prieur's air-breathing system. After the fall of France in June 1940, the group continued its researches under very restricted conditions. Movie film was made into suitable lengths by joining hundreds of rolls of ordinary 35mm cassettes. Spear-fishing provided valuable extra food. The group's first film, *Par dix-huit mètres de fond*, was completed in 1942. Cousteau at this time was also leader of a counter-intelligence group in the Resistance, for which he was later awarded the Légion d'Honneur.

In June 1943 the first automatic demand valve air breathing aqualung was perfected jointly by Cousteau and Emile Gagnan. The key patentable principle of the invention was a valve which supplies air with very slight suction from the swimmer, and an exhalation valve immediately adjacent to the inhalation valve. The inhalation and exhalation pressures were thus balanced, and the diver could breathe with very little effort. Also, because the inhalation and exhaust pressures were identical, the valve could be made very sensitive, with no risk of the air free-flowing to waste, no matter what position the diver occupied in the water. During that summer Cousteau, Dumas, and Taillez logged 500 dives between them, with a maximum depth of 60 metres.

After the end of the war the aqualung (or, in American terminology, SCUBA – the Self-Contained Underwater Breathing Apparatus) became a popular item of sports equipment, with tens of thousands of sets being sold in California alone. Sports divers today are counted in millions.

In 1944 Cousteau formed, with Taillez, the Groupe d'Etudes et Recherches Sous-Marines of the French Navy at Toulon, the first unit of its type to develop diving equipment of all kinds. Although Cousteau was not the only innovator in this fertile field, he and his teams of engineers were directly involved in many early experiments with underwater television, underwater lighting, colour photography, and cine-photography underwater, and, by the mid-1960s, the first experiments in living underwater at ambient pressure. In 1959 Cousteau launched the first modern and truly manoeuvrable small submarine, the so-called Plunging Saucer, which started a new industry.

The converted diving tender *L'Ingénieur Elie Monnier*, acquired in a derelict state at the end of the war, was Cousteau's first research ship. In 1951 he was granted leave from the French Navy to conduct scientific research, and converted a former Royal Navy minesweeper into the diving research vessel *Calypso*. Thus began a long series of cruises supported by scientific laboratories, the French Navy, the American National Geographic Society, and various private sponsors. A combination of scientific investment and commercial sponsorship, with sale of film and television rights, kept the enterprise solvent. Research and filming expeditions extended across the Indian Ocean, the Pacific coral reefs, and even beneath the Antarctic ice.

The book of *The Silent World* was published in 1953. In simple, unassuming terms, the story of his early struggles was told with photographs of the undersea world in colour. It inspired a generation of young people, who took up diving as a sport or used diving in underwater research or engineering. The story projected a simple craftsman's love of the sea. With a combination of bravery, adventure, luck, and ingenuity, Cousteau and his comrades survived and triumphed over everything – sharks, storms, gas poisoning, and underwater explosions. This amalgam of totally professional planning and seemingly artless modesty in presentation became the Cousteau trademark.

The film of the same name was a feature documentary using the most up-to-date technology, and was not intended to narrate the same story as the book. It won the Grand Prix of the 1956 Cannes Film Festival and the 1957 Oscar for feature documentaries.

In 1956 Cousteau was invited by the Comité International de Perfectionnement de L'Institut Océanographique de Monaco to become its director. The famous laboratory, founded by Prince Albert I of Monaco, had sunk into poverty. Cousteau was faced with the enormous task of attracting investment, promoting public interest, and improving both the research programmes and the public exhibits.

The appointment was controversial, since Cousteau was not, and did not claim to be, an academic. With typical energy he expanded the aquarium, attracted foreign students and scientists, and launched an ambitious series of cruises and research projects.

The initial patent of the aqualung was exploited by licensing in many countries, and a series of companies grew up marketing a range of diving gear, suits, masks, life-jackets, and commercial diving equipment for the offshore oil industry. The first experiments in underwater living were conducted in 1962 in the Bay of Marseilles at a depth of ten metres. This was followed by the construction of two underwater houses in the Red Sea in 1963, and finally a large spherical underwater habitat at a depth of 100 metres off Villefranche in 1965. The intention of this last experiment was to demonstrate to the offshore oil industry that divers could live and work for days or weeks at depths of 100–200m and conduct heavy industrial work.

Numerous countries and companies copied these projects, but the development turned out to be an evolutionary dead-end. Although the idea of living beneath the waves is fascinating, the logic of economics dictates that it is always cheaper to bring divers to the surface and store them under pressure in a deck decompression chamber between dives.

During the 1960s and 1970s television series followed one another with almost predictable success. Cousteau, who made more than 150 films, was synonymous with the sea, with research in the ocean and with an environmental consciousness that longed to save the planet from pollution. In 1973, with a fanfare of publicity, he declared himself totally opposed to spearfishing, the sport – or search for food – which had nurtured the first divers on the French Riviera in the 1930s.

During the 1970s the controversy over his position as a scientist and publicist became more intense. In August 1979 the death in a plane crash of his son and presumed successor in the underwater world, Philippe, was a terrible blow. Several projects went wrong. Managing the Cousteau commercial empire and the Oceanographic Institute in Monaco was an immense task for a man over 60. In 1972 the plan to build a huge diver-lock-out submarine, called the *Argyronete*, was abandoned amid financial recriminations and government intervention.

Criticism of Cousteau's stand on environmental issues became more acute. Put simply, the allegation was that he used the good name of science to justify his expeditions and filming, and then exploited the public's longing for simple solutions to environmental problems to make money. The BBC conducted an interview programme in the mid-1970s entitled *Will the Real Captain Cousteau Please Stand Up?* In it, science journalists interrogated Cousteau before an invited audience of environmentalists and scientists. Under this unrelenting scrutiny, Cousteau defended himself extremely well. He stated over and over again that he was not a scientist. He said that he saw himself as an engineer turned impresario, a man who could make things happen, who could give others the chance to discover truth and to change the world. At the end, the impression was that Capitaine de Corvette Jacques-Yves Cousteau knew exactly what he was doing, and was neither a hypocrite, nor self-deceiving.

Even at the end of his life Cousteau showed no signs of slowing down. He was a vociferously energetic opponent of French nuclear testing in the Pacific. He had recently commissioned a successor to *Calypso* (which sank off Singapore in 1996 after a collision with a barge): the custom-designed and ecologically sound *Calypso II.*

Cousteau's great achievement was to create the popular image of the science of the sea. His craggy, wizened face in half-lit profile was sufficient to market any product, expand the membership of any society, hype the sale of any book, promote any film. His books and films on the sea seemed to dominate the world of popular science and ecology with the same total, obliterating effect of Walt Disney in cartoon films. After a while, there was no one else left in the competition.

At the technical level many of his innovations – the aqualung, the miniature submarine, and high-quality underwater filming – were immensely creative. The underwater living experiments were a technical tour de force, even if eventually they led nowhere. Cousteau the image-maker was unique, both in the literal sense of creating moving pictures, and in the sense of touching the hearts and minds of millions with his ideas. Everybody who could read a newspaper or book or watch a television set knew that Cousteau had said the sea was important; that we must love the sea, protect it, care for it, explore it, farm it, and nurture it. He changed the way in which people saw the planet: not so much Planet Earth as Planet Water.

Cousteau is survived by the elder son, Jean-Michel, of his marriage, in 1937, to Simone Melchior, who died in 1990. The relationship between father and son had lately been soured by what Jacques-Yves saw as the latter's commercial exploitation of the Cousteau name in a Fijian eco-vacation resort. Cousteau married, secondly, in 1991, Francine Triplet, and is survived also by her and by their son and daughter.

Jacques-Yves Cousteau, underwater explorer and
film-maker, died June 25, 1997, in Paris aged 87.
He was born on June 11, 1910.

DIANA, PRINCESS OF WALES

31 AUGUST 1997

NOT SINCE THE HEYDAY of Jacqueline Kennedy Onassis had there been an international icon to match Diana, Princess of Wales. Her picture on the cover of magazines was enough to guarantee sales worldwide, and no personality in history was ever the subject of more unremitting attention on the part of the paparazzi. In that sense, the fact that she should have met her death – with her new boyfriend Dodi Fayed – while apparently seeking to escape a motorcycle pursuit by photographers carries its own cruel irony along with it.

In an age when stars have become drabber and more ordinary, she achieved unrivalled glamour and respect. She developed from being a relatively unprepossessing kindergarten teacher into a stylish and beautiful young woman, always well dressed, and beloved for her gentle and loving nature.

The most successful princesses in history have been those who loved children and cared for the sick. The Princess enjoyed a natural affinity with both children and the sick. She devoted much energy to their care, in a way entirely in tune with the age. Her warmth and kindness found many outlets, particularly in regard to those struck down with HIV. She was spontaneous in manner, happily ignoring royal protocol to bestow a kiss on a child in the crowd, and writing letters to members of the public signed 'love Diana'.

Almost from the day she emerged into public life, the British people took her to their hearts. She brought to the Royal Family not only her very English beauty, but the enthusiasm of youth, combined with an innate dignity and a good-natured sense of humour.

She was not an intellectual: neither a good passer of exams nor a noted reader. But she possessed a canny and straightforward form of common sense. She listened and she learnt, and whereas she may have found her schooldays boring, she relished her role as Princess of Wales. She loved fashion and dancing, and pop stars and groups such as Phil Collins and Spandau Ballet. In the early years of her marriage she was as excited at meeting stars like Elizabeth Taylor as they were to meet her.

Though she was born into the far from stimulating world of the conventional upper-class girl, reared in the counties of Norfolk and Northamptonshire and veering in youth towards the world of the 'Sloane Ranger', her character had great possibilities for development, and develop she did, into a figure of international importance, confident of her place on the world stage.

She was given little support, it would seem, by her own family or that into which she married. Perhaps one of the reasons that the British public loved her as they did was that they always feared for her, and were concerned that she might be unhappy, while admiring her for being a fighter who refused to give up in the face of adversity.

The world's press loved her, too. Newspapers built her up into the epitome of a fairy-tale princess. Occasionally they were fickle and turned on their creation, but it was generally more comfortable to let the world love her, and their onslaughts were accordingly short-lived. The press interest was relentless, however, and it began long before the engagement was in any sense firm. After her marriage, her every movement, her every outfit, her every mood, was the excuse for many column inches of press comment. She was a natural joy for photographers, being both photogenic and having an innate understanding of the needs of journalists. Her face could sell a million copies of any publication, and both they and she knew it. She adorned many a magazine cover by editor's choice, and once, memorably, that of *Vogue* by her own wish.

In this great love for a public figure there was bound to lurk danger. When she flourished the press supported her, but when life was dark it deserted her. In the summer of 1992, the forthcoming publication of a biography by Andrew Morton, a journalist from the lower echelons of the trade, caught the attention of Andrew Neil, the Editor of *The Sunday Times*. Several weeks of serialization damaging to the monarchy followed. Despite complaints from the Press Council and pleas from the Archbishop of Canterbury, the campaign raged on. It could be seen as a major destructive force in the Princess's life.

Diana, Princess of Wales, was born at Park House, Sandringham, as the Hon. Diana Frances Spencer. She was the third and youngest daughter of Viscount Althorp (later the 8th Earl Spencer, who died in 1992), and his first wife, the Hon. Frances Roche (later married for some years to the wallpaper heir, Peter Shand-Kydd). She became Lady Diana Spencer on the death of her grandfather in 1975.

Her Spencer forebears had been sheep farmers in Warwickshire, who settled at Althorp, Northamptonshire, in 1506. Cousins of the Spencer-Churchills, they included many connoisseurs and patrons of the arts. Having inherited a considerable fortune from Sarah, Duchess of Marlborough, they were able to spend large sums on antiquities, paintings, and sculpture.

For many generations they served their Sovereigns, and the tradition continued. The Princess's father was equerry to King George VI and to the present Queen. Both her grandmothers, the Countess Spencer and Ruth Lady Fermoy, were close members of the court of Queen Elizabeth the Queen Mother, as were no fewer than four Spencer great-aunts. To her two sons, the Princess of Wales passed strong physical Spencer traits, considerably diluting the Hanoverian strain in the Royal Family.

While the Princess's paternal ancestors were representative of the Whig oligarchy of the 18th century, she also descended through several lines from the Stuart Kings Charles II and James II, who were not ancestors of the Prince of Wales. Other paternal forebears included the great Duke of Marlborough, Sir Robert Walpole, the Marquess of Anglesey (who lost a leg at Waterloo), and the Earl of Lucan, of Balaclava fame. On her mother's side there was Irish and Scottish blood, with a sprinkling of pioneer New England stock. Her closest relationship to the Prince of Wales was that of seventh cousin once removed, through their common descent from the 3rd Duke of Devonshire.

The Princess was educated at Riddlesworth Hall in Norfolk, and then at West Heath, a boarding school in Kent. She achieved no O-level passes. Later she attended a finishing school, the Institut Alpin Videmanette at Rougemont in Switzerland, for six weeks. Her childhood was somewhat unsettled and unhappy because of the separation of her parents when she was six, and their divorce in 1969. She had more natural affinity with her father than with her mother.

During the period after leaving school, the Princess worked as a nanny, a baby-sitter, and a skivvy. She attended a cookery course in September 1978, and soon after this her father collapsed with a grave cerebral haemorrhage, from which it took him months to recover. In 1979 she worked briefly as a student teacher at Miss Vacani's dance studios. Later she was invited by friends to help at the Young England Kindergarten in Pimlico, where she was popular with the children. She worked at the kindergarten three days a week and at other times she looked after a small American boy.

In London the Princess shared a flat at Coleherne Court, Earl's Court, with three girlfriends. They found her a kind and thoughtful flatmate, keen on housework and evenings in front of the television, a lover of ballet, opera, and cinema. She loved to dance and sometimes they returned to find her dancing happily around the flat. At the time of the pre-wedding press siege, these girls were to prove staunchly loyal allies. Fortunately, they were content to spend hours in each other's company. Years later, one of them, Mrs William Bartholomew, the former Carolyn Pride, was a source for the Morton biography of the Princess.

The Prince and Princess of Wales claimed to have met in a ploughed field at Althorp where Prince Charles was staying as a guest of Lady Sarah Spencer, the Princess's elder sister, in November 1977. The accepted version of the story is that Prince Charles and Lady Sarah were romantically involved, though not deeply so. The younger sister fell in love with everything about the Prince, was keen to be Princess of Wales, and saw in him a challenge.

She knew from an early age that she would have to tread carefully, and she never put a foot wrong. It was not until the late summer of 1980 that Lady Diana Spencer's name came to the attention of the world. The Prince of Wales was nearly 32 and the subject of his eventual marriage had been of consuming interest to the media for nearly a decade. Nor had he helped his difficulty by pronouncing that he thought 30 a good age at which to marry. As November 1978 loomed, the pressure increased. But he remained a bachelor, and there were times when he looked a less than happy man.

Lady Diana's appearance on the scene refocused press attention on the Prince's bachelor state. While a discreet and low-key courtship was executed in private, Lady Diana was pursued to and from work by determined cameramen and reporters and had to resort to complicated manoeuvres to rescue the last vestiges of her privacy. Her subtle handling of the press earned her not only universal respect but the real affection of these normally hard-hearted men. At one point after she had broken down in tears, a note of apology was placed under her windscreen wiper. But the press pursuit persisted to such an extent that Lady Diana's mother wrote a letter of appeal to *The Times*. Later the Queen was obliged to complain to newspaper editors through her press secretary. The Prince proposed early in February 1981.

The engagement was announced on February 24, after which Lady Diana was better protected. From that day on she was surrounded by what she described as 'a mass of smiling faces'. Indeed the engagement was greeted with universal approval – though the Princess herself found her immediate pre-marriage days in Buckingham Palace both tense and lonely.

The Royal Wedding took place in St Paul's Cathedral on July 29, 1981, by the shared wish of both bride and groom. Prince Charles ensured that it was a 'marvellous, musical, emotional experience', with three orchestras playing and Kiri te Kanawa (soon afterwards appointed a Dame) and the Bach Choir singing. Lady Diana chose her favourite school hymn, *I vow to thee my Country*.

Many heads of state attended, including nearly all the crowned heads of Europe, President Mitterrand of France, and Mrs Nancy Reagan, wife of the then President of the United States. The King of Tonga required a special chair to be built to support his mighty frame. A last-minute absentee was King Juan Carlos of Spain, because of the decision of the Prince and Princess to embark on the royal yacht *Britannia* at Gibraltar. The wedding day was such that for a brief while it seemed that all strife was set aside, the sun blazed richly, and at the end of it, the police thanked the public for their vigilance, and the public praised the police, and, as one commentator put it, 'the world was a friendlier and easier place for everyone'.

The honeymoon was spent first at Broadlands, the home of Lord and Lady Romsey, and a favoured retreat of the Prince when he had stayed there with the late Lord Mountbatten in his youth. Then they cruised on *Britannia* in the Mediterranean. A long holiday at Balmoral followed.

Returning to London in October, the Prince and Princess took up residence at Kensington Palace and at Highgrove House in Gloucestershire. These were their homes for the next 11 years. Their first royal engagement was a 400-mile tour of Wales, the first such visit of a Princess of Wales for 113 years. The tour included a visit to Caernarfon Castle where the Prince had been invested in 1969. The Princess of Wales was given the Freedom of Cardiff, made her first public speech, and spoke a few words of Welsh. Despite the ever-present threat of incendiary devices, the tour was a resounding success.

The Princess made an immediate impact on the world of fashion. The British fashion industry, long in a precarious state, was given a welcome boost by her arrival. Her style was fresh, attractive, and original. She became the personification of current trends in British fashion, with felicitous results for the trade.

The Princess soon revealed a penchant for outfits of considerable glamour. On her first outing with her fiancé, she had arrived at Goldsmiths' Hall in a décolleté black taffeta dress, a considerable contrast to her formerly discreet image, which caused the octogenarian Lady Diana Cooper to joke: 'Wasn't that a mighty feast to set before a King?' Her wedding dress with its lavish detail and lengthy train matched the magnificence of St Paul's Cathedral and her going away outfit was chic and stylish. The fair fringe she favoured early in the marriage was widely copied for a time.

Very soon the Princess was pregnant, giving birth to a boy, Prince William of Wales, on June 21, 1982. A second son, Prince Harry, followed in September 1984.

In the early years of the marriage the Waleses normally undertook joint engagements. This was the period of the Princess's apprenticeship. But it soon became clear that of the two it was her that the public most wished to see, and Prince Charles was to some extent reduced to a male dancer supporting his glorious ballerina in her pirouettes.

While the popularity of his bride should have delighted him, it added a sense of pointlessness to his slightly frustrated life. Equally, he was irritated when he tried to make an important speech, and the next day the papers merely reported his wife's outfit. He failed to grasp that one of the things the world wanted was a recurring series of images of a young couple enjoying a happy family life. He always appeared reluctant in such photo-calls, fearing that this diminished the import of his more serious endeavours. The Princess, on the other hand, fulfilled all such demands to perfection.

The respective backgrounds of the Prince and Princess of Wales were an additional challenge in the creation of a happy family atmosphere. She had come from a broken home, while his upbringing had been formal to say the least. His early companion had been his nanny, and he lacked any close involvement with his parents.

The love of solitude to which the Prince adhered even after marriage, combined with his love of polo and hunting, inevitably left the Princess on many occasions without him. But both parents shared an adoration for their children.

Even as the world rejoiced on their wedding day, the Princess was aware that she had not entirely captured Prince Charles's heart. Yet she always felt that she would win him. He most probably felt that the marriage was akin to an arranged one, and some have said that he did not enter into it in the same spirit as his bride. When the Princess realized that Prince Charles was never entirely to reciprocate the love she felt for him, she, like many mothers, transferred much of her devotion to her sons.

The Princess celebrated her twenty-first birthday in July 1982, and that September she represented the Queen at the funeral of Princess Grace of Monaco in the cathedral at Monte Carlo.

The Princess was soon busily involved in the world of public duty. As the years went by, she evolved into a deeply committed member of the Royal Family. She swiftly became better informed – in the early days of her marriage a Fleet Street editor was surprised to hear Prince Charles explaining to her at lunch that Chancellor Kohl was the leader of West Germany. She also learnt the tricks of the royal trade, speaking easily to individual members of the public of all ages and possessing a good instinct as to what to talk about.

Yet in the early days she seldom made speeches in public, and when she did they were of the most formal sort. As she gained confidence, she began to write her own speeches, delivering them from the podium with calm assurance. She spoke of the importance of the family in everyday life, the rehabilitation of drug-users, and urged more compassion for those dying of Aids. When she and the Prince of Wales appeared together in television interviews it was not long before she was the more articulate of the two, leaving him almost monosyllabic, despite an earlier reputation for fluency.

The modern manner is for members of the Royal Family to be actively involved with any organization of which they are patron or president. Until she gave up most of her charitable commitments at the end of 1993, the Princess was never merely a figurehead, but served directly as fundraiser, promoter, chairman of meetings – and, of course, as public spokesman.

She gave her support to an enormous number of charities, in a wide range of fields. Among her key presidencies or patronages were Barnardo's; the Great Ormond Street Hospital for Children; Centrepoint; English National Ballet; RADA; the Royal Academy of Music; the Leprosy Mission; the National Aids Trust; the Royal Marsden Hospital; Help the Aged; and the National Meningitis Trust.

An exhausting round of overseas travel was also a feature of her marriage. Her first big overseas tour occurred in March and April 1983, when she accompanied

Prince Charles on a visit to Australia. The infant Prince William went with them. They travelled extensively from the Northern Territory to Canberra, through New South Wales, Tasmania, Southern Australia, Western Australia, Queensland, and Victoria. At that time the Australian Prime Minister, Bob Hawke, was a committed republican, but he was forced to concede that the Princess was 'a lovely lady'.

The Australian trip (followed on that occasion by 12 days in New Zealand) was the first of three such visits. In June they went to Canada, where there was an outbreak of 'Di-mania', a 1980s equivalent of Beatlemania.

In February 1984, the Princess made her first major solo visit abroad, to Norway to attend a gala performance of *Carmen* by the London City Ballet. Arriving in the snow, she was at once dubbed 'The Snow Princess'.

In the spring of 1985 she and the Prince of Wales went to Italy, a 17-day tour which included a visit to Sir Harold Acton at La Pietra, and to the Pope in Rome. Venice was perhaps the highlight of the tour, and here they were joined by Prince William and Prince Harry.

In October the Princess spent two days with the 1st Battalion, The Royal Hampshire Regiment (of which she was Colonel-in-Chief until she relinquished her military commitments on her divorce in 1996) in West Germany. Following their second Australian visit, the Waleses paused briefly in Fiji, and rested in Hawaii before visiting the Reagans in the United States. The White House dinner and dance was typical of the mid-Eighties bonanza-style entertainment favoured during the Reagan era, and the highlight of the evening was when the Princess accompanied John Travolta in a sensational dance to *You're the One that I Want* (from the film *Grease*), an experience which both enjoyed and which served to resurrect Travolta's flagging career.

Other destinations during these years included Austria, Japan (where there was more 'Di-mania'), the Gulf states, Portugal, and France.

In 1989 the Princess returned to the United States, this time for a less glitzy trip to New York, where she visited centres for the homeless and dying children in the Aids ward of Harlem Hospital. She was dubbed, in American parlance, 'Bigger than Gorby, Better than Bush'. There was a visit to Kuwait (where security was intense following the Salman Rushdie affair), and the United Arab Emirates. In June she and the Prince revisited Australia, and in November they went on a Far East tour, taking in Indonesia and Hong Kong.

Visiting Nigeria in 1990, the Princess saw much suffering at first hand, and pointedly shook hands with the chief of a leper colony. In May the same year she and the Prince paid the first royal visit to a Warsaw Pact country, when they travelled to Hungary. In October the Princess went alone to Washington for a ballet gala and to further understanding of Aids.

In November she and the Prince went to Japan for the enthronement of

Diana, Princess of Wales, in Paris, 1988.

Emperor Akihito (a visit surrounded by controversy in Britain). There were also visits to Brussels, to British troops in Germany, to Prague, and to Expo 92 in Seville.

Besides the birth of her two children, there were other events of significance in her years of marriage. She much encouraged the union between Prince Andrew and her friend Sarah Ferguson, and she was delighted when they married in 1986. For some years they remained close friends and confidantes, and it was a cause of distress to her when that marriage came apart in the spring of 1992.

The Duchess of York had appeared to be a good ally at court, never as glamorous as the Princess, never likely to threaten her place in the esteem of the general public, but certainly her friend. But the arrival of the Duchess of York was, in retrospect, a damaging thing for the Princess of Wales, for she began to be tarnished by the new Duchess's fun-loving and sometimes irresponsible attitude.

The two may have seemed alike in character, but they were essentially different, the Princess being a great deal more dutiful and less interested in the perks. But the Duchess of York influenced her somewhat and it was during the time when they were close that the two then Royal Highnesses prodded their friends with the tip of their ferrule at the Royal Ascot meeting, one of a number of incidents that caused Establishment eyebrows to be raised.

Each girl represented an alternative fantasy for the young: to be like the Princess of Wales was to diet rigorously and undertake regular aerobics. The Duchess of York, on the other hand, made few concessions and her attitude was more one of 'Take me as I am.' In 1988 they were both in Klosters when their friend Major Hugh Lindsay was killed in an accident skiing off-piste with the Prince of Wales. This tragedy long dampened the spirits of all three.

For many years a small circle was aware of the not altogether happy state of the Princess of Wales's marriage. Much was written about this over the years, but the situation continued until *The Sunday Times* adopted the story in 1992 and blew it up to sensational proportions. The public was left with another dream shattered, and the monarchy's image was tarnished.

The 1992 revelations suggested that the Prince and Princess of Wales had failed to establish a mutually happy rapport during their marriage. There were many obstacles to natural happiness. With nearly 13 years between them, they were almost of different generations, he being born in the late 1940s, she in the early 1960s. The Prince was always of a serious disposition, inflexible in his way of life, not noted for his willingness to accept change. The Princess was initially more light-headed, though she developed considerably in the first decade of the marriage. She certainly entered the union with a more generous heart than her husband, who did not disguise his anxiety that the taking of a wife was an additional burden in an already busy life.

Despite her enormous popularity with the public, the differences in their interests seemed to divide them increasingly as the years progressed. Though they were both energetically and successfully involved in public life, the framework of their home life gradually eroded. He began to entertain separately. She spent more time in London, frequently away from Highgrove. Their problems were the focus of more attention than any couple could bear. Not only did they have to face their respective difficulties, but they had to do so in the full blast of media attention.

The strain began to show. The Prince of Wales had resumed his earlier association with a former girlfriend, Mrs Camilla Parker-Bowles. The Princess's name was linked with those of two men nearer to her age, the Old Etonian James Gilbey and the Life Guards officer James Hewitt. There were clear signs of marital discord during a visit to India in February 1992, when the Princess spent time alone looking miserable at the Taj Mahal, and during a four-day trip to Korea in November that year, when the Prince and Princess, clearly unhappy in each other's company, were dubbed 'The Glums' by reporters.

By the end of 1992, speculation about the state of the royal marriage had come to a head, fuelled by the release of a tape of an intimate conversation between the Princess and James Gilbey. There was talk of separate living arrangements, and a suggestion that reconciliation was now impossible. In December, John Major confirmed to the House of Commons that the couple were to separate.

Separation did little to reduce public interest, particularly after the discovery in 1993 of another intimate tape recording, this time of a conversation between the Prince and Mrs Parker-Bowles. In December 1993 the Princess tearfully bowed out of public life, severing her links with most of the charities she had supported and begging to be left alone by the press. In 1994 Prince Charles admitted his long-standing and continuing relationship with Mrs Parker-Bowles in a television interview with Jonathan Dimbleby.

Despite her pleas for privacy, the Princess remained very much in the public eye. As she set about putting her life in order during the period of personal confusion that followed the separation – visiting gymnasiums one day and psychotherapists the next – her every step was dogged by photographers and reporters. Yet her relationship with the media was always more complicated than she was prepared to admit. She may have been unhappy about some of the press ambushes, and about speculation on her association with married men such as the art dealer Oliver Hoare and the England rugby captain Will Carling, but there were undoubtedly occasions when she courted the attention, in an attempt to influence perceptions of her marriage and its breakdown.

Nowhere was this more evident than in her extraordinary decision – taken without consulting the Royal Household or even her own advisers – to appear on a special edition of the BBC *Panorama* programme in November 1995. She spoke frankly about her unhappy relationship with the Royal Family, her eating disorders, and her own and her husband's adultery. She announced her desire to be seen as 'a queen of people's hearts'. On August 28, 1996, the Prince and Princess of Wales divorced.

Throughout her marital difficulties, the Princess had remained devoted to her sons. After the divorce, when she and the Prince were given joint custody, she continued to invest considerable energy in their upbringing. She was an adoring mother, and there were many images of mother and children together, the most celebrated when the children ran to their mother's arms on *Britannia* after a period apart. The devotion was reciprocated, and her boys were a great source of comfort to her.

After her divorce the Princess made a return to public life, associating herself particularly with the work of the Red Cross, and taking a leading – and sometimes controversial – role in the international campaign to ban landmines. Earlier this year she auctioned many of her dresses to raise money for charity. She also seemed to find new happiness in her private life, spending much of the past few weeks in the company of Dodi Fayed, who died with her.

When she married the Prince of Wales, Diana said on television that she saw her life as a great challenge. Realistic though she was at 20 years of age, she underestimated how great that challenge would prove and at what cost to personal happiness it would be met.

The Princess made a lasting impression on the public. On the whole, they loved her; and even when she tried their patience, she remained a source of fascination. Outwardly shy, she had no lack of inner strength and common sense. Before her marriage she cast her head down, hiding behind her fringe. After the marriage she gained confidence, the head came up, and she began to acquire that star quality that drew all eyes in crowds and preoccupied fellow lunchers in restaurants. That quality, and that strength of character, saw her through her marital difficulties, and remained with her once the marriage was over.

Soon after her marriage to the Prince of Wales she was given the Royal Family Order by the Queen, but she was never given any other honours, such as the Grand Cross of the Royal Victorian Order, which she perhaps merited. On her divorce she assumed the title Diana, Princess of Wales, and remained a member of the Royal Family. She received various foreign orders on state visits.

Her two sons survive her.

Diana, Princess of Wales, died August 31, 1997, after a car crash in Paris, aged 36.
She was born at Park House, Sandringham, on July 1, 1961.

MOTHER TERESA

5 SEPTEMBER 1997

MORE THAN ANYONE else of her time, Mother Teresa came to be regarded by millions as the embodiment of human goodness. By her compassion, humility, and, it also has to be said, shrewd eye for publicity, she raised public concern for the destitute; by devoting herself with single-minded vigour to the relief of human suffering, she galvanized individuals, both believers and non-believers, and even governments into action. Not since Albert Schweitzer has any one person had such an inspirational effect.

Mother Teresa's simplicity of purpose and approach hid a formidable personality and a determined strength of character. Despite a seemingly frail stature, she was physically strong and exercised a sometimes stern, unbending authority over her followers. Her personal philosophy was of a distinctly conservative kind, and she caused some disquiet in more liberal quarters by her highly public stance in opposition to abortion.

Her magnetism built the order she founded in Calcutta, the Missionaries of Charity, into a global movement. Without the benefit of image-makers, she captivated the attention of the international media, but was never herself captivated by it – or by the attentions of politicians. During a visit to London in 1988, she visited both Downing Street and the homeless of the capital; she praised Margaret Thatcher for supporting her sentiments, but when no progress was made against the homelessness problem, she spoke out against the Government's inaction.

Mother Teresa first became aware of the absolute deprivation of India's poor in the *bustees*, the slums of Calcutta, in the 1930s when she was involved in taking girls who were members of the Sodality of the Virgin Mary, together with some Hindu girls, to visit the sick in hospital. At the time she was a teacher at St Mary's, a Roman Catholic school in Entally, a rich residential area of Calcutta. They visited a few of the thousands of *bustees* hidden from the view of the rich residential houses and offices in Calcutta.

The contrast between the *bustees* and the oasis of beauty and security of the well-established community of the Congregation of the Loreto nuns where she lived gave a new direction to her vocation. 'I knew that I belonged to the people of the *bustees*,' she said. 'The problem was how to get there and live with them.'

It was on a train journey back to Darjeeling, on September 10, 1946 (a day now celebrated annually by her missionaries and co-workers), that Sister Teresa, as she then was, received what she described as 'the call within a call' – a directive from God, that she was to have the courage to fulfil her ambitions and work with the poorest of the poor. 'It was a command – I had to obey,' she said.

By this time she had become the Principal of St Mary's. She then began applying for permission to leave her congregation, which she dearly loved. It took two years before this was granted by the Roman Congregation. On August 16, 1948, just before her thirty-eighth birthday, she exchanged her habit for a cheap white sari with a blue border, pinned a cross on her left shoulder and with five rupees in her pocket left the safety of the convent walls.

She applied to stay with the Medical Missionary Sisters in Patna, who condensed her medical training into four hectic months. They knew she wanted to start a new congregation whose members would devote their lives to the service of the destitute. Her nuns would be expected to live exactly as the *bustee* people, and she originally planned a diet of rice and salt – the poorest food of all. The Medical Missionaries persuaded her that this would be morally wrong, for if her future congregation were to give 'their all', it was her responsibility to see that they would have a diet suited to their obligations. It was indeed sound advice which she accepted, and the food at her Home for the Destitute and Dying in Calcutta and her other missions around the world, although simple, is nutritious and adequate.

Mother Teresa – known simply as 'Mother' – was a woman of courage and spirit. She was born of Albanian parents in Skopje, christened Agnes Gonxha Bojaxhiu, and educated at the local government school. She was first inspired by the writings of Pope Pius XI and also by the letters written to the school by Jesuit missionaries who were working among the poor in India, in the archdiocese of Calcutta.

She felt called to join a religious order, and entered the congregation of Loreto nuns who worked in Bengal. Before going to India she was sent to learn the English language in Dublin. From Ireland, she went to Darjeeling, situated in the most beautiful and wealthy part of the country, and found herself completing her novitiate in the famous Loreto School, where the daughters of the rich Indians and colonials obtained the best public school education for their children. On March 24, 1931, Agnes Bojaxhiu made her first vows and took the name of Teresa.

The young Sister Teresa was transferred to St Mary's School, Entally, where she taught geography and history for 17 years. It was here that she took her final vows on May 24, 1937, and eventually became the Principal of the school.

In December 1948, after her medical training in Patna, Sister Teresa returned to Calcutta and initially stayed with the Little Sisters of the Poor. Bengal had been torn by riots resulting from the religious conflicts between Hindu and Muslim. In the city there were tens of thousands dying of starvation, tuberculosis, leprosy, and other diseases resulting from malnutrition. Teresa was not afraid, although she knew the immensity of her task, and she began work by starting a pavement school for the *bustee* children, teaching them to write using the mud and dust as a blackboard.

On March 19, 1949, a small, shy former Bengali pupil, Subhasini Das, became Mother Teresa's first postulant, and took her old name of Agnes. She was followed by nine other former students who formed the nucleus of her community, the Missionaries of Charity, which today numbers over 3,000 novices and professed nuns supported by nearly 40,000 lay co-workers operating more than 400 homes in nine countries.

The community was recognized as a new, separate order and in addition to the customary religious vows, a fourth promise was added: 'to give wholehearted, free service to the very poorest'. The majority of the sisters were from the Third World.

Unlike many other religious organizations who insist that novices should be at least second generation Christians, Mother Teresa was happy to accept girls from Indian families who wished to work with her. There were many parents who, faced with the crippling dowry prospects, were only too relieved that their daughters could be accepted into the security of such a community.

In 1952, through the Missionaries of Charity, Mother Teresa opened the Nirmal Hriday (Pure Heart) Home for Dying Destitutes. In 1965, the order was recognized as a papal congregation under the protection of the Vatican and in 1967 a Congregation of Brothers was formed. Mother Teresa was well aware that although her community was increasing at an alarming rate, it was still important that lay people should be involved with the work among the destitute, and in 1969 a constitution was drawn up in Rome to unite these co-workers into one association. There were eventually tens of thousands of lay people – including a special group called the sick and suffering co-workers – from more than 40 countries.

Mother Teresa was a tireless worker, and it was surprising that her small frame managed to keep up with the speed of her activities. 'God gives me the strength,' she said. 'There is no need to worry.' When other nuns were ordered to rest, Mother Teresa was writing letters or attending to the queues of people who would be waiting outside the parlour to tell her their problems, and ask for her advice, or answering questions to the press, who were constantly around her.

The most important part of the day was the early morning when the daily Mass was celebrated, and Mother Teresa would lead her nuns in prayer, as she did for all the services throughout the day. Sometimes she would be found alone in the chapel, sitting barefoot, her hands folded, her head bent in silent private devotion. Wherever the Missionaries of Charity worked, they tried to set up a Shishu Bhavan, a children's home, for all unwanted babies and children in need – and a Nirmal Hriday (The Place of the Pure Heart), named after the first home for the dying which was in two rooms given for her use in the Hindu temple of Kalighat. The temple to this goddess of destruction, Kali, was felt to be a fitting home for the 'place of the pure hearts'.

Mother Teresa was proud of the fact that 50 per cent of the dying were brought 'back to life' by the care of her community who, for six hours each day, washed, fed, and gave medical attention to more than one hundred dying men and women brought in from the streets of Calcutta. Whenever Mother Teresa built new homes, she would have nothing that looked too Western and, therefore, might make the building appear over-bright and expensive to the very poor, for they would then be afraid to enter and to bring those who were ill and in need.

With her fame spreading, journalists and broadcasters began trekking to her home for the destitute and dying in Calcutta. One of them was Malcolm Muggeridge, who, in 1969, made a documentary called 'Something Beautiful for God'. He described it as the most important programme he had worked on and later said the experience had caused him, 12 years later, to become a Roman Catholic. In 1971 the Vatican awarded Mother Teresa the Pope John XXIII Peace Prize and she travelled to London to open a novitiate for the training of novices of her order in Southall – the first to be established outside India.

The next year she visited Northern Ireland to set up a small community of her nuns in Belfast. But she refused to abide by the unwritten sectarian rules of the divided Northern Ireland society and withdrew them two years later. On another visit, in 1981, she condemned an IRA hunger strike as an act of violence.

A year earlier the Prince of Wales was one of the VIP visitors to her children's orphanage in Calcutta and in 1983 the Queen also came to make Mother Teresa an honorary member of the Order of Merit, the only non-British subject to be so recognized, for her work among the sick and destitute.

In spite of her international renown, Mother Teresa continued to live and work without ostentation. When she travelled she did so either alone or accompanied by just a few of her white-veiled sisters. She never deviated from her rejection of personal reward. Her philosophy was based on a simple belief in divine intervention; she forbade her co-workers from raising money in her name and relied on uninvited donations, which – as her fame spread – were not slow in coming.

With the growth of the community, there were many other activities which Mother Teresa encouraged among the poor. She arranged for food to be collected and given to thousands of destitutes – feeding 7,000 each morning at Shishu Bhavan in Calcutta. Some said the distribution of free meals made people too dependent, and that for them to make payment in kind would encourage dignity and independence.

There were medical clinics, which gave free medicines donated from many countries. Here, too, some questioned whether medical treatment should not extend to more advanced rehabilitation programmes, and that patients with long-term illnesses should learn how to become self-sufficient and take pride in earning their living. The few who were able to weave provided sheets, clothing, and bandages for the Missionary of Charity homes. But Mother Teresa was particularly insistent that money should never change hands.

The community ran family planning clinics, where only the thermometer method was used (for Mother Teresa gave credence solely to the official teaching of the Roman Catholic Church); mobile clinics for leprosy and tubercular patients; schools; malnutrition centres; and night shelters. Prison work was carried out and troubled and lonely families were visited. Mother Teresa once said: 'I have come more and more to realize that it is being unwanted that is the worst disease that any human being can ever experience.' Those who were unwanted, uncared for, and deserted were to be respected by her nuns, cared for and cherished and recognized as people with their own human dignity in their own right.

She always maintained that those in her community were really contemplatives rather than social workers, hence, although they cared for the dying, handicapped, and even minute premature aborted babies, the nuns were never to be considered a nursing order. Because she saw Christ in all people, then their work was contemplation. When she first heard that she was to receive the Nobel award she said: 'I accept the prize in the name of the poor. The prize is the recognition of the poor world. Jesus said: "I am hungry, I am naked, I am homeless." By serving the poor, I am serving Him.'

She made use of the opportunity to expound her total opposition to abortion. 'The world has given me the Nobel Prize,' she said as she was about to leave for Oslo in December 1979, 'but I ask the world for a gift – I want the abortion laws abolished. This would be a real gift.' At her request, the traditional dinner at the prize-awarding ceremony was cancelled and the money it would have cost was added to her prize money.

Mother Teresa was a hard-working and selfless woman, helped by the fact that she came of strong peasant stock and by her simple faith. She knew the meaning of loneliness by the very nature of her position. On her visit to London in 1988, she was as moved by the fate of London's homeless as she had been by the destitute of the Calcutta streets, and personally appealed to the Prime Minister for help in setting up a hostel to relieve their wants.

Speaking at the Global Forum on Human Survival in Oxford, she described abortion as the greatest threat to the future of the human race and said she would never allow a family which had practised contraception to adopt one of the orphans her missionary order cared for. She also complained that Aids victims were much more cruelly treated in Western countries than in Africa. That year she also visited the Soviet Union, China, and South Africa to set up missions among the poor.

In September 1989 she was taken to hospital in Calcutta suffering from an irregular heartbeat and a high fever and doctors fitted her with a heart-pacemaker. Seven months later the Vatican announced that she would be resigning as head of her Missionaries of Charity order on grounds of ill-health, but in September that year she abandoned her retirement plans when the mission's electoral college unexpectedly failed to agree on a successor. In December 1990 she returned to her Albanian roots, visiting Tirana, where she was awarded the Order of Maim Frasheri, the country's highest honour.

Showing little regard for her increasing frailty, she continued to work and travel. In March 1991 she was again in Albania, opening a mission there, and two months later she visited Bangladesh to survey the cyclone damage which had devastated the country. When not travelling, she remained much in evidence at her Home for the Destitute and Dying in Calcutta where, unless her fellow nuns hid her alarm clock, she would be the first to rise. 'I want to be the first to wake and see Jesus,' she would say before attending the 6 a.m. Mass, sitting indistinguishably from the other nuns on reed-mats.

In November she began a tour of her missions worldwide with a visit to Tanzania. But becoming ill on December 26 in Tijuana, Mexico, during the last leg of her journey, she was taken for treatment to the Scripps Clinic and Research Foundation in La Jolla, across the border in California. In 1993 she was admitted to hospital four times suffering from heart trouble and malaria. She underwent heart surgery but returned to Calcutta.

In 1995 she published her book *A Simple Path*, urging materialistic Westerners to ponder the value of 'prayer, meditation and silence'. But, increasingly frail, in 1996 she fell and broke her collarbone and was admitted to hospital once again. From then on she was in and out of hospital, finally facing the inevitable when in March 1997 she resigned from running the Missionaries of Charity.

Mother Teresa had her human failings: she was the spokesman for her community so that, until her retirement, one rarely heard the views expressed of any of her nuns; she was adamant in what she believed and dictatorial within her houses, which she visited regularly all over the world. In 1994 a television profile of her was broadcast on Channel 4 in which the journalist Christopher Hitchens presented her as a publicity-hungry egotist, and he followed it up with a book claiming that she promulgated 'a cult based on death, suffering and subjection'. But to most of the world she remained the 'living saint of Calcutta' and she was loved by people from all countries and all faiths. She had a magnetic aura. Crowds flocked after her and yet held her in awe.

Mother Teresa, Roman Catholic missionary and Nobel Peace Prize winner,
died September 5, 1997, aged 87. She was born in Skopje (then in Albania)
on August 27, 1910.

FRANK SINATRA

14 MAY 1998

ONE OF THE PRE-EMINENT FIGURES in American entertainment of the past 50 years, Frank Sinatra left behind a body of recorded work which set new standards in popular singing. A storyteller par excellence, blessed with a subtle sense of rhythm, he brought a rare degree of intimacy to his material; in his hands, the songs of the Gershwins, Johnny Mercer, and Rodgers and Hart sounded as if they had been written expressly for him.

His was an epic life, whose turbulent progress would have defeated the ingenuity of scriptwriters in Hollywood, where he forged a remarkably successful career as an actor in both serious and light roles. Although his signature tune, 'My Way', contained some of the most clichéd lyrics he ever uttered, it did capture Sinatra's enigmatic blend of egotism and idealism.

A friend of Presidents and – it was often alleged – of Mafia chiefs, he embodied all the virtues (and some of the vices, too) of the American century. His public displays of ill-temper, his brawls with journalists, and his carousing with the so-called 'Rat Pack' of friends and sycophants earned him a reputation as a boor; less well publicized were his many gestures of philanthropy and acts of solicitude towards friends and strangers.

Francis Albert Sinatra's upbringing in the grimy but close-knit waterfront district of Hoboken, on the other side of the Hudson from Manhattan, left a lasting imprint on his character. In later years audiences would grow accustomed to the abrupt transitions from the suave Cole Porter ballads to the coarser speaking voice and wisecracks of the blue-collar Italian-American from New Jersey. The son of a fireman-cum-part-time-boxer, he inherited much of his drive and ambition from his mother, Dolly, a local Democratic Party activist who was to be a forceful presence in his life until her death in a plane crash in 1977.

After dropping out of high school, Sinatra took manual jobs while singing in his spare time, often at Democratic functions. In his teens he borrowed $65 from his parents to buy a portable sound system which gave him an advantage over his local rivals: in later years his subtle manipulation of the microphone (inspired by the pioneering example of Bing Crosby) would become one of his prime assets. It had been hearing Crosby at a concert in 1935 that convinced Sinatra that his own professional future lay in showbusiness.

His first breakthrough came later that year when he and a trio of friends auditioned on a radio talent contest. After winning the listeners' vote, Sinatra and the trio made regular appearances on the programme as the Hoboken Four. Sinatra then struck out on his own, but another three years of dues-paying followed before he was signed up by the star trumpeter and bandleader Harry James, who vainly tried to persuade him to change his name to 'Frankie Satin'. 'From the Bottom of My Heart', Sinatra's first record with the band, was recorded in July 1939.

After six months he was poached by James's rival, the popular trombonist Tommy Dorsey. At a time when big bands dominated the airwaves, vocalists played a secondary role in solo features, but Sinatra's poised light baritone quickly made an impression on audiences. From Dorsey, Sinatra learnt much about stagecraft.

He was impressed, too, by the breath control technique that allowed the trombonist to unfurl long, legato lines. Underwater swimming exercises were one method the young singer used to extend his lung-power. The results of this rigorous self-discipline were apparent in later years, as he demonstrated his skill in extending a melodic line without apparent strain. The jazz phrasing of Billie Holiday was another significant influence.

After completing his apprenticeship with Dorsey in 1942, Sinatra embarked on a solo career which was to make him the darling of young women – the so-called 'bobby-soxers'. In spite of his gawky, undernourished frame, Sinatra was their 'Sultan of Swoon'. The best of the records he made for Columbia documented his artistic growth. Sinatra also demonstrated his commitment to quality material by recording standards such as 'Embraceable You' and 'Someone to Watch over Me'.

Hollywood beckoned. After appearances in *Reveille* with 'Beverly' and 'Higher and Higher', Sinatra joined forces with Gene Kelly in *Anchors Aweigh!* and *Take Me Out to the Ball Game*. The two men were back in navy uniform for the acclaimed adaptation of *On the Town*, released in 1949.

At the moment of his greatest successes – Columbia by this time billed him simply as 'The Voice' – Sinatra's fortunes began an equally dramatic decline. One cause lay in the turmoil of his personal life: after attracting hostile press publicity by deserting his wife, Nancy, he entered a tempestuous and short-lived marriage with the film star Ava Gardner. The quality of his vocals and his records grew more and more erratic.

One setback followed another: Sinatra parted company with Columbia and his film studio, MGM; his television show was taken off the air. Younger singers overtook him in the charts, and the internal revenue authorities were pursuing him for huge sums of unpaid tax.

But he showed his strength of character and salvaged his reputation by persuading the makers of the 1953 war epic *From Here to Eternity* to cast him as Maggio, the ill-fated GI. From the moment he had first read James Jones's novel, Sinatra had been convinced he was the right man. As he later explained: 'I knew Maggio. I went to school with him in Hoboken. I was beaten up with him. I might have been

Maggio.' His stubborn determination to win the role, and his compelling screen portrayal, were rewarded with an Oscar for best supporting actor.

Having proved himself in a serious part, Sinatra went on to give further strong performances as a heroin addict in *The Man with the Golden Arm* and as a psychotic presidential assassin in *Suddenly*. The musicals *High Society*, *Guys and Dolls*, and *Pal Joey* (which contained his timeless version of 'The Lady is a Tramp') also gave him opportunities to shine.

As he was reborn on the screen, so he entered an extraordinary phase as a vocalist, signing with Capitol Records in 1953. From being regarded as a burnt-out case he quickly re-established himself with the help of swinging jazz-influenced settings contributed first by George Siravo, then by a newcomer, Nelson Riddle. The single 'I've Got the World on a String' alerted the public to a new Sinatra, his voice deeper and more assertive. He might have lost some of the earlier finesse and precision, but the vicissitudes of the previous years had brought maturity.

Sinatra also saw the possibilities offered by the long-playing disc, then still in its infancy. Although he continued to release highly successful singles, such as 'Young at Heart', he would henceforth focus on albums, sequences of songs which would allow him to create the same sense of emotional ebb and flow as a nightclub programme. *Songs for Young Lovers* and *Swing Easy* – both released on ten-inch discs and later reissued on a single compact disc – pointed the way.

On *In the Wee Small Hours* (1955) Sinatra assembled a dozen ballads that formed a study in melancholia. With *Songs for Swingin' Lovers*, released the following year, he created what remains one of the most exuberant and sophisticated of albums. Riddle's brassy orchestrations formed the perfect foil on 'I've Got You Under My Skin', 'You Make Me Feel So Young', and 'Anything Goes'.

Over the next six years Sinatra honed and refined the formula. The travelogue *Come Fly With Me*, arranged by Billy May, gave him his biggest commercial hit to that date. *Only the Lonely* saw a return to introspection, rounded off with a treatment of the saloon song 'One for My Baby', which would become a staple of his live shows.

By the beginning of the sixties a sense of ennui had crept in, epitomized by a decidedly unfunny recording of 'Ol' McDonald'. Sinatra had long been chafing to move on from Capitol, and in 1961 he finally left to form his own company, Reprise. These were different times, however. While Sinatra's fellow 'Rat Pack' member Dean Martin liked to observe 'It's Frank's world, we only live in it', Sinatra was losing ground to a new generation and his 'ring-a-ding-ding' style seemed passé.

Despite hits for Sammy Davis Jr and Martin, Reprise was only a moderate success with record-buyers, and the label was eventually absorbed into the Warner Brothers empire. Sinatra himself struggled to achieve the consistency of his Capitol years, but as he celebrated his fiftieth birthday he turned in one of his most interesting recordings with *September of My Years*.

'Fly Me to the Moon' and 'The Best is Yet to Come' – both taken from a studio collaboration with Count Basie – showed Sinatra at his swaggering best. In 1966 the mediocre 'Strangers in the Night' surprisingly gave him the biggest single hit of his career. 'Somethin' Stupid', an equally lightweight duet with his daughter Nancy, was a hit the following year.

Sinatra remained a box-office draw at the cinema. The 1962 adaptation of Richard Condon's conspiratorial thriller *The Manchurian Candidate* had given him one of his most memorable roles. (Sinatra was so distressed by the assassination of John Kennedy that he subsequently had the film withdrawn from circulation.) In *Robin and the Seven Hoods*, an updating of the Robin Hood legend, he played an heroic Chicago gangster.

Musically, he seemed increasingly to be following trends rather than setting them. Sometimes the results were persuasive – as on the lyrical bossa nova collaboration *Francis Albert Sinatra & Antonio Carlos Jobim*. By contrast, his rendition of Simon and Garfunkel's 'Mrs Robinson' had the hallmark of a man desperately courting the wrong audience.

Soon the young would be mocking Sinatra's toupee and his self-aggrandizement on 'My Way' – the anthem that had started life as a French ballad 'Comme d'habitude'. Sinatra responded by donning more fashionable clothes and singing George Harrison's ballad 'Something' (though he could not resist ad libbing an anachronistic 'Just stick around, Jack' to the lyrics). His ill-starred marriage to the actress Mia Farrow, 30 years his junior, was seen as another symptom of a midlife crisis.

Politically, Sinatra was also out of step. Having inherited his mother's liberal politics, he had been an outspoken supporter of the civil rights movement and a member of John Kennedy's inner circle during his campaign for the White House. After JFK's election victory, Sinatra's alleged links with the Mafia were deemed an embarrassment, and he was kept at a distance. Like so many Americans of his background and generation Sinatra was disenchanted with the Democrats' leftward turn. A Nixon supporter in the 1970s, he would later become a committed Reaganite. He was awarded the President's Medal of Freedom in 1985.

Just as his fortunes had declined at the beginning of the fifties, the dawn of the seventies also seemed to find him searching for a new direction. Even so, the announcement of his retirement in March 1971 came as a surprise. Many observers were not convinced that Sinatra's decision would be permanent, and in 1973 he staged a televised comeback in the show *Ol' Blue Eyes is Back*. The next year saw a triumphant return to Madison Square Garden in a concert issued on the album *The Main Event* (though unknown to listeners at the time, some of the material was transposed from other concerts of the period).

The voice had diminished in range and intensity, but the charisma was intact.

For the rest of his career the concert arenas and casino stages would take priority as his recordings and film appearances tailed off.

His albums *Trilogy* (1980) and *LA is My Lady* (1984) received mixed reviews, although the former yielded 'New York, New York', the defiant Kander and Ebb song that was to become a regular curtain-closer. His final albums, *Duets* and *Duets II* (released in 1993 and 1994 respectively) were a curious and uneven series of virtual-reality encounters with a selection of middle-of-the road singers. The *Live in Concert* disc released for his eightieth birthday celebrations in 1995 consisted of material understood to have been recorded in 1987–88, as well as another over-dubbed duet – 'My Way' with Luciano Pavarotti.

His relations with the media were always fraught. During a tour of Australia in 1974 he had been involved in a series of altercations with hostile journalists. The ultimate assault on his reputation came in *His Way*, Kitty Kelley's biography, published in 1986 despite efforts by Sinatra's lawyers to prevent publication.

His 1976 marriage to Zeppo Marx's widow, Barbara, appeared to bring a new serenity to Sinatra's public demeanour. As the years passed, however, he had to contend with the deaths of many of his friends. The loss of Dean Martin in 1996 was a particularly harsh blow.

By that time Sinatra had not performed in public for almost two years. Even in his final concerts, and in spite of the inevitable coarsening of his voice, he was still capable of bravura displays. But he was increasingly dogged by apparent bouts of mental confusion and amnesia, despite the presence of teleprompters reminding him of the lyrics of his most famous songs. To see him lose his way on 'I Get a Kick Out of You' was a most poignant spectacle.

He is survived by his wife, Barbara, and his children, Frank Jr, Nancy, and Tina.

Frank Sinatra, singer and actor, died on May 14, 1998, aged 82.
He was born on December 12, 1915.

IRIS MURDOCH

8 FEBRUARY 1999

'IT HAS BEEN HIS FATE not to be interested in anything except everything', Iris Murdoch once wrote of one of her characters. In many ways this was her own fate, too. As a lecturer in philosophy and fellow of St Anne's College, Oxford, she shied away from the narrower analytical studies which interested such contemporaries as A. J. Ayer, and turned her attention instead to the expansive, though unfashionable, discipline of metaphysics.

Lecturing and publishing in the field of moral philosophy, she engaged with the Post-Modernist Jacques Derrida and his flanking armies of deconstructionists, arguing that fact could not be separated from value. She sought to place moral inquiry back at the heart of philosophy, embarking with Casaubon-like fervour on her extensive study *Metaphysics as a Guide to Morals* (1992), which was greeted by some critics as a ramshackle collection of essays and by others as a grand philosophical synthesis.

As a novelist, Iris Murdoch was similarly broad in her outlook, taking the 'dramas of the human heart' as her subject. Fiction, she said, was a 'hall of reflection' which can encompass every form of tragedy and comedy. She used it to chart the progress of a metaphysical battle between evil and good, usually played out within the confines of a leisured upper-middle-class society. Distrusting the constricted focus of much modern fiction, she created large casts of characters so that her novels, at their worst, spun like an emotional merry-go-round, while at their best they were persuasive and amusing commentaries on the contemporary world and the intricacies of human relationships.

She was energetically prolific, and her output seemed as much a show of stamina as of inspiration. Novels such as her 1978 Booker prizewinner *The Sea, the Sea*, or *Nuns and Soldiers* (1981), or *The Philosopher's Pupil* (1983) expanded to more than 500 pages, as she painstakingly knitted their protracted and typically mysterious plots, slowly chewing over unfashionably long descriptions and quasi-philosophical themes. Yet, although some critics suggested that adroit editorial excision would have increased the impact of her work, there were others who acclaimed her as the most accomplished novelist in post-war Britain.

Murdoch's personal beliefs were as expansive and accommodating as her fiction. She did not believe in a personal God, she said, which is why she found Buddhism especially appealing. But the religious dimension was essential to her and she bewailed the lack of faith in the modern world.

A woman of immense practical kindness, she was soft-voiced and courteous, with a warm open manner and a large capacity for sympathetic listening, which in many ways she preferred to talking. She seemed rarely to be bored by anything, taking advantage of every encounter to find out as much as possible. 'There is never a moment,' one of her friends once said, 'when she would think it inappropriate to ask: "Do you believe in God?"'

Murdoch was a familiar figure on the literary scene, youthfully pink-cheeked and with a softly enigmatic smile, dressed in her donnish clothes: woolly jerseys and tweedy A-line skirts. Although there was a natural authority and decisiveness to her conversation, her language was oddly peppered with old-fashioned schoolgirl jargon: 'Hello, old thing' and 'cheerio'.

Jean Iris Murdoch was very much a product of her benign and cultivated background. She was born in Dublin after the end of the First World War, during which her father had served as a cavalry officer. But he was a bookish, intellectual man who, on demobilization, joined the Civil Service. Her mother was also a cultured woman, who had trained as an opera singer before her early marriage. Iris was the only child, brought up as part of what she famously described as a 'perfect trinity of love'.

From the age of nine she was brought up in suburban London, but she always felt herself to be at least partly Irish, and throughout her childhood the family would spend their summer holidays there.

She was educated at the Froebel Educational Institute in London, and, from the age of 13, at a vaguely progressive school, Badminton, where she was a contemporary of Indira Gandhi.

Iris Murdoch began writing at an early age, partly, she believed, as compensation for having no siblings to play with. 'I'm the only child in search of the imaginary brother or sister. That is probably why I like to invent characters,' she once said. Her first published work appeared in a school magazine in 1933. A comic poem about a girl with 'bluebottle eyes and a sense of vocation' whose chief interest is fishing for stars in the Milky Way, it shows the vein of humour mixed with the philosophical solemnity which was to characterize her work.

In 1938 Murdoch won the Harriet Needham Exhibition to Somerville College, Oxford, where she read Mods and Greats. There she found herself mixing with such stimulating figures as Raymond Williams, Philip Larkin, Edward Heath, Denis Healey, and Roy Jenkins. Politically she was, at that time, on the far Left, and when Roy Jenkins wrote her a modest letter on some matter of party business, she penned him an impassioned reply, addressing him as 'Comrade Jenkins'. Her political preferences thereafter followed a well-trodden path. She moved to Gaitskellism in the 1950s, through the muddled attitudes of the sixties, to moderate Conservatism in the 1970s and then to Thatcherism in the 1980s.

Graduating with a first in Greats, she left Oxford to work during the war years in the Treasury under the formidable Evelyn Sharp. From there she was seconded to the United Nations Relief and Rehabilitation Administration and was sent first to Belgium and then to Austria, where, in her job in a camp for displaced people, she proved most adaptable, whether operating the switchboard or negotiating narrow roads behind the wheel of a heavy lorry.

In all this time she scarcely read a book, exhausted by the strenuous work. But passing through Brussels on the way out she had got what she described as a heady whiff of philosophy. She had met Sartre and, although previously she had considered archaeology or art history as her calling, she became fascinated by Existentialism. In Brussels she came across a bookshop owner who had pressed *L'Être et le néant* into her hands. 'It was wonderful,' Murdoch said. 'People were liberated by that book after the war, it made people happy, it was like the Gospel. Having been chained up for years, you were suddenly free and could be yourself.'

On her return to England she decided that she wanted to return to academic life and applied for and won a scholarship to pursue her studies in the United States. But as a former member of the Communist Party – which she had briefly joined under the influence of a boyfriend, Frank Thompson, who was later killed in Bulgaria – she was refused a visa. The next year, 1947, she was awarded the Sarah Smithson Studentship in philosophy at Newnham College, Cambridge, and she studied there for a year before returning to Oxford as a tutor in philosophy and fellow of St Anne's. She was to hold this post for the next 15 years.

Her first book, *Sartre: Romantic Rationalist* (1953), reflected her youthful passion for Existentialism, though intellectually she was always to remain at a distance from Sartre, and he was later to become the subject of some of her most acute criticism. She found his view of lonely, self-determining man quite inaccurate, and her collection of essays *The Sovereignty of Good* (1970) showed a widening of her work into a general attack on analytic philosophy.

Plato, however – about whom she wrote in *The Fire and the Sun* (1977) – was to remain her abiding interest, as she probed for a wider metaphysical system from which to answer the questions of philosophy.

However, as she was the first to admit – and her detractors were quick to point out – she was not a philosopher of true originality. 'Unless one is a genius, philosophy is a mug's game,' one of her fictional characters says. Only a genius, Murdoch maintained, could ever make a real contribution to the subject. At the age of 35 she turned her hand to writing novels.

In her first novel, *Under the Net* (1954) – which was actually her fourth, since she discarded two and another did not find a publisher – she harked back to Existential themes as she traced the journey of a posse of rootless individuals traipsing round London in search of their identities. But unlike Sartre's, her novels were not simply the lumbering vehicles for philosophical ideas. 'I might put in things about philosophy because I happen to know about philosophy,' she said. 'If I knew about sailing ships I would put in sailing ships.'

Once she had begun to write, Murdoch scarcely seemed to pause, producing a new novel every year or so, with perhaps a break of half-an-hour between ending one and beginning the next. She began each with a period of 'hard reflection', at the end of which every chapter would have been delineated and the characters moulded and given their names – usually improbable ones. At the end of the process, hefty shopping bags of manuscript would be presented to her publishers, Chatto & Windus, where the boast was that never a word was changed. She professed herself impervious to reviews. 'A bad review,' she used to say, 'is even less important than whether it is raining in Patagonia.'

Those who reproached her with publishing too much were perhaps missing the point: her project was one of imperfection, or imperfectibility even, as if the perfect – like the good, about which she meditated so deeply – was fundamentally beyond human achievement. If for her every novel was a fresh attempt to attain her ideal, she found each time that her ideal had moved on. She was always alert to the dangers of complacency. 'I'm in the second league,' she said, 'not among the gods like Jane Austen and Henry James and Tolstoy.'

Critics mostly felt that she was at the height of her powers in the 1960s and early 1970s, with works such as *A Severed Head* (1961), *The Italian Girl* (1964), *A Fairly Honourable Defeat* (1970), *The Black Prince* (1973), and *The Sacred and Profane Love Machine* (1974). Several of these were made into plays and films. *The Severed Head*, for instance, ran for nearly three years at the Criterion Theatre, and was made into a film starring Richard Attenborough. In 1978 she also published a collection of poems, *A Year of Birds*.

She received many honours in her life. She was appointed CBE in 1976 and advanced to DBE in 1987. She was six times shortlisted for the Booker Prize, and won it in 1978 with *The Sea, the Sea*.

In 1956 Iris Murdoch married John Bayley, later Warton Professor of English Literature and a fellow of St Catherine's College, Oxford. He looked out of his college window one day, he said, and seeing her cycling by knew at once that he would marry her. Together they lived a life of cosy intellectual companionship, haphazard domestic arrangements, and bizarre culinary creations. It was reported by friends who had them to stay early in their married life that when taking up a pot of tea in the morning, they found Iris sitting bolt up in bed with her nose in Wittgenstein, while her husband lounged at her side perusing *Woman's Own*. They were to remain constant companions throughout their long marriage, and together were familiar figures in the literary world, both dressed from their favourite 'good as new' shop. John Bayley cared for her with devotion and tenderness throughout her final years when Alzheimer's disease took an increasingly tenacious grip upon her once fine mind. He charted the cruel progress of the illness in his poignant and unflinchingly honest memoir *Iris*, published last year.

He survives her. There were no children.

Dame Iris Murdoch, DBE, novelist and philosopher, died February 8, 1999, aged 79. She was born on July 15, 1919.

* * *

STANLEY KUBRICK

7 MARCH 1999

A POWERFUL and uncompromising talent, Stanley Kubrick first came to prominence with a scathing treatment of the hypocrisies of war in *Paths of Glory* (1957) and went on to make a succession of distinctively individual films, each completely different from the one before. He could move from the outrageous black comedy of *Dr Strangelove* (1964), to the calmer, more cerebral approach of *2001: A Space Odyssey* (1968), one of his most remarkable films. Likewise he could make films as totally different as the nightmare vision of *A Clockwork Orange* and his exploration of the machinations of the 18th-century officer class in *Barry Lyndon*.

Yet there were common factors. His work was infused with a deep pessimism about his fellow creatures, whom he often portrayed as being unable to control their destiny. He had a penchant for subversive humour. Technically he was a master of his craft, with a striking visual sense and the ability to handle complicated narratives. He could work with equal facility in a number of styles, from documentary realism to the furthest flights of fantasy.

Kubrick was a meticulous director who often spent years in the preparation and shooting of a film, planning each shot with obsessive precision. This inevitably limited his output and a new film every four to five years became his norm. It also, according to his critics, produced a detached and impersonal quality, a charge particularly levelled against his later films. But it was in the nature of Kubrick's work to divide critical opinion, arousing the extremes of adulation and censure. He was a director about whom it was impossible to be neutral.

Stanley Kubrick, Tony Curtis and Laurence Olivier on the set of *Spartacus.*

He was born in the Bronx district of New York, the son of a doctor, who encouraged him to take up photography as a hobby. Infatuated with the cinema from boyhood, he got his first job at 16 as a staff photographer on the magazine *Look*. The transition from still photography to movies came in 1950 when he directed a 16-minute documentary about a boxer, *Day of the Fight*, which he sold to RKO-Pathe. There was another documentary and then, in 1953, his first feature, *Fear and Desire*, a low-budget film made with money borrowed from relatives and friends. It was virtually a one-man show, with Kubrick performing all the directing and production functions: writing the script, directing, filming, and loading the camera.

He similarly financed his next film, *Killer's Kiss* (1955), which he based on his own original screenplay about a boxer who rescues a girl from the clutches of a gangster. Less important than the banal story was Kubrick's inventive direction (again, he performed most of the other functions, too), with several touches worthy of a film-maker of far greater experience. He was now ready to move from B pictures to main features.

In partnership with the producer James B. Harris, he was able to get backing from United Artists for *The Killing* (1956), a taut thriller about a racetrack robbery. The theme, of the perfect crime that goes wrong, had been used many times in

Hollywood, but Kubrick gave it a new life with his crisp and confident handling. He also drew vivid performances from seasoned character actors such as Sterling Hayden and Elisha Cook. It was his first work to receive serious attention from reviewers.

With the release in the following year of *Paths of Glory*, Kubrick, still not yet 30, emerged at a stroke into the front rank of American directors. Set on the Western Front in the First World War, the film follows the fate of three ordinary French soldiers who are court-martialled and executed after a disastrous sortie in order to save the face of the high command. It was a triumph on all levels, as an exploration of character and motive, for its dramatic qualities and, not least, a superb piece of film-making which drew graphic contrasts between the lot of the men in the trenches and the comfortable existence of the officers commanding them.

A big critical success, *Paths of Glory* fared only moderately at the box office and since Kubrick had worked not for a salary but for a percentage of the profits, a lean time lay ahead of him. Kubrick had to wait two years for his next film. *Spartacus* (1960) was an assignment offered to him when the original director, Anthony Mann, withdrew. It was the only film in his career Kubrick did not choose to make. But he handled the conventions of the big-budget Hollywood epic with considerable flair and if he regarded the film as a chore, it is one of the more intelligent examples of the genre.

In 1961 Kubrick moved to Britain, feeling that this would offer him greater independence, and from now on his work was based in this country. His first British film, ironically, was set in the United States: *Lolita* (1962), an adaptation of Vladimir Nabokov's novel about the infatuation of a middle-aged lecturer (brilliantly played by James Mason) with a 14-year-old girl. The picture was notable for Kubrick's black humour and contained a memorably manic supporting performance from Peter Sellers.

Both black comedy and Sellers were strongly featured in Kubrick's nuclear war fantasy, *Dr Strangelove: Or How I Learned to Stop Worrying and Love the Bomb*. Sellers played three parts, including the mad doctor of the title, a latterday Nazi masterminding the American nuclear programme; and the film was a joyous amalgam of satire and farce in service of the ultimately tragic subject, the destruction of the world.

For *2001: A Space Odyssey*, Kubrick moved boldly away from traditional storytelling, with its emphasis on dialogue and character, and relied instead on the suggestive power of visual imagery. Kubrick called *2001* a 'non-verbal experience' and it is half an hour before any words are spoken. In tracing the journey of a group of astronauts towards Jupiter, years into the future, Kubrick was helped by some of the most astonishing special effects seen in the cinema up to that time.

In 1971 Kubrick made his most controversial film, *A Clockwork Orange*, a bleak view of a society dominated by mindless violence. The picture was criticized for parading what it was seeking to condemn, though the potency of Kubrick's vision (suggested by the novel by Anthony Burgess) was undeniable. Coming out in the midst of a national debate about the effects of violence on the screen, *A Clockwork Orange* was banned by several local authorities.

There could hardly be greater contrast between this film and *Barry Lyndon*, a long, elegantly mounted, but dramatically low-key version of a minor Thackeray novel of the same title. Nor was Kubrick's reputation enhanced by *The Shining* (1980), a disappointingly indulgent excursion into the horror genre, and when, after another five-year gap, he started work on a new picture, *Full Metal Jacket*, a return to form seemed overdue. In this film, which was released in 1987, Kubrick returned to the theme of the brutalizing effects of militarism and war, in what was an unsparing adaptation of a Gustav Hasford novel.

It went some way towards redeeming his reputation, though it was generally regarded as lacking the subtlety and compassion of his earlier *Paths of Glory*.

Opinion was by this time divided on Kubrick's overall merits. His detractors thought him fussy and pretentious, while to his considerable army of admirers he was simply one of the cinema's great talents. Kubrick liked to enshroud himself in mystery and at the time of his death had been working on a new film, *Eyes Wide Shut*, starring Tom Cruise and Nicole Kidman, for the past two years. It is due to be released in July.

Stanley Kubrick was three times married and is survived by his wife Christiane and by three daughters.

Stanley Kubrick, film-maker, died March 7, 1999, at his Hertfordshire home, aged 70.
He was born in New York on July 26, 1928.

YEHUDI MENUHIN

12 MARCH 1999

FEW PEOPLE HAVE ever lived so long with such fame as Yehudi Menuhin. As a child prodigy he played the violin in public from the age of seven, and was soon acclaimed as a genius; 75 years later he was still in the public eye, as much for his work for noble causes as for his music. He believed in and argued for green issues long before that term was invented.

At times, the fervour with which he espoused good works, and the sympathetic range of his ear and eye, made it seem as though he were the guardian of the human conscience. He persuaded politicians to listen to his views and sometimes even to go along with them. He was a regular contributor to the letters page of *The Times*, most recently as one of the signatories to a denunciation of the film *Hilary and Jackie*, about the cellist Jacqueline du Pré. The list of organizations of which he was founder, patron, or a committee member ran to some 15 pages. They ranged from Justice for Tibet International to groups opposed to the fluoridation of water. At one time he even ran an organic food shop in Baker Street.

He championed the young as founder of the Yehudi Menuhin School in Surrey, which numbered Nigel Kennedy among its prize pupils, and the Menuhin Music Academy in Gstaad. In 1977 he founded Live Music Now, an organization which enables young people to purchase concert tickets cheaply. As president of the Musicians International Mutual Aid Fund he helped to support the not-so-young.

Those who talked to him usually came away uplifted by the encounter. He had, one observer remarked, 'an astonishing capacity for reminding people of the more generous side of their nature'. George Steiner went further and said that Menuhin was 'probably the best-loved personality in the history of the performing arts'.

There was, though, a price to pay for the aura of saintliness which followed Yehudi Menuhin around the world from his house in Belgravia. He was mocked behind his back for his devotion to the three Ys: yoga, yoghurt, and Yehudi. Music critics were apt, especially in later years, to complain that he simply did too much; they were fond of pointing out the technical imperfections of his playing while paying tribute to its emotional content. Even as just a commentator as Desmond Shawe-Taylor – reviewing the collection of five CDs issued in 1991 to celebrate Menuhin's seventy-fifth birthday – wrote: 'Perhaps no violinist of the first order has been so continuously busy as conductor and organiser, or had quite so techni- cally chequered a career.'

Others saw deeper flaws, in the man as well as in his music. Another supposed celebration of his seventy-fifth birthday, Tony Palmer's documentary *Menuhin: A Family Portrait* for Channel 4, was considerably less welcome than the collection of CDs. Palmer's thesis was that Menuhin had spent his life in the grip of two domineering women, his mother, Marutha, and his second wife, Diana. (Menuhin's first marriage to the Australian heiress, Nora Nicholas, was, according to Palmer, a desperate and unsuccessful attempt to cut loose from Marutha's apron strings.) The film dredged up jealousy from Yehudi's sister Yaltah and suggested that he had been a poor father to his four children (two from each marriage). Interviews with all four children did little to dispel this view.

Yehudi Menuhin was deeply wounded by all this, and the scars took a long time to heal. He tried to prevent publication of the book that Palmer subsequently wrote, but succeeded only in forcing a change of publisher. Friends told the rather unworldly Menuhin that he had been foolish to trust Palmer.

On one point Tony Palmer could not be challenged: Yehudi Menuhin had a very strange upbringing. He and his two sisters were educated at home and allowed none of the usual contacts with other children and teachers. Possibly motivated by their own privations, their Russian parents were determined that the children, and especially Yehudi, should succeed at the highest level. The cost in terms of childhood pleasures was enormous: bicycles and horses were banned in case an accident could affect a finger needed to play an instrument. Yehudi's mother, who came from Tartar as well as Jewish stock, was highly selective when choosing whom her son should meet.

Yehudi Menuhin was given a toy violin when very small, but smashed it when he found that it would not 'sing'. He took his first violin lessons shortly after turning four and went to study with Louis Persinger, to whom he regularly paid tribute. His first professional engagement was in San Francisco when he was eight, and there he played Lalo's *Symphonie espagnole*. His New York debut came in 1926, and by the time he had reached 13 he had appeared in London, Berlin, and Paris. The Paris debut in 1927 with the Lamoureux Orchestra – the Lalo again and the Tchaikovsky Concerto – was particularly impressive. Menuhin stayed on to study there under the Romanian composer and violinist George Enescu, who duly became another major influence.

Enescu's earthiness and vigour provided the perfect antidote to the cerebral and isolated world of the adolescent Menuhin. It was the performance of the Beethoven Concerto, with which Menuhin became particularly associated, under Fritz Busch in New York in November 1927, that turned him into a serious player with an immediate following. Busch, at first sceptical, had declared that you don't hire Jackie Coogan to play Hamlet, but he was soon converted by Menuhin's amazing precociousness, declaring 'You can play anything with me, any time, anywhere.'

The critic Olin Downes wrote: 'Few violinists of years of experience, known to the public, have played Beethoven with as true a feeling for his form and content.'

Berlin acclaimed him in 1928, when he played with the Philharmonic under Bruno Walter; London followed a year later. His debut at the Queen's Hall on November 4 was with the LSO under Busch. *The Times* critic, though not ecstatic, was admiring.

By then, Menuhin was making his first records. He continued to study with Enescu and also with Adolf Busch. Already the depth and musicality of his performances were those of a player of much more mature years. He was truly a phenomenon.

Indeed, few violinists past or present have tackled the Bach Chaconne or the Mozart and Beethoven concertos at the age of 12 or 13 with so many insights. On his second visit to London in 1932 he was chosen to record the Elgar Concerto with the composer, a disc that has remained a classic, unsurpassed to this day.

That year he tackled Bach and Mozart under Beecham at the Albert Hall, followed by the Elgar Concerto in the second half, conducted by the composer. The performance of the 15-year-old boy with the 75-year-old composer was peculiarly moving: the reception was rapturous. *The Times* critic capitulated: 'Throughout one was impressed by the sympathy of the phrasing and the general vitality of the playing.'

Menuhin continued his international career until the war, except for a break in 1936 to study and enjoy his private life. During the war he played more than 500 concerts for the Allied troops. He also broadcast frequently, introducing the Bartók Concerto No. 2, then considered unfathomable by most people. Bartók wrote a solo sonata for Menuhin in 1942.

A studio account of the Brahms Concerto with the BBC, recorded during the war and recently resurrected from the BBC archives, shows Menuhin at this period in his most glorious form, eloquent and expansive. After the war he was the first artist to play at the Paris Opera when it reopened after the Occupation. He was also the first Jewish artist to play after the war with the Berlin Philharmonic, under Wilhelm Furtwängler (a gesture that brought him much criticism from those who felt that Furtwängler should not have remained in Germany under the Nazis). He frequently gave recitals at this time with his sisters Hephzibah and Yaltah, both accomplished pianists, and with his brother-in-law, the pianist Louis Kentner.

An experience that marked Menuhin deeply came in 1945, when he set off for Germany in the company of Benjamin Britten. They took with them, in Menuhin's own recollection, 'more or less the whole standard violin literature – concerti, sonatas, little pieces – and played it, without rehearsal, in the ruins of the Third Reich'. At Belsen they played twice in one afternoon. The prison huts had been burnt down. The surviving inmates of the camp, liberated some weeks before, had been transferred to the ss barracks, and dressed in clothing fashioned from army blankets.

It was to them that Britten and Menuhin played. 'I shall not forget that afternoon as long as I live,' the violinist later wrote. In the decades that followed, several members of that audience were to make themselves known backstage after one of his concerts.

In 1947 Yehudi Menuhin took as his second wife the ballet dancer Diana Gould, in a marriage that was to last for the rest of his life. She was handsome and tall, possibly too tall for an ideal ballerina. But that did not prevent both Diaghilev and Pavlova engaging her for their companies. 'A pity,' Diana Menuhin remarked with typical acerbity, 'they each died soon afterwards.' She would probably have been a formidable actress, but she preferred to devote her life to her husband. This she did assiduously, with little verbal restraint, guarding him whenever possible from the stream of visitors seeking his patronage.

From 1959 Menuhin made his home in London. It was about this time that he began to widen his activities. He directed, and played regularly at, the Bath Festival (1958–68), the Windsor Festival (1969–72), and the Gstaad Festival (from 1956). At Gstaad he made a second home, and there he dispensed wisdom on a wide variety of subjects. For a while he had his own chamber orchestra, which he conducted and with which he appeared as soloist.

He also began to conduct many of the major symphony orchestras of the world. His achievements in this field have perhaps been underrated. Players responded warmly to his innate musicianship, and despite obvious flaws in his baton technique, his readings often attained a notable homogeneity and strength, though his repertoire was confined. He was associate conductor and president of the Royal Philharmonic Orchestra from 1982, and principal guest conductor of the English String Orchestra from 1988.

In the meantime he interested himself in Indian music and appeared in programmes with Ravi Shankar, the celebrated sitar player. Jazz was yet another enthusiasm, and he played and recorded in a hugely popular double act with the jazz violinist Stéphane Grappelli.

In 1962 he founded the Menuhin School at Stoke d'Abernon in Surrey. There he insisted that students should be taught how to develop as rounded people, not just musicians. Pupils were trained as much in chamber music as in solo work. Many have gone on to important careers. Menuhin frequently held masterclasses at the school and it may well prove the most lasting monument to his generosity of spirit.

Menuhin's tone was rich and warm, his style overtly and spontaneously expressive, with just enough classical control for it not to become in any way effusive. Through it, he communicated with composers: Bartók was overwhelmed by

Menuhin's playing of his challenging music and composed his final major work, the *Sonata for Solo Violin*, especially for him; Walton also wrote a fine sonata.

Critics detected deficiencies both of spontaneity and technique in Menuhin's playing as his career progressed, and the violinist himself acknowledged that he had at several points in his musical life had to rethink his whole approach to his art. But no one could deny that he always enjoyed a special rapport with his audiences. As he grew older, his faithful and considerable public showed itself more than willing to make any allowances that might be needed for advancing years. Signs of technical fallibility, or of a certain loss of breadth in his playing, were more than compensated for by other, interpretative rewards.

Menuhin never lost his gift of commanding a hall's undivided attention with the spirituality of his interpretations. Well into his seventies, the now slight, even vulnerable, but wholly concentrated figure on the platform remained a potent focus of public acclaim.

Yehudi Menuhin was knighted in 1956 and appointed OM in 1987. In 1993 he was created a life peer. He is survived by Lady Menuhin and by their two sons, and by the son and daughter of his first marriage.

Lord Menuhin, OM, violinist, conductor, and philanthropist, died March 12, 1999,
aged 82. He was born in New York on April 22, 1916.

SIR ALF RAMSEY

28 APRIL 1999

SIR ALF RAMSEY has his place in the history of English football for his feat in steering his country's team to its first and, to date, only World Cup win, at Wembley in 1966. It was an achievement which owed much to his unswerving determination to do things his way, and equally to his shrewd tactical analysis, a quality not always appreciated by his critics. His refusal to be deflected by criticism revealed much of his character. It was a strength at a time when popular clamour over team changes might have led him into mistakes that would have cost England the World Cup.

As a manager Ramsey placed stress on character and workrate, rather than flair and individuality. But this was an emphasis which had its genesis in the necessity which faced him throughout his career, both at club and national level, to fashion miracles with limited assets. Thus, at Ipswich he forged a first division championship win with a team which was, in terms of its individual gifts, far from being the best in the League. And he went into the 1966 World Cup tournament without any players of really outstanding talent – no Matthews, Finney, or Lawton, and no one to match Pelé of Brazil, Eusebio of Portugal, or Beckenbauer of Germany among the foreign players of that era.

His analytic mind, his precise, almost pedantic, utterances, delivered in the estuarine Essex accents which never left him, and his stubbornness, were traits which characterized the manager; they could all be seen in the player who, perhaps typically, was a late developer.

Alfred Ernest Ramsey was born in Dagenham and educated at Becontree Heath School. He played schoolboy football to county level, but had had no approach to turn professional and was playing for a local club and harbouring an ambition to be a grocer when he joined the Army at the beginning of the war.

Wartime football was to provide him with his opportunity and he began to turn out for Southampton when stationed there with the Duke of Cornwall's Light Infantry. He began as a centre or inside forward, moving back first to half back and then finally to full back, where he began his professional career with Southampton at the end of the war.

In those days full backs were more noted for their brawn and ability to put the opposing winger onto the terraces than for any creative ability, but Ramsey brought refinement to his new position. Heavy and lacking speed, he could be exposed by fast or clever wingers, but his tactical sense enabled him to jockey them into cul-de-sacs, and his use of the ball was accurate and imaginative.

Those qualities brought Ramsey his first England cap in 1948 in the 6–0 defeat of Switzerland. But he soon lost both his club and international place to Bill Ellerington and after turning down Sheffield Wednesday he joined Tottenham Hotspur for £21,000 in 1949. It was a perfect move.

Although Spurs were then in the second division, the great 'push-and-run' side developed by Arthur Rowe was coming together. Ramsey found his true métier, his precise, intelligent passing playing an important part as the side won the second and first division championships in consecutive years. As important as his skill was his tactical input as Rowe's lieutenant, his enthusiasm for the tactical side of the game earning him the nickname 'The General' from his colleagues.

Rowe recalled before his death that Ramsey 'thirsted for tactical knowledge'. 'He wanted to know the whys and wherefores of every movement. He was an out-and-out perfectionist.'

The move to Spurs revived Ramsey's England career. Recalled in November 1949, he kept his place for the next 29 games. His penalty-taking was an asset, and he scored the goal against a FIFA XI which saved England's home unbeaten record against continental opposition in 1953. It was lost a month later in the 6–3 defeat by Hungary, the match which ended Ramsey's international career, traumatized English football, and was to have a profound effect on Ramsey's thinking, although he maintained, some would say with characteristic blindness, that goalkeeping errors had magnified the gap between the teams.

Two years later he joined Ipswich, then in the third division south, as manager, winning the divisional championship in his first season. Further success took a little longer, but when it came it was startling. Ramsey's team of virtual unknowns emulated the achievement of his playing days with Tottenham by winning the second division and then league championships in consecutive seasons.

Ipswich's successes revealed Ramsey's great abilities as manager, the capacity to get the maximum out of his players, and his tactical appreciation. Given a limited group of players (and one of limited talents), Ramsey employed them shrewdly. He developed novel tactics for those days, withdrawing his left-winger Jimmy Leadbetter to play deep as the creative linchpin of the side. And he played two big forwards, Ted Phillips and Ray Crawford, as a dual strike force, a formation which was subsequently to become increasingly familiar.

That summer of 1962, England once again flopped sadly in the World Cup, and the FA approached Ramsey to become their first full-time manager. Ramsey accepted on condition that he would be allowed to do things his way, which meant the end for the amateur selection committee. To professionals his greatest achievement, perhaps even surpassing winning the World Cup, was to bring a sense of organization and professional values to the FA.

Ramsey knew exactly what he wanted. Almost his first decision was to appoint

Alf Ramsey, 1953

the young Bobby Moore as his captain. Moore was only 22 and had played only 11
games for England. But Ramsey knew his man, and was unshakably convinced that
Moore was the bastion on which World Cup victory would be fashioned. He also
asserted from the moment of his appointment that England would win the 1966
World Cup, an astonishing statement of faith considering the glittering overseas
teams that took part in that competition. Yet Ramsey was as good as his word, in

spite of the scepticism of most critics. Not unnaturally, the media, both in the run-up to the competition and then in the faltering progress through the early rounds, took full opportunity to beat him with the rod with which he seemed to have provided them, whenever England performed below their best.

The manner of his achieving victory did not please everyone. His support for Nobby Stiles, whose place in the side was the subject of a hostile campaign after the player's bad foul on Simon in the match with France, and his tactless description of the Argentines as 'animals' after a bad tempered quarter-final, were both regarded with disfavour in some official quarters.

His ultimate decision to abandon wingers as unproductive (the famous 4–3–3 formation), taken after England's struggles in the first round of the competition, and his refusal to recall Jimmy Greaves, who dropped out at the quarter-final stage with an injury, for the final, both dismayed the romantics. But Ramsey knew what he was doing. He recognized that England had not one really world-class winger. And his preferring Hurst to the injury-prone Greaves was vindicated by Hurst's cup final hat-trick, which sealed England's victory over a strong and talented German side.

Dour though he could so often seem, on that day Ramsey provided the inspiration to his players which lifted them after Germany had equalized through a late goal by Wolfgang Weber to make the score 2–2. As England's players gathered somewhat disconsolately, awaiting play to restart for extra time, Ramsey strode out on to the Wembley turf to look at the opposition. With the same confident prescience with which he had announced his intentions before the start of the World Cup campaign, he reported back to his players: 'They're finished.' His confidence revitalized his side, who came out determined to vindicate Ramsey's faith in them. Geoff Hurst's second two goals, the first off the crossbar, whose validity will be queried again and again wherever World Cup football is discussed, the second as the crowd began to stream on to the pitch in the closing moments of the match, set the seal on a gritty and thorough England performance.

In the moment of triumph all Ramsey's faults, real and imagined, were forgotten by his critics, while the England supporters in the ground went wild. Ramsey alone remained undemonstrative. Indeed, he was the only person on the England bench who did not jump into the air at the final whistle. The day after the victory he went home to his wife and daughter to celebrate with a cup of tea in front of the fire.

Ramsey was knighted in 1967. But his bonus for winning the World Cup was not a lavish one, enabling him merely to purchase the unpretentious four-bedroom detached house in Ipswich that remained his home.

The World Cup triumph was to prove his high point, although it was to provide the basis for the tactics he was to follow at a time when his methods were shown to need modification. Victory secured through virtues of thoroughness rather than flair tended to make him stubborn when faced with the inescapable fact that qualities of a very different order were making their mark not only in South America but in European teams also. In 1969 England could manage only third place in the European championships, a placing which looks better in retrospect than it did at the time. Nevertheless, they went to Mexico to defend the World Cup in 1970 with reason for guarded optimism, many believing that the team if anything was stronger than in 1966.

However, it was to prove an ill-fated expedition, though many of the reasons for that had nothing to do with Ramsey, his selections, or his methods. Things began badly when Bobby Moore, the team captain and Ramsey's chief lieutenant, was accused of stealing a bracelet in Colombia, and was separated from the team briefly. Moore was an England hero and the affair had an unsettling effect on the team out of all proportion to its actual significance.

England progressed satisfactorily through the opening rounds, but lost in the quarter-final to West Germany, a game which brought Ramsey's management under serious scrutiny for substituting Bobby Charlton and Martin Peters when England were leading.

But it was actually the absence of England's brilliant goalkeeper Gordon Banks which was the more significant. Banks was suffering from food poisoning and could not play. His replacement, Peter Bonetti, had a poor game. It was typical of Ramsey that he thanked Bonetti for his efforts when the team left Mexico. He could be gracious at quite unexpected moments, and it was this quality which earned him the loyalty of his players.

The 1970 World Cup, which was dominated by the glorious Brazil team, was to prove the start of Ramsey's decline. He had given hostages to fortune when he said 'We have nothing to learn from Brazil', and when England lost to West Germany at Wembley in the 1972 European Championship qualifying rounds, the criticism began to mount.

His press relationships grew increasingly sour, and opposition inside the FA found its focus in the new chairman, Sir Harold Thompson, the founder of Pegasus, an amateur of the old school who resented Ramsey's disregard for the councillors' footballing knowledge.

There was also an increasing suspicion that the world had caught up with Ramsey tactically, and that his loyalty to his players was preventing him seeing the need for changes in personnel; and after England lost to Poland, a defeat which cost them qualification for the 1974 World Cup, he was sacked.

It was effectively the end of his working life, although he acted as a consultant for a time and briefly managed Birmingham City, where he had been made a director in 1977. Ramsey himself insisted it should be regarded only as a temporary step, and finding himself out of sympathy with the times, quickly resigned.

He married, in 1951, Victoria (Vickie) Phyllis Answorth, daughter of William Welch. She survives him with their daughter.

Sir Alf Ramsey, manager of the England football team,
1963–74, died on April 28, 1999, aged 79.
He was born on January 22, 1920.

* * *

RAISA GORBACHEV

20 SEPTEMBER 1999

IN BOTH DOMESTIC and international politics, Raisa Gorbachev had a public profile unmatched by any other woman in the history of the Soviet state. While she owed her fame to the fact that her husband, Mikhail Gorbachev, was the leader who initiated transformative change in the Soviet system, culminating in the dissolution of the USSR, Raisa was a person of considerable ability and charm in her own right who helped to give a human face to the hitherto unattractive Soviet leadership.

Although subject to a good deal of criticism at home for accompanying her husband on virtually all of his travels and for being elegantly dressed in a country where most women had a hard time making ends meet, Mrs Gorbachev was an excellent ambassador for her country abroad. She was respected and admired by those who really knew her, in Russia and the outside world.

Her husband came under very intense pressure from all sides as he began trying to reform the Soviet system, promoting a more and more radical transformation, and eventually presiding over its demise. The pressure would have been unbearable had he not had one person with whom he could share all his problems and on whom he could rely completely. In more than one interview he confirmed that he discussed everything with his wife. When he first said this, in an interview for American television in 1987, *Pravda* was so shocked by the suggestion that this included the highest affairs of state that it cut out the offending line.

The eldest of three children, Raisa Maksimovna Titorenko was born in Rubtsovsk in the Altai region of Siberia, and shared many of the hardships of her fellow countrymen during her childhood. Her mother, a Russian born in Siberia, learnt to read and write only after her marriage. (Raisa's maternal grandfather was a peasant who was arrested at the beginning of the 1930s; he disappeared into the Gulag and was subsequently executed.) Her father, a Ukrainian, was a railway construction worker, which meant that the family was constantly on the move; she attended many different schools in various parts of the country, and the family's numerous temporary homes in those years sometimes included carriages in railway sidings.

Raisa, a highly intelligent girl, received a gold medal in her final school year for maximum grades in all subjects and, entirely on merit, entered the philosophy faculty of Moscow University in 1949 when only 17. Although the dogmatic nature of the teaching in the last years of Stalin's life meant that the philosophical education was a very limited one, there were a few teachers with a pre-revolutionary education who provided stimulus, and many bright fellow students.

One of these was Mikhail Sergeyevich Gorbachev, whom Raisa first met in 1951. Two years later they were married, and throughout the years their partnership remained an exceptionally close and devoted one.

Raisa Gorbachev graduated with distinction from Moscow University in 1954 but stayed on in the capital for another year to be with her husband (who had begun his studies in the law faculty in 1950) while he completed his degree. The atmosphere at Moscow University changed for the better after Stalin's death in March 1953, and she always regarded these student years as among the happiest and most important of her life, even though her meagre state grant usually ran out ten days before the end of each month. In 1955 she accompanied her husband to his native region of Stavropol in southern Russia, where he began his political career, becoming First Secretary of the Communist Party for the province in 1970. Their daughter, Irina (who became a doctor) was born in Stavropol in 1957.

During the 1960s Raisa Gorbachev conducted sociological research on the way of life of the peasantry in the Stavropol region, for which she was awarded a candidate of sciences degree (the Russian equivalent of a Ph.D.). A book based on her dissertation was published in 1969. She also taught in various institutes, in particular the Stavropol Agricultural Institute, where she attained the rank of associate professor.

When Mikhail Gorbachev was appointed a Secretary of the Central Committee in 1978, the Gorbachevs took up residence in Moscow for the first time since their student years. The conditions of life this time were those enjoyed by the party elite. Raisa's interests, which included literature, art, and music, were much more intellectual than those of most of the other party bosses' wives, and she did not fit easily into that company.

It was only when her husband reached the position of heir apparent to Konstantin Chernenko in 1984 that she could emerge from the shadows and claim the attention of a wider public. She became a media sensation in Britain in December 1984 when Western journalists encountered for the first time a Politburo spouse who was not only slim and attractive but had good taste and intellectual curiosity.

Raisa Gorbachev had been to Western countries before. She visited both Italy and France with her husband as tourists in the 1970s, and these trips began the process in their minds of discarding Soviet stereotypes of the West. But the 1984 visit was not only her first to Britain and the first of a number of meetings with Margaret Thatcher – during which the British Prime Minister and the Gorbachevs established a close rapport – but also the first in which Raisa was the subject of close attention from the media.

She went down very well, but the visit saw the start of more than one myth. On a shopping trip, she bought some earrings, which were paid for in cash by the wife of the Soviet Ambassador, no doubt from an embassy fund for the expenses of visiting officials. Before long, however, this transaction had been turned into a story that was to be endlessly repeated in the world's press, about Raisa paying for the earrings with an American Express card. At the time neither of the Gorbachevs even knew what a credit card was, let alone owned one.

Similarly, there were stories about her clothes being designed in Paris, though in fact they were made by her excellent Moscow dressmaker. Sloppy journalism and Moscow rumours were exploited by political adversaries to damage her husband as he began to rock the foundations of the system in which he had grown up.

After Mikhail Gorbachev became General Secretary of the Soviet Communist Party in March 1985 (which made him de facto leader of the USSR, although it was not until 1988 that he became formal head of state and 1990 that he was accorded the title of President), Raisa came into the public eye both at home and abroad as no Soviet leader's wife had ever done before.

The male-dominated Russian society did not take kindly to seeing her on television along with her husband or performing the duties of a 'first lady', which had no part in Soviet tradition. Although she was much admired by a section of her own society, she had many critics.

She played a modest but constructive part in Soviet cultural life, visiting hospitals and schools in the manner of the spouse of a head of state in Western countries. During and after her husband's years at the top of the Soviet hierarchy, she was very active in raising money for good causes, including children suffering from leukaemia. Most of those with whom she came into direct contact had a far more favourable impression of her than the disgruntled people on the Russian street, who tended to vent upon her even more than her husband their frustrations with everyday economic conditions in the last years of the Soviet Union (which in most respects worsened during the post-Soviet period).

Abroad, she made an almost uniformly favourable impression. Her intellectual bent led her to do a good deal of homework on the countries she visited and to ask intelligent questions when she got there. One non-admirer was Nancy Reagan, who found Mrs Gorbachev excessively didactic and was discomfited by being asked when the White House was built, since she had not the faintest idea. With Barbara Bush, Raisa Gorbachev established relations of warm friendship, and she was a popular figure also in European capitals.

In the winter of 1990–91 she worked on a volume of reflections and reminiscences, based on a series of long interviews with a writer from the Stavropol region, Georgi Pryakhin. It was published under the title *I Hope* in 1991. While remaining within the boundaries of political tact, the book was quite revealing about her family background and her extreme concern about the rising tensions in Soviet society and the almost intolerable workload that her husband carried.

These memoirs were dictated before the attempted coup of August 1991. That episode, although it ended in the defeat of the putschists, was a traumatic one for Raisa Gorbachev. She was held for three days along with her husband and other members of their family under house arrest in the Crimea. She stood up to the ordeal well until they heard on the BBC Russian Service that the self-proclaimed new rulers were on their way by air to see them. Memories of a childhood in Stalin's Russia then came back, and she feared that lies that had been told about her husband's serious ill-health were about to be turned into reality. She suffered a temporary paralysis in one arm and lost the power of speech for several days. Immediately after this ordeal she began, briefly, to be viewed more sympathetically at home.

She continued, however, to be better understood and admired abroad than in Russia until severe illness struck her in July 1999. When it was diagnosed as leukaemia, and it became known that she had gone on July 25 to one of the world's leading centres for treatment of the disease, in Munster, the Russian media began to reflect a much more positive view of the couple.

As her husband abandoned his lecture tours, which are the main source of income for his Foundation for Socio-Economic and Political Studies in Moscow, and set aside all work to be constantly at her bedside, Russians began to express their admiration for the love which bound the Gorbachevs as closely together as ever after 46 years of marriage.

Raisa Gorbachev never entirely got over the trauma of house arrest. In 1993 she suffered again from temporary paralysis, but she subsequently regained much of her health and she retained her good looks and vitality. While her husband was criticized by Russians for listening too much to his wife, there were occasions when he followed his own judgment when perhaps he should have heeded her. She was strongly opposed to his standing as a candidate in the 1996 Russian presidential election, but he was determined to take part. With the media presenting the contest in stark terms – 'either Yeltsin or a return to Communism' (in the person of Gennadi Zyuganov) – Gorbachev won fewer than half a million votes.

After the break-up of their daughter's marriage, Raisa spent an increasing amount of time looking after their two granddaughters. Nevertheless, she was able to accompany her husband on most of his foreign visits throughout the 1990s, and she was always made very welcome. In May this year, shortly before her illness was diagnosed, the couple made their first visit to Australia.

Raisa Gorbachev is survived by her husband and their daughter.

Raisa Gorbachev, wife of the former Soviet President, Mikhail Gorbachev,
died of leukaemia September 20, 1999, in hospital in Munster, Germany, aged 67.
She was born in Rubtsovsk, Siberia, on January 5, 1932.

* * *

SIR STANLEY MATTHEWS

Footballer whose ability to fox his opponents dazzled crowds for decades
and earned him the game's first knighthood

23 FEBRUARY 2000

STANLEY MATTHEWS was the most famous of all English footballers, and perhaps the greatest of all wingers. Other players may have come close to matching his celebrity or his skills, but none has been held in such affection or esteem, and as a symbol of all that is best in the game he was beyond compare. His professional longevity, too, is unlikely to be challenged. He was past 50 when he played his last league game, yet he felt that he had retired several years too soon.

In his heyday, his presence in a side could add 10,000 or 20,000 to the gate for a match. In those days, before televised sport, crowds would queue all morning at the turnstiles to be sure of seeing 'the Wizard of Dribble' in action. When he returned from Blackpool to second division Stoke City in 1961, 36,000 turned out at the Victoria Ground, six times the normal attendance. He was, wrote Geoffrey Green of *The Times*, 'the Pied Piper supreme of his day. He belonged to the nation as a whole. He was Britain's most valuable and treasured export, and woe betide any full back who resorted to cruel, rough or unethical means to stop him. At once such a player became an enemy of the people.'

Matthews's play at outside right was superb, unique. He was not impressive in physique. About 5ft 9in and weighing 11 stone, he was shallow-chested and inclined to stoop. His paramount gift lay in his dribbling. He could bring a ball up almost to the feet of an opposing defender, show it to him, tempt him into the first balance-change of a tackle, and then suddenly set off in another direction at such speed that, even in his forties, none could catch him. Generally he feinted to go left and then, having thrown the defender, went outside.

That, however, will seem an oversimplification to every footballer who opposed him and to the spectators who were charmed and amazed by the almost magical skill which carried him clear past the best defenders in a quarter century of world football. To see him manipulate the ball was to see an unfathomable talent at work. 'Have you ever watched a dragonfly,' the Labour MP (and perceptive football writer) J. P. W. Mallalieu was moved to ask – 'how it hovers in one spot with its wings vibrating and then, apparently without changing gear, darts away at top speed?'

Matthews's sensitivity in control was such that he seemed almost to caress the ball with his feet, and he could sell the dummy with shoulders, hips, feet, or even, it sometimes seemed, with his eyes. His ability was instinctive, not analytical; asked once by a journalist to demonstrate his famous swerve, he replied: 'Honestly, I couldn't do it in cold blood. It just comes out of me under pressure.'

Nevertheless, football was for him as much a psychological as a physical game, the overriding aim being to dominate and demoralize the opposition. 'If I can show the man tackling me the ball by taking it close to him and then whip it past him, causing him to lunge when he thinks he has cornered me, I will soon have caused an inferiority complex from which my opponent will not easily recover,' he explained. 'A successful dribbler must develop a superiority complex in his own mind.'

In his case, that mental superiority was never arrogant or vain. On and off the field he was a modest, reserved, and courteous man. He was a scrupulously clean player who avoided physical contact; he never sought it, and his deceptive movements ensured that he rarely suffered it. 'Don't allow anybody to persuade you to play the rough stuff,' he advised young would-be footballers. 'It does not pay in the long run.' He was never booked.

It was most unusual for him to head a ball: he preferred to play football on the ground. He was sometimes accused of being reluctant to go out and win possession, and of being too keen on keeping it once he had it. But charges of selfishness are unfair. Early in his career, he admitted, his only aim had been 'to get as many goals as possible', and for a time he was the leading goalscorer at Stoke. He scored four, for instance, when his team thrashed Leeds United 8–1 in 1934, and for

England he scored three in a notable 5–4 win against Czechoslovakia at White Hart Lane in 1937. In his later years, however, he became the great provider, winning games more often by creating goals than by scoring them. He scored only 24 times in 461 post-war league appearances, but the statistics give no hint of the hundreds of scoring opportunities he selflessly made for others.

Stanley Matthews was born in Hanley, Staffordshire. His father, Jack Matthews, 'the Fighting Barber of Hanley', had a considerable local reputation as a feather-weight boxer and inspired in him what was to be a lifelong passion for physical fitness, buying him a pair of spiked running shoes for his fourth birthday and encouraging him out into the open air for breathing exercises on freezing winter mornings. Even in his eighties, Stanley Matthews was up at 6 a.m. to start his fitness regime.

It was Jack Matthews who settled his son's choice of football club. From the age of eight the boy had been an ardent fan of Port Vale, but it was his team's detested local rivals ('I hated Stoke City') that he joined after leaving school at 14. As an apprentice at Stoke he made the tea, licked stamps in the office, and played for the juniors on Saturdays for £1 a week. In his first year, at 15, he had two games for the reserves.

He signed professional forms on the first possible day: his 17th birthday. The signing fee was £10, the weekly wage £3 in summer and £5 in the season, with a £1 bonus for every win. A few weeks after his birthday, in March 1932, he played his first league match for the club, an away game against Bury. His last appearance for Stoke came more than 30 years later, when in 1965, five days past 50, he became the oldest man to take part in a first-class match.

In all he played more than 700 league games. His playing career lasted 33 years: 15 with Stoke, 14 with Blackpool, then another four back at Stoke. He won second division championship medals at 18 and 48, and in between won everything except the League championship. His first cap for England (against Wales) came in 1934, and in all (including unofficial wartime internationals) he played 84 games in an England shirt.

On his great days he won football matches on his own at the highest level. For England in that 1937 game against Czechoslovakia, for instance, he played with such effect that, though two or even three men tried to mark him, he cut open highly skilled and organized defences and won the matches virtually alone. But he once said that his own fondest memory was of beating Italy 4–0 on a blazing hot day in Turin in 1948; and what he recalled then was not so much his own perform-ance as the outstanding team – Stan Mortensen, Tommy Lawton, Wilf Mannion, Tom Finney – of which he had been a part.

Many would declare his finest performance to have been in the FA Cup Final of 1953 ('the Matthews final', as it became known) when he suddenly took up a match which Blackpool were losing 3–1 to Bolton and, imposing his skill and direction on the game in its closing stages, won the Cup for his team with a cross that allowed Bill Perry to score in the very last possible moment. Yet he played with equal brilliance on scores of occasions: for carrying a ball down the right wing of a football field against any opposition was at once his abiding urge and his supreme gift.

When he first decided to leave Stoke, public meetings were held at the town hall in the attempt to keep him there. Hoardings went up, saying 'Matthews Must Not Go!' He was, however, transferred to Blackpool in 1947, for a fee of £11,500 and a bottle of whisky. He became one of the seaside town's biggest attractions, dazzling the crowds and taking the team to two unsuccessful Wembley finals before the famous victory in Coronation year. In 1948 he won the first Footballer of the Year award.

He returned to Stoke City in 1961, giving his old club a new lease of life, and playing a considerable part in its return to the first division in the following season; he was again named Footballer of the Year. In 1965 Matthews became the first footballer to be knighted (he had been appointed CBE in 1957), and five days after his fiftieth birthday, he played his last league game, a 3–1 win against Fulham.

Shortly after retiring, he became general manager of Port Vale football club, and he went on in the next three decades to coach all over the world – in Malta, Ghana, California, Canada, and Australia. Wherever he was, he knew he had only to look at the underside of his dinner plate to be reminded of his roots in the Potteries.

In Soweto, in South Africa, he trained an all-black schoolboy team, 'Sir Stan's Men'. Those South African links brought him much pleasure, but they were not universally appreciated while apartheid held sway, and he was banned, for instance, from attending a Sportsman of the Year contest in Zimbabwe in 1985.

In 1997 he was due to be the guest of honour at a friendly game between England and South Africa at Old Trafford. Taken ill the previous day, he was unable to attend, and found himself instead one of the first patients in a new cardiology unit he himself had officially opened only a fortnight before.

Stanley Matthews married Betty Valance in 1934. They divorced in 1975, and he married Mila Winterova, who died last year. He is survived by a son and a daughter.

Sir Stanley Matthews, CBE, footballer, died on February 23, 2000, aged 85.
He was born on February 1, 1915.

BARBARA CARTLAND

Queen of the romantic novel and the world's bestselling author,
who lived in a fluffy pink world all of her own invention

21 MAY 2000

As WELL AS BEING the world's bestselling author, Barbara Cartland was the most prolific. Her output compelled a kind of breathless awe to match her prose. There was a dashing vulgarity, careless of the censure of the literati, in a performance which repeatedly and shamelessly broke the 'world record' for annual production of novels and gave her, quite absurdly, the longest entry in *Who's Who*.

She routinely turned out more than 20 novels a year, in a writing career that began in 1923. A few titles from a typical year, 1977, suggest the repetitive, mechanical nature of the exercise: *Conquered by Love*, *The Dragon and the Pearl*, *The Magic of Love*, *The Wild Unwilling Wife*, *Love Locked In*, *Rhapsody of Love*, and *Look, Listen and Love*. In her fiction there was, as another title from that year proclaimed, *No Escape from Love*.

She produced more than 650 novels besides dozens of other titles on subjects ranging across royalty, health, diet, cookery, stately homes, love, marriage, motherhood, and biography. In total she is said to have written 723 books, and she is reckoned to have sold more than a billion copies in more than 35 languages, almost exclusively to women.

She became the romantic novelist incarnate. Yet her own person, spectacularly groomed and gowned, and photographed or interviewed in sumptuous surroundings, frequently threatened to overwhelm even her own vast fictional output. Indeed on one occasion, the wedding of the Prince and Princess of Wales in 1981, her stock rose well above that merited by her work, thanks to her relationship by marriage with the Princess. The press speculated wildly and comically about what might happen if the exotically apparelled Queen of Romance turned up at such a romantic royal occasion, but she handled the matter with pristine tact, remaining reticent despite the newspapers' barbs, and declining to attend the service.

But her success, though attended by considerable publicity – of which she was by no means shy – was also the product of hard work. By the time of the arrival of the modern 'puff', in the form of remorseless exposure on television and commercial radio followed by almost simultaneous translation to celluloid, which has created commercial successes out of some novels almost before they have been read, the Cartland phenomenon was already established. The vehicle for her romantic yarns was no-nonsense prose, and she told a good story, with some reference to historical reality.

Nevertheless, she remained to the end a writer of romances in which feminine virtue found its goal in perfect married love. Vice, of the acknowledged sort to which males are prone, never infected her books. And while she herself was shrewd and successful, eminently a survivor, her productions harked back to a time when men, though dashing and even rakish (for 'experience' was a necessary component of their success with the chaste heroines), were not permitted boorishness or bad manners.

Cartland grew old in a unique style that she thought graceful and many others found grotesque. She simply refused to compromise with age, and though the focus grew softer and softer, she continued to dress like a dazzling starlet of the 1940s. Diamantes remained the old girl's best friend. She claimed that it was her hard work and gargantuan intake of vitamins that kept her in the pink, but in 1991 she sadly had to announce to a cynical world that she had stopped taking royal jelly because it was being 'pushed in sex shops as an aphrodisiac'.

Make-up was the answer to any awkward wrinkles, and so she applied it at first with a delicate powder-puff, and then in thicker and thicker coats. And having affected pink as the most feminine of colours, she stuck to it indefatigably and invariably, wearing matching hats, shoes, gowns, scarves, and frills. Like the rest of her world, her pekingese were rose-tinted, and she had a taste in Rolls-Royces shared only by Lady Penelope of *Thunderbirds*. The effect was overwhelming, amazing. Perhaps she simply did not understand the idea of caricature.

Barbara Cartland was born the daughter of Bertie Cartland and an army officer's daughter, Polly Scobell. Miss Scobell's father and mother had disapproved of the match on the grounds that the Cartlands were not landed gentry but financiers, and Birmingham financiers at that. Mrs Scobell was very much of the same opinion as Mrs Elton in Jane Austen's *Emma*: 'Birmingham ... not a place to promise much, you know. One has not great hopes from Birmingham.' Bertie's father lost a good deal of his money financing the Fishguard Railway and, though these losses would scarcely have left him indigent, he subsequently shot himself.

So Barbara's parents were left to bring up their family in no great luxury. Nevertheless, under Polly's stalwart guidance, the family had regained a life of moderate comfort by the beginning of the First World War. Then Barbara's father was killed during the Germans' Spring Offensive of 1918, having joined the Army despite being well into his thirties. Once again the family was left in straitened circumstances. Moving to London Polly opened a hat shop, and there Barbara Cartland began work, having by this time left school.

In the meantime she plunged into the social whirl of twenties London. Her good looks and vivacious character attracted numerous proposals of marriage, none of which, to her mother's exasperation, she would entertain. Nevertheless, Miss Cartland's party-going, combined with a ready ear and eye for what was going on around her, proved the making of her.

Through a friendship with a Fleet Street gossip columnist she began to earn small amounts of money for items of social news. Then she herself began to write, contributing gossipy articles to *The Daily Express*. Lord Beaverbrook soon took a personal interest in her, offering to make her the most famous woman journalist in the world if she would become his mistress. She turned him down, but he continued to help and advise her, as well as introducing her to the circle of his close friends, and obtaining invitations for her to exclusive parties. She later said that she had learnt a great deal about writing for the mass market from Beaverbrook, and for the rest of her life she remained the newspaper diarist's friend, ready to comment on almost any subject, whether or not she knew the first thing about it.

Another Canadian millionaire, the financier Sir James Dunn, was among the admirers Cartland acquired at that time. He proposed marriage to her at a glittering party at the fashionable French resort of Deauville. She refused him, too. Ironically, when she did marry Alexander McCorquodale in 1927, after turning down – she grandly estimated – 49 proposals, the marriage was very far from one of the ideal pattern familiar from her novels. It ended in divorce in 1933, and in 1936 she married Hugh McCorquodale, her first husband's first cousin. This time it was an ideally happy marriage, producing two sons: Ian, who often acted as her agent, and Glen, a stockbroker.

Cartland's first novel, *Jigsaw*, appeared in 1923, and began a steady trickle, which became a flow, which developed into a torrent. It was the writer Godfrey Winn who suggested to her that she dictate her novels, and she evolved a technique which saw her dictating between 1 p.m. and 3.30 p.m., producing with clinical efficiency a chapter a day and a novel every fortnight or so. History was the source of most of her novels, and of that, the colourful slice between the French Revolution and Waterloo provided much of her matter.

Nonetheless, her prodigious energies needed outlets in other fields too. She devised the pageant *Britain in her Industries* at the Albert Hall in 1930, and C. B. Cochran was so impressed that he arranged for it to be the finale of his first *Midnight Revue* at the London Pavilion, where it raised £12,000 for charity. Meanwhile she was busy with other glamorous events, such as motor racing at Brooklands in 1931 in a special women's race. In the same year, with Britain deep in recession, she decided that gliders might serve as cheap alternatives to aeroplanes, and she carried the first glider air mail, in her own sailplane, from Manston, Kent, to Reading.

She helped one of her brothers, Ronald Cartland, to whom she was devoted, to win a seat in Parliament, financing his election campaign with her earnings from journalism. When war came in 1939 he went to France and in May 1940 he was killed at Dunkirk, the first MP to be killed in the war; her subsequent biography of him carried a preface by Winston Churchill. Her other brother, Anthony, was killed a few days later.

Her first reaction to these events was to take refuge in Canada with her children. But she was soon to feel that she and they ought not to have privileged treatment. She returned to Britain, where she joined the Women's Voluntary Services, becoming chief welfare officer in Bedfordshire. She also worked for the St John's Ambulance Service, and for several years after the war she organized its exhibitions.

With the return of peace, Cartland was active in a host of different spheres quite apart from her writing. She supported nursing cadets, and in the 1950s helped to instigate an investigation into the housing of old people. For nine years she was a Hertfordshire county councillor. She ran a 500-acre farm. She lectured, and wrote for Sunday newspapers. She campaigned for education for gypsies and against fluoridation of water. And she lobbied for a wage for stay-at-home mothers, in the interests of maintaining the stability of family life. Whatever fashion or feminism might dictate, she retained a conviction that women long for chivalrous men and old-fashioned families – and the sales of her books show she cannot have been entirely mistaken.

The honours bestowed upon her reflected her many and various activities. She was made DSTJ in 1972 for her work with the St John's Ambulance Service. In 1981 the National Home Furnishing Association of Colorado Springs made her its Achiever of the Year. In 1991 she was created DBE. Colonel Gaddafi of Libya was said to be among her greatest fans, and certainly on Arab airport bookstalls her novels were among the few dealing with occidental erotic love that were tolerated. She herself remained fond of France, the only country, she said, 'where you can make love in the afternoon without someone hammering on the door'.

The one child of her marriage to Alexander McCorquodale, a daughter, Raine, married, first, the Earl of Dartmouth, from whom she was subsequently divorced, and secondly, in 1976, Earl Spencer, which gave Cartland a rather indirect family tie to Diana, Princess of Wales. Earl Spencer died in 1992 and in 1993 after a famous 30-day romance, his widow married Comte Jean-François Pineton de Chambrun.

Dame Barbara Cartland is survived by her daughter and two sons.

Dame Barbara Cartland, DBE, romantic novelist, was born on July 9, 1901.
She died May 22, 2000, aged 98.

SIR JOHN GIELGUD

Fastidious performer with a matchless voice, who stood centre stage
through the whole history of modern British theatre

21 MAY 2000

SIR JOHN GIELGUD was an actor who, more than any other, enshrined the spirit of English classicism. His long career was entwined with those of two other great stage knights, Laurence Olivier and Ralph Richardson, and it would be futile to claim dominance for one at the expense of the others. But they did occupy different positions in the classical commonwealth. If Olivier was its soldier and Richardson its common man, Gielgud was its priest.

To a unique degree his greatest performances coincided with the greatest plays. 'Style,' he once said, 'is knowing what sort of play you're in.' And to those who saw him as Hamlet, Mirabell, or John Worthing the experience was not simply that of witnessing a wonderful performer making the most of a wonderful part: it was to be in brain-to-brain contact with Shakespeare, Congreve, and Wilde.

As with Kean and Irving, his art was partly one of physical transformation. He entered the theatre during the epoch of the matinee idol and was able to assume romantic good looks in spite of a large nose, rapidly thinning hair, and legs that gave him acute embarrassment. What was never in doubt was the quality of his voice: an instrument of spell-binding purity, unrivalled in its speed and sensitivity of articulation. In the mouth of Hamlet it became par excellence the voice of the Renaissance; in John Worthing's, the ultimate distillation of Belgravian manners. Gielgud was a musician (good enough to play his own Bach and Chopin in the 1932 run of Rodney Ackland's *Musical Chairs*), and whatever his part, he made it sing. There were times when his rhapsodic tenor left sense behind. More often, especially in his later years, dramatic values were carried over intact into the region of chamber music: as in his duet with Richardson in David Storey's *Home* (1970), a viola to Richardson's cello.

His centre as an actor was one of the most fastidious patrician sensitivity, and it was visible in everything he played. He did not disappear into a role, in the manner of Olivier or Guinness. Rather, he approached a character by exploring different aspects of himself, and one fascination of his work was to witness the extremes to which he could bend an always recognizable personality. Some things were outside his range. He never played in dialect. He was incapable of coarseness. He lacked the muscle and animal appetite for the ultimate heavyweight roles.

But within its own compass his work was definitive: and, in the way of great actors, what he presented was not only the impersonation of a character but an insight into all human emotion. His Leontes was a revelation of jealousy itself through the portrait of one jealous man; just as his Prospero, Angelo, and Lear were essential expressions of loss, moral pride, and universal pity. Two elements were always constant: the dispassionate observer and the suffering man; a restraining combination that held even such heroes as Raskolnikov and Webster's Ferdinand on the classical rails. If marble could speak, it would have sounded like Gielgud.

Arthur John Gielgud was born in London, the youngest of three sons of Kate Terry-Lewis and Frank Gielgud, a stockbroker of Polish extraction. His great-aunt was the celebrated stage actress Ellen Terry. As a boy he was known as Jack, and at Hillside Preparatory School he played Shylock and Humpty Dumpty. After West-minster School, he at first intended to be a stage designer, and claimed he turned to acting 'only to please my parents' (who had in fact wanted him to train in architecture). He studied for the stage at Lady Benson's School and the Royal Academy of Dramatic Art, winning scholarships to both.

His professional debut was in 1921 at the Old Vic, playing a French herald in Shakespeare's *Henry V* and his first major London role was as Trofimov, the perpetual student, in Chekhov's *The Cherry Orchard*. He subsequently worked with J. B. Fagan's company in Oxford and in the West End before returning to the Old Vic in 1929 for two acclaimed seasons, including *Richard II* and the first of more than 500 *Hamlets*. His first taste of Broadway came in 1928 in Alfred Neumann's *The Patriot* and he was to return to the New York stage on many occasions. Reflecting on his early days in an interview he gave in 1991, Gielgud said: 'I spoke rather well, but rather too well, and fell in love with my own voice.'

Having established himself as a leading Shakespearean player, Gielgud returned to the West End in 1931, first as Inigo Jollifant, the 'not very interesting juvenile' in Priestley's *The Good Companions*, and then, crucially, as Richard II in Gordon Daviot's *Richard of Bordeaux* (1932). It was this performance that made Gielgud a popular star, and on which he based his career until the war.

Certainly not lacking in personal ambition, he was also ambitious for the theatre as a whole, and he made full use of his personal magnetism to help fellow artists to carry through much-needed reforms and expand the limits of popular taste. He launched the firm of Motley, three unknown girls who rose to fame as his regular designers. He seized the invitation to direct at the Old Vic in 1932 as a pretext for persuading the skinflint Lilian Baylis to pay for a fully designed production of *The Merchant of Venice* (Tyrone Guthrie said the show made Maugham and Coward seem like two Nonconformist parsons from the Midlands). He thus laid down the twin principles of design and continuous action on which modern Shakespearean production rests.

More important, he carried these reforms through in a series of West End seasons at the New Theatre and the Queen's, which set his managerial style of assembling brilliant surrounding companies, and included such landmark events as his 1934 *Hamlet*, which enjoyed an unheard-of five-month run before proceeding to New York (where it was exhaustively analyzed by Rosamond Gilder in *John Gielgud's Hamlet*); the 1935 *Romeo and Juliet*, in which he and Olivier alternated as Romeo and Mercutio; and the 1938 *Three Sisters*, an all-star ensemble production in which the main honours went to Gielgud's chosen director, Michel Saint-Denis.

As a director Gielgud could be an intimidating schoolmaster to younger members of his companies, as Alec Guinness and William Devlin found in their early years. But he was the reverse of the old-style theatrical martinet who drilled casts to fit a preconceived pattern. According to Peter Brook (a fruitful influence on Gielgud from the 1950 *Measure for Measure* to the 1968 *Oedipus*) he had no 'method' as a director. 'He is like an aircraft circling before it can land ... He will change and change indefinitely, in search of rightness ... For this reason, it has always been absolutely necessary for him to work with the best actors, and his generosity towards them in performance comes from his need for quality, which has always been infinitely more important to him than his own personal success.'

Gielgud's seasons in the 1930s blazed the trail for the permanent companies of today; but, however much some of his colleagues regretted it, Gielgud was too anti-institutional an artist ever to set up a permanent troupe of his own. It was his nature to move about within a large professional circle, forming and dissolving partnerships as he changed countries, switching between acting and directing, and rebounding – as he put it – 'between the advance guard and the rear guard' (an impulse reflecting his double theatrical inheritance from the Terrys, and the Polish side which has been tracked back to the arch-experimentalist Witkiewicz).

As one of Komisarjevsky's actors at the Barnes Theatre (where he first learnt to play Chekhov) and as an ally and patron of Saint-Denis, Gielgud was an internationalist who repeatedly lifted the English stage out of its insular rut. But any attempt to pin this label on him was at once frustrated by his engagement in the latest Noel Coward – a close friend from 1925 – when he took over the author's role in *The Vortex*.

Another close friend was Hugh (Binkie) Beaumont, the director of the once all-powerful management of H. M. Tennent, who virtually monopolized Gielgud's work on the London stage from the outbreak of war until the end of the 1950s. Beaumont's mission was to present 'the best', which, for him, usually meant glamour and high comedy. This made sense when applied to the legendary 1939 production of Gielgud and Edith Evans in *The Importance of Being Earnest*. It made less sense after the war when high comedy was at a low ebb with pieces like N. C.

Hunter's *A Day by the Sea*, in which the ever-regal Gielgud could give the impression that he was about to tip the supporting cast.

His classical career continued with undimmed distinction, particularly in the 1952 Lyric Hammersmith season, which included his definitive Mirabell and Jaffier in Peter Brook's revival of *Venice Preserv'd*. But he found no post-war counterparts to *Richard of Bordeaux* and *Musical Chairs*: and when an authentic post-war drama did finally emerge, from the new writers of the Royal Court, its scruffy, uncouth manners were not to his taste; neither were its patron saints, Brecht and Beckett.

Slower than Olivier to adapt to changing times, he remained the undisputed monarch of Tennents' Royal Family; repeating his past successes, directing operas, and making prolonged solo tours in the Shakespearean anthology *The Ages of Man*, but lacking a foothold in the modern repertory.

He made one approach to it as Julian in the 1964 Broadway production of Edward Albee's *Tiny Alice*. But it was not until 1968 that he regained the London public as the bumbling traditionalist headmaster in Alan Bennett's *40 Years On*. As a satire on his own position, it was a brilliantly disarming point of re-entry. Self-mockery was a new aspect of his talent, and one that he continued to use with devastating effect: as in Charles Wood's *Veterans*, based on his own film performance in *The Charge of the Light Brigade* (1968), and featuring the great star cooling his heels on a property horse and declaring 'I shall withdraw my labour' in the ringing voice of Henry V.

Having come to terms with the modern theatre, Gielgud showed no further inclination to coast along on his past reputation. He embarked on a series of parts in plays by David Storey, Peter Shaffer, Edward Bond, and Harold Pinter, every one of which took him into fresh emotional territory. Spooner, the crumpled poetic failure in Pinter's *No Man's Land* (1976), was one of the great creations of his life. Under-used at the National Theatre during Olivier's time, he made up the difference under Peter Hall: beginning in 1974 with a seraphic *Prospero* (appearing in almost simultaneous contrast with his portrait of the disillusioned Shakespeare in Bond's *Bingo*) and continuing with Volpone and a *Julius Caesar* in which, uniquely, Caesar emerged as the central character.

He made his final stage appearance in 1988 when, after a gap of almost a decade, he returned to the West End in Hugh Whitemore's *The Best of Friends*, which involved the 83-year-old actor in conveying an ageing process of 25 years, and playing a museum curator who sees himself as a string-pulling second-rater with no clear purpose in life. The role was at once utterly remote from his own career, and absolutely in line with his brand of verbal fastidiousness and delicate mischief: and in performance it combined total objectivity with intimate self-portraiture. When he announced that he had found life 'very interesting', and that he could leave it without regrets – 'I may pop off tomorrow' – there was no telling whether the character or the actor was speaking. This was the most unsentimental of stage farewells.

Though he may not have had, or have sought, as substantial a cinema career as Olivier and Richardson, Gielgud emerged in his later years as an effective – and very busy – character player on screen. He made his first film, *Who Is the Man?*, as early as 1924, before repeating his stage part in *The Good Companions* (1933), teaming incongruously but successfully with Peter Lorre in Hitchcock's *The Secret Agent* (1936), and playing Disraeli in *The Prime Minister* (1940).

There were glimpses of his Hamlet in Humphrey Jennings's documentary, *A Diary for Timothy* (1945), and during the post-war years he was in several Shakespeare films, among them the 1953 *Julius Caesar* (as Cassius), Olivier's *Richard III* (as Clarence), and Orson Welles's *Chimes at Midnight* (as Henry IV). From the 1960s Gielgud's films became more frequent, if not always well chosen. The important ones included *Becket* (1964), in which he played Henry II and was nominated for an Oscar; *The Charge of the Light Brigade* (1968), with his rich study of Lord Raglan; and Alain Resnais' *Providence* (1977), which contained possibly his best film performance as an embittered old writer.

His memorable cameos ranged from *Oh! What a Lovely War* (1969) to *Chariots of Fire* (1981), and he was responsible for two notable valets: in the Agatha Christie thriller *Murder on the Orient Express* (1974) and the 1981 comedy, *Arthur*, with Dudley Moore, which won him an Oscar for the Best Supporting Actor. It was a role he had originally turned down twice: 'I thought (the script) was rather smutty, rather common,' he said, bemused at the extraordinary amount of fan mail his part had elicited.

Other films included *The Elephant Man* (1980) and Richard Attenborough's epic *Gandhi* (1982). Attenborough marvelled at the way the veteran master of the stage had turned himself into 'a consummate film actor'. The reality was that film work brought Gielgud his first serious income and provided him the financial stability that is missing from a jobbing actor's life. At the age of 87 he shed his clothes for the cameras in Peter Greenaway's experimental film version of *The Tempest*, *Prospero's Books* (1991).

Of his television roles, his performance as Loomis in Simon Gray's *Quartermaine's Terms* was a memorable study in the exquisitely mannered arrogance of academic politics. Most recently he appeared in a production of *Merlin* for Channel 4 television and in 1998 had starred in *The Titchbourne Claimant* for the larger screen. A month ago he was filming the Samuel Beckett play, *Catastrophe*.

His little indiscretions – Gielgoofs as he called them – became legendary. The published ones include the day he ran into Sir Alec Guinness in Piccadilly and said, 'Alec, dear, I just can't think why you want to play big parts. Why don't you stick to the little people you do so well?' Another came with his verdict of a new portrait:

'David Hockney did a drawing of me when I was 70 and I thought that if I really looked like that, I must kill myself tomorrow.'

In 1994 he was honoured by the Globe Theatre in Shaftesbury Avenue, which was renamed the Gielgud Theatre. However, he guarded his privacy, and fought shy of gushing tributes, preferring to let his work speak for itself. He disliked the prospect of a commemoration after his death: 'I've left strict instructions for no memorial service. They have become society functions and I don't think I have the right to be commemorated at Westminster Abbey.'

Knighted in 1953 (the same year in which he was fined £10 for importuning in Chelsea), he was appointed Companion of Honour in 1977. The Order of Merit followed in 1996.

He left a record of his life and friends in the theatre in several gracefully written books, the first of which, *Early Stages*, appeared in 1939 and the last, *Backward Glances*, in 1989. His final publication was *Notes from the Gods* (1994), a collection of comments he had scribbled in programmes from his early years.

His companion of some 40 years, Martin Hensler, died last year.

Sir John Gielgud, OM, CH, actor, was born on April 14, 1904.
He died on May 21, 2000, aged 96.

SIR ALEC GUINNESS

*Versatile and self-effacing actor who turned anonymity into an art form
and himself into an international star*

5 AUGUST 2000

ALEC GUINNESS lacked many of the advantages of his theatrical peers. He could not claim Olivier's outstanding good looks and pure animal magnetism: he was bald by the time he reached 32, which emphasized his pointy, puckish ears. Unlike Gielgud he was not steeped in theatrical tradition: his childhood was disrupted and unhappy and his most vivid memory was of Nellie Wallace in music-hall at the Coliseum. He lacked Richardson's ability to be a 'card', and he certainly did not have the Richardson ruthlessness, which ensured that Ralph was never upstaged: late in his life Guinness remarked, a little ruefully, 'I'm not a very confident person, never have been.'

But he had one great gift denied the others: anonymity. On stage or on screen Olivier was always Olivier, Gielgud always Gielgud, and Richardson always Richardson. Guinness had the ability to obliterate himself completely within each character he played.

He was a master of disguise, and some of his critics claimed that he achieved this by building around himself a carapace of privacy and mystery. Such an explanation is too superficial. Guinness achieved much of his distinction by sheer graft, aided by high intelligence and a gift for acute observation.

His beginnings in the theatre before the war were uncertain. It took him two years to get a commission in the Royal Navy during the war, and his command of a rickety landing craft in the Mediterranean had its inglorious moments, as he recounted with some irony in his autobiography *Blessings in Disguise*.

In the cinema his great mentor was David Lean, who gave Guinness his first major role in *Great Expectations* and later established him as a truly international star in films such as *The Bridge on the River Kwai* and *Lawrence of Arabia*. Director and star had several well-publicised rows. But the two men needed one another.

Guinness was rare among actors in being a master of self-deprecation. He once said: 'Essentially I'm a small-part actor who's been lucky enough to play leading roles for most of his life.' For luck read good judgment. Guinness knew what was beyond his reach. After the early days his excursions into Shakespeare were comparatively rare and on the whole not very successful. He attempted *Lear* only on radio when he was well on in life. He shied away from the avant-garde, getting no closer to it than Ionesco's *Exit the King* at the Royal Court. Alec Guinness believed in the art of the possible.

Offstage Guinness usually tried to be just a face in the well-behaved crowd and generally succeeded. No breath of scandal touched his marriage of over 60 years, and he was rarely stalked by the gossip columnists. He liked good restaurants, especially the Connaught, but there again he blended into the background. He was fond of telling the story of how he handed in his coat at a hotel cloakroom and, offering to give his name, was quite pleased to be told that it would not be necessary. The coat was later handed back with the ticket still attached and on it the inscription 'Bald with glasses'.

Alec Guinness was illegitimate and no father's name appeared on his birth certificate. There have been suggestions that the man in question was a middle-aged banker called Geddes. His mother, Agnes de Cuffe, a temporary barmaid, did not admit to her son for several years that Guinness was not his real name.

She was married briefly to a self-styled 'Captain' David Stiven, who treated his stepson brutally. Agnes was little better, leaving behind her a trail of unpaid bills at cheap London hotels. Guinness had as little affection for her as John Osborne had for his monstrous mother Nellie Beatrice, although unlike Osborne he was too polite to vent his dislike in public. School was little better than home, as he moved through a succession of undistinguished South Coast establishments. By 18 he had found a modest job in a London advertising agency and cut off all relations with his mother.

He got a little training at the Fay Compton School of Dramatic Art, and plucked up the courage to write to John Gielgud, ten years older than Guinness and already an idol. Gielgud, who had been a judge at the Fay Compton end-of-term perform-ance, engaged him as Osric and Third Player for the *Hamlet* he was preparing for the New Theatre in 1934 and stuffed a few much-needed shillings in Guinness's pocket.

Guinness always claimed that it was Gielgud who launched him on his career, but an equal influence was the flamboyant Martita Hunt. She regularly told him that he had little talent, but encouraged him nonetheless and her coaching helped to get him his drama school scholarship. The two were to meet again 20 years later when Hunt played Miss Havisham in *Great Expectations*.

Guinness had a season with the Old Vic Company in 1936–37, playing a number of small roles and one quite large one, Sir Andrew Aguecheek in Tyrone Guthrie's production of *Twelfth Night*. He worked there with Michael St Denis, but Guthrie himself was to be far the greater influence.

Guthrie took him on tour with *Hamlet* to Elsinore to play before the royalty of Denmark and Sweden. His parting words before the first night were: 'Be polite to Kings and Queens if they get in your way, Alec.' Guinness, fortified by some schnapps to keep the Danish cold out, duly laid his sword on the King of Sweden's lap. Despite such indiscretions Guthrie thought his protégé good enough to play the title role, which he did under Guthrie's direction in 1938. This was reasonably well received and even drew some encouraging words from Gielgud, but it did not greatly stir the public.

By this time Alec Guinness had married Merula Salaman, a young actress whom he had met while they were appearing in André Obey's *Noah*, a St Denis production. She took him into a different world, that of cultivated and affluent Jewish society with wide connections in the arts. Guinness profited from it as he was to profit from her support for the rest of his life.

In the early days of the war Guinness tried his hand at adaptation, turning to *Great Expectations* and casting himself as Herbert Pocket. He had formed the Actors Company with George Devine and *Expectations* was staged at the Rudolph Steiner Hall in December 1939.

Guinness then appeared in a couple of contemporary plays before enlisting in the Navy. Eventually he was hauled off the lower deck and put on an officers' training course, ending up by commanding a landing craft in the Mediterranean. In between times Terence Rattigan persuaded the Admiralty to give him temporary release to play in *Flare Path* on Broadway, which was reckoned to be good wartime propaganda.

After being demobbed Guinness found himself back in London with a decent reputation from before the war but no longer of an age or with the looks to play juvenile leads. He turned his hand again to adaptation, this time *The Brothers Karamazov*, directed by Peter Brook, who was just beginning to make a name for himself as an *enfant terrible*.

At this point enter David Lean, who was planning a film of *Great Expectations*. He remembered Guinness's pre-war performance on stage as Herbert Pocket and engaged him for the same role, although the actor's screen experience had been confined to a walk-on part in a 1933 movie called *Evensong*. Pocket led to Fagin in Lean's next Dickens picture, *Oliver Twist*, and this was the part which established Guinness as a screen actor of the highest quality. He was so good that there were calls in America to ban the film on grounds of anti-Semitism.

Guinness went on to work with Lean on four other films, three of which were international successes: *Kwai*, *Lawrence of Arabia*, and *Dr Zhivago*. Finally came *A Passage to India*, Lean's last film, in 1984. Guinness knew how much he owed to Lean, especially at the beginning, but there was a price to pay. He put it delicately, as always: 'We made six films and on three we had our differences.'

Guinness also made a substantial career with Michael Balcon's Ealing Studios. *Kind Hearts and Coronets* was the first of four films there with the brilliant but undependable Robert Hamer – and by far the best. Guinness, at his own suggestion, played all eight members, male and female, of the D'Ascoyne family who are killed by Dennis Price, and so delivered eight virtuoso performances. He was later to dismiss the film as 'pretty cardboard', but *Kind Hearts* established him as a comedian of exceptional polish. Ealing quickly capitalized on this and had him working with its best directors, Charles Crichton (*The Lavender Hill Mob*) and Sandy Mackendrick (*The Man in the White Suit* and *The Ladykillers*).

This screen success began to tug him away from the classical theatre in which he had spent much of his acting life. He had played the Fool to Olivier's Lear at the New in 1947 and had not been forgiven for upstaging the master. Richardson directed him as *Richard II* at the same theatre the next year, but with only modest success. And Guinness tried his own hand at direction with *Twelfth Night*, also at the New. But he was slowly deciding that he was not really a company man and did not want to be in thrall of his more famous contemporaries.

His next major role took him back to the commercial theatre, albeit the classier end of it, as the Unidentified Guest in T. S. Eliot's *Cocktail Party*, which he played both at the Edinburgh Festival and in New York. His second *Hamlet* in 1951, which he co-directed with Frank Hauser, was not a success, despite the presence of Kenneth Tynan and other luminaries in the cast. Tynan was later to write an early and not very good study of Guinness.

Tyrone Guthrie invited him over to the newly opened Shakespeare Playhouse in Stratford, Ontario, as the first British actor to lead the company, which he did with success, Irene Worth standing at his side. After that there was little more Shakespeare on stage, apart from a *Shylock* at Chichester when he had just turned 70. There was a weird *Macbeth* at the Royal Court in 1966, given the full Brechtian treatment by Bill Gaskill and with a disastrous Lady Macbeth from an improbably cast Simone Signoret.

Once or twice during his life Alec Guinness had considered converting to Roman Catholicism and his resolve was strengthened while playing the Cardinal at the Globe in Bridget Boland's *The Prisoner*. The play, much admired in its time (1954), was a complex debate between spiritual qualities and materialism. Shortly afterwards Guinness was received into the Catholic Church, followed, independently, by his wife.

After appearing as Boniface in *Hotel Paradiso*, marvellously directed by one of his regular collaborators, Peter Glenville, Guinness left the stage for six years. The films flowed regularly – impressive ones such as *Tunes of Glory* and one or two best forgotten – and he developed a good line in little men enmeshed in political intrigue in thrillers such as *The Quiller Memorandum* and Graham Greene's *Our Man in Havana* and *The Comedians*.

Guinness was always attracted by people with secrets, and few had deeper secrets than Mrs Artminster in Simon Gray's early transvestite comedy *Wise Child* at Wyndham's in 1967. Guinness alternated between skirts and a frightening red crew-cut wig. The play shocked some of his more staid admirers, but delighted a new generation learning to live with Ortonesque humour. Alan Bennett also provided Guinness with a mischievous character in *Habeas Corpus*, and then capitalized on his ability to play spies by writing the part of Hilary (based on Kim Philby) for him in *The Old Country*. Actor and author became good friends.

Two very different roles brought Guinness huge popular acclaim when he was in his mid sixties. The first was that of George Smiley in *Tinker, Tailor, Soldier, Spy*, which kept the nation glued to its television sets in 1979 as people tried to follow the intricacies of John le Carré's plotting. This was followed by *Smiley's People* a couple of years later. The other very different role was that of Ben Obi-Wan Kenobi in George Lucas's hugely successful *Star Wars*, which also spawned a couple of sequels.

Guinness's last appearance on the stage was in *A Walk in the Woods* at the Comedy Theatre in 1988, a highly serious debate about arms control. He left the West End commenting that he had no wish to go on playing before the 'blank faces' of uncomprehending tourists. He made occasional forays into television, but they were rare; Guinness had none of the compulsion to go on appearing in cameo parts that seemed to drive Gielgud and John Mills.

He was content to live in semi-retirement near Petersfield, guarding his privacy and safe in the knowledge that within the profession he would be remembered as a great actor and, always ready to help others, the most generous of men. His memoirs, *Blessings in Disguise*, appeared in 1985; a second volume, in 1996, bore the appropriate title *My Name Escapes Me: The Diary of a Retiring Actor*. Last year he published a journal as *A Positively Final Appearance*.

Guinness was knighted in 1959, and appointed CBE in 1955 and CH in 1994. He is survived by his wife and their son.

Sir Alec Guinness, CH, CBE, actor, was born on April 2, 1914.
He died on August 5, 2000, aged 86.

DON BRADMAN

Australian maestro whose remarkable batting achievements are unlikely to be eclipsed

25 FEBRUARY 2001

IN THE WORDS of one of his Australian contemporaries, Don Bradman was the greatest cricketer ever to put boots on and walk on to a cricket field. Statistics prove the point. His batting average in all first-class cricket was 95.14, far ahead of the Indian, V. M. Merchant, who comes next on 71.22; his Test match average of 99.94 was even further ahead as his nearest rival to date, the South African, R. G. Pollock, on 60.97; while in his 96 innings in the Sheffield Shield, then Australia's main domestic competition, his average was an astronomical 110.19. He scored more triple centuries (six) and more double centuries (37) than any other batsman, and during the Australian season of 1938–39, he reeled off six successive first-class centuries, a record he shares with C. B. Fry and the South African M. J. Procter.

Moreover, although only five foot seven inches tall and slightly built, such was his timing, his footwork, and the strength of his wrists, that Bradman scored his runs at a rate which demoralized bowlers to the point of desperation. His appetite for runs, too, at any rate in the pre-Second World War period of his career, was insatiable. Where such great batsmen as J. B. Hobbs and Denis Compton were prepared, as often as not, to settle for a single hundred, Bradman continued batting with relentless and ruthless determination.

His running between the wickets was of the same voracity. No other batsman, not even the legendary W. G. Grace, has dominated the game of cricket in quite as decisive a manner.

But Bradman was not just a great batsman. In the dark days of the 1930s depression, when male unemployment in Australia afflicted one out of three families, he was an icon. Crowds would gather outside the offices of newspapers in the great cities of Sydney, Melbourne, Adelaide, and Brisbane to watch the mechanical scoreboards which had been put in place and share every run that Bradman scored. He was, for the army of the unemployed, their beacon of hope. Later on, after the Second World War, Bradman became, almost in his own person, the symbol of the return to pre-war normality and of Australian affection for, and attachment to, the British Empire. No social history of Australia can afford to neglect the impact of sport on the country's developing culture; and Bradman, in his day, was the greatest of the Australian sporting heroes.

Donald George Bradman was born on August 27, 1908, at Cootamundra, a small up-country township in New South Wales. His grandfather had escaped from the impoverished life of an East Anglian agricultural labourer at the time of the Australian gold rush of the 1850s. The search for gold proved illusory, and the Bradman family were forced back to what they knew best – working the land, poor as it was, in the inhospitable country on the River Murrumbidgee. At the age of two the child, together with his elder brother and three sisters, accompanied his parents in a move to the less intimidating climate and more fertile soil of the Southern Highlands of New South Wales. They moved to Bowral, a small town some 80 miles southwest of Sydney, and it was there that Bradman grew up.

As a child, he was never gregarious, in spite of being one of a large family. Even at school, he had few friends. One of his amusements was to entertain himself, hour after hour, by throwing a golf ball against the brickwork of a water tank by his house and trying to hit it on the rebound with a cricket stump. Little did he realize it at the time, but this boyish game was developing the concentration and co-ordination of hand and eye which were to serve him so well in his future cricketing career.

Leaving the Bowral intermediate high school at the age of 14, he soon came to the attention of the New South Wales state selectors because of the unprecedented number of runs he had made for the Bowral Cricket Club and subsequently for the Sydney grade club of St George. In 1927, at the age of 19, he was invited to play for New South Wales in a Sheffield Shield match against South Australia in Adelaide, and immediately justified his selection by scoring 118 not out, the first of his 117 first-class centuries, scored at the rate of one every three innings.

In the following year, he moved from Bowral to Sydney, became a Freemason (at a time when Masonic Protestantism dominated Sydney cricket) and was picked to play for Australia against England in the first Test match at Brisbane. He failed and was dropped. Recalled for the third Test at Melbourne, he made 79 and 112, and finished the 1928–29 Test series with an average of 66.85.

It was on the 1930 Australia tour of England that Bradman established himself as the brightest new star in the cricket firmament. It was not, as several commentators complained, a particularly elegant star, lacking as it did the elegance of a Hobbs or a Victor Trumper. He would fail, it was said, on English pitches, because he relied too much on his eye and too little on the textbook.

His response to such scepticism was devastating and immediate. He began the tour by making 236 at Worcester and 185 not out at Leicester, and in the Tests he made 131 at Trent Bridge, 254 at Lord's, 334 at Headingley, and 232 at the Oval. His aggregate for the rubber was 974 at an average of 139.14. In that one series it became clear that the young Bradman changed the balance of any game in which he was playing.

There were two consequences of this. He was lionized by the Australian press and public to the point where his colleagues started openly to criticize him. It was not just jealousy, although there was some of that. Bradman himself was not by any means an easygoing young man; he was teetotal, puritanical, and self sufficient. On his return to Australia, he left the team early and undertook a tour of the leading cities by himself. It was hardly a tactful gesture. To cap it, he became involved in a row with the Australian Board of Control over a book which he had written in violation, the Board claimed, of his contract.

The second consequence was that England devised a special form of bowling attack, designed to control Bradman's brilliance. Under the captaincy of D. R. Jardine, bodyline was launched at the Australians during the MCC tour of 1932–33. The spearhead was Larwood; support came from Voce and Bowes, and the tactic was one of open intimidation.

The English fast bowlers would aim bouncers at the batsman's body in the expectation that in defending himself, he would be caught by one of five or six short legs placed specially for the purpose or caught by one of the two deep fielders behind the square on the leg side.

Inevitably, there were injuries, and, although the tactic worked to the extent that England won this series and managed to contain Bradman to an average of 56.57, it led to a heated exchange of cables between the cricket authorities of the two countries amid threats that the tour be abandoned. Controversy and acrimony rumbled on until the British government intervened.

Not surprisingly, Bradman had disliked bodyline intensely. Although he himself was hit only once in this series, the element of personal hostility which Jardine directed towards him made for great stress.

He was helped through this by his young wife Jessie (*née* Menzies), a childhood friend whom he had married in April 1932. Even so, the strain took hold and Bradman's health suffered. By the time the 1934 Australia side to tour England was chosen there were doubts over whether he would be fit enough to go. But go he did, and he started by making another double hundred at Worcester. A spell of failures followed, but his health seemed gradually to recover and he finished the Test series with 304 at Headingley and 244 and 77 at the Oval.

Before he could return to Australia, however, his health collapsed again. This time it was appendicitis, which developed into peritonitis. For several days, while his wife was rushing to England (in so far as it was possible to 'rush' by sea), his life was in danger. The Australian press even carried a report that he had died.

Convalescence was a slow process, and Bradman played no cricket until the 1935–36 season. By that time he and his wife had moved from Sydney to Adelaide, where he had been offered a secure job in a stockbroking firm. Memories of his childhood poverty had convinced him that he should never rely on cricket alone as a source of income but learn a trade.

Once in Adelaide, Bradman was almost immediately chosen to captain South Australia, and was soon thereafter chosen to captain Australia for the Test series against England in 1936–37. Although England won the first two Tests of the series, Bradman led his side to victory in the last three with scores of 270, 212, and 169. But the series was marred by a rift within the Australia team itself, caused partly by Bradman's determined style of captaincy and partly by the dissent of a group of players of Irish Catholic origin. The Australian Board of Control was obliged at one point to intervene in support of their chosen captain.

The dispute was far from resolved on the 1938 Australia tour of England, and although Bradman himself batted up to his best form, starting with a third successive double hundred at Worcester and following with 144 in the Trent Bridge Test, 102 not out at Lord's, and 103 at Headingley, the tour was a strain, made worse by the refusal of the Australian Board to allow wives to join their husbands when it was over, a decision which Bradman himself succeeded in overturning. Bradman broke his ankle in the final Test, which was overwhelmingly won by England, and was out of action for the rest of the season.

When war was declared in 1939, he volunteered for the Royal Australian Air Force, but was soon transferred to the Army as an instructor in physical education. His muscular problems, however, caused partly by continued stress over the years, were by now severe enough for him to be invalided out in 1941. After a convalescence of nearly nine months, in his homeland of New South Wales, he returned to Adelaide with his wife and, by now, two small children. No sooner had he settled down to stockbroking, than rumours started about his employer. The rumours were well founded, the firm going bankrupt in 1945 and Bradman's employer being arrested for fraud. Bradman immediately set up his own company and showed himself to be as astute a broker as he was a cricket captain.

When the MCC arrived in Australia for the first post-war tour in 1946–47, a question mark once again hung over Don's health. There was doubt whether he would be able, or even would want, to play cricket again at the highest level.

In the event, he was back leading Australia at Brisbane and soon scarcely less prolifically than ever. Had he failed in the first Test, he might well have opted for retirement; but, helped by a controversial decision, when England had a claim for a slip catch turned down, he made 187, and a fortnight later he scored 234 in the second Test at Sydney. England were no match for Australia, and Bradman led his country for the third time to Ashes victory.

The 1948 Australian tour of England was both Bradman's farewell to international cricket and the apogee of his career. He had made up his mind that he would carry the tour through without losing a match, and this he did. But there was more to it than that. By now his speeches, at the many functions to which he was invited, were quick-witted and elegant. On the field he was still the same Bradman

– single-minded in annihilating the opposition. Off the field he was more relaxed and courteous than of yore. His only disappointment came at the Oval in what was to be his last Test innings. Needing to score only four runs to achieve a Test average of 100, he was bowled second ball, by Eric Hollies's googly, for nought. Some said, albeit soulfully, that he was so affected by the reception which crowd and the England players had given him, that his eyesight was dimmed with tears.

In 1949 Bradman was knighted, the first cricketer to be so honoured before ultimate retirement. Thereafter he confined himself to stockbroking and golf until the mid-fifties when health problems obliged him to sell his business. This left him time to take a leading part in the administration of Australian cricket, as a Test selector and twice as chairman of the Board of Control – from 1960–63 when he played a leading role in solving the problem of throwing, and from 1969 to 1972.

Bradman had four or five close English cricketing friends with whom he carried on a steady correspondence, often on technical cricketing matters, and no one ever had the best interests of the game closer to his heart. Intimidatory bowling, the change in the no ball law from back to front foot, heavy bats, and the unseemliness of Kerry Packer's World Series Cricket were anathema to him. All invitations to return to England were met with a firm refusal, and he always graciously declined when the possibility of his becoming President of the MCC was put to him. Even before the death of his wife in 1997 he had, in fact, become increasingly reclusive. For the past ten years and more, his visits to the Adelaide Oval to watch the cricket, had been few and far between, even during Test matches, and the countless pilgrims who beat a path to his door, hoping to have a word with him, were seldom successful.

He found few consolations in old age, especially when he could no longer play golf, and the loneliness of being a widower particularly distressed him. The health of his daughter went into serious decline, though his son John, who had changed his surname in 1972 to escape from his father's shadow, reverted to his patronym and became closer to him than he had ever been.

Bradman was made a Companion of the Order of Australia in 1979, and for most of the second half of the last century he would have been the people's choice as President of Australia had republicanism come the way of the country.

Sir Donald Bradman, Australia cricket captain and greatest batsman that
the game has known, was born on August 27, 1908.
He died on February 25, 2001, aged 92.

SPIKE MILLIGAN

*Goon, solo comic, and writer who contributed to Hitler's downfall
and fascinated generations of children with his fantasy fictions*

27 FEBRUARY 2002

SPIKE MILLIGAN was the outstanding comedian of his generation, first as one of
the Goons and then as a solo performer. One of the great innovators in comedy in
the last century, he was also the author of many books, which took an upside-down
and inside-out view of the world. He would take a joke, a turn of phrase, or a strange
thought and pursue its logic to the most absurd conclusions. He could create
bizarre worlds in which seemingly sensible conversations were turned on their
heads, where wild solutions were hatched out of mundane problems, and where
characters talked themselves into nonsensical knots.

Whereas each of his fellow Goons – Harry Secombe, Michael Bentine, and Peter
Sellers – had to some degree to invent a persona, Milligan seemed most to be
himself. He was naturally out-of-step with the world, convinced that his was the
sensible, obvious way. The joke, he implied, was on us: just look at it from his point
of view.

Brilliant and iconoclastic creations were spun out of the voices in his head – a
mixture of stream-of-nonsense and stream-of-conscience. But the psychological
intensity meant that he spent periods of his life as a patient in mental hospitals, and
was regarded as a crank by some for his unorthodox campaigning. 'I am condemned never to be taken seriously,' he said. The thought haunted him, and his
output of scripts, children's stories, war memoirs, novels, and comic performances
never compensated him for it.

His output was enormous. Not only did he write and star in almost all of the 157
half-hour episodes of *The Goon Show*, he also scripted eight series of his own show,
Q, for the BBC, and more than 50 assorted books of biography, verse, fiction, letters,
games, and plays.

The tradition that he created in *The Goon Show* – with Larry Stephens and Eric
Sykes also contributing to the writing – played a vital part in the post-war revitaliz-
ation of British comedy. The Goons' inspired absurdities and attacks on the Establishment made the cosy, orthodox situation comedies that had gone before sound
hopelessly outdated. Milligan's flights of surrealist fantasy, and his anarchic characters, such as Bluebottle and Eccles, paved the way for the satire movement which
swept Britain during the 1960s, and for the later television fantasies of *Monty*

607

Python's Flying Circus. Among other comedians obviously indebted to him were Billy Connolly, Ben Elton, Vic Reeves and Bob Mortimer, and even such writers as Douglas Adams.

Milligan himself had been influenced by W. C. Fields, Beachcomber, Sid Fields, Beckett, Joyce, and Groucho Marx. When he eventually met Marx, he enthused at such length about the American's genius that Groucho asked him if he could do the next 20 minutes on his own. The greatest formative influence on his life, however, was the Second World War, which had an impact on the young Milligan that can scarcely be overestimated.

Born at Ahmednagar, near Bombay, in 1918, Terence Alan Milligan was educated in a tent in the Hyderabad Sindh desert, and graduated from there through a series of Roman Catholic schools in India until the family returned to London in 1931. His father, Captain Leo Milligan, a soldier from Sligo, and his mother, Florence (*née* Kettleband), were both keen singers and semi-professional performers. Spike took after them, modelling his voice on Bing Crosby and teaching himself to play the trumpet, guitar, double bass and drums. He could never get enough of jazz.

He left school at 15 to work at Stones Engineering in Deptford, but he was sacked because he repeatedly fused the lights. Meanwhile, he had been playing with a number of jazz dance-hall bands before enlisting in the Royal Artillery at the outbreak of the Second World War. Despite his burning horror of the war itself – and he saw plenty of action to justify that – the Army gave Bombardier Milligan a heady sense of freedom and companionship. He was to describe his service in the Royal Artillery magnificently in five volumes of comic memoirs, which began with *Adolf Hitler: My Part in his Downfall* in 1971.

Milligan's war was poles apart from that of Evelyn Waugh and his patrician hero Guy Crouchback. Gunner Milligan 954024 represented those classes Waugh and Crouchback disliked and felt threatened by. The opening of *Adolf Hitler* sets the subversive tone: 'A man called Chamberlain who did Prime Minister impressions spoke on the wireless; he said: "As from eleven o'clock we are at war with Germany." (I loved the WE.) "War?" said Mother. "It must have been something we said," said Father. The people next door panicked, burnt their post office books and took in the washing.'

The experience of war shaped Milligan's comedy, and particularly its humane outrage at hypocrisy and its destructive ploys. He looked at the world and decided that it was not only absurd but harmful. Despite the comradeship, war also aggravated the manic depression he had inherited from his father, and which was very little understood at the time. He spent much of the rest of his life veering between episodes of mania and devastating bouts of depression that put him in hospital for months at a time in near suicidal despair.

Milligan's shooting war began with the landings in Algiers in November 1942, and continued until the end of the North African campaign, and beyond into Italy. In January 1944 he was nearly killed by a mortar bomb near Lauro in the hills to the northeast of Mount Vesuvius. He suffered severe shellshock, started to stammer, and suffered the first of the nervous breakdowns that were to plague him for the rest of his life.

While recuperating in Naples, he began to hone his skills as an entertainer. Mistakenly told by a doctor that he could not play the trumpet again because of a bad chest, he took up the guitar and hooked up with the jazz violinist Bill Hall and the double bassist Johnny Mulgrew to form the Bill Hall Trio. They entertained the troops until the end of the war, and when they were finally demobbed, they teamed up again on exhausting tours around Europe, for which they were paid little more (and often less) than their keep.

These were wild times for Milligan, years when he seemed afraid to stand still. Despite his emaciated physique, which he referred to disparagingly in his war diaries, he was a remarkably charismatic and good-looking young man and a success with the ladies, though many of them were left rather baffled by him. Asked by one admirer where his daft patter came from, he said: 'It arrives once a month by boat from Scandinavia. I just glue it together on the Monday.'

After splitting from Bill Hall, Spike fell in with the Ann Lenor Trio for some more touring before eventually returning home to Leathwell Road, Deptford.

Jimmy Grafton, a scriptwriter for Derek Roy on *Variety Bandbox*, encouraged him to write, and introduced him to Harry Secombe, who in turn introduced him to Peter Sellers and Michael Bentine. Though he had had little formal education, Milligan slaved away at bits of freelance scriptwriting in Grafton's attic, but it was to be several years before the BBC allowed these pub wits to air their first show, billed as *Those Crazy People, the Goons*. First broadcast on May 28, 1951, it ran for 11 series.

The weekly programme, then on the BBC Home Service, became a national institution, capturing the imagination of the country. Characters such as Neddy Seagoon, played by Secombe, Major Bloodnok, played by Sellers, and Milligan's own Eccles became the favourites of a generation. The Prince of Wales later described it as 'one of my favourite programmes', and it ran for eight years, ending in January 1960. A final performance was given in 1972 to mark the fiftieth anniversary of the BBC.

Though the show made Milligan famous, the intolerable pressure that he felt he was under at the BBC was to imperil his sanity. At one point during the third series he was taken to a hospital in Muswell Hill, put in a straitjacket, and kept in an isolation ward for three months. The pressure also cost him his marriage to June Marlowe, whom he had married in 1952 and with whom he had a son and two daughters. Milligan never forgave the BBC, though he continued, perforce, to work for it.

Not the least of his grievances was a ban on commenting on or satirizing actual events. 'All we could be was funny,' he said, 'but it had no point. We could have been lethal, but the BBC would never let us do any real voices, or anything to do with reality. That broke my heart.'

While *The Goon Show* was running successfully on BBC Radio, Milligan was also pioneering a new style of British television comedy with *A Show Called Fred*, which won him a British Academy Award in 1956, and then the Q series. Yet after *The Goon Show* came to an end, he did not find it easy to create a new role for himself. He played the part of an unemployed actor for more than a year until in 1961 Bernard Miles (later Lord Miles) gave him the part of Ben Gunn in an adaptation of *Treasure Island* at the Mermaid Theatre, London. It was the beginning of a fruitful partnership.

A whole new area of opportunity was opened up for Milligan, who was inspired to write *The Bedsitting Room* with John Antrobus. It was a success and transferred eventually to the Duke of York's Theatre in the West End. Other plays and adaptations followed, including Frank Dunlop's production of *Oblomov* with Joan Greenwood at the Lyric Hammersmith in 1964. By then Milligan had married Patricia Margaret Ridgeway (in 1962), and published his first book, *Puckoon*, about the partition of Ireland. They had one daughter.

The instant success of *Puckoon* was the beginning of a long period of creativity that was impeded only by bouts of illness, the birth of his fourth child in 1966, and the death of his wife from cancer in 1978, aged 43. Milligan was a doting but often absent father. He continued touring, writing wonderfully silly verse for his children, and flirting with film, winning the Golden Rose of Montreux for scripting and appearing in *The Marty Feldman Comedy Machine* in 1972.

Because his father had been born in Ireland, Milligan found himself, in his own phrase, 'declared a stateless person' in 1960. He considered the official decision both inexplicable and deeply wounding. Although he became a citizen of the Irish Republic, and later considered Australian citizenship, official rulings had a habit of bringing him into conflict with authority. He was not a man to be pigeonholed.

Never easily dissuaded from his point of view, Milligan became a passionate defender of the rights of the downtrodden of all kinds. His love of animals led him to smash a window at the Hayward Gallery in 1972 in protest at an exhibition which proposed to electrocute 20 catfish as a work of art. In 1974 he again took direct action by shooting an airgun at a 16-year-old youth whom he suspected of vandalizing a children's playground at the back of his North London home. He was given a conditional discharge.

Other campaigns had conspicuous successes. As well as one of the founders of the Finchley Society, he was a member of the Victorian Society and his enthusiasm

Spike Milligan and the model Celia Hammond led a march from Lincoln's Inn Fields to Downing St on October 4th 1970. It was organized by the League Against Cruel Sports of which Milligan was a patron.

for old buildings and fittings led to the retention of the Victorian lamp standards on Constitution Hill outside Buckingham Palace, which the Department of the Environment had wished to remove. In the early 1970s he also spent three years personally restoring an oak carving of elves in Kensington Gardens.

He became an increasingly ardent advocate of causes ranging from CND to the ban on the slaughter of seal pups. He was a member of the World Wide Fund for Nature and Greenpeace; he was fiercely opposed to pornography and smoking (even though as a young man he smoked like a chimney), and he was a compulsive letter-writer.

No issue was too trivial to catch his attention, whether it was defecating dogs, useless town councils, over-hanging hedges, or leaky Biros, the last of which inspired a memorable letter to Harold Wilson. He found allies for these causes in people as disparate as Robert Graves, Prince Charles, Elton John, Paul Getty, Eric Sykes, Ronnie Scott, Paul and Linda McCartney, and Michael Foot.

When he wrote to *The Times* in 1990 to ask the paper to make sure his obituary was ready ('as I have not been feeling well lately'), he added that his 'most recent exploit was trying to save Rye Hospital' ('Yours ailing, Spike').

With his almost total recall (which make his memoirs such vivid reading), Milligan was a formidable opponent in an argument. His solutions to problems – expelling all children who encourage others to smoke at school, for instance – often seemed drastic, but there was an iron logic behind them. And his outrage was genuine.

Despite having four children of his own from his three marriages, and two other children, Milligan was obsessed by population growth. When Tony Blair became Prime Minister in 1997, Milligan wrote to him with a modest proposal to help to remedy the crisis: a moratorium on births for five years.

Like a man refusing to be beaten by impossible odds, Milligan never let go of his hard-won beliefs and principles. He lived his life like a precocious child, took great pleasure in his own children, and continued to write in a youthful, zany way until his death. His books on animals for children, including *Milliganimals* (1968), *Milligan's Ark* (1971), and *Condensed Animals* (1991), are among his most lasting works, and *Badjelly the Witch* (1973) has had generations of young readers quivering. He also painted in both oils and watercolours.

A vulnerable and honest man, Milligan could at the same time be ruthless, obstinate, and awkward. He claimed to be a misanthrope, but it was exploiters, manipulators and fools he hated, not mankind in general.

He received many awards, including a Lifetime Achievement Award for comedy in 1994, the year he was appointed honorary CBE. He was advanced to Hon. KBE in 2000.

Spike Milligan is survived by his wife, Shelagh Sinclair, and by his children.

Spike Milligan, comedian and writer, was born in Ahmednagar,
India, on April 16, 1918. He died in Rye, East Sussex,
on February 27, 2002, aged 83.

CHRISTIAAN BARNARD

Bold and skilful surgeon who carried out the world's first human heart transplant operation and relished the celebrity it brought him

2 SEPTEMBER 2001

CHRISTIAAN BARNARD made history in December 1967 when he performed the world's first human heart transplant operation at Groote Schuur Hospital in Cape Town. The recipient, Louis Washkansky, a Lithuanian-born dentist in his fifties, lived on for just 18 days, aided by the heart which came from a young woman who had died in a car crash, but Barnard's fame was secure. Like the American astronauts at around the same time, he became not just a popular hero, but an icon of progress and scientific advance.

Seven years later he was the first surgeon to perform a double heart transplant – what became known as the 'piggy-back' technique – by giving a second heart to assist an ailing original. Then, in 1977, he pioneered a third operation in which he planted the heart of a baboon inside the chest wall of a woman patient to assist her own faltering heart.

All three procedures brought him both acclaim and controversy: while the world applauded his boldness and skill, it also argued about the ethics of such operations. He was widely seen as a medical maverick, somewhere between God and Frankenstein, hailed or reviled for his apparent power over this most mystical of human organs. Critics called him a 'surgical opportunist', and debate raged over the definition of death. Was a human being dead when brain activity ceased, even though his heart continued beating? If so, was it permissible to remove the organ and give it to someone else?

Although it irked him that he was far from British and American research centres, Barnard was in many ways fortunate to be working relatively unsupervised in South Africa, rather than in the more cautious and regulated atmosphere of the United States (where Norman Shumway had been undertaking at Stanford in California much the same preparations as he had). Free of the disapproving scrutiny of jealous peers and fastidious medical ethicists, Barnard was in many respects a law unto himself.

Having identified Washkansky as a potential recipient in November 1967, Barnard had to wait for a donor to be found. Although very much a guinea-pig, Washkansky, who had diabetes and incurable heart disease, was felt to have an 80 per cent chance of surviving the operation at the time. The alternative was certain death. 'For a dying man it is not a difficult decision because he knows he is at the end,' said Barnard later. 'If a lion chases you to the bank of a river filled with crocodiles, you will leap into the water convinced you have a chance to swim to the other side. But you would never accept such odds if there were no lion.'

The first potential donor was a black South African. Barnard was prepared to operate, but his colleagues counselled that if the experiment went awry he would go down in history as an Afrikaner Mengele. A few days later his opportunity came when Denise Darvall, a white woman, was fatally injured in a car accident less than a mile from Groote Schuur.

As she lay on a life-support machine, Barnard prepared to move into uncharted territory. Neglecting to inform his superiors of what he was about to do, he said a prayer, switched off her life-support machine and, as her heartbeat faded away, made an incision. After he had carefully stitched Darvall's heart into Washkansky's chest, there were several unnerving minutes as it lay inert before he applied an electrical stimulus. The beating began, and Barnard became a household name.

Undeterred by Washkansky's death 18 days later from double pneumonia as a result of his suppressed immune system, Barnard almost immediately went ahead with a second transplant. This time the patient left hospital and resumed an active life before his body rejected the donated organ. Nevertheless, he had lived for 19 months after the operation. Barnard's fifth and sixth patients survived for nearly 13 and 24 years respectively.

Christiaan Neething Barnard was born at Beaufort West, a small town in the heart of the Karoo plateau in Cape Province. His father was a pastor of the Dutch Reform Church. Driven by an overriding ambition, inherited from his mother, a church organist who had high hopes for all her children, Christiaan developed into a young man in a hurry, a trait he never lost. Typical of his obsession to go places fast was the fact that he crammed the six years' work normally required for a Ph.D. into a two-year crash course. He received his medical training at Cape Town University, where he qualified in 1946, and initially went into family practice.

After a varied career in South Africa he went to Minnesota University in Minneapolis in the late 1950s to work with Professor Wangensteen and Professor Lillehei, two of the leading heart surgeons of the day. In due course he returned to Cape Town, complete with the first heart-lung machine to be installed in an African hospital. It had been donated by the United States Government. He was soon established as a skilled cardiac surgeon, successfully handling hundreds of patients with valvular disease. His became known as one of the best heart surgery units in the world. In the operating theatre he proved to be somewhat temperamental and in public he adored attention, but no one could question the surgical results. He developed a technique to correct the infant cardiac killer known as 'transportation of the great vessels', and by 1962 his team had developed a successful artificial mitral heart valve.

All was now set for a new era in South Africa of what was technically known as open-heart surgery. Barnard had spent many years experimenting with heart transplantation, mainly with dogs. During 1967 he spent three months in the United States acquainting himself with the latest thinking before launching into his pioneering operation.

The real challenge in heart transplantation was not the technical difficulty of the surgery, but the danger of rejection. As Barnard himself put it: 'The big battle in a heart transplant was not going to be in placing a new heart in a human being, but in getting it to stay there.' That was why his opposite numbers in Britain had decided that heart transplantation must only be used with the utmost discretion until more was known about overcoming rejection. Britain imposed a moratorium on heart transplants between 1970 and 1979 because of the poor survival rate.

Barnard's own university gave him every facility for research, appointing him Professor of Surgical Science in 1968, but his natural impatience meant that his overriding interest was always in the operating theatre, and in practice rather than theory.

Variations on heart transplantation were tried after the original operation: the putting in of an auxiliary heart to act in tandem with the patient's failing heart, and the use of the baboon's heart, among them. Their transitory success did not daunt Barnard.

Though he had in some ways turned to his advantage the years of working in relative isolation from the critical and stimulating atmosphere of the great medical research centres of Britain or the United States, he relished all the more the international renown which came with the first transplant operation. He became a frequent participant at international conferences, and enjoyed meeting world figures, from the Pope to presidents, to Sophia Loren: he was the centre of attention wherever he went.

Tall, slim, and athletic, with a flashing smile and the good looks of a film star, he was a man of great charm and personality. Catapulted to international celebrity and frequently photographed in the company of beautiful women, he soon acquired a parallel reputation as a dashing socialite. He graced the covers of magazines and toured the world.

Some described him as the playboy of cardiac surgery. Though not unjustified, the description does not paint a wholly fair picture of an able surgeon who was intensely devoted to his craft and desperately keen to provide new hearts for old. He worked hard, and contributed significantly to the understanding of the contribution of surgery to the amelioration of the failing heart.

By the late 1970s Barnard was becoming increasingly affected by rheumatoid arthritis in his hands, from which he had suffered for some years, and in 1983 he was forced to retire from active surgery. He established a heart research team in

Oklahoma City which also inquired into the ageing process. He divided his time between there and his farm in South Africa, and also spent time in Switzerland.

For many years he contributed a weekly newspaper column to the *Cape Times*, which was both readable and stimulating. Earlier, in 1969, he had published a volume of autobiography, *One Life*, donating his royalties to the Chris Barnard Fund, which has since supported research into heart disease and organ transplantation in Cape Town. A further, sometimes sensational volume, *The Second Life*, appeared 20 years later, and he also wrote a number of other books dealing with heart trouble, arthritis, and euthanasia as well as several racy airport novels, including a thriller about organ transplants.

At home in South Africa he lived on a 32,000-acre sheep farm and game preserve in the area where he grew up, reintroducing wildebeest and springbok. He continued to live in the public eye. In 1986 he endorsed an 'anti-ageing' cream which turned out to be dubious and was withdrawn from the American market the following year. Although his endorsement was lucrative, it tarnished his medical reputation.

He attracted further controversy when he entered the rows which followed the death of Diana, Princess of Wales, with whom he had been on friendly terms. He claimed that her life could have been saved if she had been taken straight to hospital rather than treated at the scene of the accident in Paris.

Barnard was sometimes criticized for not fighting harder against apartheid, a failing he came to regret. 'I opposed it whenever I could,' he said, but admitted that 'I didn't stick my neck out'. He did, however, use non-white nurses to assist in his operations – a first in South Africa – and once transplanted the heart of a white woman into a black man. He treated hundreds of patients around the world free of charge.

Last year he left South Africa, announcing that the invasive and hostile attitude of the country's tabloid press and its interest in his complicated private life was too much to bear. He went to live in Vienna.

He was married three times. From his first marriage, which ended in divorce in 1970, he had a daughter and a son (who committed suicide in 1984). He had two sons by his second wife Barbara Zoellner, from whom he was divorced in 1982. His third wife, whom he married in 1988, was Karin Setzkorn, a model by whom he had a son and a daughter; they divorced in 1999.

Professor Christiaan Barnard, heart surgeon, was born on November 8, 1922.
He died on September 2, 2001, aged 78.

QUEEN ELIZABETH
THE QUEEN MOTHER

30 MARCH 2002

THE WIFE OF King George VI was the first non-royal queen consort since Catherine Parr in the 16th century, and the first non-royal mother of a sovereign since Anne Hyde in the 17th. But these achievements – interesting as they may be for the record book – say nothing of the individual, whose achievements were of a quite different order.

By virtue of qualities peculiarly her own, not the least of which was an extraordinary, even awe-inspiring, longevity, Queen Elizabeth came to occupy a special position in the country and throughout the world. As queen consort from 1936 to 1952, she was immensely popular and an incalculable asset to the monarchy. As queen mother she was, if possible, more popular still, and continued to make an outstanding contribution to the work of the Royal Family.

It was not in her nature to behave as though her privileged position was a crushing burden. By temperament an enjoyer of life, she entered into everything she did with gusto, and never forgot what she owed to people whose lives were less comfortable, pleasant, and interesting than her own. With this attitude, she could turn even an intrinsically tedious occasion into a party. As a *Times* leader once said of her: 'She lays a foundation stone as though she has discovered a new and delightful way of spending an afternoon.'

When she married Albert, Duke of York in 1923 she had no reason to imagine that he would ever be king. But 13 years later, she was more than equal to the double challenge of supporting him in a role for which, in many ways, he seemed to be unfitted, and of making a success of her own role as first lady. Though it is absurd to suggest that the monarchy itself was seriously endangered by Edward VIII's abdication, it is true that, but for her, the institution might, at that time, have suffered some loss of glamour and prestige, if only temporarily.

Without doubt it was her devotion and strength of character that enabled the new king to rise above the natural disadvantages of a stammer, and almost crippling shyness, to become a competent and, in time, a well-loved monarch. At the same time she took to her new position with apparently effortless ease, showing from the first the star quality that was never to desert her.

During the Second World War, Queen Elizabeth was unchallenged as the woman to whom people looked for inspiration. If she had not been there, the monarchy might have been comprehensively upstaged by Winston Churchill (however unwillingly, on his part). Her conduct during the war showed her at her brilliant best, and deepened the affection and respect in which she was already held.

By contrast with his father, King George VI was able, with the help of Queen Elizabeth, to give his children a home life that was as warm and intimate as any in the land; and it is immensely to the credit of both parents that they never thought of sending their daughters to invidious and probably unhappy safety overseas during the war.

On the education of her children Queen Elizabeth's instincts were conservative. As a result, the princesses Elizabeth and Margaret were not sent to school but taught by governesses. It may be argued that after 1945 her essential conservatism may have somewhat delayed the process of evolution and adaptation of the royal household that the times required. But her relatively old-fashioned views never cost her any popularity, partly because they were widely shared in the community, but also because her personal charm prevailed over any criticism.

However, behind the famous smile was a character that was tough as well as sweet and gracious. Without this toughness she could not have achieved what she did. In general, her strength was exerted to good ends, and helped to make her a unique public personality, whose service to the monarchy was second to none in the 20th century.

Elizabeth Angela Marguerite Bowes Lyon's exact place of birth remains a mystery, although it was probably in London. It was always assumed to have been at St Paul's, Walden Bury, the Hertfordshire home of her parents, the 14th Earl and Countess of Strathmore and Kinghorne, whose ninth child she was, but she herself denied it without ever elaborating on where precisely she entered the world. Lord Strathmore was a dignified but unremarkable backwoods peer. Lady Strathmore, daughter of a parson with ducal (Portland) connections, was the more forceful parent.

Elizabeth and her younger brother, David, were respectively 17 and 19 years younger than their eldest sister, and their mother used to say that they might have been her grandchildren. Their upbringing and education had a distinctly Victorian flavour.

The future queen's early life was passed in an almost royal routine, alternating between the estate in Hertfordshire, with its Queen Anne house, a big London house in Grosvenor Gardens, and the historic seat of the family, Glamis Castle, which was used largely for holidays and shooting parties.

A pretty child with striking eyes, she early showed the companionable disposition which was later to win her so many friends, as well as the not entirely friendly description of 'a simple, chattering, sweet-hearted, little round-faced woman in pink'. (Her other distinctive dress colour was to be powder-blue.) As with most young women of her class, there were no plans for her to have a career beyond that of marriage. Her education was at home, apart from brief attendance at 'select classes for girls' at a school in Sloane Street. For the rest, her childhood before 1914 was more or less happy and carefree.

War changed all this and brought her into contact with harsher realities. Personal sorrows struck her family. One of her brothers, Fergus, was killed, and another, Michael, taken prisoner. The circle of friends which had gathered annually for the three-month holiday at Glamis was similarly reduced. But the war had positive value for Lady Elizabeth. The drawing-room at Glamis was converted into a convalescent home for wounded Australian soldiers discharged from Dundee Infirmary; their presence gave her an opportunity for service, which she relished.

With the inventiveness of youth she and David improvised trivial comforts for the soldiers, ran errands for them, and entertained them with stories and games. With her beguiling ways she became immensely popular with them – as later with a worldwide public. It was also good for her to find, at an impressionable age, that she could get on with men from backgrounds of which she had absolutely no knowledge. She liked to listen to what they had to say, and in return talked to them about herself without embarrassment or condescension.

But when the war ended she returned to the conventional round. She belatedly 'came out' (though she was never actually presented at court) and then threw herself into the social activities appropriate to a girl of her standing. She loved parties and was known as one of the best dancers in London, though she never became a familiar name to the readers of social gossip columns. Her reputation as a charming, eligible girl was confined to a fairly limited circle. She seemed to have no desire for early marriage and turned down a number of proposals before coming of age.

The first post-war meeting with her future husband, Albert, Duke of York, took place in 1920 at a party given by his father's friend, Lord Farquhar (later – posthumously – exposed as a crook). Soon the duke was visiting Glamis and beginning his long courtship, which was not to end until his third proposal was accepted by Elizabeth at St Paul's, Walden Bury, on January 14, 1923. Joyfully, he sent a telegram to his mother – 'ALL RIGHT BERTIE'. It was, indeed, a providential moment for him, and not for him only.

They were married in Westminster Abbey on April 26, 1923. It was the first marriage of a sovereign's son for nearly half-a-century, and popular enthusiasm vindicated the decision to hold it in Westminster Abbey rather than in the privacy of a Chapel Royal. Queen Alexandra attended – one of her last public appearances – as did her sister, the Dowager Empress of Russia. The Archbishop of York preached a somewhat wordy sermon. In the afternoon the couple drove away to Polesden Lacey, which had been lent to them by Mrs (Maggie) Greville, who later favoured the Royal Family with substantial legacies.

Before there was any question of her becoming a royal personage, Elizabeth had been described by an observer, at a British Embassy ball in Paris, in these words: 'The most charming sight there was Lady Elizabeth Bowes Lyon, a bewitching little figure in rose colour, which set off her lovely eyes and dark eyebrows to perfection. She seemed to me the incarnation of fresh, happy, English girlhood.' (She would have corrected the word 'English'.) It was not expected, in 1923, that a royal duchess should necessarily become an active public figure. All the same, Elizabeth began to undertake engagements in her own right. The first were modest enough, connected with local organizations or charities that friends persuaded her to support. But national presidencies and patronages followed.

Her most important work at this time was done out of the public eye in helping her husband to fight his natural handicaps. Her easy, relaxed temperament was balm to him, and the change in his bearing was soon noticed. With her encouragement he set about tackling the worst obstacle to his performance in public, his stammer. Visiting the Australian speech therapist Lionel Logue in 1926, he began a course of treatment which certainly improved, though it could never completely eliminate, what had seemed to be an insuperable problem.

She fitted well into the tightly knit family circle of King George V, who astonished other members of his family by treating her unpunctuality – particularly at meals, where it would normally have driven him to fury – as a venial fault. She was fond of him and, unlike his own children, never afraid of him.

During the winter of 1924–25, she accompanied her husband on a visit to East Africa and the Sudan, which was largely recreational, but broadened their horizons. On safari in Kenya she was no mere spectator of the Duke's marksmanship, but did a lot of shooting herself with a 0.275 Rigby rifle.

The birth of her first daughter on April 21, 1926, was a highly popular event. The child was given her mother's first Christian name, which could also be seen as a gesture to England's, though not Scotland's, past. The second daughter, Margaret – or Margaret Rose, as she was always known at the time – was born four years later, on August 21, 1930.

At first the Yorks could hardly compete with the dashing Prince of Wales as a royal attraction. He was the star, while they were essentially only members of the supporting cast. In 1927, however, they had an opportunity to shine on their own, when they went on a world tour which included state visits to New Zealand and Australia.

For a time during their visit to New Zealand the Duchess was out of action with a throat infection, but this was almost a blessing, however disguised. It pleased her that the Duke was able to cope on his own, and that the undiminished enthusiasm with which he was greeted relieved him of the suspicion that the crowds had previously turned out to see only his wife.

In Australia, the Duchess's good humour and informality made a strong appeal. She bore the turbulent welcome of crowds as cheerfully as she bore the extremes of temperature. At a ball at Government House, Melbourne, she insisted on dancing with a man whom she had met as a wounded officer at Glamis during the war.

After this tour the couple returned to a more settled existence. Their first married home had been the White Lodge in Richmond Park, but in 1927 they took up residence at No. 145 Piccadilly, which remained their London address until they moved to Buckingham Palace. In 1931 the King gave them the Royal Lodge in Windsor Park, which was expanded and done up for their benefit; it became their favourite home.

As the years passed and the Prince of Wales remained unmarried, the prospect that their elder daughter might one day succeed to the throne came to seem less remote. But any idea that the Duke of York might be called to it himself was still beyond the wildest speculation.

With George V's death in January 1936, however, the crisis which produced this result became imminent. Already aware of the new King's attachment to Wallis Simpson, the Yorks soon realized that it was much more than a passing affair: that he was, in fact, determined to marry her, and that if he could not marry her as king, he would abdicate forthwith.

The Yorks were genuinely distraught, he doubting his capacity to do the job of monarch, she anxious on his behalf and not at all wanting him to be exposed to such a test. But when it became apparent that the British and Dominion governments would not accept Mrs Simpson as queen, or even as the king's morganatic wife, Edward bowed to constitutional necessity and promptly abdicated. In his farewell broadcast he made a graceful reference to his brother and to the happy family life that he enjoyed.

So far as the State was concerned, the transition was perfectly smooth. The constitutional crisis ended the moment Edward signed the instrument of abdication, and the fairy-story appeal of the monarchy was doubly enhanced: by the Yorks' brave assumption of office for duty's sake and by Edward's renunciation of it for love.

But the new King and Queen did not see it that way. In their view, Edward had let the monarchy down, and the woman who had inveigled him into doing so was beyond the pale. As a result, a family feud developed and the Duke and Duchess of Windsor (as the former king and his wife became) entered upon a life of exile, with the duchess denied the title 'Royal Highness' to the end of her days. Queen Elizabeth's relentless disapproval of the Duchess of Windsor arose from the belief that the duchess's behaviour had imposed an intolerable strain on King George VI and had eventually contributed to his early death.

The new king, though much improved since his marriage, was still painfully conscious of his limitations and inadequacies, more especially by comparison with his elder brother. When he told Queen Mary that Edward was abdicating, he broke down and (in his own words) 'sobbed like a child'. The new Queen accepted her destiny with a serene self-confidence. In her first letter to the Archbishop of Canterbury she wrote: 'I can hardly believe that we have been called to the tremendous task and (I am writing to you quite intimately) the curious thing is that we are not afraid.' It was certainly true of her, and her courage was vital in sustaining the King.

She made few public appearances between her husband's accession and the Coronation on May 12, 1937. In this she acquitted herself with dignity and reverence, and people were touched also by her air of youthfulness. She was the youngest queen consort since George III's wife, Queen Charlotte, had been crowned in 1761. As the crown was placed on Queen Elizabeth's head, Winston Churchill (who had been a staunch and romantic supporter of Edward VIII) turned to his wife, his eyes full of tears, and said: 'You were right; I see now the "other one" wouldn't have done.'

With the dark clouds of war gathering on the horizon, Neville Chamberlain's policy of appeasement was tried and failed. Queen Elizabeth and her husband were enthusiastic supporters of the policy, to the extent of appearing with Chamberlain on the balcony of Buckingham Palace after his return from signing the Munich agreement, even though the agreement was to be the subject of a party vote in the House of Commons. This extraordinary constitutional lapse escaped censure because the royal couple were reflecting overwhelming popular sentiment at the time.

Earlier in 1938 they had paid a successful state visit to France, which had to be postponed from June to July because of the sudden death of Queen Elizabeth's mother. In Paris the Queen chose to wear white as a mark of mourning, and her all-white trousseau was much admired, as was her appearance for the first time in crinoline dresses inspired by Winterhalter portraits of the young Queen Victoria. She also benefited, then as later, by being able to converse with a fair degree of ease in French.

In the spring and early summer of 1939 they undertook a more ambitious journey, first to Canada and then to the United States. After landing at Quebec in mid-May they travelled across Canada to the Pacific coast, everywhere evoking loyal demonstrations. Returning eastwards they made history by entering the United States, at Niagara, on June 9. In Washington a senator congratulated the King on being 'a great Queen-picker'.

While staying with the Roosevelts at Hyde Park the Queen was able to talk to her daughters in England by transatlantic telephone, a novel experience for both her and them.

At about this time Sir Harold Nicolson wrote of her in his diary: 'She really does manage to convey to each individual in the crowd that he or she has had a personal greeting. It is due, I think, to the brilliance of her eyes. But she is in truth one of the most amazing Queens since Cleopatra.'

During the Second World War she came into her own, more especially, of course, after the fall of France, when invasion seemed imminent. At this time a number of people sent their children out of the country, and the possibility of sending the princesses to Canada was, in fact, discussed. But the King and Queen decided firmly against it, realizing that in a supreme national emergency it was quite wrong for children of the rich and privileged to be made invidiously safe; also that it was desirable, in any case, for their family to stay together.

The Queen's attitude was summed up in words that are, justly, the most famous of her life: 'The Princesses would never leave without me, and I couldn't leave without the King, and the King will never leave.'

The children lived at Windsor during the war, which meant that their lives were considerably more at risk than those of many children from poor families, who were removed to remote parts of the country. The King and Queen normally slept at Windsor, but drove into London for the day. Buckingham Palace was hit several times by bombs, which enabled the Queen, as she put it, to 'look the East End in the face'. The East End of London and other blitzed areas were able to look her in the face when she and the King visited them after raids. Her combination of glamour, serenity, friendliness, and genuine sympathy made her uniquely effective in lifting people's spirits.

She did not, however, go around wearing any of the uniforms that were available to women in the war effort, though she could have worn any or all of them if she had wished. Her essentially feminine nature recoiled from the somewhat Amazonian connotations of a uniform, and she continued to dress in her usual style.

But in 1943 'Chips' Channon detected a change in her walk, which may have been associated with the slight amplification of figure that came to her in middle age. As she entered St Paul's for a service to celebrate the victory in Tunisia, she was, he wrote, as ever 'gracious and smiling', but also 'leaning back, a new walk she has acquired'.

She and the King were sympathetic towards sovereigns and governments in exile. In particular, they treated General de Gaulle with an understanding and consideration that he did not, as a rule, receive from the British Government. Their kindness was handsomely acknowledged in his memoirs, and in later years he never failed to show special regard for the Queen Mother in her widowhood.

They were unable to return President Roosevelt's hospitality, because he did not visit Britain during the war. But Mrs Roosevelt stayed at Buckingham Palace in 1942 and suffered acutely from the cold there, since there was limited electric heating even in rooms with windows patched-up after bombing. She was also served simple wartime food on gold and silver plates, perhaps a studied attempt to emphasize the truth that the Royal Family had submitted themselves to all the rigours of wartime austerity.

The Queen also had the bulldog courage of that slightly unrealistic type which the British people are not ashamed to display in moments of dire peril and have no aversion to seeing reflected in their leaders. Thus she practised with both .303 rifle and .38 service revolver in the grounds of Buckingham Palace, telling Sir Harold Nicolson, who had expressed surprise at this martial activity from one so diminutive, 'Yes, I shall not go down like the others,' referring, perhaps not entirely fairly, to the capitulation of the monarchs of the continent in the face of the German onslaught.

The victory of Labour in the 1945 general election restored the monarchy to its normal position of unchallenged prestige. Churchill, who in spite of himself had in some ways eclipsed the sovereign, was replaced by the uncharismatic Clement Attlee. Yet Attlee was no less of a traditionalist than Churchill, and he and his colleagues showed, like Ramsay MacDonald and the first Labour Government, that they yielded to none in reverence for the throne.

Queen Elizabeth was not the one to contemplate making any unnecessary concessions to the spirit of the age, and shrewdly judged that virtually none were, in fact, necessary, since politicians and press were equally reluctant to demand any. The pre-war royal routines, including some that were beginning to seem out of date even then – such as the presentation of debutantes at Buckingham Palace – were brought back without significant modification.

Between February and May 1947 the King and Queen toured the Union of South Africa. The visit was stage-managed by the country's illustrious prime minister, Field Marshal J. C. Smuts, who must have hoped that it would serve to counteract the appeal of the Nationalist party. Although it was embarrassing for the Royal Family to have to leave Britain en route for a land of sunshine when the British people were experiencing one of the worst winters on record, with the added misery of fuel shortage, the tour went ahead on firm ministerial advice and was, on the face of it, a triumphant success. The Queen's part in it was from first to last outstanding, and when speaking to Afrikaners resentful of England she would sometimes imply, a little speciously, that as a Scotswoman she could understand their feelings.

Soon after her arrival in Cape Town she returned to the family of President Kruger a family Bible of his that had fallen into British hands during the Boer War. And at Bloemfontein she called on the octogenarian widow of President Steyn of the Orange Free State. But along with such conciliatory gestures to former enemies, she also showed to the full her appreciation of those South Africans who had fought beside Britain in two world wars, more especially wounded veterans.

Travelling in a white and gold train, the royal party visited Southern Rhodesia and the three British protectorates of Bechuanaland, Basutoland, and Swaziland, as well as most parts of the South African Union. They saw all the sights of the region, including the Victoria Falls and any amount of wildlife, and it meant much to the King and Queen that they had their daughters with them on such a spectacular trip.

Before they re-embarked for home (they travelled both ways by sea, in the Royal Navy's most modern battleship, HMS *Vanguard*), the Queen received an honorary doctorate from Smuts himself as Chancellor of the University of Cape Town. In acknowledging it, she made her only speech of the tour, in which she listed the qualities to which academics should aspire as honesty, justice, and resolve, all needing to be sustained by religious faith. The speech was highly praised. However, conversation was her natural medium, and her supreme gift was for putting people at their ease in informal talk.

In July 1947 the King and Queen announced the engagement of their elder daughter, Princess Elizabeth, to Lieutenant Philip Mountbatten, and the wedding took place in Westminster Abbey on November 20 with a show of pageantry that brightened the rather dreary post-war scene. Within a year the Queen was able to celebrate the birth of her first, and perhaps favourite, grandchild, Prince Charles.

Meanwhile, she and the King had celebrated their Silver Wedding, on April 26, 1948. Publicly, the day was marked by a service at St Paul's, followed by a 20-mile drive through the streets of London in the afternoon. In the evening she and the King appeared on the balcony of Buckingham Palace, and were repeatedly called back by an enthusiastic crowd.

But in November the King was diagnosed as suffering from incipient arteriosclerosis and a projected tour of Australia and New Zealand had to be postponed. In the event, it never occurred, because the King's health, never robust, was entering an irreversible decline. In September 1951 he was found to have lung cancer and his left lung was removed. He seemed to recover from the operation, while looking much aged. But during the night of February 5–6, 1952, after a day's shooting at Sandringham, he died in his sleep.

His death left Queen Elizabeth a widow in her early fifties, faced with the challenge of adapting herself to a new life. Beyond question, she was profoundly sad to lose her husband. Despite her initial reluctance to marry him, she had become a most loving as well as a most devoted wife, and they were a very close couple. All the same, the task of supporting him had been quite a strain and inevitably involved some cramping of her own style. Now that she was alone, it was some compensation for her loss of private happiness that her public role became less difficult and demanding.

Without wishing in any way to stand in her daughter's light, she showed no desire to withdraw into the traditional reclusion of a dowager. The title that she chose for herself, Queen Elizabeth The Queen Mother – with its curious and somewhat unyielding repetition of the royal title, had an unmistakably assertive ring. She remained a star, as she had been as queen consort – the more so, perhaps, for being able at last to perform on her own.

And she continued to live in style. In London her residence was Clarence House. Out of London she had the use of her old home, Royal Lodge, at Windsor, while on the Balmoral estate Birkhall was placed at her disposal. In addition, she soon acquired a dilapidated castle overlooking the Pentland Firth, did it up and renamed it the Castle of Mey – visited, at most, for a few weeks every year. Later, another castle, Walmer, was added to her residences, when, in 1978, she became Lord Warden of the Cinque Ports in succession to Sir Robert Menzies.

Her widowhood was clouded by a family crisis. When the King died she asked Group Captain Peter Townsend, a much decorated Battle of Britain fighter ace who had been an equerry since March 1944, to stay on as comptroller of her household. Townsend was already estranged from his wife; he was therefore romantically footloose and a likely focus of romantic thoughts. It was hardly surprising that he and Princess Margaret fell in love with each other.

The affair trailed on until October 1955 with Townsend meanwhile getting divorced and being rusticated for a time in Brussels. By then the princess was free to marry without her sister's consent, though it was made clear that if she married Townsend she would have to forfeit her royal title and perquisites. In the end she renounced him, 'mindful of the Church's teaching' and of her 'duty to the Commonwealth'. Five years later she married Antony Armstrong Jones, who became Lord Snowdon, and from whom, in 1978, she was divorced.

These events must have caused the Queen Mother, an Anglican traditionalist, a lot of distress. Yet she was also adaptable and worldly wise.

It was noteworthy that some of her best friends were divorcees and when the Snowdons' divorce occurred she appeared to accept it with equanimity, remaining on good terms with her daughter's ex-husband.

As Queen Mother she travelled far more than she had ever done as Queen. In 1954 she revisited the United States to receive money which had been raised there in commemoration of her husband. She also received an honorary doctorate at Columbia University in New York, where the citation described her as 'a noble Queen, whose quiet and constant courage in time of great stress sustained a nation and inspired a world'; and in Washington she was a guest of the Eisenhowers at the White House. Thereafter her peregrinations were unremitting. Canada she visited nine times, Southern Rhodesia (now Zimbabwe) four times, Australia and New Zealand twice, Northern Rhodesia (Zambia) and Nyasaland (Malawi) twice, Uganda twice, as well as Kenya, Tunisia, Jamaica and other places in the Caribbean, Cyprus, and Iran. In Europe, she was a frequent visitor to France, and she went several times to Italy. Germany, though never her favourite country, was visited too.

Nearer home, she was seen in the Channel Islands and the Isle of Man. And, of course, she visited every part of the United Kingdom itself, including Northern Ireland, to which she was particularly devoted. When the Queen was out of the country she would often act as a Counsellor of State, or carry out investitures.

One of the posts that gave her most satisfaction was the chancellorship of London University, which she held from 1955 to 1980. In this she showed her capacity to disarm even radical lecturers and students, and it must have been a tribute to her, as well as to her grand-daughter, that when she eventually stood down Princess Anne was elected to succeed her by a convincing majority, in a secret ballot, against strong competition.

Among recreations, none meant more to the Queen Mother than racing. Her passion for National Hunt racing made her the most popular owner in the land by a long way. Both through her understanding and love of horses and her immense enjoyment of steeplechasing and its world, she became, over half a century, the embodiment of the sport, as well as its greatest ambassador. As such, she helped to transform the image of National Hunt racing and enhance its prestige.

Yet it all came about by accident. Whoever made the seating plan for the Royal Ascot dinner at Windsor Castle on June 15, 1949, must take the responsibility. Lord Mildmay, that idol of National Hunt racing, later tragically lost in a bathing accident, happened to be seated between Queen Elizabeth and her daughter, then Princess Elizabeth. It was he who suggested that they should try their luck at owning a steeplechaser. There was a ready response. Mildmay would find a suitable horse to be trained by Peter Cazalet. It was Monaveen. Owned in partnership, he was the first of the Queen Mother's more than 450 winners.

Monaveen had to be put down in 1950. But he had fired the Queen Mother's ambition to go into racing and register her subsequently famous blue colours with buff stripes. The first horse to carry these successfully was Manicou, who appropriately triumphed in the King George VI Chase on Boxing Day, 1950. There followed many more important winners, including Laffy (1962 Ulster Harp National); Makaldar (1965 Mackeson Hurdle); Inch Arran (1973 Topham Trophy); Tammuz (1975 Schweppes Gold Trophy); Insular (1986 Imperial Cup); Special Cargo – one of her special favourites (1984 Whitbread Gold Cup and three times in a row successful 1984–86 in the Grand Military Gold Cup which his owner also captured with The Argonaut in 1990 and Norman Conqueror in 1996).

The Queen Mother's most prolific jockey was David Mould who, between 1966 and 1973, rode 106 of her winners. Her big disappointments came in the Grand National, particularly when Devon Loch looked a certain success in 1956 but slipped on the run-in. Against that, she had a remarkable steeplechaser in Game

Spirit who ran up an astonishing 21 victories between 1971 and 1976. His name, above that of any of her horses, perhaps most fittingly represented her own character.

Another outdoor sport that she much enjoyed was fishing, particularly salmon-fishing. She was very fond of gardens, as was her brother Sir David Bowes Lyon – whose death in 1961, while staying with her at Birkhall, was a great blow to her – but she did not do much active gardening herself. She was, however, an energetic walker.

During a time when royal patronage of the arts was not very conspicuous, she was the principal exception. Advised by Kenneth Clark, she became a modest collector of relatively modern paintings, including works by Augustus John, Sickert, Wilson Steer, Matthew Smith, and Paul Nash. She also bought a Monet that had belonged to Clemenceau, and it was at her invitation that John Piper produced his series of drawings and water-colours of Windsor.

In 1964 she had an emergency operation for appendicitis, and two years later underwent a colostomy. But her basically strong constitution enabled her to weather these vicissitudes and throughout the 1960s and 1970s she maintained an extensive diary of royal engagements. Among other things she was occupied by her patronage of no fewer than 300 charities and was colonel-in-chief of 13 regular regiments, eight of them in the British Army and five in the forces of Commonwealth countries.

Among these her colonelcies of both the Black Watch and the Black Watch of Canada emphasized her ties with Scotland. She was also honorary colonel of three Territorial Army units: the Royal Yeomanry, the London Scottish Regiment, and the Inns of Court Regiment and was commandant-in-chief of Women in the Royal Navy and RAF and was patron of the Women's Royal Army Corps Association.

In the summer of 1980, on the occasion of her eightieth birthday, she drove to St Paul's in a landau with Prince Charles through cheering crowds. Her ninetieth birthday was the cause for even more extended congratulations. Though she had specifically asked that no fuss be made, there were celebrations in Scotland, Wales, and England lasting well over a month. These included a recorded concert featuring works especially commissioned by young composers, organized by the Prince of Wales to raise funds for his charitable trust. In his foreword to the recording, the Queen Mother's favourite grandson described it as: 'a wonderful reason for commissioning some new music: to celebrate a very special occasion and an even more special grandmother'. On the day itself a crowd of 4,000 stood for hours outside Clarence House with the temperature in the nineties, waiting for her to appear.

But clouds were gathering again over the personal lives of members of the Royal Family. The marriage of her granddaughter Princess Anne had already failed in the

1980s. Now, in quick succession in the early 1990s, the marriage of her second grandson, the Duke of York, foundered and was closely followed by the separation of the Prince and Princess of Wales. Both events were accompanied by unsparing reporting of details of private conflicts and sexual infidelities that would have been undreamt of a generation earlier.

The disintegration of the Prince of Wales's marriage affected the Queen Mother deeply and, given her predilection for her eldest grandson, involved her in undoubted partisanship. Relations between the Queen Mother and the Princess of Wales had never been good. Under the pressure of the publicity which accompanied the painful steps towards the dissolution of the heir to the throne's marriage, they cooled even further. But, though a staunch churchwoman to whom divorce was anathema, the Queen Mother studiously avoided giving any public hint of her feelings.

At this time the popularity of the Royal Family was sinking to its lowest level during the present reign. The indulged lives of the younger generation, with their seemingly incessant round of parties and beach or skiing holidays, grated on a British people which was having to tighten its belt in the worst economic recession since the war. Even the Queen, with her untaxed millions, found that the nation's sympathy had its limits when a part of Windsor Castle was destroyed by fire, and the initial assumption appeared to be that the public would pay. A spate of unprecedented royal-bashing was unleashed in the popular press.

The Queen Mother alone escaped censure. Her popularity continued undimmed. A public appeal, launched in 1990, for a monument to celebrate her life with an ornamental gate (named the Queen Elizabeth Gate) at Hyde Park raised the necessary £2 million within two years. This quite confounded her own sensitivities about the wisdom of such an appeal in a time of recession.

Almost to the end the Queen Mother demonstrated remarkable robustness, both physical and mental, in her round of duties. In May 1992, when verging on her ninety-second birthday, she insisted on unveiling a statue of Bomber Command's wartime leader, Air Chief Marshal Sir Arthur Harris, at St Clement Dane's Church in the Strand. This was in spite of the fact that she had been advised that there might be demonstrations of a more than merely vociferous character. In the event there were, but in spite of all the shouting and paint-throwing she delivered a speech of tribute to Bomber Command's dead, in a clear and resolute voice.

Physical frailty was hinted at in her absence from Royal Ascot in the following year. Yet, in July of the same year, on a day of brilliant sunshine, she appeared much recovered when she strolled through the Queen Elizabeth Gate on its official opening by her daughter, the Queen. During her later years there were the occasional health scares which are generally associated with those many years her junior. At 95 and then 97, she underwent hip replacement operations.

The Queen Mother was to live to play the central role in a celebration which, perhaps more than any other, summed up her life of unstinting service to the British people – the fiftieth anniversary of VE day on May 8, 1995. In a moving echo of the original ceremony in 1945, though this time without Winston Churchill and King George VI at her side, she stepped out onto the balcony of Buckingham Palace, followed by both her daughters, to wave to the 400,000 strong crowd which thronged the Mall. Joining in with them in the singing of some of the old wartime favourites, this astonishingly sprightly 94-year-old seemed more than ever a symbol of the nation's fortitude in dark years of adversity.

By the time of her centenary in August 2000, the Royal Family was recovering some, though certainly not all, of its popularity. There were several reasons for this. The Princess of Wales was dead, killed in a high-speed car crash in a Paris underpass. It was an event which led to a powerful, if ultimately short-lived, outpouring of public grief, particularly among the young – especially young women – to whom, it seemed, she had been such an icon. More broadly, the awkward position of the Prince of Wales at that time reminded people that he was, after all, another human being and was no more to be protected from the grief of such a tragedy than anyone else. The censure attaching to his relationship with his paramour, Camilla Parker-Bowles, gradually abated.

A return visit to St Paul's Cathedral on July 11 marked the start of the Queen Mother's hundredth birthday celebrations. Almost all of her descendants, as well as distant relations and in-laws from several European royal families, were present to hear the Archbishop of Canterbury lead the nation in tribute to her. Meanwhile, members of parliament heard the Prime Minister's congratulation in the form of a Humble Address in the House of Commons.

Certainly, there were words and actions of dissent. A Channel 4 television programme made insinuations about her steely nature and extravagant lifestyle, but they made no great impact on the population at large. Dissident Irish Republicans tried to disrupt a colourful parade that was part military and part fun held at Horse Guards on July 19 through a series of security alerts which paralyzed most of London's rail, underground, and bus routes.

With no precedent for celebrating such longevity in the Royal Family, her advisers had dreamt up the colourful occasion, which was an effervescent and eccentric 90-minute spectacular involving more than 7,000 participants, from schoolchildren to holders of the Victoria Cross. On her birthday itself, August 4, 2000, the Queen Mother, like all centenarians, received a personally signed card from the monarch. Standing outside Clarence House beside the Prince of Wales, she struggled for a moment with the envelope until her equerry stepped forward to slit it open with a ceremonial sword. Touchingly, it was signed 'Lilibet', Queen Elizabeth II's childhood pet name.

Meanwhile, the crowds had gathered in their thousands and, escorted by the Prince of Wales, the Queen Mother travelled in an open landau, garlanded with flowers in her racing colours of blue and buff, to Buckingham Palace for a celebratory lunch with the extended family. But before sitting down there was, much to the delight of the crowds, time for a wave from the balcony.

Certainly it was a tribute to her person that while the popularity of lesser royals ebbed and flowed, hers seemed to remain constant. Her role always as consort but never monarch had given her a detachment from any constitutional entanglements. There was also a genuine public admiration of the behaviour of a queen who, having been widowed at a relatively young age, had not, as she might well have done, retired into pampered seclusion, but had continued to make a positive and colourful contribution to public life. Above all, she gave the impression always of making herself available to people and of placing herself and her time at their disposal.

Astonishingly, to those who might have imagined that her hundredth birthday would be her last, she courageously negotiated another 12 months, at the end of which she was able to celebrate her one hundred and first. She did so shortly after having had a blood transfusion which, though it had seemed to be a prognostication of irreversible decline, left her evidently much invigorated.

On August 4, 2001, she entertained a dozen of her closest family to lunch at Clarence House, and when she rounded off the birthday celebrations with a visit to the Royal Ballet at Covent Garden, it was not so much her health which gave cause for concern, as that of Princess Margaret, who attended her in a wheelchair, visibly a shadow of her formerly vivacious self.

As the year drew on Princess Margaret could be seen to be in palpable decline. In 2002, while the Queen Mother made a very slow recovery from a cold caught over the Christmas period, it began to seem to be a distinct possibility that her daughter might precede her to the grave. And, indeed, the Queen Mother was herself still struggling against the effects of a chest infection which, worryingly to those around her, continued to confine her to bed, when the death of Princess Margaret was made known on February 9.

What her private feelings were in a moment of such painful bereavement cannot be known. In a spirit which was characteristic of her, she declared that she would travel from Sandringham to her daughter's funeral service at St George's Chapel, Windsor, and she did. Even a fall in her sitting room at Sandringham two days before, as a result of which she sustained a cut arm, could not shake this resolve, despite the Queen's efforts to dissuade her.

The Queen, her elder daughter, survives her.

Queen Elizabeth The Queen Mother was born in London on August 4, 1900.
She died on March 30, 2002, aged 101.

BARBARA CASTLE

Labour firebrand who introduced child benefit and the Breathalyser – and launched
a brave but doomed attempt at trade union reform

3 MAY 2002

FOR MORE THAN 20 YEARS Barbara Castle was Britain's best-known woman politician. As a minister she was astute, accomplished, combative, and controversial, her successes eclipsing memories of Margaret Bondfield, Ellen Wilkinson, and Florence Horsburgh, the only three previous women Cabinet ministers. She was the favourite of party activists, frequently topping the poll in the constituency section of the national executive. Ladbroke's regularly took bets on her becoming the first woman Prime Minister. This alerted some of her political opponents to the possibility of having a woman at No. 10 and, to that extent, Castle, to her dismay, was sometimes said to have played a part in the election of Margaret Thatcher as Conservative leader and the longest-serving twentieth-century inhabitant of No. 10.

Barbara Castle was an easily identifiable figure from the moment she arrived at the Commons in the Labour landslide of 1945. Her temperament matched the fiery colour of her hair. Inevitably, the popular papers called her the Red Queen as she exhibited from her backbench seat below the gangway a pent-up fury about the slow pace of socialist reform. She had joined the Independent Labour Party when she was 16 and her fundamental beliefs never changed.

She once summed up her nature as being constitutionally incapable of turning down a challenge, however risky, and claimed that once she was embroiled in anything she had to try to make it work. This attitude was responsible for some of her greatest achievements: equal pay, the introduction of seat belts, the state earnings-related pension scheme (Serps), equal pension rights for women, child benefit, the statutory right to belong to a trade union – and, of course, the Breathalyser. 'I suppose the Breathalyser's what I shall be remembered for', she used to say.

Unfortunately her self-confessed inability to resist a challenge means that she will be remembered also for her brave but forlorn bid to reform the trade unions, a move which almost ended her career and at one time endangered the position of her ally and patron, Harold Wilson. Her plan in 1969 to modernize the unions and stop unofficial strikes caused alarm even among her traditional friends on the Left. Opposition in the Parliamentary Labour Party, mobilized by James Callaghan and the late Douglas Houghton, proved too strong: the vital elements of her scheme were abandoned when the Chief Whip, Robert Mellish, told the Cabinet her Bill would never get through the Commons. That failure cost Castle any chance she might have had of becoming the first woman Prime Minister.

This was one of her few misjudgments about her party: her ministerial career was almost entirely successful. Although she was a woman operating in what was largely a male environment she hated being credited with a masculine mind. She managed to dominate most of her civil servants and colleagues without losing her essential femininity. She demanded to be taken for what she was and not for what she was born, though she was not above tears when all else had failed.

She was a socialist from childhood. Her father, Frank Betts, a tax inspector, was an enthusiastic propagandist for the ILP and it was not surprising that her first election address, written when she was six, consisted of a ten-word promise: 'Dear citizens, vote for me, I will give you houses.'

Betts was an unusual tax inspector. He was a voracious reader and Castle maintained that she was brought up in an aura of Greek plays, Irish ballads, medieval romances, and Icelandic sagas – with Betts teaching himself various foreign languages at the breakfast table. His wife, Annie, was in the same mould. She was a milliner who became a William Morris socialist, and Castle's early memories included dancing round the maypole every spring in her family's series of neglected gardens.

The gardens were numerous because of her father's profession. The Inland Revenue believed in keeping tax inspectors on the move and, though Castle was born in Chesterfield, her father was soon posted to Hull and on to Pontefract before moving to Bradford, where Castle went to Bradford Girls' Grammar School and won a scholarship to St Hugh's College, Oxford.

She fell in love with Oxford, but then began to hate it. She thought her college dull and stifling. She went up to read French but soon switched to philosophy, politics, and economics, as she had decided her future lay in journalism or politics. She found Oxford in the early 1930s a mixture of sexual discrimination and sexual frustration. She found a welcome lack of discrimination in the Labour Club, where she became a leading figure, to the neglect of her studies. Her general unhappiness was reflected in her degree. She went down with a third.

By then her family had moved on to Hyde in Cheshire. She had no money and no prospects. The only job she could find was selling crystallized fruits in a Manchester department store, dressed improbably as Little Nell. She was considered bright enough to be transferred to the store's London headquarters; but there her ideas were thought too bright altogether, and she was sacked. She was saved from despair by the great love of her life, William Mellor, a former Editor of the *Daily Herald*.

She had met Mellor through the Socialist League. The attraction was immediate. Mellor, married, with a child, was in no position to marry her immediately and made this clear. Frank Betts told Barbara appreciatively: 'I never expected a man to come and tell me his intentions towards my daughter were strictly dishonourable.'

Mellor, 22 years older than she was, dominated their relationship. He launched a local government magazine and she became its secretary. Then, in 1937, he became Editor of a new magazine. It was called *Tribune*. The magazine was the brainchild of George Strauss, Aneurin Bevan, and Sir Stafford Cripps – who provided most of its finance. Castle wrote a column for it in conjunction with a new friend, Michael Foot. But Mellor soon ceased to be Editor and in 1942 he died from a duodenal ulcer. Castle was desolate but next year she went as a delegate to her first Labour Party conference. The conference changed her life. It brought her fame, a job, and a husband.

She spoke on the Beveridge Report and her speech was a sensation. The next day her picture was on the front page of the *Daily Mirror* and she was hailed as 'The Voice of Youth' (she was actually 32). The paper immediately appointed her its housing correspondent. The night editor who made the all-important decision to make her the *Mirror*'s main story was Ted Castle. His first marriage had broken up and they began meeting regularly. He was also a leftwinger and they shared speaking engagements. In July 1944, with the V1s falling on London, they were married. Nye Bevan and Jennie Lee were two of the four guests at their wedding breakfast at the Savoy.

The marriage lasted until Ted Castle's death 34 years later. In one way, their partnership was difficult. Ted Castle was a talented journalist who longed to be a politician but his only successful bid to get a constituency to fight ended in 1953 in a by-election defeat. He had to be content with a local government aldermanship, an appointment as Member of the European Parliament and a belated life peerage. This was probably just as well. In the Commons he would never have been more than a run-of-the-mill backbencher, while his wife – with many of the characteristics of a leading actress – always seemed destined to be a star. It nevertheless proved to be a successful marriage, despite their failure to have children, which Barbara Castle always described as the greatest sorrow of her life. Ted Castle's death in 1979 was an event from which she never fully recovered.

He was at her side during her triumphs and occasional disasters and never more so than during the 1945 general election. Her *Mirror* column and more platform successes brought her the chance to fight one of the two Blackburn seats, where she was selected after the constituency's women revolted against an all-male list. Her husband chauffeured and encouraged her throughout an exhilarating but exhausting campaign which she duly won.

In the Commons she lined up automatically with the Left. She was one of the Labour MPs who supported Dick Crossman's 1947 amendment calling on the Attlee

Government to recast its foreign policy. She backed the new Keep Left Group. None of this prevented her political advancement. Cripps appointed her his PPS at the Board of Trade and his successor, Harold Wilson, retained her in the post and began an association which lasted 40 years.

In 1950 she was elected to the women's section of her party's national executive. Showing considerable courage, she decided to stand the next year for one of the seven seats in the constituency section. To her astonishment, she came second, only Bevan being ahead of her. The following year the leftwingers won six of the seven seats and the Bevanite movement became a reality.

The Bevanites were a curious organization: despite right-wing allegations, they never truly developed into a party within a party. They were not tightly knit. Most of them mistrusted each other. Bevan himself, with a tendency to indolence, had no talent for conspiracy, unlike his front man, Ian Mikardo. Castle once summed up her leader: 'Bevan wanted Bevanism without the Bevanites. He hated teamwork.' But while Bevanism may have helped Castle's popularity with party members, it did not appear to have helped her in her constituency, where she scraped in at the 1955 election by just over 500 votes.

The next Parliament was not her happiest. She spoke largely on colonial affairs, concentrating on apartheid in South Africa, the Hola camp massacre in Kenya, and the struggle for Enosis in Cyprus. It was a visit to Cyprus, where she was interpreted as having been critical of British troops, that got her into trouble with the right-wing press. She even launched a libel action against Christopher Chataway (which she lost), but she rode the storm, increasing her majority at Blackburn in 1959.

Then, in 1960, Wilson stood against Gaitskell for the party leadership and Castle nominated him. Predictably, Wilson lost and, just as predictably, Gaitskell dropped Castle from her post as front-bench spokesman on Ministry of Works affairs. But, when Gaitskell died in 1963, Wilson replaced him and Castle's star rose again. Once Labour won the 1964 election, Wilson made her Minister of Overseas Development. After nearly 20 years spent almost entirely on the back benches, Castle was in the Cabinet.

Office gave her the fulfilment her restless spirit demanded. Her civil servants appreciated the battles she won to obtain aid for developing countries. Even her enemies, who were plentiful by this time, were forced to admire the burning social conscience which caused the Cabinet and the Treasury to give more to her department than they ever intended.

Promotion came soon. Wilson appointed her Minister of Transport in 1965, using an advertising slogan of the time to flatter her by saying that he needed 'a tiger in the tank'. But at first her appointment was ridiculed, as she had never held a driving licence, though this was not for want of effort. Michael Foot had once given her lessons, but after a series of near disasters, including being expelled from the Regent's Park circuit as a danger to other road users, both decided that regard for each other's safety demanded an end to the experiment.

She took advantage of preparatory work done by Tom Fraser, her predecessor, and produced no fewer than four White Papers before introducing her Transport Bill. This set up three new state bodies – the National Freight Corporation, the National Bus Company, and the Scottish Transport Group. The Bill was an impressive achievement, though it failed in her original hope of solving the problem of the railways, where it soon became clear that there was no core of profitable lines and that continuing and increasing subsidies would be needed.

Her most spectacular act was the introduction of the Breathalyser. She was denounced by sections of the liquor trade, but fewer road deaths, reliably attributed to the consequent change in driving habits, made it one of the most beneficial acts of her career. At the time, she was against random breath testing, but later, as a backbencher, she reversed her position.

Her time at Transport was a golden period. No section of new motorway was opened without a photograph of her. In 1967 she was voted the best-known member of the Cabinet after Wilson, and people began to talk of her, with some reason, as Wilson's successor. When she was promoted in 1968 to become Secretary of State for Employment and Productivity, with the rank and additional title of First Secretary, she seemed the Prime Minister's closest colleague.

But her new post, which carried such promise, always contained the possibility of disaster. Ray Gunter had famously described the old Ministry of Labour – before Castle renamed and reshaped it – as 'the bed of nails'. On the night of her appointment she wrote in her diary: 'I am under no illusion that I may be committing political suicide.' In her case she was nearly right.

Castle's first inheritance was a Prices and Incomes Bill about which she had reservations. She believed in the policy as a whole but her trouble was that large sections of the Labour movement did not. At the 1968 party conference a resolution to abandon the policy was carried by five million votes to just over a million. Castle ignored the warning. She came top of the voting for the executive's constituency section and, encouraged by this, she returned to London determined to do something about the unions.

Wilson, harried by unofficial strikes, had set up a royal commission under Lord Donovan in an effort to find a solution. The report was on Castle's desk. She accepted the general tenor of the report, which was fairly acceptable to the unions, but she went well beyond it. With her advisers she produced her own plan to delay and possibly defuse unofficial strikes. It called for pre-strike ballots, a 28-day conciliation period, and settlements to be imposed where unofficial action came from inter-union disputes. It also proposed penalties – the hated penal clauses – if the new rules were breached.

At her husband's suggestion, she called the White Paper outlining her proposals 'In Place of Strife', an obvious echo of the title of Aneurin Bevan's book *In Place of Fear*. If she hoped by this to gain left-wing support, she failed. Her proposals produced more strife in her party than anything since the dispute over nuclear disarmament.

But Wilson was captivated by her plan. He saw it as a vote-winner and believed it could get through the Commons. He was soon disabused. In the spring of 1969, when it was debated in the House, 55 Labour MPs voted against it and some 40 abstained. Worse was to come.

Three weeks later, at a meeting of the national executive, James Callaghan, then Home Secretary, opposed the scheme. With the active help of Douglas Houghton, his old colleague from the tax officers' union who was now chairman of the Parliamentary Labour Party, he worked diligently to organize opposition. By this he risked being sacked from the Cabinet, but Wilson, fearful of union reaction, held back. Castle realized the danger, calling Callaghan 'the snake lurking in the grass'. They had been old opponents when on different wings of the party. Now they became outright enemies and remained so for the rest of their careers.

Wilson, who had hoped for a short, quick Bill, found himself bogged down. His Cabinet was divided. He began to display irritation, petulance, and, it was said, some evidence of fear at Cabinet meetings. His position seemed in genuine danger, and supporters of Callaghan and Jenkins began seriously to weigh up their chances for the succession. But they could never combine and Wilson scraped through.

But the plan to tackle the unions did not. Robert Mellish, the new Chief Whip, announced it would never get through the Commons. Castle's original backers, including Peter Shore, Wilson's particular protégé, and Roy Jenkins, the Chancellor, withdrew their support. Wilson and Castle were isolated. The Prime Minister railed against the deserters, calling them 'the weak sisters'. The decisive meeting with the TUC ended with the unions offering 'a solemn and binding undertaking' – later a much derided phrase – to intervene in unofficial strikes.

In fact, the unions kept to the agreement pretty well and unofficial strikes were reduced. But that was not the way Parliament, the press, and the public saw it. The next day many papers carried the headline 'Surrender'. And that was the impression which remained at the 1970 general election.

Castle was shattered by the experience. There was some consolation soon afterwards when her Equal Pay Bill got through Parliament, but her defeat by the unions haunted her. Eventually there was grudging admission by some of her opponents that perhaps they would have done better to accept the reforms proposed by Castle rather than wait for the swingeing limitations imposed by Margaret Thatcher. But this acknowledgement came too late to revive any chance she might have had of becoming the first woman Prime Minister or even the first woman Foreign Secretary. She was even voted out of the Shadow Cabinet.

Wilson, somewhat to his surprise, won a narrow victory in the first election of 1974 and Castle, equally to her surprise, was recalled to Government as Secretary of State for Health and Social Security. It was Wilson's tribute to her loyalty as well as testimony to her undiminished energy.

She repaid his confidence by showing all her old spirit in her new post. She launched an ambitious pensions plan and fought a series of battles with the hospital consultants in a bid to phase out pay-beds. She considered that her main achievement was the introduction of the Child Benefit Act, switching the male tax allowance for children directly to the mothers. This was in its final stages in 1976 when Wilson resigned. Callaghan sent for her almost immediately and said he wanted her post in order to make way for younger people. She said she was tempted to say: 'Why not start with yourself?' She was 66; he was 64.

She had realized her Commons career was coming to an end but wanted to see her Child Benefit Act through its final stages. She was devastated by her sudden dismissal. She felt she had been 'discarded like a piece of old junk'.

She sat out the rest of the Parliament and then, to general surprise, she left Westminster in 1979 and was elected to the European Parliament. She had been a consistent opponent of entry into what was then still called the Common Market and had campaigned in the 1975 referendum for Britain to leave. Now she came to work in Strasbourg herself. Though she could never be described as *communautaire*, she gradually relaxed her outright opposition.

While she continued to maintain that Britain had entered on the wrong terms, she now believed that her country should try to change the European Union from within. She became quite a figure at Strasbourg, leading the British Labour MPs and becoming vice-chairman of the Socialist Group. When she retired from the Parliament in 1989 she moved almost immediately to another – to the House of Lords as Baroness Castle of Blackburn.

Although she spoke occasionally in the Upper House her activities tended to diminish. Her eyesight was failing and so was a little of her spirit – which made the cruel caricature of her in David Hare's play *The Absence of War* (1993) all the more hurtful. Despite voting for John Prescott in the 1994 leadership election, she initially became reconciled to the prospect of a Blair Government.

But before long she grew restive under the regime of new Labour. Although Tony Blair had put in an appreciated appearance at her eighty-fifth birthday party at Brighton in 1995, her attitude towards the leadership had by the following year become distinctly more critical. Just as in 1943 she had seized the headlines with a fiery speech calling on her leaders to show boldness in introducing the welfare state, so more than half a century later at Blackpool in 1996 she repeated the performance with another firework display that the party leadership could well have done without.

Within a few days of her eighty-sixth birthday, she had to be helped to the rostrum. But she soon proved that she knew how to use her frailty to her own advantage. She achieved what must have been a record for a speaker from the floor. She not only gained a standing ovation at the end of her speech but she also received one before she even reached the microphone.

In the early days of the Blair leadership she had been careful to support it – 'anything for a Labour Government, dear', was the view she expressed in private – but she became increasingly anxious about the way new Labour was developing. Her apprehensions surfaced at the 1995 conference when she pleaded eloquently for more money to be spent on pensions. She savaged Gordon Brown and Harriet Harman as effectively as she had assailed other leaders in the past. It was a Bevanite speech from one of the last survivors of the Bevanites.

By her last days, she was almost completely blind. This did not prevent her from enjoying being entertained at luncheons in London. 'Read me the menu, dear, but don't tell me the prices,' she would say. *Tribune* remained one of her great interests. It brought back memories of her first lover, Will Mellor, and her first triumphs. Recently she attended a lunch – at the Gay Hussar, inevitably – to produce ideas for invigorating the paper. Her idea was for a greater role for herself. She never underrated her worth. But blindness meant that she could never play the active role she wanted again.

In her last days she would refer often to her husband, Ted. She had had other lovers, and so had he. But this apparently open marriage did not seem to diminish their relationship. When they entertained she insisted on giving Ted his role as the head of the household. 'Of course Ted will carve,' was her introduction to many a meal. For a woman so conscious of her appearance, her blindness must have had an added terror. But to the end she was never less than beautifully dressed.

She is survived by her nephews and nieces, to whom she was devoted.

*Baroness Castle of Blackburn, PC, former Labour Government Minister,
was born on October 6, 1910. She died on May 3, 2002, aged 91.*

ALISTAIR COOKE

The ultimate professional, whose evergreen 'Letter from America' embraced
most of the key events in post-war American history

30 MARCH 2004

THE BEST-KNOWN BROADCASTER of his age, Alistair Cooke was also the most accomplished practitioner, at least in a studio in front of the microphone. His *Letter from America*, which went out weekly from 1946 until this month, was easily the longest-running BBC programme. It spanned the history of America, from the days of recovery after the Second World War, through the McCarthyite period of the Cold War and the turbulent 1960s, when Cooke personally witnessed the assassination of Bobby Kennedy, to the attacks of September 11, 2001, and the second gulf war.

Letter from America had its critics – who regarded it as altogether too bland and soft in the predominantly rose-coloured view it presented of the United States – but even among its detractors there was no denying the sheer professionalism with which it was done.

Cooke's technique – and this was true also of his written journalism – was always to approach his subject at a tangent, moving from some far-off periphery to the core of what he wanted to say. On the air this turned him into a natural story-teller, the master of the pause and the deliberate hesitation, with the matchless gift of sounding entirely spontaneous when he was, of course, reading from a prepared script.

This was a facility that did not serve him quite so well on television, where he could appear rather measured and mannered. His 13-part series *America*, for the BBC in 1972, was an enormous commercial success but did not enjoy anything like the critical acclaim accorded to Kenneth Clark's celebrated *Civilisation*: on the contrary, it was heavily attacked, by academics in particular. Nevertheless, the secondary television sales from it, and the accompanying book, which sold 2.8 million copies in hardback, made Cooke's fortune.

His consequent renown also brought him an invitation to address a joint session of the US Congress as part of American Bicentennial celebrations in 1974. The previous year he had been appointed an honorary KBE (he had been an American citizen since 1941) on the nomination of Edward Heath.

What faithful British listeners to *Letter from America* seldom realized was that its sole author and originator enjoyed an almost equal fame in the country of his adoption, though there it was based on television appearances rather than on radio. From the early 1950s to the early 1960s when he presented *Omnibus* – a kind of *Panorama* of the arts for the CBS network – to the 22 years from 1971 to 1993 when he topped and tailed *Masterpiece Theatre* for PBS (the Public Broadcasting Service), Cooke was a familiar face to generations of cultivated Americans. He was the proto-type mid-Atlantic man: perceived in Britain as the best sort of sophisticated Ameri-can and in the United States as the very model of an English gentleman (only the more quizzical of his friends occasionally wondered whether this constituted something of an identity crisis).

Alfred Alistair Cooke – as he became when he added 'Alistair' to his formerly single Christian name, by deed poll on his twenty-second birthday – was the son of a Lancashire Methodist lay preacher and an Irish mother and, although born in Salford, was brought up largely in Blackpool, to where his parents (both of whom suffered from lung trouble) had moved to take advantage of the sea breezes.

He broke free of the strict Nonconformist constraints of his family background – no alcoholic drink was permitted in the house and no games were to be played on Sundays – by winning a scholarship to what became Blackpool Grammar School. The headmaster there was a tremendous snob but also had a genuine regard for English literature. It was largely thanks to his influence and inspiration that the young Cooke won an exhibition to Jesus College, Cambridge, where he came under the competing influences of Sir Arthur Quiller-Couch and I. A. Richards.

On one occasion Cooke read an essay on the Romantic poets as Quiller-Couch was dressing for dinner. He was proud of the piece, and slightly disconcerted to have Q walking in and out in search of his clothes. When he had finished, Q pro-nounced in his too-contrived style: 'Cooke, you must learn to murder your dar-lings.' After a while he did, so that although his undergraduate writing often tried too hard to keep up with William Empson, who also wrote theatre, book, and film reviews in Cambridge, Cooke's later writing was admirably straightforward.

He took a first in Part I of the English tripos and a second in Part II, a disparity perhaps to be explained by his editorship in his last year of *Granta* – where he worked with William Empson, Jacob Bronowski, and Michael Redgrave – and his part in founding a university drama company, the Mummers. He got an early foothold, too, in professional journalism when in 1929 he was appointed Cam-bridge drama critic of *The Manchester Guardian*. He also wrote for both *The Nation* and *The Athenaeum* (both of them later incorporated into *The New Statesman*).

In 1931 he organized a visit to Germany by a group of friends calling themselves the Oxford and Cambridge Players, and saw Hitler in full spate outside the Braunhaus. But Cooke was so politically naive that he was more interested in Hitler's rhetorical devices than in his message.

He was in no way afflicted by diffidence, and wrote to the BBC asking to be put before the microphone to give talks on theatre, literary criticism, or poetry even before he was 23 (perhaps redeemingly, in the same letter he also suggested that he might draw caricatures for *Radio Times*). The BBC, however, declined the offer of his services at that stage, so he spent a year at teaching college in Cambridge. 'Has skill as an actor, a facile pen, and is a good draughtsman. Literary tastes, but eclectic rather than original. Could be of great service to a school if he could control his egoism,' read his assessor's report.

Then, in 1932, the course of his whole future life was determined when he was selected as one of the Commonwealth Fellows annually sent by the Harkness Fund to the United States.

While in America, where he studied drama at Yale and linguistics at Harvard, Cooke met Charlie Chaplin, who took a great shine to him. They worked together on a film script about Napoleon, and although the project was abortive, the association did Cooke's standing no harm. In 1934 it probably played its part in persuading the BBC to appoint him its film critic.

To the annoyance of the cinema trade, which thought he was much too high-brow, Cooke held the post for nearly three years. It was not, however, in delivering weekly film reviews that he made his first serious impact. That came when he presented a series of eight programmes called *I Hear America Singing* on the BBC's Home Service. A compilation of American jazz records (some of which he had mysteriously managed to borrow from the Library of Congress), this hit series first fully revealed Cooke's natural gifts as a fluent, impromptu-sounding broadcaster.

Slightly surprisingly, in the wake of this great success, he immediately decided to return to the United States. In 1934, while still on his Commonwealth Fellowship, he had married his first wife, Ruth Emerson (a great-grandniece of Ralph Waldo Emerson); but he seems also to have shrewdly spotted a gap in the journalistic market.

While working as the BBC's film critic, he had broadcast a regular *Letter from London* for the American network NBC, and almost from the start he appears to have aspired to do the same in reverse for the BBC. At first he had to be content with being merely one of the contributors to an already running feature known as *American Commentary*, and although he formally suggested the notion of a weekly 'American Letter' as early as 1940, it was not accepted until February 1946. (For the first three years it went under that title, before becoming *Letter from America*.)

The intervening years were not the happiest in Cooke's career. He did some written journalism as a special correspondent for *The Times* between 1938 and 1941, and when that came to an end he became a US-based feature writer on the *Daily Herald* as well as doing some tabloid journalism for the *Daily Sketch*. The truth was that he was not at that time a very popular figure, at least among English people and Anglophiles in New York. Inevitably, questions were raised about an able-bodied young man in his early thirties choosing to work in a neutral country abroad when back at home his countrymen were under direct threat; and these questions were amplified in 1941, when at one of the lowest points of the war, Cooke took out naturalization papers as an American citizen.

For a time he became something of a pariah, and the official British Information Services were even instructed to withdraw all assistance from him. In retrospect, such treatment may seem harsh, but then Cooke was not uncalculating: as early as 1938 he had advised a young man who worked with him on *I Hear America Singing* to emigrate to the United States as soon as possible on the ground that 'there is going to be a terrible war in Europe'.

In the event, largely as a result of America's own entry into the war in December 1941, the cloud passed. Cooke undertook a tour of the US in 1943 to report on the effect of war on various trades and professions, and became a mainstay of the BBC's *American Commentary*. The only criticism of him back at Broadcasting House in London arose from what was officially called his 'tendency to be allusive and glib'. He was, of course, deliberately pioneering a new style of broadcasting, speaking as if in conversation, and this inevitably involved a certain inconsequentiality – which was later to become his trademark.

In 1945 Cooke was given an opportunity to relaunch his career as a fully fledged print journalist. A cable from the Editor of *The Manchester Guardian* to his hotel in San Francisco, where he had gone for the BBC to cover the birth of the United Nations, asked him to file also to that great liberal voice of provincial England.

Cooke, who had been without a newspaper connection since his contract with the *Daily Herald* expired in 1944, was delighted to accept, and soon – since the creation of the UN was of great interest to *The Manchester Guardian's* idealistic readers – he found himself filing up to 4,000 words a day. It was the beginning of an association that was to endure, though not without its troubles, for 27 years.

In 1948 Cooke became the paper's chief American correspondent at a salary of $14,000 a year. The figure was reliably reported barely to have changed by the time he laid down his burden in the autumn of 1972, and he once wryly remarked that there were two British institutions (*The Guardian* and the BBC) for which no one worked unless they were totally indifferent to money – and he, in his innocence, had joined both.

By the mid-1940s, however, Cooke was already fairly prosperous. His first marriage had broken up, and in 1946 he married a widow, Jane Hawkes, with two children. She was a talented painter and soon he was able to move back into the apartment block on Fifth Avenue that he had left on his divorce in 1944. His real break, however, came in 1952 when in New York he was given a Peabody Award, recognizing the contribution he had made to international understanding, through the first six years of *Letter from America*.

So charmed was his largely media audience by his witty and urbane speech of acceptance that in no time the American television networks were competing for his services. cbs won with its invitation to host the weekly arts programme *Omnibus*, which he did for a decade and more.

Television fame almost immediately brought him remunerative invitations to join the American lecture circuit, and this was an art-form in which, with his undergraduate actor's background, he was thoroughly adept. Although he did not become really rich until the publication of *Alistair Cooke's America* in 1973, his account of the Hiss case, *A Generation on Trial* (1950), established his reputation with the American public as a serious writer. He subsequently published a succession of books – though most of them were no more than potboilers (many of them collections of his *Letters from America*). Among the best of his books was *Six Men* (1978), a slim collection of half a dozen essays on individuals he respected, including Charlie Chaplin, Adlai Stevenson (in some ways his ideal of the civilized man in public life), and H. L. Mencken (the *Baltimore Sun* columnist whom he regarded as his journalistic mentor). Another such collection, *Memories of the Great and the Good*, appeared in 1999.

Politically, Cooke seemed to move to the right as he grew older. The young man who had been drawn to America by his admiration for Franklin Roosevelt and the New Deal ended up by being fêted in the Reagan White House. He took up golf in the 1950s, and since he tended to play with rich and prosperous business executives, this may have had its impact on his political attitudes.

But the real criticism of his broadcasting output was that he had a habit of ignoring things that upset him. No one listening even regularly to *Letter from America* would have been able even to tell how badly the fabric of American society was torn by the Vietnam War, to sense the passions involved in the civil rights struggle (which he criticized as ill-thought-out), or to appreciate the tensions that provoked the race riots of the late 1960s. His favourite viewpoint – and once or twice in his more reflective speeches he came close to admitting this – was that of the benign onlooker sitting under the trees watching the people dance.

Perhaps it was symptomatic of a general failing when at the end of 1996, in his eighty-ninth year, he stumbled into controversy by casually remarking in a broadcast that he found it surprising that only four per cent of American women military personnel complained of being subjected to attempted or actual rape – adding, for good inconsequential measure, that '96 per cent of the men showed remarkable restraint'. Even in a less politically correct society than America, this provoked indignant criticism: the proverbial storm promptly broke over Cooke's head.

Again, it was probably symptomatic that the burden of his defence was that he had been brought up in the tradition of gallantry, and that he was now too old to change his ways.

The storm passed, though, and his slightly weary, slightly wheezy tones continued to be heard each week by an admiring audience until three weeks ago, when the BBC announced, apparently rather to his chagrin, that his last *Letter* had been broadcast. He was speaking, it sometimes seemed, not only from another continent, but from another age.

Alistair Cooke, journalist and broadcaster, was born in Salford
on November 20, 1908. He died in New York at midnight
on March 29–30, 2004, aged 95.

* * *

RONALD REAGAN

President of the United States whose optimism gave America new pride and
whose vision brought the Cold War to an end

5 JUNE 2004

RONALD REAGAN manifestly lived the American dream in which he so fervently believed. He rose from the humblest origins to become a minor Hollywood star, Governor of California for two terms, and finally America's fortieth President. His presidency was controversial and marked by some signal failures as well as achievements, but he handsomely won two presidential elections and was one of the few presidents to leave office better loved than when he was sworn in.

As President, he will be primarily remembered for hastening the end of the Cold War – or even, some claim, for winning it. He did this by ordering the largest peacetime military build-up in United States history and by the development of the Strategic Defence Initiative or 'Star Wars' programme, which was designed to shield America from incoming missiles.

This policy of 'peace through strength' made clear to an economically faltering Soviet Union that the arms race was unwinnable, and two crucial nuclear arms reduction treaties ensued. By the time Reagan left office, the threat of nuclear war between the West and the Communist bloc had greatly diminished. Reagan's foreign policy in other areas, however, notably the Middle East and Central America, was far less successful.

Domestically, Reagan's two great achievements were to restore America's pride and confidence after Vietnam, Watergate, and the 'malaise' of Jimmy Carter's presidency, and fundamentally to change the terms of the political debate by advancing what was, in 1980, the almost heretical notion that government was part of the problem, not the solution. Twenty-four years later, that notion has been embraced by all but the most liberal of America's politicians.

Reagan presided over the longest expansion in the US economy since the Second World War; but it came at considerable long-term cost. He cut taxes, but failed to cut spending, and in the course of his presidency America went from being the world's leading creditor nation to its most prominent debtor, driving up interest rates abroad and bequeathing a huge burden of debt to the next generation of Americans.

The other major blot on Reagan's presidency was the Iran–Contra scandal. With his blessing, US arms were secretly shipped to Iran in an attempt to secure the freedom of US hostages in Lebanon. White House aides then diverted the proceeds from those arms sales to the Nicaraguan Contras, in defiance of a congressional ban on such support. Reagan denied knowing of the diversion, but on this matter he was, for once, not convincing, and in any case he had no answer to the charge of appalling judgment and slack management.

Ronald Reagan had no claim to be considered an intellectual, and for a long time the elites in Washington and other world capitals found it hard to take the former actor seriously. He fell asleep during an audience with the Pope, gave himself a famously light workload, culled jokes and anecdotes from the *Reader's Digest*, and even in interviews tended to be lost without his 'cue cards'. Once, believing a radio microphone was switched off, he jokingly announced that 'the bombing begins in five minutes', and late in his presidency it was revealed that his wife, Nancy, had consulted an astrologer about propitious dates for major policy ventures.

Yet Reagan brought other talents to the presidency that more than compensated for such shortcomings and eccentricities. He had in view a few basic and immutable goals, which gave his Administration an unusual clarity of purpose – the unleashing of America's entrepreneurial spirit by lowering taxes and reducing the role of government, and the restoration of the United States' international pre-eminence by strengthening its military forces and confronting Communism.

He was an uplifting speaker who took over a demoralized country and convinced it that its best days were still to come. He was adept at sensing and articulating the nation's mood, most notably following the Challenger space shuttle disaster of 1986. He restored lustre and dignity to the presidency, but above all he was immensely likeable. Democrats dubbed him 'the Teflon President' because no dirt ever stuck to him, and that was perhaps because he was always so genial and optimistic. He also had a fine line in self-deprecating humour. In a farewell speech he said he planned to 'lean back, kick up my feet and take a long nap,' then added: 'Come to think of it, things won't be that different after all.'

The publication in 2003 of a selection of his letters, written both in office and in the years before and after, showed him at his best. Whether writing to friends or political opponents, to young children, activists, or members of his own family, he showed himself to be principled, witty, and thoughtful, even meditative. His religious faith clearly guided him in his attempt to do the right thing, and he remained courteous and considerate to those who opposed him.

On a personal level, however, Reagan was an enigma. He was a friendly man who had practically no close friends except his wife, Nancy. He forgot the names of senior officials, and was remote even from his four children, one of whom – Patti, his daughter from his second marriage – openly rebelled against his conservatism.

Edmund Morris, his official biographer, once called him 'the most mysterious man I have ever confronted. It is impossible to understand him.'

Although he lacked close friends, Reagan had an ideological soulmate in Margaret Thatcher, whom he first met in London in 1975 before either of them was in supreme office. While he was President and she was Prime Minister, the so-called 'special relationship' between Britain and the US blossomed. Most obviously, he gave Britain vital logistical and material support during the Falklands conflict of 1982. She welcomed the deployment of American cruise missiles on British soil, and in 1986 she allowed Britain to be used as a base for the bombing of Libya. Their one serious argument was over the US invasion of Grenada, a member of the Commonwealth, in 1983, but the last document Reagan signed as President was a letter of appreciation to Baroness Thatcher, and in 1989 he received an honorary knighthood from the Queen.

Ronald Reagan, Mikhail Gorbachev, and Margaret Thatcher were the three dominant figures of the 1980s. History may well place the man who was sometimes unkindly called 'the acting President' in the first rank of those who have occupied the White House. At the very least he will be one of the most prominent in the second division.

Ronald Wilson Reagan was born in a rented flat above the only bank in the tiny Illinois town of Tampico. His Irish-American father, Jack, was an unsuccessful shoe salesman and an alcoholic, and moved his family endlessly around Illinois in the search for work. He finally managed to become part-owner of a shoe shop in the town of Dixon, but the shop went broke in the Depression.

Despite his family's poverty, Reagan decided he wanted to attend a small Christian institution called Eureka College after leaving school, partly because his girl-

President Ronald Reagan riding with the Queen at Windsor, 1982.

friend was going there, but also to continue playing football. He was awarded one of its scholarships for needy students, and met the rest of his costs by working as a summer lifeguard. His academic record was mediocre, but it was at Eureka that he developed a passion for acting.

He graduated at the height of the Depression, when a quarter of all Americans were out of work, but managed to persuade a radio station in Davenport, Iowa, to employ him as a sports commentator. Within three months he was transferred to a sister station in the state capital of Des Moines, where he spent the next four years.

One of his jobs was to provide colourful commentaries on the Chicago Cubs' baseball games as if he was actually sitting in Wrigley Field. He was, in fact, sitting in Des Moines reading ticker-tape accounts of each pitch.

In 1937 Reagan followed the Cubs to Los Angeles for their spring training. A friend introduced him to a Hollywood agent, who was impressed by his voice and physique and persuaded Warner Brothers to give him a screen test. That was the start of a 29-year acting career during which he made 53 films and became a minor star or, in his own characteristic words, 'the Errol Flynn of the B movies'.

He believed his finest film was *King's Row*, in which he played a man who regained consciousness to find his legs amputated. 'Where's the rest of me?' he cried. It was Reagan's most memorable screen line and later, as an aspiring politician, he used it as the title of an autobiography designed to show he was more than a mere actor.

In another big film, *Knute Rockne – All American*, he played George Gipp, the legendary football player who urged his team-mates just before his death to 'win one for the Gipper'. Reagan retained and revelled in the nickname, and half a century later used the same line to urge Americans to elect Vice-President George Bush to succeed him.

In 1940 Reagan married Jane Wyman, an actress also under contract to Warners. They had two children, one of them adopted, but they divorced in 1948 because, she claimed, he had become obsessed with political activities. During the war Reagan was excused from active service because of poor eyesight, and instead made air force training films.

After the war he rose to become president of the Screen Actors Guild, and battled against Communist infiltration of Hollywood. He did not engage in McCarthyite witch-hunts, however, and defended one young actress against charges of Communist sympathies. Her name was Nancy Davis, and she subsequently became his second wife.

Reagan had long been a staunch New Deal Democrat, and had been greatly inspired by President Roosevelt's 'fireside chats' during the Depression, but his battles with Communist infiltrators made him rethink his political allegiance. So, too, did a four-month filming stint in post-war England, during which, he later wrote: 'I saw first-hand how the welfare state sapped incentive to work.'

In 1954, with his Hollywood career fading, he agreed to host a new television show sponsored by General Electric and to give pep talks at General Electric plants around the country. He spent eight years doing that, and his talks gradually developed into a robust denunciation of big government.

During 1960, though still a registered Democrat, he campaigned for Richard Nixon.

In 1962 he joined the Republican Party, and two years later he agreed to be co-chairman of Barry Goldwater's presidential campaign in California, delivering a 30-minute speech on his behalf on national television on the eve of polling day.

The Goldwater candidature was submerged by the campaign for the incumbent President, Lyndon Johnson, but Reagan's contribution had been noticed by a group of wealthy Republicans who liked not only his conservative views but also his attractive demeanour and talent for television. They persuaded him to run against Pat Brown, the Democratic Governor of California, in 1966. He presented himself as an outsider determined to bring California's bloated government down to size, and romped to victory with 58 per cent of the vote. He was 55.

Reagan's governorship was a dress rehearsal for his presidency. He trumped a hostile Democratic legislature by appealing directly to the people. He set broad goals but left the actual implementation to subordinates. His rhetoric was considerably more robust than his actions. He failed to reduce the state's bureaucracy significantly, and actually approved one of California's largest tax increases, though this was followed by successive cuts.

Generally, though, his governorship was considered a success, and in 1976, two years after leaving the governor's mansion, he mounted his first serious bid for the presidency (there had been an abortive effort in 1968). He was challenging the incumbent President Ford for the Republican nomination – but not an elected President, since Ford had taken the White House as a result of Nixon's disgrace.

Reagan campaigned on his favourite conservative themes of smaller government, lower taxes, and greater individual liberty, and fell just 70 votes short of the 1,140 he needed for victory at the Republican convention in Kansas City.

Had he won, he might have been President when oil prices doubled, and could well have been ousted – like the luckless Carter – after just one term. As it was, he emerged as front-runner for the Republicans' 1980 nomination. He won it, and then handsomely defeated President Carter on polling day by carrying 44 states – and his coat-tails were long enough to give the Republicans control of the Senate. At 69 Ronald Reagan became America's oldest president. He told the nation in his inauguration speech that it was 'time to reawaken this industrial giant, to get government back within its means, and to lighten our punitive tax burden'.

As America's fortieth president, Reagan enjoyed one immediate, auspicious piece of good fortune. Within minutes of his speech, Iran freed the 52 Americans who had been held hostage for 444 days in Tehran. That was by design: President Carter had caused great offence to the Iranian authorities the previous spring when a botched effort had been made to rescue the hostages in a desert raid with helicopters.

But less than three months after he took the presidential oath of office, fortune seemed to cease to smile on the new President. As he was leaving the Washington Hilton Hotel off Connecticut Avenue, Reagan was shot in the chest by a crazed gunman. 'Honey, I forgot to duck,' he joked to his wife as he waited for surgery.

Equally characteristic was his wisecrack to the surgeons as he was about to undergo sedation: 'I hope you're all Republicans.' Spared the assassination of yet another national leader, the nation gave thanks for the President's survival, and from that moment on his political position was probably impregnable.

During the following eight years Reagan had to return to hospital for the removal of polyps from his colon, treatment of skin and intestinal cancer, and for prostate surgery, but he invariably managed to project an image of rude good health. This impression was reinforced by frequent photographs of him riding and chopping wood during regular visits to his Californian ranch. And although it was increasingly apparent within the White House that he was becoming hard of hearing, his infectious optimism overwhelmed any impression of disability.

The attempt on his life was undoubtedly politically helpful. Reagan's good-humoured courage boosted his popularity, and it may well have helped him to win congressional approval for a 25 per cent tax cut in July 1981. For this he carried the day in the nominally hostile House of Representatives, largely thanks to the votes of 40 conservative southern Democrats (known as the 'boll weevils') who defied their party leaders. In 1986 he pushed another major Bill through Congress which cut the number of income tax bands from 14 to 3, reducing the top rate from 70 to 33 per cent and reversing past governments' attempts at social engineering.

Reagan passionately believed that lower taxes would stimulate economic activity and, over time, generate greater revenues – a theory known as 'supply-side' economics. During his eight years in office the United States created roughly 17 million new jobs, and the gross national product nearly doubled. Yet the sustained economic expansion was fuelled by more than just tax cuts. Reagan tended to forget the $100 billion tax increase he had been obliged to endorse in 1982. Oil prices, which had doubled during the late 1970s, fell steadily during the 1980s, and America was emerging from its deepest recession since the 1930s. Despite the prosperity he appeared to bring in his wake, Reagan was unable to balance the budget. Effectively he was replacing the old liberal policy of 'tax and spend' with one of 'borrow and spend'.

For the truth was that while he was cutting taxes he was greatly increasing defence expenditure and failing to make the deep cuts required elsewhere in the federal budget. The national debt nearly tripled while he was in the White House, from $900 billion to nearly $2,700 billion, and the trade deficit quadrupled. By the time he left office, interest repayments on that debt amounted to 14 per cent of the total budget, and the debt was growing by roughly $200 billion a year. What more than anything else enabled him to achieve his aim of cutting back government interventionism was his success in placing his successors in a fiscal straitjacket.

Reagan himself recognized his inability to cut government spending, calling it 'one of my greatest disappointments' and blaming it consistently on Congress. Yet an estimated 92 per cent of the federal spending contained in the six key budgets of the Reagan years was proposed by the White House, not by Congress. For all of Reagan's conservative rhetoric, the federal government continued to expand during his time in office, and federal spending continued to rise as a percentage of GNP.

Reagan had inherited from Carter not just a stagnant economy, but a demoralized system of military defence, whose capabilities were thought by some to be in danger of being overtaken by the Soviet Union. He embarked on a massive military build-up, and in the autumn of 1983 America began deploying cruise and Pershing II missiles in Britain and other European countries to counter the threat of Soviet ss-20s. These deployments were bitterly resisted by nuclear disarmament activists, who not only derailed the whole process in West Germany but pitched much-publicized protest camps outside Greenham Common and other US bases in the United Kingdom.

In the same year, Reagan labelled the Soviet Union an 'evil empire' that would eventually be consigned to the 'ash heap of history', and launched the Strategic Defence Initiative – the development of a space-based 'shield' intended to intercept and destroy incoming missiles.

From the outset, Moscow bitterly opposed this Star Wars programme. It argued that it would begin a fresh arms race in space – which the Soviet Union was in no position to fund – and undermine the principle of mutually-assured destruction that deterred either superpower from launching a nuclear strike against the other.

Reagan, however, maintained that the initiative was purely defensive, and that the US could successfully negotiate nuclear arms agreements with Moscow only from a position of strength.

He got nowhere with successive Soviet leaders Brezhnev, Andropov, and Chernenko – all hardliners – but with Mikhail Gorbachev's accession in 1985 a remarkable thaw began in US–Soviet relations.

The two men first met at their so-called 'fireside summit' in Geneva that November. They established a good personal rapport and agreed that they must try to end the arms race. The following year they met again in Reykjavik. They came close to an astonishing agreement to eliminate all nuclear weapons, but the talks collapsed when Gorbachev again insisted that America must abandon the Strategic Defence Initiative.

In 1987, however, Gorbachev made a triumphant visit to Washington to sign the Intermediate-range Nuclear Forces Treaty, eliminating all Soviet and American medium-range missiles in Europe. This was the first treaty that had ever actually reduced the size of the superpowers' nuclear arsenals, and by the time Reagan left the White House in January 1989 he and Gorbachev had laid the groundwork for the first Strategic Arms Reduction Treaty, cutting US and Soviet long-range nuclear missiles by roughly a third. (Presidents Bush and Gorbachev finally signed the START I agreement in 1991.) There is no doubt that Reagan's military build-up contributed to the pressures on Gorbachev and to the ending of the Cold War. Reagan himself was certain of its importance. 'The Soviet economy was a basket case, in part because of enormous expenditures on arms,' he wrote in his memoirs. Gorbachev 'had to know that the quality of American technology, after reasserting itself beginning in 1981, was now overwhelmingly superior to his. He had to know we could outspend the Soviets on weapons as long as we wanted to.'

One of Reagan's last overseas trips was to Moscow, the first by a US President in 14 years. He and Gorbachev did a 'walkabout' in Red Square. They dined at the Gorbachev dacha outside Moscow. Reagan was permitted to give a lecture at Moscow State University, and was mobbed by enthusiastic Muscovites during a visit to Arbat

Street. In his farewell address as President, Reagan proclaimed a 'new closeness' in US–Soviet relations, and in his memoirs he wrote: 'There was a chemistry between me and Gorbachev that produced something very close to a friendship.'

But Reagan's intense hostility towards Communism also led to his highly controversial interventions in both Nicaragua and in the tiny Caribbean island of Grenada. In Nicaragua the Sandinistas had taken power in 1979, and Reagan feared that they were trying to export their revolution and arms to other places – in particular to El Salvador and the other Central American republics. He battled with Congress throughout most of his presidency over how openly, and to what extent, the US should support Nicaragua's anti-Sandinista 'Contras', men he liked to call 'freedom fighters'.

In 1983 Reagan ordered an invasion of Grenada, where an extreme left-wing faction had seized power and Cuban workers were building a suspiciously huge new airstrip.

This was one of the very few occasions on which Reagan and Thatcher openly disagreed. She got wind of the invasion just before it started and telephoned the President, who was in a Cabinet meeting. 'As soon as I heard her voice I knew she was very angry,' he wrote later. She 'asked me in the strongest language to call off the operation. Grenada, she reminded me, was part of the British Commonwealth, and the United States had no business interfering in its affairs.'

But the area of foreign policy that really bedevilled Reagan, and ultimately led to the greatest embarrassment of his presidency, was the Middle East. In 1982 he sent US Marines into Beirut to supervise an agreed PLO withdrawal from that city and the subsequent withdrawals of Israeli and Syrian forces from Lebanon. The Marines instead found themselves caught in an intractable conflict. In April 1983 a terrorist attack on the US Embassy in Beirut killed 16 Americans, and in October that year 241 Marines died in a suicide bombing of their Beirut barracks. Early the following year Reagan ordered the evacuation of all US forces from Beirut.

In November 1984, with the economy recovering and Reagan proclaiming that it was 'morning in America', he won a landslide re-election victory over Carter's former Vice-President, Walter Mondale, carrying every state except Mondale's native Minnesota and the District of Columbia. It was a significant triumph, but did not insulate him against controversy. Halfway through his second term he and his Administration were shaken by the Iran–Contra scandal.

This began in 1985 when Israeli sources told the Administration that moderates within the Iranian Government wanted to rebuild relations with Washington in anticipation of Ayatollah Khomeini's death. They were prepared to use their influence to secure the release of six American hostages held by Hezbollah guerrillas in Lebanon, but in return wanted small shipments of US arms to enhance their prestige within the Government.

Despite the strong opposition of George Schultz, his Secretary of State, and Casper Weinberger, his Defence Secretary, Reagan agreed to allow Israel secretly to ship us arms to Iran. Over the following months three hostages were released, but in November 1986 a small Beirut magazine reported that America was trading arms for hostages.

In the ensuing furore it also emerged that Oliver North, a member of Reagan's National Security Council staff, had diverted some of the proceeds of the arms sales to the Nicaraguan 'Contras' to circumvent a congressional ban on such assistance. Colonel North and Admiral John Poindexter, the National Security Adviser, were both dismissed. Reagan insisted he had not known of the diversion.

At best he was guilty of negligence, and at worst of complicity in an illegal act, but the truth was never conclusively established.

Reagan's Vice-President, George Bush, was elected President in November 1988.

Reagan left the Oval Office on January 20, after Colin Powell, his new National Security Adviser, had reported 'the world is quiet today'. One of his last acts was to scribble Bush a good luck note on paper headed 'Don't Let the Turkeys Get You Down'. He returned to California, where he and Nancy divided their time between Los Angeles and the ranch in the mountains near Santa Barbara that he so adored.

Reagan kept a low profile in retirement, though he addressed the Republican 1992 convention at Houston, scoring a great hit on its opening night with a characteristically engaging speech. He was held in great affection by the party that he had done so much to rehabilitate after Watergate, but even though his views on current issues were rarely offered or solicited, he gradually became an elder statesman whose dignity was obvious to all.

He announced he had Alzheimer's disease in a letter to America on November 5, 1994. 'I now begin the journey that will lead me into the sunset of my life,' he wrote. 'When the Lord calls me home, whenever that may be, I will leave with the greatest love for this country and eternal optimism for its future.' He was unable to appear in public during the late stages of his illness, but was reconciled with his children.

He is survived by his wife, Nancy, whom he married in 1952, and their son and daughter, and by a son from his first marriage.

Ronald Reagan, President of the United States, 1981–89,
was born on February 6, 1911. He died
on June 5, 2004, aged 93.

FRANCIS CRICK

Biologist whose discovery of DNA *in 1953 unlocked the 'secret of life' but
who continued his voyage of scientific discovery*

28 JULY 2004

TO THE PUBLIC, Francis Crick was one of the men who, with the American J. D. Watson, discovered the structure of DNA and received a Nobel prize for it. To his colleagues and students, he was one of the most distinguished and influential biologists of the 20th century, as well as one of the most flamboyant. Scientists would tell stories about Crick the way politicians once told stories about Churchill. This public image was not one that Crick wholeheartedly relished.

He had cultivated much of his persona to cut a dash in the world of molecular biology, where his true worth was known; he did not much care that it provided so prominent a mark in the public eye. Yet Crick was an original, looking at the world in ways his colleagues could often hardly fathom.

Francis Harry Compton Crick was born in 1916 in Northampton, the son of Harry Crick. He was educated at Mill Hill School and University College, London, where he graduated in physics in 1937. He became a research student there, but before he could finish his work for a thesis the Second World War began and he became a member of the Admiralty's mine design department.

During his time there he became aware that his real interests lay in biology rather than physics, and when he returned to civilian life in 1947 he decided to enter some field of biological research. He obtained a research studentship from the Medical Research Council and joined the Strangeways Institute in Cambridge, which made a speciality of research in cell biology. Soon he realized that he wanted to work at a more fundamental level.

In 1949 he joined M. F. Perutz and J. C. Kendrew in the Cavendish Laboratory, becoming the third member of the newly founded Medical Research Council Unit which later developed into the Medical Research Council Laboratory of Molecular Biology.

He remained a member of the staff of the council throughout the rest of his career.

His major discovery, made in 1953 in close collaboration with his American colleague J. D. Watson, and based on the experimental work of M. H. F. Wilkins, Rosalind Franklin, and E. Chargaff, was the double-helical structure of deoxyribonucleic acid (DNA), the substance which, in almost every living cell, is the repository of the hereditary information that determines the characteristics of the organism.

Crick and Watson reasoned their way to the structure of DNA on only the barest of the evidence provided by others. They built models again and again. 'The important thing is to ignore data, which complicates life,' James Watson wrote to Crick in 1954. The first piece of the puzzle fell obediently into place. Crick then proposed that there must be small molecular tags, each type of which read the appropriate codeword on a gene and carried one sort of amino acid to the site where the protein was being assembled.

The structure of DNA showed that it could carry long messages; it seemed that it would be neat if those messages described the chains of amino acids that form proteins, but it would take another eight years, a lot of false starts and the resources of most of the large biological laboratories in the world to begin the translation of the language in which the message was written.

Giving as it did an immediate insight into the way in which the information is stored and passed on from generation to generation, the discovery of the double-helix structure of DNA was immediately recognized as perhaps the most important single contribution of the century to fundamental biology, and it gave Crick and Watson an international reputation almost overnight. The significance of the work was later recognized by the award of the Nobel Prize for Medicine jointly to Crick, Watson, and Wilkins in 1962, the *annus mirabilis* for molecular biologists, which saw five of them invited simultaneously to Stockholm to receive the same honour.

The structure of DNA was, however, only one of a whole series of major contributions to our understanding of the molecular basis of living organisms made by Crick throughout his career. Earlier on he had worked in the field of the X-ray analysis of proteins, as a critic of existing methodologies and an originator of new theoretical approaches. After the DNA structure, he was responsible for the formulation of the so-called 'central dogma' that biological information, stored in nucleic acids and passed on by their replication, is transformed into protein molecules, but that the reverse transformation never occurs.

He played a leading part in the work that led to the elucidation in detail of the genetic code by means of which biological information is recorded. He was largely responsible for several concepts underlying the understanding of the mechanism by which biological information is translated into protein molecules, especially the idea of a 'messenger' carrying information from one part of the cell to another, and for the 'adapter hypothesis' which explains the way in which specific protein molecules corresponding to that information are assembled. Both of these fundamental concepts were confirmed by experiment.

Later he became interested in problems of cell differentiation. It is a significant illustration of the rapid development of the field of molecular biology into more and more complex biological systems, a development in which Crick himself had played a leading part, that the division of the MRC Laboratory of which he was joint head (with S. Brenner) was in 1969 renamed the Division of Cell Biology, when only 20 years before he had abandoned the classical field of cell biology in favour of what then seemed a more fundamental approach.

Crick's great power as a scientist would have manifested itself in whatever field he had chosen to work; it derived from an individual and characteristic intellectual style. He had an unusual capacity for concentrated thought, and he argued with clarity and ruthlessness. Interminable discussions with his colleagues were a major element in his method of work, and he impressed them as having more sheer intellectual ability than anyone else they had met.

In all things a realist, he was well aware of his own power, and sometimes showed it. Some thought this arrogance, but he was the first to recognize, and go on record, when he happened to have been wrong. He seldom did experiments with his own hands, being for the most part a theoretician, pushing new ideas to the limit, but insisting that the hypotheses to which they led be checked against experimental evidence.

He had a deeper mathematical and physical insight than anyone else working in the field, and he was capable of discussing in depth almost any part of it. He was a determined reductionist and atheist who went on record as saying that one of his principal motives in entering biology was to try to show that the apparently mysterious phenomena of life could be explained in terms of physics and chemistry.

He spent much time discussing with experimentalists the significance of their results, often interpreting these for them and telling them what experiments to do next. These characteristics did not always endear him to his colleagues, but they made him an intellectual leader of the highly productive field of molecular biology during the four decades which followed the discovery of the structure of DNA.

Crick was not afraid to court controversy. In 1981 he published *Life Itself*, in which he suggested that life on Earth might have been planted as micro organisms by a more advanced, alien civilization. He called his theory Panspermia ('seed everywhere'), but although he insisted that it was merely a hypothesis, it attracted much caustic comment from other scientists. Crick conceded in an interview in 1995 that the book might perhaps have been a mistake, but defended his right to air the hypothesis. 'Panspermia was just an idea, something to be considered. The book was actually quite reserved about the whole thing. Of course, if you only glanced at it, you could have gotten the idea that I was a bit nutty.'

It was of a piece with Crick's love of shock tactics. In 1967 he had joined Graham Greene and the Beatles among many others who signed a full-page advertisement in *The Times* proclaiming the law against marijuana to be 'immoral in principle and unworkable in practice'.

In his later years Crick was based at the Salk Institute in La Jolla, California, and it was in San Diego that he died. At the Salk, he turned his attention to unravelling the workings of the brain. His last major work (again, an affair of some controversy), *The Astonishing Hypothesis: The Scientific Search for the Soul* (1994), argued that it was high time to think scientifically about the intractable problem of consciousness. Although not going so far as to propose a fully developed solution to the mystery, he made several suggestions about what a biological explanation for consciousness might be like. It was no surprise that he came down in favour of determinism. 'Awareness neurons,' he wrote, would perhaps one day be found, just as the structure of DNA had been discovered.

Though a man of wide-ranging interests, his only real passions were in science and in attacking all forms of religion. Besides the Nobel prize his many other honours included fellowship of the Royal Society (1959), the Lasker Award (1960), and the Prix Charles Leopold Mayer of the French Académie des Sciences (1961). He was a Fellow, and later an honorary Fellow, of Churchill College, Cambridge, and a director of the Salk Institute. In 1991 he was appointed a member of the Order of Merit.

Crick married in 1940 Ruth Doreen Dodd. This marriage was dissolved, and in 1949 he married Odile Speed. He is survived by her, by their two daughters, and by a son of his first marriage.

Francis Crick, OM, FRS, biologist, was born on June 8, 1916.
He died on July 28, 2004, aged 88.

YASSIR ARAFAT

Palestinian leader who inspired his people's struggle for a homeland
but lacked the political clout to make their dream a reality

11 NOVEMBER 2004

A TIRELESS POLITICIAN, administrator, and, in the opinion of some, an exhi-
bitionist and opportunist, for more than 40 years Yassir Arafat inspired his people
to remain hopeful for eventual freedom from Israeli occupation. He also won
almost universal recognition for his Palestine Liberation Organization (PLO) as the
sole representative of the Palestinian nation. In 1994 he was awarded the Nobel
Prize for Peace, jointly with the Israeli Foreign Minister, Shimon Peres, and the
Israeli Prime Minister, Yitzhak Rabin.

In the end, however, he would take his dream of a Palestinian state to his grave,
and at the time of his death the prospect of it seemed as remote as ever. After the
Oslo peace agreement of 1993, which gave a measure of autonomy to the occupied
territories of the West Bank and the Gaza Strip, he failed to convince Israel that the
guerrilla leader had changed into a statesman. Not only did he fail to curb the
terrorism of such rival organizations as Hamas and Islamic Jihad against Israeli
civilians, but evidence suggested that he was complicit in similar atrocities carried
out by al-Aqsa Martyrs Brigades, a branch of his own Fatah movement which he
financed. Subsequently, when negotiations ground to a complete halt in 2001 and
Arafat was put under house arrest by Israel in Ramallah in the West Bank, he did
not allow any political institutions or individual leaders to emerge from his shadow
to replace him.

By then, his closest aides appeared to have alienated the people they were supposed to represent. Having spent many years with him in exile in Jordan, Lebanon,
and Tunisia, his circle were commonly referred to as 'the Tunisians', while suspected involvement in illicit financial deals sullied their reputations further.
Younger candidates for leadership, who had spent all their lives in the occupied
territories and thought they understood Israel better, were marginalized.

Mohammed Abdel-Rauf Arafat al-Qudwa al-Husseini, the sixth child of his
father's first marriage, resisted being drawn on the details of his life, preferring,
instead, to surround his circumstances with myths to suit the political needs of the
moment. Accordingly, he claimed that he was born in Jerusalem, even though his
early education records in Egypt show him to have been born in Cairo, where his
father had transferred his mercantile business two years earlier.

659

On his father's side, he was a member of the prominent al-Husseini clan of Gaza, and his mother was one of the Abu Sauds of Jerusalem, counting as minor aristocracy in the old city. Contrary to another claim, he was not related to the notorious Haj Amin al-Husseini, the Grand Mufti of Jerusalem who advocated alliance with Nazi Germany during the Second World War and who led the Palestinian government in exile after 1948.

Arafat's mother died in 1933, when he was four. He was sent with an infant brother to Jerusalem to spend three years at the home of a maternal uncle. In 1937, shortly after his father took an Egyptian wife, he was taken back to Cairo. There he had a comfortable and relatively uneventful upbringing, emotionally attached to Palestine, which he visited regularly, but immersed in the political and social culture of wartime Cairo: pro-German, anti-monarchist, and increasingly Islamic. It was there, at Farouk Secondary School, that he gained the nickname Yassir (carefree). For the rest of his life, he spoke Arabic with an Egyptian accent.

In November 1947, the UN voted to partition Palestine between Arabs and Jews, a plan which assigned territory on the basis of 44 per cent to 56 per cent. Arab states and the leaders of the Palestinian Arabs rejected the plan. In May the following year the UK ended its mandate, and Jewish leaders proclaimed the State of Israel. War broke out between the the new state and a number of Arab armies, resulting in the heavy defeat of the latter. By the time a ceasefire was obtained in January 1949, the Jewish State had expanded its lands and occupied roughly 75 per cent of Palestine. The Arabs felt humiliated and began a new era of turmoil and revolution. (In December 1949 Jordan annexed the area known as the West Bank.) Traumatized, young Arafat first decided to seek a new life by applying to study in Texas. But he changed his mind after savouring the attraction of political activity among school pupils, and entered King Fouad I University (now Cairo University) to study civil engineering in the autumn of 1949. But clearly he was not interested in his subject, for it took him seven years to obtain a poor degree.

In contrast, he was quite successful in getting elected to a number of student posts, at first in the faculty of engineering as an Egyptian supporter of the Muslim Brotherhood, but later in the Palestinian Students' League. The association with the Brothers introduced him to urban guerrilla warfare and made him an explosives expert, so that, at the time of the invasion of the Suez Canal zone by the forces of Israel, Britain, and France in 1956, he was called up into the Egyptian Army as a bomb-disposal officer.

This was after spending three months in prison after an abortive attempt, in October 1954, on the life of Colonel Nasser, the strongman of the Egyptian regime that had overthrown King Farouk.

There is no evidence that Arafat took part in any operations against Israel from the Gaza Strip, then ruled by Egypt, though he later claimed such activity. It does, however, seem that he was active in uncovering salvageable weapons on the Second World War battlefield of El Alamein to send to Gaza.

Recollections of his friends and family in those years portray him as an over-active young man who was 'a compulsive doer' and a 'showman', without scruples about telling lies. He was totally possessed by the idea of recovering the lost terri-tories, but soon came to the conclusion that, whereas support from Arab govern-ments was to be usefully sought, in the last resort the Palestinians could rely only on themselves.

Arafat's first job after graduation in 1956 was at a cement factory near Cairo, but he hated the work and also found the atmosphere of Egypt unsuitable to his ambitions as a Palestinian political activist. He founded another Palestinian student union to enable him to organize protests in the Gaza Strip, but he was still restless. He also needed money. In 1958, after a visit to Iraq, which had just toppled its monarchy, he decided, with several other Palestinians, to emigrate to Kuwait, a largely undeveloped backwater.

Despite its appalling heat and humidity, Kuwait offered several advantages.

It left its growing Palestinian community to its own devices, and it provided the newcomers with travel documents; at this juncture he formally became 'Yassir Arafat'. Kuwait also paid well. Arafat became the owner of four cars, had holidays in Europe, widened his circle, and founded a new publication: *Falastinuna* (Our Palestine), advocating armed struggle. The periodical was soon published in Beirut, attracted donations from supporters in many countries and formed the nucleus of the guerrilla movement al-Fatah (Victory) in 1959. Arafat's full-time career as a guerrilla began five years later, when he assumed the nom de guerre Abu Ammar (after one of the disciples of the Prophet Muhammad) and sold his larger cars to drive to Lebanon in a Volkswagen to set up base there.

There then began a period of rapid expansion, with Fatah gaining some 200 full-time guerrillas by the time of its first successful attack, in January 1965, on an Israeli irrigation pipeline from Jordan. The boastful publicity allowed Arafat by a willing Arab press made him a hero of the masses, and radical Third World coun-tries such as China joined his financiers, though Arafat himself occasionally spent months in Lebanese and Syrian jails. In 1966 Fatah was admitted to the member-ship of the Palestine Liberation Organization, at the time an ineffectual body spon-sored by Egypt.

The defeat of Egypt, Syria, and Jordan in the Six-Day War of June 1967 stunned the Arab world and discredited its governments. But it catapulted Arafat to the highest position within the Palestinian national movement. He was elected the PLO's chairman in 1969, in succession to the Egyptian client, Ahmad Shukairi. 'They chose a man who could work 24 hours a day,' Arafat said after his election by the Palestine National Council, the Palestinian 'parliament' in exile. Thenceforth, the person of Arafat was out of bounds to his enemies within Arab governments, though his closest associates could be murdered with impunity.

After an unsuccessful, clandestine journey to the West Bank, newly occupied by Israel, to recruit guerrillas, Arafat stepped up raids on Israel from Jordan, bringing harsh retaliation by Israel.

In 1970 King Hussain of Jordan found the situation intolerable and used the Beduin troops of his army to suppress the PLO inside the country.

The operations, from September 1970 to July 1971, were carried out with treachery and brutality on both sides – so much so, indeed, that some 70 Palestinian guerrillas surrendered to Israel rather than risk falling into Jordanian hands.

The bitterness that followed turned the streets of the Near East and Europe into a battleground for terrorists and hit squads, beginning with the assassination in Cairo in 1971 of the Jordanian Prime Minister, Wasfi al-Tal, by Palestinians calling themselves Black September Commandos.

It was later admitted that Black September had been set up by Salah Khalaf, or Abu Iyad, Arafat's second-in-command, out of Force 17, Arafat's personal bodyguard. They were under strict orders from Arafat not to betray any links with the PLO.

Among other acts, Black September carried out the abduction of Israeli athletes at the Munich Olympics of 1972. Nine Israelis died in a German operation to rescue them. While such acts were condemned worldwide as despicable, they were privately acknowledged to be effective by some Israeli officials. For example, General Aharon Yariv, head of Israel's military intelligence and under orders to exact revenge for Munich, prophesied that the atrocity would ensure a place on the political map for the PLO: 'They think in strategic terms better than we do,' he wrote.

Reduced in numbers but more popular among Palestinians, Fatah set up new camps in Syria and Lebanon, and began to mount raids into Israel from Lebanon's southern region, provoking numerous Israeli incursions into that country.

The Arab-Israeli Yom Kippur War of October 1973 left the Palestinians largely unaffected, though it made the 'victorious' Egyptians less receptive to Palestinian requests. By 1975 Fatah and other Palestinian guerrilla groups were so established in Lebanon that they were being accused of being 'a state within a state' and were portrayed as a big factor in the outbreak of war between leftist Muslims and rightist Christians. At that point Arafat committed one of the most serious mistakes of his career. He sided with the Muslims and provided a pretext for President Assad of Syria, who wanted to control him, to send client Palestinians and the Syrian Army to confront him. Thousands of Palestinians died and Fatah was confined to small areas in south Lebanon.

Nevertheless, the PLO was now recognized, by the declaration of the Arab summit of Rabat in 1973, as 'the sole representative of the Palestinian people' and Arafat himself was received in many parts of the world as a head of state. After November 1974, when he was invited to address the general assembly of the UN, Arafat tried to project the image of a statesman who was taking steps towards the recognition of Israel. However, he still demanded the creation of a unitary, secular state of Palestine in which Arabs and Jews lived as equals. When Ayatollah Khomeini came to power in Iran in 1979, Arafat was received as a hero in Tehran.

The Camp David accords of 1978 shook the Arab world. Egypt, the most powerful Arab state, was recovering its own lands in return for vague promises from Israel to grant autonomy to the Palestinians and discuss their future in five years' time.

Arafat prevented King Hussain, with whom he had earlier made peace, from co-operating in the US-brokered scheme, and played a prominent part in the expulsion of Egypt from the Arab League.

Another great setback befell the PLO in 1982, when Israel's Likud-led Government invaded Lebanon, surrounded Beirut, and forced the expulsion of the guerrillas from that country. Arafat, who had largely been blamed for provoking the invasion by attacking northern Israel, was able to escape alive only thanks to the intercession of Western powers. The PLO's headquarters had to be transferred to Tunis and its guerrillas dispersed all over the Arab world. The Palestinian refugees of the camps of Sabra and Chatila were massacred when Israel allowed Lebanese Christian militiamen into them.

A string of Palestinian terrorist attacks in Europe in the mid-1980s, in which Fatah was thought to be implicated, caused the US to end the dialogue it had begun with the PLO in 1988. But a popular war of attrition, the intifada uprising, which began on the streets of the occupied territories in 1988, came to the PLO's rescue and neutralized Israeli pressure on the United States to ignore the Palestinians' demands for a homeland. A realization that the PLO did exert influence over Palestinian public opinion, together with the growing power of Islamic activists in the territories, caused President Bush to press Israel to agree to the indirect participation of the PLO in the peace talks of 1991, held in Madrid. The Palestinian delegates from inside the occupied territories were allowed secretly to be approved by the PLO and were clearly accountable to it. This was despite Arafat's support for the Iraqi dictator Saddam Hussein in his invasion of Kuwait the previous year, which had further isolated him in the Arab world and caused the PLO to lose the bulk of its income from the rich Arab states of the Gulf.

The formal peace talks seemed to have reached stalemate and Arafat's authority was fading. There then occurred an event as extraordinary as it was symbolic. In April 1992, while on one of his many flights around the Arab world, Arafat crashed in the Libyan desert when a sandstorm brought down his small aircraft in a remote region near the Chad border. Three members of the crew were killed, but Arafat, battered and bruised, was rescued, stumbling around the desert with ten other survivors.

This was not the first time he had escaped death by a whisker. A year later he made a political resurrection almost as astonishing. In August 1993 the PLO and the new Labour Government of Israel suddenly announced a breakthrough. Secret negotiations in a series of country houses in Norway had enabled them to agree on the setting up of a Palestinian Authority, initially under the PLO, in the Gaza Strip and around the town of Jericho in the West Bank. Further negotiations about the future of East Jerusalem and other disputed issues would be held no later than the summer of 1995, and a 'final status' in the relationship between Israel and the Palestinians would be achieved inside five years.

There were those who believed that Arafat's fear of a rival leadership rising from within the occupied territories to marginalize him had played a crucial part in persuading him to participate in the Oslo talks. In any event, the news electrified the world. But for Arafat it was a dangerous gamble. What if Israel were not forthcoming in future negotiations and kept the other half of the territories under occupation? Syria and Jordan, too, felt sidelined, sensing that Israel was now under less pressure to sue for peace with them. Syria began to give new support to Arafat's unrealistic detractors among the Palestinians.

After the televised celebration on the lawn of the White House in Washington in September 1993, when Arafat and the Israeli leader Yitzhak Rabin shook hands, and after an embarrassing tantrum in Cairo in May 1994 when Arafat would not sign the proposed map of autonomous Jericho despite the visible anger of President Mubarak, the two areas were handed over to the control of the PLO. Israeli occupation forces withdrew, and some 900,000 Palestinians greeted Palestinian policemen on their streets.

Unforeseen factors then came into play in the form of Jewish and Palestinian terrorism. Yitzhak Rabin, Prime Minister of Israel, was assassinated by a Jewish extremist in November 1995. Islamist opponents of the peace treaty among the Palestinians resorted to suicide bombings in Israel, and these discredited the succeeding Government of Shimon Peres. In the general election of May 1996 Israel narrowly voted for Benjamin Netanyahu to lead a right-wing Government that, while claiming that it wanted peace with the Palestinians, promised to expand the Jewish settlements in the remaining occupied territories.

The last bout of negotiations in which Arafat participated was held with Ehud Barak, the Labour Prime Minister, in the US and Egypt under the chairmanship of President Clinton, with both Barak and Clinton eager to make concessions as they approached the end of their terms. Although this is disputed by the Palestinians, the Israelis said that they were prepared to offer the Palestinians 97.5 per cent of the occupied territories of 1967 and compensate them for the remainder, East Jerusalem, with land out of Israel elsewhere.

But Arafat refused. He wanted both the return of East Jerusalem and the right of several million Palestinian refugees and their descendants from 1948 to return to their former homes or lands in Israel. The US, under the new Republican Administration of George W. Bush, refused to enter any more talks with Arafat and, while a new intifada in the territories further enraged Israeli public opinion, the new, right-wing Government of the Likud party under Ariel Sharon put a complete end to Arafat's journeyings abroad. He was put under house arrest in a building in Ramallah in the West Bank.

For the last years of his life Arafat was a virtual prisoner in his Ramallah compound, refused permission by the Israelis to travel around the Palestinian territories and afraid to go abroad least he be prevented from returning.

It was a time of disillusion. Already there was growing discontent among Palestinians with his capricious leadership, the perceived corruption of those around him, and his failure to allow a more transparent framework of government.

Younger Palestinians, especially, were angered by the lavish lifestyle of those who had built villas in Gaza; many also wanted the Palestinian Authority to spend more money on desperately needed social services.

The European Union, which since the Oslo accords had provided the bulk of foreign aid and budgetary support to the Palestinian Authority, also demanded that Arafat account for the huge sums that were still deposited in his personal account.

Rumours that the Israelis provided a slush fund for him in a bank account also fuelled the discontent, and Arafat had to concede a full investigation which concluded that 40 per cent of all the funds received by the Palestinian Authority had been misappropriated.

Younger Palestinians also chafed at Arafat's vacillating leadership, which was eclipsed by the uncompromising militancy of Hamas and Islamic Jihad. Arafat was torn between trying to retain authority by covert support for Palestinian militancy, while nominally condemning suicide bombings and, at moments of tension, arresting dozens of Palestinian leaders in response to Israeli and Western calls for a curb on terrorism. Most were usually quickly released.

In May 2003, under intense pressure from the US and Egypt, Arafat agreed to allow the secretary-general of the PLO, Mahmoud Abbas, whose nom de guerre was Abu Mazen, to become Prime Minister, with the aim of curbing the terrorist networks and reforming the Palestinian Authority from within. But Arafat refused to give Abu Mazen control of the numerous security organizations he had created, or even to allow him control of the Palestinian Authority's finances. Abu Mazen resigned in September and was succeeded by the pliant Ahmad Qureia who also found his attempts to govern thwarted by Arafat. He submitted his resignation, but it was not accepted.

Until his virtual imprisonment, Arafat had been one of the most 'nomadic' of all the international statesmen of the late twentieth century. He travelled constantly to meet foreign leaders and Palestinian communities. He had great charisma in personal encounters, though he lacked it in public.

In late 1991, Arafat announced that he had secretly married Suha Tawil, a wealthy Christian woman 33 years his junior who had converted to Islam. Mrs Arafat's frequent shopping trips to Paris, however, did not help her husband's reputation for probity, and disappointed many more Palestinians. She and their daughter survive him.

Yassir Arafat, President of the Palestinian National Authority,
was born on August 4, 1929.
He died on November 11, 2004, aged 75.

* * *

POPE JOHN PAUL II

2 APRIL 2005

POPE JOHN PAUL II was without doubt one of the most striking, interesting, and influential figures of our times. This was an impression that grew ever stronger in his extraordinary old age. The visible pain and frailty of his final years gave frequent rise to speculation of a possible retirement: and yet these were the years in which not only the inner strength but also the radicalism of this supposedly conservative figure became most apparent.

A tireless missionary, he was the first pope to visit all the inhabited continents of the world, drawing the largest crowds in history. He was the first to be fully at ease with the modern media, spreading the Christian message through television interviews, the internet, books of his personal writings, and compact discs. He was the first officially to visit a synagogue or mosque, and the first to travel to Britain and Ireland. And he was the only Pope to have acknowledged publicly the Church's failings over two millennia.

For much of his reign, John Paul II was – not only for the secular world but also for many Roman Catholics – a figure of paradox. He was, it was said, a social progressive but an ecclesiological reactionary; a pastoral bishop who had been deeply influenced by the Second Vatican Council but who then – or so some critics volubly asserted – directed his entire pontificate towards a restoration of the Catholicism of the preconciliar period.

He was a defender of liberty wherever the rights of men and women were denied by despotic regimes, but his opponents soon began to claim that he himself silenced dissent among bishops and clergy quite as ruthlessly as any secular dictator. It seemed to many that he was wholly out of touch with the secular realities amid which he lived; yet few of his contemporaries had shown a more profound and subtle understanding of the nature of the historical forces that were to sweep away the post-war division of Europe, between the capitalist West and the communist East.

Partly, these conflicting perceptions were based on a tendency to judge him by criteria which were either theologically superficial or wholly secular. The paradoxes were more apparent than real.

Those, for instance, who saw a contradiction in a Pope who forbade his clergy to become involved in politics and yet who exercised an apparently direct political influence in his native Poland, failed to understand how his influence operated within a national culture that had a spiritual dimension from which the Marxist state was, in the nature of things, wholly disconnected.

The political levers of power were never directly an object of his concern: and yet many of those in the Solidarity Movement who did confront the Polish secular state were motivated by a Catholic humanism in which the dignity of beings made in the image of God was central, and which had been powerfully revitalized by their compatriot's charismatic evangelical presence.

Karol Wojtyla's anti-Communism was thus no merely ideological phenomenon but derived from the same source as his entire critique of modern secularist culture.

His thinking had evolved both as a result of his professional career as an academic philosopher and from the circumstances of his pastoral experience as priest and bishop. He believed that the secular mind – in both East and West – had installed cultures deeply inimical to the flourishing of the human personality.

The enemy, for him, was anything which obscured man's nature as an essentially moral being – from relativism in moral philosophy to totalitarianism in politics.

Man's vocation was to become what God intended him to be: the drama of every human life was the struggle against evil, both personal and social.

This interaction between philosophy and pastoral reality can be seen in his early theological focus on human sexuality. Modern secular thinking was focused on the norm of personal gratification – Wojtyla's personalist norm focused on the imperative to avoid using others. We had, he wrote, to meet the freedom of another person and depend on it. This could be done only within the context of permanent commitment, not as a means of confining the human personality but, on the contrary, as the only means by which sexuality can be truly liberated.

By the end of his life, it was quite widely felt that John Paul had won the intellectual argument within the Church. Though there were still those who perceived him as a reactionary Pope who had sought to reverse the advances inaugurated by the Second Vatican Council, there were as many others who argued – if perhaps less loudly – that it was he who, in the end, was the council's most definitive interpreter and advocate. In the view of the distinguished American Jesuit theologian Cardinal Avery Dulles, for instance, John Paul II had, more than any other single individual, succeeded in comprehensively restating the contours of Catholic faith in the light of Vatican II and in relation to postconciliar developments in the Church and in the world.

This had certainly been his intention from the beginning. After his election, he told the assembled cardinals that his 'first task and definitive duty' was to complete the implementation of the Second Vatican Council. But he consistently refused to accept the view of some postconciliar radicals that Vatican II represented a dramatic break with Catholic tradition.

'If anyone reads the council,' he declared in February 2000, 'presuming that it marked a break with the past, while in reality it placed itself in line with the faith of all time, he definitely has gone astray.'

It is part of the achievement of his pontificate that this understanding has been widely accepted. An indication of how far opinion had shifted came with the publication in 1992 of the *Catechism of the Catholic Church*. Although it was largely the work of other hands, it was nevertheless a central part of John Paul's own project.

The Catechism had at first been seen by progressives as an irrelevant and essentially anti-conciliar document. But this analysis was proved false as this weighty volume became a massive best-seller and the undisputed touchstone of Catholic doctrine, of which it had effectively re-established the objective and systematic character after decades of intellectual instability. Here, as so often elsewhere, John Paul II may be said to have reunited the See of Peter with the *sensus fidelium*, the deepest instinct of Catholic believers.

Karol Jozef Wojtyla was born in southern Poland as the nation was emerging from 150 years of foreign domination. The youngest son of Karol Wojtyla, a retired captain in the Austro-Hungarian Army, and Emilia Kaczorowska, a cabinet-maker's daughter, he was baptized on June 20, 1920.

The future Pope's early life was marked by dramatic personal loss. When he was barely nine years old, his mother died, aged 45, from kidney failure. Three years later, his beloved brother, Edmund, a doctor 13 years his senior, died after contracting scarlet fever from a patient.

At 16, Wojtyla's passionate and precocious interest in Polish literature drove him into amateur theatre. Working closely with a local avant-garde director, he wrote, produced, and acted in a series of experimental plays. In 1938, after coming top of his secondary school class, Wojtyla moved with his father to Poland's cultural capital, Cracow, to study Polish language and literature at the ancient Jagiellonian University.

The following year Hitler's Germany invaded Poland. The Second World War saw Wojtyla's university professors sent to Sachsenhausen, while he himself was forced to work in a stone quarry to avoid deportation. The experience inspired him to become a lifelong champion of workers' rights. He continued to write prolifically, producing a number of religiously themed plays, novels, and poems. He also organized and acted in clandestine theatre performances, at some risk to his life.

February 18, 1941 marked the third and greatest personal loss of Wojtyla's youth.

Returning home from the quarry, he found his father dead. The 20-year-old was taken in by family friends and began to live a life of intense prayer, guided by a mystical Cracow tailor, Jan Tyranowski. Sensing in himself an 'interior illumination', he decided to sacrifice his promising literary career to train for the priesthood.

In the autumn of 1942, he presented himself at Cracow's underground seminary and was accepted. For the next three years he led a double life as a worker-seminarian, studying philosophy during night shifts at a chemical plant. If discovered by the Nazis, he faced execution by firing squad or deportation to Auschwitz. On August 4, 1944, as the Germans began to lose their grip on Poland, the underground seminarians took refuge in the home of Cardinal Adam Stefan Sapieha, the Prince Archbishop of Cracow. Wojtyla narrowly avoided capture, hiding in the basement as the Gestapo swept the upper floors of his house.

In January 1945 the Red Army liberated Poland, making it possible for Wojtyla to pursue his studies openly at the reopened major seminary of Cracow and the theology faculty of the Jagiellonian University. He was ordained the following year, on All Saints Day, by Cardinal Sapieha and celebrated his first Mass in the crypt of Cracow's Royal Cathedral, which houses the remains of Poland's great leaders. The setting, he said later, expressed his 'special spiritual bond with the history of Poland'.

A fortnight after his ordination, Father Wojtyla left Poland, for the first time in his life, to study at the Angelicum University in Rome. Under the tutelage of the French Dominican theologian Father Garrigou Lagrange, Wojtyla wrote a thesis on St John of the Cross's understanding of faith. His two-year course allowed him to 'learn Rome' and discover the 'universal dimension of the Church'. In the holidays, he travelled around Italy and northern Europe, ministering to immigrant Polish workers in the coal mines of Belgium and meeting priests working as manual labourers in inner-city Paris.

In June 1948 Father Wojtyla passed his doctoral examination, but failed to collect his degree because he could not afford to print his thesis. He returned in the same month to Poland to work as a curate and teacher of religion in a rural parish. Less than a year later, he was transferred to the parish of St Florian in Cracow to begin a student chaplaincy. A 'little family' of students quickly gathered around the charismatic young priest, who defied the Communist regime, and clerical convention, by leading mountain retreats and canoeing trips and giving weekly talks on religion.

He saw these as a way of combating the aggressive atheism of Poland's dictatorship and, by 1953, they had evolved into a two-volume anti-Communist catechism, circulated furtively among seminarians and Catholic intellectuals. During this period, Wojtyla also produced his most successful plays *Our God's Brother* and *The Jeweller's Shop*, and his best long poem, *The Quarry*.

In September 1951, Wojtyla began a second doctorate at the Jagiellonian University, which he gained in January 1954. In October of the same year, he was appointed to the philosophy department of the Catholic University of Lublin, where he lectured on the philosophical ethics of Max Scheler, Immanuel Kant, and Thomas Aquinas. In December 1956 he took the chair of ethics at the university and began a lecture programme on sexual ethics that culminated in 1960 in the daringly frank book, *Love and Responsibility*.

In July 1958 Pope Pius XII named Wojtyla auxiliary bishop of Cracow. He was consecrated on September 28, a few months before Pope John XXIII convoked the Second Vatican Council. Bishop Wojtyla anticipated many of the ecumenical council's themes in an essay to the preparatory committee, in which he urged that the 'inalienable liberty and responsibility of the person' be the basis of all council documents. He also called for a special declaration on religious liberty, which he hoped could be used against the repressive Polish regime. He appealed for the Church to become a bulwark for human rights, not just for its own flock but for everyone.

Bishop Wojtyla went behind the Iron Curtain in October 1962 for the first session of the council. Over the next three years, he contributed to debates on liturgical reform, Revelation, the nature of the Church, dialogue with the world, and religious freedom.

Throughout, he sided with the progressive bishops of Northern and Central Europe.

Shortly before he left for Rome, the See of Cracow fell vacant. For the next year and a half it remained empty as the Church sought to find a candidate acceptable both to Rome and the Communist regime. In 1963 the Primate of Poland, Cardinal Stefan Wyszynski, reluctantly nominated Bishop Wojtyla (apparently his eighth choice). The regime allowed his name to go forward, believing that Wojtyla was an apolitical intellectual, who would counter Wyszynski's aggressive Polish nationalism. On December 10, 1963, Pope Paul VI named Wojtyla Metropolitan Archbishop of Cracow. On March 8, 1964, he was installed at the Royal Cathedral.

At 43, he was the youngest bishop in Poland and, after Cardinal Wyszynski, the second most powerful.

As archbishop, Wojtyla found new and more effective ways to undermine the Communists' grip on Polish society. By the time he became Pope, he had created almost 20 new parishes, each involving a struggle with the regime. He held secret ordinations, smuggled Catholic literature, protected the independence of the Church press, and created a network of lay synods, which gave Catholics a channel for community activism outside government control. In 1966 his campaign took on a national dimension when he joined Cardinal Wyszynski in a celebration of the millennium of Christianity in Poland.

Wojtyla's election to the College of Cardinals in June 1967, at the unusually early age of 46, intensified his involvement in international Catholic affairs. He made speaking tours of the US, Canada, and Australia, and frequent trips to Rome (when the regime allowed), attending synods of bishops and sitting on Vatican committees for liturgy, the clergy, and Catholic education. He became a trusted adviser to Pope Paul VI, playing an important role in the development of *Humanae Vitae*, the Pope's controversial encyclical prohibiting artificial contraception.

In 1976 Pope Paul gave Wojtyla his most explicit seal of approval, inviting him to preach the Lenten retreat at the Vatican. Wojtyla prepared his sermons in less than two weeks, but the Pope was deeply impressed by the insight of his reflections on the Church's place in liberal, democratic societies. The meditations were later published as *Sign of Contradiction*, introducing Wojtyla's thought to a new, worldwide audience.

Catholicism experienced a double blow two years later when the death of Paul VI was followed quickly by that of his successor, John Paul I, just 33 days after election. When the cardinals met again in Rome, it resulted in what had seemed unthinkable: the election of a non-Italian pope. The Italian favourite, Cardinal Giovanni Benelli, the Archbishop of Florence, performed strongly in the opening ballots. But as the conclave progressed, the cardinals became convinced of the need to elect a non-Italian. Cardinal Wojtyla had the backing of the influential Archbishop of Vienna, Cardinal Franz Konig, who had met the Polish bishop during trips behind the Iron Curtain. In the seventh vote, Wojtyla overtook Benelli; in the eighth vote he achieved the necessary two-thirds majority.

The Vatican Secretary of State, Cardinal Jean Villot, stood before Wojtyla's desk and asked, in Latin, whether he accepted the nomination. Wojtyla replied: 'In the obedience of faith before Christ my Lord, abandoning myself to the Mother of Christ and the Church, and conscious of the great difficulties, I accept.' He was then asked to choose a name. In honour of his predecessors, he said he would be known as John Paul II. The College of Cardinals burst into applause at the choice.

Unlike John Paul I, Wojtyla was not overawed by his election: he refused any assistance in donning the white papal robes and stood rather than sat to receive the homage of the cardinals.

At 58, Cardinal Wojtyla became the youngest Pope of the century, the first Slav to hold the office, and the first non-Italian for almost 500 years. A collective gasp swept St Peter's Square, and the watching world, when the election was announced.

Moments later, in his first public appearance as Pope, John Paul II broke with custom by addressing the crowd in Italian, introducing himself to his bewildered new diocese as 'a man called from a far country to start anew on this road of history and of the Church'.

John Paul II was solemnly inaugurated Pope at St Peter's Basilica on October 22.

In his first homily, he proclaimed a bold evangelical message to the world, setting out in the clearest possible terms the scale on which he conceived the challenges ahead for himself and for the Church: 'Do not be afraid! Open wide the doors for Christ. To His saving power open the boundaries of states, economic, and political systems, the vast fields of culture, civilisation, and development. Do not be afraid!' The final words became the leitmotif of his pontificate.

The following year, in his first encyclical, *Redemptor Hominis* (The Redeemer of Man), John Paul II expounded in more detail his distinctive Christian humanism, and identified seven key tasks for the years ahead: to alert the world to the significance of the year 2000; to challenge Communism's denial of religious freedom; to establish the moral foundations of a free society; to oversee the full implementation of Vatican II; to restore unity within the Catholic Church; to pursue full Christian unity; and dialogue with world religions.

Hours after John Paul II's election, Cardinal Wyszynski had taken the new Pope aside and told him God had chosen him to lead the Church into the third millennium. The prophecy left a deep impression on him and his first encyclical focused on the coming millennium from the opening paragraph. The Church was living, he wrote, in a new season of expectation, looking forward to a renewal of faith 2,000 years after the birth of Christ.

Wyszinski's prophecy was confirmed, for John Paul II, on May 12, 1981, when the Pope survived an assassination attempt, having been shot in St Peter's Square by a Turk, Mehmet Ali Agca. The assassin's bullet came within a fraction of ending his life, leading him to say later that 'one hand fired the gun and another guided the bullet'. Agca, who acquired the gun in Bulgaria, was widely thought at the time to have acted on Moscow's orders. John Paul II attributed his miracle escape to Our Lady of Fatima, on whose feast day the attack fell. 'In the designs of Providence there are no mere coincidences,' he said at the Portuguese shrine the following year. The coming millennium was, he later said, the 'hermeneutical key' to his pontificate.

Karol Wojtyla did not come to the papacy with an explicit plan for dismantling the Communist bloc. But by relentlessly focusing on human rights, particularly the primary right to religious freedom, he attacked the heart of the Communist project – its claim to be the twentieth century's true humanism and true liberator. In June 1979 he took the message to his homeland. During a nine-day pilgrimage to Poland, in which he addressed a rapturous third of his countrymen, he chastised the Polish regime for repressing the country's deep religious heritage.

Speaking to an estimated million people in Warsaw's Victory Square, with Poland's Prime Minister, Edward Gierek, watching anxiously from a hotel, he proclaimed that 'without Christ' it was impossible to understand the history of Poland. His visit left the nation stirred and eager to enact the national moral renewal for which he had called. Barely a year later, the Polish Government sanctioned the Communist bloc's first independent, self-governing trade union, Solidarity.

John Paul II was informed in December 1980 that the Soviet Union was massing troops on the Polish border in order to crush Solidarity. He wrote a bold letter to the Soviet leader, Leonid Brezhnev, urging him not to invade. The danger passed, but a year later Poland's military dictator, General Wojciech Jaruzelski, declared martial law and arrested the Solidarity leadership. Leading prayers in the Vatican, the Pope pleaded with the general to put 'an end to the shedding of Polish blood'. What happened in Poland, he said, was 'important not only for a single country but for the history of the world'.

His intuition was confirmed over the next eight years as the Communist bloc unravelled. The year of the fall of the Berlin Wall, and of the first free election in Poland, 1989, was John Paul's *annus mirabilis*, and was capped by the December visit of a humbled Mikhail Gorbachev to the Vatican. John Paul told the leader of the Soviet Union (who considered the Pope 'a providential man') that their meeting was 'a singularly meaningful event, a sign of the times and a sign that is rich with promise'. Interpretations of the Pope's role in the collapse of European Communism would vary wildly, but there was wide agreement that he was indispensable in shaping the revolution of conscience that had preceded, and made possible, the non-violent political revolution of 1989.

With Communism vanquished, John Paul II sensed that the newborn democracies of Eastern Europe faced massive new challenges. The first task, he believed, was to build a free society upon solid ethical foundations. In a trio of major encyclicals, beginning in 1991 with *Centesimus Annus* (The Hundredth Year), he offered a blueprint. The encyclical argued that democratic societies had to be grounded in a respect for the fundamental freedom and dignity of the human person.

A democracy without values easily turned into open or thinly disguised totalitarianism, John Paul wrote. Communism's error was to reduce human beings to economic units. Without fundamental values, capitalism would do the same.

He further elaborated his vision in the landmark 1993 encyclical *Veritatis Splendor* (The Splendour of Truth), on the fundamentals of the Church's moral teaching. The encyclical evaluated the modern crisis of moral relativism, linking the recognition of universal moral norms to democratic equality, the defence of the socially marginal, the just distribution of wealth, and integrity in government.

His third effort to establish the moral basis of life in democratic societies was the 1995 encyclical *Evangelium Vitae* (The Gospel of Life), which argued that democracies risked self-destruction if moral wrongs were legally defended as rights. Democracies that denied the inalienable right to life from conception until natural death were tyrant states, creating a pervasive culture of death in which abortion, euthanasia, and the death penalty were actively promoted. He appealed for the creation of a new culture of life, which defended the dignity of every human life.

It was a message that too often went unheeded. In the last years of his pontificate John Paul repeatedly warned Europeans that they were losing contact with their Christian heritage. He was bitterly disappointed that the European Union's proposed constitution contained no reference to the Church's critical role in forming Europe's identity. Europe was, he said, witnessing a 'silent apostasy', which would have grave consequences for Church and society.

If this was John Paul II's challenge to the world, his challenge to the Catholic Church was to absorb fully the teachings of Vatican II before the coming of the year 2000. Many Catholics, he believed, had failed to grasp the council's true meaning. Vatican II was not, he said, a political struggle between conservative and progressive factions in the Church hierarchy. It was a major religious event aimed at strengthening the evangelical and apostolic life of the Church for the next millennium.

In his first encyclical, he had sought to draw a line under the bitter infighting that followed the council, warning Catholics against making thoughtless criticisms, and calling theologians to close collaboration with the Magisterium.

His comments were interpreted as signalling a crackdown on dissenting Catholic theologians, a view given credence in December 1979 when he disciplined the outspoken liberal theologian Hans Küng.

Over the next 20 years, in moves that met with incomprehension outside the Church and bitterness from some within it, a half dozen more theologians would be disciplined. To those who raised concerns about academic freedom, the Pope could respond in uncompromising terms: 'Within the ecclesial community, theological discussion takes place within the framework of faith. Dissent from Church doctrine remains what it is, dissent; as such it may not be proposed or received on an equal footing with the Church's authentic teaching.'

The Pope's greatest intellectual confrontation of this kind came in 1979 on his first visit to Latin America. With revolutionary tumult sweeping the continent, Catholic theologians were demanding that the Church ally itself with the poor in a Marxist-influenced struggle for justice. In a crucial and controversial speech to the Latin American bishops, John Paul argued that such liberation theologies reduced the Kingdom of God to a political, secularized kingdom. The Church was committed to the poor, but did not need to have recourse to ideological systems in order to love, defend, and collaborate in the liberation of man.

The Pope's concern to secure the legacy of Vatican II also took more positive forms, however. In 1983 he produced the long-awaited revised *Code of Canon Law* and, in 1992, issued the universal *Catechism of the Catholic Church*, which became an international best-seller. And while his detractors accused him of being autocratic, and of centralizing ecclesial authority excessively in Rome, he spent more time meeting the Church's bishops than any other Pope in modern history, demonstrating thereby his commitment to Vatican II's doctrine of episcopal collegiality, which he felt would always be strong enough to overcome any risk of serious division in the Church.

John Paul also encouraged the growth of so-called 'new movements' in the Church, dynamic, predominantly lay, groups, which flourished under his pontificate as never before. He promoted them vigorously, seeing them as a response to John XXIII's vision of a 'new Pentecost'. There were those, including some bishops, who saw the movements as undermining established structures, but here, at least, this supposedly authoritarian pontiff seemed content, in the words of one commentator, to allow a 'holy anarchy' within the Church.

John Paul II's openness in these areas revealed the radical way in which he conceived the office of Pope. There were those in the Church whose understanding of lay participation, or episcopal collegiality, undoubtedly differed from his, but even his critics would concede that John Paul brought a new style of leadership to the Vatican, shunning the anonymous bureaucratic style of previous Popes for a highly visible and personal ministry that was both pastorally and evangelically assertive. The purpose of the papacy, he believed, was not to seek worldly power, but to present the Gospel to the world. As he explained in his 1990 encyclical *Redemptoris Missio* (The Mission of the Redeemer): 'The Church proposes; she imposes nothing.'

He believed that this mission demanded that he travel the world preaching the Gospel. His energetic, relentless journeys made him the most recognized Pope in history. Millions saw him in person and millions more on television as he made whistle-stop, tarmac-kissing, handshaking, baby-hugging, crowd-blessing tours of the five inhabited continents. His innovatory World Youth Days drew millions of young people, including the largest crowd ever recorded anywhere, at Manila in

1995. He used every available medium to spread his message, becoming the first pontiff to publish a personal book, the best-selling *Crossing the Threshold of Hope*, which was translated into more than 40 languages. In 2003 he published a cycle of poems, which offered an intimate insight into his inner life. In *The Roman Triptych* he meditated on his pontificate and imagined the conclave that would elect his successor.

The Pope's tireless commitment to worldwide mission highlighted a transformation taking place in the Catholic Church. While Mass attendances and the number of vocations were declining in the West, there was rapid expansion in the developing world, particularly in parts of Africa and Asia. During John Paul's pontificate the number of Catholics in the world increased by more than 40 per cent, from 757 million in 1978 to 1.06 billion at the end of 2001. Growth in Africa during the same period was some 150 per cent, and in Asia 60 per cent.

John Paul's travels also allowed him to exercise a distinctive style of international diplomacy. He sought to challenge and embarrass repressive regimes during his visits, by emphasizing the inalienable dignity and the rights of every human being. The approach scored notable successes in Chile, Nicaragua, the Philippines, Nigeria, and Cuba. He built a unique moral profile in world affairs through his regular audiences at the Vatican. Determined to become the voice of those who cannot speak or who are silenced, he insistently called for world peace, condemning conflicts as far apart as the Falkland Islands, the Balkans, and the Gulf.

The first ever papal pilgrimage to England, in 1982, at the height of the Falklands conflict, was a golden opportunity for John Paul II to show his commitment to the quest for Christian unity. The historic prayer service at Canterbury Cathedral with the Archbishop of Canterbury, Robert Runcie, marked the highest point of relations between the Anglican and Catholic Churches since the Reformation. Hopes of imminent unity, however, were shattered when the Church of England opted to ordain women to the priesthood. John Paul II insisted – to the chagrin of a vocal minority of Catholics – that the Church had no authority whatsoever to ordain women. By the end of the 1980s, the Pope and the Anglican primate frankly acknowledged that they saw no solution to the impasse.

John Paul placed more hope in the reunion of the Catholic and Orthodox Churches.

His first steps towards unity came in 1979 with a visit to the Oecumenical Patriarch of Constantinople and formal dialogue between Orthodox and Catholic theologians. By December 1987, when he received the Patriarch on a five-day pilgrimage to Rome, he could state that there were no theological reasons why the two Churches could not become one.

But it was politics, rather than theology, that disappointed the Pope's millen-

nial hope for unity. After the collapse of Communism, a resurgent Russian Orthodox Church complained of Catholic proselytizing and was deeply angered by the
decision to create Catholic administrative territories in the former Soviet Union
without prior consultation. Although he never fulfilled his dream to visit Moscow,
John Paul travelled to Athens in May 2001, where he offered an apology for Catholic
aggression to the Greek Orthodox leader, Archbishop Christodoulos. A month
later, he visited Ukraine, the world's main Catholic-Orthodox flashpoint. Although
his visit eased tensions, it did not bring the unity between the two sister Churches
which he so desired.

John Paul II, however, remained convinced that unity was God's will for the
Church. He expressed this powerfully in his 1995 encyclical *Ut Unum Sint* (That
They May be One), when he affirmed the Catholic Church's irrevocable commitment to unity. In a remarkable passage, he asked Orthodox, Anglican, and Protestant Christians to help him to redesign the papacy as an office of unity for the
whole Church of Christ.

Unity among Christians was not enough; the Pope sought harmony and understanding among all the world's religions. To this end, he called a historic meeting
of religious leaders to pray for peace in Assisi in October 1986. A year earlier he
had addressed 80,000 Muslim youths on the importance of peaceful coexistence
between Christianity and Islam. In May 2001 he became the first pontiff officially
to visit a mosque, in Damascus.

But it was Christianity's relationship with Judaism that most captivated him. In
April 1986 he became the first Pope to visit Rome's synagogue, where he said that
the Jews were still God's chosen people and called them Christianity's 'privileged
elder brothers'. This new relationship between the two faiths was consolidated in
1993, when Israel and the Holy See forged a landmark agreement leading to full
diplomatic relations.

Five years later the Vatican published a document asking forgiveness for 2,000
years of Catholic anti-Judaism. But it was John Paul II's visit to the Holy Land in
March 2000 that truly marked a break with two millennia of Christian-Jewish
hostility. At the end of the week-long visit, which included a stop at Jerusalem's
Holocaust museum, the Pope placed a prayer in the Western Wall, regretting
Christian hostility to Jews and hoping for 'a new era of fraternal dialogue in the
third millennium'.

The trip to Israel forced many observers to reassess an extraordinary pontificate.

Over the preceding two decades, John Paul II had become the longest-serving
Pope of the twentieth century. He had made more than 100 foreign pilgrimages,
delivering some 3,000 addresses to hundreds of millions of men, women, and
children. He had written more than a dozen encyclicals and three dozen apostolic

letters. He had canonized more people than all the other Popes in history combined. He had held general audiences attended in all by more than 16 million people. He had created more than 200 new cardinals and 3,000 bishops, and established diplomatic relations with more than 60 countries.

This astonishing work rate took its toll. From the mid-1990s, the Pope's health deteriorated and the ebullient, dashing figure of the 1980s became a visibly strained old man. The Pope, he said, as he battled with ill-health in the last decade of his life, 'had to suffer' in order to purify the Church for the third millennium. But despite his physical limitations, he continued to enjoy life. 'It is wonderful to be able to give oneself to the very end for the sake of the Kingdom of God,' he said in a 1999 message to older people.

On Christmas Eve 1999 John Paul II walked through the Holy Door of St Peter's, signalling the start of the Great Jubilee of the Year 2000. The jubilee, which he had looked forward to since his election, would, he predicted, herald a new springtime of Christian life. The surprises of the pontificate were not yet over.

In January, he knelt side-by-side with the Archbishop of Canterbury and a Greek Orthodox Metropolitan for the opening of the Holy Door of St Paul's Outside the Walls. In February, he received more than 20,000 sick and terminally ill people in St Peter's Square for a special Mass.

In March he held a day of pardon in which he asked God's forgiveness for the sins of Catholics over the past 2,000 years. He hoped that the ceremony would lead to a purification of memory and prepare the Church to bring the Gospel to the people of the new millennium. In May he revealed the third secret of the Fatima visionaries, which predicted the 1981 attempt on his life. In the same month, he celebrated the world's first ecumenical commemoration of the twentieth century's 13,000 Christian martyrs.

In August the Pope preached to the largest gathering in European history. More than two million young people from 160 countries were present for the closing World Youth Day Mass in Rome. The pontiff challenged his young congregation to 'set the world ablaze' with Christian fervour. In September, he beatified two predecessors, Pius IX, who called the First Vatican Council, and John XXIII, who called the second. The following month he led the world's bishops in a collective consecration of the new millennium to the Blessed Virgin Mary. In November, at a jubilee gathering of politicians, he declared St Thomas More patron of statesmen.

On January 6, 2001, after a year of special events for Catholics from all professions and states of life, he marked the end of the Jubilee Year by shutting the Holy Doors. On the same day, he signed the apostolic letter, *Novo Millennio Ineunte* (At the Beginning of the New Millennium), which exhorted the Church to deepen its commitment to prayer and mission. The Jubilee Year, the Pope wrote, had given the Church a special time to reflect on its condition, three decades after the Second

Vatican Council. The council, which he termed 'the great grace bestowed on the Church in the twentieth century', was a 'sure compass' showing the Church's direction in the new millennium.

In February 2001 John Paul II brought the depleted College of Cardinals back to full strength, adding 43 new members at the largest consistory in the Church's history. The consistory consolidated the Pope's influence over the conclave which would elect his successor, but raised eyebrows by the inclusion of both moderates and hardliners. Studied closely, the nominations reflected John Paul's global strategy for creating a dynamic and evangelically assertive Church and his disregard for the conventional labels of church politics.

He consolidated his vision of a reinvigorated Church in his 2003 encyclical on the Church and the Eucharist, *Ecclesia de Eucharistia*, in which he appealed for a return to traditional Eucharistic devotions. A year earlier he had boldly introduced five new meditations for the rosary, a prayer that had changed little since the 15th century, and he encouraged Catholics to confess their sins regularly. These interventions highlighted the Pope's belief that prayer and sacramental life were the key to the renewal of the Church.

Almost to the end of the Pope's life there was no let-up in his gruelling schedule. He was on a four-day trip to Slovakia in September 2003 when his health appeared to deteriorate dramatically. Shortly after his return from that trip, in what was widely regarded as an acknowledgment that the end was near, he named 31 more cardinals, further strengthening the body that would elect his successor.

Yet, almost two months later, though terribly frail, he was there to install those new cardinals at a consistory many had feared he would not live to see. The previous Sunday, in fulfilment of a cherished desire, he had beatified Mother Teresa at a Mass attended by 300,000 people in St Peter's Square.

That same week, John Paul II had reached a milestone passed by only three of his predecessors, in celebrating his silver jubilee as Pope. He will be remembered not least for the strength of faith and of purpose that sustained him through those long, exhausting years. But he deserves to be remembered, too, as a man who participated in the great political and intellectual conflicts of the late twentieth century; who defended the human rights of millions around the world; who set out a compelling vision of moral life in an age of relativism; who injected new urgency into the Christian faith. A prophet of the new millennium, he should be acknowledged, even by his critics, as one of the great Popes of the last.

Karol Wojtyla, Pope John Paul II, was born on May 18, 1920.
He died on April 2, 2005, aged 84.

ACKNOWLEDGEMENTS

This book would not have been possible, of course, without the work of *The Times* obituarists whose work is collected here, or without the efforts of my predecessors, the nine obituaries editors of *The Times* from 1920 to 1999: Frederick Lowndes, H. B. Walton, J. H. Filmer, Colin Watson, Peter Strafford, T. E. Utley, John Grigg, John Higgins and Anthony Howard. I would also like to thank past and present *Times* colleagues who were roped in at one stage or another and whose efforts made the task of editing the book much easier: Angus Clarke, Maria Cleminson, Justine Cohen, Lisa Cotton, Daniel Crewe, Peter Davies, Tim Martin, Catharine Morris, Liam Parker, Victoria Walker, Patrick West and Sandra White. I am particularly grateful to Judith Heywood, who oversaw the editing and processing of vast amounts of text – and found all the photographs; to Nick Mays in *The Times* archive who assembled much of the historical material I have used in the introduction; to Andrew Sims in *The Times* picture library; and to Isabel Sheehy, Martin Toseland and Edwin Moore at HarperCollins.

HarperCollins would like to thank Mark Holland at Gales; David Pickering for copyediting and Hazel Mills for proofreading.

Ian Brunskill,
Obituaries Editor of *The Times*

INDEX

Page numbers in *italics* refer to photographs.